Financial Management
An Irish Text

THIRD EDITION

Thomas Power, Stephen Walsh
and Paul O'Meara

GILL & MACMILLAN

Gill & Macmillan Ltd
Hume Avenue
Park West
Dublin 12
with associated companies throughout the world
www.gillmacmillan.ie

© Tom Power, Stephen Walsh and Paul O'Meara 2009
978 07171 4554 6
Index compiled by Cover to Cover
Print origination in Ireland by Carole Lynch

The paper used in this book comes from the wood pulp of managed forests. For every tree felled, at least one tree is planted, thereby renewing natural resources.

We would like to acknowledge Roger Acton, Rory Kelleher, Dr Eleanor O'Higgins,
Dr John Teeling, Chris Johns and the *Sunday Business Post*
for permission to reproduce articles in the book.

The author and publisher have made every effort to trace all copyright holders,
but if any have been inadvertently overlooked we would be pleased to make
the necessary arrangement at the first opportunity.

To Anne, Jack, Molly, Ellen and Maura
(Jack and Paddy – accountants from different spheres – RIP). P.O'M.

To Tracy and Cathal. T.P.

To my late father and mother, Joe and Kate. S.W.

Contents

Preface

The first edition of this textbook was published in 2001. The rationale behind its publication was to provide a textbook that students could understand in a subject area that students from all backgrounds find very difficult. Corporate financial management is the essential ingredient in a textbook of this nature because most students from all backgrounds find themselves working in corporations of one sort or another. The main theme of the first edition was value creation because this should be the objective of all organisations (public or private). Nine years on and the same theme of shareholder (stakeholder) value is at the heart of the third edition. Finance is a most exciting and challenging area of study and it is of course ever-changing. With the most recent turmoil in financial markets involving the sub-prime mortgage markets and the credit crunch, the third edition of this text has been expanded to include a theoretical discussion of some of the important concepts involved.

MAIN CHANGES TO THE THIRD EDITION:

- Part 1 is now titled Introduction to Financial Management. Because of the recent turmoil in financial markets, chapter 1 An Overview of Finance has been expanded to include a theoretical discussion on money markets and interest rates and the yield curve. It also incorporates an overview of the key paradigms in finance.
- Part 2 of the text is now titled Fundamental Concepts in Finance – Risk and Return, and includes chapters on the fundamental principles in finance. These include chapters on the time value of money, introduction to bonds and portfolio theory and the capital asset pricing model and portfolio performance taking account of risk.
- We have amalgamated three chapters into part 3 titled Valuations. Included here are chapters on dividend policy and mergers and acquisitions.
- Part 4 discusses strategic financial decisions, including chapters on investment appraisal, also including an intuitive discussion on real options, financial forecasting and planning, the cost of capital and capital structure.
- One of the main objectives of this third edition is to categorise more strongly the main sources of finance. Part 5 is now titled Long-term Sources of Finance and has chapters on raising equity and the bond market. Part 6 has chapters on short- and medium-term sources of finance.
- In the new Part 7, Special Topics on Finance is divided into two chapters. Chapter 19 is an examination of risk management including the essentials of international financial management and derivatives and chapter 20 is a discussion on loans and mortgages.

Target audience

This book is mainly designed for undergraduate students of commerce, accounting and finance, business studies, business management, economics, banking, valuations/property, as well as for M.B.A. and M.Sc. students where finance is a subject. It is expected that students will have completed some introductory course in financial accounting and basic mathematics. However, the book does review some basic accounting concepts in Chapter 2.

In addition, practitioners will find this book very useful because it encompasses concepts and material they work with on a daily basis. Finally, students who take professional examinations will find this book essential reading material. These include:

- Institute of Chartered Accountants in Ireland
- Society of Chartered Surveyors
- Chartered Institute of Bankers
- Chartered Institute of Public Accountants
- Chartered Institute of Management Accountancy
- Chartered Association of Certified Accountants
- Diploma in Financial Management (ACCA).

Pedagogical guide

The structure of this book is such that individual lecturers can customise it to suit their own individual styles without lack of continuity. It can, for example, be customised to suit **short courses** in finance. Of course, the book is also suitable for more advanced and detailed courses. We have included a comprehensive reference and additional reading material for students who want to advance their knowledge of the areas in greater depth.

The lay-out of this book is designed principally to enhance student learning. These include:

- Each chapter begins with a set of learning objectives to be achieved by the student.
- Each chapter ends with a comprehensive executive summary.
- Many chapters incorporate newspaper vignettes, which bring real world examples into the text. These are taken mostly from *The Irish Times*, so they mainly involve Irish case studies.
- About 400 end of chapter questions. These include general review and concept questions and computational and mathematical questions and problems, which we know from our experience students like to get their teeth into.
- Each chapter contains worked answers and solutions to illustrate various themes.
- References and further additional material is provided for students who want to explore certain topics in more detail.
- A glossary of finance and investment terms is provided at the end of the book.

For the lecturer

A website which includes:
- Solutions to all end of chapter questions and problems. This forms an effective solutions manual.
- PowerPoint presentation material (in colour) covering all of the main issues presented in the text. This includes graphs, tables, etc.
- A new section containing additional questions and solutions for each of the chapters in the text.

For the student

- Access to all PowerPoint presentations.

Acknowledgments

Special thanks to Anne Russell at Dublin Institute of Technology for her input on the Irish corporate tax system.

Colleagues at Dublin Institute of Technology and Athlone Institute of Technology, in particular Enda Keegan, Frank Conway, Paul Prendergast, Bernadette Shannon, and past and present students.

Of course, writing a textbook of this nature relies heavily on capturing the time-honoured principles in finance. This would not have been possible without the inspiration of dozens of authors, academics and researchers. We have endeavoured to capture their contribution in the lists of further reading that are provided. We would like to thank, without implicating, all those scholars.

We also owe a great debt of gratitude to our many legions of students down through the years for the many perceptive observations they made on previous editions.

Finally we would like to thank all the editorial staff at Gill & Macmillan, in particular Marion O'Brien, Emma Farrell and Aoife O'Kelly, for their many comments and suggestions.

Part 1

Introduction to Financial Management

1
An Overview of Finance

CHAPTER OBJECTIVES

Having studied this chapter the student will be able to:

1. appreciate the objectives of financial management
2. understand the role of the financial manager
3. distinguish between the different forms of business organisations
4. understand the concept of shareholder value
5. recognise that ethical business behaviour will have long-term profitability gains
6. appreciate the importance of interest rates
7. understand the factors that affect the level of interest rates
8. explain the yield curve.

INTRODUCTION

Reading the quality newspapers on a day-to-day basis one notices a staggering amount of information on finance. We see news reports about companies taking over other companies, companies issuing their end-of-year financial reports, football clubs negotiating contracts with players, governments selling off utilities and supporting their currencies, and many more. All of these business stories involve finance and the amount of money involved is quite staggering. People involved in organisations must understand the basic principles of financial management.

This chapter introduces the fundamental principles of finance – recognising that finance also involves the study of investment markets. For example, if one works in the money and capital markets dealing with stocks, bonds, mutual funds, pension funds, etc., a sound understanding of financial management is necessary because investments of this nature will require an understanding of the financial performance of the firm. In addition, investment advice from stockbrokers to their clients presupposes an understanding of financial management. Furthermore, financial managers will require an understanding of how markets view companies and how security prices are set.

The basic theme running throughout this text is value creation. The emphasis is clearly on valuation and its companion, net present value. Net present value (NPV) represents the excess of market value over cost and is what creates wealth and value. If the market value of an investment is greater than its cost then value is created. Consequently, NPV is treated as the most fundamental principle in finance.

1.1 What is finance?

Finance is about managing money. You can readily appreciate this if you think of the basic issues to be considered in setting up a business. Your first consideration (after you have put your business plan together) will be to determine how much cash you will need to finance the business. This is the budgeting process, which involves assessing the firm's long-term investment projects. It is at this stage that we begin the discussion on the most fundamental principle in finance – net present value (NPV). Investment projects are undertaken when their market value is greater than their cost. This will involve an assessment of the future timing and risk of future cash flow generated by these investments. We develop these themes in detail throughout this book.

You will then need to consider where this cash will come from, i.e. will you have sufficient savings of your own to fund the operation or will you need to bring in outside investment in the form of a partnership or loans from financial institutions? This is the **capital structure decision**, which is crucial for the financial manager to get right if he/she is to maximise the return on investment to the owners.

Managing the day-to-day working capital (stock, cash, debtors and creditors) will absorb considerable time, but decisions made here will have a huge bearing on the company's profitability and liquidity. These issues are discussed in the chapters on **working capital**.

There is however one overriding consideration included in all of these decisions (budgeting, capital structure and working capital), and that is that these investments must be managed in a way that maximises the owner's wealth. We discuss this briefly next.

1.2 The role of the financial manager

While the role of the financial accountant in firms is to provide a profit and loss account (an account of the profits or losses over the recent past) and a snapshot of the fiscal position of the firm's assets and liabilities recorded in the company's balance sheet, the role of the financial manager is quite different.

Although the function of the financial accountant is an important one, the information provided is historical. However, since the value of all assets is the extent to which these assets can generate cash flows both now and in the future – companies only succeed by looking to the future. This is the role of the financial manger and it involves making decisions that affect the future of the firm. This involves assessing long-term investment projects, how these projects are funded and an assessment of the day-to-day working capital requirements. The primary role of the financial manger is to make these investments while adding value (wealth) to shareholders.

1.3 Maximising shareholder value

Emanating from the US in the 1990s and increasingly taking a foothold in Europe is the concept of value creation. Shareholders are the owners of corporations. They elect directors who in turn appoint managers to run the company. It seems reasonable that shareholders will want managers to manage the company in such a way as to maximise shareholders' wealth. The wealth of shareholders is the number of shares they hold multiplied by the market price of the share. Therefore shareholder value maximisation means maximising the price of the company's shares. It is not surprising therefore that a system of compensation packages which remunerate managers and employees based on value creation has developed. We will return to this concept and look at how we can best calculate value added in later chapters.

Nevertheless, the idea that maximising shareholder value should be the sole consideration in business seems insidious. Surely there are other and perhaps more important goals of business, such as the maximisation of employee welfare, and the reduction of pollution. Proponents of value creation will insist that maximising share price benefits everybody in society and society itself.[1]

Share ownership is increasing because of the proliferation of growth in pension funds, life insurance companies and unit-linked funds. This is why, particularly in the US, pension funds and mutual fund managers are seeking out companies that are adopting shareholder value added financial systems. With the advent of the internet and e-commerce more and more individuals are trading in stocks and shares online, sometimes for very short periods such as a day (day trading). Around the world share ownership is increasing because of government commitment to the privatisation of public utilities. Therefore, because more and more people are now becoming shareholders, maximising share price can increase the wealth of many more people.

1.4 What maximises share price?

The value of a share, indeed the value of any financial asset, depends on the ability of a company to generate cash flows both now and in the future. In finance, 'cash is king'. Cash is what is used by companies to invest in value-creating projects and to pay dividends.

Shareholder value is maximised by generating cash flow and not necessarily by maximising profits. The remuneration package of company executives will depend on how successful they are at maximising shareholder value. **Profit maximisation should not necessarily be a goal of financial management**. For example, developing a new product may involve a lot of time, money, risk and effort. It will reduce short-term profitability. However, if the future cash flows of the project are more than enough to offset the initial capital outlay, then shareholder wealth will increase. Concentrating on short-term profitability may destroy shareholder value.

The **timing** of cash flows is also important in enhancing shareholder value. Cash received sooner is more valuable because it can be reinvested in the company to generate more cash or paid to shareholders as dividends.[2] Finally, investors will pay more for shares that are less risky. Therefore reducing the **riskiness of the expected cash flows** can enhance share price (shareholder wealth).

To summarise, maximising shareholder wealth means maximising share price. The price (or value) of a share depends on:

1. the ability of the company (i.e. share) to generate cash flow
2. the timing of these cash flows
3. the riskiness of these cash flows.

Therefore to maximise share price (i.e. to maximise shareholder value) requires:

1. generating as much cash flow as possible
2. getting these cash flows into the company as quickly as possible and
3. doing all this while minimising risk.

1.5 What doesn't maximise share price?

Shareholders appoint directors who in turn appoint managers. Managers act as agents for owners. Managers are assumed to make decisions that enhance shareholder value. Sometimes, however, managers make decisions that suit themselves at the expense of shareholders. Agency theory deals with the conflict of interest between managers and their shareholders, and between shareholders and creditors. Agents work on behalf of others. The people agents represent are called principals. For example senior management and the board of directors of the Smurfit Group act as agents for their shareholders or principals. The directors and management have a legal and ethical responsibility to enhance their shareholders' interests, i.e. shareholder value. An agency cost is any benefit a manager receives from a company that is not part of the manager's remuneration package and which does not enhance shareholder value. For example agency costs may include golf in the afternoon, fancy offices and the use of luxurious company cars where smaller, less expensive ones would do, the use of company helicopters and perhaps jets (see Box 1.1).

Another example of an agency cost is managers deciding not to embark on projects that are risky, even though such projects may be potentially lucrative if they pay off. Managers will have a lot more to lose (they may lose their jobs) than individual shareholders who may have only a small proportion of their capital tied up in the company. Agency costs also include the expenditure incurred by shareholders designed to investigate and control managerial actions, such as audit costs on internal control. In addition, agency costs involve the appointment of outside specialists to the board of directors in order to limit and control the actions of managers. Controlling agency costs is difficult, particularly for large companies where individual shareholders will not have the power to control managers who are not acting in the best interests of their shareholders. There are a number of ways that agency costs can be reduced:

1. One way to reduce agency costs is the threat of takeovers. A **takeover** is likely to replace inefficient and wasteful managers. If managers are only interested in **lining their own pockets** at the expense of shareholders, the threat of a takeover is likely to ensure that such managers will be replaced after the takeover.
2. **Stock options** may be a means of synchronising the interests of managers with those of shareholders. Stock options are increasingly becoming a part of employee and management remuneration packages. Managers are more likely to act in the interest of shareholder wealth maximisation if they are themselves significant shareholders.
3. Finally, **pension fund managers** who control large blocks of shares in companies can take action to deal with the agency problem:

(a) Action against managers of companies (in the form of advice, or the imposition of outside directors on the board of management) if their actions are in conflict with shareholders' interests. This is the best course of action for fund managers to take.

(b) They could exit the market by selling their shares in the company. However, because they hold such large portfolios of shares, selling those shares would depress the market price.

Box 1.1 Top Irish executives take home world-class salaries

Ireland's publicly quoted companies might be small by international standards but their top executives take home salaries and bonuses on a par with their global peers, according to a survey just published.

A new report from Hewitt Associates shows that the directors of Ireland's quoted companies achieved an average 12 per cent rise in their basic pay last year, and a 'staggering' 30 per cent increase when bonuses and other benefits are included.

By comparison, the average rate of increase on fixed salaries for executives in the US was about 4 per cent, while the European figures ranged from 3.5 per cent to 7.5 per cent depending on the country.

The figures were compiled up to May 2008 and are sure to stir debate from shareholder groups and pension funds about the level of pay increases awarded to directors here.

The average remuneration for the highest paid director – usually the chief executive – was €1.3 million, according to Hewitt's analysis.

Hewitt avoided listing out the individual payments made to all directors of Irish plcs but it said the average total remuneration paid to directors ranged from €496,000 for the lower quartile of the 69 companies surveyed to €2 million for the upper quartile.

This reflects the different size of the companies, according to Hewitt.

Hewitt director Rachael Ingle said the pay increases were high by international standards but added that they were likely to moderate significantly this year given the economic downturn.

'Our expectation would be that it will come down again to 5 or 6 per cent for fixed pay this year,' she said. 'There's going to be significant pressure in the current economic climate.'

Hewitt found that about 40 per cent of a director's pay is now made up of bonuses and performance-related payments.

This percentage is about 50 per cent for the larger cap companies and about 15 per cent for the market tiddlers.

Hewitt's research shows that more and more Irish public companies are now opting for long-term incentive plans for their executives instead of share option schemes.

About 35 per cent of the companies now use LTIPs to reward directors compared with 20 per cent in 2006.

The LTIPs generally involve the issuing of free shares if certain targets are met, while share options involves granting stock at an attractive price which vests at a date in the future.

→

The decline of stock market valuations over the past couple of years has resulted in many stock options now being under water, and therefore less attractive as a motivational tool for executives.

A change in accounting standards in recent years also forced companies to calculate the cost of the share options and list that figure in their accounts.

'Hewitt believes LTIPs are a better mechanism for reward,' Ingle said.

'Not only are they more cost effective but they also offer more value to shareholders concerned about dilution of shares.

'They more accurately reflect business performance outside market trends, offering more positive returns for the employee. We expect to see a greater shift towards LTIPs over the next few years.'

Aer Lingus chief executive Dermot Mannion has benefited from an LTIP scheme and executives at IAWS have been offered a 10-year scheme following its merger with Swiss food group Hiestand.

While CEOs and other executive directors achieved double-digit increases in their salaries, Hewitt's study found that non-executive directors got an average rise of 6 per cent while executive chairman were given an average 5 per cent boost in fees.

More than 25 per cent of Dublin listed companies granted share options to non-executive directors, a practice that is frowned upon in the UK as being against corporate governance best practice.

Ingle said this probably reflected a US influence at some of the companies listed here, given that the practice is more common across the Atlantic.

'In the US it's standard practice so maybe some of the Irish companies are taking their influence from there and some are taking it from the UK, where it's not seen as good practice,' she said. 'It's a mix of influences at play.'

Hewitt's survey illustrates the pecking order among executive directors. Finance directors (FD) generally get about two-thirds of the pay awarded to the CEO with the next layer of director getting about 60 per cent.

'The chief operating officer seems to be coming more to the fore than in the past and a lot of companies seem to be equalising their [COOS] pay with the FD, who traditionally would have been considered the number two,' she said.

'In the US, the culture is very different. The CEO is the emperor and the difference could be three to five times that of the next best paid director.'

According to Ingle, Irish directors are paid more than their equivalents in the UK, when the relative size of the company is taken into account.

'They're bigger fish in a smaller pond here,' Mr Ingle said. 'It's a smaller market with a smaller pool of people so Irish companies have to pay more to get the right people.'

Called the *Report on Irish Directors' Remuneration 2008*, the study looked at the pay of directors at all 69 Irish listed companies, including those on the IEX junior market.

The report found that earnings per share is no longer the only means used to measure performance.

Return on capital employed and other measures are now being used by public companies here.

The Irish Times, 22 August 2008

Figure 1.1 illustrates the major factors affecting share prices. These are broadly divided into **internal** and **external** factors, and the impact of the business/economic environment.

Figure 1.1 Major factors affecting share value

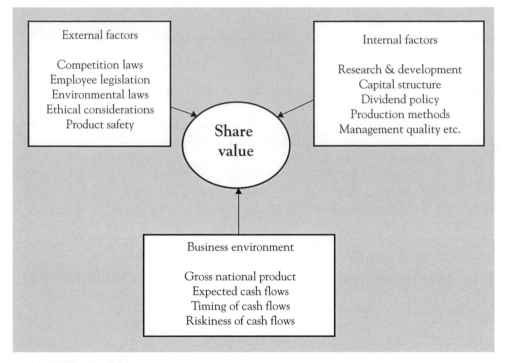

1.6 Summary of key paradigms

1.6.1. Risk v return

We live in a risky world. By crossing the road we run the risk of being knocked down by a car, a bus or a cyclist. If we want to avoid any chance of being run over by traffic we could stay indoors all our lives. Doing this increases the risk of dying younger because of a lack of exercise. Risk is the chance that some unfavourable event will occur. The old saying 'A bird in the hand is worth two in the bush' goes to the heart of understanding human nature. We all prefer to have things now rather than later. To sacrifice consumption today we will require a greater amount of consumption in the future. You will need more in the future if you are to delay current consumption. The extra consumption demanded is the real rate of interest. This real rate of interest excludes the effects of inflation. Risk-averse investors tend to avoid additional risk unless they are compensated for taking on the additional risk. This is the risk–return relationship. To get a return greater than the real rate of return, an investor will incur more risk. No investor would buy a risky security if they were not compensated for the risk. This is why asset returns must fluctuate with risk. Because many securities have more than the risk-free amount of risk, the only way that these securities can be sold is to offer a higher amount of interest.

1.6.2 The time value of money

Money received today is worth more than money received in the future. Which would you prefer: €100 today or €100 in twelve months' time? Not a difficult decision to make. The value of an asset is the present value of the cash flows that asset generates both now and in the future. An investment is worthwhile if the present value of these cash flows is greater than the initial cost of the investment.

1.6.3 Asymmetric information

In business, if everybody knows the same thing then both investors and managers have the same information. This is called **symmetric information**. It assumes that investors and insiders have the same information. However, this may not be the case. Insiders (managers) will often have better information than that which outsiders (investors) have. This is called **asymmetric information**. An insurance agent, for example, who sells car insurance may not know the extent to which the car owner will take the necessary steps to protect his car against theft. It is also reasonable to assume that the insiders (managers) of an organisation will have different information about the future of the firm than outsiders. This will have important implications for the capital structure of the firm – the proportion of debt and equity in the capital structure. To illustrate the point, consider two firms. Firm A has a new investment opportunity that will increase the value of the firm. Firm A managers believe that this new investment opportunity will generate cash flows, the present value of which will be greater than the cost. Hence a positive NPV project. To fund this new investment opportunity Firm A will need to raise new capital. How should it raise this capital? Suppose it funds the new investment by selling shares. When the profits from this investment materialise the new investors will share in the wealth creation. If the firm had not issued new stock the original shareholders and managers would get to keep all of the profits created themselves. Therefore, asymmetric information explains why firms with positive future prospects should avoid selling shares and instead fund investments with debt capital or internal sources of funds. So, a company that has financing options and decides to issue debt to fund an investment sends a signal to the market that its prospects are good and its stock price will rise.

1.7 Ethics in business

Ethical issues challenge the function of business and financial management. These include the civil rights of employees and consumers, environmental pollution concerns, workplace health and safety issues, ethical responsibilities of management towards shareholders, fair employment opportunities, product safety, ethical advertising standards, bribery and corruption and insider dealing.

There is a fundamental shift throughout the world to have big business incorporate ethical issues in their investment policies. A move in Britain to have pension fund trustees look beyond a simple narrow financial focus will have repercussions in Ireland (see Box 1.2).

Box 1.2 Ethics takes centre stage in pension market

The business and financial world has recently become the target for campaigners, sometimes violent, who do not like what it does with its power and money.

Last year witnessed increased opposition to big business at a number of points throughout the world, including the well-organised demonstrations at the World Trade Organisation in Seattle as well as more violent bomb threats against investors in certain companies.

While these activists hit the headlines, a much more fundamental and peaceful shift is underway behind the scenes particularly in Britain. We in Ireland would do well to take notice of emerging developments.

From 3 July this year British pension fund trustees will have to move beyond their traditional, narrow financial focus and inform their members about the ethics that lie behind their investment policies.

The significance of this development should not be underestimated. Already the largest fund management groups are organising to monitor companies they invest in on issues ranging from energy use to labour conditions in their factories. It has been predicted that stg £100 billion of pension fund money will soon be invested according to some kind of ethical criteria.

Most major consulting actuary firms have already set up teams to look at socially responsible investment (SRI).

Also, all the major institutions are now trying to decide how to provide these services to their customers.

The impetus for this dramatic development came originally from local authorities and others concerned about where their members' savings were going. For years, such pension trustees were reading about whether they were legally allowed to discriminate between the company investments on anything other than financial grounds. The traditional view was that trustees' fiduciary duties prevented them from worrying about what the companies were doing, or how they were doing it.

The only issue to guide investment decisions was supposedly the duty to maximise financial returns for members.

During the 1990s this dictum was diluted. While trustees still had to look after members' money as best they could, as long as financial returns were not threatened they could discriminate on social and environmental grounds.

This approach mirrored the traditional ethical investment stance avoiding activities such as arms, tobacco and alcohol manufacturing, and gambling.

But the new pensions regulation moves the argument on well beyond that exclusionary approach to what has become known as 'engagement'.

Following an amendment to the 1995 British Pensions Act, trustees must declare, in their annual statement of investment principles: 'The extent (if at all) to which social, environmental or ethical considerations are taken into account in the selection, the extent and realisation of investments; and their policy (if any) directing the exercise of rights (including voting rights) attaching to investments.'

Ministers have made it clear that this is not intended to drive investments away from unpopular sectors. Instead it is based on two notions: the right of pension scheme

⟶

members to know where their money is being invested; and the view that responsible businesses will be more profitable in the long term. This latter view is reflected in the ethical statement which has been drawn up by Hermes, the investment manager in charge of BT's stg £29 billion fund which is the largest in Britain and the first leading company to respond to the new regulation.

BT's fund managers will be required to consider that 'the company run in the long-term interests of its shareholders will need to manage effectively relationships with employees, suppliers and customers, to behave ethically and to have regard for the environment and society as a whole'.

This injunction is similar to the approach to be taken by the third largest British fund, the University Superannuation Scheme.

The US finally caved in last December after a long campaign by its lecturer members, and agreed to 'engage' companies about their non-financial policies and performance.

Other funds would follow suit over the next few months, but it will be some time after 3 July this year before the full impact on the business world is felt.

It is expected that trustees are taking the view that they need to respond positively to this development. They will need to because they will be targeted by dissatisfied members if they stick to the position that ethics have no place in fund management. And in the nervous world of pensions, there is also likely to be concern in some trustees' minds about their legal liability if members can be shown in a few years' time that funds which do take ethics seriously have performed better.

As a result, chief executives and finance directors are going to find themselves facing questions about their carbon dioxide emissions and human rights policies – not from campaigners whose job it is to go on about these things, but from pension fund managers.

For years companies have complained that market pressure for short-term results prevented them from taking environmental and social issues more seriously. Chief executives have frequently promised that they would be able to improve their green performance if only analysts and fund managers understood the issues and the importance of addressing subjects such as global warming or Third World labour conditions.

This argument will no longer apply. There might be some concerns regarding costs in that adding new dimensions to investment managers' research responsibilities will clearly add to costs at a time when the industry is seeking to pare expenses in pursuit of better returns for funds.

However it is possible to track indices which take account of ethical issues. And since the end of last year, investors have been able to follow the Dow Jones Sustainability Index, comprising international companies leading the field in pursuit of sustainable development. Also, while remembering that the new regulation is supposed to be about engagement, fund managers should continue to raise social and environmental issues in routine company meetings along with more mainstream issues such as investment, cost-cutting and dividend policy.

The new pensions regulation in Britain will make trustees take social and environmental issues seriously. This is clearly a welcome development in a world that is becoming increasingly conscious of the environment.

$\longrightarrow$

> While there are a number of smaller-scale funds operating within Ireland that could be described as socially and environmentally responsible, the fact is we have not yet become alive to the demands and the opportunities such a departure will present. A new challenge has now been posed to fund managers and indeed government in Ireland to keep abreast of these exciting initiatives.
>
> Roger Acton (head of ACCA Ireland), *Sunday Business Post*, 7 May 2000

There have been many examples of unethical business behaviour. Many of these have involved the collusion of the world of politics and business. In the late 1990s the Irish Government set up several inquiries to investigate unethical practices. These included how some of Ireland's financial institutions were involved in successful attempts to allow some investors to avoid paying deposit interest retention tax (the so called DIRT Inquiry presided over by the Dáil's Public Accounts Committee). (See Box 1.3.)

Box 1.3 Learning to recognise the law and ethics divide

Always tell the truth. That way you don't have to remember anything, declared Mark Twain.

The often contradictory memories of events recounted to the different tribunals and inquiries in Ireland suggest some witnesses have failed to take Mark Twain's advice.

An interesting example is the inquiry by the Dáil Committee of Public Accounts into DIRT. Did or did not AIB Bank have a tacit agreement with the Revenue to ignore a tax liability of up to €127.1 million? As the cat and mouse game between politicians, bankers, Revenue and barristers is played out, it is obvious the issue is being treated primarily as one of legal compliance, rather than of value systems and integrity.

Even if AIB had an amnesty from the Revenue, does that excuse its behaviour and attitude? The crux is that AIB, indeed all the banks with bogus foreign accounts, aided and abetted tax evaders. With or without Revenue agreement, their behaviour could be deemed unethical. This is the core issue, even if there is room for argument about personal responsibility of those involved.

The explanations – indeed justifications – of the behaviour of the banks and their bogus account holders typify the rationalisations often heard when unethical choices have been made: for example, 'everybody else does it' or 'if we don't do it, someone else will'. Defence of unethical behaviour on the basis of its frequent occurrence or that you will lose out to a competitor is not acceptable ethical reasoning.

'It doesn't really hurt anyone' is another justification. Tax evasion, social welfare fraud and false compensation claims fall into this category. This is because the victims of these transgressions are usually faceless, for example Dublin Corporation or insurance companies.

'The system is unfair' – tax evasion in the 1980s has been justified by way of the 'crucifying' tax rates prevailing at the time. Moreover, those who facilitated bogus foreign accounts to evade taxes have actually defended this practice on the basis that there would have been a flight of capital out of the State had they not acted as they did.

⟶

'We'll wait until the lawyers tell us it's wrong' – the philosophy of those appearing before the different inquiries with their teams of legal advisers. This attempts to equate law with ethics, not always a perfect match. There are many situations where behaviour is perfectly legal but totally unethical, for example, when banks forgive large debts or influential debtors under political pressure but relentlessly pursue smaller less powerful debtors, the moral reasoning used is at a low level.

In fact, an element considered to influence ethical judgment and action is the maturity in moral reasoning attained by the individual. Lawrence Kohlberg, an American psychologist, has devised a theoretical framework that describes development in moral reasoning.

Kohlberg's theory consists of six stages of moral reasoning. The stages are sequential and invariable in their order.

At the first two stages, the person accepts good/bad or right/wrong as being externally imposed by some authority figure. In childhood, it is the parents, in adulthood, it may be the boss. At the first stage, the person 'has a punishment and obedience orientation' and does what is expected by the authority figure to avoid punishment. In business life, this childish orientation is paralleled by the mentality that nothing is wrong if you can get away with it and avoid punishment.

At the second stage, 'instrumental purpose and exchange', the individual has stepped outside him/herself to an awareness that others too have needs. In fact, the person realises that s/he can trade in the satisfaction of these needs. For instance, an employee can be encouraged to sell high margin but unsuitable products to a vulnerable class of customers. The seller might make a high rate of commission. At this development stage, the incentive of the remuneration is the main consideration of employee and employer.

At the third and fourth stages, the individual takes up group expectations as standards of moral behaviour. Conformity to the norms of one's family, or social, professional or ethnic/national groups is given as the reason for choosing one behaviour over another.

At stage three, 'good' behaviour is used to gain approval from those to whom one has an emotional or social dependency relationship. This involves the mutual maintenance of trust, loyalty, respect and gratitude to consolidate such relationships. At stage three reasoning, an employee may mis-sell products under the direction of a manager in order to retain good working relationships with the superior, and with peers engaged in the same practice for the same reasons. Of course, these practices might be disapproved of by those outside the workplace, creating a conflict of moral judgment.

In stage four, the basis of approved behaviour moves to obligations to society and the common good. The rationale for moral behaviour is to keep the institution going, to avoid a break-down in the system 'if everyone did it'. Those who have reached this stage might refuse to mis-sell products because it could harm consumers and thereby, society.

The fifth and sixth stages involve 'principled thinking', when people see beyond law for the sake of law and order, or social norms. Instead, principles guide moral behaviour. At stage five, the emphasis is still on rules and laws, but these should protect people's rights. So, an employee refusing to mis-sell products at this point would justify the refusal on the grounds that it violates the rights of customers to know the full truth.

→

Stage six thinking appeals to universal ethical principles. These tend to be abstract, dealing with justice, equality of human rights, respect for the dignity of human beings and the concept that human beings are ends in themselves, not instruments. At this stage, the person will have the insight to grasp complexity, the existence of conflicting principles, and the difficulty of resolving them.

For example companies setting up in countries where child labour and corruption are rampant have a conflict between providing indirect support for regimes which violate human rights and freedoms, and providing a livelihood, food and shelter for the citizens of those regimes.

According to Kohlberg's research, fewer than 20% of the population achieved principled thinking: most stop at stage five.

Kohlberg considers the higher stages morally preferable to lower ones. Of course, a high moral reasoning level does not guarantee moral conduct, since other factors, such as personality and organisational culture, influence behaviour. But research studies have found a moderate relationship between lower moral reasoning stages and behaviour, ranging from delinquency and fraud, to cheating at exams.

Moral reasoning stages are measurable through psychometric tests, although they are rarely used as an assessment instrument in Ireland. Had they been used, who knows? The Irish taxpayer might have been deprived of the hours of riveting entertainment showing at all the tribunals and inquiries.

Dr Eleanor O'Higgins (UCD), *The Irish Times*, 1 November 1999

At the time of writing, there is an ongoing tribunal of inquiry into payments made to politicians in the planning process. Elected county councillors have the power to zone designated lands for commercial and residential development.

While these have all been high-profile cases, companies and management must be made to understand that **ethical business behaviour can have long-term profitability gains.** It will avoid the possibility of hefty legal expenses, gain more business from customers who support ethical business policies, and it will attract high-calibre employees.

1.8 Forms of business organisation

There are three main legal forms of business organisation: sole proprietorship, partnerships and limited liability companies.

1.8.1 Sole trader

Sole proprietorship is the most prevalent form of business organisation in Ireland and around the world. This is a business formed and owned by one individual. The general features of sole proprietorship are:

- It is independent, easily and inexpensively formed.
- It avoids corporation tax and profits are taxed at the rate of personal income tax.
- There are no requirements under the Companies Act for disclosure to the public of its accounts.

- It has the limitations that it doesn't have access to large sums of capital and has unlimited liability.
- The life of a sole proprietorship is legally limited to the life of the founder.

1.8.2 Partnership

A partnership exists whenever two to twenty persons carry on a business with the view of making a profit. It has the following characteristics:

- Partnerships can be formal when formed under a written deed of partnership, or informal oral agreements.
- It can easily be formed and is relatively inexpensive.
- The liability of the partners is unlimited.
- It can be in two forms: (a) **general partnership** where each partner contributes an agreed amount, and (b) **limited partnership** where some of the partners are liable for all the debts of the firm and other partner(s) are liable only for their financial contribution to the firm.
- General partnerships can be dissolved after a fixed term or after the completion of a specific venture for which the partnership was set up in the first place, the bankruptcy or death of a partner, legally on the grounds of insanity, misconduct of a partner, or viability of the business. Limited partnerships cannot be dissolved on the death, bankruptcy or lunacy of a limited partner.
- Profits are taxed at the appropriate income tax rate.

1.8.3 Limited liability company or the corporation

A limited liability company is a legal entity separate from its owners. The formation of a limited liability company takes the following form:

- The articles of association: The rules governing the organisation are set out by the owners in a contract known as the articles of association. These govern the internal workings of the company. They set out the relative rights and duties of the management of the company and its shareholders. The main elements of the articles of association include:
  (a) the authorised share capital of the company and its division into shares
  (b) the voting rights of these shares
  (c) powers of directors
  (d) meeting of the shareholders and procedures at such meetings.
- Memorandum of association: The document governing the relationship between the company and others is set out in the memorandum of association. The main contents of the memorandum are:
  (a) the name of the company. If the company is a public company, the words **public limited company (plc)** should be included in the name. If it is a private company the word **Limited** or **Ltd** should be included.
  (b) the main areas of activity in which the group intends to operate

(c)   the authorised or nominal share of capital

(d)   a statement that the liability of the members is limited.

These documents, together with a list of the directors, are sent to the registrar of companies, and if everything is in order, he/she will issue a certificate of incorporation.

The fact that the corporation is a separate legal entity (from its owners) means that it can have unlimited life and will continue after the life of its owners. Transferability of ownership is easier than in a partnership or a sole proprietorship because the ownership of a limited liability company can be divided into a number of shares which are more easily transferred. Easier transferability of shares improves liquidity, which means that it is easier to convert shares (assets) into cash. The liability of a limited liability company is, as the name suggests, limited. The risk borne by the investors of a corporation is limited, which means that investors cannot lose more than the amount they invested when buying the shares. The ability of a corporation to attract capital is greater than that of a partnership or a sole trader. Consequently, growth opportunities for corporations are better.

1.9 Financial markets

A principal role of the financial manger is to raise funds to finance the firm's investments. While much of these funds can be sourced internally from retained profits, most companies will find it necessary to seek external capital. Knowledge of financial markets is therefore necessary.

The financial system consists of markets and institutions that match buyers of funds (investors) and sellers of funds (savers). For the economy as a whole, savings and investments are key to long-term economic prosperity. An economy that saves a large slice of its GDP has more funds available for investment and this raises the country's capital and productivity.

Financial markets are the institutions where those who have surplus funds (savings) can supply these funds to others who have a deficit (borrowers). There are two types of financial market – capital markets and money markets.

1.9.1 Capital markets

When companies and governments need to raise money for long periods of time (greater than a year) they do so in the capital markets.

The two capital markets that are most relevant are the bond market and the stock market.

The Bond Market

A company can fund its investments with two types of capital – **debt capital** and **equity capital**. When it wants to raise debt capital it borrows money from the public by issuing bonds. A bond is an IOU or a certificate of indebtedness. This certificate (also known as a **security**) will specify the terms and conditions of the loan and all obligations of the borrower. These include the time in which the loan will be repaid (date of maturity), the periodic rate of interest to be paid and the subsequent repayment of the principal or the amount borrowed. This bond can be held by the buyer until the maturity date or sold on the bond market at some time before the date of maturity – this is the liquidity function of the financial system. These bonds or securities have value because the owner or bearer has the right to be paid the amount that is specified on the certificate. Therefore a bearer has the right to sell the security to another party for cash. The new owner could also trade or sell the security to someone else.

There are thousands of different types of bond traded in the market. When corporations, governments and local authorities need money for investment (e.g. to build factories, roads, schools, hospitals, etc.) they will usually sell bonds.

Characteristics of bonds:
1. The maturity date of the bond (when the principal has to be paid) can be short, a few months, or as long as 30 years. The interest rate on a bond depends on the date to maturity. Long-term bonds are riskier because the holders have to wait longer for payment. To compensate for this higher risk, long-term bonds usually pay higher interest rates.
2. There is the possibility that bond holders may fail to pay the interest (and/or principal) on the debt. This is the bond's credit risk. If the probability of default is high, those who buy bonds will seek higher interest payments to compensate for this higher risk. It's usually agreed that governments don't 'go broke', therefore they don't default and therefore have low credit risk with commensurate interest. However, this is not always the case and governments can go broke as was the case with Russia in 1999 (see Box 1.4). Note that the interest rate paid on corporate bonds will vary with the risk attached to that bond. Rating agencies assess the creditworthiness of bonds and apply a rating. For bonds that have very high credit ratings and little chance of default a rating of AAA is assigned. Other bonds may be rated AA, A or BBB. Bonds that are rated below BBB are referred to as **junk bonds** because they are not investment grade and are too risky. Features that investors like about bonds will tend to lower the interest rate and features that investors don't like will tend to raise interest rates.

Box 1.4 Open your eyes to the risks

Novice investors have been left penniless by the spectacular collapse of the International Securities Trading Corporation (ISTC) a high-flying finance company that fell to earth in the global credit crunch.

They all invested at least €50,000 each in two ISTC bonds managed by Friends First, believing their capital was guaranteed.

Two sisters – one 55, the other 70 – put their life savings of €300,000 into the ISTC creative Step UP bond last week, including a substantial lump sum that the older woman took from her pension fund when she retired.

The bonds are now worthless, however, making ISTC the biggest disaster in Irish investment history. ISTC raised €165m from investors in the largest share placement ever by a private Irish company. ISTC attracted money from wealthy businessmen as well as from 125 individuals who invested €43m through the Friends First bonds.

→

ISTC used the cash to raise debt finance to lend to banks and other financial institutions that needed to borrow money – the same market that sparked the crisis at Northern Rock last September.

As the crisis spread throughout the global financial system, however, the value of ISTC's investments plummeted, forcing a fire sale of the company. Under the deal, investors in Friends First bonds will get nothing.

In the wake of the ISTC disaster many investors have concerns about how secure their assets are.

Aren't bonds a safe bet?

Bonds are often seen as a safe bet between low-yielding deposits and risky equities. They pay fixed returns – useful for those seeking a steady income – and their values do not fluctuate as much as stocks and shares.

Investors, though, take too much for granted. Bonds issued by companies – or banks in the case of ISTC – are the riskiest. Those issued by governments are safer, but not entirely risk-free.

Governments have been known to default on their debts as happened in Russia in 1998. Bonds can also lose their value when interest rates are rising. Investors should examine the credit rating of the bonds they are buying, ensuring they are of investment grade. People can lose money on bonds. They are traded in the same way as equities, so their values can go up and down. There's also the risk of default.

www.timesonline.ie/money, *The Sunday Times*, 9 March 2008, extract by Niall Brady

The Stock Market

Another way for companies to raise money for their investments is through the stock market or **equity finance**. A company's stock represents ownership of the company and is therefore a claim on the cash flows generated by the company. While the owner of the stock is a part owner, the holder of a bond is a creditor. As part owner the stock holder participates in the success of the company, whereas the bond holder is just paid the interest on their loan. If the company gets into trouble the interest on debt is fixed and must be paid before shareholders get anything. Because stocks are higher risk the return on stocks must be higher than interest paid on bonds.

When corporations raise new equity they do so by selling stock on the **primary market**. The corporation receives the funds from the sale. **Secondary markets** are markets where existing securities are traded among investors. An investor who decides to sell 1,000 shares in Intel, for example, will do so on the secondary market.

Security exchanges are organisations that facilitate the trade of stocks and bonds among investors. Companies may wish to list their shares or bonds on an organised exchange such as the Dublin Stock Exchange, the London Stock Exchange or the New York Stock Exchange so that they can be traded. In contrast to the organised exchanges that have physical locations, the over-the-counter (**OTC**) market has no physical location and trading in securities is conducted electronically. The OTC is a network of dealers worldwide that hold an inventory of securities for sale. If you wanted to buy a security you would shop around with dealers who hold the security. The biggest and most significant OTC market is the NASDAQ.

It's important here to distinguish between financial markets and financial institutions. **Financial markets** are organisations that facilitate the trade of securities. **Financial institutions** are organisations that channel funds from savers to borrowers.

1.9.2 Money markets

Cash flows in companies, governments and other organisations seldom occur at the same time. Cash flowing in seldom occurs at the same time as cash flowing out. Companies' cash inflows may be greater than their cash outflows, in which case they will have surplus cash. At other times cash outflows may be greater than cash inflows and cash deficits occur. Similarly, government tax revenues typically occur near the end of the fiscal year, while government expenditure occurs all year round. In this case governments will need to raise cash in the short term and repay it when tax receipts are collected. To solve these problems of cash flows occurring at different times, money markets have developed. Raising money for short-term purposes (maturities of one year or less) is conducted in the money markets. Remember, holding excess cash has an opportunity cost in terms of lost interest income. Those who will need to buy money market securities include governments, companies and financial institutions. Most transactions conducted in the money markets are by telephone and computers.

The term **money market** is a misnomer because money is not traded. Money market securities are very liquid and can be sold for cash quickly. Hence the term money markets. Buyers of securities in money markets will only buy from well-established, large and reputable issuers. If a company had excess cash and wanted to sell that excess cash to another company for a few days, it simply would not have time to check out the reputation and credit risk of the issuer. Because it is only the large and reputable issuers in the market, the risk involved in money market transactions is low.

Examples of some money market instruments follow:

Commercial Paper: Commercial paper is a short-term IOU. It is only issued by large corporations with strong credit ratings and issued to other large firms, pension funds, and to banks. Most commercial paper matures within 40 days and usually doesn't pay interest – they are issued at a discount and the return comes in the way of an increase in price.

Treasury Bills: to refinance previously issued government securities that come due each week, governments issue treasury bills or **T-bills**. This is the most liquid debt security issued by governments. T-bills will have maturity dates of 12 months or less. The risk of default is zero because governments can simply print more if they run out of cash. In addition, because of the short-tem nature of T-bills inflation risk is low. For these reasons, T-bills are close to being risk free and consequently the yield from T-bills is low. T-bills are sold at a discount which means that they do not pay interest. They are sold for less than they are worth at maturity.

Inter-bank lending: By law, commercial banks are required to keep a proportion of their assets in cash form. The reason for this is to maintain confidence in the banking system. Banks with excess cash over their required level can lend this excess cash to other banks whose cash is below the required level, usually for a period of 1 day. Banks could borrow from the central banks but they may not want to alert the central banks to any liquidity problems. The interest rate in this market is closely watched because it will influence the central banks' money supply. This is done indirectly by the central banks buying or selling government securities.

Repurchase Agreements: Repurchase agreements (**repos**) operate when a firm sells securities with an agreement to buy that same security back at some specified future date. Repos are short term, with maturities between 3 and 15 days. Long-term repos are available with maturities up to six months. Holders of government securities usually participate in this market. This essentially makes the repo a collateralised loan and therefore low risk. Any coupons paid on repos during the period of time the repo buyer owns the security are paid to the seller.

Repurchase agreements are sometimes used by central banks to release money into the banking system.

Bankers' Acceptances: This is an order to the bank by the drawer to pay a specified person (the bearer) a specified amount at a given date. In this sense it is like a post-dated cheque. For example, suppose a company wanted to buy some machinery from Hong Kong. The Hong Kong firm might not want to ship the machinery without being paid because it might not know enough about the UK firm. For the same reasons the UK firm is reluctant to send money to Hong Kong in advance of receiving the machinery. By issuing a bankers' acceptance this stand-off can be resolved because the bankers' acceptance is a promise to pay the shipper if any problems occur.

This characteristic makes bankers' acceptances a money market instrument. Bank acceptances sell at a discount to their face value. Bankers acceptances rates are the rates in which they trade.

1.9.3 Financial asset markets and real asset markets.

So far we have looked at the principle financial markets – capital markets and money markets. Real asset markets or physical (tangible) asset markets deal with real assets such as automobiles and real estate. Financial assets are pieces of paper that allow the owners of these financial assets to a contractual claim on the underlying real assets. For example, if you own a Smurfit corporate bond (or share) this gives you a claim on the cash flows generated by Smurfit's real assets. Mortgage markets deal with loans that are secured on real estate. Mortgages are a financial asset like bonds and shares.

As a general point, financial markets need to be efficient. An efficient transfer system from those who are net savers to those who need to access money is essential for any market economy. If construction companies and governments did not have access to money there would be no houses built. If transportation companies did not have access to financial markets there would be no public transport. In short, efficient economies need efficient financial markets.

1.10 Interest rates

When buyers and sellers of money come together in the money markets the price of money is determined. This is the interest rate or the rental price of money.

The interest rate or the price of money is determined by many factors that determine the supply of money and the demand for money. If the supply of money is restricted, the price of money rises, other things being equal. However, what this analysis does not tell us is why individual firms will pay different interest rates on their borrowed funds. What are the specific factors that determine the interest rate paid by particular firms?

The interest rate prevailing at any particular time is the **nominal interest rate**. This nominal rate is comprised of several components. These are:

1.10.1 The Real Rate of Interest

By lending money the lender postpones opportunities to spend that money during the period it is loaned. Investment opportunities for the lenders during this loan period are lost. The compensation paid by the borrower to the lender for this lost opportunity is the real rate of interest or the basic rate of return required to satisfy the lender for this lost opportunity.

Additions to this real rate of interest are called **premiums**. Some of the major premiums are:

1. **A premium for inflation.** The effect of rising prices is that it reduces the purchasing power of the money in your pocket. For this reason money received in the future is less valuable than money in your hand. Because of inflation the money that lenders receive when their loan is repaid will not purchase as much as when the loan was made. If lenders anticipate inflation they will demand additional returns (interest) to compensate for this additional risk. Note that the inflation premium will be the average *expected* rate of inflation during the life of the security.

   The real rate of interest plus the inflation risk premium is the nominal risk-free rate.

$$\text{real interest rate} + \text{inflation risk premium} = \text{nominal risk-free rate}$$

Example

An investor buys a €1,000 short-term government bond with a maturity of one year and is paid 6 per cent interest. The investor will receive €1,060 at the end of the year. However, let's suppose inflation is 10 per cent during the year. If the price of a cappuccino at the beginning of the year is €1, it will cost €1.10 at the end of the year. At the beginning of the year €1,000 would have bought 1,000 cups of cappuccino. At the end of the year, €1,060 would have bought 963 cappuccinos. So in real terms the investor is worse off.

2. **The default risk premium.** A default on a loan happens when the borrower fails to pay the interest and the principal when it is due. If a borrower has a suspect history or has had financial difficulties in the past, the lender faces the risk that the borrower will

default. Corporations that issue bonds will receive a credit rating. The lower the credit rating the higher the default risk premium and therefore the higher the interest rate.

3. **Liquidity risk premium.** Liquid assets are assets that can be converted into cash quickly without loss in value. Lenders can sell loans to others. The easier it is to sell loans the more liquid the loan is. Liquidity is something that is desirable by investors. Illiquid loans will pay a higher interest to compensate lenders for the hassle of having to hold the loan until maturity. The liquidity risk premium is the interest that lenders need to compensate for illiquidity.

4. **The maturity risk premium.** If interest rates go up, the price of long-term bonds will go down. Lenders that have made loans at the original rate will be trapped in receiving the original (lower) rate of interest. New loans that are made will receive the new and higher interest rate. This interest rate risk is more pronounced the longer the date to maturity. If lenders perceive that interest rates will rise in the future, they will increase the interest charged on the loan to compensate for this interest rate risk. Of course, interest rates can be expected to go up or down and consequently the interest rate risk can go up or down. This doubt as to the direction of interest rates will make lenders adjust the current interest rate in order to compensate themselves for this risk.

However, while short-term bonds do not have exposure to interest rate risk (because of the short maturity), they are exposed to reinvestment rate risk. When short-term bonds mature and are reinvested in other short-term bonds when interest rates are lower, then the interest income will decline. For example, if short-term rates were 10% an investor would receive an interest income of €100,000 on a €1m investment. If after reinvesting, interest rates had fallen to 5%, interest income would have been €50,000. If the money had been reinvested in long-term debt, then the income would have been preserved. Of course, the trade-off is that while interest income would have been preserved, the principal is still exposed to maturity risk (unlike short-term bonds).

1.10.2 Nominal interest rates

The quoted prevailing rate of interest is the nominal interest rate. The nominal interest rate is the real interest rate plus all of the premiums discussed above. The following equation shows the relationships of various components:

$$N = k + INFL + LP + DRP + MRP \qquad (1.1)$$

Where
N = the nominal rate of interest (the rate quoted)
k = real rate of interest
INFL = inflation risk premium
LP = liquidity risk premium
DRP = default risk premium
MRP = market risk premium

Note that nominal interest rates will vary over time because the real rate of interest and the premiums will vary causing market rates to fluctuate. In addition, if the European

Central Bank intervenes in the markets to change the money supply this will also lead to fluctuations in the rate of interest.

1.11 The term structure of interest rates – the yield curve

Interest rates on long-term bonds will be higher than interest rates on short-term bonds. The reason, as discussed above, is that long-term investments have greater risks than short-term investments. Consequently the price of long-term bonds will be affected more by changes in interest rates than will the price of short-term bonds. If market interest rates go up – the price of bonds will fall. If market interest rates fall – the price of bonds will rise. Bond prices will change more depending on the length of the term to maturity.

Example

Suppose an investor buys a bond for €100 with a yield of 10%, and say that after a few years €100 bonds are being issued that yield 12%. The consequence is that no investor will pay €100 for the old bond that pays 10%. The price of the old bond must fall to a price that yields 12%.

The relationship between the yield (return) and maturity is referred to as the **term structure of interest rates**. This relationship between short-term and long-term bonds (the term structure of interest rates) is important both to borrowers who need to decide whether to issue long or short securities and for investors who will have to decide whether to buy short- or long-term securities.

A yield curve depicts graphically the interest rates for securities in the time remaining to maturity. The interest rates on a particular security are plotted with various maturity dates.

Historically, long-term rates have been above short-term rates in most years. Consequently, the shape of the yield curve will be upward sloping or normal. It's described as **normal** because interest rate risk is lower for short-term securities, i.e. lower market risk premiums. If short-term rates are high and investors expect them to decline then the yield curve will be abnormal or downward sloping. This was the case in the 1980s when short-term rates were very high (principally because of very high rates of inflation) but most investors took the view that monetary authorities would implement appropriate macroeconomic policies that would eradicate the cause of high inflation and that the long-term prognosis for interest rates would be below short-term rates.

An example of Irish, UK and US yield curves is depicted in Figure 1.2[3]. Flat yield curves (i.e. when short-term rates are not much below long-term rates) may indicate that the economy is going to slow down. The European Central Bank may have pushed up short-term rates to curb inflation which in turn slows economic activity. Long-term inflationary expectations are reduced and long-term rates fall.

Figure 1.2.

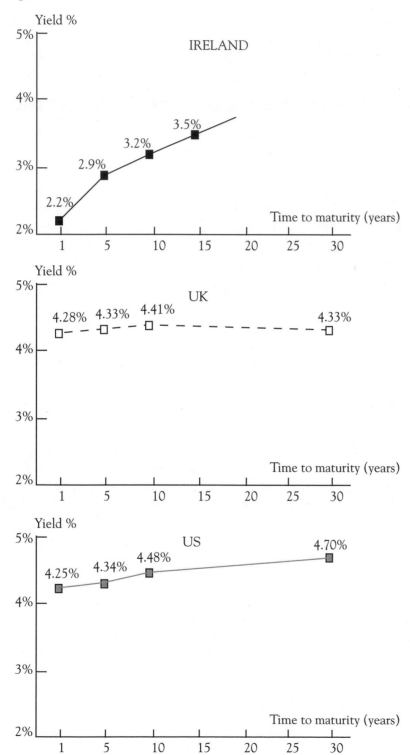

1.12 Theories that determine the shape of the yield curve

The Pure Expectations Theory: According to this theory the yield curve only depends on expectations about the future direction of interest rates. Long-term rates are simply a weighted average of the interested rates expected during the life span of the maturity. For example, if interest rates for next year are expected to be 8% and 10% for the subsequent year, then the two-year rate will be 9% (8% + 10%) / 2 = 9%.

Similarly, the rate on a four-year loan will be the geometric average of the four one-year rates that are expected over the next four years.

Example

If you borrow money from the bank for a period of four years, the bank may expect inflation to increase for each of the four years. Consequently, the lending institution may predict the annual rates of interest and the estimated long-term rates as follows:

Table 1.1 Pure expectations theory and estimated long-term rates

Year	Expected Annual Rate	Expected Average Interest Rate
2007	5%	5%
2008	6%	5.5%
2009	7%	6%
2010	8%	6.5%

This theory therefore assumes that bond prices are determined solely by expectations on future interest rates. This would imply that investors do not perceive long-term bonds as being riskier than short-term bonds. In other words, the pure expectations theory implies that the maturity risk premium is zero. However, most evidence points to the view that long-term bonds are riskier than short-term bonds and that a positive maturity risk premium does exist. The required rate of return for longer term bonds is greater than that for short-term bonds to compensate for the higher maturity risk. This theory is known as the Liquidity Preference Theory.

The Liquidity Preference Theory: The theory that long-term bonds will yield more than short-term bonds holds that lenders will prefer to make short-term loans and borrowers will prefer to take out long-term loans. Therefore to encourage lenders to make long-term loans, borrowers must pay an interest premium. The intuition behind this is risk aversion by borrowers. Borrowers prefer to borrow long term because of risk aversion. By borrowing long term at a fixed rate, investors may miss out on the opportunity of gaining from a reduction in short-term rates but this is better than the risk of interest rates rising to the point where the investor cannot afford the cost of these rising interest rates.

So for this reason borrowers prefer to borrow long term with fixed interest loans. Lenders, on the other hand, prefer to make short-term loans. In other words, the liquidity preference theory holds that lenders prefer to lend short-term because these securities can be converted into cash (are more liquid) without the possibility of loss in value. This reduces risk and therefore lenders will accept lower yields on short-term securities. Borrowers prefer to hold long-term debt because short-term debt exposes them to the possibility of having to repay the debt if short-term rates rise. Therefore borrowers, all else being equal, will pay a premium for long-term funds. Thus a maturity risk premium exists and this maturity risk increases with time to maturity. So, an upward sloping yield curve exists.

Another reason why lenders prefer to make short-term loans is that it is more difficult to forecast what the financial position of the borrower will be in 10 or 15 years time. Therefore short-term loans will allow lenders to reconsider the terms of the loans if general market business conditions or the financial health of the borrower has deteriorated.

In summary, expectations about future interest rates are the most important factor determining the shape of the yield curve. However, the slope of the yield curve will change because of investors' expectations about future interest rates **and** because of the existence of a maturity risk premium.

Market Segmentation Theory: Some financial analysts subscribe to another theory called the market segmentation theory. This theory holds that there is clear market segmentation for funds between those who trade in short-term bonds and those who trade in long-term bonds. The supply and demand for short-term bonds will determine the price (interest rate) for short-term bonds and the supply and demand for long-term bonds will determine the price (interest rate) for long-term bonds. In this sense there is no connection between the yield on short-term and long-term bonds, and it doesn't explain the shape of the yield curve because it doesn't provide any particular reason why long-tem rates will be above short-term rates.

1.12.1 Review of the theories

- **The pure expectations theory:** Long-term rates are an average of expected short-term rates from now to maturity. These short-term rates are influenced by expected inflation rates.
- **The liquidity preference theory:** Lenders prefer to hold securities that are short-term because they are more liquid and borrowers (who are assumed to be risk averse) prefer to borrow long term because of the risk of having to pay back short term if short-term rates rise.
- **Interest rate risk:** If interest rates change the value of bonds will fluctuate. This interest rate risk increases with time to maturity and so a premium is paid by borrowers on long-term loans to compensate for the increased risk.
- **Market segmentation theory:** The market for short-term and long-term bonds are segmented and the supply and demand for each types of security determines their price.

SUMMARY

- Finance is about managing money. The most fundamental principle in finance is net present value – is the market value of an investment greater than its cost?
- Finance also involves the study of the investment market.
- Shareholders will want management to manage the company so that shareholder wealth is maximised.
- Cash is king – the value of any financial asset depends on the ability of the asset to generate cash flows both now and in the future.
- Profit maximisation should not necessarily be a goal of financial management.
- Cash received sooner is more valuable.
- Reducing the riskiness of cash flows increases share value.
- Agency theory deals with the conflict of interest between managers and shareholders.
- Ethical issues challenge the function of business and financial management.
- There are three legal forms of business organisation: partnership, limited liability companies and sole proprietorship.
- Financial markets are numerous, with the two main markets being capital markets and money markets.
- Capital markets are for long-term debt and company shares.
- The nominal or the quoted interest rate is the real risk-free rate plus premiums that reflect inflation, default risk, maturity risk and liquidity risk.
- The relationship between the interest rate paid on securities and their maturity dates is referred to as the **term structure** of interest rates.
- The shape of the yield curve depends on expectations about the future direction of interest rates and the risk associated with different maturity dates.
- If the inflation rate is expected to increase the yield curve will be upward sloping or normal. The yield curve will be downward sloping or inverted if inflation is expected to decline.

WEB LINKS

www.financewise.com
Comprehensive data on financial matters from around the world.

www.thecorporatelibrary.com
Information on compensation, board ratings and comparative data, corporate governance.

www.forbes.com
Intelligent investing.

QUESTIONS

1. What is finance?
2. Explain the link between the study of finance and the study of investment markets.
3. What do you understand by the term 'shareholder value'?
4. Should profit maximisation be an objective of financial management? Explain your answer.
5. In finance, 'Cash is king.' Discuss.
6. Illustrate and outline the factors influencing share value.
7. Define agency theory. What is an 'agent' and what are 'agency costs'? How can agency costs impinge on the primary goal of 'wealth maximisation'?
8. Define (a) sole trader, (b) partnership and (c) corporation.
9. Describe the legal and ethical challenges that face the financial manager.
10. For class discussion: Should managers be interested only in the maximisation of shareholder wealth or should they also be interested in the welfare of society at large?
11. Why are financial markets so important? What services do they provide? If there is a lack of confidence in the financial system what impact would this have on the wellbeing of the economy?
12. Under what circumstances would an investor use a money market fund?
13.♦ Why do long-term interest rates differ from short-term rates?
14.♦ If the risk-free rate of interest is 4% and the expected rate of inflation is 3% in the current year and 5% during the next two years, what is the yield on a three-year treasury security? Assume no maturity risk premium.
15. A one-year treasury bond yields 6%. If the market anticipates that in one year from now one-year treasury bonds will yield 7%, what is the yield today on two-year treasury securities?
16. What is the default risk premium if the real rate of interest is 5% and the expected rate of inflation is 3%, the liquidity risk premium is 1%, the maturity risk premium is 5% and the nominal rate is 17%?
17.♦ How would the yield curve for a private corporation differ from the yield curve of the government?
18. Explain the pure expectations theory and the liquidity preference theory in describing the yield curve.
19. Evaluate the consequences if long-term rates were not an average of expected short-term rates.

NOTES

1. See 'The Goals of the Corporation', in *Financial Management: Theory and Practice*, 9th edn, Brigham, Gapenski and Ehrhardt, Chapter 1.
2. See 'Theory of the Firm, Managerial Behaviour, Agency Costs and Ownership Structure', M.C. Jensen and W.J. Meckling in the *Journal of Financial Economics*, October 1976.
3. Yield curves taken with kind permission from: *Fundamentals of Investment: An Irish Perspective* by Brian O'Loughlin and Frank O'Brien, Gill & Macmillan 2006.

2

Financial Statements and Cash Flow

CHAPTER OBJECTIVES

At the end of this chapter the student will be able to:

1. understand the relevant features of financial statements
2. appreciate the distinction between cash flow and profitability
3. understand the concepts of operating cash flow and free cash flow
4. understand that operating performance is measured by reference to free cash flow.

INTRODUCTION

This chapter examines financial statements and cash flow. Chapter 1 emphasised that shareholder value maximisation depends on the generation of cash flow. The starting point in forecasting future cash flows begins in the financial statements. This chapter does not deal with the preparation of financial statements. It emphasises that financial statements provide information for management in their decision-making.

2.1 The balance sheet

A balance sheet is a list of a company's assets, liabilities and equity at any one point in time. It is a snapshot of the company. The reader might like to draw up his/her own balance sheet by making a list of his/her assets and liabilities. Assets are what you own (e.g. cash, property, books, etc.) or what is owed to you (people who owe you money). Liabilities are what you owe to other people (loans to the bank or building society, to your class mate). The difference between the value of your assets and your liabilities is your equity or net worth.

This is expressed in the balance sheet equation:

$$\textbf{Assets = Liabilities + Equity} \tag{2.1}$$

Balance sheets are divided into five sections:

1. Fixed assets
2. Current assets
3. Current liabilities

4. Long-term debt
5. Equity.

Figure 2.1 shows how the balance sheet is constructed. On the left-hand side is a list of the assets and on the right-hand side is a list of the company's liabilities and equity.

Figure 2.1 The balance sheet

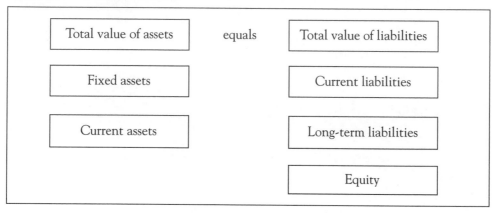

The balance sheet of a hypothetical company Genesis Ltd is provided in Table 2.1. The current year (2008) and the previous year's (2007) data is provided.

2.1.1 Fixed assets

Fixed assets are assets that are expected to provide a benefit to the firm for more than one year. They are held for long-term use in the business. For example, plant and machinery is described as a tangible fixed asset. Similarly, intangible fixed assets such as trademarks and patents have a life that can span over many years. Genesis Ltd has fixed assets of €2,640,000 at book value.

2.1.2 Current assets

On the other hand, current assets have a life of less than one year. It is expected that current assets will be converted into cash within one year. For example, stock would normally be sold within a year. The exception of course is stock that has remained unsold during the year. In this case, the closing stock would be carried forward to the following year. Cash and debtors (or accounts receivable) are also current assets. Genesis has €1,747,000 in current assets. This is made up of €890,000 in stock, which is what the company has produced but has not sold to its customers. It has €850,000 in debtors. This is what customers owe to Genesis.[1] It has cash of €7,000.[2]

Table 2.1 Balance sheet as at 31 December 2008(€000)

	2008	2007
Fixed assets		
Plant and machinery (net)	2,640	1,923
Current assets		
Stock	890	830
Debtors	850	630
Short-term investments		130
Cash	7	70
	1,747	1,660
Amounts falling due within one year (current liabilities)		
Creditors	120	60
Bank overdraft	220	120
	340	180
Net current assets	1,407	1,480
Total assets *less* current liabilities	4,047	3,403
Amounts falling due after more than one year		
Long-term debt	1,700	1,160
Capital and reserves		
Preference shares	80	80
Ordinary shares	220	220
Retained earnings	2,047	1,943
	4,047	3,403

2.1.3 Current liabilities

Current liabilities have a life of less than one year. In other words, it is expected that they will be paid within 12 months. Creditors are companies and individuals to whom the firm owes money. Genesis owes suppliers €120,000 for materials it purchased on credit.[3] It has a bank overdraft of €220,000.[4] This is a short-term loan which is repayable to the bank within a year.

2.1.4 Net working capital

Net working capital (NWC) is current assets minus current liabilities:

$$\text{Net working capital} = \text{Current assets} - \text{Current liabilities} \qquad (2.2)$$

NWC is positive when current assets are greater than current liabilities. This would be the normal case for healthy companies. For Genesis, this is €1,747,000 – €340,000 = €1,407,000. This is sometimes shown as **net current assets**.

2.1.5 Long-term liabilities

Any debt that is not due within the year is a long-term liability. Firms borrow in the long term from a number of different sources and for different reasons.[5] Genesis has €1,700,000 in long-term debt. The figure on the balance sheet refers only to the principal or the actual amount borrowed. The interest paid on the debt appears in the profit and loss account, which we discuss in the next section.

2.1.6 Shareholders' equity (or net worth)

The difference between the value of the firm's assets and the firm's liabilities is the company's equity. In a sense, this figure makes the balance sheet balance. This is depicted in equation 2.1 and is referred to as the balance sheet equation. Genesis has a net worth of €2,347,000.

The equity section shows preference shares, ordinary shares and retained earnings. A fixed rate of dividends is paid on preference shares and they have priority on dividend payments over ordinary shareholders. The ordinary share capital is the original investment made by the shareholders. This is the **book value** of their investment. The **market value** of their investment will depend on the market price of the shares. We discuss this in more detail in Chapter 8.

The figure for retained earnings is the sum of all the earnings that have been available to ordinary shareholders since the inception of the business *less* all dividends paid to ordinary shareholders since its inception. This amounts to €2,047,000 for Genesis. **This does not constitute cash**. Earnings retained by the company over the years will have been invested in various projects by the company or may have been used to pay off some outstanding debts.

2.2 The profit and loss account or income statement

The profit and loss account is a summary of the performance of the firm over a certain period – a year or a quarter of a year. The profit and loss account equation is:

$$\textbf{Income (profit) = Revenue – Expenses} \qquad (2.3)$$

Revenues are the gross income (sales) of the company. Expenses represent the costs incurred in generating this revenue. The profit and loss account of Genesis is given in Table 2.2.

Table 2.2 Genesis Ltd

Profit and loss account for the year ended 31 December 2008	(€000)	
	2008	2007
Turnover	6,000	5,700
Cost of sales	3,260	3,104
Gross profit	2,740	2,596
Selling and distribution	1,086	1,034
Administration	923	879
Depreciation	162	155
Profit before interest and tax (PBIT)	569	528
Interest paid	180	120
Profit before taxation (PBT)	389	408
Taxation (30%)	117	125
Profit after tax (PAT)	272	283
Preference dividends	8	8
Profit available for ordinary shareholders	264	275
Ordinary dividends	160	170
Retained earnings	104	105

2.2.1 Turnover

This is the revenue or sales generated by Genesis, which came to €6,000,000.

2.2.2 Cost of goods sold

This represents the direct costs of the goods sold, e.g. direct labour, materials and direct overheads. These costs come to 54.3% of sales income. Deducting the cost of sales from sales we get gross profit which equals €2,740,000.

2.2.3 Selling, distribution and administration

These include salaries paid to sales people, marketing expenses, insurance and other office expenses. This figure is deducted from gross profit. The total for Genesis is €2,009,000.

2.2.4 Depreciation

Assets generate sales. Depreciation is that part of a fixed asset consumed when generating the sales. It is an expense and like all expenses will be entered as expenses in the profit and loss account.

2.2.5 Operating profit

Having deducted the cost of goods sold, selling, distribution, administration and depreciation expenses from gross profit we are left with profit before interest and tax (PBIT) or **operating profit**. This is an extremely significant figure, as we shall see later on in the chapter. Genesis's operating income is €569,000.

2.2.6 Profit before tax

The interest paid on the company's borrowings is deducted from the operating profit to arrive at the profit before taxes (PBT). For Genesis this is €389,000.

2.2.7 Profit after tax (PAT)

Having deducted all operating expenses and financing costs, we are left with net profit (income) or profit after tax. The PAT for Genesis is €272,000.

2.2.8 Preference dividends

Once the net profit has been determined, the preference shareholders receive their dividends. What is left is profit available for the ordinary shareholders. Preference dividends to Genesis's preference shareholders came to €8,000.

2.2.9 Ordinary dividends

Dividend policy is discussed in Chapter 9 but, in a nutshell, a company can pay out all of the remaining profit (after paying preference shareholders their dividends), or reinvest the profits in the company, or lay out some of the earnings and reinvest the remainder.[6] Retained earnings are that proportion of the profit after tax that is retained (reinvested) in the firm. The rest is paid out as dividends to the ordinary shareholders. Of the €264,000 profit after tax and preference dividends for Genesis, €160,000 (60%) is given to shareholders as dividends, while the remainder €104,000 (40%) is retained in the company. For convenience we have rounded off these figures.

2.3 Statement of cash flows

Although companies can make large profits during the year, the amount of cash the company reports in its balance sheet may be the same at the end of the year as it was at the beginning of the year – it may even be less. The net profit made during the year is not always kept as cash. It can be used in a variety of ways. For example, it could be used to purchase fixed assets, to finance an increase in debtors or stock, or to pay dividends to its shareholders. The statement of cash flows shows how cash flows into and out of a business over a period. The statement of cash flows is constructed by distinguishing between cash flow and income in the profit and loss account, and by comparing the changes in the balance sheet between the beginning and the end of the accounting period. Have a look at Genesis's cash flow for the year 2008 in Table 2.3.

Table 2.3 Statement of cash flows for 2008 – Genesis Ltd

Operating profit	€569
Depreciation	€162
Increase in stocks	€(60)
Increase in debtors	€(220)
Increase in creditors	€60
Operating cash flow before interest and tax	€511
Less Servicing of finance	
Interest paid	€(180)
Less	
Taxation paid	€(117)
Net cash flow before investing and financing	€214
Less Dividend payments	€(168)
Capital expenditure	
Purchase of fixed assets[7]	€(879)
Net cash flow before financing	€(833)
Financing activities	
Sale of short-term investments	€130
Increase in long-term debt	€540
Decrease in cash during the year	€(163)
Summary of change in cash[8]	
Change in cash	€(163)
Cash at the beginning	€(50)
Cash at the end	€(213)

2.3.1 Depreciation

Net profit is arrived at after depreciation is calculated and deducted as an expense. Depreciation is included with all the other expenses, administration, distribution, etc. There is one important distinction between depreciation and these other expenses – **depreciation does not involve a movement of cash**. The financial manager does not sign a cheque for depreciation. Therefore, since depreciation does not involve the movement of cash (it is a non-cash expense), it must be added back to net profit when calculating the company's cash flow.

2.3.2 Changes in current assets and current liabilities

Any changes in the company's balance sheet during the year will indicate changes in the company's cash flow.

An increase in current assets (except cash) will decrease cash. A decrease in current assets increases cash balances. Buying additional stock, for instance, will mean that the company will have to use some of its cash balance to pay for the additional inventory. On the other hand, if stock decreases from one year to the next, the company must be selling more stock than it is buying and so cash will be increasing. In addition, an increase in accounts payable (creditors) will mean the company is getting more time to pay its bills, which saves cash. A decrease in creditors will mean a reduction in cash. These changes along with depreciation are referred to as changes in operating activities.

2.3.3 Servicing of finance

Interest on debt involves a cash outlay, as does taxation paid on company profits.

2.3.4 Changes in fixed assets

Buying fixed assets will reduce cash and the sale of fixed assets will increase cash. These are investing activities.

2.3.5 Changes in share capital and borrowings

Selling additional shares or bonds will increase cash. On the other hand, the company could use some of its cash to buy back shares,[9] pay dividends to its shareholders or pay off some of its outstanding debt.

2.4 Importance of the statement of cash flows

The cash flow statement is probably the most important financial statement because of the information that it provides. The financial manager will need to know if the company is generating sufficient cash flow to finance additional fixed assets to generate further growth and repay debt. Genesis's net profit (profit after tax) is €272,000. Adding the non-cash charge for depreciation (€162,000) to the net profit gives the net cash flow of €434,000. However, it has used €220,000 to finance increases in working capital[10] to give a net cash flow from operations of €214,000. This figure (net cash flow from operations) is a hugely important figure in finance. Companies can report net profits but simultaneously have negative operational cash flow. As we will see in Chapter 11, profits can be manipulated in a variety of ways but it is not possible to manipulate operational cash flow. **So in this respect the cash flow from operational activities can be much more reliable in assessing the financial 'wellbeing' of a company.**

Genesis purchased fixed assets (gross) €879,000 in 2008. The company raised an additional €540,000 in borrowings and €130,000 by selling short-term investments. It paid out €168,000 in dividends to preferred and ordinary shareholders. Considering all these activities we find that Genesis's cash outflows were greater than its cash inflows by €163,000. The good news from the cash flow statement is that it has a positive cash flow from operating activities. However, it purchased additional fixed assets while borrowing heavily and paying out cash to shareholders. This situation could have long-term repercussions for Genesis.

2.5 Operating performance

In the opening chapter, we said that one of the primary goals of financial management is shareholder wealth maximisation. Shareholders are the owners of companies and they appoint directors to direct the operations. Directors in turn appoint managers to run the company by investing shareholders' money in a way that maximises shareholder value. Managers will in turn be compensated by reference to how successful they have been in meeting this objective. However, it would only be fair to assess managers' performance by looking at the operating income they have generated with the assets they have under their control. In other words, operating profit (profit before interest and tax) is the appropriate yardstick. Companies will have different capital structures (debt in relation to equity) and consequently different interest payments. The capital structure decision is a decision taken outside the realm of operational management. Consequently, an inappropriate capital structure could wipe out an otherwise impressive operating profit. Similarly, companies can have different tax structures. Therefore it would be unfair to compare two companies with different tax structures by looking at their profit after tax. Profit after tax is an unsound way of evaluating the performance of a company's employees and operating managers.

2.6 Net operating profit after tax (NOPAT)

The best measure of a company's operating performance is net operating profit after tax.[11] It would be unfair to measure the performance of managers and employees alike by looking at net profit because this figure is calculated after interest is paid on debt. The amount of debt a company takes on is a decision taken by the directors of the company. In other words, a good operating performance by managers and employees could be destroyed by interest payments. NOPAT is the after-tax profit earned if the company had no debt.

Net operating profit after tax is defined as:

$$\text{NOPAT} = \text{PBIT}(1-T) \qquad (2.4)$$

where PBIT is profit before interest and tax, and T is the corporation tax rate the company pays on its profits, in this case 30%.

For Genesis the NOPAT = €569,000(1 − 0.3) = €398,300.

2.7 Calculating free cash flow[12]

The concept of free cash flow is a crucially important concept in finance, a concept we will return to in Chapter 8 on company valuations.

We have already noted that net cash flow is net profit *plus* any non-cash flow items like depreciation. However, some of this cash flow must be used to replace fixed assets and working capital (operating capital) in order to continue and expand operations. Therefore **free cash flow** refers to what is left (free) to distribute to shareholders and lenders. Therefore increasing shareholder value means increasing free cash flow.

The first step in calculating free cash flow is to define and distinguish between operating and non-operating assets. Operating assets are assets used to operate the business. Operating assets are divided into operating working capital (cash, debtors, stock) and operating fixed assets (plant and machinery). Non-operating assets will include marketable securities, investments in land for future use and subsidiaries, etc. The current assets included in operating working capital are those that *do not pay interest*. Companies will tend to hold a certain amount of cash for operating purposes as well as minimum amounts of stock and debtors. Investments in, say, marketable securities are excluded because these are decisions made by the directors of the company and are not part of core operations.

The current liabilities included in operating working capital are those that *do not charge interest*. These include creditors and accruals. Bank overdrafts and short-term loans are excluded in calculating net operating working capital because they are treated as investment capital.

Therefore

$$\text{Total operating capital} = \text{Net operating working capital} + \text{Net fixed assets} \qquad (2.5)$$

and

$$\text{Net operating working capital} = (\text{Stock} + \text{debtors} + \text{cash}) - (\text{Creditors} + \text{accruals}) \quad (2.6)$$

For Genesis we have

Net operating working capital =(€890,000 + €850,000 + €7,000) – (€120,000) = €1,627,000

and

Net fixed assets = €2,640,000, which gives

Total operating capital (2008) = €1,627,000 + €2,640,000 = €4,267,000

For the year 2007 the total operating capital is

Net operating working capital = (€830,000 + €630,000 + €70,000) – (€60,000) = €1,470,000

Net fixed assets = €1,923,000. This gives

Total operating capital (2007) = €1,470,000 + €1,923,000 = €3,393,000[13]

The increase in total net operating capital from the year 2007 to 2008 is €874,000. A summary of the change in total net operating working capital is given in Table 2.4.

Table 2.4 Summary of changes in total net operating capital

(Genesis Ltd)	2008	2007
	€	€
Plant & machinery	2,640	1,923
Stock	890	830
Debtors	850	630
Cash	7	70
Creditors	(120)	(60)
	4,267	3,393
	Change of €874,000	

2.8 Operating cash flow

Operating cash flow is NOPAT *plus* non-cash adjustments such as depreciation.

$$\textbf{Operating cash flow = NOPAT + Depreciation} \qquad (2.7)$$

For Genesis this is

$$\text{NOPAT + Depreciation}$$
$$= €398,300 + €162,000 = €560,300$$

Remember that free cash flow is operating cash flow *less* any gross investment in operating capital, i.e. in net operating working capital and in net fixed assets.

Free cash flow = Operating cash flow – Gross investment in operating capital   (2.8)

where
$$\textbf{Gross investment in operating capital =}$$
$$\textbf{Net investment in operating capital + Depreciation} \qquad (2.9)$$

For Genesis

Gross investment in operating capital = Net investment in operating capital + Depreciation

$$€1,036,000 = €874,000 + €162,000$$

Therefore free cash flow is

$$\text{Free cash flow = Operating cash flow – Gross investment in operating capital}$$
$$€(475,700) = €560,300 - 1,036,000$$

There are two alternative definitions of free cash flow, both providing the same result:

1. **Free cash flow (FCF) = NOPAT − Net investment in operating capital**   (2.10)

Equation 2.10 gives the same result as equation 2.8:

Free cash flow (FCF) = NOPAT − Net investment in operating capital
$$(€475,700) = €398,300 − €874,000$$

2. **Free cash flow** $= \begin{pmatrix} \textbf{Operating} \\ \textbf{cash flow} \end{pmatrix} - \begin{pmatrix} \textbf{Expenditure} \\ \textbf{on fixed assets} \end{pmatrix} + \begin{pmatrix} \textbf{Increase in} \\ \textbf{operating} \\ \textbf{working capital} \end{pmatrix}$ (2.11)

Equation 2.11 gives the same result as equations 2.10 and 2.8:

Free cash flow $= \begin{pmatrix} \text{Operating} \\ \text{cash flow} \end{pmatrix} - \begin{pmatrix} \text{Expenditure} \\ \text{on fixed assets} \end{pmatrix} + \begin{pmatrix} \text{Increase in} \\ \text{operating} \\ \text{working capital} \end{pmatrix}$

$$(€475,700) = €560,300 − (€879,000 + €157,000)$$

Equation 2.11 can be shown in tabular format as

Free cash flow =	
Operating cash flow	€560,300
Less Expenditure on fixed assets	€(879,000)
Plus Increase in operating working capital	€(157,000)
= Free cash flow	€(475,700)

The investments it made during the year in operating capital have wiped out the positive NOPAT. Free cash flow is what is left over for investors. Not only was there nothing left over but also additional investor capital was provided in the form of debt capital. There are two points to remember here:

1. If the NOPAT is negative, it probably spells something fundamentally wrong with operations.
2. **A negative free cash flow is not always a bad sign.** In fact, it might prove to be very positive. If the additional investments in operating capital are used for positive NPV projects, it will add value to the firm in the form of higher free cash flows in the future. In fact, many so called growth companies have positive NOPAT but negative free cash flows. This is because they are at the growth stage of their business cycle and will incur significant expenditures to launch their product.

SUMMARY

- Balance sheets are lists of companies' assets and liabilities.
- The profit and loss account is a statement of the financial performance over a period.
- The statement of cash flow is a summary of the number of euros that came into the business and the number of euros that went out of the business.
- Cash flow is important because investors know that it is cash flow (not profits as reported on the profit and loss account) that will pay creditors, dividends and fund additional investment projects.
- Net operating capital is the amount of capital that the company needs to continue operations.
- Net operating profit after tax (NOPAT) is the profit after tax that a company would have if it had no debt. It excludes the impact of financing activities and is therefore a better measure of the operating performance of the operating managers and employees.
- Free cash flow is the amount of cash that is available for distribution to shareholders and investors. Maximising free cash flow maximises shareholder value.

WEB LINKS

www.fool.com/features/1996sp0708a.htm#4

www.reportgallery.com
Links to company financial statements classified by stock exchange, by industry and by sector. These include Irish companies quoted on US exchanges. Most Irish company reports are located on the World Wide Web.

QUESTIONS

1. Explain each of the following terms:
    (a) the five sections of the balance sheet
    (b) the income statement
    (c) the cash flow statement
    (d) net worth
    (e) net operating working capital
    (f) total operating working capital
    (g) net cash flow
    (h) NOPAT.
2. ♦ Explain the significance of the difference between NOPAT and PAT.
3. Explain operating cash flow and net cash flow.
4. The figures shown on the profit and loss account may not represent the cash position of the company at the end of the year. Why? Discuss.
5. If a company's free cash flow is negative, is this a bad sign? What about operating cash flow?
6. How would you explain a negative change in net working capital during the year?
7. ♦ Lexus Ltd has €30,000 in fixed assets, €10,000 in current assets, €3,000 in current liabilities, €15,000 in debentures. Calculate the net worth and net working capital.

8. Sales for Quirkie & Co. for the year just ended came to €1,000,000. Costs incurred amounted to €600,000. Depreciation on fixed assets was €10,000 and interest charges came to €5,000. Calculate the net profit assuming taxation of 15%. If it pays out 10% in dividends, what is the addition to retained earnings?

9.♦ Sales for the year amounted to €1,000,000. The cost of goods sold was €600,000. Depreciation was €12,000 and interest charges came to €5,000. Tax was at the rate of 15%. Calculate the operating cash flow.

10. The following information is provided from the profit and loss account and balance sheet of Dominican Limited for the year 2007.

Sales	€100,000
Cost of sales	€60,000
Administration expenses	€5,000
Depreciation	€7,000
Interest paid	€12,000
Taxation	€6,000
Dividends	€6,500
Ordinary shares issued during the year	€2,000
Redeemed long-term debt	€6,000

Calculate: (a) The operating cash flow for the year 2007.
               (b) The cash flow to shareholders.
               (c) Cash flow to creditors.

11. The total assets of Alpha Ltd is €4,000,000. It has to pay creditors €3,600,000 during the year. Calculate the value of shareholders' funds.

12.♦ The following information is available from the accounts of Alexis Ltd:

Sales	€1,000,000
Cost of sales	€600,000
Depreciation	€10,000
Interest charges	€3,000
Dividends paid	€4,000
Change in fixed assets (net) during the year	€30,000
Change in current assets	€6,000
Change in current liabilities	€2,500
Taxation (15%)	

Calculate: (a) the net profit; (b) operating cash flow; (c) free cash flow

13.♦ A company's profit after tax for the year was €1m and its profit before interest and tax was €3m. The company's corporate tax rate is 15%. How much did it pay in interest charges?

14. The profit before interest and tax of O'Keeffe Ltd is €600,000. The company's tax rate is 20% and it has no debt. Depreciation of fixed assets was €100,000. Calculate the company's net cash flow and its operating cash flow.

15. The financial statements of Beta Ltd are as follows:

Profit and loss account for year ended 31 December

	2008	2007
Turnover	€1,500	€1,000
Cost of sales	€1,200	€800
Gross profit	€300	€200
Depreciation	€35	€25
Profit before interest and taxes	€265	€175
Interest	€27	€17
Profit before taxes	€238	€158
Taxes (20%)	€48	€32
Profit after tax	€190	€126
Ordinary dividends	€139	€88

Balance sheet as at 31 December	2008	2007
Fixed assets (net)	€400	€260
Current assets		
Stock	€225	€250
Debtors	€200	€125
Cash	€16	€11
Total current assets	€441	€386
Current liabilities		
Creditors	€148	€95
Short-term debt	€85	€53
Accrued expenses	€90	€65
Total current liabilities	€323	€213
Net working capital	€118	€173
Net total assets	€518	€433
Long-term debt	€185	€185
Ordinary share capital	€60	€60
Retained earnings	€273	€188
	€518	€433

Calculate
(a) NOPAT for 2008.
(b) Net operating working capital for 2007 and 2008.
(c) Total operating capital for 2007 and 2008.
(d) Free cash flow for 2008.

NOTES

1. The management of debtors or accounts receivable is explored in Chapter 17.
2. The appropriate or optimum amount of cash a company should hold is discussed in Chapter 16 on cash management.
3. The management of inventory and accounts payable (creditors) is discussed in Chapter 17.
4. Sources of short-term finance are discussed in Chapter 16.
5. The amount of money borrowed by firms is a crucial decision in financial management and is discussed in detail in Chapter 13.
6. There is another option and that is to repurchase some of the shares. Share purchase is discussed in Chapter 9.
7. There was a net increase in fixed assets of €2,640 − €1,923 = €717. This is the net increase *after* the deduction for this year's depreciation. Therefore, the depreciation expense should be added back in to show the total increase in *gross* fixed assets.
8. Remember that an **overdraft** is seen as **negative** cash. So therefore the opening cash is €70 − €120 (overdraft) = €50. Cash at the end of the year is €7 − €220 (overdraft) = €213.
9. Share buy-backs are discussed in Chapter 9.
10. Cash used for increases in stock €(60,000) + cash used to finance increases in debtors €(220,000) *less* an increase in cash from an increase in creditors €60,000 = €220,000.
11. Remember PAT is profit **after** tax and after interest is paid on company debt. NOPAT is profit after tax but **before** interest is paid on debt.
12. There are different methods used in calculating **free cash flow**. The general method used here is that used by Brigham, Gapenski and Ehrhardt, *Financial Management − Theory and Practice*.
13. We do not include the figure for short-term investments because these are investments made, which do not impact on operations. This is an asset which is not under the control of the operating managers.

3

Financial Statement Analysis

CHAPTER OBJECTIVES

Having completed this chapter the student will be able to:

1. interpret from financial statements:
   (a) the ability of companies to meet their short-term financial obligations – liquidity ratios
   (b) how efficiently the company is using their assets – asset management ratios
   (c) the extent to which the firm uses debt finance to fund their operations – gearing ratios
   (d) the overall effect of liquidity, asset management and gearing on company profitability – profitability ratios.

2. and:
   (a) show how the most important ratio in business, the return on equity (ROE) is affected by asset turnover, the profit margin and gearing – the Du Pont formula
   (b) show how liquidity, asset management, gearing and profitability affect market valuation – company valuation ratios
   (c) assess the trends in financial ratios over periods of time – trend analysis
   (d) introduce the concepts of market value added (MVA) and economic value added (EVA)
   (e) understand the difficulties in making international accounting comparisons
   (f) highlight the weaknesses of ratio analysis.

INTRODUCTION

Financial statements provide a wealth of information about the financial health and state of affairs of companies. As we saw in Chapter 1, the principal purpose of management is to maximise company value. Financial analysis will help in this regard by comparing and evaluating trends over time. Financial performance is often measured by using financial ratios. Ratio analysis is concerned with quantifying the relationship between key variables in a company's financial statements. The information provided by ratio analysis is used by different groups of people including management, employees, creditors, banks and the suppliers of goods and services. Information unlocked from company financial statements using financial analysis will show the ability the company has:

1. in meeting its day-to-day financial obligations (liquidity)
2. in calculating the rate of return it is getting from its capital invested (profitability)
3. in establishing the efficiency with which it is using its assets and the extent to which it has used borrowed funds to finance its operations (gearing).

In this chapter financial ratios will be calculated using hypothetical data.

3.1 Solvency–liquidity ratios

Solvency refers to the ability of a firm to pay its liabilities as they fall due. In other words, a firm must have sufficient liquid assets to meet its financial obligations. A liquid asset is one that can be quickly converted into cash, without loss in value.
   A firm is liquid if

(a) the company's total assets exceed its total liabilities – a positive **net worth**. This is long-term solvency
(b) the firm is able to pay all its short-term debts as they fall due. If its short-term assets exceed its short-term liabilities – short-term solvency.

3.1.1 The current ratio

Short-term (current) liabilities refer to less than one year. Therefore, in balance sheets the heading 'amounts falling due within one year' refers to short-term debt, whereas 'amounts falling due after more than one year' refers to long-term debt. Short-term liabilities consist of accounts payable, bank overdrafts, short-term loans, current maturities of long-term debt, accrued taxes (taxes due), and other accrued expenses such as wages.
   Current assets are those that can be quickly converted into cash. Current assets normally include stocks, accounts receivable (debtors), marketable securities and cash.
   The ratio of current assets to current (short-term) liabilities is referred to as the current ratio. The current ratio is calculated by dividing current assets by current liabilities:

$$\text{Current ratio} = \frac{\text{Current assets}}{\text{Current liabilities}} \qquad (3.1)$$

At this stage it is important to point out that ratios on their own do not mean anything because a ratio is simply one number divided by another. We need to look behind the figures and analyse what items make up the assets and liabilities that constitute the ratio. We need to look at the trends in the company's ratios over a number of years to see if they are improving or not. Finally, we need to compare our company's ratios with ratios of similar companies in the same industry – this is known as **benchmarking**.
   The data given in Tables 3.1, 3.2 and 3.3 is taken from a hypothetical company Genesis Ltd, which published its accounts as at 31 December 2008.

Table 3.1 Genesis Ltd

Balance sheet as at 31 December 2008	€000s	
	2008	2007
Fixed assets		
Plant and machinery (net)	2,640	1,923
Current assets		
Stock	890	830
Debtors	850	630
Short-term investments	130	
Cash	7	70
	1,747	1,660
Amounts falling due within one year (current liabilities)		
Creditors	120	60
Bank overdraft	220	120
	340	180
Net current assets	1,407	1,480
Total assets *less* current liabilities	4,047	3,403
Amounts falling due after more than one year		
Long-term debt	1,700	1,160
Capital and reserves		
Preference shares	80	80
Ordinary shares	220	220
Retained earnings	2,047	1,943
	4,047	3,403

We can see from the balance sheet for the year 2008 that Genesis has €1,747 in current assets and €340 in current liabilities. The current ratio is got by dividing current assets by current liabilities:

	2008	2007	Industry average
Current ratio	$\dfrac{€1,747}{€340} = 5.14$ times	$\dfrac{€1,660}{€180} = 9.2$ times	6 times

This means it has €5.14 in short-term assets for every €1 in current liabilities, which is lower than the average. Is this good or bad? To answer this question we need to consider the following:

(a) What type of company we are looking at? For example, the current liabilities of food stores are usually greater than their current assets. They don't hold a great deal of stock (perishable goods), don't usually provide credit, but they get the usual credit terms from their suppliers. Because cash flows into the shop on a daily basis, they can feel confident of meeting their short-term debts. On the other hand, manufacturers will usually have lots of cash tied up in raw materials, work in progress and finished goods, and will provide whatever the usual credit terms are to their customers (debtors). At the same time, the demand for cash will come from employees (wages), the banks (in the form of interest payments) and their suppliers (creditors). Therefore, manufacturers will need to have more in current assets than current liabilities. How much more depends on the length of the **conversion cycle** or the **working capital cycle.** The conversion cycle estimates the length of time it takes to convert raw materials back into cash. The longer this time period, the greater the need for a higher current ratio. For example a heavy engineering company's conversion cycle could be nine to twelve months and it will therefore need a high current ratio, whereas a bakery products company will need a lower current ratio.

(b) A high current ratio does not necessarily mean that a company is liquid and a low current ratio does not necessarily mean that it is illiquid. An example should illustrate this point.

Example 3.1 Current ratios and liquidity

Firms A and firm B have the same current ratio but they have quite different liquidity profiles:

Current assets:	Firm A (€)	Firm B (€)
Stocks	20,000	10,000
Debtors	5,000	15,000
Cash	5,000	5,000
	30,000	30,000
Current liabilities	15,000	15,000
Current ratio	2:1	2:1

Firm B will have an inflow of cash from debtors of €15,000, while firm A, over the same period, will have an inflow of cash from debtors of just €5,000. The current ratio, on its own, doesn't show this.

(a) Look at the ratio over a period. Is it improving or disimproving? Later on in this chapter we consider how this is done in the section on trend analysis.

(b) Who is asking the question? For example, if **suppliers** were thinking of extending credit to a company, they would like to see a high current ratio. If current liabilities are rising faster than current assets, the current ratio will fall and this could spell trouble for suppliers. From the point of view of a **shareholder**, a high current ratio may not be good. Recently, for example, Fyffes plc had a lot of money tied up in non-productive assets such as excess cash. With interest rates so low, shareholders were not happy with the rate of return they were getting. They demanded that the company use the cash to invest in a suitable acquisition so those shareholders would see a higher rate of return. The situation was resolved when the company reduced its cash holding by making an acquisition.

(c) Industry average ratios: If a firm's ratios are far removed from the industry average then this should act as a clear warning signal for management. Corrective and radical action may be needed. **However, reaching industry average ratios should not necessarily be the ultimate objective of management.** Some companies will exceed the industry average while other good companies may be below the industry average. A falling current ratio, for example, could mean that the company is very proficient in just-in-time stock control or it could mean that its stock control is very poor and so the company may be unable to meet orders and therefore sales. Genesis is below the industry average, which would indicate a relatively weak liquidity position. But at a ratio of 5.13:1, Genesis could liquidate their current assets at only 19.5% of their book value to pay off their current creditors in full (1 ÷ 5.13 = 19.5%). It is often said that a current ratio of 2:1 should be the target. There is no scientific basis for this assertion except to say that it does seem to be a ratio which companies work towards, and in this sense it gains some validity.

3.1.2 Quick ratio or acid test ratio

The quick or acid test ratio is calculated by deducting inventories (stocks) from current assets and dividing the remainder by current liabilities. Stocks are usually the least liquid of a company's current assets because if the demand for a company's product falls off, then stocks won't be sold and are therefore not liquid.

$$\text{Quick ratio} \quad = \quad \frac{\text{Current assets } \textit{less} \text{ stock}}{\text{Current liabilities}} \qquad (3.2)$$

	2008	2007	Industry average
Quick ratio	$\dfrac{(€1,747 - €890)}{€340} = 2.52$ times	$\dfrac{(€1,660 - €830)}{€180} = 4.6$ times	3 times

This means that, excluding stocks, for every €2.52 the company has in short-term assets it owes €1 to its creditors. In practice, companies will aim for a ratio of 1:1 (i.e. liquid assets are sufficient to cover short-term liabilities) but again, like the current ratio, a quick ratio of less than 1:1 does not necessarily spell disaster. For example, if a firm has liquid assets of €2,500 and current liabilities of €5,000 (a quick ratio of 0.5:1), the company would appear to have liquidity problems. Like the current ratio, the composition of liquid assets and current liabilities is important. Liquid assets could consist of €2,000 in cash and €500 in debtors, while the current liabilities could comprise €2,000 in creditors due in three months, and tax due of €3,000 to be paid in nine months' time. The firm will be able to meet its short-term obligations and will probably be able to generate enough cash flow in the remaining six months to cover its tax liability.

Genesis has a quick ratio less than the average for other firms in the same industry. However, if Genesis can collect accounts receivable (debtors) on time, it will be able to pay off current liabilities without having to liquidate its stock. The question to ask ourselves here is **what would happen if all the company's creditors asked for immediate payment**. Faced with this situation, the company would look to those assets that could easily be turned into cash within a short space of time (a day or a week). It may not be possible to sell off stocks in this space of time (if at all), particularly if it is a manufacturing company. However, some businesses such as retailers may be able to realise all of their assets including stocks.

3.1.3 Creditors payment period

Like the current ratio, we must look behind the quick ratio and ask how likely is it that company creditors will look for immediate payment. We can calculate on average how long it is taking the company to pay its creditors. How many days is the company allowed from the people it owes money to, before it has to pay them? To find this out we calculate a new ratio called the creditors payment period.

$$\text{Creditors payment period} = \frac{\text{Trade creditors}}{\text{Cost of sales}} \times \text{Number of days in the accounting period} \quad (3.3)$$

If the accounting period is one year, then we will use 365 as the number of days in the period.

	2008	2007	Industry average
Creditors payment period	$\frac{€120}{€3,260} \times 365 = 13$ days	$\frac{€60}{€3,104} \times 365 = 7$ days	20 days

This means that based on cost of sales the company is taking 13 days on average to pay its creditors. Genesis is not taking as long a period to pay its creditors as are other companies in the industry. This may mean that there is a demand for a shorter payment period from Genesis's customers. This puts pressure on company liquidity.[1]

3.1.4 Working capital to sales ratio

Working capital is defined as current assets less current liabilities. This working capital to sales ratio gives an indication of the capital necessary to fund the operation on a day-to-day basis. It tells us how much the company needs in working capital to fund every €100 in sales. It is calculated as

$$\text{Working capital ratio} = \frac{\text{Current assets } \textit{less} \text{ current liabilities}}{\text{Turnover (sales)}} \quad (3.4)$$

So, if the working capital ratio is given as €20 for every €100 in sales, a €100,000 order means that it will require €20,000 in working capital to fund the order. The sales figure will provide an indication of the cash flow for the company. If sales are increasing and the working capital ratio is static, the company is in danger of going into liquidation (the company doesn't have enough cash to meet the increased level of activity undertaken). This situation is known as **overtrading**.[2]

A declining working capital ratio would indicate a danger of overtrading. The working capital ratio for Genesis is

	2008	2007	Industry average
Working capital ratio	$\dfrac{€1,407}{€6,000} = 0.23{:}1$	$\dfrac{€1,480}{€5,700} = 0.26{:}1$	0.21:1

Genesis's working capital ratio is slightly higher than the average for the industry, and is getting worse, which means:

1. it needs more working capital for every €100 in sales than the industry average
2. it may need to reduce its working capital requirements. By cutting the amount of cash tied up in stocks and debtors and increasing the number of days before it pays its creditors (creditors payment period), it is possible to use the same amount of cash to fund an increasing amount of sales.

3.1.5 Other liquidity ratios

We briefly discuss two additional liquidity ratios. A creditor who needs payment very soon might be interested in the cash ratio:

$$\text{Cash ratio} = \frac{\text{Cash}}{\text{Current liabilities}} \qquad (3.5)$$

Short-term creditors of Genesis will be worried about its very poor cash ratio:

2008

$$\text{Cash ratio} \quad \frac{€7}{€340} = 2\%$$

In addition, consider how long the company would be able to survive, if for some reason (perhaps because of a lost export market) cash inflows began to dry up. To calculate the time involved we can use the ratio[3]

$$\textbf{Interval measure} = \frac{\textbf{Current assets}}{\textbf{Average daily operating costs}} \qquad (3.6)$$

Total operating costs for Genesis (excluding interest charges and depreciation – we don't include depreciation because it is a non-cash item, and interest payments are excluded because we are only concerned with operating costs) is €5,269. Average daily operating costs is €5,269/365 = €14.4. Therefore

$$2008$$

$$\text{Interval measure}\quad \frac{€1,747}{€14.4} = 121 \text{ days}$$

Genesis could hang on for about 4 months.

3.1.6 Long-term solvency

The long-term solvency of a company can be gauged by answering the following question:

Do the company's total assets exceed its total liabilities?

The difference between total assets and total liabilities is called **net worth**. If the reader added up all his/her assets (everything he/she owns or is owed) and deducted all his/her liabilities (all his/her debts), the result would be his/her individual net worth. Another name for this is the company's **net book value** or **shareholders' funds**. Positive net worth occurs when total assets are greater than total liabilities. Companies and individuals can suffer from the same problem. If the value of your mortgage is greater than the value of your house (if total liabilities are greater than total assets), there is negative net worth or negative equity. The net worth of Genesis for 2008 is €2,267. However, some practices need attention when using net worth as a measure of liquidity. These include the methods used in the revaluation of fixed assets and the provision for liabilities and charges. Appendix 3A provides a discussion of some of these practices.

3.2 Debt management ratios – gearing/leverage ratios

These ratios attempt to answer the following question:

To what extent is the company in debt?

Gearing or leverage is the proportion of debt the company has in its capital structure. Gearing can be calculated in different ways. This is because there are different definitions of what debt is. Debt can be defined as:

1. long-term loans only
2. long-term and short-term loans
3. net debt (all loans *less* cash and short-term deposits)
4. total debt (short and long-term bank loans *plus* current liabilities and long-term liabilities).

The first three definitions are concerned with **formal, interest-bearing** debt. These are loans from financial institutions and individuals and are referred to as **financial gearing/ leverage**. The final definition includes all money owed by the company, both to financial institutions and to all other creditors including trade creditors, the government (tax due) and money owed to shareholders in the form of dividend payments due. This is referred to as the total debt ratio. Interested parties will have their own favoured way of calculating gearing. Financial institutions will obviously be more interested in the first three definitions of debt, while management and business analysts will be more concerned with the total debt ratio. The debt ratios are calculated as follows:

1. **Long-term loans ratio** $= \dfrac{\text{Long-term loans}}{\text{Capital employed}} \times 100$ (3.7)

This shows the proportion of long-term capital that has been borrowed.
Capital employed = Total assets *less* Current liabilities.

	2008	2007
$\dfrac{\text{Long-term loans}}{\text{Capital employed}} \times 100$	$\dfrac{€1,700}{€4,047} \times 100 = 42\%$	$\dfrac{€1,160}{€3,403} \times 100 = 34\%$

2. **Long-term loans to equity ratio** $= \dfrac{\text{Long-term loans}}{\text{Equity}}$ (3.8)

	2008	2007
$\dfrac{\text{Long-term loans}}{\text{Equity}}$	$\dfrac{€1,700}{€2,267} = 75\%$	$\dfrac{€1,160}{€2,163} = 54\%$

This is the proportion of long-term loans to equity. In 2008, long-term loans were 75% of the firm's equity. This ratio is also referred to as the debt to equity ratio.

3. **Net debt** $= \dfrac{\text{Formal debt } less \text{ cash and short-term deposits}}{\text{Capital employed}} \times 100$ (3.9)

	2008	2007
Net debt	$\dfrac{(€1,700 + €220) - (€7)}{€4,047} = 47\%$	$\dfrac{(€1,160 + €120) - (€70)}{€3,403} = 36\%$

Some companies may have cash balances and overdrafts. Consequently, by paying off their overdrafts with cash they could significantly reduce their gearing. This is the definition of gearing used mainly by financial analysts.

4. **Total debt ratio** $= \dfrac{\text{Total debt}}{\text{Capital employed}} \times 100$ (3.10)

	2008	2007
Total debt	$\dfrac{(€1,700 + €340)}{€4,047} = 50\%$	$\dfrac{(€1,160 + €180)}{€3,403} = 39\%$

This ratio shows the extent of companies' total indebtedness. (Note that all gearing figures need to be adjusted for **goodwill**. Appendix 3B, using the Kerry Group as an example, shows how the adjustment is made.)

For Genesis, the ratio of total debt to total capital employed is 50%. This may act as a warning signal to the management of Genesis because

1. borrowing more money may be difficult unless they can raise more equity
2. company creditors may be worried about Genesis's ability to pay.

Finally, financial leverage has an important implication for shareholder wealth maximisation. If a company earns more on investments that have been financed with borrowed funds than it pays in interest, then the return on equity (shareholder return) is enhanced or geared. The implications of capital structure are explored in Chapter 13. Appendix 3D at the end of this chapter gives an example illustrating the **gearing effect**.

3.2.1 Interest cover ratio

In addition to finding the extent to which the company is in debt, of more importance is the ability the company has in financing its debt. In other words, we need an answer to the following question:

Does the company have the ability to pay interest on its debt?

The interest cover ratio is calculated by dividing **profit before interest and taxes** by **interest payable**.[4]

$$\text{Interest cover ratio} = \frac{\text{PBIT (Operating profit)}}{\text{Interest payable}} \qquad (3.11)$$

Table 3.2 Genesis Ltd

Profit and loss account for the year ended 31 December 2008 (€000)		
	2008	2007
Turnover	6,000	5,700
Cost of sales	3,260	3,104
Gross profit	2,740	2,596
Selling and distribution	1,086	1,034
Administration	923	879
Depreciation	162	155
Profit before interest and tax (PBIT)	569	528
Interest	180	120
Profit before taxation (PBT)	389	408
Taxation (30%)	117	123
Profit after tax (PAT)	272	285
Preference dividends	8	8
Profit available for ordinary shareholders	264	277
Ordinary dividends	160	170
Retained earnings	104	107

The interest cover data for Genesis Ltd:

	2008	2007	Industry average
Interest cover	$\dfrac{€569}{€180}$ = 3.2 times	$\dfrac{€528}{€120}$ = 4.4 times	5 times

It measures the number of times the firm's operating income covers its interest payments. Put another way, it measures the extent the firm's operating income can decline before it is unable to meet its annual interest costs. The ratio has deteriorated and is below the industry average and should act as a warning signal to the management of Genesis.[5]

The riskier the company, the higher this ratio should be. High levels of financial risk (high borrowings) and low interest cover can be a signal of future solvency problems for a company.

3.2.2 Fixed-charge coverage ratio

Many companies lease assets. These are fixed charges which, when added to interest charges, provide a more comprehensive view of a firm's long-term solvency.

$$\text{Fixed-charge coverage ratio} \quad = \quad \frac{\text{(PBIT + Lease payments)}}{\text{(Interest charges + Lease payments)}} \qquad (3.12)$$

A note to the accounts of Genesis shows that lease payments amount to €30 million. Therefore the fixed-charge coverage ratio for Genesis is

	2008	2007	Industry average
Fixed-charge coverage	$\dfrac{€569 + €30}{€180 + €30}$ = 2.85 times	$\dfrac{€528 + €30}{€120 + €30}$ = 3.72 times	5 times

The ratio got worse, and like the last two ratios is below the industry average and simply reinforces the view that the company may encounter difficulties if it tries to increase its debt.

3.2.3 Cash interest cover ratio

Because interest is paid out of cash, it is necessary to find out the ability of the company to pay interest from operational cash flow. How many times does operational cash flow cover interest payments? We introduced cash flow statements in Chapter 2. The cash flow statement of Genesis is given in Table 3.3.

Table 3.3 Genesis Ltd statement of cash flows for 2008

Operating profit	€569
Depreciation	€162
Increase in stocks	€(60)
Increase in debtors	€(220)
Increase in creditors	€60
Operating cash flow before interest and tax	€511
Less Servicing of finance	
Interest paid	€(180)
Less	
Taxation paid	€(117)
Net cash flow before investing and financing	€214
Less Dividend Payments	€(168)
Capital expenditure	
Purchase of fixed assets	€(879)[6]
Net cash flow before financing	€(833)
Financing activities	
Sale of short-term investments	€130
Increase in long-term debt	€540
Decrease in cash during the year	€(163)
Summary of change in cash[7]	
Change in cash	€(163)
Cash at the beginning	€(50)
Cash at the end	€(213)

The number of times interest payments are covered by operational cash flow is

$$\text{Cash interest cover} = \frac{\text{Operational cash flow}}{\text{Interest payments}} \quad (3.13)$$

For Genesis the cash interest cover is

	2008	Industry average
Cash interest cover	$\frac{€511}{€180} = 2.8$ times	4.2 times

The operational cash flow is only just covering the interest bill 2.8 times. This is lower than the industry average, and it could result in liquidity problems.

When calculating interest cover we should remember that the interest reported in the profit and loss account is usually **net** interest after deducting interest receivable. Should this be included when calculating interest cover? Appendix 3C, using Unidare plc as an example, illustrates how interest receivable is treated.

3.3 Asset management ratios or efficiency ratios

These ratios measure the efficiency with which the company is utilising its assets. It is important that companies have the right amount of investment tied up in assets. Assets generate sales that in turn generate profits. It follows therefore that if a company does not have enough investment in assets it will lose sales, reduce cash inflow and adversely affect liquidity and profitability. On the other hand, if it has too much money tied up in assets, then its capital costs will be too high which will adversely affect cash inflow, liquidity and profitability. Therefore it is important to have the correct amount of investment in assets. It should not be too high or too low.

3.3.1 Stock turnover ratio

The stock turnover ratio is defined as sales divided by stock (inventories)

$$\text{Stock turnover ratio} = \frac{\text{Sales}}{\text{Stock}} \qquad (3.14)$$

	2008	2007	Industry average
Stock turnover ratio	$\frac{€6,000}{€890} = 6.7$ times	$\frac{€5,700}{€830} = 6.9$ times	7.5 times

This means that each item of stock is sold out or restocked (turned over) 6.7 times a year. Genesis's stock turn is below the industry average, which suggests too much stock. This suggests that too much investment (cash) is tied up in stocks, which are not being sold and therefore are not being converted back into cash. If this continues and stocks continue to increase then the company will find itself short of cash to pay creditors and to service its debts. So too much investment tied up in stock is unproductive and yields a low or zero rate of return.[8]

Because the sales figure is given at market prices (units sold × sales or market price) and the stock figure is usually given at cost price, the stock turnover figure is therefore overstated. It would be preferable to use the **cost of sales** as the numerator.

$$\text{Stock turnover} = \frac{\text{Cost of sales}}{\text{Stock}} \qquad (3.15)$$

	2008	2007	Industry average
Stock turnover	$\frac{€3,260}{€890} = 3.6$ times	$\frac{€3,104}{€830} = 3.7$ times	5 times

An alternative calculation shows how many days' sales the stock held represents.

$$\text{Stock turnover ratio} = \frac{\text{Stock}}{\text{Cost of sales}} \times 365 \qquad (3.16)$$

	2008	2007	Industry average
Stock turnover (days' sales)	$\dfrac{€890}{€3,260} \times 365 = 99$ days	$\dfrac{€830}{€3,104} \times 365 = 98$ days	70 days

Sometimes average stock (opening stock + closing stock + 2) is used. This might be preferred because sales occur over the entire year whereas stock is for one point at the end of the year. Preferably, if stock figures are given for each month of the year, then we could calculate the stock turn by summing the twelve months' stock and dividing by twelve. If this isn't possible, take the sum of the opening and closing stock and divide by 2.

$$\text{Stock turnover ratio} = \frac{\text{Average stock}}{\text{Cost of goods sold}} \times 365$$

The lower the stock relative to sales, the less capital is tied up. Stocks should be held to a minimum provided there is enough stock to meet customer requirements. A low turnover multiple or a high number of days' stock held (as it is for Genesis) might be an indication of:

- a fall-off in demand for the firm's product
- overproduction
- slow moving stock
- inefficiency in stock control.

3.3.2 Debtors collection period or average collection period

This ratio is an estimate of the number of days, on average, it takes for the people who owe you money (debtors) to pay. It is calculated by taking accounts receivable (debtors) and dividing by the average daily sales to find the number of days' sales that are tied up in debtors.

$$\text{Debtors collection period (DCP)} = \frac{\text{Debtors}}{\text{Average credit sales per day}} = \frac{\text{Debtors}}{\text{Annual credit sales}} \times 365 \qquad (3.17)$$

	2008	2007	Industry average
Debtors collection period	$\dfrac{€850}{€6,000} \times 365 = 52$ days	$\dfrac{€630}{€5,700} \times 365 = 40$ days	40 days

In 2008, Genesis waited on average 52 days before it received payment from its debtors. This is a deterioration from the previous year and is well above the industry average. Too much cash is tied up in debtors and is not being converted back into cash quickly enough. This situation is contributing to Genesis's poor liquidity position, as illustrated in the quick ratio and the interest cover ratios.[9]

It is useful to evaluate the debtors collection period with the credit terms being offered by the company. If the debtors collection period is greater than the credit terms given, then customers are not paying their bills on time.

The management of Genesis should watch this ratio because if the DCP is greater than the credit terms given:

- the customer may be in financial trouble if s/he is not paying his/her bills on time
- Genesis is not getting the cash in from its customers and this will put pressure on its liquidity position.

Genesis may have to resort to borrowing, which adds to its capital costs.

3.3.3 Fixed asset turnover ratio

This ratio measures how efficiently the company is using its fixed assets. It is calculated by dividing sales by net fixed assets.

$$\text{Fixed asset turnover} = \frac{\text{Sales}}{\text{Net fixed assets}} = \text{Times} \qquad (3.18)$$

	2008	2007	Industry average
Fixed asset turnover	$\frac{€6,000}{€2,640} = 2.27$ times	$\frac{€5,700}{€1,923} = 3$ times	3 times

This measures the amount of sales a company generates with the amount of money it has tied up in fixed assets. In the case of Genesis, for every €100 in fixed assets the company generates €227 in sales. The worrying aspect is that it has deteriorated from the previous year. The company's assets are generating less income, which results in weaker cash flows and more liquidity worries.

Financial statements are drawn up on the **historical cost** basis of accounting. This means that the assets shown on balance sheets reflect the historical costs of the assets. Inflation causes fixed assets purchased in the past to be understated in current terms. Therefore, if we are comparing the fixed asset turnover of an old firm, which would have purchased its fixed assets at a low price in the past, with a new firm, which would have acquired its fixed assets recently, it is probable that the old firm would have a higher fixed asset turnover ratio. Making comparisons is therefore difficult. Nothing can be done about this until the accountancy profession comes up with a way of dealing with inflation and makes accounting statements deal with current values.

3.3.4 Total asset turnover

This ratio measures the efficiency with which a company is utilising all of its assets.

$$\text{Total asset turnover} = \frac{\text{Sales}}{\text{Total assets}} = \text{Times} \qquad (3.19)$$

	2008	2007	Industry average
Total asset turnover	$\dfrac{€6,000}{€4,387} = 1.4$ times	$\dfrac{€5,700}{€3,583} = 1.6$ times	2 times

Is Genesis generating sufficient sales to justify capital invested in assets? It is below the industry average and efforts should be made to increase sales or reduce the investments tied up in assets.

3.4 Profitability ratios

Most of the ratios we have looked at so far have been calculated by using data from the balance sheet. Profitability ratios use data taken from the profit and loss account and the balance sheet. In calculating rates of return, profit figures (from the profit and loss account) are compared with various investment figures taken from the balance sheet. An outline profit and loss account and balance sheet shown in Table 3.4 provides different definitions of what profit means. Comparing these definitions of profit with the different definitions we find for investment in the balance sheet, we can calculate the rate of return the company is making on its investments. This is what profitability is. It calculates the percentage rate of return the company makes on different measures of investments. For example, if shareholders want to know the rate of return they are getting on their investment, the appropriate profit figure to use is profit for ordinary shareholders. This is divided into the appropriate investment figure from the balance sheet, which is shareholders' funds. A business analyst might be more interested in the rate of return on all capital employed, in which case the appropriate profit figure is profit before interest and tax and the appropriate balance sheet figure is total assets. These ratios will be calculated in sections 3.4.5 and 3.4.7.

Profitability ratios, like the other ratios, are of little use on their own. We must look at trends and industry averages. In addition, for profitability ratios, a comparison with other rates of return in the investment markets would be very useful, e.g. gilts, bonds, cash, currencies and equities.

Table 3.4 Different definitions of profit and investment – calculating return

Profit and loss account	Balance sheet
Gross profit	Fixed assets
Profit before interest and tax (PBIT)	Current assets
Profit before tax (PBT)	Amounts falling due within one year
Profit after tax (PAT)	= Current liabilities
Profit for ordinary shareholders (PFO)	Capital employed (net total assets)
	Amounts falling due after more than one year
	Long-term loans
	Total assets less total liabilities
	= Net worth
	= Shareholders' funds

3.4.1 Gross profit margin

The gross profit margin measures the profit remaining after the costs of goods sold have been deducted from sales. The ratio is

$$\text{Gross profit margin} = \frac{\text{Gross profit}}{\text{Sales}} \times 100 \qquad (3.20)$$

	2008	2007	Industry average
Gross profit margin	$\frac{€2,740}{€6,000} = 46\%$	$\frac{€2,596}{€5,700} = 46\%$	50%

This ratio indicates that Genesis's cost of goods and services sold came to 54% of sales income. This left 46% of total sales income for other uses.

3.4.2 Operating profit margin

The operating profit margin is a measure of the costs of goods sold plus all other operating expenses. Operating profit is profit before interest and tax. It is calculated as follows:

$$\text{Operating profit margin} = \frac{\text{Profit before interest and tax}}{\text{Sales}} \times 100 \qquad (3.21)$$

For Genesis the operating profit margin is

	2008	2007	Industry average
Operating profit margin =	$\frac{€569}{€6,000} = 9.5\%$	$\frac{€528}{€5,700} = 9.3\%$	10%

Therefore, for Genesis, 9.5% of sales revenue remains after all operating expenses have been deducted. This ratio is useful when comparing companies with different tax and gearing structures. This is because the profit figure is taken before interest and tax.

3.4.3 Operating profit margin after taxes

Like many things in life, taxes have to be paid. Because of this certainty, a better measure of company profitability is the operating profit margin after taxes. In the previous chapter we defined net operating profit after taxes (NOPAT) as PBIT(1 − T) = €569 (1 − 0.3) = €398. The operating profit margin after the tax ratio is calculated is

$$\text{Operating profit margin after taxes} = \frac{\text{NOPAT}}{\text{Sales}} \times 100 \qquad (3.22)$$

The ratios for Genesis are

	2008	2007	Industry average
Operating profit margin after taxes	$\dfrac{€398}{€6,000} = 6.6\%$	$\dfrac{€370}{€5,700} = 6.5\%$	6.7%

Therefore, after all operating costs and taxes have been subtracted, Genesis is left with about 6.6 cents for every €1 of sales. **The operating profit margin after taxes is the true measure of the profitability of the company's operations.**

3.4.4 Net profit margin on sales

This measures the profit per one euro of sales. It measures the return the company generates for every €1 in sales. It is calculated as follows:

$$\text{Net profit margin} = \frac{\text{Profit for ordinary shareholders}}{\text{Sales}} \times 100 \qquad (3.23)$$

	2008	2007	Industry average
Net profit margin	$\dfrac{€264}{€6,000} = 4.4\%$	$\dfrac{€277}{€5,700} = 4.8\%$	4.8%

So from an accounting point of view, Genesis generates 4.8 cents profit on every €1 in sales.

The company's net margin on sales is lower than the average ratio for its competitors. This may indicate:

(a) the cost ratios of Genesis are too high or sales prices are too low.
(b) too much debt capital (remember that the profit figure used in this ratio is profit **after** interest has been paid on debt). Therefore if two companies have identical operating results in terms of sales, operating costs and operating profit, they will have different profit **after** tax figures if one firm has a greater amount of debt capital. And as we have seen earlier, the company with the low net margin may end up with a higher return on equity because of its greater use of debt (see Appendix 3D).

3.4.5 Raw earnings ratio

This ratio is useful because it illustrates the return on the company's total assets before the effect of gearing and taxes. The profit figure we use is profit before interest and tax (PBIT). We use profit before interest and tax for a number of reasons.

(a) Since the denominator includes debt, the numerator must be the profit figure before interest is paid on that debt.
(b) It is necessary to use PBIT when comparing companies with different capital structures. This is because interest is paid on profits **before** tax, while dividends are paid on profits **after** tax.

(c)   Tax regulations can change from year to year. Therefore, if we want to compare a company's performance from one year to another, we must be consistent and use profit before any tax deductions.

$$\text{Raw earnings (RE)} = \frac{\text{PBIT}}{\text{Total assets}} \qquad (3.24)$$

	2008	2007	Industry average
RE	$\dfrac{€569}{€4,387} = 13\%$	$\dfrac{€528}{€3,583} = 14.7\%$	18%

What do these figures mean? Genesis is currently making a return of 13% on its total assets employed. This means that for every €100 in capital employed it is making a profit (a return) of €13. Is this good or bad? To answer this question we would need to know:

(a)   What are the industry comparisons?
(b)   What have been the trends in the company's own raw earnings over the years?
(c)   How does it compare with other market returns, e.g. gilts etc?

3.4.6 Return on total assets

This measures the return on total assets after interest and taxes have been paid, and after any dividends due to preferred stockholders have been paid.

$$\text{Return on total assets (ROTA)} = \frac{\text{Profit for ordinary shareholders}}{\text{Total assets}} \times 100 \qquad (3.25)$$

For Genesis the ROTA is

	2008	2007	Industry average
ROCE	$\dfrac{€264}{€4,387} = 6\%$	$\dfrac{€277}{€3,583} = 7.7\%$	8%

Genesis's ROTA is below the industry average because of its lower operating profit ratio and because it has a high level of debt in its capital structure. The high gearing will result in high interest charges and subsequently lower profit after tax.

3.4.7 Return on equity (ROE)

This ratio measures the return that ordinary shareholders get on their investment.

Taking the income available for ordinary shareholders and dividing it by equity gives the ROE.

$$\text{Return on equity (ROE)} = \frac{\text{Profit for ordinary shareholders}}{\text{Equity}} \qquad (3.26)$$

	2008	2007	Industry average
ROE	$\dfrac{€264}{€2,267} = 11.6\%$	$\dfrac{€277}{€2,163} = 12.8\%$	12.8%

Ordinary shareholders get an 11.6% return on every €100 invested. With equities providing investors with high returns on their investments, this will be a cause for concern for Genesis stockholders. This may be reflected in the market price for Genesis shares. **Interestingly the ROE is greater than the ROTA because of the use of debt.** As explained in Appendix 3D, the use of debt can increase the return on equity because of its tax advantages, and because of the higher return required to compensate for the additional risk. This **gearing effect** will become more apparent after studying the following section on the Du Pont formula.

3.5 Ratio pyramids – the Du Pont system

This system of ratio pyramids brings all the ratios we have already calculated together and it shows how they are interrelated. It was first developed by the Du Pont organisation in America, hence its name. Ratio pyramids have the following characteristics:

1. They provide a reference for management to plan their overall profitability.
2. The ratios are interdependent and so the effects of a change in one ratio can be traced against changes in other ratios.
3. They show how the return on equity is affected by asset turnover, the profit margin and gearing.

The Du Pont equation is given as

$$\textbf{Return on assets} = \textbf{Net margin} \times \textbf{Total asset turnover} \qquad (3.27)$$

$$\frac{\text{Net profit}}{\text{Total assets}} = \frac{\text{Net profit}}{\text{Sales}} \times \frac{\text{Sales}}{\text{Total assets}}$$

This equation is illustrated in the modified Du Pont chart in Figure 3.1. You can read the chart as follows:

1. The various costs are added together to give total costs.
2. Total costs are then subtracted from sales to give net profit.
3. Net profit is then divided by sales to give the net margin. Note that from a management point of view if the net margin is low it may be because the individual costs may be too high (by industry comparisons). The management can set in motion measures that will tackle this high cost structure, and so increase the profit margin.
4. On the other side of the chart, we calculate total assets (fixed assets + current assets).
5. Total assets are then divided into sales to give the number of times Genesis **turns over** its assets each year. In Genesis's case this is 1.36 times. For every €100 in total assets the company generates €136 in sales.

6. Finally, multiply the net profit margin by the total asset turnover to get the return on assets. This is the Du Pont equation.

Figure 3.1 Modified Du Pont chart for Genesis

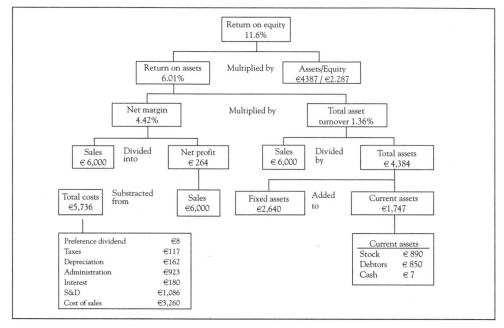

Genesis made €4.42 in net profit on every €100 in sales, a net margin of 4.42%. It turned over its assets 1.36 times in the year. Therefore, it generated a return of 6.01% on its total assets. So, in 2008 the Du Pont equation gives the following answer:

$$\text{Return on assets} = \text{Net margin} \times \text{Total asset turnover}$$

$$\frac{\text{Net profit}}{\text{Total assets}} = \frac{\text{Net profit}}{\text{Sales}} \times \frac{\text{Sales}}{\text{Total assets}}$$

$$6.01\% = 4.42\% \times 1.36$$

Supermarkets and general convenience shops would have a high total asset turnover because of the frequency with which they sell food and drink. However, they would have low net profit margins. On the other hand, heavy engineering firms would have low asset turnover but high profit margins.

In addition, the chart in Figure 3.1 shows how the return on equity (ROE) is affected by asset efficiency, net profit margin and gearing. Remember that if the company finances all of its assets with equity capital only, then the return on assets (ROA) would equal the return on equity (ROE). This is because total assets would equal total equity:

$$\text{ROA} = \frac{\text{Net profit}}{\text{Total assets}} = \frac{\text{Net profit}}{\text{Total equity}} = \text{ROE} \qquad (3.28)$$

However, if the company finances part of its total assets with debt, then the return on equity must be greater than the return on assets. In fact, the ROA is the product of the net profit margin, total asset turnover, and the **equity multiplier**. The equity multiplier is the ratio of total assets to common equity:

$$\text{Equity multiplier} = \frac{\text{Total assets}}{\text{Common equity}} \qquad (3.29)$$

For Genesis, the equity multiplier is

$$\text{Equity multiplier} = \frac{€4,387}{€2,267} = 1.94$$

The company finances every €194 of total assets with €100 of equity. Therefore the modified Du Pont equation which gives the ROE is

$$\text{ROE} = \text{Net margin} \times \text{Total asset turnover} \times \text{Equity multiplier}$$

$$\frac{\textbf{Net profit}}{\textbf{Equity}} = \frac{\textbf{Net profit}}{\textbf{Sales}} \times \frac{\textbf{Sales}}{\textbf{Total assets}} \times \frac{\textbf{Total assets}}{\textbf{Equity}} \qquad (3.30)$$

For Genesis, this works out as

$$11.6\% = \frac{€264}{€6,000} \times \frac{€6,000}{€4,387} \times \frac{€4,387}{€2,247}$$

$$11.6\% = 4.42\% \times 1.36 \times 1.94 \text{ (allowing for rounding)}$$

Obviously, if the firm were financed totally with equity, the equity multiplier would be equal to 1. Why? Remember from Chapter 2 the accounting equation

$$\text{Assets} = \text{Equity capital} + \text{Debt capital}$$

If all assets are financed by equity, with **no** debt, then the equity multiplier must be equal to 1:

$$\text{Equity multiplier} = \frac{\text{Total assets}}{\text{Common equity}} = 1$$

Therefore, if the equity multiplier is 1, the ROE must be the product of the net margin and the asset turnover ratio:

$$\text{Modified Du Pont equation}$$
$$\text{ROE} = \text{Net margin} \times \text{Total asset turnover} \times \text{Equity multiplier}$$

$$\frac{\text{Net profit}}{\text{Equity}} = \frac{\text{Net profit}}{\text{Sales}} \times \frac{\text{Sales}}{\text{Total assets}} \times \frac{\text{Total assets}}{\text{Equity}}$$

$$6.01\% = \frac{€264}{€6,000} \times \frac{€6,000}{€4,387} \times \frac{1}{1}$$

$$6.01\% = 4.42\% \times 136$$

However, the equity multiplier for Genesis is 1.94 and this has the effect of increasing the ROE from 6.01% to 11.6%. **Shareholder value (ROE)** has been **geared up** by the use of debt capital.

The return on equity could also be derived by dividing the return on total assets by the equity fraction. The equity fraction is the proportion of equity in the capital structure. For Genesis, the equity fraction is €2,267/€4,387 = 52%. Therefore

$$\text{ROE} = \frac{\text{ROTA}}{\text{Equity fraction}} = \frac{6.01\%}{0.52} = 11.6\%$$

Looked at this way, **the Du Pont formula can be used by management to see how they can improve performance and hence shareholder value.** This means assessing the two ratios that make up the overall return on total assets and the company's use of debt.

3.6 Market valuation – maximising shareholder value

These ratios compare the book value of a company to its market value. The book value is the same as net worth. Taking all the company's assets and deducting all its liabilities, we are left with the company's net worth. The ratios we have already calculated – liquidity, asset efficiency, debt management and profitability – will determine what the book value is. If these ratios are good then this will be reflected in the book value. The book value will in turn be reflected in the market value of the company's shares. Financial management's primary goal is to maximise shareholders' wealth.

This is achieved by maximising the difference between the market value of shareholders' investment and the amount of capital supplied by shareholders. This difference is referred to as **market value added**.

| **Market value added (MVA)** | **=** | **Market value of equity** | *minus* | **Equity capital supplied by shareholders** | (3.31) |

The market value of equity is **the number of shares multiplied by the market price per share**. Equity capital supplied by shareholders is **total common equity *plus* reserves**.[10]

Example 3.2 Market value added – Unidare plc[11]

MVA calculation
Price per share	€2.35
Number of shares	19.8m
Market value	€46.53m
Equity + reserves	€34.55m

Unidare's MVA is therefore €46.53m *minus* €34.55m which equals €11.98m or 1.35 times shareholders' funds. Maximising this figure will enhance shareholder value.

A different form of the MVA ratio is the market to book ratio. In a sense, this ratio incorporates all the ratios we have already calculated and is a final overall assessment of company performance. It is calculated by taking the market capitalisation and dividing it by the shareholders' funds.

$$\text{Market to book ratio} = \frac{\text{Market capitalisation}}{\text{Shareholders' funds}} \qquad (3.32)$$

Genesis's market price is given at €5 per share. It has 520,000 shares in issue. This means that Genesis is valued at a slight premium to shareholders' investment. Each €100 share investment in Genesis is valued in the market at €146.

Obviously, companies will want to achieve a minimum ratio of 1:1 and preferably higher.

Table 3.5 Genesis Ltd market:book ratio

Market price	Number of shares	Market capitalisation	Shareholders' funds	Market: book ratio
€5	520,000	€2,600,000	€2,267,000	$\dfrac{€2,600,000}{€2,267,000} = 1.146{:}1$

3.7 Economic value added

Closely related to market value added is economic value added (EVA). It is a measure of how the firm has added to shareholder value. The profit and loss account shows what is left for ordinary shareholders after tax has been paid to the government and interest has been paid to the providers of debt capital. This is an accounting definition of what profit means. This definition only accounts for the cost of debt capital. However, if we were to deduct the cost of all capital including the cost of equity capital, we would be left with a true economic profit. As we will see in Chapter 13, equity capital has a cost because equity shareholders will require a rate of return to satisfy them for the risk they take in investing in the company. For shareholders there is an opportunity cost involved in their decision to buy equity. Shareholders give up the opportunity to invest funds elsewhere, of equal risk, where they could earn a rate of return. The cost of equity capital is the rate of return required to satisfy the providers of equity capital. What's left after tax and interest on debt has been paid is retained earnings. This belongs to equity shareholders. If all or part of this is distributed to the shareholders in the form of a dividend (shareholders' return), income tax will have to be paid by those who receive the dividend. Therefore, from the company's position this reduces the cost of equity capital. Therefore it is the after-tax cost of capital which is important.

EVA = PBIT (1–T) – (Total capital supplied by shareholders) (After-tax cost of capital)(3.33)

Suppose that the after-tax cost of capital for Genesis is 12% (calculation of after-tax cost of capital will be given in Chapter 13). The operating profit to be used in EVA calculations is NOPAT, which is equal to PBIT (1 – T) discussed in Chapter 2. Therefore for Genesis, EVA is

$$EVA = €569 (1 - 0.3) - (€2,267)(0.12) = €398 - €272 = €126$$

This suggests that Genesis has added €126,000 to shareholder wealth during 2008.

Emanating from the US, EVA is the new mantra in shareholder wealth maximisation. EVA differs from other corporate performance yardsticks (e.g. earnings per share) by charging profit for the cost of all capital employed, including equity capital. According to its proponents, by concentrating on EVA management can carry out its functions in a way consistent with maximising shareholder value. While a full discussion is beyond the scope of this book, we will return to its main theme in other chapters throughout the book.

3.8 Trend analysis

Ratios are useful, not on their own, but if they are seen over periods. Trends will provide clues as to whether the situation will improve or get worse. Trend analysis plots a ratio over time. Figure 3.2 illustrates the trend in the ROTA of Genesis from 1998 to 2006.

Fig. 3.2 Return on total assets 1998–2006

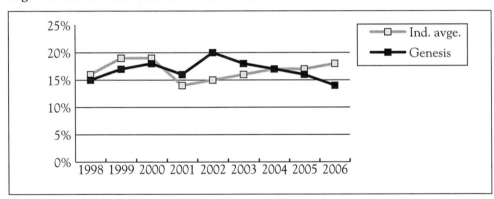

Financial analysts plot trends in ratios over time. To the financial analyst, the resulting graph is a very useful tool in spotting strengths and weaknesses.

3.9 Horizontal analysis

This involves comparing one year's figures with another and calculating the percentage change.[12] Tables 3.6 and 3.7 provide a horizontal analysis for Genesis, followed by an analysis of the results.

Table 3.6 Genesis horizontal analysis – profit and loss account

	2007	2008	% change
Turnover	5,700	6,000	5.2
Cost of sales	3,104	3,259	4.8
Gross profit	2,596	2,740	5.5
Administration	879	923	5.0
			→

	2007	2008	% change
Selling and distribution	1,034	1,086	5.0
Depreciation	155	162	4.5
Interest	120	180	50.0
PBIT	528	569	7.7
Taxation	125	117	(6.41)
PAT	285	272	(4.5)
Profit for ordinary shareholders (PFO)	275	264	(4.0)
Ordinary dividends	170	160	(5.8)
Retained earnings	105	104	(0.009)
Turnover	5,700	6,000	5.2

Table 3.7 Genesis Ltd horizontal analysis – balance sheet

	2007	2008	% Change
Fixed assets	1,923	2,640	37
Current assets	1,660	1,747	5.2
Cash	70	7	(91)
Debtors	630	850	34
Stock	830	890	7.2
Short-term investments	130	0	(100)
Current liabilities			
Creditors	60	120	100
Bank overdraft	120	220	83
Working capital (net current assets)	1,480	1,407	(4.9)
Total assets less current liabilities			
(capital employed)	3,403	4,047	18.9
Long-term debt	1,160	1,700	46
Shareholders' funds	2,163	2,267	4.8

Horizontal statement analysis

1. Sales increased by 5.2% during the year while cost of sales increased by 4.8%. This has led directly to a 5.5% increase in the gross profit.
2. However, because the long-term debt (46%) and the bank overdraft (83%) have increased, interest payments increases (50%) have wiped out the gain in gross profit.
3. Consequently, PAT and retained earnings have fallen.
4. As a result, shareholders have suffered a fall in dividend income.
5. While sales have increased (5%), working capital has decreased (4.9%). The working capital ratio is deteriorating and the consequence could be overtrading. Of particular

concern to the management of Genesis will be the increase in stocks of 7.2%, while sales have increased by only 5%.

3.10 Common size statements (vertical analysis)

Items in the profit and loss account are expressed as percentages of sales. This tells us what percentage of sales income is profit and costs. Similarly, each item in the balance sheet is expressed as a percentage of capital employed or, alternatively, total assets. Tables 3.8 and 3.9 provide common size statements for Genesis followed by a common size statement analysis.

Table 3.8 Genesis Ltd common size statement – profit and loss account for the year end 31 December 2008

	2008	2007	2008 Industry average
Turnover	100%	100%	100%
Cost of sales	54.4%	54.4%	55%
Gross profit	45.6%	45.5%	45%
Operating expenses:			
Selling and distribution	18.1%	18.1%	16%
Administration	15.3%	15.4%	15.2%
Depreciation	2.7%	2.7%	2.6%
Profit before interest and tax (PBIT)	9.48%	9.26%	11.2%
Interest	3%	2.1%	1.2%
Profit before taxation (PBT)	6.48%	7.15%	10%
Taxation (30%)	1.95%	2.1%	2.0%
Profit after tax (PAT)	4.53%	5%	8.0%
Preference dividends	.0013%	.0014%	.1%
Profit available for ordinary shareholders	4.4%	4.8%	7.9%
Ordinary dividends	2.6%	3.0%	4.1%
Retained earnings	1.75%	1.9%	3.8%

Table 3.9 Genesis Ltd common size statement – balance sheet as at 31 December 2008

	2008	2007	2008 industry average
Fixed assets			
Plant and machinery (net)	65.20%	56.50%	60.0%
Current assets			
Cash	.0002%	.0205%	3.2%
Debtors	21.00 %	18.50%	17.0%
Stock	22.00 %	24.40%	19.1%
Short-term investments	–	.038%	1.0%
	43.00 %	42.95%	40.2%
Amounts falling due within one year (current liabilities)			
Creditors	3.0%	1.76%	3.5%
Bank overdraft	5.4%	3.50%	3.4%
	8.4%	5.26%	6.9%
Net current assets	34.7%	43.49%	33.3%
Total assets less current liabilities	100%	100%	100%
Amounts falling due after more than one year			
Long-term debt	42.00%	34.00%	33.00%
Preference shares	1.9 %	2.35%	.2 %
Capital and reserves			
Ordinary shares	5.4 %	6.4 %	7.8 %
Retained earnings	50.5 %	57.00%	59.2 %
	100%	100%	100%

Common size statement analysis

1. PBIT is below the average because selling/distribution costs are above the average.
2. Interest costs are higher than the average because of the company's greater reliance on borrowed funds, both short-term (bank overdraft) and long-term (debentures).
3. Taxation is currently lower because of lower PBIT.
4. Consequently, PAT and profit for ordinary shareholders are lower than the industry average.
5. The debtors figure is higher and this will have cash flow consequences. This is one of the contributory factors giving it a significantly lower end of year cash figure.
6. Stock accounts for 22% of total capital employed, above the industry average of 19%. The management of Genesis should now question why this is happening, and develop a policy to resolve the problem.

Using a method called **sensitivity testing**, we can measure how sensitive the overall return on investment is to changes in the individual cost ratios. We defer a discussion of this to Appendix 3E at the end of the chapter.

3.11 International accounting practices – accounting in different countries

Accounting is not a standardised exercise internationally. Consequently, because different accounting standards apply in different countries, it is very difficult for investors to make cross-border comparisons. The main reasons for this are:

- In Ireland, for example, net book value of assets is cost *less* accumulated depreciation. In other countries, an effort is made to try to make the asset values reflect current market values.
- Differences occur in the treatment of goodwill, leases, research and development costs and pension plans.
- Historical and political factors: Commonwealth countries have a legacy of UK accounting practices. French accounting practices have been influenced by the German occupation. Japanese accounting is a hybrid of UK and US practices. In addition, there will be increasing demands for a common European accounting practice because of the single currency.
- Ownership: In Germany and Japan the banks are the key source of both debt and equity capital. In the UK and US, the public capital markets are most important in raising capital. Therefore, there is a greater demand for more information from accounts in the US and the UK than there is in Germany and Japan who use very conservative reporting practices.

3.12 Limitations of ratio analysis

- Creative accounting can have the effect of manipulating profits:
  (a) A change in the method used could have a serious impact on reported profits.
  (b) Reducing **paper** charges (charges that don't require an invoice) made to the profit and loss account. Examples of **paper** charges are depreciation and provisions.
  (c) Long-term contracts. Some companies have contracts which span several accounting periods. Construction companies are examples. When should the revenue from such contracts be recognised in the profit and loss account? This is usually done on a percentage completion basis. Different ways of calculating the percentage of contract completion will give different turnover figures.
  (d) Raising short-term loans to reduce balances to creditors.
- Many large companies operate different divisions in different industries, and therefore industry comparisons are made difficult.
- The effect of inflation may be ignored. For example a volume increase in sales of, say, 5% could constitute a decline in real terms if inflation is running at a rate greater than 5%.
- Seasonal factors may distort figures. Company end of year figures may not reflect the position throughout the year.

- Generalising ratios. A high current ratio may be good or it may be bad. It may indicate a strong liquidity position but it may also indicate that the company is holding too much cash, which is unproductive.
- Financial ratios do not tell us to what extent a company's revenue is
  - (a) tied to one key product. This is important because while a single product company might be more focused in its operations, a lack of diversification increases the company's risk.
  - (b) tied to a single key customer. What happens to company performance if the customer goes elsewhere?
  - (c) dependent on a single supplier. Any problems with this supplier will lead to shortages of essential raw materials.
  - (d) dependent on the legal and regulatory environment – the legal framework surrounding the regulation of, for example, the telecommunications industry, the tobacco industry and the banking sector.

SUMMARY

Information from financial statements is used by different groups of people. Shareholders use financial statements to see if their original investment in the company has increased in value. The providers of debt finance will want to know if the company can service their debts, as will suppliers of raw materials and services. The users of financial statements will require a proper financial assessment, which will include ratio analysis, trend analysis, common size statements, Du Pont and sensitivity analysis.

This chapter discussed the techniques used to answer these questions. The principal areas discussed were:

- Liquidity ratios – current and acid test ratios, and creditors collection period.
- Profitability ratios – gross and net margin, return on capital employed, return on total assets and return on equity.
- Debt management ratios or how efficiently the company is utilising its assets – stock turnover, debtors collection period, fixed asset turnover and total asset turnover.
- Debt management ratios – gearing ratios and the ability of the company to finance its debt.
- Trend analysis to plot the performance of a company over time.
- The concept of market value added and economic value added.
- How all the ratios combine to give the most important ratio in business – return on equity (ROE).
- The Du Pont system – showing how the pyramid of ratios interrelates to give the shareholder value – the return on equity.
- The limitations of ratio analysis.

WEB LINKS

http://finance.yahoo.com
This gives information on ratios for companies.

www.annualreports.com
Gives links to financial statements.

www.cfonet.com/html/articles/cfo/1998/98Jatist.html
Thousands of articles from CFO magazine including Economic Value Added (EVA).

www.annualreports.com
Company profiles.

QUESTIONS

1. Explain the following:
    (a) Liquidity ratios
    (b) Debt management ratios
    (c) Asset management ratios
    (d) Profitability ratios
    (e) Trend analysis
    (f) Comparative ratios
    (g) Du Pont formula.
2. ✦ The stock turnover ratios are more important for a manufacturing company than they are for a service company. Explain.
3. You are employed as a business analyst in a manufacturing company. The company's managing director brings you into his office and states: 'The current asset to current liabilities ratio has increased. Total assets are generating less sales than the previous year. I also notice that sales have not increased, and neither have the fixed asset turnover ratio and quick ratio. What's going on?'
4. ✦ Explain the impact inflation has on ratio analysis.
5. Ratios on their own don't mean anything – they are simply one number divided by another. Therefore, it is important to use some **benchmark** when analysing ratios. Explain and outline any significant problems there might be in this approach.
6. At the end of the month, a company pays off some of its creditors. What happens the current ratio if initially it is (a) >1 and (b) <1?
7. Explain the relationship between the ROE and the ROA.
8. ✦ The profit and loss account of Dunmore Ltd is reproduced below. Construct a common size income statement.

Dunmore Ltd profit and loss account for year ended 31 December 2007

Sales	€400
Cost of sales	€260
Depreciation	€40
Profit before interest and tax	€100
Interest	€20
Profit before tax	€80
Tax 15%	€12
Profit after tax	€62
Dividends	€20
Retained earnings	€42

9. ✦ The balance sheet and profit and loss account of Doyle Ltd for the year ended 31 December 2007 is as follows:

Balance sheet	€(000)	Profit and Loss account	
Fixed assets			
Plant & machinery (net)	€180	Sales	€126
Current assets		Cost of sales	€80
Stock	€9	Depreciation	€18
Debtors	€9	PBIT	€28
Cash	€6	Interest	€15
	€24	PBT	€13
Current liabilities		Tax (20%)	€3
Creditors	€6	PAT	€10
Short-term loans	€40		
	€46		
Net working capital	(€22)		
Net total assets	€158		
Financed by			
Debentures	€70		
Ordinary shares	€30		
Retained earnings	€58		
	€158		

(a) Calculate the following ratios:
  (i) Liquidity (current and acid test)
  (ii) Stock turnover
  (iii) Debtor turnover
  (iv) Days sales outstanding
  (v) Cash ratio
  (vi) Times interest earned
  (vii) Total debt ratio.

(b) Using the Du Pont identity, calculate the ROE and break it down into its different parts.

10. The balance sheet and income statement of Alpha Ltd is provided below and you are asked to calculate the various ratios that follow.

Profit and loss account	2008	2007
Turnover (net)	€100	€70
Cost of sales	€75	€48
Selling and admin. expenses	€8	€15
Depreciation	€1	€1
Profit before interest and tax	€16	€6
Interest	€2	€3
Profit before tax	€14	€3
Tax	€3	€0.6
Profit after tax	€11	€2.4
Balance sheet		
Fixed assets (net)	€20	€17
Current assets		
Stock	€10	€12
Debtors	€9	€5
Cash	€2	€3
Total current assets	€21	€20
Current liabilities		
Creditors	€3	€2
Short-term debt	€3	€2
Accruals	€4	€4
Total current liabilities	€10	€8
Working capital	€11	€12
Total net assets	€31	€29
Long-term debt	€9	€15
Ordinary shares	€1	€1
Retained earnings	€21	€13
	€31	€29

(a) Gross profit margin
(b) Operating profit margin
(c) Net profit margin
(d) Total asset turnover
(e) Fixed asset turnover
(f) Debtors turnover
(g) Stock turnover

(h) Current ratio
(i) Creditors payment period
(j) Debt ratio and equity multiplier
(k) TIE ratio
(l) ROE
(m) ROA.

11. Using the information from the balance sheet and income statement of Alpha Ltd, prepare a common size income statement and balance sheet.

12. From the information contained in the balance sheet and income statement of Alpha Ltd, construct a Du Pont analysis.

13.♦ Market to book ratios don't always tell the full story. Explain.

14. (a) Is it always good news when the current ratio increases?
     (b) If a firm has a low asset turnover ratio what does this mean and how can it be rectified?

15. The balance sheet and profit and loss account of Harry Murphy's DIY is as follows:

Balance sheet as at 31 December 2007 (€000)

Fixed assets (net)	€280
Current assets	
Stock	€300
Debtors	€120
Cash	€90
Total current assets	€510
Current liabilities	
Creditors	€100
Short-term loans	€90
Accruals	€40
Total current liabilities	€230
Working capital	€280
Total net assets	€560
Long-term debt	€50
Ordinary share capital	€230
Retained earnings	€280
	€560

Profit and loss account for the year ended 31 December 2007 (€000)

Net turnover	€1,600
Cost of goods sold	€1,280
Sales, general & distribution expenses	€140
Depreciation	€20
Profit before interest and tax	€160

Interest	€9
Profit before tax	€151
Tax	€23
Profit after tax	€128

The average financial ratios for the industry are as follows:

Fixed asset turnover	7x	Sales to stock	11x
Total asset turnover	3x	Debtors collection period	25 days
Net margin	4%	Times interest earned	6x
ROTA	10%	Current ratio	2.5x
ROE	13%	Gearing (debt: TA)	35%

As a financial analyst you are asked to prepare a report on the performance of Murphy's DIY which should include:
(a) a ratio analysis
(b) a Du Pont equation
(c) a comparison of Murphy's DIY with the industry average.

16. South East Manufacturing Ltd has total assets of €2m and an operating profit (PBIT/TA) of 25% on total assets. What would be the difference in the ROE if the company financed its operations with gearing of 40% or 100% equity? (Assume interest on debt of 5% and a corporation tax rate of 15%.)

17.♦ The net profit margin of Compu-Vision Ltd is 3% and the company's ROE is 16% and ROA = 11%. Calculate the equity multiplier.

18. Companies in the same industry will use standardised ratios that are meaningful and useful for that industry only. For example, hotels might use an income:cost per room ratio. Give examples of how different industries might use different ratios to standardise financial information.

19. Net income for the year is €100,000. The interest charges amount to €20,000 and depreciation charged is €5,000. Calculate the cash coverage ratio assuming a tax rate of 15%.

20. Express Cargo Ltd has a gearing ratio of 40%. The amount due in less than one year is €1,000 and it has a current ratio of 1.5. Its net profit margin is 6% on sales of €5,000. The company's ROE is 18%. How much does the company have invested in fixed assets?

APPENDIX 3A
Practices we need to look out for when using net worth as a measure of company liquidity

• Revaluation of assets
If assets are revalued, the increase in value is added to the asset figure in the balance sheet. For the balance sheet to balance (recall the balance sheet equation where assets equal capital *plus* liabilities) an equal amount should be added to the capital section of the balance sheet, since any increase in value belongs to the shareholders.

Example Revaluation of assets and net worth

A company has tangible fixed assets of €1m and share capital of €1m. In 2000 the company bought property for €100,000 which it paid for out of its share capital. In 2004 it decided to revalue its property portfolio and since property prices have been rising it is now valued at €400,000. The company decides to incorporate this into its balance sheet:

Balance sheet before revaluation		Balance sheet after revaluation
Fixed assets	€1m	€1.4m
Share capital	€1m	€1m
Revaluation reserve		€0.4m

Asset revaluation is not an exact science and not all companies revalue their assets. One should ask therefore if the company's positive net worth is due to asset revaluation. The possibility arises that some companies may revalue their assets simply to show a positive net worth. One should ask who carried out the valuation and what method of valuation was used.

- Provisions for liabilities and charges

In their accounts, companies make provisions for possible future liabilities. Provisions that relate to a reduction of an asset are deducted from that asset. For example, bad debt provisions are deducted from debtors in the balance sheet. Other provisions relate to potential losses and are shown on the balance as **provision for liabilities and charges**. It is with these that potential difficulties can arise because some companies will use this technique to **window dress** their accounts. For example, companies will not like disclosing bumper year profits because markets prefer steady non-volatile growth in earnings. If the market expects profits of €50 million and the company reports profits of €60 million, then the market will expect profits of €70 million the following year. Therefore, reporting higher than expected profits can generate unrealistic expectations about the company. To prevent this happening the company can camouflage its profits by increasing its provision for liabilities and charges. This will have the effect of lowering its reported net worth.

APPENDIX 3B
Adjusting gearing figures for goodwill

All gearing figures need to be adjusted for goodwill. Goodwill is the difference between the purchase price of an asset and its book value. If, for example, the book value of a company's assets is €100m and if the company is sold for €150m, goodwill is equal to €50m. Writing off goodwill reduces the gearing ratio as it reduces the capital and reserves. When looking at trends in a company's performance or inter-company comparisons, it is preferable to add back the figure for goodwill. The following example is taken from Kerry Group plc (1997).

Capital and reserves	€445,421
Goodwill reserve	€(357,357)
	€88,064

Kerry's long-term debt is given in note 14 to their accounts at €261,782. Total assets *less* current liabilities are given at €374,376. This is adjusted for the goodwill written off through reserves. Therefore the two gearing percentages are:*

Adjusted

*261,782 ÷ 731,733 = 36%

Unadjusted

€261,782 ÷ 374,376 = 70%

*€731,733 = €374,376 + Goodwill reserve €357,357

APPENDIX 3C
Interest cover and interest receivable

When calculating interest cover we should remember that the interest reported in the profit and loss account is usually net interest after deducting interest receivable. Should this be included when calculating interest cover? If interest receivable is a normal part of a company's profits then we should include it in calculating interest cover. If, on the other hand, interest received is not a normal part of business income then we should not include it in interest cover calculations.

Example Unidare plc

Note 7 to Unidare's annual report 1997 shows net interest expense as follows:

Net interest expense:
     Interest payable:
     Borrowings wholly repayable within five years:

– bank overdraft and loan	(€734)
– finance lease	(€9)
Interest receivable	€615
	(€128)

Profit before interest and tax for Unidare was €7,003 (000)

Interest cover (Unidare)

Including interest receivable
€7,618/€734 = 10.3 times

Excluding interest receivable
€7,003/€734 = 9.5 times

APPENDIX 3D
Why is gearing/leverage important?

Financial leverage has an important implication:
* If a company earns more on investments that have been financed with borrowed funds than it pays in interest, then the return on equity is enhanced or **geared**.

Example Gearing and return on equity

A company which has assets of €1m is financed totally with equity. It has no borrowed funds. The financial results of its first year of trading are:

Operating profit	€200,000
Taxation	€40,000
Profit after tax	€160,000

Therefore the return on equity (ROE) = PAT ÷ Equity = €160,000/€1m = 16%. For every €100 in equity the company makes €16 in profits after tax.

The company then decides to expand its business and invest a further €1m. This time it borrows the €1m from the bank at an interest rate of 7%. This additional investment of €1m generates the same amount of operating profit €200,000. A summary of its new financial position is as follows:

Operating profit	€400,000
Less interest	€70,000
Profit before tax (PBT)	€330,000
Taxation (20%)	€66,000
Profit after tax (PAT)	€264,000

Therefore the new return on equity = €264,000 ÷ €1m = 26.4%.

Therefore by using debt the company has **geared up** the return to equity shareholders. There are two reasons for this.

1. The interest paid on debt is tax deductible. In the above example the company pays €70,000 to the bank in interest charges. The corporation (company) tax rate is 20% on company profits. This tax is paid on €330,000, not €400,000. Therefore the company shareholders have an extra bonus of €14,000 (€70,000 × 20%).
2. Buying shares in a company is riskier than lending the company money. People and institutions that lend money to companies have a prior call on the company's assets. This means that they must be paid the interest on their loans before shareholders receive any return in the form of dividends. Banks, financial institutions and debenture holders must be paid the interest they are due. If this is not forthcoming, they have a right to enforce payment by forcing liquidation. On the other hand, shareholders will only be paid a dividend if the company directors decide that it is in the best interests of the firm. Therefore, because shareholders carry a greater risk, they require a higher rate of return to compensate for this higher risk.

In the above example, shareholders enhanced their return when the company increased the level of debt in the capital structure. The more gearing, the higher the return on equity. So why not have 100% gearing? The answer to this question depends on the overall level of risk attached to the firm. A firm has two types of risk associated with it:

- Business risk which relates to the type of business environment in which the company operates. The operations of a business will inherently face a certain amount of risk. This will relate to the type of business environment the business is in, e.g. the level of competition in the industry, industrial relations history etc., and on the level of operating leverage. Operating leverage refers to the proportion of total costs that are fixed. If a high proportion of a company's total costs are fixed, it will mean the company has high business risk. Capital intensive firms usually have high levels of fixed costs. This type of risk is business risk. Obviously some industries will face less business risk than others. Market share and profit margins will be tight in companies with high business risk. Any downturn in the company's fortunes (a fall-off in sales) could have serious implications for the company's profitability and survival. As we will see in Chapter 13, by using debt the company isolates business risk on to one type of investor – the ordinary shareholders.
- Financial risk refers to the level of debt the company has in its capital structure – its gearing. A company with a high level of debt has a high financial risk. The risk arises because interest on debt must be paid, whereas dividends do not have to be paid to equity shareholders.

A **general rule** is that companies with high business risk should carry low financial risk. Companies in very competitive environments should not carry high levels of debt. A company operating in a very competitive environment (high business risk) and therefore tight profit margins, runs the risk of going out of business if there is a slow-down in the economy or if there is a fall-off in the demand for its product or service because this will cut already tight profit margins. If a company has high operating leverage, a small change in sales will result in a large change in the return shareholders get on their investment. Interest on debt must be paid regardless of the amount of profits. A further example will help illustrate how financial leverage affects risk and return. Table 3D analyses two companies that are identical except for the way they are financed. Firm U (ungeared) has no debt, whereas firm G (geared) is financed half with equity and half with debt at 7% interest. Both companies have assets of €1,000 and sales of €1,000. Their **expected** operating profit (PBIT) is €400. However, things could turn out to be not what was expected. There could be a bad year for sales. Operating profit could be lower, and in the second column of the table, we see operating profit declining from €400 to €50 under bad conditions. Under normal, (expected/good) conditions, firm G will provide a return to its equity shareholders of 51.1% versus only 28% for firm U. However, financial gearing can cut both ways. If sales are lower and costs higher than expected, the return on assets will be lower than expected. The geared firm's return on equity falls faster than that for the ungeared firm. Under the bad conditions, the debt-free firm still shows a profit, but the geared firm shows a very low profit and return on equity. The geared firm needs cash to service its debt while the ungeared firm does not. Firm G must pay €35 in interest regardless of the levels of sales and profitability. If the economy is in recession, the firm is unlikely to be able to generate additional sales income to meet the interest payments. If the company doesn't have sufficient cash resources to meet the interest payment on its debt, it will either go into liquidation or it can try to raise additional equity capital. The latter option could prove to be very difficult when the firm is running at a loss. Selling shares does not prove attractive to potential shareholders when all the company wants to do is use the money raised to pay interest to banks and lower its debt:equity ratio. (A more detailed discussion of this will be given in Chapter 13.)

Table 3D Financial gearing and return on equity

Firm U (ungeared)		
Total assets	€1,000	
Financed by:		
Debt	€0	
Equity	€1,000	
	Good conditions	**Poor conditions**
Sales	€1,000	€500
Operating costs	€600	€450
Operating profit (profit before interest and tax)	€400	€50
Interest	–	–
Profit before tax (PBT)	€400	€50
Tax (30%)	€120	€15
Profit after tax	€280	€35
Return on Equity (ROE)	28%	3.5%

Geared firm (G)		
Total assets	€1,000	
Financed by:		
Debt (7%)	€500	
Equity	€500	
	Good conditions	**Poor conditions**
Sales	€1,000	€500
Operating costs	€600	€450
Operating profit	€400	€50
Interest	€35	€35
Profit before tax	€365	€15
Taxation (30%)	€109.5	€4.5
Profit after tax	€255.5	€10.5
Return on equity	51.1%	2.1%

To summarise:
- Firms with high debt ratios have higher than expected returns when the economy is normal, but they can suffer losses when the economy goes into recession.
- Firms with low debt ratios are less risky but they forgo the opportunity of **gearing up** their return on equity.

APPENDIX 3E
Sensitivity testing

Sensitivity testing can help us understand how Genesis can improve its overall performance. By assuming possible improvements in the company's cost ratios and/or improvements in sale price, we can trace the impact of these changes in the company's overall return on total assets and shareholders' investments.

Explanation

1 Ratio	2 Old value %	3 Change by %	4 New PBIT/ sales	5 New ROI %	6 % change ROI	7 New PBIT a	8 Interest a	9 PBT a	10 Tax %	11 New PAT a
Cost of sales/ Sales	54.4	(2)	10.56	14.37	11.3	663.6	180	453.6	30	317.5
S + D/ Sales	18.1	(2)	9.84	13.4	3.9	590.4	180	410.4	30	287.28
Admin./ Sales	15.3	(5)	10.2	14	8.5	612	180	432	30	303
Sales/ Total assets	1.36	5	14	20	110	882	180	702	30	491

12 Pref. div.	13 New PFO a	14 New PFO/ sales %	15 Asset turn times	16 New ROTA %	17 % change onROTA	18 New equity	19 New multiplier	20 New ROE	21 Old EOE	22 % change
8	309.5	5.2	1.36	7	17	2066.8	2.12	14.9	11.6	28
8	279.9	4.7	1.36	6.3	5.3	2055	2.13	13.4	10.5	28
8	295	5	1.36	6.7	11.4	2061	2.12	14.3	10.5	35
8	483	7.6	1.43	11	83	2716	1.6	17.8	10.5	69

To help explain the sensitivity test, take the cost of sales ratio.

Cost of sales ratio
- The old value is 54.4%, given in the vertical analysis above.

- Reducing this by 2% increases the PBIT by 2%, and we get a new PBIT/sales of 10.56% (54.4% × .02 = 1.09 + 9.48% =10.56%).
- The new ROI is the product of the new PBIT/sales ratio and the old asset turnover ratio (10.56 × 1.36 = 14.37). This constitutes an 11.3% increase from the old ROI, which was 12.9%.
- The new PBIT is €633.6 (€6,000 × 10.56% = €633).
- Interest is deducted of €180 and this gives a profit before tax of €453.6.
- Tax of 30% is deducted, giving a profit after tax of €317.5.
- Preference dividends (€8) are deducted leaving €309.5 for ordinary shareholders.
- The new PFO/sales ratio is €309.5/€6,000 = 5.2%.
- Multiplying the new PFO/sales ratio by the original asset turnover ratio of 1.36, gives the new return on total assets of 7% (1.36 × 5.2%). This constitutes an increase in the old ROTA of 17%.
- Profit for ordinary shareholders has increased from €264 to €309.5. The dividend pay-out ratio is 60% and 40% is added to retained earnings. Therefore €309.5 × 0.4 = €123.8 is added to retained earnings. This gives a new equity figure of €123.8 + €1,943 = €2,066.8.
- Total assets of €4,387 when divided by the new equity figure of €2,066.8 gives the new equity multiplier of 2.12
- Therefore, the new return on equity is 14.8% (2.12 × 7%), which constitutes an increase in the old ROE of 27%.

Sales/total assets
(Assumptions: an increase of 5% in selling price and no change in volume)

- The original asset turnover ratio is 1.36 times.
- Before any changes are made, €9.48 in every €100 sales income is operating profit. The other €90.52 goes to pay the operating costs. Given an increase of 5% in selling price, **and no other changes,** the operating costs as a percentage of sales falls to 86% (90.5 divided by 1.05). Therefore, the new PBIT/sales ratio is the residual 14% (100% *minus* 86%).
- Therefore the new sales to total asset ratio is 1.43 (6,000 × 1.05)/€4,387.
- The new ROI is now 20% (1.43 × 14%). This is an increase of 55% on the original ROI of 12.9%.
- The new PBIT figure is €882 (€6,000 × 1.05 = €6,300 × 0.14).
- Deducting interest, tax and preference dividends gives a profit for ordinary shareholders of €483 and a new PFO/sales of 7.6% (483/6,300).
- The new ROTA is 11% (7.6% × new asset turn ratio of 1.43), which is a huge 82% increase in the ROTA (i.e. the original ROTA was 6.01%). **This shows the importance of price in the overall calculations.**
- Adding the increase in retained earnings (€483 × 0.4 = €193.2) gives the new equity figure of (€193.2 + €1,943 = €2,136.2) and a new equity multiplier of €4,387 ÷ €2,136.2 = 2.05.
- Consequently, the new ROE is 11% × 2.05 = 22.5%, or a 94% increase (from the original 11.6%).

Sensitivity testing can be performed for cost reductions (and/or price increases) or cost increases (and/or price reductions). In reality, it may be difficult, or impossible, in some situations to cut costs or increase prices. Even if costs can be reduced, it might have productivity side effects particularly in the area of labour relations and motivation. Nevertheless, sensitivity testing provides us with a useful tool in financial analysis.

NOTES

1. Sometimes cost of sales means different things to different companies, so turnover is often used instead of cost of sales in creditors payment period calculations.
2. A more detailed analysis of working capital and overtrading is given in Chapter 11.
3. The term interval measure is used by Ross, Westerfield & Jordan in 'Working with Financial Statements', *Fundamentals of Corporate Finance*.
4. The profit before interest and tax figure may include **exceptional items**. These are once-off items, so when we calculate interest cover it is important to exclude exceptional items in the calculation:

Interest cover = PBIT less exceptional items/interest payments

5. Because interest is paid before tax is deducted, the numerator is PBIT because the full amount of operating income is available for interest payments.
6. There was a net increase in fixed assets of €2,460 *minus* €1,923 = €537. This is the net increase **after** the deduction for this year's depreciation. Therefore, the depreciation expense should be added back in to show the total increase in **gross** fixed assets.
7. Remember that an **overdraft** is seen as **negative** cash. So therefore the opening cash is €70 *minus* €120 (overdraft) = €50. Cash at the end of the year is €7 *minus* €220 (overdraft) = €213.
8. A more detailed discussion on this topic is provided in Chapter 17 on inventory and credit management.
9. The reader might find it useful to refer to Chapter 16 on working capital.
10. In calculating MVA and market to book ratios, the following issues will need to be considered:
    (a) Goodwill: goodwill arising on acquisition should be amortised over its life. Assets are reduced by the amount of goodwill and reserves by the same amount. Using this method, profits are not affected and balance sheet totals are reduced. Rates of return on assets and equity will therefore increase because of this artificial reduction in assets. This will have the effect of enhancing the market to book ratio.
    (b) Revaluation of fixed assets. What effect will a company's revaluation policy have on valuation ratios? The increase in asset values will be matched by an increase in reserves. The revaluation does not affect the profit and loss account, as it is not a realised profit. The consequence of this is that the return on assets and the return on equity will get worse. This will not boost market to book ratios.
    (c) Pension funds. Surpluses or deficits in pension funds will impact on the company's value.

11. The share price and the number of shares were extracted from *The Irish Stock Manual 2000*. For simplicity, the share price is taken as the average between the high and low prices on offer for 1998. Shareholder funds is that reported in their balance sheet in 1998.

12. It is usual to extend this analysis to several years.

Part 2

Fundamental Concepts in Finance –
Risk and Return

4

The Time Value of Money

CHAPTER OBJECTIVES

At the end of this chapter the student should be able to:

1. understand the concept of the time value of money
2. distinguish between simple and compound interest calculations and when to use each
3. understand the concept of discounting
4. understand the difference between the nominal and effective rates of interest
5. calculate the effective rate of interest from the nominal rate and vice versa
6. understand the difference between fixed and variable rates of interest
7. understand the concept of annuities
8. distinguish between present value and future value of an annuity
9. calculate the value of each of the four variables in both the present value and future value of an annuity formula, i.e. present/future value, interest rate, number of payments, periodic payments.

INTRODUCTION

If you were offered the following option:

* €10,000 now or
* €10,000 in ten years' time

which would you choose?

It is almost certainly the case that your answer would be €10,000 now.

Why would everyone choose the first option? There are a number of possible reasons:

* risk of default, i.e. perhaps in ten years' time the person/institution offering the €10,000 will have disappeared and you won't get the money;
* inflation over the next ten years will eat into the value of €10,000 and will be far less valuable then than now.

Let's exclude these two possibilities, i.e. the €10,000 is guaranteed with no default risk and inflation is guaranteed to be zero for the next ten years.

The third and most important reason why you would choose the €10,000 now is because money has a **time value**, i.e. money now is more desirable and valuable than the same amount at some date in the future. A simple rationale for this is that if you have the money now you could place it in a demand deposit account paying, say, 5% p.a. and have instant access to it. In technical terms you are receiving a **return** and have a **liquid** asset. If you left it there for ten years it would be worth a lot more than €10,000 (€16,288.94 – see below). Alternatively you could remove the interest each year, consume it and still leave the €10,000 intact.

Likewise if you are offered an investment which pays €10,000 in ten years' time, you won't pay €10,000 for it now. You will pay a sum less than that. Why? Because you want to make a return on your investment and you want to be rewarded for forgoing access to your money (i.e. liquidity).

4.1 Simple interest

Interest is the amount paid on a periodic basis on a savings account (or charged on a loan). It is usually calculated as a percentage of the amount (principal) in the account at the beginning of the period. Savers may choose to take the interest from the account at the end of each period. In this case the principal will remain intact at its original value. The interest earned over n periods of time by the saver, in this case, is referred to as simple interest and can be calculated from 4.1 below:

$$I = PV.k.n \qquad\qquad (4.1)$$

where I = interest earned
            PV = present value (original principal)
            k = interest rate per period
            n = number of interest periods.

The value of any one of the four variables can be calculated from the other three.

If interest is taken from the account at the end of each period and held in a non-interest bearing form, e.g. a shoebox under the bed, the amount the saver will have after n periods is the original principal *plus* the simple interest.

$$FV = PV + I \qquad\qquad (4.2)$$

where FV = Future value

This can be written as $FV = PV + PV.k.n$

or

$$FV = PV (1 + k.n) \qquad\qquad (4.3)$$

where PV = present value

FV = future value
  k = interest rate per period
  n = number of interest periods/fraction of interest period.

Example 4.1 Future value using simple interest

Suppose €1,000 was deposited into an account paying 8% p.a. and left for 5 years. If the interest is withdrawn each year and held in a non-interest bearing form, then the total amount that the saver has at the end of 5 years is, from 4.3 above:

$$FV = 1,000(1 + (0.08). 5) = 1,400$$

While this is a somewhat artificial situation it is useful as a comparison with the equivalent compound interest calculation (see example 4.6 below).

    If the principal is left in the account for less than a full interest period, then the interest is normally calculated as a fraction of the interest for the full period, e.g. if interest is paid annually and the saver withdraws the money after six months, the interest would be half of the stated annual rate.

    Any one of the parameters in 4.3 can be calculated if the other three are known, through simple algebraic manipulation. The following examples assume that money is deposited for less than a full year.

Example 4.2 Solving for future value

A lady places €5,000 in a deposit account which pays 8% p.a. Interest is paid on a pro rata basis if left in the account for less than one year. If she closes the account 3 months later, how much money will she get?

Here   PV = 5,000
               k = 0.08k
               n = $^1/_4$

Using 4.3 $FV = 5,000 (1 + (0.08).(^1/_4)) = 5,100$

Example 4.3 Solving for present value

Suppose the same lady as above wished to have €5,600 after 3 months. How much would she have to put on deposit now?

Here   FV = 5,600
               k = 0.08
               n = $^1/_4$

Using 4.3 $5,600 = PV (1 + (0.08) . (^1/_4))$

$$PV = \frac{5{,}600}{(1 + (0.08) \cdot (^1/4))} = 5{,}490.20$$

Example 4.4 Solving for the time factor

A lady places €5,000 in a deposit account which pays 8% p.a. Interest is paid on a pro rata basis on money on deposit for less than a year. How long will it take before she can withdraw €5,250?

Here   PV = 5,000
         FV = 5,250
          k = 0.08

Using 4.3 $5{,}250 = 5{,}000 (1 + (0.08).n) = 5{,}100$

$$n = \frac{\dfrac{5{,}250}{5{,}000} - 1}{0.08} = 0.625$$

The answer above is expressed as a fraction of a year. To convert it into days or months simply multiply it by 365 or 12, e.g. $0.625 \times 365 = 228$ days.

Example 4.5 Solving for the interest rate

A lady wishes to have €5,300 in six months' time. If she places €5,000 in a deposit account now, what annual rate of interest must she earn to reach her target? Assume that interest is paid on a pro rata basis if left in the account for less than one year.

Here   PV = 5,000
         FV = 5,300
          n = $^1/2$

Using 4.3 $5{,}300 = 5{,}000 (1 + k.(^1/2))$

$$k = \frac{\dfrac{5{,}300}{5{,}000} - 1}{^1/2} = 0.12 = 12\%$$

4.2 Compound interest

The saver may choose to leave the interest in an account, in which case it is added to the principal at the end of each interest period. Interest is then earned on both the original principal and the interest earned to date. The fund is said to earn interest on a compound basis i.e. compound interest.

The value of the savings fund after n periods can be calculated from 4.4 below

$$FV = PV\,(1 + k)^n \qquad\qquad (4.4)$$

where   PV   = present value (original principal)
           FV   = future value
           k   = interest rate per period
           n   = number of interest periods.

Example 4.6 Compound interest

How much is in an account after five years if €1,000 is deposited and the fund earns interest at the rate of 8% p.a.?

Using 4.4 above $FV = 1,000\,(1.08)^5 = 1,469.33$

Note that the future value here is substantially greater than the value in example 4.1, which used simple interest. This illustrates the value of compounding. Section 4.4 below shows that the more frequent the interest compounding, the greater is the final value of the investment.

     Any one of the parameters in 4.4 can be calculated if the other three are known, through simple algebraic manipulation. Example 4.6 above showed how to calculate FV. The calculation of PV is left until section 4.3. The calculation of n and k are shown in examples 4.7 and 4.8 below. The value of n can be found using logarithms.

Example 4.7 Finding the time factor

A man deposits €5,000 into an account paying 8% p.a. compound. How long will it take for the value to grow to €8,000?

Here   PV   = 5,000
           FV   = 8,000
           k   = 0.08

The value of n can be found using logarithms.

From 4.4 $8,000 = 5,000\,(1.08)^n$

Through algebraic manipulation this can be reduced to

$$n \times \log 1.08 \;=\; \log \frac{8,000}{5,000} = \log 1.6$$

$$n = \frac{\log 1.6}{\log 1.08} = 6.11$$

Thus it takes a little over 6 years to reach the target of €8,000.

Example 4.8 Finding the interest rate

A man deposits €5,000 into an account. He wishes to have €8,000 ten years later. What annual rate of interest must the account pay?

Here   PV = 5,000
         FV = 8,000
          n = 10.

From 4.4 $8,000 = 5,000 (1 + k)^{10}$
    This reduces to

$$(1 + k)^{10} = 1.6$$
$$1 + k = (1.6)^{1/10} = 1.0481$$
$$k = 0.0481 = 4.81\%$$

In order to avoid repetitive calculations, the compound interest tables (Table A2.1) shown in Appendix 2 can be used. The columns give the rate of interest per period, while the rows give the number of periods. The entries in the body of the table show the value of a €1 investment for the specified period of time at the specified rate of interest per period. Thus to find the value of a €1 investment for 5 years at 6% p.a., simply read the relevant entry from the table, i.e. 1.3382 (the future value is €1.3382). The future value of any other investment amount is got by multiplying it by 1.3382, e.g. the value of a €6,000 investment at 6% p.a. for 5 years is found thus:

$$€6,000 \times 1.3382 = €8,029.2$$

4.3 Discounting and present value

Discounting is basically the opposite of compounding.

Discounting arises because **money has a time value**. As pointed out at the start of this chapter, money is worth more now than in the future if only because it can be invested and can earn a return.

Let's look at a simple example, first without discounting and then using a discounting approach.

Suppose an investment costs €500 now and pays €250 at the end of each of the next three years. Is this a good investment? Assume there is no default risk and there is no inflation in the economy over the three years. It looks like a good investment. The investor receives €750 over three years for a €500 outlay now. This looks like a 50% return over three years.

The above is misleading. It **may** be a good investment – this depends on the rate of interest in the economy.

Suppose the investor borrowed to buy the investment and suppose the bank charged an annual interest rate of 10%.

The investor's bank account might look like this:

Time	Borrow	Interest	Repay	Balance
0	500			– 500
1		50	250	– 300
2		30	250	– 80
3		8	250	162

This is a good investment. The investor ends up with €162 at the end of the third year.

Now repeat this exercise where the rate of interest charged by the bank is 30% p.a.

Time	Borrow	Interest	Repay	Balance
0	500			– 500
1		150	250	– 400
2		120	250	– 270
3		81	250	– 101

Now the investor makes a loss. The message here is that the value of the investment depends crucially on the rate of interest.

The figures of €162 profit and €101 loss might be termed the net terminal value of this investment.

Now look at this investment from a different perspective. Suppose the bank charges 10% p.a. on borrowed funds. How much could the investor borrow from the bank using this investment as security?

The €250 receivable in one year's time could support a borrowing of

$$\frac{€250}{1.1} = €227.27$$

In other words if the investor borrowed €227.27 from the bank today, he could discharge this debt in one year's time with a payment of €250.

Likewise the receipts of €250 at the end of the second and third years could support borrowings of

$$\frac{€250}{(1.1)^2} \text{ and } \frac{€250}{(1.1)^3} = €206.61 \text{ and } €187.83 \text{ respectively.}$$

The three future receipts could together support a borrowing of €621.71 in total. Since the investment only costs €500 to buy, the investor can take a profit of €121.71 now.

The three numbers represent the discounted values or present values of future receipts. The sum of €621.71 is the total discounted or present value of the future stream of income and the net present value (see Chapter 12 of the investment is €121.71.

The student should now re-do the above calculation where the rate of interest is 30% on borrowed funds. This will show that the present value of the future receipts is €454.03 and the net present value of the investment is – €45.97.

Again it is clear that as the rate of interest increases, the present value of a future receipt decreases and vice versa.

The discounted or present value of a future sum can be calculated by inverting 4.4 above, i.e.

$$PV = \frac{FV}{(1 + k)^n} \tag{4.5}$$

Example 4.9 Finding the discounted value of a future receipt

An investment bond (bonds are dealt with in detail in Chapter 5) is due to pay €8,000 in five years' time. How much is it worth today if the rate of interest on such investments is 12% p.a.?

Using 4.5 above

$$PV = \frac{8,000}{(1.12)^5} = 4,539.41$$

Discounting is the fundamental basis of discounted cash flow analysis as discussed in Chapter 12 and the mathematics of bond market investment as discussed in Chapter 5.

Each of the other parameters in 4.5 can be calculated from the other three. This is not shown here as the approach is similar to that used in the compounding formula.

Just as in the case of compounding, a set of mathematical tables may be used to avoid repetitive calculations in discounting. The discount tables shown in the appendix (Table A2.2) can be used. The columns give the rate of interest per period, while the rows give the number of periods. The entries in the body of the table show the value today of a €1 receipt at a specified time in the future for a specified rate of interest per period. Thus to find today's value of €1 in 5 years' time where the rate of interest in the market is 6% p.a., simply read the relevant entry from the table, i.e. 0.7473, and the present value is €0.7473, i.e. just under 75 cent. The present value of any other future amount is got by multiplying it by 0.7473, e.g. the value of a €6,000 receipt in 5 years where the appropriate rate of interest is 6% p.a. is found by

$$6,000 \times 0.7473 = €4,483.80$$

4.4 Nominal and effective rate of interest

Banks normally quote a rate of interest on an annual basis but may charge interest to the account more often than once a year. Likewise interest may be added to a savings account more often than once a year. The stated/advertised rate is referred to as the nominal rate. The actual rate that the borrower pays or the actual rate that the saver earns will be greater than the nominal rate if compounding takes place more often than once a year. The actual rate is referred to as the effective rate of interest or annual percentage rate (APR). In practice the APR may also include other costs such as set-up charges, etc. These are ignored here for simplicity. The APR can be calculated from 4.6 below:

$$\text{Effective rate of interest } = \left(1 + \frac{j_m}{m}\right)^m - 1 \qquad (4.6)$$

where jm = nominal rate of interest compounded m times per year.

Example 4.10 Effective rate of interest

(a) What is the effective rate of interest if the nominal rate of interest is 9% p.a. and interest is compounded quarterly?
Using formula 4.6

$$\text{Effective rate of interest } = \left(1 + \frac{0.09}{4}\right)^4 - 1 = 0.093 = 9.3\%$$

(b) What is the effective rate of interest p.a. if the nominal rate is 15% p.a. and interest is compounded monthly?

$$\text{Effective rate of interest } = \left(1 + \frac{0.15}{12}\right)^{12} - 1 = 0.1608 = 16.08\%$$

(c) At what nominal rate of interest compounded monthly must €1,000 be invested in order to double itself in eight years?
Here   PV = 1,000
       FV = 2,000
        n = 96 months
        k = unknown, where k = monthly rate

Solve for k from formula 4.4 above.

$$2,000 = 1,000\,(1 + k)^{96}$$
$$2 = (1 + k)^{96}$$
$$2^{1/96} = 1 + k$$
$$1.007246412 = 1 + k$$
$$0.007246412 = k$$

This gives k = 0.007246412

The nominal rate is therefore $12 \times 0.007246412 = 0.086956 = 8.7\%$

4.5 Fixed versus variable rates of interest

Banks may offer savers or borrowers an option to receive or pay a fixed rather than a variable rate of interest. In times of rising interest rates borrowers are protected by fixed rates, but they do not get the benefit if rates fall. The opposite applies to savers.

Whether choosing a fixed rate over a variable rate is an efficient decision or not is really only answerable after the event. With a fixed rate borrowers are opting for certainty over uncertainty.

Example 4.11 Fixed and variable rates of interest

What fixed rate of interest p.a. payable for five years provides an equivalent compound investment return to a variable rate structure paying interest as follows?

Year	Rate of interest
1	10
2	12
3	14
4	9
5	15

The fixed rate is that which would produce the same future value after 5 years as the variable rate structure.

Future value using variable rates
Let the initial investment be €1,000

$$FV = 1,000 \ (1.1).(1.12).(1.14).(1.09).(1.15) = 1,760.52$$

Future value using fixed rates
$1,760.52 = 1,000 \ (1 + k)^5$
where k = fixed rate of interest p.a.
Solving the above equation gives k = 11.98%

$$\text{Check } 1,000 \ (1.1198)^5 = €1,760.77$$

Example 4.12 Fixed versus variable rate

What fixed nominal rate of interest p.a. compounded monthly would be equivalent to a variable rate structure over three years if the variable rate was

(a) 10% p.a. compounded quarterly in the first year?
(b) 12% p.a. compounded monthly in the second year?
(c) 14% p.a. compounded half-yearly in the third year?

Variable rate
Let initial investment = €1,000

$$FV = 1,000 \ (1.025)^4 \ (1.01)^{12} \ (1.07)^2 = 1,424.03$$

Fixed rate
$$1,424.03 = 1,000 \ (1+k)^{36} \text{ where k = } \mathbf{monthly} \text{ rate of interest}$$

Solving the equation gives k = 0.0098676
Nominal annual rate = $12 \times 0.0098676 = 0.1184 = 11.84\%$

4.6 Continuous streams of payments

Continuous regular streams of payments are a feature of many financial arrangements, either formally or informally.

- A young lady wishes to save in order to decorate her apartment and decides that she can afford to save €300 per month. She may be interested in knowing how long it will take to reach a certain target figure or she may wish to know how much she will have saved after a certain period of time.
- Her brother wants to buy a new car. He does so by borrowing from a finance company. He will be interested in knowing what his regular repayment will be or how long it will take to pay off the loan.

The two examples illustrate the two principal driving forces of a continuous stream of payments, either a future value (FV) to be reached or a present value (PV), here a loan, to be paid off. The present value of a stream of payments also arises in relation to investment appraisal (see Chapter 12).

Future value of annuity

Using the example of the young lady saving to decorate her apartment, she lodges €300 into an account at the end of each month. The account pays a monthly interest rate of 0.5%. How much has she got in the account after three years, i.e. 36 deposits?

Each of the payments will earn compound interest at the same interest rate, but for a different length of time. The first payment will earn interest for 35 months, the second for 34 months and so on. The second last payment will earn one month's interest and the last deposit will earn no interest, if the account is valued at the end of the third year. The total value is therefore the sum of the 36 deposits *plus* the compound interest on each one. This can be calculated as follows:

FV @ time 36 = 300 $(1.005)^{35}$ + 300 $(1.005)^{34}$ + . . . + . . . 300$(1.005)^1$ + 300

Calculating the value of this stream would involve 36 calculations. However, since the terms form a geometric progression, it can be easily shown that the sum is given by 4.7 below.

$$FV = P_t \left[\frac{(1 + k)^n - 1}{k} \right]$$
(4.7)

where   FV = future value
Pt = periodic payment
k   = interest rate per compounding period
n   = number of payments.

Note that the fund is valued just as the last payment is being made and so the last payment earns no interest.

The stream of payments in this example forms an ordinary simple annuity. The conditions for an **ordinary simple annuity** in the future value case are:

- the rate of interest is paid at the same frequency as the payments are being made (here monthly)
- the interest is added to the account at the same time as the payments are being made (here at the end of the month)
- the fund is valued just at the point when the last payment is being made (here at the end of the 36th month).

Any one of the four variables can be calculated given the other three. Calculation of the number of payments required, i.e. n, requires the use of logarithms, while the calculation of the rate of interest requires a trial and error approach. The technique of linear interpolation can be used to find the value of k (see example 4.14 below).

In the example above, if payments had been made at the start of each month and the fund is valued at the end of the 36th month, then each payment earns an additional one month's interest. The value from the formula above would be multiplied by (1.005) or (1 + k) in the general case. This is referred to as a simple annuity due.

Example 4.13 Future value of an ordinary simple annuity

Solving for the future value

A young lady is saving to decorate her apartment. She lodges €300 into an account at the end of each month. The account pays a monthly interest rate of 0.5%. How much has she got in the account after three years?

Using 4.7 above

$$FV = 300 \left[\frac{(1.005)^{36} - 1}{0.005} \right] = 11{,}800.83$$

Annuity tables – future value

4.7 involves the calculation of the following:

$$\frac{(1+k)^n - 1}{k}$$

This is a repetitive calculation, differing only in the value of the two parameters, n and k. In order to avoid such repetitive calculations, a set of annuity tables is provided in the Appendix. There are two sets, one for future value and the other for present value. The entries in the body of the future value annuity table (Table A2.4) give the future value, after n periods, of a regular stream of €1 deposits for n periods into an account paying k% per period, e.g. €1 invested at the end of each year for 12 years into an account paying 8% p.a. has a value at the end of the 12th year of €18.98, according to the tables.

This annuity factor, 18.98, can then be used to find the value of any other equal deposit for the same period at the same rate of interest, e.g. if the deposit had been €50, then the future value at the end of the 12th year is €50 × 18.98 = €949.

Each row represents a different time period and each column represents a different rate of interest.

Solving for the periodic payment

If one wished to set a target of €10,000, and wanted to know the size of the monthly deposit required, it can be solved from the expression. (The interest rate and the term are as above.)

$$10,000 = P_t \left[\frac{(1.005)^{36} - 1}{0.005} \right]$$

The value is solved by simple algebraic manipulation and is €254.22.

Solving for the number of payments

If one wished to know how long it would take to reach a target of €10,000 with payments of €300 per month, it can be solved from the expression

$$10,000 = 300 \left[\frac{(1.005)^{n} - 1}{0.005} \right]$$

The value is solved using logarithms.

$$(1.005)^{n} = \frac{10,000 \times 0.005}{300} + 1 = 1.166667$$

$$n \times \log(1.005) = \log 1.166667$$

$$n = \frac{\log 1.166667}{\log(1.005)} = 30.9$$

This can be interpreted as 30 full deposits and one final deposit at the end of the 31st month less than €300. It will not be equal to 0.9 of €300 since the relationship between P_t and n in 4.7 is not linear. In some instances there may be no need for a final smaller payment since the interest alone will carry the fund value over the target in the last month. This is covered in the end of chapter questions.

Since the monthly rate of interest is small in the above example, a different example is used to illustrate the calculation of the rate of interest.

Example 4.14 Solving for the rate of interest

A company has to repay a loan of €600,000 in eight years' time. It sets up a fund and deposits €50,000 at the end of each year for the eight years. Calculate, using the technique of linear interpolation, the annual rate of interest which the company must earn on the fund in order to pay off the loan in the time required. Answer to one place of decimals.

Using 4.7

$$600,000 = 50,000 \left[\frac{(1 + k)^8 - 1}{k} \right]$$

Since k appears in the formula above and below the line, there is no simple algebraic manipulation which can isolate it on one side of the equation. It must be solved by trial and error.

A number of trial values of k are inserted into the equation above. This is continued until two rates produce values either side of the target of €600,000.

Since the answer will be approximated between these two rates, the nearer they are, the more accurate the answer will be. All examples in this chapter (and in Chapters 5 and 15) approximate the answer to one place of decimals using the technique of linear interpolation between two interest rates which are one percentage point apart.

Using k = 10% produces FV = €571,794.41. This leaves the fund short of the target, therefore the rate of interest must be higher than 10%.

Using k = 11% produces FV = €592,971.71. This still leaves the fund short of the target, therefore the rate of interest must be higher than 11%.

Using k = 12% produces FV = €614,984.66. This is above the target and so the required rate is below 12%.

The rate is therefore between 11% and 12%. The answer can be approximated using linear interpolation.

A quicker way to locate the two discount rates is to divide the FV by the P_t in formula 4.7. This gives the value of the expression in brackets. In this example it equals 12.

Now, using the n = 8 row in table A2.4 in Appendix 2 (the FV of an ordinary simple annuity), locate the interest rate that gives a value near to 12. A rate of 10% gives a value of 11.436, while a rate of 12% gives a value of 12.3. This tells us that the answer is between 10% and 12% and suggests that it might be close to 11%.

The technique of linear interpolation assumes that the future value rises in a linear fashion as the rate of interest is increased. While the true relationship is non-linear, the assumption of linearity is a reasonable approximation for small changes in the rate of interest.

A one percentage point rise in k from 11% causes the future value to rise by €22,012.95 (614,984.66 − 592,971.71). What fraction of a 1 per cent increase in k from 11% would cause the future value to rise by €7,028.29 (600,000.00 − 592,971.71)? This is calculated as follows:

$$\frac{x}{1} = \frac{7{,}028.29}{22{,}012.95} = 0.3$$

The answer is therefore approximated as 11.3%. This can be checked by using 11.3% as the value of k in 4.7 and calculating FV. This produces FV = 599,486.51 which is €13.49 short of the target. To complete the answer, k should be increased to 11.4% and FV recalculated. This produces FV = 601,674.96, which is significantly above the target. The answer is therefore k = 11.3% correct to one place of decimals.

(Linear interpolation is discussed and explained in more detail in Chapter 5.)

Present value of annuity

Using the example of the young man wishing to buy a new car, he reckons that he can repay €350 per month off a loan. The bank charges interest at the rate of 0.7% per month. He wishes to pay the loan off over a period of three years. How much can he afford to borrow?

Each of the monthly payments could itself pay off a small loan. For example, the payment of €350 in one month's time could pay off a loan taken out today. The bank would lend an amount of money so that when interest is added to it for one month, the debt to the bank would be €350 and the loan would be cleared with the single payment. The amount the bank would lend is simply the present value or discounted value of €350 payable in one month's time. This can be solved using 4.5 above.

$$PV = \frac{FV}{(1 + k)^n}$$

$$PV = \frac{350}{(1.007)^1} = 347.57$$

The bank would therefore lend the man €347.57 today which would be repaid in one month's time at €350.

Likewise the bank would lend a second amount which would be repaid in two months' time with a payment of €350. The amount of this loan can be calculated as

$$PV = \frac{350}{(1.007)^2} = €345.15$$

The 36 repayments can therefore be seen as repaying a succession of different loans, each one smaller as the payment period is further out into the future. The total that could be borrowed is therefore

$$PV = \frac{350}{(1.007)^1} + \frac{350}{(1.007)^2} \ldots + \ldots \frac{350}{(1.007)^{35}} + \frac{350}{(1.007)^{36}}$$

This involves 37 calculations. However since the terms form a geometric progression, it can easily be shown that the sum is given by 4.8 below

$$PV = P_t \left[\frac{1 - (1 + k)^{-n}}{k} \right] \tag{4.8}$$

where
  PV = present value
  Pt = periodic payment
  k   = interest rate per discounting period
  n   = number of payments.

Note that the loan is valued at the start of the month but the first payment is made at the end of the month.

   This stream of payments in this example forms an **ordinary simple annuity**. The conditions for an ordinary simple annuity in the present value case are:

• the rate of interest is paid at the same frequency as the payments are being made (here monthly)
• the interest is added to the account at the same time as the payments are being made (here at the end of the month)
• payments start at the end of the first interest period or one period after the loan is taken out (here at the end of the 1st month).

Any one of the four variables can be calculated given the other three. Calculation of the number of payments required, i.e. n, requires the use of logarithms, while the calculation of the rate of interest requires a trial and error approach. The technique of linear interpolation can be used to find the value of k (see example 4.16 below).

   In the example above, if the repayments had started at the beginning of the first month, one month's interest is saved and so a larger loan could be taken out. The value from the formula above would be multiplied by (1.005) or (1 + k) in the general case. This is referred to as a simple annuity due. This would be unusual in a lending situation but could arise in an investment appraisal situation (see Chapter 12).

Example 4.15 Present value of an ordinary simple annuity

Solving for the present value

A young man wishing to buy a new car reckons that he can repay €350 per month off a loan. The bank charges interest at the rate of 0.7% per month. He wishes to pay off the loan over a period of three years. How much can he afford to borrow?

Using 4.8, the PV can be solved as

$$PV = 350 \left[\frac{1 - (1.007)^{-36}}{0.007} \right]$$

This produces an answer of €11,103.63.

Annuity tables – present value

Formula 4.8 involves the calculation of the following

$$\frac{1 - (1 + k)^{-n}}{k}$$

This is a repetitive calculation, differing only in the value of the two parameters, n and k. Similar to the case of the future value, there is a set of annuity tables to obviate the need for such calculations in the present value case. The entries in the body of the present value annuity table (Table A2.3) give the present value of a regular stream of €1 payments for n periods where the discount rate is k% per period, e.g. a €1 repayment each year for 12 years against a loan which is charging interest at 8% p.a. can support a loan size of €7.54 today, according to the tables. This annuity factor, 7.54, can then be used to find the value of any other equal payment stream for the same period at the same rate of interest, e.g. if the repayment had been €50, then the present value is €50 x 7.54 = €377.

Each row represents a different time period and each column represents a different rate of interest.

Solving for the periodic payment

Suppose the man wished to borrow €12,000 and wanted to know what the monthly repayments would be. The interest rate and term of the loan are as above.

Using 4.8

$$12,000 = Pt \left[\frac{1 - (1.007)^{-36}}{0.007} \right]$$

This produces an answer of = €378.25

Solving for the number of payments

Suppose the man can only afford to repay €300 per month and wants to borrow €12,000. How long would it take to clear the loan? The interest rate is as before.

Using 4.8

$$12,000 = 300 \left[\frac{1 - (1.007)^{-n}}{0.007} \right]$$

The solution requires the use of logarithms. The procedure is similar to that in the future case and is not reproduced here. The answer works out at n = 47.09. This can be interpreted as 47 monthly payments of €300 and a final smaller payment one month later. The final smaller payment will not be 0.09 of €300, since the relationship between P_t and n is not linear. Alternatively the loan could be cleared on the 47th month by increasing the €300 payment. The increased size of the 47th payment or the size of the 48th payment can be calculated by using the outstanding balance formula. This is discussed in Chapter 20.

Calculation of the rate of interest from 4.8 requires the use of linear interpolation. This is shown in the example below.

Example 4.16 Solving for the rate of interest

A company is repaying a loan of €800,000 with annual repayments of €120,000 over a period of twelve years, with the first repayment made one year after the loan is taken out. Calculate, using the technique of linear interpolation, the annual rate of interest which is being charged on the loan. Answer to one place of decimals.

Using 4.8

$$800,000 = 120,000 \left[\frac{1 - (1 + k)^{-12}}{k} \right]$$

As before, trial values of k are inserted into the equation above.

Using k = 10% produces PV = €817,643.02. This means that at a rate of interest of 10%, 12 annual payments of €120,000 would pay off a loan of €817,643.02. Since the loan is only €800,000, the rate of interest must be above 10%.

Using k = 11% produces PV = €779,082.74. This is below the loan size and so the required rate is below 11%.

The rate is therefore between 10% and 11%. The answer can be approximated using linear interpolation.

The technique of linear interpolation assumes that the present value falls in a linear fashion as the rate of interest is increased. While the true relationship is non-linear, the assumption of linearity is a reasonable approximation for small changes in the rate of interest.

A one percentage point rise in k from 10% causes the present value to fall by €38,560.28 (817,643.02 – 779,082.74). What fraction of a one per cent increase in k from 10% would cause the present value to fall by €17,643.02 (817,643.02 – 800,000.00)? This is calculated as follows:

$$\frac{x}{1} = \frac{17,643.02}{38,560.28} = 0.46$$

The answer is therefore approximated as 10.5%. This can be checked by using 10.5% as the value of k in 4.8 and calculating PV. This produces PV = 797,995.72 which is €2,004.28 short of the given loan size. To complete the answer k should be reduced to 10.4% and PV recalculated. This produces PV = 801,865.31 which is just €1,865.31 above the loan size. The answer is therefore k = 10.4% correct to one place of decimals.

SUMMARY

- Money has a time value, i.e. money received now is worth more than the same amount received at a time in the future.
- Money invested for a period of time grows in value at a compound rate.
- The process of discounting is used to find the present-day equivalent (present value) of a future sum.
- The higher the discount factor, the lower the present value of a future receipt.
- The annual effective rate of interest is higher than the nominal/stated rate if compounding takes place more often than once a year.
- Fixed rates of interest protect borrowers against the possibility of increased interest charges, but prevent them from benefiting if interest rates fall.
- Many financial arrangements involve a continuous stream of regular payments. This may be in the context of repaying a loan or receiving a pension or other payment.
- Loan repayments can often be treated as an ordinary simple annuity, where the loan size will equal the present value of the repayment stream discounted at the appropriate rate of interest.
- Regular savings contributions can often be treated as an ordinary simple annuity, where the value of the fund at a point in the future can be found as the future value of the stream of contributions.

QUESTIONS

1. What is the effective rate of interest p.a. if the nominal rate of interest is 12% and interest is compounded quarterly?
2. ♦ If a savings account stands at €10,000 today, and no deposits have been made into it for the past seven years, how much was in it seven years ago if interest was earned at
   (a) 12% p.a. compounded monthly for the seven years?
   (b) 12% p.a. compounded monthly for the past four years and 10% p.a. compounded half-yearly for the previous three years?
3. At what nominal rate of interest p.a. compounded quarterly must €1,000 be invested in order to double itself in four years?
4. (a) A loan of €45,000 is to be repaid with equal monthly payments (except the last) of €400 starting one month after the loan is taken out. The interest rate is 6% p.a. compounded monthly. Find the number of €400 payments.
   (b) If the bank required that the above loan be repaid ten years after it is taken out, what is the size of the equal monthly payment, starting one month after the loan is taken out, required to clear the loan?
5. If a savings account stands at €8,000 today, and no deposits have been made into it for the past five years, how much was in it five years ago if interest was earned at
   (a) 9% p.a. compounded monthly for the five years?
   (b) 9% p.a. compounded monthly for the past three years and 12% p.a. compounded quarterly for the previous two years?
6. ♦ A loan of €8,000 with interest at 1.1% per month is to be repaid over seven years with equal monthly payments starting one month after the loan is taken out.

Calculate the amount of interest which will be paid over the life of the loan.

7.♦ A family wishes to have €15,000 in three years' time in order to undertake some refurbishment on their home. They place €5,000 into a fund today paying interest at 12% p.a. compounded monthly. They intend to deposit a fixed amount into the fund at the end of each month starting at the end of the current month. The fund pays interest on a simple interest basis on money on deposit for part of a month.

(a) What size must this monthly deposit be in order to have €15,000 in three years' time?

(b) Suppose the family only made the initial deposit of €5,000 and the first 30 of the intended 36 monthly deposits. How long would it take the fund to grow to €15,000?

(c) Going back to (a) above, suppose after two years the family realised that they would need €18,000 rather than €15,000 at the end of the third year and decided to increase the size of the monthly deposits in the third year to a new equal value. What would this new monthly deposit have to be?

8. A family decide to set up a fund to provide assistance towards a third-level education for their newborn child. They deposit a single amount of money, on the day the child is born, into a fund paying interest at 12% p.a. compounded quarterly. The fund will allow the child to withdraw €1,000 on a quarterly basis for a total of 16 quarters, starting on her 17th birthday. What single deposit is required to establish the fund on the day of the child's birth?

9.♦ A farmer is buying a parcel of land from a neighbour. The seller wants either €200,000 immediately or €100,000 now and €30,000 at the end of each year for 5 years. Which option should the buyer choose if the rate of interest is

(a) 14.4% p.a. compounded monthly and is expected to remain so for 5 years?

(b) 14.4 % p.a. compounded monthly for the first two years, expected to rise to 15.6% p.a. compounded monthly for the third year, and to fall to 13.2% p.a. compounded quarterly for the last two years?

10. Joe is made redundant on his 50th birthday and receives a lump sum payment of €40,000. He finds another job and decides to invest the €40,000 into a fund paying interest at 1.2% per month. He retires from the new job on his 60th birthday and receives a lump sum payment of €10,000. He deposits this immediately into the same fund. He decides to make 180 equal monthly withdrawals from the fund, starting one month after his 60th birthday, so as to exhaust the fund with the last withdrawal.

(a) Find the size of the monthly withdrawals.

(b) Suppose Joe was forced to withdraw €15,000 from the fund on his 55th birthday to cover an unforeseen expense, but otherwise the conditions are similar to part (a) above. Calculate the size of the monthly withdrawals.

11. (a) A family wishes to have €25,000 in three years' time to build an extension to their home. They intend to deposit a fixed amount at the end of each month, starting at the end of the current month, into a fund paying interest at 13.2% p.a. compounded monthly. Interest is paid on a simple interest basis on money on deposit for a fraction of a month. Find the size of the monthly deposit.

(b) Suppose the family in part (a) above won €10,000 in a lottery at the end of the first year and placed this amount into the fund immediately.

    (i) How long would it now take to reach the target of €25,000 if they continued with the existing monthly deposits?

    (ii) If they decide to stick with the three-year plan, and to reduce their monthly deposits in the second and third year to a new equal value, what size would these deposits be in order to reach the target of €25,000 at the end of the third year?

12. Jean is buying a business from the current owner. The owner wants €260,000 now or €100,000 now and a further €40,000 at the end of each year for the next four years and €60,000 five years from now. Which payment option should Jean choose if the rate of interest is

    (a) 14% p.a. compounded quarterly and expected to remain so?

    (b) 14% p.a. compounded quarterly at present, but expected to fall to 12% p.a. compounded monthly after two years and to 9% p.a. compounded monthly one year later?

13. (a) A family wishes to have €30,000 in four years' time to build an extension to their home. They intend to deposit a fixed amount at the end of each month, starting at the end of the current month, into a fund paying interest at 10.8% p.a. compounded monthly. Interest is paid on a simple interest basis on money on deposit for a fraction of a month. Find the size of the monthly deposit.

    (b) Suppose the family in part (a) above won €12,000 in a lottery at the end of the second year and placed this amount into the fund immediately.

        (i) How long would it now take to reach the target of €30,000 if they continued with the existing monthly deposits?

        (ii) If they decide to stick with the four-year plan, and to reduce their monthly deposits in the third and fourth year to a new equal value, what size would these deposits be in order to reach the target of €30,000 at the end of the fourth year?

14. A tenant renting an office from a landlord for five years beginning today is offered the following rental options:

    (a) €30,000 p.a. payable annually in advance (i.e. at the beginning of each year) or

    (b) €28,000 p.a. payable annually in advance *plus* 10% of annual turnover payable in arrears (i.e. at the end of each year). Turnover is forecast as follows:

Year	Turnover (€000)
1	20
2	25
3	30
4	35
5	40

Which option should the tenant choose if the current rate of interest is

(a) 12% p.a. compounded monthly and expected to remain so?

(b) 12% p.a. compounded monthly, but is expected to increase to 14% compounded quarterly after two years?

15.♦ A loan of €700,000 is repaid with annual payments of €100,000 over a period of 10 years, the first payment one year after the loan is taken out. Using the technique of linear interpolation, calculate the rate of interest (to one place of decimals) which is being charged on the loan.

16.♦ A company has a loan of €14,000 at a variable rate of interest. The loan is to be repaid within four years. It agrees to pay back €4,000 at the end of the first year, €5,000 at the end of the second year and €6,000 at the end of the third year. What single payment at the end of the fourth year will clear the loan if the rate of interest changes as follows:

Year	Rate of interest
1	15% p.a. compounded monthly?
2	12% p.a. compounded monthly?
3	9% p.a. compounded monthly?
4	12% p.a. compounded quarterly?

17. Explain the concept of the 'time value of money'.
18. Define the following:
   • Nominal rate of interest
   • Effective rate of interest
   • Ordinary simple annuity.
19. Distinguish between a fixed and variable rate of interest. What are the advantages and disadvantages of each?
20. Explain the purpose of discounting.

5
Introduction to Bonds

CHAPTER OBJECTIVES

At the end of this chapter the student should understand:

1. the defining features of a fixed interest bond
   - face/nominal value
   - redemption value
   - coupon
   - redemption date
2. the defining features of a discount bond
3. the defining features of a perpetual bond
4. the defining features of a stepped-interest bond
5. the relationship between bond prices and yield
6. and be able to calculate the yield measures
   - gross redemption yield
   - net redemption yield
   - gross flat/income/running yield
   - net flat/income/running yield.

INTRODUCTION

This chapter provides an introduction to the mathematics of bonds and investment in the bond market. Chapter 15 deals with more advanced aspects of bonds and describes the structure and operation of the Irish Government bond market.

There are four underlying investment assets in a developed economy:

- equity
- bonds
- property/real estate
- cash and related investments.

Bonds represent, after equity, the largest asset category in institutional portfolios, though typically not in individual investors' portfolios. Bonds can be viewed both from the issuer's and the investor's point of view. For the issuer they represent a funding mechanism, e.g.

a company raising capital to undertake a research and development project or a government raising funds to meet a budget deficit. For the investor they represent a (relatively low-risk) investment opportunity. The issuer will obviously attempt to issue the bond at the lowest possible cost to itself while the investor will be looking to generate the maximum return possible.

5.1 Definition of a bond

A bond is basically a paper asset through which the issuer agrees to pay the purchaser some amount(s) of money at some agreed date(s) in the future, in exchange for a sum of money now.

There is an enormous range of bond types available to the investor. This topic deals with the simplest types. The basic bond is one with a fixed coupon and a fixed redemption date. Section 5.4 describes some variations on the basic type.

5.2 Defining features of a bond

The key defining features of a bond are

- Nominal or face value
  This is a notional amount which is used to calculate the periodic interest payment. It is normally a round figure such as €100 or €1,000 and represents the basic amount against which the % coupon is paid. It is usually the same as the redemption value.
- Redemption value
  This is the amount which will be repaid on the redemption date. It is typically €100 or €1,000.
- Coupon
  This is the periodic (e.g. annual or semi-annual) interest payment. It is expressed as a percentage of the face value. In the case of a fixed interest bond it does not change over the life of the bond. Note that the coupon rate and the market rate of interest are unrelated after issue. In the case of a floating rate bond, the coupon rate is adjusted periodically to reflect current market rates of interest. The rate is expressed as a margin over some reference rate e.g. EURIBOR. As the reference rate changes the coupon rate on the bond changes, normally at the end of each period, e.g. quarterly. This chapter is primarily concerned with fixed interest bonds.
- Redemption date
  This is the date on which the redemption value of the bond is to be paid.

5.3 Fixed coupon and fixed redemption date bond

The most typical bond is one which pays both a regular coupon and a final redemption value. Thus a bond with a nominal and redemption value of €1,000 and an annual coupon of 12% with 10 years to run to maturity will pay €120 p.a. for ten years and €1,000 at the end of the tenth year.

Figure 5.1 Typical fixed coupon and redemption date bond

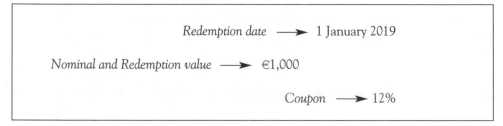

The above bond is issued on, say, 1 January 2009 and is redeemable by the issuer on 1 January 2019, at a redemption value of €1,000. It pays an annual coupon of €120 (12% of €1,000) on 1 January (unless otherwise indicated) each year up to and including 2019.

5.4 Alternatives to the fixed coupon and redemption bond

5.4.1 Pure discount bond/zero coupon bond

- The basic feature of a discount bond is that the value at redemption date is greater than the price at issue. There may be a coupon paid periodically in addition to the discount. If a coupon is paid, it will typically be below the going market rate for similar bonds. The investor is compensated by the capital bonus at redemption. In a pure discount bond the coupon is zero. In other words, the only return to the purchaser is in the form of a capital bonus or gain at the redemption date. A pure discount bond is often referred to as a zero coupon bond or simply a zero.
- A pure discount bond (zero coupon bond) may be used where the issuer could be faced with cash flow problems in the early years of the debt if annual interest payments had to be made. The solution is to issue a bond in which the interest 'accrues' and is effectively paid as a single sum together with the capital sum on redemption.
- Zero coupon bonds are particularly useful in financing a project which will not generate a cash inflow for some time, e.g. a property development with a construction period of, say, 2 years. The cash inflow will not arise until the development is sold or starts to generate a rent roll.

Figure 5.2 Typical zero coupon bond

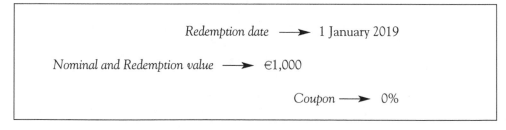

The above bond is issued on, say, 1 January 2009 and is redeemable by the issuer on 1 January 2019, at a redemption value of €1,000. Since it does not pay any annual coupon, it is sold by the issuer to the investor at a discount to its redemption value for a price of, say, €600. The investor receives a capital gain on redemption of €400 or two-thirds of the price paid.

Example 5.1 Zero coupon bond

A company wishes to raise €30 million to fund a new project. It wishes to do so through the issue of a five-year zero coupon bond. The redemption yield on a five-year government gilt is 7% p.a. The market will require, say, a 2% p.a. margin over the government gilt to reflect the additional risk. What is the sum repayable by the company at the end of 5 years?

Solution
The implicit annual interest rate is 7% + 2% = 9%. The amount repayable is the amount borrowed plus rolled-up interest

$$= €30 \text{ million } (1.09)^5 = €46.16 \text{ million}$$

Note that the interest is calculated on a compounding rather than on a simple basis.

Another way to look at this is that the company issues a zero coupon bond with a redemption value of €46.16 million at a price of €30 million, i.e. at a discount of 35%.

5.4.2 Irredeemable bond

An irredeemable bond is one where there is no redemption date and so no redemption value is paid. These are also called perpetual bonds. The coupon is calculated as a percentage of the Nominal or Face value.

This type of bond is not issued very frequently. In practice, there may be an interest enhancement for a number of years after, which it may be redeemed for a nominal sum.

Figure 5.3 Typical perpetual bond

Redemption date ⟶ Undated

Nominal and Redemption value ⟶ €1,000

Coupon ⟶ 12%

The above bond is issued on, say, 1 January 2009 and pays an annual coupon of €120 (12% of €1,000) on 1 January (unless otherwise indicated) each year in perpetuity.

5.4.3 Callable bond/dual redemption-dated bond

Bonds may be issued with a range of redemption dates within which the issuer is free to call the bond in, i.e. to pay the investors the redemption value. No further coupon payments are made.

The decision to redeem the bond will depend on the relationship between the coupon rate on the bond and the market rate of interest at any time during the callable period. If the market rate is lower than the coupon rate, it makes economic sense to redeem the bond early and to reissue at the lower market rate.

Example 5.2 Callable bond

A 12% coupon bond with €100 face value and redemption value is issued on 1 January 2009. The final redemption date is 1 January 2019, but the issuer has an option to call the bond at any time after 31 December 2014. If the issuer raises €20 million at issue, the annual interest charge is €2.4 million. If after 6 years the market rate of interest on similar investments (i.e. four-year bonds since the bond now has only 4 years to go to the final maturity date) is 14%, the issuer will leave the bond in the market. If, however, the market rate of interest has fallen to 10% on four-year bonds and the issuer believes that the market could hold an issue of €20 million, he would be expected to redeem the bond immediately and reissue a new four-year bond (total value €20 million) at a coupon of 10% thus reducing the annual interest charge to €2 million. The proceeds from the new issue would be used to redeem the existing bond.

5.4.4 Stepped-interest bond

This is a bond where the coupon rises over the life of the bond in a pre-determined manner.

Like the discount bond, it holds down the rate of interest payable by the issuer in the early years. Here, however, the purchaser is compensated by higher rates of interest in the later years, e.g. the coupon is set at 3% for the first 3 years rising by 2% each year for the remainder of the life of the bond.

A stepped-interest bond may be used with the coupon set at zero up to the point at which the project that is being funded starts to produce a positive cash flow, say three years after issue, and then stepped up to a level consistent with the expected cash flow from the project.

The derivation of the true annual cost of finance for a stepped-interest bond is discussed in Chapter 15.

5.4.5 Stripped zero coupon bonds

These are bonds which are issued such that the amount due for redemption is spread over a number of years. They are effectively a series of differently dated bonds. They may be used to fund, say, a property development where the development is sold off in phases over a number of years. The amount and maturity of each strip would be set to coincide with the expected value and date of each sale.

5.5 Comparison of coupon bond and pure discount bond

Two important distinctions arise between these two main types of bond, viz. reinvestment risk and relative volatility. While these are problems for the investor rather than the issuer they may be reflected in the yield required at the time of issue.

Reinvestment risk refers to the rate of interest at which coupon income from a bond can be reinvested in the financial markets. While the bond may have been issued at a coupon rate of 10%, the rate of interest may have fallen before the coupon income is paid and the investor is forced to reinvest at a lower rate. The holder of the zero coupon bond has a guaranteed (ignoring default risk) return over the whole period.

Volatility refers to the change in the value of a bond as the market yield changes. If the yield rises, the value of the bond falls and vice versa (see section 5.7). This holds for both coupon and pure discount bonds. However, for given maturity dates, lower coupon bonds are more volatile than higher coupon bonds (see Chapter 15, section 15.3). Thus the pure discount bond is more volatile than the coupon bond.

These two factors may affect the price that investors are prepared to pay for the bond at issue and hence the required yield.

5.6 Bond yields

Two main yields are used to track the bond market:

- redemption yield
- flat yield.

5.6.1 Redemption yield

The redemption yield includes coupon income flow and capital or redemption value. It is basically the internal rate of return.

The gross redemption yield is defined as the discount rate which equates the present value of the gross future cash flow with the price paid. Section 5.8 below discusses its derivation in detail.

5.6.2 Flat yield

This is also called the income yield or running yield. It includes only the annual coupon income flow. It is calculated as

$$\frac{\textbf{Annual income}}{\textbf{Current price}} \times 100 \qquad\qquad (5.1)$$

The gross flat yield is calculated using the gross coupon income while the net flat yield uses the coupon income net of the appropriate tax deduction.

The flat yield is comparable to the dividend yield on equity.

5.7 Pricing a bond

This section deals with the pricing of a bond at a coupon date, i.e. just after a coupon has been paid and the next one is not due until one period (year) from now. Chapter 15, section 15.1, discusses pricing between coupon dates.

5.7.1 Pricing a coupon and redemption bond at a coupon date

Example 5.3

Suppose the following are the parameters of the bond:

- Purchase date 1 March 2009
- Redemption date 1 March 2019
- Annual coupon is 8% of nominal value
- Nominal and redemption value is €1,000
- Annual coupon payments start on 1 March 2010.

The cash flow from the bond is as follows:

Table 5.1 Cash flow from bond

Date	Cash flow €
01/03/09	Purchase
01/03/10	80
01/03/11	80
01/03/12	80
01/03/13	80
01/03/14	80
01/03/15	80
01/03/16	80
01/03/17	80
01/03/18	80
01/03/19	1080

The investor pays a sum of money now to generate an annual income of €80 at the end of each of the next ten years and a final payment of €1,000 in ten years' time.

How much should the investor pay?

This depends on the rate of return the investor wishes to receive. Suppose a bank deposit account was paying 8% p.a. now. The investor may wish for a 2% premium over this to reflect the fact that his/her money is tied up for ten years and to reflect reinvestment risk (see Section 5.5). Thus the investor wishes for a 10% p.a. return over the ten-year period. The price is derived by discounting the future cash inflow by 10% p.a. This can be calculated individually for each cash inflow or alternatively by using two financial formulae.

Calculating the present values individually produces the following:

Table 5.2 Present value of cash flow @ 10% discount rate

Date	Cash flow €	PV of cash flow €
01/03/09	Purchase	
01/03/10	80	72.73
01/03/11	80	66.12
01/03/12	80	60.11
01/03/13	80	54.64
01/03/14	80	49.67
01/03/15	80	45.16
01/03/16	80	41.05
01/03/17	80	37.32
01/03/18	80	33.93
01/03/19	1080	416.39
Total		877.11

Taking the €80 receivable on 1 March 2014 as an example, the present value can be calculated as

$$PV = \frac{80}{(1.10)^5} = 49.67$$

or by using the present value tables contained in the Appendix

$$PV = 80 \times 0.6209 = 49.67$$

Alternatively the following formula can be used

$$PV = Pt \left(\frac{1 - (1 + k)^{-n}}{k} \right) + \frac{\text{Redemption value}}{(1 + k)^n} \qquad (5.2)$$

where
- PV = present value (price)
- Pt = annual coupon payment
- k = interest rate per annum
- n = number of payment periods

The first part of this formula is the present value of an ordinary simple annuity and the second part is a discounted value of a future receipt.

Using 10% p.a. as the required return, the fair price to pay is €877.11. If the investor pays more than this, then the return is less than 10% p.a. If the investor pays less than this, the return is above 10% p.a.

5.7.2 Pricing a zero-coupon bond at a coupon date

Example 5.4

Since a zero-coupon bond does not pay any regular interest income to the holder, the pricing formula is simply the second part of 5.2 above.

$$PV = \frac{\text{Redemption value}}{(1 + k)^n} \tag{5.3}$$

where   PV = present value (price)
        k   = interest rate per annum
        n   = number of years to redemption.

Suppose a bond has a redemption value of €1,000 and a redemption date of 1 March 2016. Today's date is 1 March 2009. The yield on similar bonds in the market is 6% p.a. Find the price of the bond.

$$PV = \frac{€1,000}{(1.06)^7} = €665.06$$

5.7.3 Pricing a perpetual bond at a coupon date

Since a perpetual bond does not pay any final redemption value, the price is simply the present value of the infinite series of coupon payments, i.e. the first part of 5.2 above with n = ∞

$$PV = Pt \frac{1 - (1 + k)^{-n}}{k}$$

but since n is infinite, this collapses to

$$PV = \frac{Pt}{k} \tag{5.4}$$

where   PV = present value
        Pt = annual coupon payment
        k   = interest rate per annum.

Example 5.5

A perpetual bond pays an annual coupon of 5% of a nominal value of €1,000. The yield in the market for such investments is 7% p.a. The next coupon is due one year from today. Find the price of the bond.

$$PV = \frac{€50}{0.07} = €714.29$$

5.8 Deriving the gross redemption yield from the price

The gross redemption yield can be calculated from the price through a process of trial and error. The future cash flow is discounted at different rates until two discount rates produce answers either side of the price. Since the answer will be approximated between these two rates, the nearer they are, the more accurate will be the answer.

The examples below approximate the answer to one place of decimals using the technique of linear interpolation between two discount rates which are one percentage point apart.

Example 5.6 Deriving the gross redemption yield

Suppose a bond has the following parameters:

- Purchase date 1 March 2009
- Redemption date 1 March 2019
- Annual coupon is 8% of nominal value
- Nominal and redemption values are €1,000
- Annual coupon payments start on 1 March 2010.

The bond is selling at a price of €800. What is the GRY on the bond?

Solution
The future cash flow is discounted until two answers, one above €800 and the other below €800, are found using discount rates which are one percentage point apart.

Following trial and error discount rates of 11% and 12% produces present values of €823.32 and €773.99 respectively.

Table 5.3 Present value of future coupon and redemption payments

| | Discount rate 12% | | | Discount rate 11% | |
Date	Cash flow	PV of cash flow	Date	Cash flow	PV of cash flow
01/03/2009			01/03/2009		
01/03/2010	80	71.43	01/03/2010	80	72.07
01/03/2011	80	63.78	01/03/2011	80	64.93
01/03/2012	80	56.94	01/03/2012	80	58.50
01/03/2013	80	50.84	01/03/2013	80	52.70
01/03/2014	80	45.39	01/03/2014	80	47.48
01/03/2015	80	40.53	01/03/2015	80	42.77
01/03/2016	80	36.19	01/03/2016	80	38.53
01/03/2017	80	32.31	01/03/2017	80	34.71
01/03/2018	80	28.85	01/03/2018	80	31.27
01/03/2019	1080	347.73	01/03/2019	1080	380.36
Total		773.99	Total		823.32

Note that the present values can be calculated individually as above or using the present value of an ordinary simply annuity formula and the compound discount formula i.e.

$$PV = 80 \left(\frac{1 - (1.11)^{-10}}{0.11} \right) + \frac{1,000}{(1.11)^{10}} = 823.32$$

and similarly for 12%.

These answers can be interpreted as follows:

If an investor paid a price of €773.99 for the bond she would be getting a gross redemption yield of 12% while if she paid €823.32 she would be getting a gross redemption yield of 11%. **Clearly the higher the price paid, the lower is the yield and vice versa.** In this example, the price paid is €800 so the investor is getting a yield somewhere between 11% and 12%. The answer can be approximated using linear interpolation.

Figure 5.4 Calculating a bond yield using linear interpretation

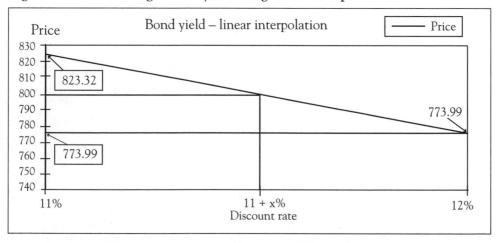

The technique of linear interpolation assumes that the price of the bond falls in a linear fashion as the GRY is increased. While the true relationship is non-linear, the assumption of linearity is a reasonable approximation for small changes in the GRY.

Discount rate	Price
11%	823.32
11 + x%	800.00
12%	773.99

A one percentage point rise in the GRY causes the bond price to fall by €49.33(823.32 – 773.99). What fraction of a 1 per cent increase in the GRY would cause the price to fall by €23.32 (823.32 – 800)? This is calculated as follows:

$$\frac{x}{1} = \frac{23.32}{49.33} = 0.47 \cong 0.5$$

where x = interest rate increase required to decrease price by 23.32.

Therefore GRY is estimated at 11.5%.

5.9 Deriving the net redemption yield from the gross redemption yield

The gross redemption yield is the most often used and published measure of bond market return. Many investors are subject to tax on the coupon income from government bonds and so the net redemption yield is the relevant measure.

It is important to note that the net redemption yield is **not** simply equal to the gross redemption yield × (1 – tax rate).

Example 5.7

Suppose the bond referred to in example 5.6 is currently selling at a gross redemption yield of 11%. What is the net redemption yield to a 20% taxpayer?

Solution
The price is first calculated as above.
   Price @ GRY of 11% = €823.32

The net redemption yield is found by equating the present value of the future net receipts from the bond with this price of €823.32. This is done, as before, through a process of trial and error, i.e. the future net cash flow is discounted at varying rates, until two answers, one above €823.32 and the other below €823.32 are found, using discount rates which are one percentage point apart.

The net cash flow from the bond is €80 per annum less tax at 20%, i.e. €80 – (0.20 x €80) or 0.80 x €80 = €64 for 10 years plus €1,000 at the end of the tenth year. This is shown in Table 5.4 below.

Following trial and error, discount rates of 9% and 10% produce present values of €833.14 and €778.79 respectively, see Table 5.4 below.

Table 5.4 Solving for the net redemption yield

| Date | Discount rate 9% | | Date | Discount rate 10% | |
	Cash flow	PV of cash flow		Cash flow	PV of cash flow
01/03/2009			01/03/2009		
01/03/2010	64	58.72	01/03/2010	64	58.18
01/03/2011	64	53.87	01/03/2011	64	52.89
01/03/2012	64	49.42	01/03/2012	64	48.08
01/03/2013	64	45.34	01/03/2013	64	43.71
01/03/2014	64	41.60	01/03/2014	64	39.74
01/03/2015	64	38.16	01/03/2015	64	36.13
01/03/2016	64	35.01	01/03/2016	64	32.84
01/03/2017	64	32.12	01/03/2017	64	29.86
01/03/2018	64	29.47	01/03/2018	64	27.14
01/03/2019	1064	449.45	01/03/2019	1064	410.22
Total		833.14	Total		778.79

Note: There may be a small rounding error in the totals as the totals are calculated by formula, rather than as the sum of the entries in the columns.

Note that the present values can be calculated individually as shown above or using the present value of an ordinary simple annuity formula and the compound discount formula, i.e.

$$ PV = 64 \ \left(\frac{1 - (1.09)^{-10}}{0.09} \right) + \frac{1000}{(1.09)^{10}} = 833.14 $$

and similarly for 10%.

The answer to the first part of the formula above can be got from the annuity tables with k = 9% and n = 10 years. The answer to the second part can be obtained from the discount tables with k = 9% and n = 10 years.

These answers can be interpreted as follows:

If an investor paid a price of €778.79 for the bond she would be getting a net redemption yield of 10% while if she paid €833.14 she would be getting a net redemption yield of 9%. **Clearly the higher the price paid, the lower the yield and vice versa.**

In this example, the price paid is €823.32 so the investor is getting a yield somewhere between 9% and 10%, but very close to 9%. The answer can be approximated using linear interpolation.

A one percentage point rise in the NRY from 9% causes the bond price to fall by €54.35 (833.14 − 778.79). What fraction of a 1 per cent increase in the NRY from 9% would cause price to fall by €9.82 (833.14 − 823.32)? This is calculated as follows:

$$
\begin{array}{cc}
\text{Discount rate} & \text{Price } \euro \\
9\% & 833.14 \\
9 + x\% & 823.32 \\
10\% & 778.79
\end{array}
$$

$$\frac{x}{1} = \frac{9.82}{54.35} = 0.18 \approx 0.2$$

where x = fractional interest rate increase required to decrease price by 9.82 at this point.

Therefore NRY to a 20% taxpayer is estimated at 9 + 0.2%, i.e. 9.2%.

Example 5.8

A government bond with face value of €100 has eight more years to run. It pays an annual coupon of 10% on 1 March and has just paid this year's coupon. Today's date is 1 March 2009. The redemption value is tax-free, but the coupon income is subject to tax at the holder's marginal rate. It is currently selling at a gross redemption yield of 7% p.a. Calculate the net redemption yield on the bond to a 21% taxpayer.

Solution
The price must first be calculated.
  Price @ GRY of 7% = 117.91.
  The coupon income is €10 less tax at 21% = €7.90.
  The net cash flow from the bond is €10 per annum less tax at 21%, i.e. €10 – (0.21 x €10) or 0.79 x €10 = €7.90 for 8 years plus €100 at the end of the eighth year. This is shown in Table 5.5 below.
  Following trial and error, discount rates of 6% and 5% produce present values of €111.80 and €118.74 respectively, see Table 5.5 below.

Table 5.5 Solving for the net redemption yield

Discount rate 6%			Discount rate 5%		
Date	Cash flow	PV of cash flow	Date	Cash flow	PV of cash flow
01/03/09			01/03/09		
01/03/10	7.90	7.45	01/03/10	7.90	7.52
01/03/11	7.90	7.03	01/03/11	7.90	7.17
01/03/12	7.90	6.63	01/03/12	7.90	6.82
01/03/13	7.90	6.26	01/03/13	7.90	6.50
01/03/14	7.90	5.90	01/03/14	7.90	6.19
01/03/15	7.90	5.57	01/03/15	7.90	5.90
01/03/16	7.90	5.25	01/03/16	7.90	5.61
01/03/17	107.90	67.70	01/03/17	107.90	73.03
Total		111.80	Total		118.74

Note: There may be a small rounding error in the totals as totals are calculated by formula, rather than as the sum of the entries in the columns.

Note: The present values can be calculated individually as shown above or using the formulas as above, i.e.

$$PV = 7.90 \left[\frac{1 - (1.05)^{-8}}{0.05} \right] + \frac{100}{(1.05)^8} = 118.74$$

and similarly for 6%.

The answer to the first part of the formula above can be got from the annuity tables with $k = 5\%$ and $n = 8$ years. The answer to the second part can be got from the discount tables with $k = 5\%$ and $n = 8$ years.

These answers can be interpreted as follows:

If an investor paid a price of €111.80 for the bond she would be getting a net redemption yield of 6% while if she paid €118.74 she would be getting a net redemption yield of 5%. As before, the higher the price paid, the lower the yield and vice versa.

In this example, the price paid is €117.91 so the investor is getting a yield somewhere between 5% and 6%. The answer can be approximated using linear interpolation.

A one percentage point rise in the NRY from 5% causes the bond price to fall by €6.94 (118.74 − 111.80). What fraction of a 1 per cent increase in the NRY from 5% would cause the price to fall by €0.83 (118.74 − 117.91)? This is calculated as follows

Discount rate	Price
5%	118.74
5+x%	117.91
6%	111.80

$$\frac{x}{1} = \frac{0.83}{6.94} = 0.12 \cong 0.1$$

where x = fractional interest rate increase required to decrease price by 0.83 at this point.

Therefore NRY to a 21% taxpayer is estimated at 5 + 0.1%, i.e. 5.1%.

Thus if two investors, one tax exempt and the other liable to taxation on the coupon income from the bond at a rate of 21%, pay €117.91 for the bond, the first is receiving a (gross) redemption yield of 7% while the second is receiving a (net) redemption yield of 5.1%.

5.10 Calculating the net redemption yield at different tax rates

Example 5.9

A government bond with face value and redemption value of €100 has ten years to run. It pays a gross annual coupon of 9% on 1 September each year. Today's date is 1 September 2009. It has just paid the annual coupon. The redemption value is tax-free, but the coupon income is subject to tax at the holder's marginal rate. It is currently selling at a net redemption yield of 8% to a taxpayer @ a tax rate of 41%. Calculate the net redemption yield on the bond to a taxpayer @ a tax rate of 20%.

Solution

First find the current price, using the formula. Note that the coupon income is €9 less tax at 41% = €5.31.

$$PV = 5.31 \left(\frac{1 - (1.08)^{-10}}{0.08} \right) + \frac{100}{(1.08)^{10}} = 81.95$$

Price @ NRY of 8% (@ tax rate of 41%) = 81.95

If two investors are paying the same price for a bond but one faces a higher taxation rate than the other, then the net redemption yield will be higher for the lower taxpayer. Therefore the answer in this case must be above 8%.

The coupon income to the second investor is €9 less tax at 20% = €7.20.

The net cash flow from the bond is €9 per annum less tax at 20%, i.e. €9 - (0.20 x €9) or 0.80 x €9 = €7.20 for 10 years plus €100 at the end of the tenth year. This is shown in Table 5.6 below.

Following trial and error, discount rates of 11% and 10% produce present values of €77.62 and €82.79 respectively, see Table 5.6 below.

Table 5.6 Solving for the net redemption yield

	Discount rate 11%			Discount rate 10%	
Date	Cash flow	PV of cash flow	Date	Cash flow	PV of cash flow
01/09/09			01/09/09		
01/09/10	7.20	6.49	01/09/10	7.20	6.55
01/09/11	7.20	5.84	01/09/11	7.20	5.95
01/09/12	7.20	5.26	01/09/12	7.20	5.41
01/09/13	7.20	4.74	01/09/13	7.20	4.92
01/09/14	7.20	4.27	01/09/14	7.20	4.47
01/09/15	7.20	3.85	01/09/15	7.20	4.06
01/09/16	7.20	3.47	01/09/16	7.20	3.69
01/09/17	7.20	3.12	01/09/17	7.20	3.36
01/09/18	7.20	2.81	01/09/18	7.20	3.05
01/09/19	107.20	37.75	01/09/19	107.20	41.33
Total		77.62	Total		82.79

Note: There may be a small rounding error in the totals as totals are calculated by formula, rather than as the sum of the entries in the columns.

Note that the present values can be calculated individually as shown above or using the formula above i.e.

$$PV = 7.20 \left(\frac{1 - (1.10)^{-10}}{0.10} \right) + \frac{100}{(1.10)^{10}} = 82.79$$

and similarly for 11%.

The answer to the first part of the formula above can be obtained from the annuity tables with $k = 10\%$ and $n = 10$ years. The answer to the second part can be found from the discount tables with $k = 10\%$ and $n = 10$ years.

These answers can be interpreted as follows:

If an investor paid a price of €77.62 for the bond she would be getting a net redemption yield of 11%, while if she paid €82.79 she would be getting a net redemption yield of 10%. As before, the higher the price paid, the lower the yield and vice versa.

In this example, the price paid is €81.95 so the investor is getting a yield somewhere between 10% and 11%. The answer can be approximated using linear interpolation.

A one percentage point rise in the NRY from 10% causes the bond price to fall by €5.17 (82.79 – 77.62). What fraction of a 1 per cent increase in the NRY from 10% would cause the price to fall by €0.84 (82.79 – 81.95)? This is calculated as follows

Discount rate	Price
10%	82.24
10 + x%	80.95
11%	77.09

$$\frac{x}{1} = \frac{0.84}{5.17} = 0.16 \cong 0.2$$

where x = fractional interest rate increase required to decrease price by €0.84 at this point.

Therefore NRY to a 20% taxpayer is estimated at 10 + 0.2%, i.e. 10.2%.

Thus, if two investors, one liable to taxation on the coupon income from the bond at a rate of 41% and the other liable to taxation on the coupon income from the bond at a rate of 20%, pay €81.95 for the bond, the first is receiving a (net) redemption yield of 8% while the second is receiving a (net) redemption yield of 10.2%.

5.11 Calculating the gross and net income yield

The terms 'income yield', 'running yield' and 'flat yield' are used interchangeably. This yield is based on the annual coupon income flow only. It is calculated as

$$\frac{\text{Annual income}}{\text{Current price}} \times 100 \tag{5.5}$$

The gross income yield is calculated using the gross coupon income while the net income yield uses the coupon income net of the appropriate tax deduction.

It is similar in concept to the dividend yield on equity.

Example 5.10

- Purchase date 1 March 2009
- Redemption date 1 March 2019
- Annual coupon is 8% of nominal value
- Nominal and redemption value is €1,000
- Annual coupon payments start 1 March 2010
- Coupon income is subject to tax at the holder's marginal rate
- Redemption value is tax-free

Suppose the bond is selling for a price of €900. Calculate
(a)   the gross income yield
(b)   the net income yield to a 20% taxpayer
(c)   the net income yield to a 41% taxpayer

Solution
(a)   The gross annual coupon is €80.

$$\text{Gross income yield} = \frac{80}{900} \times 100 = 8.89\%$$

(b)   The net annual coupon is €80 less tax at 20% = €64.00.

$$\text{Net income yield} = \frac{64.00}{900} \times 100 = 7.11\%$$
$$(\text{@ 20\% tax})$$

(c) The net annual coupon is €80 less tax at 41% = €47.20.

$$\text{Net income yield} = \frac{47.20}{900} \times 100 = 5.24\%$$
$$(\text{@ 41\% tax})$$

Note that net income yield = gross income yield x (1 – tax rate).

SUMMARY

- A bond is a paper asset, where the issuer agrees to pay the purchaser a sum or sums of money at a specific time(s) in the future.
- Fixed interest bonds and fixed redemption dated bonds are the principal generic types of bond.
- A discount bond is sold for less than its redemption value.
- In a discount bond, the annual coupon payment is typically below the going market rate at the time of issue.
- In a zero coupon bond, the only return to the investor is in the form of a capital gain at redemption.
- A callable bond will normally be 'called' as early as possible if the coupon rate on the bond is above the current market rate.

- The gross redemption yield is the main yield used to compare bonds.
- The gross redemption yield is defined as the discount rate which equates the present value of the future gross income stream with the price paid.
- The flat yield on a bond is comparable to the dividend yield on equity.
- Bonds are priced by discounting the future cash flow at the appropriate discount rate.

QUESTIONS

1.♦ A government bond with face value of €100 has eight more years to run. It pays an annual coupon of 12% and has just paid this year's coupon. The redemption value is tax-free, but the coupon income is subject to tax at the holder's marginal rate. It is currently selling at a gross redemption yield of 9% p.a. Calculate the net redemption yield on the bond to a 24% taxpayer. (Answer to one place of decimals.)

2.♦ A government bond with face value of €100 has six years to run. It pays an annual coupon of 9% on 1 September each year to the holder of the bond at the close of trading on 31 August in that year. It has just paid the annual coupon. The redemption value is tax-free, but the coupon income is subject to tax at the holder's marginal rate. It is currently selling at a net redemption yield of 8% to a taxpayer @ a tax rate of 42%. Calculate the net redemption yield on the bond to a taxpayer at a tax rate of 20%. (Give your answer to one decimal place.)

3.♦ A government bond with face value of €100 has eight more years to run. It pays an annual coupon of 9% and has just paid this year's coupon. The redemption value is tax-free, but the coupon income is subject to tax at the holder's marginal rate. It is currently selling at a net redemption yield of 5% p.a. to a 44% taxpayer. Calculate
   (a) the gross income yield on the bond
   (b) the net income yield on the bond to a 22% taxpayer.

4. A government bond with face value of €100 has nine years to run. It pays an annual coupon of 8% and has just paid this year's coupon. The redemption value is tax-free, but the coupon income is subject to tax at the holder's marginal rate. It is currently selling at a net redemption yield of 6% to a taxpayer at a tax rate of 44%.
   (a) Calculate the net redemption yield on the bond to a taxpayer at a tax rate of 22%. (Give your answer to one decimal place.)
   (b) Using the same information as in (a) above, calculate the gross income yield on the bond.

5. A government bond with face value of €100 has twelve more years to run. It pays an annual coupon of 8% and has just paid this year's coupon. The redemption value is tax-free, but the coupon income is subject to tax at the holder's marginal rate. It is currently selling at a gross redemption yield of 12% p.a. Calculate the net redemption yield on the bond to a 26% taxpayer. (Answer to one place of decimals.)

6. A government bond with face value of €100 has ten more years to run. It pays an annual coupon of 12% and has just paid this year's coupon. The redemption value is tax-free, but the coupon income is subject to tax at the holder's marginal rate. It is currently selling at a gross redemption yield of 10% p.a. Calculate the net redemption yield on the bond to a 26% taxpayer. (Answer to one place of decimals.)

7. Explain the relationship between price and yield.

8. Define gross redemption yield.
9. Define net redemption yield.
10. Explain what is meant by a discount bond. Why might it be attractive to an issuer?
11. Explain what is meant by a stepped-interest bond. Why might it be attractive to an issuer?
12. Explain what is meant by an irredeemable bond.
13. Explain what is meant by the flat yield on a bond. Why is it a relevant measure?

6

Portfolio Theory and the Capital Asset Pricing Model

CHAPTER OBJECTIVES

At the end of this chapter the student should be able to:

1. calculate two-asset portfolio expected returns and standard deviations from discrete probability distributions
2. understand the impact of covariance and correlation on portfolio selection
3. identify efficient portfolios using indifference curves and the capital market line
4. explain the nature and significance of the capital market line
5. discuss the significance of systematic and unsystematic risk and the capital asset pricing model
6. calculate the required rate of return of a security using the capital asset pricing model
7. have an awareness of empirical research on the reliability of the capital asset pricing model in practice
8. briefly explain the arbitrage pricing model (APM)

INTRODUCTION

One of the earliest theories associated with efficient investment was that of Charles H. Dow, and it was known as Dow Theory. Dow, who was the editor of the *Wall Street Journal*, started to compile daily averages of share prices in 1897. Even today the Dow Jones index is one of the best known stock market performance indices in the world.

The birth of modern portfolio theory began with an article written by Harry Markowitz in 1952. A portfolio is a collection of two or more assets, and the idea of identifying portfolios which give the highest return for a given level of risk was developed by Markowitz. In this chapter we will focus on financial securities such as ordinary shares in companies, but the fundamental techniques have a wider application in areas associated with reducing corporate risk, by having a diversity of projects in a company or producing a product range instead of just one product, etc.

The chapter is broken down into three sections: the basic statistical analysis of risk and return; the application of Markowitz theory using indifference analysis; and finally considering the capital asset pricing model (CAPM) developed by William Sharpe in 1963, which gives us a way of valuing securities according to their level of risk.

6.1 Risk and return

The portfolio mantra is 'maximise return and minimise risk' and in this section we will look at the statistical measures of risk (standard deviation/variance) and return (average or expected value). Both of these measures will be based on discrete probabilities. The expected return, variance and standard deviation of security 'a' are given by the following

$$\text{Expected value (EV)} = \Sigma Pa = \bar{a} \tag{6.1}$$

$$\text{Variance } (\sigma^2_a) = \Sigma P(a - \bar{a})^2 \tag{6.2}$$

$$\text{Standard deviation } (\sigma_a) = \sqrt{\Sigma P(a - \bar{a})^2} \tag{6.3}$$

where P is the probability of the various outcomes and a is the associated outcome.

Example 6.1

Securities A and B have the following returns and associated probabilities.

Probability (P)	Return for A	Return for B
0.1	15%	10%
0.8	25%	30%
0.1	35%	50%

Probability (P)	Return for A	P × a
0.1	15%	1.5%
0.8	25%	20%
0.1	35%	3.5%
	Expected value of return ΣPa =	25%

The expected value return on security A is 25%.

The expected return on security B is (0.1)(10%) + (0.8)(30%) + (0.1)(50%) = 30%.

On the basis of expected values, investment B offers, on average, a higher return, but in choosing B the level of risk is ignored. The definition of risk that is often used in finance literature is based on the variability of return from the expected value. Statistical measures of variability are the variance or standard deviation of returns. The variance of return is the weighted sum of squared deviations from the expected return.

Squaring deviations ensures that positive and negative deviations from the expected value contribute equally to the measure of variability regardless of sign.

The variance formula is $\Sigma P (a - \bar{a})^2$ and the standard deviation is the square root of the variance.

The variance of the expected return for each security is as follows

Probability (P)	Return for A	Mean deviation $(a - \bar{a})$	$P(a - \bar{a})^2$
0.1	15%	−10	0.1× 100%
0.8	25%	0	0.8 × 0%
0.1	35%	10	0.1 × 100%
		Variance $\Sigma P(a - \bar{a})^2$ =	20%

The variance is 20% and the standard deviation of A (σ_a) is = $\sqrt{20\%}$ = 4.472%

$$\sigma^2_b = (0.1)(10 - 30)^2 + (0.8)(30 - 30)^2 + (0.1)(50 - 30)^2 = 80\%,$$
$$\text{and } (\sigma_b) = \sqrt{80} = 8.944\%$$

The variability score for B is larger, indicating a higher degree of risk.

If these investments are mutually exclusive, i.e. only one can be chosen, then a better measure of risk is the coefficient of variation (CV), i.e.

$$CV = \sigma /EV \tag{6.4}$$

This risk measure takes on board the relative values of both expected value and variability.

$$CV \text{ of A} = 4.472/25 = 0.17888 \text{ and for B} = 8.944/30 = 0.29813$$

B has the higher risk measure and therefore the higher risk.

In financial markets it has been observed that the returns on securities have a normal distribution and therefore there is an equal probability of returns being above or below the expected value (mean). Because of this the variance becomes a very strong measure of risk.

The term **mean variance efficient** is used to describe an investment with the highest expected return for a given level of risk and the lowest risk for a given level of return.

6.2 Covariance and correlation

In the previous examples the investor was confined to choosing either A or B. Now let us assume investments are not mutually exclusive and can be combined into a two-asset portfolio. By combining the above investments in a portfolio, with 50% invested in A and 50% invested in B, the average return will be

$$(0.5)(25\%) + (0.5)(30\%) = 27.5\%$$

The expected return of a portfolio is simply a weighted average of the expected returns of the individual investments.

However, when you combine investments into a portfolio it is important to look at more than the individual variance factors of the two securities. It is necessary to quantify the extent to which the two securities move up or down together, and this is measured by their covariance.

The covariance of A and B is

$$Cov_{ab} = \Sigma P(a - \bar{a})(b - \bar{b}) \tag{6.5}$$

Using the example above the covariance of A and B is found as follows

Probability	a	b	$a - \bar{a}$	$b - \bar{b}$	$P(a - \bar{a})(b - \bar{b})$
0.1	15%	10%	−10%	−20%	(0.1)(−10)(−20)
0.8	25%	25%	0%	0%	(0.8)(0)(0)
0.1	35%	50%	10%	20%	0.1(10)(20)
				Covariance =	40%

A positive covariance indicates that the returns of the two securities move in the same direction. If the result were negative it would imply the returns were moving in opposite directions. The problem with covariances is that it is difficult to compare them with each other, as their magnitude does not tell the full story. However, if they are used as an input into the correlation formula, results are then comparable as the correlation coefficient scale has a strictly limited range from −1 to +1.

The correlation coefficient for A and B is

$$r_{ab} = \frac{Cov_{ab}}{\sigma_a \sigma_b} \tag{6.6}$$

The formula can be easily rearranged to express the covariance $Cov_{ab} = r_{ab}\sigma_a\sigma_b$.

In the example above
$$r_{ab} = \frac{40}{(4.472)(8.944)} = +1$$

This is an example of perfect positive correlation and indicates that the returns of the two securities rise and fall together. Correlation can only take on values from +1 to −1.

- A positive result means returns tend to move together.
- A negative result means returns tend to move in opposite directions (the most extreme example being a value of −1).
- If the correlation coefficient has a value of zero then the securities are independent and have no relationship with each other.

In reality the correlation coefficient between returns on investments tends to lie between 0 and +1 and in a two-asset portfolio there is normally a partial reduction of risk. Negative correlation is not necessary for risk reduction, but values close to +1 are considered to have higher risk. Correlation values typically hover close to 0.5 as all stocks on the Irish stock exchange are affected by many of the same variables, such as interest rates and the performance of the Irish economy, etc. This is, however, sufficiently far away from a value of 1.0 to deliver diversification benefits. The correlation between shares in the same sector would be higher. For example, shares in Allied Irish Bank and Bank of Ireland would have a higher correlation than shares in Allied Irish Bank and Ryanair.

When a portfolio is made up of just two assets, then the expression for the variance of the portfolio is given by

$$\sigma^2_{a+b} = \sigma^2_a W^2_1 + \sigma^2_b W^2_2 + 2W_1 W_2 r_{ab}\sigma_a\sigma_b \qquad (6.7)$$

where W_1 and W_2 are the weighted proportions invested in A and B. This is a formula that on first sight may send students for a strong cup of coffee! The first two terms deal with the risk of the individual investments and the third term considers the way in which the returns of each pair of investments co-vary. The most important part of the formula is the value of the correlation coefficient r_{ab}.

The standard deviation of a two-asset portfolio is simply the square root of the variance formula.

$$\sqrt{\sigma^2_{a+b} = \sigma^2_a W^2_1 + \sigma^2_b W^2_2 + 2W_1 W_2 r_{ab}\sigma_a\sigma_b}$$

If the previous example is used with an equal investment in A and B (i.e. W_1 and W_2 = 0.5) and we change the value of r_{ab} from +1 to 0 to −1, the following results are obtained

If r_{ab} = +1 then σ^2_{a+b} = (20)(0.5)^2 + (80)(0.5)^2 + 2(0.5)(0.5)(1)(4.472)(8.944) = 45%
$$\sigma_{a+b} = \sqrt{45\%} = 6.71\%$$

If r_{ab} = 0 then σ^2_{a+b} = (20)(0.5)^2 + (80)(0.5)^2 + 2(0.5)(0.5)(0)(4.472)(8.944) = 25%
$$\sigma_{a+b} = \sqrt{25\%} = 5\%$$

If r_{ab} = −1 then σ^2_{a+b} = (20)(0.5)^2 + (80)(0.5)^2 + 2(0.5)(0.5) (−1)(4.472)(8.944) = 5%
$$\sigma_{a+b} = \sqrt{5\%} = 2.24\%$$

From the results it can be seen that the variability is highest when there is perfect positive correlation, lower when there is none and lowest when there is perfect negative correlation. Perfect negative correlation does not occur between the returns on two investments in the real world, although it is useful to know the theoretical extremes. Returns on investments in the same industry tend to have high positive correlation, whilst the returns on investments in different industries tend to have low positive correlation. For this reason investors prefer to invest in different industries to create a well-diversified portfolio, to ensure that the maximum risk reduction effect is obtained. In general, the risk of a two-asset portfolio will depend on the risk of the constituent investments in isolation, the correlation between them and the proportion in which the investments are mixed.

Box 6.1 Strength in diversity

Pension funds should diversify into asset classes that have a low correlation with equities, in order to provide pension funds with greater diversification and an 'optimal' portfolio allocation, according to pension consultants Hewitt Associates. In a survey conducted by the firm amongst diversified pension funds from fund managers KBC

$\longrightarrow$

Asset Management, Irish Life and Eagle Star, it was found that diversification into assets such as commodities and emerging market equities, in addition to more traditional equity and bond funds, resulted in a more 'efficient' portfolio or better risk-return profile for investors.

Betty O'Reilly, an investment consultant with Hewitt, says investment managers are now looking at alternatives, including categories or 'themes' such as alternative energy, active currency, emerging markets, commodities, private equity, hedge funds, unconstrained or high-performance equities, together with any number of satellite themes such as water, infrastructure and forestry.

Fiona Reddan, *The Irish Times*, 1 August 2008

6.3 Markowitz and modern portfolio theory

6.3.1 Indifference curves

The attitudes of investors to risk can be shown graphically with indifference (utility) curves. Along any indifference curve there is an equal level of utility available to the investor. The usual trade off between risk and return occurs. The indifference curve slopes upward at an increasing rate because of the increasing rate of marginal substitution, i.e. by taking on more risk units, progressively larger units of return are required to compensate the investor and keep utility constant. These curves are often viewed as an elegant but impractical treatment of risk and in practice it is very difficult to derive indifference curves for individual decision-makers. Ignoring these practical difficulties, investor attitudes to risk may differ; they do act rationally, and are not prepared to expose themselves to higher levels of risk without the possibility of higher returns.

Figure 6.1 Indifference curves

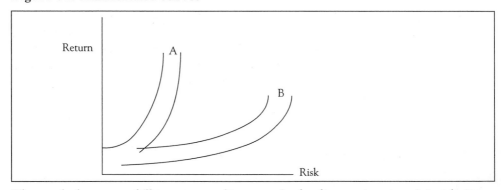

The graph shows two different types of investor. In the diagram investor **A** is risk averse and demands greater compensation in the form of increased return for a relatively small increase in risk. Investor **B** is not as conservative and more open to taking risks for relatively smaller compensation. This difference in attitude to risk is reflected in the slopes of the two curves.

Having looked at investor preferences Markowitz turned his attention to the availability of investments that existed in the real world. Earlier it was shown that by diversifying and avoiding positively correlated investments risk levels are reduced. Markowitz studied combinations of many shares in different portfolios and found the existence of an egg-shaped cluster of portfolios (known as the envelope curve). While investors could position themselves anywhere inside the cluster of possible portfolios, it was evident that some of them were more efficient than others.

A portfolio is **mean-variance efficient** if it offers the maximum return for a given level of risk, or the minimum risk for a given level of return. The most efficient portfolios lie on the portfolio efficiency frontier, as can be seen on the curve AB in the diagram below. Markowitz developed a technique called quadratic programming to find this efficient frontier. If the indifference curve map of an individual is superimposed on the envelope curve (the shaded area in the diagram), the optimum portfolio is found where the highest indifference curve touches the efficient frontier at a tangent (portfolio **M**).

Figure 6.2 Market portfolio position M

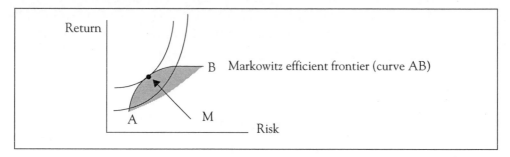

Portfolio **M** contains a proportion of all the securities on the market, i.e. shares, bonds, gold, property and rare paintings, etc. Clearly no individual can hold the market portfolio, but a good approximation might be the FT100, the Standard & Poors 500 or the FTSE Actuaries All-Share Index, which contains about 900 shares.

James Tobin extended Markowitz's analysis in 1958 by including risk-free securities into any portfolio. If risk-free securities (R_f) are introduced such as post office savings or government gilts, then the efficient set of portfolios can become a straight line. This line is known as the **Capital Market Line (CML)** and it supersedes the old efficient frontier. This line is found by pivoting a line clockwise from R_f on the Y-axis, until it reaches a point of tangency with the efficient frontier (**M**).

Figure 6.3 Capital market line and efficient portfolios

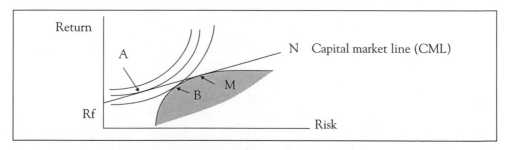

Portfolio **M** represents the optimal combination of risky securities. The capital market line (CML) is the line joining the points R_f, **M** and **N**. Investors will vary their attitudes to risk but will all find their optimal return/risk combination somewhere on the line joining these two investments. The investor only deals in portfolio **M** or R_f.

The major assumption behind the CML is that investors can borrow and lend at the risk-free rate of return. Investors can now move along the CML by splitting their investment between risk-free assets and the market portfolio **M**.

Without the existence of risk-free securities the investor in the diagram above would locate at point **B**, but because they are available the investor is located at point **A**.

Portfolio **A** represents the investor's preference for a larger proportion of total investment in risk-free assets than in the market portfolio **M**, and this is an example of a person who is somewhat risk averse, i.e. the position of portfolio **A** is closer to R_f than **M**.

If the investor likes to take a risk, then portfolios such as **N** are available. In this case the investor borrows at the risk-free rate and has more than 100% of their investment in portfolio **M**.

Investor **N** is risk-seeking compared to investor **A** and can achieve a higher expected return by leveraging the investment, but at a higher risk as measured by the standard deviation.

The capital market line indicates for a given level of risk, the return the investor should expect on the stock exchange. It is often referred to as giving the market price of risk.

6.4 The equation of the capital market line (CML)

The formula for the **CML** is expressed by a general linear equation of the form $y = a + bx$ where **a** is the risk-free rate of return and **b** represents the increase in the return as the risk increases, i.e. the slope of the risk/return line.

Figure 6.4 Capital market line

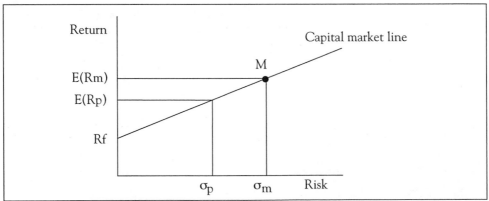

R_f = risk-free rate of return
$E(R_m)$ = the expected return for the market portfolio
$E(R_p)$ = the expected return for any portfolio on the **CML**
σ_m = the risk (standard deviation) of returns in portfolio **M**
σ_p = the risk (standard deviation) of returns in any portfolio on the **CML**.

The slope of the **CML** can be expressed as

$$\frac{(E(R_m) - R_f)}{\sigma_m} \tag{6.8}$$

This slope indicates the change in return due to a change in risk in moving from **Rf** to **M** and this represents the extent to which the required returns from a portfolio should exceed the risk-free rate of return, to compensate the investors for risk.

The equation of the **CML** can be expressed as

$$E(R_p) = R_f + \frac{(E(R_m) - R_f)\sigma_p}{\sigma_m} \tag{6.9}$$

The expression additional to the risk-free rate represents the risk premium the investor requires as compensation for accepting portfolio risk. This risk premium includes both business risk and financial risk. This equation forms the basis of the capital asset pricing model.

6.5 Practical problems in applying portfolio theory

Portfolio theory is not a practical method of project appraisal for financial managers. It does, however, introduce the concept of risk reduction through diversification. In trying to apply portfolio theory in practice, the following problems exist.

1. Investors cannot borrow at the risk-free rate.
2. Identification of the market portfolio **M** involves finding out returns and risks for all investments, which is more or less impossible in practice.
3. The market portfolio is not static over time.
4. The transaction costs associated with constructing **M** would be too expensive for a small investor.
5. The techniques rely on past data to predict future risk and return, complicated calculations and the generation of indifference curves for individual utility preferences.

Some of the problems mentioned above can be overcome by investing in unit trusts or stock exchange index tracker funds as a proxy for the ideal market portfolio **M**.

While the Markowitz model provides a relatively simple solution for investment criteria in the two-asset case, it becomes much more complicated when the number of assets becomes larger. The calculation of covariances in combinations of two is based on $N(N-1)/2$ where N is the number of securities. In the case of a portfolio of 100 securities, it is necessary to calculate $N(N-1)/2$ or $100 \times 99/2 = 4,950$ covariances. These difficult calculations, although relatively easy with a computer today, stimulated other approaches to investment management. The capital asset pricing model (**CAPM**) was one such new approach developed by William Sharpe in 1964. Sharpe's model was a single-index model that relates the returns on each security to the returns of a common index. In Ireland, this could be represented by the ISEQ overall index and the major advantage of the model is that it reduces the number of calculations required, as you do not have to calculate the relationship between all pairs of securities being considered.

Both Sharpe and Markowitz were awarded the Nobel Prize for Economics in 1990.Before explaining the **CAPM** it is important to understand the difference between systematic and unsystematic risk.

6.6 Systematic and unsystematic risk

Total risk of an investment (as considered in portfolio theory) under the CAPM can be broken down into systematic and unsystematic risk. Unsystematic risk, which is also known as diversifiable or specific risk, is that part of risk that can be eliminated by holding a well-diversified portfolio. Examples of unsystematic risk include the nature of the business a company is involved in (oil exploration or food retailing), operational risk, financial risk and industrial relations problems which exist within the company, etc. In a portfolio such random factors tend to cancel as the number of investments in the portfolio increases. The risk associated with an asset that cannot be eliminated by diversification is systematic risk (also known as non-diversifiable or market risk). Systematic risk relates to the market and economy as a whole and its impact on investment, for example the impact which interest rate changes, inflation changes, taxation changes or exchange rate changes have on a company. Since these factors cause returns to move in the same direction they cannot cancel out and therefore systematic (market) risk remains present in all portfolios. Some investments will be more sensitive to market factors than others and will therefore have a higher systematic risk.

Figure 6.5 Systematic and unsystematic risk

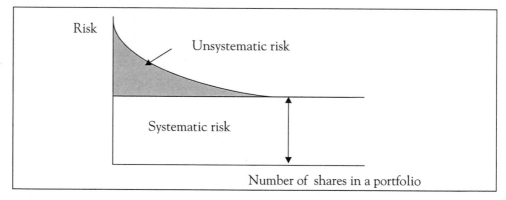

Solnick (1974) found that substantial reduction in the risk of a portfolio occurred as the number of different shares held in a portfolio approached 20. After that the reduction in risk was quite modest. A well-diversified portfolio is easily achieved by buying into a unit trust or a tracker fund. The systematic risk associated with any security will vary and the **CAPM** tries to determine a fair price for an individual security by measuring its systematic risk. Systematic risk must be accepted by any investor, unless investment is entirely focused on risk-free opportunities. In return for accepting systematic risk, an investor will expect to earn a return which is higher than the return on risk-free investment. The influence of **CAPM** on the world of finance has been enormous over the past 30 years. Its far-reaching consequences changed the way portfolios were constructed for pension and insurance funds around the world. It has given the world of finance an alternative method of calculating the cost of capital for a firm and the required rate of return on projects.

6.7 The capital asset pricing model

This economic model is based on a set of assumptions:

1. All unsystematic risk is eliminated as the investor holds a well-diversified portfolio of securities.
2. Investors can borrow and lend at the risk-free rate.
3. Investors act rationally and try to maximise utility.
4. There is perfect information available in the market to investors.
5. Capital markets are perfectly competitive.

Sharpe's basic observation was that shares tend to move with the market, and that there was a linear relationship between the market as a whole and any individual security.

A statistical analysis of historical returns from an individual security and from the average market return would indicate if such a linear relationship exists. A series of comparative figures could be prepared over time of the return of a company's shares and the average return of the market as a whole. The results can be drawn on a scatter diagram and using regression analysis a line of best fit could be drawn. This line is called the characteristic line and the slope of this line is the share's beta (β), which indicates the sensitivity of the share's return to the return on the market.

Figure 6.6 Security characteristic line

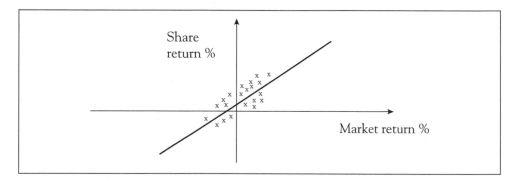

From the diagram, the return from the share and the return from the market tend to move together, i.e. they are positively correlated. The return from the share may be higher or lower than the market return and this is because the systematic risk of the individual share differs from that of the market.

CAPM tries to measure this individual systematic risk, known as beta (β). The most popular way of calculating beta is to observe the historical relationship between returns and assume that the covariance will persist into the future. This is called ex-post analysis. A share's beta factor is the measure of the volatility of its returns relative to the market. The beta factor of the market as a whole is 1.0. A company's beta factor is simply a yardstick against which the risk of other companies can be measured. Beta is calculated as the ratio of the covariance of an individual securities return with the return of the market ($\mathbf{Cov_{sm}}$) and the variance of the market (σ^2_m).

$$\beta = \frac{Cov_{sm}}{\sigma^2_m} \qquad\qquad (6.10)$$

Using regression formula based on the x- and y-axis (market x and the individual share y) the covariance of $xy = n\Sigma xy - \Sigma x\Sigma y$ and the variance of $x = n\Sigma x^2 - (\Sigma x)^2$.

This beta formula can also be written

$$\beta r = \frac{r_{sm}\,\sigma_s\sigma_m}{\sigma^2_m} \qquad \text{or} \qquad \frac{r_{sm}\,\sigma_s}{\sigma_m}$$

Example 6.2 Beta formula

Shares of a company have a covariance of 7.5 with the market whereas the market has a variance of 4.5. What is the beta of the company's shares?

Solution
$7.5/4.5 = 1.67$

This ratio is easily calculated using the regression statistics on a spreadsheet or manually as the next example shows.

Example 6.3 Calculation of a beta coefficient

The normal way of measuring β factors for an individual company is to use regression analysis to examine the relationship between percentage returns of the particular company and the returns of the market portfolio. In the example that follows the ISEQ index is used to represent the market.

The formula for beta is $\beta = \dfrac{Cov_{sm}}{\sigma^2m}$

Again this can also be written as $\beta = \dfrac{n\Sigma xy - \Sigma x\Sigma y}{n\Sigma x^2 - (\Sigma x)^2}$

Where x represents the market and y represents the individual share.

The following figures relate to the monthly observations of the % return of the ISEQ index and the % return of a particular share each month over the past six months.

Month	ISEQ Index % (X)	Share % (Y)
January	5	4
February	-10	-8
March	12	9.6
April	3	2.4
May	-4	-3.2
June	7	5.6

Calculate the slope (systematic risk or beta factor) of the share.

Solution

$$\beta = \frac{n\Sigma xy - \Sigma x \Sigma y}{n\Sigma x^2 - (\Sigma x)^2} \qquad \text{or} \qquad \frac{\text{Covariance xy}}{\text{Variance x}}$$

$$\beta = \frac{n\Sigma xy - \Sigma x \Sigma y}{n\Sigma x^2 - (\Sigma x)^2} = \frac{6(274.4) - (13)(10.4)}{6(343) - 13^2} = 0.8$$

The CAPM assumes that unsystematic risk can be cancelled out by diversification. The CAPM also uses the principle that the returns on shares in the market are expected to be higher than the returns of risk-free investments. The difference between the market return and risk-free return is called the **excess return**. The capital asset pricing model can be stated as follows:

$$E(R_s) = R_f + [E(R_m) - R_f]\beta_s \qquad (6.11)$$

This is also known as the equation for the security market line.
R_f = risk-free rate of return, $E(R_m)$ = the expected return for the market portfolio $E(R_s)$ = the expected return for share s, and β_s is the beta coefficient for share s.

The CAPM provides the required return based on the perceived systematic risk of an investment. It also contends that the systematic risk-return relationship is positive (the higher the risk the higher the return) and linear.

In the equation, the systematic risk as measured by β_s is compared with the risk and return of the market and the risk-free rate of return to calculate a required return of share s and hence a fair price for share s.

The risk-free rate can be approximated by taking the return on short-term government bonds or post office savings. The return for the market is difficult to calculate and is usually approximated by using stock exchange indices as a representation of the market.

The excess return or market risk premium of $(E(R_m) - R_f)$ has traditionally been estimated by academics at between 8% and 9%,on an arithmetic average basis. However more recent studies by Dimson, Marsh and Staunton indicate the risk premium has fallen substantially in recent years and they suggest it is only 3% to 4%. A recent study by Barclays Capital notes that the premium in the UK has been 2.4% over the past decade. According to Dimson *et al.*, most financial professionals regard the equity risk premium as the single most important number in finance.

Example 6.4 CAPM *formula application*

Company A has a share beta of 1.5. The risk-free rate is 4% and the expected market return is 12%. What is the expected return of company A's share?

Solution
Expected return = 4% + (12% − 4%) 1.5 = 16%. This also represents the cost of equity. The application of the CAPM in the calculation of the cost of capital and an appropriate target rate of return for business risk is explored in greater detail in Chapter 13.

Example 6.5 *Identifying efficient investments with CAPM*

A company is considering investing in different projects with the following data available.

Project	A	B	C
Expected return	14%	12%	17%
Correlation of returns with the market	0.62	0.75	0.58
Standard deviation of returns	3.7%	4.1%	6.5%

The expected return is 15%, the standard deviation of market returns is 4.8% and the risk-free rate of return is 8%.
   Which of the projects should be undertaken?

Solution
First find beta = $\dfrac{r_{sm}\sigma_s}{\sigma_m}$

Project	A	B	C
Beta	$\dfrac{0.62 \times 3.7 = 0.48}{4.8}$	$\dfrac{0.75 \times 4.1 = 0.64}{4.8}$	$\dfrac{0.58 \times 6.5 = 0.79}{4.8}$

CAPM required return A = 8% + (15 − 8%).48 = 11.36 and expected is 14%.
CAPM required return B = 8% + (15 − 8%).64 = 12.48 and expected is 12%.
CAPM required return C = 8% + (15 − 8%).79 = 13.53 and expected is 17%.

Therefore projects A and C should be undertaken and project B is inefficient. If the choices are mutually exclusive then the one with the highest abnormal return should be chosen. In this case project C.

6.8 CAPM and portfolios

Just as an individual security has a beta factor, so too has a portfolio of securities. The beta factor of a portfolio is the weighted average of the beta factors of the securities that make up a portfolio.

Example 6.6 CAPM and portfolios

A portfolio consisting of four securities has information as follows.

Security	No. of shares	Beta	Share price
A	60,000	1.16	€4.29
B	80,000	1.28	€2.92
C	100,000	0.90	€2.17
D	125,000	1.50	€3.14

The current market rate of return is 15% per annum and the risk-free rate is 6%. Find the overall portfolio beta and the expected return for the portfolio.

Solution

Market value	Beta	Market value × beta
€257,400	1.16	298,584
€233,600	1.28	299,008
€217,000	0.90	195,300
€382,500	1.50	588,750
€1,100,500		1,381,642

Beta as a whole = 1,381,642/1,100,500 = 1.26
Expected return on the portfolio = 6% + 1.26(15% − 6%) = 17.34%

A beta value of 1.0 is the yardstick against which all share betas are measured. The beta value of a share is normally between 0 and 2.5.

- If a share has a beta value greater than 1.0, it will be classified as an **aggressive** share. In a bull market it would rise faster than the market average and in a bear market it would fall more than the market average.
- If a share has a beta value less than 1.0, it will be classified as a **defensive** share. In a bull market it would rise slower than the market average and in a bear market it would fall less than the market average.
- A beta value of 1.0 would simply follow the market.

This information could be used by investors to identify portfolio selection to suit their risk profile or possibly to identify shares that were incorrectly priced on the basis of beta level and returns. Analysts often advise when it is a good time to buy, sell or hold certain shares. The CAPM is one method analysts can use to help them reach their conclusions. They can calculate the expected return and the required return for each share. The required return is subtracted from the expected return to give what is known as an **alpha value** (abnormal return) for each share.

Example 6.7 The alpha value

Suppose we are considering two investments, Mutt plc and Jeff plc. Their beta values and expected returns are as follows

	Beta value	Expected return
Mutt plc	1.5	18%
Jeff plc	1.1	18%

The market return is 14% and the risk-free rate of return is 4%. What are the alpha values and which investment would you recommend?

Solution

	Expected return	Required return	Alpha value
Mutt plc	18%	4% + (14% – 4%)1.5 = 19%	–1%
Jeff plc	18%	4% + (14% – 4%)1.1 = 15%	+3%

Sell shares in Mutt plc as it has a negative alpha and the expected return does not compensate the investors for the level of systematic risk. Buy shares in Jeff plc (positive alpha value) as the expected return more than compensates the investors for the level of systematic risk. If CAPM correctly reflects the risk-return relationship and the market is efficient, then the alpha values reflect a temporary abnormal return. Arbitrage profit-taking would ensure that any existing alpha values would move toward zero.

Alpha can be determined algebraically by the equation

$$E(R_s) = R_f + [E(R_m) - R_f)]\beta_s + \alpha$$

where the expected value of alpha is zero. A selection of shares with generally positive alpha values will result in above expected performance of the share portfolio and investors will be interested in the factors that drive alpha and in ascertaining measures which might reflect positive alpha values.

6.9 General comment

Beta factors for a company are calculated statistically from past observed returns. The London Business School *Risk Management Service* is published quarterly, using monthly returns from the previous last five years to calculate each quoted share's beta. Statistically, the reliability of the beta value will increase as the number of data included in its calculation increases. However, standard regression techniques tend to overestimate high betas (>1) and underestimate low betas (<1). The reason for this is that the CAPM has difficulty in dealing with seasonal factors observed in stock markets over the years (the January effect, etc.).

There has been great debate on the validity of CAPM and a lot of empirical research has been carried out. Much of this research has focused on beta and its stability over time. While empirical evidence on individual betas has been inconclusive, there is general agreement that the betas of shares display high levels of stability over time. The idea behind such portfolio betas being stable is based on the actual changes in individual betas tending to cancel each other out to some degree. Tests have also been carried out on the security market line using regression analysis, the most celebrated being the work done by Fama and Macbeth (1973). Their work suggested that a linear relationship does exist between risk and return: however, the CAPM and systematic risk measures do not fully explain the expected returns of individual securities.

Roll (1977) suggested that it was impossible to empirically test the CAPM, as the true market portfolio cannot be ascertained. The stock exchange indices are a poor substitute for the market as it fails to include all possible investments (bond foreign currency, property, antiques etc.). The consequence of this leaves CAPM difficult to prove or disprove.

CAPM is seen as a very useful model. However, critics believe that the relationship between risk and return is more complex than the linear model assumed by Sharpe. One model that could replace the CAPM is the arbitrage pricing model (APM) developed by Stephen Ross in 1976.

6.10 Arbitrage pricing model (APM)

When CAPM was developed it was based on a single index in that the return from a security is a function of just one factor, its beta value.

$$E(R_s) = R_f + [E(R_m) - R_f)]\beta_s$$

Instead of looking at a single factor influencing the return on each security, the APM assumes that the return is based on a number of independent factors (a form of multiple regression analysis). The actual return on any security is of the form

$$E(R_j) = R_f + b_1 factor_1 + b_2 factor_2 + b_3 factor_3 + b_4 factor_4 \ldots \text{etc.}$$

The factors involved in the APM were not identified by Ross in his original paper. He also suggested some securities are considered more sensitive to some factors than others. Further research done by Roll, Ross and Chen showed that there were four dominant factors.

1. The level of industrial activity specific to the company sector.
2. The rate of inflation.
3. The spread between short-term and long-term interest rates.
4. The spread between the yield of low and high risk corporate bonds.

The disadvantage of this form of analysis is its relative complexity and although the problem of finding the market portfolio is avoided, you now have to identify the sensitivities of the factors involved. Finding the relevant individual factors and the appropriate sensitivities of such factors for an individual share is extremely difficult. This has meant that the APM has not been widely adopted by the investment community as a practical decision-making tool.

CAPM remains the standard model used by investment practitioners and no other model has improved on its usefulness in explaining risk return relationships. The CAPM is generally considered somewhat superior to the dividend valuation model in calculating the cost of equity.

SUMMARY

- Investment risk and return can be measured by standard deviation and expected value statistics.
- When combining investments in a two-asset portfolio a key determinant of risk is the level of correlation that exists between the investments.
- Markowitz's portfolio theory provides a framework to identify the most efficient portfolio of risky and risk-free investments.
- The risk of an investment can be broken down into systematic and unsystematic risk.
- Unsystematic risk can be eliminated by holding a well diversified number of investments.
- The CAPM tries to measure systematic risk (beta factor) assuming a linear relationship between an individual share's returns and those of the market.
- The CAPM provides the required return of an investment based on the perceived systematic risk of the investment.
- Empirical tests neither prove nor disprove the validity of the CAPM, but it does provide a good understanding of the relationship between systematic risk and the required rate of return of investments.

WEB LINKS

http://www.londonstockexchange.com
London Stock Exchange

http://www.ise.ie
Irish Stock Exchange

http://finance.yahoo.com/
Yahoo finance pages

QUESTIONS

1. Explain the terms expected value, standard deviation and correlation and comment on their application in portfolio theory.

2. What is the Capital Market Line?
3. What is the difference between systematic and unsystematic risk?
4. What is the beta factor of a share and how can it help an investor choose what shares to invest in?
5. Has diversification at a company level any value to a company's ordinary shareholders?
6.♦ The ISEQ index at the end of 2007 and 2008 was 4750 and 5150 respectively. The dividend yield for 2008 was 4% and government bonds are currently yielding 4%. The price of shares in a company quoted on the index was €1.67 and €1.90 at the end of 2007 and 2008 respectively with a dividend pay out of 4c. The company has a beta of 0.97.
    (a) Was the return satisfactory on this share using the CAPM?
    (b) Comment on any weaknesses in your analysis.
7.♦ Summerhill Flynn plc has identified two quoted shares, which they believe will exhibit negative correlation in their possible returns over the next year as follows:

Economic state	Probability	High stool	Low stool
A	0.30	25%	14%
B	0.45	22%	18%
C	0.25	12%	20%

    (a) Calculate the expected return, variance and standard deviation of each security.
    (b) Calculate the covariance between the two securities and the correlation coefficient.
    (c) Construct a portfolio consisting of 70% by value of High stool and 30% Low stool. Calculate the expected return, variance and standard deviation of this portfolio.
8.♦ Three possible investments have been identified by Indecisive plc. The company wants to invest an equal sum in two of these investments and the following information is available.

	M	N	O
Expected return	15%	18%	17%
Standard deviation	2.4%	6.2%	4.3%
Covariance of returns			
M & N 12.2%			
M & O 8.1%			
N & O – 4.5%			

    (a) Estimate the correlation coefficient between each of the three possible portfolio combinations and explain the implications of these coefficients for portfolio risk.
    (b) Which of the three possible combinations would you consider the most efficient on the basis of mean-variance efficiency?

9. ♦ Sheila Takya has €800,000 to invest for a year, on which she is seeking a return of at least 16%.

She has identified the following possible non-divisible investments.

Project	Investment needed	Percentage return mean	Standard deviation
1	€500,000	14%	3%
2	€300,000	17%	4%
3	€500,000	20%	8%
4	€500,000	24%	7%

Unused cash of €100,000 or more can be invested in the money market (MM), to earn a mean return of 14% and a standard deviation of 3%.

Correlation coefficients between the returns on various investments have been estimated as follows:

	Market	MM	Projects 1	2	3	4
Market	1	0.8	0.7	0.7	0.8	0.8
MM	0.8	1	0.4	0.4	0.5	0.5
Project 2	0.7	0.4	0.7	1	0.6	0.5

Advise this person using portfolio theory on the most efficient use of the €800,000, assuming that all of the funds must be invested for one year.

10. K. Bambury plc is about to invest an equal sum in each of two companies from a choice of three available. The companies are in different industries and the data on risk and return over the past six years is given below:

Company	Average annual returns	Standard deviation of return
Groucho	11%	17%
Harpo	20%	29%
Zippo	14%	21%

The correlation coefficient between returns is as follows:

Groucho and Harpo   0.00
Groucho and Zippo   0.40
Harpo and Zippo   0.62

Estimate which of the portfolios is the most efficient.

11. ♦ Mount Temple plc has diversified into five different industries. The return of each investment is not correlated with the return of any other investment. The estimated return of the five investments is as follows:

Investment	Risk (SD%)	Return %
1	8	14
2	10	16
3	7	12
4	4	9
5	16	22

Estimate the risk and return of the portfolio of five investments and explain the significance of your result.

12.◆ The following figures relate to the monthly observations of the % return of the ISEQ index and the % return of a particular share over the past year.

Month	ISEQ	Share
Jan	+ 1	−0.5
Feb	−1	−2.0
Mar	+1.2	0
Apr	−2	−2.4
May	−1.5	+1.1
Jun	+0.5	−0.5
Jul	+1.1	−0.6
Aug	+1.3	+1.6
Sept	0	+0.4
Oct	+2	+1.5
Nov	+2.5	+2
Dec	+0.6	+0.2

(a) Calculate the slope (the beta or systematic risk measure) of the share.

$$\beta = \frac{n\Sigma xy - \Sigma x \Sigma y}{n\Sigma x^2 - (\Sigma x)^2} \quad or \quad \frac{\text{Covariance xy}}{\text{Variance x}}$$

(b) If the risk-free rate is 6% and the expected return for the ISEQ was 12%, what would be the expected return for this share?

13. Patty O'Dors plc has €50 million to invest that is currently earning 6% in short-term money market deposits. It is considering investing in one of three projects available. A consultant has estimated the risk/return data for the three projects as follows:

	A	B	C
Investment €million	35	40	28
Correlation of returns with the market	0.76	0.63	0.58
Standard deviation of returns	8.4%	4.6%	14.3%
Expected rate of return	15%	11%	17%

Market return per annum is 15%, market standard deviation of returns is 6.9%, and the risk-free rate of return is 6% per annum.

(a) Evaluate which project should be selected using the capital asset pricing model.

(b) The profitability index for project 2 was later calculated at 1.3, based on equal cash flows of €16 million per year from this project for four years. What does this imply about the accuracy of the beta coefficient estimated for the project?

14.◆ Joe King plc has a project with a four-year life and an initial outlay of €12 million. The project would generate annual cash flows of €5.3 million each year for the four years. The risk-free rate of return is 6% and the expected market rate of return is 11%. If the profitability index of the project is 1.4, what beta value has been applied to this project?

15. The following data is available about four potential investments:

Share	Forecasted return	Share standard Deviation	Covariance with market
A	16%	6.3%	32%
B	12%	4.8%	19%
C	14%	4.7%	24%
D	19%	6.9%	43%

The market return is 14.5%, the market standard deviation is 5% and the risk-free rate is 6%. Estimate the alpha values for each share.

16.◆ B. Wilderd is considering a portfolio of shares as follows:

Share	Beta	Expected return	Standard deviation	Investment Value
A	1.4	16%	7%	€3.8 million
B	0	6%	2%	€5.2 million
C	0.7	10%	5%	€6.1 million
D	1.1	13%	13%	€2.9 million

Calculate the weighted average beta and the required return of this portfolio using the capital asset pricing model, assuming the risk-free rate is 5.5%. If the expected market return is 12.5%, is the portfolio efficient?

7

Portfolio Performance Taking Account of Risk

CHAPTER OBJECTIVES

At the end of this chapter the student should:

1. understand the importance of taking explicit account of risk in portfolio selection, performance and evaluation
2. understand the concept of **safety-first** criteria as they relate to portfolio selection
3. understand and be able to apply numerically the three safety-first criteria detailed in this chapter, viz. Roy, Kataoka and Telser
4. understand the concept of **risk-adjusted** portfolio return measures
5. understand and be able to apply numerically the four risk-adjusted portfolio performance evaluation techniques detailed in this chapter, viz. Sharpe, Treynor, Jensen and the differential (total risk) return measure.

INTRODUCTION

Investment selection and performance evaluation tend to focus primarily on return only, i.e. investors base their perception of the attractiveness of different funds/portfolios on the level of return achieved over, say, a three- to five-year period. The level of risk inherent in a portfolio is often addressed by the potential investor through the advertised risk stance of the fund, e.g. a risk-averse investor may choose a capital-guaranteed fund or a low-risk equity fund, while a risk-taking investor may opt for an aggressively managed equity fund.

This chapter deals with a number of approaches to investment evaluation and fund selection which specifically and explicitly address the issue of risk.

Two specific approaches are dealt with:

- safety-first investment criteria
- risk-adjusted return measures.

7.1 Safety-first investment selection criteria

Suppose the following return information on fund performance over a 30-year period is available for three funds – no other information is available:

Fund	A	B	C
Average annual return (%)	8	10	13

If you were investing in one fund, which one would you choose?

Most investors would choose fund C since, on average, it has paid the highest return over the past 30 years.

Now suppose that information is also available on the standard deviation of returns.

Fund	A	B	C
Average annual return (%)	8	10	13
Standard deviation (%)	4	9	15

Which fund would you now choose?

The answer is no longer as clear cut. Different investors would choose different funds reflecting their attitude to risk.

Safety-first investment selection criteria may assist investors in making a choice as to the most desirable fund to invest in.

The basis of this approach to investment selection is to attempt to limit the risk of unacceptable or unsatisfactory out-turns.

Clearly the investor cannot control the return on an investment, but may be anxious to avoid a disaster or avoid making losses. Investors may give primacy to the avoidance of unsatisfactory out-turns over and above expected returns.

Take a simple example. Suppose a family has a stock of wealth of €500,000 which it can invest in order to earn a return, but has no other income. The family requires an absolute minimum of €35,000 each year to live on. A 7% return on its investment will meet its minimum requirement. A return above 7% is a bonus and will allow it to do many more things: take a holiday, decorate the house, etc. Nowhere, however, is it guaranteed a 7% return. The family is most concerned with avoiding disaster and less concerned with the potential for extra returns. It therefore wishes to invest in a fund that is **least likely** to underperform its minimum requirement, i.e. achieve a 7% return.

There are three main approaches to safety-first investment selection, each called after the author who devised the approach. These are:

- Roy
- Kataoka
- Telser.

The basis of each of the approaches, together with a numerical example, is given below. Further examples are given at the end of the chapter.

Note: In order to keep the mathematics simple, it is assumed that the portfolio returns are normally distributed. An alternative approach where this condition is not met is suggested.

7.1.1. Roy's criterion

The basis of this approach is to minimise the probability that the portfolio return is below some specified lower limit, i.e.

$$\text{Minimise prob. } (R_p < R_1) \qquad (7.1)$$

where
R_p = the portfolio return, and
R_l = the lower limit or lowest acceptable return.

The best portfolio is the one that has the lowest probability of producing a return below the specified level R_l.

Here the investor **subjectively** selects a lower acceptable return R_l, say, 7%, below which she does not want the portfolio return to go. The criterion then **objectively** selects the preferred portfolio on the basis that it has the least chance of falling below R_l.

Note: Since the lower limit is a subjective choice by the investor, different investors will choose different lower limits and Roy's criterion will select a different preferred portfolio for each investor.

Assuming that the distribution of portfolio returns is normal, the best portfolio is the one where R_l is the maximum number of standard deviations below the mean.

Figure 7.1 Distribution of portfolio returns

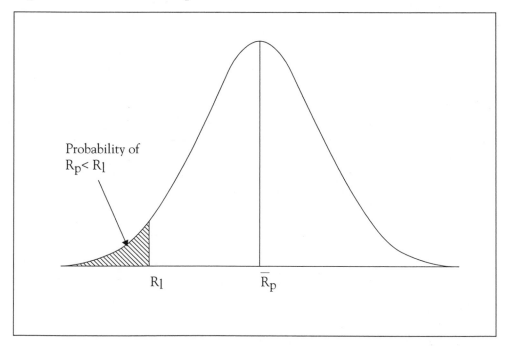

The best portfolio is one where $\overline{R}_p - R_l$ = maximum number of standard deviations (σ).

Example 7.1 Roy's safety-first criterion

Let 2% be the minimum desired return.

Fund	A	B	C
Mean return	6	9	11
Standard deviation (σ)	2	4	6

What Roy's criterion establishes is the probability of getting a return below the lower limit (in this case 2%) based on the historical mean and standard deviation of the returns from the portfolio. In the case of fund C, for example, the mean return is 11% and the standard deviation is 6%. To get a return of 2% means falling 9 percentage points (11 − 2) below the mean. This is 1.5 standard deviations below the mean. The probability of this occurring in a normal distribution can be read off from the standard normal distribution table provided in the Appendix and is 6.7%. The results for all three funds are shown below.

Fund	A	B	C
Mean return	6	9	11
Standard deviation (σ)	2	4	6
Difference from 2% (σ)	−2	−1.75	−1.5
Probability of return < 2%	2.28%	4.01%	6.68%

A has a 2.28% chance of delivering a return of 2% or less (i.e. about once in 44 years), B has a 4.01% chance of such a return (about once in every 25 years), while C has a 6.68% chance (once in 15 years). Therefore A is the preferred portfolio.

   As discussed above, different investors may set different lower limits.

Example 7.2 Roy's safety-first criterion

Let 4% be the minimum desired return and repeat the analysis above.

Fund	A	B	C
Mean return	6	9	11
Standard deviation (σ)	2	4	6
Difference from 4% (σ)	−1.0	−1.25	−1.17
Probability of return < 4%	15.87%	10.56%	12.10%

Here B has the least chance of delivering a return below 4% (about once every 9 to 10 years) compared to A (about once every 6 years) and C (little over once in 8 years) and so B is the preferred portfolio.

7.1.2 Kataoka's criterion

The basis of this approach is to maximise the lower limit subject to the probability that the portfolio return, being less than the lower limit, is not greater than some specified value.

Unlike Roy's criterion, where the investor specifies a minimum acceptable **return** level, in Kataoka's criterion, the **subjective** input by the investor is in the form of an acceptable **risk** level. In other words, the investor accepts that in a certain percentage of the time (investment periods) the return will fall below some level, let's call it a **floor**. He is prepared to accept that once in, say, every 20 periods (5% of the time) or once in every 15 periods (7% of the time) the return will fall below the floor. Each fund will have a different floor below which it falls, say, 7% of the time. The **objective** selection criterion is then to identify the fund which produces the highest floor.

Let α = specified risk level

Criterion is

Maximise R_l

Subject to probability $(R_p < R_l) \leq \alpha$ (7.2)

The subjective selection is α, i.e. a risk level acceptable to the investor.

Objective criterion is to select the portfolio with the highest possible lower value (floor) satisfying the constraint.

Let α = 10%. This means that the investor is prepared to accept a 1 in 10 chance of falling below some floor level.

Once again assuming that the returns from the portfolio are normally distributed, a number can be derived below which the return from the fund will fall only 10% of the time (and, by definition, above which the return will lie 90% of the time). From the standard normal distribution tables it can be seen that the bottom 10% of the distribution (10% in the left-hand tail of the distribution) occurs at 1.28 standard deviations below the mean. This holds for all normal distributions. Thus the value of R_l can be calculated for each fund as 1.28 standard deviations below the mean, i.e.

$$R_l = \overline{R}_p - 1.28\sigma$$

Figure 7.2 Distribution of portfolio returns

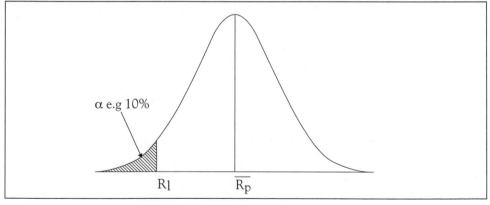

The best portfolio is the one with highest value of R_l.

The objective then is to select the portfolio which allows the highest value of R_l.

Example 7.3 Kataoka's safety-first criterion

Using the same data as in Example 7.1 above and letting α = 10%.

Portfolio		A	B	C
$\overline{R_p}$		6	9	11
σ_p		2	4	6
R_l (Note 1)	=	3.44	3.88	3.32

The results indicate that 10% of the time fund A will fall below 3.44% return, fund B will fall below 3.88%, while fund C will fall below 3.32%. Since fund B produces the highest floor, it is the preferred portfolio.

Example 7.4 Kataoka's safety-first criterion

Suppose α was set at 25%. The relevant figure from the normal distribution tables which cuts off the bottom 25% is 0.67.

Portfolio		A	B	C
$\overline{R_p}$		6	9	11
σ_p		2	4	6
R_l (Note 2)	=	4.66	6.31	6.98

The results now indicate that 25% of the time fund A will fall below 4.66%, fund B will fall below 6.2%, while fund C will fall below 6.98%. Since fund C produces the highest floor, it is the preferred portfolio.

The reader should be clear regarding a critical difference between Roy's and Kataoka's criteria. In the case of Roy, the investor **subjectively** selects a minimum percentage **return** and objectively selects the preferred portfolio on the basis of the lowest risk of not meeting this desired return. In the case of Kataoka, the investor **subjectively** selects an 'acceptable' **risk** level (percentage) and objectively selects the preferred portfolio on the basis of the **highest minimum return** consistent with this risk level.

7.1.3 Telser's criterion

The basis of this approach is to revert back to the intuitively appealing criteria of selecting the portfolio with the highest average return, provided it obeys a safety constraint. The constraint is effectively a combination of Roy and Kataoka $\Rightarrow$ that the probability of a return below some floor is not greater than some specified level.

Criterion is:

$$\text{Maximise } \overline{R}_p$$

$$\text{Subject to probability } (R_p < R_l) \leq \alpha \tag{7.3}$$

Here there are two subjective decisions:
⇒   Choice of acceptable risk level = α
⇒   Choice of acceptable lower limit = R_l

The **objective** criterion is to select that portfolio with the highest expected return satisfying the constraint. The constraint effectively operates as a filter. Only those funds meeting the constraint qualify for consideration. Of those that qualify, the preferred portfolio is simply the one which has delivered the highest average return in the past.

Example 7.5 Telser's safety-first criterion

Using the same data as in Example 7.1 above, let R_l = 2% (minimum desired return), and α = 10% (acceptable risk level).

Fund	A	B	C
Mean return	6	9	11
Standard deviation (σ)	2	4	6
Difference from 2% (σ)	−2	−1.75	−1.5
Probability of return < 2%	2.28%	4.01%	6.68%
Obeys constraint?	Yes	Yes	Yes

All funds pass the constraint since they all have a less than 10% chance of falling below a 2% return in any period. While fund C is one and a half times more likely than fund B, and three times as likely as fund A, to fall below a 2% return, it falls within the acceptable risk tolerance level (of 10% likelihood) and it therefore qualifies for consideration. Of the qualifying funds (here A, B and C), fund C has the highest average return and is therefore the preferred portfolio.

Example 7.6 Telser's safety-first criterion

Now let R_l = 4% (minimum desired return), and let = 12% (acceptable risk level).

Fund	A	B	C
Mean return	6	9	11
Standard deviation (σ)	2	4	6
Difference from 4% (σ)	−1	−1.25	−1.17
Probability of return <4%	15.87%	10.56%	12.1%
Obeys constraint?	No	Yes	No

Now only fund B meets the constraint and is chosen ahead of fund C (which fails the constraint) despite the fact that it has a lower average return. Fund B is therefore the preferred portfolio.[3]

Summary of the three approaches

The key differences between the approaches are:

- Roy's approach gives primacy to keeping the risk of **bad** out-turns to a minimum, where 'bad' is determined by the investor.
- Kataoka's approach is to explicitly recognise and quantify what is an acceptable risk level and then to select on the basis of the portfolio having the highest 'worst' out-turn consistent with the risk level.
- Telser's approach is to revert to the intuitively appealing selection criteria of highest average return, but forcing adherence to a constraint that sets both an explicit level of risk and a worst out-turn.

Non-normally distributed returns

In the case where returns are not normally distributed, the investor could attempt to determine the functional form of the distribution and adapt the analysis above to fit the distribution. Alternatively the investor could have recourse to Tychebyshev's inequality,[4] which offers an approach which is independent of the functional form of the distribution but is much weaker or less convincing in terms of the results. A simple, though not mathematically robust, alternative, utilising the logic of each of the three criteria is offered here.

Roy's criterion: The basis of the suggested approach is simply to count the number of returns which have fallen below the specified lower limit and to express these as a percentage of the total. The fund with the lowest percentage falling below the lower limit is the preferred fund.

Kataoka's criterion: Once again an acceptable risk level is chosen, say 10%. Each fund's returns are ranked and the return on the fund just above the bottom 10% represents the target lower limit. The fund with the highest lower limit is the preferred fund.

Telser's criterion: A lower limit and an acceptable risk level are specified. Following the approach in Roy's criterion set out above, the percentage falling below the lower limit is calculated. If this percentage is lower than the specified risk level, then the fund qualifies for consideration. The fund with the highest average return from among the qualifying funds is the preferred one.

7.2 Risk-adjusted return measures

Performance evaluation and analysis based only on return achieved is somewhat crude and limited. Evaluation techniques tend to be primarily concerned with comparing the return on one portfolio with the return on some other portfolio. This could be with a benchmark fund, e.g. an appropriate mixed asset fund for the type of investor, the performance of competitor funds or with market indices such as the ISEQ for an Irish equity fund, the FTSE 100 for a UK equity fund, the index of the Irish bond market for a fixed-interest fund, etc. This, however, is unsatisfactory if one wishes to reflect the level of risk carried by the fund manager. Comparisons should be made between portfolios of similar risk levels or, if different risk levels exist, then comparisons can be made by developing an explicit risk/return trade-off.

The measures set out below address the issue of the level of return achieved for the amount of risk taken. There are two broad approaches, one which measures the return per unit of risk taken and the other which measures the **differential** return on a fund, where differential refers to the additional (positive or negative) return compared to that which would have been achieved by following a naive investment strategy.[5]

Return per unit of risk measures

There are two measures of this type differing in their definition of risk. These are:

- the Sharpe measure
- the Treynor measure.

Measures of risk
The two measures of risk used are:

- Total risk: normally measured by standard deviation of returns and denoted by σ_p.
- Non-diversifiable risk: normally measured by the β coefficient of the fund/portfolio.

7.2.1 The Sharpe measure

This is sometimes referred to as the excess return to variability measure and is measured by the formula

$$\frac{(\overline{R_p} - R_f)}{\sigma_p} \qquad (7.4)$$

where

$\overline{R}_p$ = the average return on the portfolio
R_f = the return on the risk-free asset
σ_p = the standard deviation of the portfolio returns.

The logic of the measure is quite straightforward. Every fund should expect to earn a return of the risk-free rate plus something more. How much more depends on the level of risk taken. The ratio allows an analysis as to whether the amount of return over and above the risk-free rate (excess return) is sufficient to compensate for the additional risk taken.

Example 7.7 The Sharpe measure

The risk-free rate of return was 5% p.a. over a certain period of time. Fund A had an average return of 12% and a standard deviation of 6%, while fund B had an average return of 15% and a standard deviation of 9% over the same period. This says that fund A earned a return 7 percentage points above the risk-free asset by taking on a risk level of 6% while fund B earned a return 10 percentage points above the risk-free asset by taking on a risk level of 9%.

The Sharpe measure for the two funds is

Fund A $\dfrac{(12-5)}{6} = 1.17$

Fund B $\dfrac{(15-5)}{9} = 1.11$

Fund A earned 1.17% return for each 1% of risk carried, while fund B earned 1.11% return for each 1% of risk carried. While fund A is paying a lower return on average than fund B, it is delivering a greater return for the level of risk attached and is therefore the preferred fund.

7.2.2 The Treynor measure

The logic is broadly similar to that of Sharpe and measures the excess return to non-diversifiable risk. It is measured by the formula

$$\frac{(\overline{R_a} - R_f)}{\beta_a} \qquad (7.5)$$

where
R_a = the average return on an individual asset/portfolio
R_f = the return on the risk-free asset
β_a = the risk of the asset/portfolio as measured by its β value.

Example 7.8 The Treynor measure

The risk-free rate of return was 5% p.a. over a certain period of time. The market average return was 11% p.a. Fund A had an average return of 12% and a β of 1.2, while fund B had an average return of 10% and a β of 0.8 over the same period.

The market average return was 6% p.a. above the risk-free rate. Fund A earned a return 7 percentage points above the risk-free asset by taking on a risk level which was 120% of the market average, while fund B earned a return 5 percentage points above the risk-free asset by taking on a risk level which was 80% of the market average.

The Treynor measure for the two funds and the market average is

Market average $\dfrac{(11-5)}{1} = 6$

Fund A $\dfrac{(12-5)}{1.2} = 5.83$

Fund B $\dfrac{(10-5)}{0.8} = 6.25$

Since the market portfolio has a β value of 1, any fund carrying a greater risk than the market average ($\beta > 1$) should have an excess return higher than the market average, and any fund carrying lesser risk than the market average ($\beta < 1$) should have an excess return lower than the market average. Fund A earned an excess return of 5.83% when the risk level is neutralised to the market average, while fund B earned an excess return of 6.25% when the risk level is neutralised to the market average. Fund A is therefore paying an excess return lower than the market average and lower than fund B, while fund B is paying an excess return greater than the market average and greater than fund A when account is taken of the risk inherent in each fund. Fund B is therefore the preferred fund.

Differential return measures

There are two measures of this type, differing in their definition of risk. These are:

- differential return (total risk) measure
- the Jensen (β risk) measure.

The basis of this approach is the assumption that the investor has an alternative investment strategy of investing in a combination of the market portfolio and borrowing/lending at the risk-free rate, i.e. the investor can choose a risk level through a combination of the risk-free asset and the market portfolio – **the naive strategy**. The investor through, say, stock selection, may receive a return which differs from that which would have been achieved by the naive strategy. This differential return can be calculated and analysed to determine the fund manager's stock-picking ability.

As shown in Chapter 6, all combinations of the market portfolio and the risk-free asset lie on a straight line intercepting the return axis at the risk-free rate.

Figure 7.3 Differential return measures

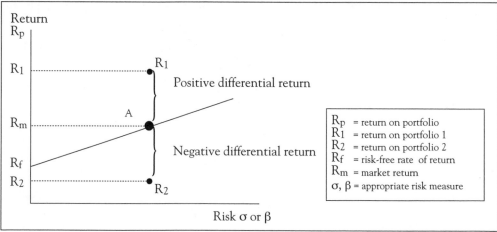

Any portfolio with a return above the line has achieved a positive differential, while any fund with a return below the line has achieved a negative differential. This relationship can be drawn with risk measured by either total risk or β risk (the CAPM).

Differential return (total risk) measure

The slope of the line connecting the market portfolio and the risk-free rate is

$$\frac{E(R_m) - R_f}{\sigma_m} \qquad (7.6)$$

where
$E(R_m)$ = the expected return on the market portfolio
R_f = the return on the risk-free asset
σ_m = the standard deviation of the returns on the market.

The equation of the line is: $E(R_i) = R_f + ((E(R_m) - R_f)/\sigma_m) \times \sigma_i$

where
$E(R_i)$ = the expected return on an individual asset/portfolio
σ_i = the standard deviation of the returns on an individual asset/portfolio.

This can be rewritten: $E(R_i) = R_f + (E(R_m) - R_f) \times \dfrac{\sigma_i}{\sigma_m}$

This form of the equation allows the ratio of the total risk of the asset/portfolio to the total risk of the market to be explicitly recognised.

Example 7.9 The differential return (total risk) measure

The risk-free rate of return was 5% p.a. over a certain period of time. The market average return was 10% p.a. and the standard deviation of market returns was 7%, while fund A had an average return of 13% and a standard deviation of 9% over the same period.

The expected return on fund A is $5 + (10 - 5) \times \dfrac{9}{7} = 11.43\%$

This says that a fund such as Fund A, which has taken $\dfrac{9}{7}$ (1.28 times) of the market risk, could have received:

Rf = 5% plus 9/7 of the market risk premium (10% − 5%)

= 5% + 9/7 × (10 − 5)% = 11.43% through a naive investment strategy

The actual return on fund A was 13%.

The differential return is therefore 13% − 11.43% = 1.57%.

Fund A has therefore achieved a return of 1.57% above that which could have been achieved by simply borrowing at the risk-free rate and investing in the market portfolio.

7.2.3 The Jensen measure

This is sometimes referred to as Jensen's alpha and is broadly similar to the previous measure except that the measure of risk used is β rather than total risk.

The formula for calculating the expected return on a fund is the CAPM.

$$E(R_i) = R_f + \beta_i (E (R_m) - R_f) \tag{7.7}$$

Example 7.10 The Jensen measure

The risk-free rate of return was 5% p.a. over a certain period of time. The market average return was 11% p.a., while fund A had an average return of 12% and a β of 1.2 over the same period.

The expected return on fund A is

$$5 + 1.2(11 - 5) = 12.2\%$$

The actual return on fund A was 12%.

The differential return is therefore 12% − 12.2% = − 0.2%.

Fund A has therefore achieved a return 0.2% below that which could have been achieved by simply borrowing at the risk-free rate and investing in the market portfolio.

SUMMARY

- This chapter has set out two approaches to portfolio performance evaluation and selection when account is explicitly taken of risk. They are safety-first investment criteria and risk-adjusted return measures.
- There are three main approaches to safety-first investment selection.
- Roy's criterion is to select a minimum return level and minimise the risk of failing to reach this.
- Kataoka's criterion is to specifically accept a risk level and select the portfolio which offers the highest minimum return (floor) consistent with that risk level.
- Telser's criterion is to revert to the intuitively appealing selection criterion of highest average return, but forcing adherence to a constraint which recognises both an acceptable risk level and a minimum desired return level.
- The chapter also deals with the issue of risk-adjusted portfolio return analysis. Four measures are discussed:
  (a) the Sharpe measure
  (b) the Treynor measure
  (c) the differential return to total risk measure
  (d) the Jensen measure.
- The Sharpe and Treynor measures neutralise the risk across different portfolios and compare the adjusted return. The measures differ in their concept of risk, with Sharpe using total risk and Treynor using β risk.
- The other two measures compare the return achieved to that achievable through a naive investment strategy. The differential return may be positive or negative. The

measures differ in their concept of risk, the first using total risk and the Jensen measure using β risk, i.e. the CAPM.

QUESTIONS

1.◆ The table below shows the average return on three unit-linked funds over a 30-year period together with the standard deviation of returns:

Fund	A	B	C
Average return (%)	13	17	21
Standard deviation (%)	5	9	12

Adopting a **safety-first** approach to the investment selection, which of the funds would be chosen by an investor adopting:
(a) Roy's criterion (lower acceptable return, R_l = 7%)
(b) Kataoka's criterion (risk level, α = 13%)
(c) Telser's criterion (R_l = 7%, α = 13%)?

2.◆ The table below shows the average return on three unit-linked funds over a 40-year period together with the standard deviation of returns:

Fund	A	B	C
Average return (%)	12	15	20
Standard deviation (%)	4	7	10

Adopting a **safety-first** approach to the investment selection, which is the most desirable fund, under
• Roy's criterion (lower acceptable return, R_l = 5%)
• Kataoka's criterion (risk level, α= 8%)
• Telser's criterion (R_l = 5%, α = 8%)?

3. The table below shows the average annual return on three unit-linked funds over a 35-year period together with the standard deviation of returns:

Fund	A	B	C
Average annual return (%)	13	17	19
Standard deviation of return (%)	5	8	10

Which of the funds would be chosen by an investor adopting
(a) Roy's criterion (lower acceptable return, R_l = 6%)
(b) Kataoka's criterion (α = 10%)
(c) Telser's criterion (R_l = 6%, α = 10%)?

4.◆ The risk-free rate of return was 4% p.a. over a certain period of time. Fund A had an average return of 11% and a standard deviation of 5%, while fund B had an average return of 14% and a standard deviation of 7% over the same period. Calculate the Sharpe measure for the two funds and indicate which fund would be preferred on this measure.

5.♦ The risk-free rate of return was 6% p.a. over a certain period of time. The market average return was 9% p.a. Fund A had an average return of 13% and a β of 1.1, while fund B had an average return of 14% and a β of 1.2 over the same period. Calculate the Treynor measure for the market and for the two funds and indicate which fund would be preferred on this measure.

6.♦ The risk-free rate of return was 6% p.a. over a certain period of time. The market average return was 11% p.a. and the standard deviation of market returns was 5%. Fund A had an average return of 16% and a standard deviation of 8% over the same period, while fund B had an average return of 9% and a standard deviation of 6% over the same period. Calculate the differential return (total risk) measure for the two funds and indicate which fund would be preferred.

7.♦ The risk-free rate of return was 7% p.a. over a certain period of time. The market average return was 10% p.a. Fund A had an average return of 11% and a β of 1.4 over the same period, while fund B had an average return of 13% and a β of 1.6 over the same period. Calculate the Jensen measure for the two funds and indicate which fund would be preferred.

8. Explain clearly the basis of the three safety-first approaches shown below, indicating the key differences between them:
   (a) Roy's criterion
   (b) Kataoka's criterion
   (c) Telser's criterion.

9. Discuss the main approaches to risk-adjusted portfolio performance, indicating the differences between the various measures.

NOTES

1. R_l is calculated as $R_l = \bar{R}_p - 1.28\sigma_p$
2. R_l is calculated as $R_l = \bar{R}_p - 0.67\sigma_p$
3. The mathematics used in Telser is the same as that used in Roy. The difference is that in Roy it is the fund with the lowest probability of falling below the minimum acceptable return which is chosen, while in Telser it is the fund with the highest average return so long as the calculated probability is not greater than the specified risk tolerance level.
4. This is discussed in most advanced statistics or investment textbooks. See, for example, Elton and Gruber.
5. A naive investment strategy is one where the investor invests in a combination of the risk-free asset and the market portfolio.

Part 3

Valuations

8

Share and Company Valuations

CHAPTER OBJECTIVES

At the end of this chapter, the student will be able to calculate the price of common stock using:

1. the zero growth dividend formula
2. the constant growth formula
3. the non-constant growth formula

and be able to:

4. calculate the value of common stock using the P/E ratio
5. calculate the value of common stock using balance sheet methods
6. understand how to value companies using the free cash flow method.

INTRODUCTION

In Chapter 4 we discussed the concept of the time value of money – how to value future cash. In Chapter 5, we described bond values as the present value of future interest payments plus the present value of bonds at maturity. Similarly, we value common stocks in the same way as we value other assets by using the discounted cash flow formula.

8.1 Share value and cash flow

The cash flow to a holder of a common share is a stream of dividends:

Value of share = P_0 = Present value (PV) of expected future dividends (8.1)

Imagine that you purchase a share today for €2 and you expect to sell it in one year's time for €3. You also expect to receive a dividend of 20 cents over the next year. Therefore, the rate of return (r) you expect to receive from holding this share is 60%:

$$r = \frac{P_1 - P_0 + D_1}{P_0}$$

$$= \frac{€3 - €2 + €0.2}{€2} = 60\%$$

where P_1 = price of share at end of the first period
  P_0 = current price of the share
  D_1 = expected dividend at the end of the first period.

Therefore, the expected return on the share is the dividend received *plus* the expected gain in the price of the share, divided by the original price.

Similarly, if you were given the expected rate of return of a security of similar risk, you can predict the current price:

$$P_O = \frac{D_1 + P_1}{1 + r} = \frac{3.2}{1.6} = €2$$

But what determines the price of the share at the end of the year (P_1)?

How much will you receive in one year's time when you sell the share? The answer of course depends on what dividends any future investor will expect to receive from this share. Therefore the price of a share in one year's time will be the present value of expected future dividends received on that share during year 2 *plus* the expected share price at the end of year 2. The price of the share at the end of year 2 will be the expected dividends received from that share during year 3 *plus* the expected share price at the end of year 3 and so on. Therefore, the current value of a share is the present value of the future dividend stream as shown in equation 8.1. This is the generalised dividend valuation model or the **going concern** assumption model. Provided a company does not go into liquidation or is consequently acquired by another company, common shares can last for ever. We don't have to worry about terminal value. As we move further into the future the present value of cash flows approaches zero. Therefore, today's price can be expressed as shown in equation 8.1.

Example 8.1 *Share valuation*

Suppose you are considering the purchase of CRH shares which are currently trading at €19 a share and which will pay 19 cents in dividends a year. Security analysts expect the share to trade at €29 in one year's time. Will you buy the share at this price? To make a decision you will need to calculate the present values of expected future cash flows, which consist of the dividend payments and the expected share price in one year's time. However, before you can do this you will need to know what the required rate of return is on equity of similar risk. Suppose the rate of return you require to compensate for the risk involved in investing in this type of share is 10%.

Solution
The value of the share today is the expected value of the future cash flows:

$$PV = P_0 = \frac{D_1}{(1 + k_e)} + \frac{P_1}{(1 + k_e)} = \frac{0.19}{1.1} + \frac{29}{1.1} = €26.5$$

where   PV = present value
       P_0 = intrinsic or theoretical value of the share
       D_1 = dividend received during the year
       k_e = the required rate of return on equity capital.

Alternatively, the total rate of return is

$$\frac{29.0 - 19.0 + 0.19}{19.0} = 53.6\%$$

This is a much greater return than you require.

Therefore you would choose to buy it because the present value of the shares is €26.5, which is greater than the current value of €19. You believe the share is undervalued. You believe it is worth €26 whereas it is selling for €19. As far as you are concerned CRH shares offer a higher rate of return than similar securities of similar risk. However, this may be just how **you** feel about risk and return. Other investors may not be as optimistic about the future cash flows and they may therefore place a **higher risk** on them, which require **a higher rate of return, thus lowering the market price**.

8.1.1 What if a company never pays a dividend?

Equation 8.1 says that the current value of a share is equal to the present value of the expected future dividend stream. But what if a company has an official policy of never paying dividends and in addition has no liquidation value. Does this share have a value? Think what would happen if you tried to sell this share. No rational investor would buy it. The company would be taking in all of this money from investors without ever giving any of it back. Therefore it has no value. This type of security doesn't exist. What we generally mean when we say that companies don't pay dividends is that they currently don't pay dividends. A buyer of this type of share will expect the company to pay dividends someday. Companies that currently don't pay dividends are called growth stocks (although new research would indicate that there is no such thing as a growth industry – see Box 8.1), because their value emanates from capital gains. Other companies are known as income shares because their value derives from dividend income. With growth shares, investors are happy to forgo current income for future capital gains. The share price of growth stocks will increase because the date of the expected dividend payment gets closer.

There are also companies that pay irregular dividends, i.e. the dividends can be different every year. In the following section, we examine share valuation based on different assumptions regarding dividend growth.

Box 8.1 The devil is in the detail

BOOK REVIEW *The Granularity of Growth: Making Choices That Drive Enduring Company Performance* by Patrick Viguerie, Sven Smit, Mehrdad Baghai; Wiley Publications. Authors argue leaders of large institutions should avoid taking an averaged view of their businesses and should manage them with greater focus at a more detailed level, while continuing to take advantage of their scale, writes Stefan Stern

There is no such thing as a growth industry.

No, this is not the latest doom-laden forecast for 2008. It is the penetrating insight offered by three management consultants – two from McKinsey, the other a former McKinsey partner – in this thought-provoking new book.

Too often people speak in the most general terms about market trends. 'The world's ageing population will generate increasing demand for healthcare,' we might say, or 'You have to invest in the booming Chinese economy'.

But closer analysis reveals these sweeping remarks do not help you to understand how businesses actually make money.

'Most discussions of megatrends take place at a very broad and superficial level,' Viguerie, Smit and Baghai argue.

'That may be fine for financial commentators on TV or casual dinner-party chat, but it's not much use if you happen to be the CEO of a large company trying to make decisions about where to compete or to allocate resources.'

Consider a customer walking into a branch of Starbucks. Will he or she simply order 'a cup of coffee'? Unlikely. The customer makes a specific and deliberate choice. In economies and product categories, this effect is magnified on an industrial scale.

So, the authors say, managers' understanding of markets has to go much deeper, down to a 'granular' level.

'We believe that the leaders of large institutions need to avoid taking an averaged view of all their businesses; instead, they should manage them with greater focus at a more detailed level, while continuing to take advantage of their scale,' the authors write.

McKinsey has hired a team of data analysts based in India to carry out what the firm calls 'granular growth decompositions' – a detailed study of the way companies make money.

They have separated this revenue generation into three main categories: mergers and acquisitions; 'portfolio momentum' or growth in revenue achieved in the markets where a business competes; and 'share gain' or achieving a greater share of a given market.

Their findings are pretty startling. For one thing, M&A does not seem to be an inevitably value-destroying route. Indeed, the coming slowdown could be a great time to make some smart acquisitions, the authors say.

Second, 'portfolio momentum' is of supreme importance. This vital measure of strategic performance reveals the wisdom of decisions taken many years earlier.

The authors quote approvingly the candid thoughts of an ex-CEO of Shell, Lo van Wachem: 'The actual revenue I realise today is grossly dependent on the energy reserves

→

acquired and explored by the two CEOs before me, and CEOs two generations after me will reap the rewards of my efforts.'

Third, agonising over market share can be a waste of time, however important we believe it to be. Have 'superior insights' or 'truly distinctive capabilities' instead, they advise.

'If you don't, you'll find your competitors' execution soon matches yours, and your market-share performance will take a dive . . . stalling your growth programme.'

McKinsey's analysis has confirmed the authors in their belief that a business's success depends heavily on the markets in which it operates.

'So the next time a company announces stellar performance, it's worth taking a closer look to see how much of its growth came from better steering, and how much from a favourable tailwind,' they write. 'What is driving performance: execution or strategic choices?'

Practically, a company like Procter and Gamble seems to have taken the granularity message on board. Its skilful brand management embodies this. And yet, P&G's rival Unilever arguably tripped up in recent years by cannibalising its own brands, getting its granules in a twist.

So 'going granular' is not easy. And doesn't it all sound rather time-consuming? It needn't be so. 'In our experience . . . the critical issues affecting growth are brought to light immediately, making the dialogue between the executive board and the business unit much more specific,' the authors say.

'In most cases, the number of issues discussed doesn't increase, but the specificity and quality of those issues rises dramatically.'

In 2008, you can stop worrying so much about market share and get to grips with choice market granules instead – (*Financial Times* service).

The Irish Times, Monday 31 December 2007

8.2 Zero growth

What is the value of a share in a company where dividends are expected to remain constant, i.e. zero growth? Here $D_1 = D_2 = D_3$ . . . etc. The value of the share is the constant dividend divided by the required rate of return:

$$P_0 = \frac{D_1}{(1+ke)} + \frac{D_2}{(1+ke)^2} + \frac{D_3}{(1+ke)^3} + \ldots \frac{D}{(1+ke)^\infty}$$

Therefore, because the dividend is always the same the value of a zero growth stock is a perpetuity. The constant dividend is divided by the required rate of return on equity.

Example 8.2 Valuing zero growth stocks

$$P_0 = \frac{D}{ke}$$

What is the value of a share that pays a constant dividend of €4 if the required rate of return is 10%?

Solution

Using equation 8.1

$$P_0 = \frac{4}{0.1} = €40$$

Therefore we would expect to sell the share for €40.

8.3 Constant growth stocks

Remember that dividends are paid out of earnings. In turn, earnings will be determined by the margin that companies make on their sales that in turn will be influenced by the growth rate in the economy. This will vary from company to company but, on average, dividend growth will continue at roughly the same rate of growth as nominal GDP. Companies may have an explicit goal of a constant growth in dividends.[1] Therefore if a company has just paid a dividend and if that dividend grows at a constant rate (g), then the next dividend will be

$$D_1 = D_0 (1 + g)$$

where D_1 = next dividend to be paid
D_0 = dividend just paid
g = constant growth rate.

If g is constant, equation 8.1 can be modified to:

$$P_0 = \frac{D_0 (1 + g)}{(1 + ke)} + \frac{D_0 (1 + g)^2}{(1 + ke)^2} + \frac{D_0 (1 + g)^3}{(1 + ke)^3} + \ldots \frac{D_0 (1 + g)^\infty}{(1 + ke)^\infty} \tag{8.2}$$

Provided the growth rate is less than the discount rate we can rearrange the above equation (8.2) as

$$P_0 = \frac{D_0 (1 + g)}{ke - g} \quad \Rightarrow \quad \frac{D_1}{ke - g} \tag{8.3}$$

where $\Rightarrow$ means 'is the same as'.

This is **Gordon's growth model**.[2] (For a full exposition of the dividend growth model proof, see Appendix 13A.)

Note that if the growth rate is greater than the discount rate the present values of the expected dividend stream will get larger and larger. This would give us a share price that is infinite, and since no share price is infinite, it would not make sense for the growth rate g to be larger than the discount rate K_e. We discuss this in more detail in section 8.3.1 below.

Example 8.3 Constant growth stock

Pioneer Company Ltd has just paid a dividend of €2 per share and dividends at the company are expected to grow at a steady rate of 7% per annum. What is the present value of the share if the required rate of return is 12%?

Solution

First, we find the expected value of the dividend at the end of the first year, D_1.

$$D_1 = D_0 (1 + g)$$
$$= €2 (1+.07)$$
$$= €2.14$$

Remember that the dividend just paid of €2 (D_0) is **only** used to determine D_1 because the value of a share is the present value of expected **future** dividends.

We can now use equation 8.3 to find the expected price (present value) of the share P_0.

$$P_0 = \frac{€2.14}{(0.12 - 0.07)} = €42.8$$

8.3.1 Points to remember about the dividend growth rate g

- In Chapter 9, we will discuss dividend policy in more detail, but for now you should understand that for strategic reasons companies may pursue a constant dividend growth rate.
- For equation 8.3 to hold, it is necessary for K_e to be greater than g. If it were the case that the growth rate g was greater than the cost of equity K_e, the present value of the dividend stream would become infinite. No share has an infinite price. When K_e is greater than g the PV of each dividend $D_0 (1 + g)/1 + K_e$ gets smaller and smaller while the euro amount of each dividend $D_0 (1 + g)$ gets bigger and bigger. If g is greater than K_e, the PV of successive dividend payments would get progressively bigger and this just would not make sense. Note that it is however possible that some companies, in the initial stage of their development, can have supernormal growth rates and this can lead to g being greater than K_e.
- The longer-term growth rate can also be estimated by looking at the dividend payout ratio, which is the ratio of dividends to earnings per share (EPS).

Example 8.4 Estimating dividend growth rates

(a) Using the dividend payout ratio.
   Consider a company that pays 60% of net earnings in cash dividends, i.e.

$$\text{Payout ratio} = \frac{\text{Dividends}}{\text{Earnings per share}} = 60\%$$

This means that it retains 40% of earnings for reinvestment purposes.[3] The **reinvestment ratio** is

$$1 - \frac{\text{Dividends}}{\text{EPS}} = 1 - 0.6 = 0.4$$

Suppose the return on equity (ROE) is 12%, i.e.

$$\text{ROE} = \frac{\text{EPS}}{\text{Equity}} = 12\%$$

If the ROE is 12% and the company reinvests 40% of earnings then the company's equity will increase by 4.8%

$$= (0.12)\,(0.4) = 4.8\%$$

Therefore, if the company follows a constant dividend policy, dividends will grow at 4.8%, i.e.

Growth rate g = (Reinvestment ratio)(ROE) = (0.4)(0.12) = 4.8%

(b) Using past changes in dividends to forecast future dividends.
The dividends (cents per share) paid by the XYZ Group between 2003 and 2007 were:

Year	Dividends
2003	12.7
2004	14.3
2005	16.8
2006	19
2007	20.1

The average growth rate is found using the equation

$$g = \sqrt[n]{\frac{FV}{PV}} - 1 \tag{8.4}$$

where PV = earliest accruing dividend
FV = most recent dividend
n = number of intervals between the dividend payments – in this case four.

Therefore, assuming a required rate of return of 15%, XYZ's dividend growth rate from 2003 to 2007 is

$$g = \sqrt[4]{\frac{€20.1}{€12.7}} - 1$$

$$g = \sqrt[4]{1.58} - 1$$

$$g = 1.12 - 1 = 0.121 = 12.1\%$$

To find the expected current value of AIB stock if dividends grow at a constant rate of 12.1% a year and where the most recent paid dividend is €0.21 and the expected return is 15%:

$$P_0 = \frac{D_0 (1 + g)}{(ke - g)}$$

$$P_0 = \frac{€.21(1 + 0.121)}{(0.15 - 0.1221)}$$

$$P_0 = €8.1$$

Therefore, the expected value of XYZ stock is €8.10 **if** the assumptions made are correct.

Note, however, that it is not advisable to use the constant growth formula for stocks that have high current growth rates because they are unlikely to be sustained.

8.4 Non-constant or supernormal growth

In the last section, we saw how companies settle down at some stage of their life cycle and tend to grow at a constant rate. In the initial start-up phase, some companies grow at above average growth rates and then begin to level off. In addition, some companies may experience a particular period when the dividend stream is either very high or very low due to either a successful investment expansion programme or an economic recession. Furthermore, some companies have a competitive advantage because of effective barriers of entry to the industry in which they operate. For example, the estimated cost of building a new wafer fabrication plant at Intel is huge, which effectively makes it very difficult for would-be competitors to enter the microchip industry.

To illustrate a company that goes through different phases of growth we use the following example.

Example 8.5 Non-constant growth

Currach Eanach plc has just paid a dividend of 12 cents per share. Because of favourable economic conditions and a rapid expansion programme, dividends are expected to grow at an annual rate of 15% for the next three years. After the third year, company sales and earnings will fall off and dividends are expected to grow at 8% per annum. The company's required rate of return is 10%. Find the value of Currach Eanach's shares.

Solution
To find the value of a non-constant growth share such as Currach Eanach's we take the following steps:

1. Determine the present value of the dividends during the non-constant growth phase.
2. Find the constant growth rate and use it to find the present value of the dividend stream (including the price of the shares at the end of the non-constant growth phase) after the non-constant growth phase.
3. Add the present values got in steps 1 and 2 to find the theoretical value of the share.

1. Find the expected dividends during the three years of supernormal growth.
   (a) First dividend $D_1 = 12(1 + 0.15) = 13.8$ (Note 4)
   (b) Second dividend $D_2 = D_1 (1 + g) = 13.8(1.15) = 15.8$
   (c) Third dividend $D_3 = D_2 (1 + g) = 15.87(1.15) = 18.25$.
2. The present value of the stream of dividends during the constant growth phase is got using Gordon's growth model which gives us the share price at the end of the **third** period. The fourth year dividends are then discounted back **one time period** to the third year. The third year price is then discounted back to year zero and this is added to the present value of the dividends received from the first three years to find the theoretical current price.
   First, find the dividend for the fourth year:

$$D_4 = D_3 (1 + .08) = (€.1825) (1.08) = €.1971$$

The price of the share the investor would expect to receive at the end of the non-constant growth period P_3 is

$$P_3 = \frac{D_4}{ke - g} = \frac{€.1971}{0.02} = €9.85$$

In other words the value of the share at the end of year 3 is €9.85.[5]

Figure 8.1 Finding the value of a supernormal growth stock

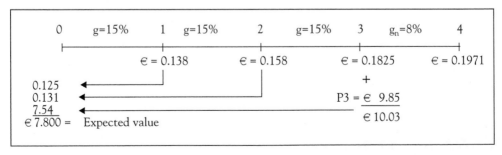

Now discount €9.85 + the third year dividend of €0.1825 = €10.03 back three periods to find its present value.

Finally, the sum of the present values provides us with an estimate of the current expected value of the stock. This is €7.8 and is illustrated in Figure 8.1.

8.5 Price earnings method

The dividend valuation models (DVMs) are the most rigorous means of valuing stocks. The difficulty is that it is not always easy to come up with the relevant information on, for example, growth rates and discount rates.

In Chapter 14 we introduce various stock market ratios. We will see how, using the P/E ratio, the market values €1 in earnings. If a company's earnings per share is 10 cents and the share price is €2, investors are prepared to pay 20 times historic earnings for the share. This is the historic price earnings ratio (PER):

$$PER = \frac{\text{Current market price of share}}{\text{EPS}} \qquad (8.5)$$

Firms in the same industry are expected to have similar P/E ratios in the long run. We can estimate the value of a company's shares using the P/E ratio.

In the late 1990s, there were significant increases in share prices that resulted in market valuations breaching historic norms. In July 1998 for example the market traded at 18.9 times current earnings compared to a ten-year average of 14.1 times.[6] We will talk more about market valuations in Chapter 14.

8.5.1 How to interpret P/E ratios

- High P/E ratios may signify that investors place a low risk on these shares and are therefore willing to pay a higher price for them.
- High P/E ratios may indicate high growth prospects.
- High PEs may indicate that the company has had poor financial results but investors expect the company to improve its performance.
- The weakness of using industry average P/E ratios is that firm-specific factors, which might lead to a company's P/E ratio being above or below the industry average, are ignored.
- The financial pages of quality newspapers give the PEs of quoted companies. However, these are based on historic earnings. It would be more useful from an investor's point of view if future earnings were used in the calculation. Instead of using a historic P/E ratio we can use a prospective PER (price earnings ratio) which includes next year's expected earnings:

Recall the dividend growth model.

$$P_0 = \frac{D_1}{Ke - g}$$

Divide both sides by next year's earnings E_1

$$\frac{P_0}{E_1} = \frac{\dfrac{D_1}{E_1}}{ke - g}$$

Here the PE multiple rises if g rises, and falls if K_e increases. $\dfrac{D_1}{E_1}$ is the payout ratio. If this rises, less earnings are reinvested in the firm and so g will fall. Therefore, the PER may not increase.

Example 8.6 *Valuation using the prospective PER*

Murphy Engineering Ltd's required rate of return is 12%. The company reinvests 60% of its earnings. Next year the company expects dividends to grow by 5%. What PE multiple would you attach to this share?

Solution

$$\frac{P_0}{E_1} = \frac{D_1/E_1}{ke - g} = \frac{0.4}{0.07} = 5.7 \text{ times}$$

Now if the growth rate falls to 3% and the required rate of return increases to 14% the prospective PER becomes

$$\frac{0.4}{0.14 - 0.03} = 3.6 \text{ times}$$

P/E ratios are difficult to interpret because of the difficulty of comparing the earnings of different companies. For example, different methods of calculating depreciating and valuing stock will lead to different profits figures.[7]

8.6 Valuation using the balance sheet

A balance sheet is a list of a company's assets and liabilities. We can apply two methods to value a business using a balance sheet – the net asset value and liquidation value.

8.6.1 *Net asset value (NAV)*

This is sometimes referred to as a company's net worth or shareholders' funds. NAV is simply calculated by adding up the company's assets and deducting all liabilities. For example the NAV of Ryanair Holdings plc for 1999 as shown in their balance sheet is €250,964,000.

To find the book values per share simply divide the NAV by the number of shares.

$$\text{Book value per share} = \frac{\text{NAV}}{\text{Number of shares issued}} \tag{8.6}$$

The company had 164,759,808 shares in issue on 31 March 1999. Therefore the book value per share is €250,964,000/164,759,808 = €1.52.

The market values not only the company's net assets but also the income flow derived from these assets and also other intangible assets not included in the balance sheet such as brand names, management quality, etc. For this reason net asset values act as a starting point **only** in the overall valuation process.

8.6.2 Liquidation value

Liquidation values are based on market (realisable) values and not book values. Liquidation values are based on what the assets would realistically make on the open market. The liquidation value of a liability is the money it takes to pay off that liability.

Example 8.7 Liquidation value

ABC Ltd's liquidation values are as follows (€000)	
Freehold property	100
Fixed asset value@	
70% of book value	20
Current assets valued @	
80% of book value	150
Total asset value	270
Less Current liabilities	200
Loans	50
Total liabilities	250
Net assets	20

Assuming 100 shares, the liquidation value per share is 20/100 = 20c.

8.7 Valuing the entire company using free cash flows

Some companies don't currently pay dividends. In addition, some companies are private, which means they do not have a market value for their shares. Cash flow valuation methods are a means of valuing such companies. Remember, cash is king. While companies can enhance and manipulate profits (see Chapter 11) this is not possible to do with reported cash flow. The wealth of a shareholder depends on the company's ability to generate cash flow, or more precisely free cash flow. You will recall from Chapter 2 that free cash flow is what is left for shareholders after all the necessary investments (to sustain the company) have been made in total operating capital.

Example 8.8 Company valuation using free cash flow

The financial statements of Brandon Ltd for 2008 (actual) to 2012 (projected) are given in Tables 8.1 and 8.2.

Table 8.1 Profit and loss account (actual and projected) for Brandon Ltd 2008–2012

	Actual 2008 €m	Projected 2009 €m	2010 €m	2011 €m	2012 €m
Turnover	1,662.8	2,258.8	2,381.8	2,450.6	2,638.8
PBIT	74.2	84.6	95.4	90.8	92.2
Interest	(24.2)	(26.2)	(26.4)	(26.6)	(19.2)
PBT	50	58.4	69	64.2	73
Taxation	7.5	8.8	10.35	9.6	10.9
PAT	42.5	49.6	58.65	54.6	62.1

Table 8.2 Balance sheet (actual and projected) for Brandon Ltd

	Actual 2008 €m	Projected 2009 €m	2010 €m	2011 €m	2012 €m
Fixed assets	398.6	463	456.8	452.2	486
Current assets					
Stock	126.6	124.8	140.8	147.6	157
Debtors	227.2	254.0	259.8	252.8	255.8
Marketable securities	9.8	11.4	10.4	10.2	8.8
Cash	49.8	116	117.6	166.2	124.8
	413.4	506.2	528.6	576.8	546.4
Current liabilities					
Creditors	192.36	339.8	292.68	290.08	288.96
Accruals	128.28	84.2	122.32	124.32	123.8
	320.64	424	415	414.4	412.76
NWC	92.77	82.2	113.6	162.4	133.64
Total NA	491.36	545.2	570.4	614.6	619.64
Financed by					
Long-term debt	204.8	260.6	256.4	263.8	106.2
Share capital	244.1	234.6	279	296.8	453.2
Retained earnings	42.46	50	35	54	60.24
	491.36	545.2	570.4	614.6	619.64

Table 8.3 Calculating Brandon's expected future free cash flow

		Actual		Projected		
		2008	2009	2010	2011	2012
		€m	€m	€m	€m	€m
Note 1	Operating net fixed assets	398.6	463	456.8	452.2	486
Note 2	Net operating working capital	82.96	70.8	103.2	152.4	124.84
Note 3	Total net operating capital required	481.56	533.8	560	604.4	610.84
Note 4	Total net new investment in operating capital		52.24	26.2	44.4	6.44
Note 5	Net operating profit after taxes (NOPAT) = PBIT (1 − Tax rate)		71.9	81.09	77.18	78.37
Note 6	Less total net new investment in operating capital		52.24	26.2	44.4	6.44
Note 7	Free cash flow		19.66	54.89	32.74	71.93

Note 1: Net fixed assets as per balance sheet.

Note 2: Remember from Chapter 2 that net operating working capital = (Stock + Debtors + Cash) *minus* (Creditors + Accruals). In other words, net operating working capital is operating current assets *less* operating current liabilities. Therefore, for Brandon Ltd we leave out marketable securities. These are **financial assets** and are not part of the operating requirements.

Note 3: This is the sum of net operating fixed assets and net operating working capital.

Note 4: This is the net addition to operating assets. So for example for 2009 the net addition to operating assets is €533.8 *less* €481.56 = €52.24.

Note 5: This is net operating profit after tax. The tax rate is 15%, therefore for 2009 the PBIT (1 − tax rate) = €84.6(1 − 0.15) = €71.9m. This is operating profit after taxes (NOPAT).

Note 6: This is NOPAT *less* the net investment in total operating capital. So while in 2009 the company has projected €71.9m in net operating profit after taxes, it will invest €52.24m in operating capital. This leaves €19.66m in free cash flow for shareholders. Value added economics suggests that performance-related bonuses and pay be related to **free cash flow** and not on accounting measures of profit.

Turnover at Brandon is expected to grow at a non-constant growth rate up to 2012. After 2012 a constant growth rate of 8% is expected. The company's required rate of return is 10%. We can calculate the company's value using the free cash flow calculated in Table 8.3.

The value of a business is the present value of the free cash flow up to the horizon period (H) *plus* the present value at the horizon period.

The horizon value refers to the first year of constant growth, where the NPV of growth opportunities is zero.[8] The horizon value is the value of operations at the end of the forecast period. It is what the company's operating assets are worth at the end of the forecast period. The horizon period is **the time** when the firm enters into **competitive equilibrium**. Attempts to expand sales will meet with fierce competition from competitors who have **caught up** in terms of efficiency in the market place. The horizon period is the time when the competition catches up.

Up to this point, the present value of investment opportunities is greater than the cost of capital. This is the **growth stage** of the business cycle. When more and more businesses enter the industry and when the industry becomes more efficient and competitive, the present value of investment opportunities becomes zero.

The following steps are taken:
1. Calculate the free cash flow. Remember from Chapter 2 that free cash flow is net operating profit after tax *minus* net investment in operating capital.
2. Find the present values of the free cash flows for the non-constant growth period – up to 2012.
3. Use the constant growth formula to calculate the horizon value (H) at the end of 2012. Next, calculate the present values of all subsequent years back to 2012. Then the total year 2012 value is discounted back to the year 2008 to find its present value.
4. Finally, summing the present value of the free cash flow during the non-constant growth period *plus* the present value of the horizon value gets the value of the firm.

The overall market value of the company is derived as follows:
(a) The value of the company at the horizon period

$$V_H = PV = \frac{FCF_H\,(1+g)}{ke-g} \tag{8.7}$$

where V_H = horizon value
FCF_H = free cash flow at horizon period

Therefore the value of the operation at the end of 20X5 is

$$V_H = PV = \frac{FCF\,(1+g)}{Ke-g} = \frac{€71.93\,(1.08)}{0.1-0.08} = \frac{€77.7}{0.02} = €3{,}885m$$

This is what Brandon would expect to receive if it sold its operations at the end of 2012.

In addition, the total cash flow at the end of 2012 is the sum of the expected free cash flow at the end of 2012 *plus* the expected value of operations at the end of 2012:

$$€71.93m + €3{,}885m = €3{,}956.93$$

(b) The present value of the FCF for the non-constant growth periods are

Year	FCF	Discount	PV
2009	19.66	1.1	€17.87
2010	54.89	$(1.1)^2$	€45.36
2011	32.74	$(1.1)^3$	€24.59
Total PV			€87.82

(c) Present value of horizon period

$$\frac{€3,956.93}{(1.1)^4} = €2,702.58$$

(d) Therefore the total value of FCF and the total value of operations as at 2008 is

$$\begin{bmatrix} \text{Total present value} \\ \text{of operations }_{2008} \end{bmatrix} = \begin{bmatrix} \text{Present value of non-constant} \\ \text{growth period} \end{bmatrix} + \begin{bmatrix} \text{Present value of} \\ \text{horizon period} \end{bmatrix}$$

This is

$$[€2,790.4] = [€87.82] + [2,702.58]$$

Figure 8.2 illustrates these figures using a PV time line.

Figure 8.2 Valuation of whole company using free cash flows and non-constant growth rates

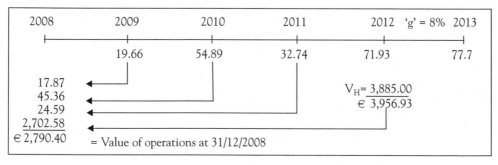

The total value of any company is the value of its operating assets *plus* the value of its non-operating assets.

$$\text{Total value of operations} = \begin{bmatrix} \text{Value of operating} \\ \text{activities} \end{bmatrix} + \begin{bmatrix} \text{Value of non-operating} \\ \text{activities} \end{bmatrix} \quad (8.8)$$

The value of Brandon's non-operating assets at the end of 2008 is €9.8m (i.e. Brandon's marketable securities) and the value of its operating activities is €2,790.4m. Therefore the overall value of Brandon Ltd as at the end of 2008 is

$$\text{Total value of operations} = [€2,790.4m] + [€9.8m] = €2,800.2m$$

Remember, a company will finance its operations with equity or debt, or a combination of both. Therefore the total value of operations *minus* the value of the company's debt must equal the value of the company's equity.

Deducting the total value of the company's debt, i.e. €204.8m, we get the market value of its equity as at the end of 2008. This is the total value of operations *less* the total value of debt:

Market value of equity = Total value of operations − Total value of debt   (8.9)

For Brandon Ltd this is

$$\text{Market value of equity} = €2,800.2\text{m} - €204.8\text{m} = €2,595.4\text{m}$$

The **book value of equity** at the end of 2008 is €286.56m, which represents the shareholders' actual investment in the company. By deducting this from the market value of equity, we get the **market value added**. This is the value added to shareholders' investments by management and employees. Table 8.4 gives a summary of the valuations for Brandon Ltd.

Market value added = Market value of equity − Book value of equity   (8.10)

Therefore, Brandon's market value added is

Market value added		Market value of equity		Book value of equity
€2,308.84m	=	€2,595.40m	−	€286.56m

Table 8.4 Valuation summary of Brandon Ltd as at 31/12/2008 (€m)

Present value of FCFs for non-constant growth period	87.82
Plus	
Total present value of FCFs for constant growth period (i.e. horizon value)	2,702.58
Equals	
Present value of operating activities	2,790.4
Plus	
Value of non-operating activities	9.8
Total value of operations	2,800.2
Less	
Value of debt	204.8
Equals	
Market value of equity	2,595.4
Less	
Shareholders' investment	286.56
Equals	
Market value added	2,308.84

8.8 Standard valuation methods and hi-tech stocks

For a while in 2000 dot.com stocks became a password to instant financial success (see Box 8.2). What do the standard valuation methods tell us about the valuation of hi-tech stocks?

Box 8.2 Flocking to the dot.com party

Dot.com has become a password to instant success in Western equity markets. Since the arrival of Netscape on the market five years ago, the market has been flooded with new technology stocks that have fundamentally distorted market performance.

In 1998/99, for instance, the value of Internet stocks soared 400 per cent against just short of 20 per cent of the more traditional US indices – the Dow Jones and the Standard and Poor's 500.

That explains the rush by more traditional media companies and others to reinvent themselves as dot.com. In Ireland, two dramatic examples have been Independent News and Media, whose shares have jumped 36% from €7.96 to €10.80 in the 10 days since it announced the provision of Internet access via television to cable customers, and Fyffes, whose business-to-business web service has seen the share shake off the blues which dogged it for so long and rise from €1.65 to €3.85. This week BSkyB showed even newish media companies are not immune to the need to upgrade on technology. Announcing an interim loss of £61.5 million sterling compared with a profit of £53.2 million in the previous year, its stock surged by more than 20 per cent on the day to record highs.

Why? Quite simple. The market could not have cared less what the results said once the company announced it was to invest £250 million sterling to boost its presence online.

The same strategy has already bolstered the fortunes of two other media giants – Reuters and Pearson.

If only turning a profit were so easy.

Business Briefing, *The Irish Times*, 12 February 2000

As we have seen in this chapter the value of a share is the expected value of the future dividends received from that share as in the equation 8.1:

$$P_o = \frac{D_1}{(1 + ke)} + \frac{D_2}{(1 + ke)^2} + \frac{D_3}{(1 + ke)^2} + \frac{D}{(1 + ke)^\infty}$$

If, according to equation 8.1, an investor concludes that the stock's price exceeds a reasonable valuation but goes ahead and buys it anyway, the investor would be following the bigger fool theory – you believe that the stock is overpriced but you also believe that there is a bigger fool out there who will buy the share at an even higher price from you when you decide to sell.

There have been many examples of the bigger fool theory down through the ages.[9] More recently, the global market crash of 1987 was preceded, among other reasons, by the bigger fool theory. In 2008, billions were wiped off the value of Ireland's quoted financial stocks. The biggest losers were Anglo Irish Bank, Bank of Ireland and Allied Irish Banks, who suffered a huge drop in market capitalisation. This fall-out in financial stocks was mirrored globally.

The bigger fool theory describes speculative investments and doesn't fit with the dividend valuation models (DVMs) described earlier. Unrealistic expectations are applied to valuations. Many of these so-called new economy stocks are valued on unrealistic assessments of sales growth – not on free cash flow or even profits. (See Box 8.3.)

Box 8.3 Don't be last one left with fool's stock

Can I pose a few questions? Are we in a bubble? Is the bubble bursting? The answer to each of these questions must be yes. As an interested observer there is no doubt in my mind that: (a) the stock market is still in a bubble despite recent corrections; (b) Irish house prices are in a bubble; and (c) the Irish economy is demonstrating many of the characteristics of a bubble. . . . Even some of the most risk friendly speculators must shudder at some of the valuations now being applied to assets . . .

The price of a share is equal to the present value of the sum of all future expectations. Bubbles happen when unrealistic expectations are applied to valuations.

I do not understand the current valuation model that values a company only on a multiple of sales. Don't worry about profit or return on investment.

This so called enterprise valuation model simply won't work. One example illustrates the madness of current expectations. A recent successful stock market launch in Britain resulted in a market value that could only be justified by either of the following:

- Annual sales growth of 65% at a 25% margin or
- Annual sales growth of 50% with a 40% net margin.

What are the chances of either occurring? None whatsoever. A quick look at almost all the Irish tech stock valuations should cause you to ponder. In fact, it should cause you to head for the door. . . .

Bubbles do not have to explode. Like a slow puncture, markets can decline over time. Rallies are followed by declines with subsequent peaks usually lower.

Is this what is happening? I believe it is. It is now old fashioned to think that investment must earn a return. Any venture in bricks, clicks or intellectual property rights must cover the cost of the investment and make a margin to cover profit. Profit for many seems an outdated concept. Business ventures must make a profit otherwise capital will flow to other areas. Does that make sense? It should because that's what happens.

How can you have billion dollar values on companies with small sales, no profits and only vague hopes of making profits in the future? The answer is 'the greater fool theory'. Almost every buyer of bubble stocks cares little about the business or its prospects. They expect to sell on their shares at a higher price. Buyers believe there is a greater fool out there willing to pay a higher price to buy shares, which they in turn can sell on.

$\longrightarrow$

As long as the 'pass the parcel' games continue, the markets can rise. Day trading[10] is grist to this mill.

Look at today's business pages; look at the valuations placed on certain new economy companies. The future is obvious – share prices will fall. Most new economy ventures will fall. Investors will lose their money. The few that succeed will be the Ges, Exxons and IBMs of the future.

Extracted from an article written by John Teeling, chairman of Cooley Distilleries as well as a member of oil and mineral resource companies, *The Irish Times*, 19 May 2000.

SUMMARY

- Valuing common stock is more difficult than valuing bonds because (a) cash flows are not explicit, (b) it is difficult to find an appropriate rate of return and (c) a common share's life is for ever.
- The value of a common stock is the present value of the future dividend stream.
- A zero growth stock suggests that future dividends are constant, i.e. $D_1 = D_2 = D_3$ etc.
- The value of a constant growth stock is

$$Po = D_1 (1 + g)/(ke - g) = D_1/ke - g$$

- Companies go through different phases during their business cycle from initial accelerated growth to moderate growth and finally no growth. These phases signify different dividend growths. Summing the discounted values of dividends at each stage of growth gets the market price of such a stock. This is the supernormal growth model.
- The PER is used to measure companies that don't have a market price.
- NAV is a measure of a company's book value. This is total assets *less* total liabilities, which is the company's net worth or shareholders' funds.
- Liquidation value is used to value assets below their book value or assets with poor earnings capacity.
- The cash flow valuation model is used to value companies that don't pay dividends.

WEB LINKS

www.ise.ie
Link to Irish Stock Exchange.

www.123world.com/stockexchanges
Links to world stock exchanges.

www.barra.com
Information on company valuations.

www.discountdividendmodel.com
A calculator for estimating stock values.

www.finance.yahoo.com
For company and market information.

QUESTIONS

1. Why is valuing common shares more difficult than valuing bonds?
2. Why is liquidation value more dependable than book value?
3. ♦ The value of a common share depends on expected dividends. Why therefore can't companies increase shareholder value by simply increasing dividends?
4. Do share values reflect the long-term performance or short-term performance of a company?
5. In the dividend valuation model (DVM), why is the cost of equity assumed to be greater than the growth in dividends g? Illustrate your answer diagrammatically.
6. Why is g (growth in dividends) in DVM assumed to be constant?
7. Is there any value in a share that will never pay a dividend and has no liquidation value?
8. How do share prices reach their equilibrium position?
9. ♦ The following is an estimate of dividends that will be paid on a particular share: year 1 = €1, year 2 = €1.5, year 3 = €2. It is expected that after this dividends will grow at a constant rate of 4% p.a. The company's cost of capital is 8%. Calculate: (a) the current price of the share P_O, (b) the price of the share in one year's time at P_1, (c) the capital gain between P_O and P_1, (d) the dividend yield at P_O, and (e) draw a time line valuation of the shares.
10. Boherbawn Investments Ltd's current share price is €30. It has just paid a dividend of €2 per share. The company is now stabilised and it expects dividends to grow at a constant rate into the future. The company's cost of capital is 10% and it is expected to remain at that level. Calculate Boherbawn's expected stock price in four years' time.
11. Bolton Ltd shares are selling for €50 per share. The next dividend payment is due in one year's time and this is expected to be €2 per share and the expected share price in one year's time is €60. Calculate the shareholders' expected rate of return?
12. What does a negative dividend mean?
13. 'The value of stocks is determined by dividend income and not by capital gains.' Evaluate this statement.
14. ♦ The end of year dividend on common stock of Mountjoy Ltd is expected to be €5 per share and the shares are expected to sell for €60 per share. Calculate the current share price if the expected rate of return is 10%.
15. Garbh Eoin Quarrying Ltd has just paid a €5 per share dividend to its common shareholders. There have been some concerns about financial irregularities in addition to environmental concerns associated with the company. Because of this, the dividend growth rate is expected to be just 3%. Calculate the expected value of the price of Garbh Eoin shares, if its cost of capital is 15%. Would you buy a stock whose share price was expected to decline?
16. ♦ You are considering the following three investment opportunities. Stock A provides dividends of €5 per share for ever. Stock B is expected to provide a dividend of €6 next year. Dividend growth is expected to be 5% per annum thereafter. Stock C will pay a dividend of €2 next year and dividend growth is expected to be 15% for the following 4 years and zero thereafter. The cost of capital is 8% for each share. Which

share is the most valuable?

17. Flybynight Airlines is experiencing rapid growth with dividends expected to grow by 12% during the next two years, 14% in year 3, and at a constant rate of 5% thereafter. Flybynight has just paid a dividend of €1.20 per share. The market capitalisation rate is 10%. Calculate the value of stock today.

18.♦ Yesteryear has just paid a dividend of €3 per share. The company doesn't expect to be able to continue the payout and it expects to reduce the payout by 10% next year and thereafter. The company's cost of capital is 14%. Calculate the share price.

19.♦ Elm Co., a drugs manufacturing company, has never paid a dividend. The company has a cost of capital of 12% and a free cash flow of €200,000. The FCF is expected to grow at a constant rate of 5%. The company has debentures of €500,000. You are required to calculate the overall value of the firm.

NOTES

1. This is discussed in Chapter 6.
2. M.J. Gordon and E. Shapiro, 'Capital Equipment Analysis: The Required Rate of Profit', *Management Science*, 3 October 1956.
3. We discuss earnings per share (EPS) in detail in Chapter 14, but for the moment remember that EPS is profit for ordinary shareholders divided by the number of ordinary shares and ranking for dividend.
4. Note that D_0 is 12 cents and it is only used to estimate D_1. D_0 has already been paid and does not therefore enter the equation because we are dealing with the present values of **future** cash flows.
5. €9.85 is a year 3 cash flow because this is the expected price of the share at the end of year 3.
6. Source: *Irish Equity Market Forecasts*, Davy Research, July 1998.
7. Creative forms of accounting will be discussed in Chapter 11.
8. This general definition is used by Brealey and Myers in *Principles of Corporate Finance*, 6th edn. Chapter 4, 'The Common Value of Stock', deals with the meaning of the **horizon period**.
9. See John Kenneth Galbraith, *A Short History of Financial Euphoria*, Whittle Books.
10. Day trading is the practice of buying and selling securities on the same day.

9
Dividend Policy

CHAPTER OBJECTIVES

At the end of this chapter the student should:

1. understand what dividends are
2. know the sequence of events in dividend payments
3. know why companies need to have a dividend policy
4. be able to analyse the controversy about dividend policy. Does dividend policy affect shareholder value?
5. understand how companies determine the level of dividends paid out at any one time
6. be able to assess the alternatives to cash dividends.

INTRODUCTION

Dividends are cash payments out of profits to shareholders and are therefore a major cash outlay for many corporations. How much of the company's retained earnings (profit for ordinary shareholders) will be paid to shareholders (if any) and how much will be ploughed back into the company's investment plans? This is the dividend policy decision. What is of greater importance is the effect this policy decision will have on shareholder wealth. We will explore this question later on in the chapter. However, why is it necessary to have a planned dividend policy at all? The answer is that shareholders don't like surprises. Companies are reluctant to pay out substantial cash dividends if they know that they cannot repeat it the following year. If shareholders don't get the dividend they expect, they can react by selling their shares and driving down the share price. Therefore companies try to plan their dividend payouts and by doing so help stabilise share prices.

In addition, dividend policy can impact on companies' investment plans. If a company has a high dividend payout policy, any investment plans the company has earmarked to be financed by retained earnings may have to be put on hold. Therefore, dividend policy must be taken into account along with the company's investment and capital expenditure decisions.

9.1 Dividend payments sequence

Irish public limited companies usually pay dividends twice a year every six months. An interim dividend is paid relating to the first six months of trading, followed by a final dividend after the end of the financial year. Dividends are usually expressed as: (a) dividends per share (euro per share); (b) dividend yield (see Chapter 14), dividends as a percentage of the market price; or as (c) the dividend payout, which is dividends as a percentage of earnings.

Table 9.1 Kerry Group consolidated profit and loss account 1997 (extract)

Profit after taxation and attributable to ordinary shareholders	€64,632
Dividends: paid (interim)	€2,392
proposed	€4,817

(Note that the word 'proposed' is used which means that the directors are proposing a final dividend but it is up to the shareholders at the group's AGM to decide whether it should be paid or not.)

The dividend payout is 11.2%.

The board of directors decides when the company will pay a dividend. The following is the sequence of events leading up to the actual payment.

1. *Declaration date*: on this date the board declares a dividend to be paid on a certain date in the future.
2. *Date of record*: When shares are sold it takes time to process the paperwork and to record the change of ownership. This is the date the holder of the share must be on record in order to receive a dividend.
3. *Ex-dividend date*: Because it takes time to process the buying and selling of shares and to make sure that the dividends go to the right people, the stock exchange establishes an ex-dividend date. This is generally four working days before the date of record. This means that if you buy a share before this date you are entitled to the dividend – the share is said to **trade with dividend** or **cum dividend**. Investors who buy the share on or after this date will not be entitled to the dividend – the share will trade **ex-dividend**. The ex-dividend date is important for two reasons: (a) it determines who is entitled to the dividend; and (b) the value of the share will fall by roughly the amount of the dividend. Therefore, if a share has a market value of €5 cum dividend and if a €1 dividend is declared on that share, then the ex-dividend price will fall to roughly €4. Because dividends are taxed as income, the actual ex-dividend price of the share will be influenced by the individual investor's marginal tax rates.
4. *Payment date*: The cheques are posted to the investors.

We should note, however, that this process is likely to become much simpler because of technological developments, particularly with the electronic transfer of funds.

9.2 The dividend policy debate

In the opening chapter of this book, we said that the overriding consideration of financial management is to maximise shareholder value. In this section we will set out to evaluate the effect dividend policy has on shareholder wealth. Remember that the dividend policy decision is whether to pay out cash now or invest the cash and pay it out later. How much of the company's retained earnings should be paid out now (if any) and how much should be reinvested? What effect does this decision have on shareholder value? There are essentially three schools of thought in answer to this question. The first states that dividend policy has no effect on shareholder value. This is the irrelevancy argument and was first developed by Franco Modigliani and Robert Miller. The second school suggests that an increase in dividend payout ratio increases shareholder value – the bird in the hand theory. The third school of thought states that an increase in dividend payout ratio reduces shareholder value – the tax differential theory. The main arguments are outlined below along with some real world resolutions to the debate.

9.2.1 The irrelevancy argument in perfect capital markets

The value of a firm is determined by the earning power of its assets, not how these earnings are distributed. You can slice a cake into many pieces but it doesn't change the size of the cake. Similarly, a company's dividend policy has no effect on the price of a company's shares and no effect on the overall value of the firm. Modligiani and Miller (MM) assumes perfect capital markets (see Chapter 13) and ignores taxes and commission costs.

Example 9.1 Irrelevance of dividend policy

Boyvale Ltd has the following capital structure:	
Balance sheet (market values)	€
Fixed assets	600,000
Cash	400,000
	1,000,000
Financed by:	
100,000 ordinary shares	1,000,000

The market value of Boyvale shares is 1,000,000/€100,000 = €10. The company has decided to pay the €400,000 as a cash dividend, or €400,000/100,000 shares = €4 per share. Ignoring taxes, commission costs and other market imperfections, does this policy decision affect shareholder value?

After paying out the cash dividend each share is worth €600,000/100,000 shares = €6 per share. Therefore the share price has fallen but the value of the shareholders' holdings hasn't changed. A shareholder with 100 shares before the dividend payment was worth 100 × €10 = €1,000. After the dividend payment her worth is now 100 × €6 = €600. However, she also has €4 cash dividend per share which is worth 100 × €4 = €400. So her total wealth is now €600 + €400 = €1,000. To further illustrate, MM's irrelevancy argument understands that any shareholder can create his/her own **home-made dividend**. Suppose, for example, that Boyvale decided not to pay a dividend. Our shareholder in the above example could, if she desired, sell 40 of her 100 shares at €10 per share in order to generate €400 in cash. Her overall wealth won't have changed because she now has €400 in cash *plus* €600 in shares, giving her a total value of €1,000.

The criticism of MM is that their assumptions are unrealistic. However, remember that the validity of a theory is determined by its ability to predict and explain, and not in the realism of its assumptions. In particular, they assumed perfect capital markets, rational investors, and no taxes and commission costs. The next two theories try to incorporate these real world factors.

Example 9.2 The dividend irrelevancy argument and present value

MM assumed no risk. Assume that the interest rate or the rate at which cash can be invested is 5%. Now assume that the company has €20,000 available to pay out in cash dividends to its shareholders. Alternatively, it can reinvest the €20,000 in the company. If it pays out the €20,000 as a cash dividend today, the present value of this option is €20,000. If it reinvests the €20,000 for 3 years it produces a capital gain of €20,000 $(1.05)^3 = €23,152$. This has a present value of €20,000. Therefore the firm's policy decision of high payout versus low payout gives the same present value.

9.2.2 The bird in the hand theory

This theory states that investors prefer to receive dividends now (a bird in the hand), instead of having company earnings invested in the firm in the expectation of future capital gains (two in the bush). Dividends are in the hand while capital gains are in the bush. There is a certainty about cash dividends, whereas there is an uncertainty about capital gains. The risk attached to capital gains is greater than the risk attached to near dividends. Therefore we can conclude that high payout ratios reduce risk and therefore reduce the cost of equity.[1] Consequently, companies with high payout ratios will be more popular and will therefore have higher share prices and higher company valuations. Furthermore, issuing new shares to increase dividends will incur commission and flotation costs, which will have the effect of lowering share value.

This is different from MM. The critical conclusion of the bird in the hand theory is that dividend policy affects company risk and therefore the cost of equity. For MM, the cost of equity is independent of dividend policy, and company risk (and therefore investors' required rate of return) depends on the company's operational cash flows that depend on the company's investment and borrowing policies and not on dividend policy. Proponents of MM would say that while it is true that cash dividends are less risky, this is so because the cash is in the bank. The investor could achieve a similar outcome if she sold some shares and put the money in the bank.

9.2.3 Tax differential theory

Irish tax laws are such that tax rates on dividend income are higher than tax rates on capital gains. This would be the case in most countries. Shareholders should prefer capital gains to dividends because most investors would have unused capital gains allowances, while our personal allowances are usually used up. The tax rate in Ireland on capital gains is 30%, whereas dividend income will be taxed at rates according to the individual investor's marginal tax rate, which is greater than 20%. Depending on marginal tax rates, this could be 22% or 44% (at the time of writing). From a tax point of view it would make sense for a company to plough back its earnings into the business where subsequent earnings growth would lead to higher share prices (capital gains) which would be subject to lower capital gains tax. Company dividend policy should be for low dividend payouts, which will result in lower taxes, and investors will therefore be willing to pay more for low payout shares. Note that, according to this theory, a low payout will lower the risk and consequently lower the cost of equity.

9.3 Resolutions to the dividend controversy

9.3.1 The information (signalling) content of dividends

There is a lot of empirical evidence to suggest that share prices rise when dividends are unexpectedly increased and fall when they are unexpectedly reduced. This would suggest that high payouts are best. However, MM argued that share prices change because of the information content of dividends and not because of changes in dividend payout ratios per se. In other words, a dividend cut is a signal that management is not confident about the future and that current dividends cannot be maintained. The risk attached to expected future dividends rises, the cost of equity rises and the share price falls. In addition, an unexpected increase in dividends is a signal from management that it is confident about the future prospects of the company and that current dividends can be maintained. This reduces the risk attached to expected future dividend payments, the cost of equity is reduced and share values rise. Briefly, we can be sceptical about the quality of the earnings reported by the company, unless these earnings are backed up by appropriate dividends.

9.3.2 Clientele effect

There are also real world examples of investors attracted to particular companies because of their dividend policy. This clientele effect suggests that young investors, for example, will prefer shares that grow in value from capital gains and that they will sacrifice current income in the form of cash dividends for future capital gains. Therefore they look for companies that retain earnings and with low dividend payouts. Similarly, other groups, e.g. retired pensioners, will seek out companies with high payout policies because they may prefer current income.

Therefore companies with a low payout policy will attract certain groups and companies with a high payout will attract other groups. A change in dividend policy attracts a different clientele. The supply and demand for high payout shares will determine the share's equilibrium price. If demand for these shares exceeds the supply, the share price will rise. Low dividend payout companies will then be enticed to switch their dividend policy to a high payout until the dividend market is in equilibrium and all the clientele are satisfied. As long as there are enough high dividend payout companies to satisfy high yield investors, a company cannot increase its share price by increasing its dividend.

9.4 Dividends as a residual of profits

Having examined the theoretical approaches to dividend policy and looked at some empirical evidence, we can now look at how companies decide on the actual dividends they pay to their shareholders.

In principle, companies should reinvest retained earnings in projects as long as these projects give a rate of return greater than the company's cost of capital, i.e. a positive net present value. In other words, dividends should not be the main focus of attention, but what should be of primary consideration is the amount of retained earnings available for profitable investment opportunities. Earnings should not be retained unless the company can earn a rate of return greater than shareholders can get for themselves by reinvesting their dividends in investments of equal risk. However, companies adopting this policy must make sure that they maintain their optimal capital structure (Chapter 13) by adding an appropriate amount of borrowed funds to their equity. Otherwise they would have an inappropriate amount of equity, which would therefore increase the cost of capital and lower the share price.

Example 9.3 Residual dividend theory

Hexel Construction Ltd has just earned profits after tax of €1m. The company's cost of capital is 10% and its optimal debt:equity ratio is 40%. The company's investment managers have listed three projects, all with yield rates greater than the company's cost of capital.

Project	Cost (€)
A	100,000
B	150,000
C	300,000

The total finance required for all three projects is therefore €550,000. To maintain its optimal debt equity ratio of 40%, it will need to borrow €220,000, i.e. 40%. Therefore the amount of residual profits is €670,000 (i.e. €1m *minus* €330,000), and this is what is paid to shareholders as a cash dividend.

Table 9.2 Residual dividend policy – Hexel Construction

Total finance required	€550,000
Capital structure	40% debt and 60% equity
Borrowings	40% × €550,000 = €220,000
Equity investment	60% × €550,000 = €330,000
Total earnings	€1,000,000
Dividends	€1,000,000 *less* €330,000 = €670,000

By following the residual dividend theory the amount of dividends paid out can be expressed as

$$
\begin{aligned}
\text{Dividends} &= \begin{pmatrix} \text{Profit for ordinary} \\ \text{shareholders} \end{pmatrix} - \begin{pmatrix} \text{Retained earnings} \\ \text{required to finance} \\ \text{new projects} \end{pmatrix} \\
&= \begin{pmatrix} \text{Profit for ordinary} \\ \text{shareholders} \end{pmatrix} - \left[\begin{pmatrix} \text{Percentage of equity} \\ \text{in the capital structure} \end{pmatrix} \begin{pmatrix} \text{Total finance} \\ \text{required} \end{pmatrix} \right]
\end{aligned}
$$

In the above example the dividends paid = €1,000,000 *less* (60% × €550,000) = €670,000.

9.5 Dividend stability

The residual policy, if adopted, could result in unstable dividends. In years when earnings are high and profitable investment opportunities are low, dividends will be high. When earnings are low and profitable investments are high, dividends may be zero. However, shareholders may prefer stable cash dividends. As we have already seen, cutting dividends may send the wrong signal to the market about the future prospects of the firm and share prices may drop. An optimal dividend policy is about balancing the needs of shareholders against the need for internal sources of finance. With this in mind, public companies tend to adopt a policy of stable dividends. In other words, most publicly quoted companies do not follow the residual dividend approach to dividend policy.

9.6 Summary of factors when firms decide on dividend policy

The long-run policy of firms is to decide on a percentage of earnings that they will pay out of earnings – their target payout ratio. This is done after considering the following factors:

(a) Avoid cutting dividends.
(b) Don't reject positive NPV projects so as to pay a dividend.
(c) Avoid issuing new equity to pay a dividend.
(d) In deciding what dividend to pay, the company should maintain its target debt:equity ratio.

9.7 Factors influencing dividend policy

Directors of companies are not free to decide on whatever dividends they wish to pay out. There are certain restrictions placed on them by external and internal forces:

*   **Providers of debt capital**: People and institutions that loan money to a company will expect to be paid interest on their loans out of the cash tank of the company. This is the same cash tank from which shareholders expect to be paid cash dividends. Therefore, before investors provide loans to companies, they may place restrictions on excessive cash dividends.
*   **Legal restrictions**: Companies cannot pay dividends out of legal capital, which is defined as the par value of existing shares. This means that companies can only pay

dividends from retained earnings, i.e. accumulated profits. Companies that make losses in any particular year can still pay dividends, provided it comes out of profits retained from previous years. This gives some protection to creditors by preventing shareholders withdrawing capital originally provided by shareholders. If this rule did not exist, any company who got into financial difficulties could liquidate their assets and distribute the proceeds to their shareholders, leaving their creditors (debt providers) in the lurch.

- **Shortage of cash**: Dividends are paid out of cash and any shortage of cash may mean that dividends are not paid. However, if a company has a planned dividend policy and if shareholders expect a dividend payment, a shortage of cash may lead to higher company borrowing.
- **Investment opportunities**: A company's dividend payout ratio will depend on its investment plans. If a company has profitable investment plans, it will tend towards a low payout ratio. Conversely, if profitable investment opportunities are scarce, it will normally have a high payout ratio.
- **Cost of issuing new equity shares**: Companies can finance their investments from (a) retained earnings, (b) issuing new shares and/or (c) borrowing. If the cost of issuing new shares (commission costs, flotation costs, etc.) is higher than the cost of retained earnings (see Chapter 13), this will favour a low dividend payout.
- **Ownership and control**: Directors may be concerned about losing control of their company and they may be reluctant to issue new shares to finance their investment plans. Therefore they depend on retained earnings as a source of finance and consequently opt for a low dividend payout.

9.8 Alternatives to cash dividends

9.8.1 Share or scrip dividends

This is a payment to existing shareholders which dilutes the value of each outstanding share. Share dividends are usually expressed as a percentage. For example a 20% scrip dividend would mean that all existing shareholders would receive one new share for every five shares they already hold.

Example 9.4 Share dividends

The balance sheet of Dodgy Ltd is as follows:	
Balance sheet (extract)	€000
Net assets	6,000
Financed by	
Share capital	
100,000 @ €1 per share	100
Share premium account	900
Retained earnings	5,000
	6,000

The company announces a 20% share dividend. The principal use of the share premium account is to pay bonus share issues. In all, 20,000 new shares are issued to existing shareholders. The balance sheet after the scrip dividend shows the share premium account reduced by €20,000. No cash has changed hands. The overall financial effect is nil. The overall value of the firm is unaffected although it is cut into a further 20,000 pieces. The book value of the shares will, however, fall because there are more shares in issue.

Dodgy Ltd balance sheet (after scrip issue)	
	€000
Net assets	6,000
Financed by	
Share capital 120,000 @ €1 each	120
Share premium a/c	880
Retained earnings	5,000
	6,000
Book value of the shares before scrip dividend	6,000,000/100,000 = €60
Book value of the shares after the issue	6,000,000/120,000 = €50

When shareholders receive a share dividend, they can either hold on to them or sell them for cash. This opens up the possibility for the shareholder of making a profit. **An enhanced scrip dividend** is where the shares offered are worth more than the cash dividend. **Special dividends** are the same as normal dividends but are usually bigger and paid on a once-off basis.

9.8.2 Share splits

These are similar to share dividends in that they both increase the number of shares outstanding and neither increases the overall value of equity outstanding. The difference is that while share dividends are issued instead of a cash dividend, share splits are used to bring share prices into what is believed by management to be a realistic trading range. Companies may find that their share price has grown to such a high price that demand for their share has fallen. To correct this and to bring the share into a more popular trading range, the company can split its stock.[2] This is usually expressed as a ratio, e.g. a 3 for 1 share split indicates that three new shares will be issued for every one share already in issue.

9.8.3 Share repurchases

A company can pay cash to its shareholders in either of two ways:

- cash dividend, or
- share repurchase.

A company that has a large amount of unwanted cash (i.e. after paying a cash dividend and after all profitable projects have been identified) will see its debt:equity ratio change in favour of high cost equity. This increases the overall cost of capital. To avoid this the company will give back this cash to its shareholders by buying back some of their shares. This is a share repurchase.

A share repurchase reduces the number of shares outstanding but doesn't affect the company's earnings. Therefore earnings per share (EPS) rises. However, the P/E ratio is not affected because the share price follows exactly the rise in the EPS. Therefore share repurchase has no effect on company value. In Box 9.1 the author suggests that while share repurchases are popular in financial markets the messages they convey are inferior to that of increased dividends.

Example 9.5 Share repurchase

XYZ Ltd expects to earn €2m in the current year. The company has 1,000,000 shares outstanding, which have a current market price of €10. It is proposing to pay out €1m to its shareholders by way of a share repurchase. It will buy back the shares at a 10% premium to the current market price, i.e. at €11. This means that it will buy back 1,000,000/€11 = 90,909 shares.

The EPS before the repurchase = €2,000,000/1,000,000 = €2
The P/E ratio = €10/€2 = 5
The EPS after repurchasing = €2,000,000/909,091 = €2.2
The expected price after repurchase = (EPS) × (P/E) = €2.2 × 5 = €11
The market value of the company before the share repurchase was 1,000,000 shares × €10 = €10,000,000
In addition, the market value of the company after the share repurchase is 909,091 × €11 = €10,000,000.

The actual impact of share repurchases on P/E ratios depends on the market's reaction to the buy-back. If it views the share repurchase as positive, then the P/E ratio may rise. On the other hand if it views it unfavourably, then the P/E ratio may fall. Whatever the outcome for investors there is one sure winner and that is the brokers who manage the transaction (see Box 9.2).

Box 9.1 Dividends matter and they always will

Serious Money: The Standard & Poor's 500 recently celebrated its 50th birthday, an event that has been accompanied by an unprecedented upturn in corporate profits that has seen earnings per share (EPS), advance at double-digit levels in each of the last 19 quarters. Operating cash flows have reached more than $1 trillion (€745 billion) yielding the corporate sector more than ample internal funds to finance growth opportunities.

However, management has been extraordinarily frugal in the amount of money it has been willing to invest in value-creating projects and cash distributions to shareholders have soared. Corporate America has returned more than $1 trillion to owners over the past two years as reinvestment rates have dropped to record lows.

$\longrightarrow$

The buy-and-hold advocates of the 1990s bull market purported that stock prices always go up in the long run and that cash distributions are of little consequence.

The historical evidence says that cash distributions account for the bulk of stock market returns in the long run and capital gains in real terms have been decidedly pedestrian. Indeed, real stock prices did not make a new high until 1958 following the infamous peak of 1929 and the apex in 1968 was not surpassed until 1992. The message to be learned must be that fundamentals always win over long horizons.

Cash distributions have advanced sharply in recent years, increasing by 19 per cent per annum to more than $650 billion in the past 12 months.

As cash distributions have reached record levels, corporate America has increasingly used share repurchases as the method of payout, despite the Bush regime's equalisation of tax rates on capital gains and dividend income. Share repurchases by S&P 500 firms have increased by almost 27 per cent per annum over the past five years, while dividend payments have risen at a much more modest rate of almost 10 per cent.

Are share repurchases that good relative to old-fashioned dividends? The answer is No, but the investment community's focus on earnings growth suggests otherwise.

The misguided thinking is best illustrated by way of a simple example. Suppose a firm with 10,000 shares is currently priced at $10 per share or a market capitalisation of $100,000, which consists of an operating business worth $90,000 and excess cash of $10,000. Assume that the firm is earning profits of $6,000 on its core business and interest income of $250 at a deposit rate of 2.5 per cent.

The firm decides to distribute the excess cash of $10,000 to shareholders through the repurchase of shares. The shares are repurchased at $10 a share, which reduces cash and firm value by the said amount. The number of shares drops to 9,000 and the stock price remains exactly the same but the price/earnings (p/e)multiple drops from 16 to 15.

Why does the p/e multiple fall? The value of the firm before the buyback includes the operating business, which is valued at 15 times, and the excess cash, which at an interest rate of 2.5 per cent is valued at 50 times. The p/e multiple of 16 times is a weighted average of the two components. Once the excess cash is distributed to shareholders, the p/e multiple drops to that of the operating business.

The example excludes some of the more important tenets of financial theory - taxes and bankruptcy costs were not considered. The optimal mix of debt and equity involves a trade-off between the marginal tax savings provided by more borrowings and the marginal costs associated with an increased probability of financial distress. The distribution of excess cash should cause share prices to rise – albeit by a small amount – due to a more appropriate mix of debt and equity.

Dividends have historically been the primary delivery vehicle that have ensured that management has not wasted excess cash in value-destroying projects. Furthermore, historical evidence shows companies rarely increase dividends unless management believes that it can be maintained in the long run. Consequently, dividends reflect a company's earnings power.

Share repurchases on the other hand, reflect temporary increases in profitability and move in tandem with the economic cycle. Furthermore, unlike a dividend increase, management is not obliged to complete a buyback programme. Additionally, buybacks

→

do not represent a permanent distribution of excess cash. Repurchased shares remain available for reissue to fund stock options or acquisitions.

Share repurchases are much-loved in today's financial markets yet the message conveyed to investors is vastly inferior to that of increased dividends. Dividends have been an important component of stock returns through time. They matter – always have and always will.

Charlie Fell, *The Irish Times*, 13 April 2007
Charlie Fell is an independent consultant and lectures in finance and investment in UCD and the Institute of Bankers in Ireland.

Features of a share buy-back

- A share repurchase may act as a signal to the market that the shares are undervalued and that the company sees its own shares as a good investment.
- A buy-back may also be seen as an indication by management that it is not prepared to use shareholders' money on wasteful investments.
- There may be an excess supply of shares on the market so a share repurchase can keep the share price solid. When share prices went into free fall in October 1987 (black Monday, 19 October), many large American corporations announced share buy-backs, which helped to slow down the drop in prices.
- A share buy-back is treated as a capital gain by the individual shareholder and will therefore receive more favourable tax treatment than if the shareholder received a cash dividend.
- Shares that are bought back from shareholders are held as **treasury shares**.
- Share buy-backs cost the company and shareholders money.

Box 9.2 Who wins in a share buy-back?

When companies go into the market and buy back shares, there are usually mixed feelings.

Is it a sign that the company simply doesn't have any ideas on how to spend excess money? Or more positively, is it a genuine mechanism to put some money back into shareholders' pockets while simultaneously boosting earnings per share?

Whatever the benefits for shareholders, when shares are bought or sold there is one sure-fire winner – the brokers who handle the deal.

Bank of Ireland's broking subsidiary Davy and London broking blueblood Cazenove handled the bank's recent €342 million buy-back of 52 million shares. How much did all this realise for Davy and Cazenove in terms of fees and commissions?

That's hard to gauge as fund managers are notoriously coy about telling people like 'Current Account' what sort of arrangement they have with stockbrokers.

But even a commission of 0.5% would have given Davy and Cazenove commission of €1.7million on shares they bought from institutions for Bank of Ireland – not to mention the fee they would have negotiated with the bank itself to handle the buy-back.

'Current Account – An inside track on business', *The Irish Times*, 9 May 1999

SUMMARY

- Dividend policy is a decision taken by management to determine what proportion of a company's earnings is paid out to shareholders over time.
- In a world of no taxes and other imperfections, dividend policy is irrelevant and makes no difference to shareholder wealth.
- Income tax paid on dividends and flotation costs of new issue favour a low dividend payout and therefore increasing dividend payouts will lower shareholder value.
- The bird in the hand theory states that cash dividends are less risky than future potential capital gains. Therefore, high payouts can raise shareholder value.
- The information content of dividends and the clientele effect suggests that there are some groups of investors who prefer a high payout and others that prefer a low payout. Therefore, dividend policy will be determined by the financial needs of shareholders.
- The theoretical approach as to what is the optimal dividend policy is inconclusive. Empirically the fact that companies pay substantial dividends can be seen as evidence that that is what shareholders want.
- The residual dividend theory suggests that the amount of earnings retained within the firm is important and the amount paid as dividends should not be the principal issue.
- There are certain restrictions placed on the directors of companies when it comes to paying dividends.
- A scrip dividend occurs when shareholders receive additional shares in proportion to their existing holdings instead of a normal cash dividend.
- A company with excess cash can give it back to shareholders via a share repurchase. These may have a tax advantage over cash dividends.

WEB LINK

www.cfonews.com
Worldwide corporate news.

QUESTIONS

1. Explain dividend irrelevance theory; bird in the hand theory; tax differential theory.
2. Define optimal dividend policy.
3. Would it be rational for a company to pay out dividends and issue new equity during the same year?
4. What effect do scrip dividends have on the market price of a share? Would it increase the market value of the firm?
5. How might clientele effects influence dividend policy?
6. Can a change in a company's dividend policy send a signal to shareholders? Explain.
7. 'Dividends are important but dividend policy is irrelevant.' Discuss.
8. James Ltd has just issued its annual report, which showed a profit for ordinary shareholders of €100,000. It has declared a dividend of €20,000. Calculate the payout ratio.
9. ◆ Is it sensible to have a residual dividend policy?

10.◆ A company has 100,000 shares in issue and pays an €8 per share as a cash dividend. The company's profit after tax and after all preference dividends have been paid is €2,000,000. It has a P/E ratio of 10. Calculate: (a) share price; (b) the payout ratio.

11.◆ Murphy Construction Ltd has just announced end of year profits after tax of €100,000. The company maintains a debt:equity ratio of 60% debt and 40% equity. It follows a residual dividend policy. The company has positive NPV projects for the coming financial year of €200,000.
   (a) How much can Murphy spend on capital projects while maintaining its capital structure?
   (b) How much will Murphy pay in dividends?

12. Decies Ltd has a capital structure consisting of 60% debt and 40% equity. Its capital budget is €3.6m and the company estimates that its earnings for the year will be €1.8m. Calculate the company's payout ratio if it follows a residual dividend policy.

13.◆ How can dividend policy be irrelevant if share prices rise following an increase in dividend payments?

14. Divine Ltd has a cost of capital of 10%. The company is to pay a current year dividend of 20 cents, but in two years time the company is to close down. It will distribute the proceeds of liquidation via a cash dividend. The proceeds of the sale are expected to be €1m. In addition, there will be 100,000 shares outstanding. Calculate:
   (a) the current share price
   (b) the amount received in dividends in each of the two years if you would prefer to receive the same amount in both years. Assume that you own 1% of the shares. (Home-made dividend.) Ignore taxes.

15. If dividends attract more tax than capital gains, why pay any dividends at all?

16. The Athlone company paid a dividend of 80 cents a share, which was an increase of 10% over the last year's pre-split dividend. The dividend just paid of 80 cents was after a 4-for-1 stock split. Calculate the dividend per share for last year.

17. Why would a firm decide to pay a scrip dividend instead of a cash dividend? Explain the difference between a share dividend and a share split.

18.◆ The balance sheet of Garbh Eoin Ltd is as follows:

Balance sheet (market values as at 6/5/2009	
Fixed assets	200,000
Cash	30,000
	230,000
Financed by	
10,000 shares	230,000

The company declared a dividend of €3 per share and the shares go ex-dividend on 7/5/2009. Calculate the value of the shares on 7/5/2009. Ignore taxes.

19. Alternatively, suppose the company in question 18 decided to repurchase €12,000 worth of shares. Ignoring taxation, show how the effect of a repurchase is the same as a cash dividend.

20. Use the concept of present value to explain the 'bird-in-the-hand' theory.

NOTES

1. Recall from Chapter 8 the constant share growth valuation model:
   $P = D/K - g$ and therefore $K = D/P + g$. So K is reduced because investors value €1 of dividends (D/P, the dividend yield is less risky) more than €1 of capital gains (the g component).
2. There is little empirical evidence to support the notion that shares trade within an optimum trading range. However, there is a belief that the market value of companies will suffer if their shares do not trade within this range. If the share price is above the upper limit of this range, demand for these shares will fall, the share price will fall and consequently so will the market value of the firm. For example, if the top of the trading range is 100, a doubling of the number of shares will halve the price of the shares to 50, leaving the overall market value of the firm unaffected. However, because of the lower price additional demand might shift the price above 50, thereby increasing the overall market value of the firm.

10

Mergers and Acquisitions

CHAPTER OBJECTIVES

At the end of this chapter the student will be able to:

1. distinguish between the different types of takeover
2. understand how mergers/acquisitions are grouped
3. understand the rationale for mergers
4. analyse mergers.

INTRODUCTION

The total acquisition activity in Ireland in 2008 came to €8.6 billion. This included acquisitions, disposals, mergers, management buy-outs and management buy-ins. The most acquisitive company of the year was Cement Roadstone Holdings, the construction group, which accounted for circa 40% of the value of the top 10 acquisitions of Irish companies in 2008. Irish companies such as Jefferson Smurfit, the Kerry Group and CRH have become significant international businesses because of merger and acquisition activity.

Table 10.1 2008 Top ten acquisitions by Irish companies

Acquirer	Target	Sector	Consideration
1 Global Radio	GCap Media	Media and Publishing	€473m
2 CRH	Pavestone Group LP	Construction and Property	€348m
3 CRH	My Home Industries (50% stake)	Construction and Property	€290m
4 Aryzta (IA WS)	Hierstand Holdings (33% stake)	Food and Drink	€235.2m
5 Aryzta (IA WS)	Hierstand Holdings (36% stake)	Food and Drink	€225m
6 AIB	Bulgarian Credit Bank	Financial Services	€216m
7 Glanbia	Optimum Nutrition	Food and Drink	€214m
8 CRH	Yati Group (26% stake)	Construction and Property	€197m
9 CRH	Ancon Building Products	Construction and Property	€109m
10 Aergo Capital	Safair Technical Ltd	Financial Services	€109m
Source: Chapman Flood Mazars (CFM) Acquisitions Survey 2003			

Table 10.1 gives the 2008 top ten acquisitions by Irish companies.

From a legal point of view, mergers are different from acquisitions. A merger is a combination of two separate companies, which merge into a new entity via the exchange of shares. An acquisition is where one company acquires shares in another company for cash and the acquired company loses its identity. Mergers fall into different categories, but whatever the category they generate lots of interest, controversy and lots of money for many people involved. This chapter sets out to explain some of the main issues involved.

10.1 Legal forms of acquisition

When one group of shareholders takes control from another group of shareholders, it is referred to as a takeover. A takeover can be accomplished by:

1. acquisition or merger
2. proxy contests, or
3. going private transaction.

10.1.1 Merger or acquisition

For one company to acquire another there are three legal mechanisms available:

(a) The merger or complete consolidation of one company by another
    A merger is the complete assimilation of one company by another. The **bidder**, or the acquiring firm, acquires all the assets and liabilities of the acquired firm. The bidder retains its name and the acquired firm will no longer exist after the merger. A consolidation is exactly the same as a merger except that neither the acquiring firm nor the acquired firm will legally exist after the consolidation. An entirely new firm will be created with a new name and a new identity. The main disadvantage of a merger/consolidation is that it must get the approval of usually two-thirds of the shareholders of each firm, which may not be easily obtained.

(b) Acquisition of shares
    The acquiring firm can buy up a firm's voting shares with a combination of cash, stock, etc. A public statement made by the acquiring company to the shareholders of the target firm can accomplish this. This is referred to as a **tender offer**. The offer can be withdrawn if sufficient voting shares are not acquired. In a share acquisition, no shareholder meeting is required. The shareholders can choose whether or not to tender their shares. It can be effective, particularly if there is hostility on the part of the target firm's management, because the bid goes directly to the shareholders and bypasses management.

(c) Acquisition of a company's assets
    A company can acquire another company by effectively buying all of its assets. This will require agreement by the target firm's shareholders.

10.1.2 Proxy contests

A proxy is the right to cast somebody else's vote. A group of (usually unhappy) shareholders can gain the proxies of a sufficient number of other shareholders and through a proxy contest can vote in new directors and therefore gain control of the company.

10.1.3 Going private transactions

In a going private transaction all the publicly owned shares are bought by a small group of private shareholders. The small group of investors is usually the management and such transactions have become known as management buy-outs (MBOs). Because it is common for such transactions to be financed largely by borrowed funds, they are referred to as leveraged buy-outs (LBOs).

Figure 10.1 Forms of takeover

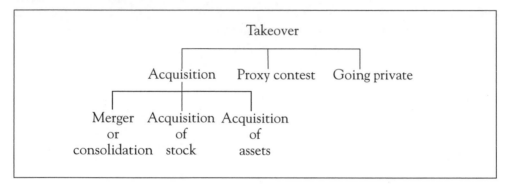

10.2 Types of mergers/acquisitions

Mergers and acquisitions are usually grouped into the following three types:

1. Horizontal
    This type of merger occurs when firms in the same line of business combine, e.g. two banks combining (Lloyd's with TSB in Britain) or two retailers (Sainsbury's with Texas Homecare). Another example is the Chrysler/Daimler-Benz merger in 1998.

2. Vertical Merger
    This involves the combination of firms at different stages of the production process. For example, the acquisition by an airline company of a group of travel agents would be a vertical merger.

3. Conglomerate merger
    This occurs when firms that are not related to each other combine. The combination of a food producer with a car manufacturer would be an example. Sometimes the motivation for such mergers is diversification and the possibility of risk reduction. Conglomerate mergers were all the rage in the 1960s and 1970s. The 1980s were spent

breaking up most of the conglomerate mergers formed in the previous two decades and the 1980s were characterised by LBOs and junk bond acquisitions. The 1990s has been characterised by strategic alliances because of the growth of the global economy.

10.3 Rationale for mergers

The level of merger/acquisition activity in the 1980s and 1990s has been enormous. Obviously there are reasons behind this phenomenal growth in merger activity. The following is a list of some of the motives behind the mergers.

10.3.1 Synergy

The idea behind this motive is that the combined entity will be greater than the sum of the parts that make up the entity. Synergy is sometimes expressed as $2 + 2 = 5$. In other words, the merger will be beneficial if the combined value of the two firms will be greater than the sum of the values of the individual firms. Suppose that firm A wants to acquire firm B to form a new entity called firm C. The merger will make sense if the value of firm C (Vc) is greater than the combined value of firm A (Va) and firm B (Vb). It is important to estimate only the incremental cash flows that will occur from the acquisition. That is, if

$$Vc > Va + Vb$$

Therefore the difference between the combined values of the two firms and the value of the new entity (V) is the net incremental gain from the merger.

$$\textbf{Net incremental gain from merger} = \textbf{V} = \textbf{V}_c - (\textbf{V}_a + \textbf{V}_b) \qquad (10.1)$$

If V is > 0 there is synergy. If < 0 there is no incremental gain and the merger does not make financial sense.

The value of firm B to firm A is the value of firm B *plus* the incremental gain V. If we denote the value of firm B to firm A as $V_b{}^*$, then the value of firm B to firm A is

$$\textbf{Value of firm B to firm A} = \textbf{V}_b{}^* = \textbf{V} + \textbf{V}_b \qquad (10.2)$$

To determine the financial merits of an acquisition we will therefore need to determine the incremental gains that can be made. The incremental gains are the incremental cash flows arising from the acquisition. In other words, we must determine the cash flows of the combined entity and compare them to the cash flows that the two firms generate when operating separately. We will return to this later on in the chapter.

10.3.2 Economies of scale

Synergy occurs because of economies of scale. Economies of scale begin to set in when the average cost of production falls as the firm increases in size. Reductions in average cost per unit occur because of:

(a) operating economies from rationalisation of manufacturing capacity, management, production, distribution and administration

(b) increased market power, which is one of the most important driving forces behind merger activity. A firm can acquire another firm to become a dominant player in the market. This reduces competition and leads to higher profits. This is not a socially desirable rationale for mergers and the regulatory authorities will monitor such acquisitions very carefully.

(c) differential efficiency, which occurs if the management of the acquiring firm is more efficient and it increases the efficiency to which the assets of the firm taken over are put.

(d) lower financing costs because a merged firm will generally be able to borrow funds more cheaply than the separate firms could. This is because from a lender's point of view the merged firm is less risky. As separate firms, firm A cannot guarantee firm B's debts and vice versa. If the two firms merge, the combined firm AB is less risky because one part of the business effectively guarantees the other part's debt. There is a mutual guarantee that makes the debt of the combined firm less risky.

10.3.3 Market entry

If a company decides to enter a new market, it may decide that the best way (and the most cost-efficient way) to penetrate the new market is by means of an acquisition of a company already established in that market. This is referred to as growth by acquisition. It may be much more difficult and costly to grow into a market organically (by the firm's own efforts). In addition, a new entry into the market will mean more competition, which could depress prices and profits. It would make more sense therefore for the company to enter a new market by acquisition. However the competition authority may take a dim view of any acquisition if it is seen as an attempt to monopolise the market (see Box 10.1).

Box 10.1 Competition Authority blocks Breeo sale

Kerry Group's proposed €165 million acquisition of Breeo Foods has been blocked by the Competition Authority.

The authority said that it had decided to prohibit the deal on the grounds that it would 'substantially lessen competition' in the Irish food market.

Both companies are involved in distribution of consumer foods such as cooked meats, cheese, spreads, chilled juice, fresh dairy products and pre-packed sandwiches.

The decision was made by the Competition Authority in accordance with section 22(3)(b) of the Competition Act 2002.

Breeo, which is owned by Reox Holdings, includes the Dairygold, Galtee, Shaws, Roscrea, Mitchelstown, Calvita and Sno brands. The acquisition also includes Breeo Foods's chilled-foods distribution service.

The Competition Authority's ruling follows a full investigation by the authority's Mergers Division.

It is only the third time that the Competition Authority has blocked a proposed merger since the provisions of the Competition Act regarding merger control came into effect in January 2003.

$\longrightarrow$

> Reox Holdings said it was disappointed by today's decision but said it would continue to build on Breeo's position in the market.
>
> 'We are naturally disappointed at the Competition Authority's decision as we believe that the sale of the business to Kerry Foods was a good proposition for the Breeo business, its shareholders and staff, Irish consumers and the consumer foods market in this country. We will review the detail of the Competition Authority's decision over the next number of days,' said Reox chairman Flor Riordan.
>
> IrishTimes.com, 29 August 2008

10.3.4 Tax advantages

In the US, tax considerations have been a powerful consideration in mergers and acquisitions. In the US tax losses in any particular year can be used to reduce taxable profits in later years. Therefore profitable firms can acquire firms with large accumulated losses, which can be turned into a tax saving after the merger. Furthermore, mergers provide a way of minimising taxes when disposing of surplus funds. If a company has free cash flow, it can dispose of it in any one of four different ways (provided there are no internal positive net present value projects). First, it can distribute the surplus cash to the shareholders, in which case the shareholders are subject to tax liabilities. Second, the company can repurchase its own shares, but this incurs capital gains tax for the shareholders. Third, it can invest the money in short-term marketable investments, but the rates of return are usually very low, particularly in a low interest rate environment. Finally, using the surplus funds to purchase another company will avoid all the tax considerations of dividends and share repurchase.

10.4 Company: market value and book value

Companies can be seen as acquisition targets because the market is undervaluing their shares. If the book value of a company's assets is greater than the market value of the company's shares, then the company may be seen as an acquisition target. In other words, it may be cheaper to buy existing companies than build new plants.

10.4.1 Break-up value

Break-up value is the value of each individual part of the business if they were sold off separately. If this is greater than the market value, the firm becomes an acquisition target. Buying the company and subsequently selling off the company in individual parts makes an incremental gain.

10.4.2 Managerial motives

Not all the motives for merger/acquisition activity are based on economic rationale. Many decisions are made as a result of the personal motivations of managers. These may be described as egotistical motives for mergers (empire building). The larger the firm one manages, the more prestigious it is. In addition, it can be the case than managerial salaries are based on turnover and profits. The bigger the company, the bigger the manager's salary.

10.4.3 Eliminating inefficiencies

Some companies can be undervalued because of poor management of resources, which leads to the inability to embark on ways to increase sales and improve cost to sales ratios and hence improve profits. Better management, via a takeover, can exploit the various opportunities that exist within the company. Greater efficiencies can help drive profit growth.

10.4.4 Risk arbitrage and other third party motives

Arbitrage is the process of buying and selling the same securities in different markets at different prices and thus making a profit. Risk arbitrage is the process of buying (speculating) in securities of companies that are likely takeover targets. This is a speculative process and vast amounts of money can be made if the individuals concerned can get in and out of the market at the right time with minimum cost. There is, however, scope for illegal insider trading and some famous risk arbitrageurs, like the American Ivan Boesky, have gone to jail for such actions.

In addition, many advisers and investment bankers can make substantial fee income during the acquisition process. Advice is provided on the rules and regulations regarding takeovers, finance, defence tactics, etc.

10.5 Questionable motives for mergers

There are certain financial consequences of mergers that happen regardless of whether a merger takes place or not. Sometimes these consequences are given as rational motives for mergers. We look at two of those – the effect on earnings per share and diversification.

10.5.1 Increasing EPS

Mergers can create an illusion of gains in the form of growth in EPS. This can lead investors to believe that the firm is financially better off than it actually is. An example will illustrate.

Rathgormac takes over Cluain Fhia. The financial position before the merger is set out in the first two columns in Table 10.2. The assumption is that the merger makes no economic gains, i.e. no additional value. Therefore, the firms are worth the same, when merged, as they are as separate units.

Rathgormac will exchange one of its shares for 1.5 shares in Cluain Fhia in a share for share exchange, i.e. (€30/€20 = 1.5). Therefore, the total number of shares issued by Rathgormac will be 133 (200/1.5).

After the merger the market value of the combined firms is the sum of the values of the two firms before the merger, i.e. €10,000. The earnings per share of the merged firms is now €1.20 (€400/333) or a 20% increase. **This is despite the fact that there is no real gain made by the merger**. However, the P/E ratio falls. Why? Remember that the total market value of the merged entity is the same as the sum of the values of the two firms. This is as it should be. The market has not been fooled by the 20% increase in the EPS.

Therefore the market price reflects this and therefore it does not change. Consequently the P/E ratio must fall. On the other hand, if investors see the 20% increase in earnings as an indication of real growth, the price of Rathgormac's shares will rise, as will the P/E ratio. This is **EPS growth illusion** or magic. For it to work, shareholders in both companies must get something for nothing. This is unlikely. **Companies can increase their EPS by buying companies with a lower P/E ratio than their own.** Their EPS will rise despite the fact that there is no economic gain from the merger. The management of the acquiring firm will promise higher earnings through better management and greater operational efficiencies. If the market believes this, then it will still place a high P/E ratio on the acquiring firm. In other words, the value of the acquiring firm goes up and shareholders are happy. But these shareholders have been fooled. The increase in value has been achieved by an illusion of earnings growth and not by any significant managerial acrobatics or operational efficiencies. Growth in EPS has been achieved by buying a company with a lower PER. In the long run EPS will fall because you are not increasing value by implementing any operational efficiency. In other words, you cannot keep fooling investors all the time.

Table 10.2 Mergers and EPS growth illusion

	Rathgormac	Cluain Fhia	Rathgormac post-merger
EPS	€1	€1	€1.20
Price per share	€30	€20	€30
P/E ratio	30	20	25
Number of shares	200	200	333
Earnings	€200	€200	€400
Value	€6,000	€4,000	€10,000

10.5.2 Diversification

Diversification is sometimes used as a rationale for acquisitions. The argument goes as follows. Diversification reduces risk. Mergers can be seen as diversification in order to reduce risk. In other words, if income comes from a variety of sources and markets, then the cash flows will be less risky and less volatile. They achieve the same income and return but with lower risk. A reduction in risk is therefore a gain from the merger. Therefore investors will be prepared to pay a premium for diversified firms.

But does diversification increase value? And will investors be prepared to pay a premium for diversified firms? The answer to both these questions is no. The simple answer is that mergers don't do anything that shareholders can't do for themselves. In fact, diversification is cheaper and easier for shareholders to do themselves than it is for the company. In other words, shareholders can get all the diversification they need by buying shares in as many companies as they want. Therefore they will not be prepared to pay a premium for a share in a merged company just for the benefit of diversification – they can achieve the benefits of diversification more easily and more cheaply themselves.

10.6 Merger gains and costs

An economic incremental gain is made when the two firms are worth more together than they are apart. From equation 10.1, we learned that an economic gain is made when the combined value of firm A and firm B is greater than the sum of the value of firm A and firm B:[1]

$$\text{Incremental gain} = V = V_c - (V_a + V_b)$$

where
V_a = value of firm A
V_b = value of firm B
V_c = combined value of firm A and firm B.

Also, the value of firm B to firm A is

$$V_b^* = V_b + V$$

where

$$V_b^* = \text{value of firm B to firm A}$$

The net present value to A of a merger with B is the difference between the gains from the merger and the costs incurred. In other words

$$\text{NPV} = V_b^* - \text{Cost} \qquad (10.3)$$

The merger should go ahead if the NPV is positive.

10.6.1 Cash acquisitions

Suppose that firm A has a value of €300 and firm B has a market value of €100. A merger between the two would allow an incremental value (gain) of €100. Therefore

$$V = €100$$
$$V_a = €300$$
$$V_b = €100$$

Suppose that a sale is agreed and firm A agrees to buy firm B for €175 cash. The €175 cash paid is the cost of the acquisition. This means that firm A agrees to pay a premium of €75 (€175 − €100) for firm B.

Note that the overall merger gain V is €100 and the shareholders of firm B have amassed €75 of this.

Therefore, if the overall gain from the merger is €100 and firm B's shareholders receive €75 of this, then the incremental gain to firm A's shareholders is €25. In other words, the value of firm B to firm A is

$$V_b^* = V + V_b = €200$$

Therefore if firm A pays €175 in cash to acquire firm B, the NPV of the cash acquisition is

$$NPV = V_b^* - cost$$
$$= €200 - €175 = €25$$

Therefore the acquisition is profitable.

Suppose that the number of shares in issue before the merger is 20 with a price per share of €15. After the merger the value of the merged entity is the pre-merger value of firm A €300 *plus* the NPV of €25 = €325. Therefore the value of each share outstanding is €325/20 = €16.25. This represents a gain of €1.25.

10.6.2 Stock acquisition

With cash payments the shareholders in the target company receive cash payments and they are no longer part of the new company. The cost of the acquisition is the cash paid to pay off the shareholders in the target company.

If the merger is in the form of a share for share exchange, no cash changes hands. The shareholders of the target company remain as shareholders of the newly formed merged company. The value of the merger will simply be the sum of the pre-merger values of firm A and firm B *plus* the incremental value or the gains from the merger:

$$V_c = V_a + V_b + ØV$$
$$€300 + €100 + €100 = €500$$

Example 10.1 Mergers via stock acquisitions

The cost of the acquisition for firm A is €175 worth of firm A stock. If the price of firm A shares is €15, firm A will give up €175/€15 = 11.7 shares. The number of shares in issue after the merger is now 20 + 11.7 = 31.7 shares, giving each share a value of €500/31.7 = €15.77.

How much does the merger cost firm A? Firm A gave €175 worth of its shares to firm B's shareholders. Firm B's shareholders now have 11.7 shares in the new company after the merger. These shares are now valued at €15.77 each. Therefore the gain to B's shareholders is 11.7 × €15.77 = €185. The gain for B's shareholders is a loss to the shareholders in firm A. The overall value of firm B to firm A we estimated to be €200. The cost of the acquisition is €185. Firm A must give €185 of the overall gain to the shareholders of firm B. Therefore the NPV of the merger is

$$NPV = V_b^* - Cost$$
$$= €200 - €185 = €15$$

10.6.3 Comparing cash and stock acquisitions

In the above example, firm B shareholders share in the NPV of the merger because they become shareholders in the new company. With the cash acquisition, firm A shareholders get to keep all of the NPV. In a share for share exchange the cost of the merger will depend on the gains made from the acquisition. This is because the shareholders in the target firm will become shareholders in the merged firm, and the shareholders in the acquiring firm must share the gains made from the merger with the shareholders of the target firm. Therefore, if shares are used to buy a company, the cost will usually be higher. If cash is used to finance an acquisition, the shareholders in the target firm will not benefit from the incremental gains arising from the merger. Incidentally, if firm A overvalued firm B, perhaps because it miscalculated some of firm B's strengths, and makes an offer that is too much, then firm A's shareholders will benefit from this because it will share this loss with the shareholders of firm B if the offer is on a share for share basis. Of course this would not be the case if it were a cash offer. Finally, a cash payment will not affect the voting control of the merged entity, whereas if shares are used, control of the company after the merger may be affected.

10.7 Discounted cash flow analysis in valuing the target firm

Here we discuss a common method used in valuing a target firm.[2] To use the DCF analysis to value the target firm, it will first be necessary to estimate the incremental free cash flows that are expected to result from the merger. This is similar to the corporate valuation model we discussed in Chapter 8 and Chapter 11.

Table 10.3 shows the pro-forma cash flow statement for Southside Ltd, which is seen as a possible target by Northside Ltd. These are projected estimates of Southside Ltd's cash flow after any merger takes place. The cash flow includes all synergistic impacts of the merger. Southside Ltd would become a subsidiary of Northside Ltd.

Table 10.3 Pro forma statement of Southside Ltd

	2007 €m	2008 €m	2009 €m	2010 €m	2011 €m
1. Net turnover	100	120	150	160	170
2. Cost of goods sold	70	84	105	112	119
3. S, G & A expenses	10	12	15	16	17
4. Depreciation	5	5	6	6	7
5. PBIT	15	19	24	26	27
6. Interest	4	5	6	7	7
7. PBT	11	14	18	19	20
8. Taxation (20%)	2.2	2.8	3.6	3.8	4
9. PAT	8.8	11.2	14.4	15.2	16
10. + depreciation	5	5	6	6	7
11. Cash flow	13.8	16.2	20.4	21.2	23
12. Less earnings retained for growth	4	5	5	6	6
13. + horizon value					367
14. Net cash flow	9.8	11.2	15.4	15.2	384

The method used here to value the target firm is the **equity residual method**. The residual cash flows are what is left over for the acquiring company's shareholders.

Depreciation is added back in on line 11 to estimate the firm's cash flow. Some of the cash flows generated by Southside Ltd will be used by Southside to replace obsolete assets, and additional equity funds will be required to expand Northside's new subsidiary. Therefore some of the cash flows generated by Southside will be used to finance asset replacement and fund growth opportunities. The rest will belong to the shareholders of Northside Ltd.

In this example we have projected cash flows up to 2011, but of course we can assume that Northside will operate Southside as a subsidiary for ever. Therefore, we must estimate Southside's cash flows **beyond** 2011. From Chapter 8 we remember how to estimate this 'horizon value' using the constant growth formula. We assume that Southside's cash flows will grow at a constant rate of 8% after 2011. Note that the appropriate cost of capital to use is Southside's, which we assume to be 13%. Therefore the value of Southside at the end of 2011 (or the present value of all cash flows after 2011) is €367m:

$$V_{2011} = \frac{CF_{2012}}{Ke - g} = \frac{(€23 - €6)(1.08)}{0.13 - 0.08} = €367m$$

On line 14 are the cash flows that belong to the shareholders of Northside. These are the cash flows that Northside Ltd uses to estimate the valuation of the proposed merger. Note that we used 13% as the discount rate in estimating the value of operations at 2011. The cash flows on line 14 represent equity because they are taken after interest and taxes have been deducted. Therefore the appropriate cost of capital is the cost of equity capital rather than a general weighted cost of capital. Besides, in any acquisition process it is the owners of the company that are being bought out and not the creditors. Consequently, in merger valuations the appropriate valuation is the value of the target firm's equity. Therefore the appropriate cost of capital is the cost of equity capital.

We can use the CAPM to estimate Southside's cost of equity capital of 13%. Assume that Southside's post-merger beta doesn't change and stays at its pre-merger value of 1.5. If the risk-free rate is 7% and the market risk premium is 4%, then Southside's cost of equity capital is calculated as

$$K_e = K_f + (R_m)\beta = 7\% + (4\%)1.5 = 13\%$$

Therefore the value of Southside as at the end of 2007 is the present value of expected future cash flows discounted at 13%

$$V2007 = \frac{9.8}{(1.13)^1} + \frac{11.2}{(1.13)^2} + \frac{15.4}{(1.13)^3} + \frac{15.2}{(1.13)^4} + \frac{367}{(1.13)^5} = €236.6m$$

This is the value of Southside to Northside at the end of 2007. This is the maximum price that Northside will pay for the acquisition.

10.8 Hostile and friendly takeovers

Having put together the analysis of the possible takeover target (e.g. the DCF analysis) and having decided on the method of payment, the management of the acquiring firm will need to decide how it is going to approach the target firm's management. If the target firm's management is receptive to the proposed merger, a statement will be issued to the shareholders of both companies encouraging acceptance of the deal. This is a so-called friendly merger.

However, mergers sometimes involve less than friendly transactions when the target firm resists the approaches of its suitor. If the management of the target firm, for whatever reason (maybe they feel the price being offered is too low), rejects the offer, then the acquiring firm will appeal directly to the target firm's shareholders and ask them to tender their shares for the price being offered. The management of the target firm will encourage their shareholders to reject the offer on the grounds that the price is too low. This is called a **hostile takeover** bid. One of the first stages in a hostile takeover is the **dawn raid**. This is where the acquiring firm buys up shares in the target firm with such alacrity that the acquiring firm will have built up a substantial holding of the target firm's shares before the target firm's management has time to react. Prices are usually offered at substantial premiums to the previous day's closing price.

Note that the rules governing takeovers require that any individual or company that holds a 30% stake in a company must make a mandatory bid for all the target company's shares. This is designed to prevent a predator buying the company on the cheap. Thirty per cent is a substantial holding, making it very difficult for anyone else to launch a bid. In order to avoid making a mandatory bid, many individuals or companies hold 29.9% of the shares. This is the maximum amount they can hold without making a formal bid for all the shares.

The target firm in a hostile bid may embark on a series of defensive strategies to repel the acquiring firm's advances. The various defensive tactics involved include:

1. **Press releases** and mail shots to their shareholders outlining their view. Of course this might be the self-interest of management and not in the shareholders' interests.
2. **Targeted repurchase**. The target firm purchases its own stock from a specific investor at a substantial premium. These very high premiums can be seen as a bribe to eliminate hostile bidders. In America they are referred to as **greenmail**.
3. **White knight**. This is where the target firm invites a second bid from a friendly company to compete with the hostile bidder.
4. **White squire**. This is somebody who is on the side of the target firm who will buy enough shares in the target firm to prevent the merger.
5. **Poison pills**. This is tantamount to economic suicide in order to make a hostile takeover impossible. Poison pills can take different forms. For example, shareholders may be allowed to buy shares at a large discount should the bid be successful. These are sometimes called **share rights plans**.
6. **Golden parachutes**. This is where managers get lucrative payouts if the bid is successful. This could make the potential bid unfeasible.
7. **Employee share ownership plans (ESOPs)**. Employees are given share ownership, which makes it more difficult for the bidder to take over.

8. **Crown jewels**. Target firms will often threaten to sell off valuable company assets when faced with a hostile takeover – sometimes referred to as the **scorched earth** strategy. This might involve a lock-up which is an option granted to perhaps a white knight to purchase the crown jewels at a set price in the context of a hostile bid.
9. **Pac-man defence**. Here the target firm makes a counter bid for the hostile bidder.

10.9 Leveraged buy-outs

The two main differences between a merger and a leveraged buy-out are:

(a) Most of the purchase price is financed with debt.
(b) After the LBO, the company goes private (it is no longer traded on the stock exchange).

Where the existing management is involved, the LBO is called a management buy-out or MBO. The debt is financed by the acquired company's operations. An analysis of the cash flows of the acquired company is carried out (similar to that in Table 10.3). All earnings and cash flows will be retained in the business to pay off the debt. After a number of years the entire debt is paid off and the shareholders are left with a substantial increase in their original investment. Sometimes after the company has been made strong and profitable, the management will plan to make it public again. Substantial profits can be made from LBOs. The risks of course are very high because of the highly leveraged means of financing the LBO. But along with high risk come high returns. The most successful LBO merchants in 1980s America, Kohlberg Kravis Roberts & Co. (KKR), were reputed to have made in the region of 50% annual return on their investments in LBOs.

    The first MBO of an Irish public company was the Candover-backed buy-out of Clondalkin. For a brief assessment and case study see Box 10.2.

Box 10.2   Clondalkin management buy-out set to succeed

The first management buy-out (MBO) of an Irish public company – the €385 million Candover-backed buy-out of Clondalkin – seems assured of success after more than 35% of Clondalkin's shareholders gave irrevocable acceptances to the €9.10 a share offer from Edgemeade, the vehicle for the management bid.

    The total cost of the buy-out rises to €475 million when Clondalkin's debt at the end of June is taken into account.

    Assuming the offer succeeds, a 44-strong management team will end up owning 19% of Edgemead, with Candover putting up €122 million in equity finance for its 81% stake.[3]

    Clondalkin chairman Mr Henry Lund said that each of the executives involved in the MBO group was investing the proceeds from their Clondalkin shares and share options. He added that the management group would be investing on a roughly pro rata basis as Candover, with an unspecified discount reflecting the expertise the management group is providing to the new private company.

$\longrightarrow$

Despite this discount, it looks like the management group is investing in the order of €25 million for its 19% stake . . .

About one quarter of the cost of the buy-out and €90.6 million in assumed debt will be covered by the equity component, with a further 50% in senior debt and 25% in mezzanine finance coming from a group of banks including AIB, Warbourg Dillon Read and Lehman Brothers.

Clondalkin management first began exploring the possibility of a buy-out after the stock market slumped in August last year in the wake of the Asian crisis.

Unlike front-line industrial shares like CRH, which have rallied strongly since that slump, Clondalkin shares have suffered as sentiment towards small/mid-capitalisation companies turned negative.

The movement of industrial funds out of Irish stocks into European shares following the introduction of the single currency was another major factor which affected shares like Clondalkin.

Mr Lund was exasperated at the market's treatment of his company's shares, given the strength of the group's earnings over the past 15 years. 'CRH shares have risen 148% since last year's crash. We are up 48% even though our earnings growth was the same. If we had risen 148% since August last year, our shares would be at €19 now and we wouldn't be doing this.'

But the management's offer to take Clondalkin private is not cheap, with the €9.10 offer to shareholders equivalent to 12 times historic earnings per share and 7.5 times earnings before interest, tax and depreciation.

'We couldn't cheapskate this deal. There's always some scepticism about management buy-outs and Warburgh and Candover told us we had to offer a full price up front. This was a one-shot opportunity and, to be credible, we had to come up with our best offer straight away. . .

We have sufficient facilities for bold-on acquisitions and will be able to fund acquisitions up to €100m . . .half of our growth has come through acquisitions in the past 15 years and we want to maintain that pattern. . .

The difference between us and a stock market company is that we can take a long-term view and are not driven by six month earnings per share growth and share prices.'

Extract from *The Irish Times*, Brendan McGrath, 9 November 1999

10.9.1 Junk bonds

Up to the 1980s institutional investors such as pension funds and insurance companies generally did not tend to invest their funds in risky projects. It was very difficult for risk-taking companies to find the type of capital to fund their operations. This was all to change in the 1980s when American investment bankers such as Drexel Burnham Lambert sold the idea of high rewards compensating for the high risk. The junk bond industry was born. They were high-risk high-yield bonds sold to investors to fund risky companies that were in trouble, mergers and leveraged buy-outs. Some of these mergers and LBOs were financed with 95% debt. Obviously the risk of not being able to generate sufficient cash flows to finance the debt was very high. Because of this there were many calls to ban the junk bond market. Many of the investments took a hammering because of their inability to generate the cash flows to repay the debt. The default risk on these bonds increased and the market dried up in the early 1990s. However, the default risk on junk bonds has now fallen and the market is healthier than previously. But don't forget that many junk bond deals were successful, such as those used by Ted Turner to finance the development of CNN.

10.10 Winners and losers

Who are the winners and losers in acquisitions and mergers? The evidence suggests that value is created, but the question is how is: this added value distributed?

(a) **Shareholders**. Most empirical research suggests that the shareholders of the target firm benefit most from a merger. First, the target firm's shareholders benefit if two or more firms are competing for the merger, thus pushing up the share price. Second, the management of the acquiring firm may be more concerned with the idea of managing a larger organisation and in return may be willing to surrender all of the added value to the shareholders of the target firm. Therefore, the evidence suggests that the added value created because of mergers is captured almost entirely by the shareholders of the target firm.

(b) **Employees**. Cost-cutting can often follow mergers in an effort to boost profits and shareholder value. Unfortunately these cost cuts can result in redundancies.

(c) **Financial institutions**. As mentioned earlier, some advisers and financial institutions benefit greatly from mergers because of the fees they receive.

(d) **Society.** The general economy will suffer from merger activity if these mergers result in monopoly power. However, the monopoly commission will monitor such mergers to see if such monopoly power develops. On the other hand, greater efficiencies and better management may result in lower prices of goods and services.

10.11 Divestitures and spin-offs

Companies can, in addition to buying other companies, sell part of their own company. This is referred to as a divestiture. The sale could be to another firm or a new company is created and the shares in the new company are distributed to the parent company's shareholders. This is referred to as a spin-off. The parent company's shareholders will become the owners of the divested division. Sometimes divestitures occur because of anti-trust legislation where the government wants to break up the company (e.g. Microsoft). AT & T paid about $8bn for the computer group NCR in 1990. It subsequently discovered that it didn't 'fit in' (no synergy) with AT & T's core business and it was sold off. Markets generally react positively to spin-offs because management time can be devoted to managing operations that they know best. In addition, shareholders will be content in the knowledge that management will not be tempted to invest in projects in a part of the business that is doing badly.

Governments around the world are undergoing programmes of privatisation, which is an example of divestitures. At the time of writing, there are government proposals to break up CIÉ and spin off the company into its constituent parts – Dublin Bus, Bus Éireann and Iarnrod Éireann. Telecommunications, electric utilities and airlines have undergone significant worldwide privatisation.

Carve-outs are similar to spin-offs except that the shares are sold in a public offering. In other words, shares are sold to the public instead of to the existing shareholders.

Box 10.3 outlines how companies that indulge in mergers and acquisitions feasts may become bloated by unnecessary activities.

Box 10.3 Weight-loss schemes can help bloated companies

After an MA binge, simplifying your firm's structure by offloading unnecessary subsidiaries will yield many benefits, writes George Maloney.

Companies that have indulged in the mergers and acquisitions feast over the last few years may now find that their once-trim corporate structures are bloated by unnecessary subsidiaries.

As well as being costly and time-consuming, maintaining these dormant or inactive subsidiaries can pose serious risks to the health of a group and its directors. It is difficult to assess just how obese corporate group structures have become, but anecdotal evidence from the UK is alarming. Recent analysis of the FTSE 100 indicates up to 50 per cent of entities within plcs could be dormant or inactive.

In many cases, directors simply do not know how many dormant subsidiaries lurk within their corporate structures, the reasons for their existence or the risks contained within them.

This corporate memory loss can frequently occur in large groups built up through MA activity as senior managers move on or are replaced. A wide geographic spread or diversity of operations can make the problem worse.

In some cases, dormant entities are justified for tax reasons or because they protect a name, brand, trademark or some other form of non-transferable intellectual property. Others are harmless in isolation but are costly and time-consuming because the parent company must file annual returns for each of them, incorporate them into its consolidated accounts and provide details on inter-company capital distributions.

The most frequent risks posed by a dormant entity are contingent liabilities, such as legacy property lease covenants, long-forgotten guarantees for products or services or legacy employee claims. Once identified, the company can mitigate or remove these liabilities by negotiating a settlement with the parties involved and then seek to wind up the subsidiary.

Dormant subsidiaries can also pose personal risks to company directors. Directors must have full knowledge and control of all entities and are ultimately liable for the corporate governance of these entities. By doing nothing, directors expose themselves and the group to accusations of complacency, incompetence or, in the worst case, negligence.

This may ultimately result in action being taken by the Director of Corporate Enforcement or the Companies Office.

$\longrightarrow$

> As well as minimising risk, a simplified group structure brings many immediate rewards. Cost savings alone from reduced regulatory compliance and management time mean that corporate structure simplification projects often pay for themselves within two years. The review may also reveal long-forgotten assets that can be realised or distributed up to trading entities where the asset can be put to better use.
>
> There are also longer-term benefits for the company that chooses to lose weight. A simplified structure results in a more efficient use of capital and a stronger balance sheet. The greater transparency will improve its image and communication with its stakeholders, most importantly shareholders, lenders and credit-rating agencies.
>
> Finally, in the event of future MA opportunities, it will be able to realise the highest value for its shareholders or obtain cheaper finance with which to fund acquisitions.
>
> There has never been a better time to consider shedding that excess weight. Losing weight is hard work but the results make it all worthwhile.
>
> *The Irish Times*, 13 June 2008
> George Maloney is a partner at Baker Tilly Ryan Glennon.

SUMMARY

- A takeover can be achieved in one of three ways: (a) acquisition or merger; (b) proxy contests; (c) going private.
- Horizontal mergers develop when two firms in the same industry combine.
- A vertical merger occurs when a firm combines with one of its suppliers or customers.
- A conglomerate merger occurs when firms in unrelated industries combine.
- Synergy is the idea that the combined entity will be greater than the combined value of the parts that make up the entity.
- Economies of scale are a motive for mergers. Economies of scale set in when the average cost of production falls as size increases.
- Growth by acquisition may be more advantageous than organic growth.
- Growth in EPS should not be a motive for mergers.
- Merging to reduce risk by diversification does not make economic sense.
- In an acquisition paid for with stock the target firm's shareholders share in the NPV because they are now part of the merged firm. With a cash acquisition the target firm's shareholders get to keep all of the NPV.
- Discounted cash flows are a method used in evaluating a merger.
- With a leveraged buy-out most of the purchase price is financed with debt and the company goes private.

WEB LINKS

www.mazars.ie
For information on mergers and acquisitions in Ireland.

www.mergerstat.com
For information on global merger activity.

QUESTIONS

1. Define the following terms:
   (a) horizontal merger, vertical merger, conglomerate merger, friendly merger, hostile merger, target company, operating merger, financial merger.
   (b) the DCF method used to evaluate a merger.
   (c) greenmail, white knight, golden parachute, crown jewels, tender offer, shark repellants, poison pill.
   (d) leveraged buy-out.
   (e) junk bonds.

2. ' Mergers take advantage of economies of scale.' Explain.

3. Diversification is sometimes used as a rationale for mergers. Is this a correct reason for mergers?

4. Does merging to increase EPS make economic sense?

5.♦ Empirical evidence suggests that the shareholders of acquiring firms benefit very little from takeovers. Discuss some reasons for this phenomenon.

6. What are the possible difficulties that result from mergers?

7.♦ Many companies split up voluntarily. What are the main reasons?

8. Evaluate the gain and cost of a merger financed by (a) cash and (b) stock.

9. Firm A is considering the acquisition of firm B. The purchase price has been estimated at €11m. Both firms generate annual cash flows of €1m per annum into perpetuity. The management of firm A believes that synergistic benefits of €500,000 will result from the merger. The appropriate cost of capital is 10%. Should the acquisition go ahead?

10.♦ Murphy Corporation is considering the acquisition of Patterson plc. The following information is available on Patterson:

Expected dividend (year end)	€1.50 per share
Dividend growth	6%
Beta	0.8

If Murphy acquires Patterson it is expected that synergies will lead to an increase in dividend growth to 7% per annum instead of the current 6%. Furthermore, because Murphy plans additional investments in Patterson and because this investment will be financed with debt, it is estimated that Patterson's beta will increase to 1.1. The risk-free rate of interest is 7% and the market risk premium is 8%.
Calculate:
(a) Patterson's share price before the acquisition.
(b) The value of Patterson to Murphy and the possible purchase price.

11. McMurrow Airlines wants to acquire Celtic Airlines and operate it as a subsidiary. McMurrow has estimated the following post-merger information on Celtic Airlines:

	2001	2002	2003	2004
Net turnover	€800	€1,000	€1,200	€1,500
Expenses	€70	€90	€100	€120
Interest	€30	€32	€35	€40

The debt ratio of Celtic will increase after the merger therefore adding to the financial risk and consequently increasing Celtic's beta to 1.4. McMurrow also estimates that Celtic's gross profit percentage will be 30% and the new post-merger consolidated corporation tax rate will be 25%. Having completed its analysis McMurrow believes that a terminal growth rate of 6% is achievable on Celtic's cash flows after 2004.

Calculate the value of Celtic Airlines to McMurrow. (Note: use the CAPM to evaluate the appropriate cost of capital. The risk-free rate is 9% and the market risk premium is 3%.) Depreciation funds are not available to the shareholders by McMurrow.

12. Pike Electronics wants to acquire Electric Power Ltd for €1m. Having carried out an analysis of the proposed acquisition, Pike estimates that the merger will generate incremental cash flows of €120,000 annually for about 12 years. It is also estimated that the cost of capital for this acquisition will be 10%. Should Pike Electronics acquire Electric Power?

13. Smiley wants to acquire Wiley. Both are in the same line of business and both generate annual cash flows of €100 into perpetuity. The cost of equity capital for both firms is 12%. Synergy is expected to add a total of €10 to the merged firm. Calculate the value of Wiley to Smiley.

14.♦ The following information is available for two firms X and Y:

	Firm X	Firm Y
Number of shares	1,000,000	2,500,000
Share price	€50	€40
Gearing	0%	0%

X wants to acquire Y and estimates that synergy will add €1m to a merged firm. Y has agreed but wants to be paid €50 a share. Should X agree to the purchase price?

15. Kuncrete Ltd wants to acquire Concrete Ltd. Kuncrete has a market capitalisation valuation of €100m and Concrete has a market capitalisation valuation of €80m. They are both all equity firms. Kuncrete expects synergy to increase its incremental after-tax cash flows by €2m per annum into the future. Kuncrete needs advice on the possible payment mechanism of any possible deal. There are two options (a) a cash payment of €85m or (b) a share for share exchange involving 45% of Kuncrete's shares. Advise Kuncrete on the alternatives. Concrete's cost of equity is 8%.

16. Decies Ltd wishes to acquire Premier Ltd. Decies Ltd has 1,000 shares in issue with a current market price of €20, while Premier has 700 shares in issue with a current market price of €10. Decies Ltd has estimated that the value of the acquisition in terms of synergistic incremental gains would be €3,000.

   (a) If Premier wants cash of €11 per share, what is the NPV of the merger? What will the share price be after the merger?

   (b) If, on the other hand, Decies offers 10 of its shares for every 15 shares in Premier, what will the price of the share be in the merged firm? What is the NPV of the merged firm?

   (c) Under which option (cash or stock) are the shareholders better off?

NOTES

1. The NPV method is used extensively in academic literature. For a more detailed description of this method, see Ross, Westerfield & Jordan, *Fundamentals of Corporate Finance*, and Brealey & Myers, *Principles of Corporate Finance*.
2. Although there are a number of methods used in DCF analysis of mergers, the free cash flow and DCF method used here is the clearest and most rigorous, and is used by Brigham, Gapenski & Ehrhardt, op. cit.
3. Candover is a venture capital company.

Part 4

Long-term Financial Strategy

11

Financial Forecasting and Planning

CHAPTER OBJECTIVES

At the end of this chapter the student should be able to:

1. understand the importance of financial forecasting and planning
2. construct pro forma income statements and balance sheets
3. discuss the weaknesses of accounting-based management
4. understand how shareholder wealth is maximised via the maximisation of free cash flows
5. evaluate the valuation of an entire company using free cash flows
6. understand the concepts of economic value added and market value added.

INTRODUCTION

The primary objective of financial management is maximising shareholder value. Wealth creation occurs when investments generate returns that are greater than the cost of capital used for the investments. The first step in the management process of maximising shareholder value is a coherent corporate plan. This will include the short-term, medium-term and long-term objectives of the firm. Financial planning involves the conversion of the corporate plan into quantitative terms. The financial plan will involve projected financial statements (pro forma) that analyse the effect the corporate plan will have on projected profits. A strategic corporate plan ensures:

1. Money needed for investment purposes will be available. This will include money needed for fixed assets, stock, debtors, research and development, etc. Raising funds will take time. A financial plan will estimate the future financial needs and will therefore provide the necessary time for management to source the required finance.
2. Financial plans can be used to forecast free cash flows (FCF). If the cash flows arising from the business plans are insufficient to cover dividend payments, increases in net working capital and fixed assets (i.e. negative FCF), then management must reappraise its capital structure by borrowing or issuing additional shares.
3. Financial planning will allow for unexpected changes in economic conditions in which the plan is based. Forecasting is important because business decisions are based on forecasts of expected and unexpected situations that a business will be exposed to in

the future. Sensitivity analysis deals with unexpected events occurring by factoring in different scenarios like changes in interest rates, currency fluctuations and domestic or international demand side shocks to the economy. Failure to anticipate future events can have devastating effects on company performance.

This chapter looks at two approaches to financial forecasting and planning. The first approach is based on traditional accounting information. We refer to this as **accounting-based management.** We follow this with a look at the weaknesses of accounting-based management as a financial planning tool.

The second approach emphasises that the essence of financial planning is to maximise shareholder value. This approach to financial planning is called **value-based management,** and it is used to overcome the weaknesses of accounting-based management.

11.1 Financial forecasting

Financial forecasting involves making projections about future events. This begins with the budgeting process, which identifies the assets that are required and what revenues will be generated from the use of these assets. Chapter 12 analyses how capital budgets are prepared and how they are accepted or rejected. In this chapter we examine how a budget, once accepted, is implemented. Remember budgets are plans that have been converted into quantitative terms. Capital budgets cover investments in fixed assets. Operating budgets are those that deal with day-to-day activities. The principal operating budget is the sales budget.

11.1.1 The financial planning process

Financial planning is designed to ensure that companies meet their investment objectives. The process begins with the sales forecast. Because all other budgets will depend on the volume of activity in sales, the sales budget is the most important budget of all.

Sales forecasts

The projected financial forecasts (pro forma statements) require accurate sales forecasts. However, forecasting sales is difficult. The following factors will need to be considered:

- Economic conditions. Economic factors such as inflation, interest rates and growth rates in GDP will impact on the market in which the firm sells its product.
- Production capacity. The forecasted sales figure may be constrained because of a lack of production capacity.
- Estimating the number of customers who will not pay their debts.
- Estimating the effect sales projections will have on cash balances. As we will see later on in the chapter, it is possible to run out of cash during periods of high sales growth as it is during periods of low sales growth.
- Competition. Identifying the level of competition in the market may have the effect of making sensible projections out of crazy sales forecasts. Allied to this should be a realistic assessment of anticipated market share the firm expects to achieve.

- Advertising campaigns and terms of credit also affect sales and these will be imputed in the sales forecast.

Getting the sales forecast accurate is crucial. An overly optimistic forecast will mean too much investment in fixed assets and inventory and high storage costs.

Underestimating demand for the product will mean losing customers and market share. The consequences will lower share prices and lower shareholder value.

Forecasting sales – historical average growth rates

Before discussing how companies forecast sales growth, it is important to note that growth in itself should not be an appropriate corporate goal. Consider a company whose sales growth is rapid. In order to expand production to meet demand, the company invests additional cash in plant and equipment. Still unable to meet the additional demand, over-utilisation of its plant and equipment will result in failure and break-down. In their efforts to expand production, more cash is invested in stock, raw materials and accounts receivable. Soon the company runs out of cash and it goes into liquidation. The good news in all of this is that demand for the company product is high and this is reflected in the sales growth forecast. The bad news is that poor financial planning failed to identify the increased financial needs required to fund the sales growth. Consequently, **an important aspect of financial planning is to ensure that a firm does not run out of cash**.

11.2 Financial forecasting – pro forma statements

11.2.1 The per cent of sales method

Once the sales forecast has been completed, we must then forecast the effect the forecasted growth in sales will have on the balance sheet and income statement. In other words, we must construct a pro forma profit and loss account and balance sheet. The financial planning model we describe here is the per cent of sales method. The items on the profit and loss account and balance sheet are divided into two groups – those that vary directly with sales and those that do not. We will then be able to measure the amount of additional financing the company needs to support the increase in sales.

Using the per cent of sales approach, the following steps are taken:

1. Forecast the estimated sales.
2. Calculate as a percentage of current sales each item on the profit and loss account and balance sheet that varies with sales.

Example 11.1 Pro forma statement using the per cent of sales approach

The profit and loss account of Parnell Ltd is as shown in Table 11.1.

Table 11.1 Parnell Ltd profit and loss account for year end 2007

Turnover	€5,000
Operating costs (70% of sales)	€3,500
Profit before tax (PBT)	€1,500
Tax (20%)	€300
Profit after tax (PAT)	€1,200
Dividends	€300
Retained earnings (RE)	€900

Parnell Ltd has projected an increase in sales of 20% for the next twelve months. Therefore anticipated sales will be €5,000 × 1.2 = €6,000. If costs remain at 70% of sales, we forecast costs at €6,000 × 0.7 = €4,200. We will also assume that Parnell Ltd will maintain a constant dividend payout ratio of 25%, i.e. €300/€1,200

$$\text{Dividend payout ratio} = \frac{\text{Ordinary dividends}}{\text{Profit after tax}} \qquad (11.1)$$

Therefore the percentage of retained earnings to profit after tax is 75% or €900/€1,200. **This is the retention ratio.**

$$\text{Retention ratio} = \frac{\text{Retained earnings}}{\text{Profit after tax}} \qquad (11.2)$$

The pro forma profit and loss account of Parnell Ltd is shown in Table 11.2.

Table 11.2 Parnell Ltd pro forma profit and loss account for year end 2008

Sales	€6,000
Costs	€4,200
Profit before tax (PBT)	€1,800
Tax (20%)	€360
Profit after tax (PAT)	€1,440
Dividends	€360
Retained earnings	€1,080

Note that this is a simplified example and we have lumped all costs including depreciation and interest payments together in a single figure. We will relax this assumption in a more detailed example later on in the chapter.

11.3 Pro forma balance sheet

To prepare a pro forma balance sheet we take each item on the balance sheet and decide which items vary directly with sales and those that don't.

The balance sheet of Parnell Ltd is given in Table 11.3.

Table 11.3 Parnell Ltd balance sheet for year end 2007

Fixed assets	€7,200	(144% of sales) note 1
Current assets		
Stock	€2,400	(48% of sales) note 2
Debtors	€1,760	(35.2% of sales) note 3
Cash	€640	(12.8% of sales) note 4
	€4,800	(2.4 x) note 5
Less current liabilities		
Creditors	€1,200	(24% of sales) note 6
Short-term loan	€400	note 7
	€1,600	
Net working capital	€3,200	
Net total assets	€10,400	
Financed by		
Debentures	€3,200	
Ordinary share capital	€2,200	
Retained earnings	€5,000	
	€10,400	

Note 1: This is €5,000 × 1.44 = €7,200. The assumption here is that the company is operating at full capacity, i.e. no excess capacity. Therefore any increase in sales will require additional investment in fixed assets. We will relax the full capacity assumption in the next section to allow for expansion in sales without additional investment in fixed assets. Note that even if plant and machinery is operating at full capacity, it may be possible to expand production by running additional shifts or by increasing the speed of use of existing machinery.

Note 2: It is reasonable to assume that as sales increase the company will require more stock to support the increase in sales. For Parnell Ltd the ratio of stock to sales is

$$\frac{€2,400}{€5,000} = 48\%$$

We will discuss stock management in Chapter 17, but assuming no change in inventory management, the forecasted stock for the year 2008 is €6,000 × 0.48 = €2,880.

Note 3: Debtors/accounts receivable
These are assumed to change proportionately with sales. Parnell's 2007 debtors to sales percentage is

$$\frac{€1,760}{€5,000} = 35.2\%$$

Therefore the forecasted debtors figure for the year 2008 is €2,112 (€6,000 × 0.352).

Note 4: The amount of cash needed to support the level of sales is expected to remain at the year 2007 level, which is

$$\frac{€640}{€5,000} = 12.8\%$$

Therefore Parnell forecasts a cash balance of €768 (€6,000 × 0.128) for the year 2008.

Note 5: Parnell has total assets of €7,200 (fixed assets) *plus* €4,800 (current assets) = €12,000. The total assets to sales ratio is therefore

$$\frac{€12,000}{€5,000} = 2.4\text{ x} \quad (x = times)$$

So Parnell currently needs €2.4 in total assets to generate €1 in sales. This is referred to as the **capital intensity ratio**.

$$\text{Capital intensity ratio} = \frac{\text{Total assets}}{\text{Sales}} \qquad (11.3)$$

Note 6: Of course to increase total asset investments to meet an increase in sales requires an increase in funds to finance this increase in investment. Therefore, on the 'financed by' section of the balance sheet we will show accounts payable varying with sales. As the volume of sales increases, the company will place more orders for materials with its suppliers. Therefore, accounts payable will change with sales. So part of the increase in investments in total assets would be financed 'spontaneously' with increases in accounts payable. Items in the balance sheet that increase spontaneously with increases in sales are called **spontaneously generated funds**. In 2007 accounts payable as a percentage of sales is

$$\frac{€1,200}{€5,000} = 24\%$$

Therefore we project Parnell's accounts payable in 2008 to be €1,440 (€6,000 × 0.24).

Note 7: Short-term loans, debentures and ordinary share capital will not vary spontaneously with sales. These are decisions taken by company management. Retained earnings will not vary spontaneously with sales, but it will change with sales. It will depend on profit after tax and the dividend payout ratio adopted by management.

We can now construct Parnell's pro forma balance sheet for the year 2007 based on the projections we have already discussed. This is shown in Table 11.4.

11.4 Additional financial needs (AFN)

The AFN are the additional funds the company needs if the increase in assets required to finance the increase in sales is greater than the spontaneously generated funds produced from the sales increase. Parnell requires an additional €1,440 in fixed asset investment *plus* an additional €960 in current assets for a total additional financial requirement of €2,400.

Part of this would come from spontaneous increases in accounts receivable of €240 and part from the profit after tax that is not paid out as dividends, i.e. retained earnings of €1,080. Therefore Parnell Ltd will require additional financing of €1,080:

Increase in total assets (€2,400) = increase in creditors (€240) *plus* increase in retained earnings (€1,080) *plus* AFN (€1,080).

The AFN figure of €1,080 is what makes the balance sheet balance.

11.4.1 Financing the AFN

The benefit of financial planning models is that it allows management to investigate the various options it has. For example, Parnell could plan to raise the AFN of €1,080 by additional borrowing or by issuing additional shares. On the other hand, Parnell may have a policy of not borrowing any additional funds and not issuing any additional equity. In this case, the forecasted 20% increase in sales will not be feasible and planned growth is scrapped. In the next section on value-based management we will discuss the effect of growth on key financial ratios. For example, Parnell's net working capital in 2007 was €3,200 (€4,800 − €1,600). The projections based on a 20% growth rate show the current assets will increase by €960 and current liabilities will increase by €240. This means it can raise an additional €720 (€960 − €240) in short-term loans and maintain its net working capital of €3,200 (€5,760 − €2,560). The remaining additional funds required of €360 (€1,080 − €720) can be financed as management sees fit.

Table 11.4 Parnell Ltd pro forma balance sheet for year end 2008

	2008	Change from 2007
Fixed assets	€8,640	€1,440
Current assets		
Stock	€2,880	€480
Debtors	€2,112	€352
Cash	€768	€128
	€5,760	€960
Total assets	€14,400	€2,400
Financed by		
Current liabilities		
Creditors	€1,440	€240
Short-term loan	€400	—
	€1,840	€240
Working capital	€3,920	€720
Net total assets	€12,560	
Long-term loans	€3,200	—
Share capital	€2,200	
Retained earnings	€6,080	€1,080
	€13,320	
AFN	€1,080	€1,080
	€14,400	

11.4.2 *Capacity utilisation*

In formulating the pro forma statements we assumed that Parnell Ltd was operating at full capacity and therefore any increases in sales growth was followed by an increase in fixed assets. However, some companies may, because of economies of scale, build excess capacity. Therefore any increase in sales and production can be accomplished without additions to fixed assets. If the capital intensity ratio is low, sales can increase without much additional external capital. A high capital intensity ratio will mean that additions to production output will lead to high levels of external finance.

11.5 AFN – the equation approach

As we have seen, pro forma statements are used to forecast capital requirements. The equation approach is a simpler method and can be used if the ratios are expected to remain constant and if a rough measure of capital requirements is required. The following formula is used to forecast the additional financial needs:

$$ \text{AFN} = \frac{A}{S_0} \, S - \frac{L}{S_0} \, S - [NS_1(1 - d)] \qquad (11.4) $$

where AFN = additional funds needed

A = assets that are linked directly to sales

S_0 = sales during the last year (in Parnell's case, 2007)

S = change in sales, i.e. projected sales for 2008 *minus* previous year's sales 2007

L = liabilities that change spontaneously with sales

$NS_1(1 - d)$ = increase in retained earnings where N net margin = the net profit divided by sales or profit per €1 of sales. d is the dividend payout ratio

S_1 = sales in the projected period (2008)

Applying this equation to Parnell Ltd, we find the AFN as

$$ \text{AFN} = \frac{€12,000}{€5,000} \, €1,000 - \frac{€1,200}{€5,000} \, €1,000 - [0.24 \times €6,000 \times (1 - 0.25)] $$

$$ = (€2,400 - €240) - (€1,080) = €1,080 $$

We get the same answer using the equation approach as we did the tableau method. However, we can't assume that this will always be the case. The formula method assumes that:

1. assets increase in proportion to sales.
2. liabilities such as accounts payable will grow at the same rate to sales. However a change in a company's credit policy may alter this.
3. the net profit margin remains the same as sales grow. This would be unlikely.

11.6 Lumpy assets

In some industries, growth can only be accommodated by large discrete increases in fixed assets. An increase in capacity can only happen in lumpy increases in assets. This is illustrated in Figure 11.1. We assume that the minimum and most economically efficient investment in fixed assets is €1,400m. This produces enough output to generate sales of €1,000m. To increase sales beyond this point would require a total investment in plant of €2,100m. So any small increase in sales beyond the €1,000m mark will require a large financial investment.

Figure 11.1 Lumpy assets

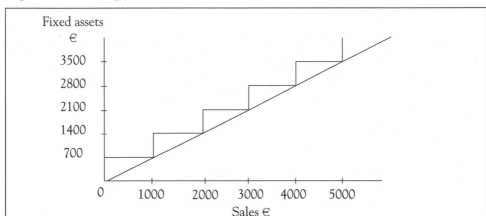

11.7 Maximum internal growth rates

What is the growth rate a firm can achieve without recourse to external funds?

This is the growth rate in sales that can be achieved with internal financing only and where the AFN is zero. Algebraically this is computed as

$$\text{Internal growth rate} = \frac{\text{ROA}(1-d)}{1-\text{ROA}(1-d)} \qquad (11.5)$$

where

ROA = return on assets (in Parnell's case this is profit after tax of €1,200 divided by total assets of €12,000=10%
d=dividend payout ratio (for Parnell this is the dividends of €300 divided by the profit after-tax figure €1,200 which is = 25%).

This results in an internal growth rate of

$$\frac{0.10(1-0.25)}{1-0.10(1-0.25)} = \frac{0.075}{0.925} = 8.1\%$$

Therefore Parnell Ltd can grow at 8.1% per annum without requiring external finance.

11.8 Maximum sustainable growth rate

This is the growth rate that can be achieved without recourse to additional external equity financing while keeping a constant debt to equity ratio. We will discuss the reasons why companies might want to avoid selling additional equity shares in Chapter 14. The principal reasons are the costs involved and the existing shareholders may not want to share the profits of the company with new shareholders. Why companies will want to maintain a particular debt/equity relationship is discussed in Chapter 13. The algebraic formula to ascertain this sustainable growth rate is

$$\text{Sustainable growth rate} = \frac{\text{ROE}(1 - d)}{1 - \text{ROE}(1 - d)} \qquad (11.6)$$

where ROE = return on equity (for Parnell this is PAT of €1,200 divided by equity of €7,200 which is 16.6%) and $(1 - d)$ is the retention ratio.

Therefore Parnell's sustainable growth rate is

$$\frac{0.166(1-0.25)}{1-0.166(1-0.25)} = \frac{0.1245}{0.8755} = 14.2\ \%$$

Therefore, Parnell can grow at 14.2% without issuing additional equity.

Of course, growth rates will attract more companies into the industry, forcing growth rates down. Therefore the long-term sustainable growth rate will be affected by economic factors. For example:

- An increase in the profit margin will increase the return on equity and therefore increase the sustainable growth rate.
- Total asset efficiency: the more sales generated per €1 of assets, the higher the return on equity and therefore the higher the sustainable growth.
- Financial gearing: a higher proportion of debt relative to equity in the firm's capital structure reduces the need for equity and therefore increases the sustainable growth rate.
- Dividend policy: a reduction in the dividend payout increases retained earnings and therefore the greater the maximum sustainable growth rate.

Finally, **if actual growth exceeds the sustainable growth rate, the company will run short of cash.** If growth exceeds the sustainable growth rate, the company must increase its profit margin, increase its asset efficiency (i.e. generate more sales per €1 of assets), increase its gearing, increase the retention ratio (i.e. keep more earnings for reinvestment), or it will have to sell new equity shares.

Example 11.2 Sustainable growth rates

A company has the following characteristics:

1. Total assets = €100
2. Total equity = 60%

3. Total debt = 40%
4. Debt to equity ratio of 0.66
5. An dividend payout ratio of 35%
6. An asset turnover ratio of 1.3
7. A net profit margin of 4%.

The company wants to expand its sales growth beyond its sustainable level to 12%. Calculate:

(a) the sustainable growth rate.
(b) the increase in the net profit margin necessary to fund the increase in the sustainable growth level to 12%.

Solution
(a) First, we calculate the return on equity. Remember in Chapter 3, on financial statement analysis, we defined the ROE, using the Du Pont formula, as

ROE =	Net profit margin	×	asset turnover	×	equity multiplier
ROE =	4%	×	1.3	×	1.66
ROE =	8.63%				

(Note: the equity multiplier can be calculated as 1+ the debt equity ratio).[1]

The dividend payout ratio d is 35%. Therefore the sustainable growth rate is

$$\text{Sustainable growth rate} = \frac{ROE(1 - d)}{1 - ROE(1 - d)}$$

$$= \frac{0.0863(1 - 0.35)}{1 - 0.0863(1 - 0.35)}$$

$$= \frac{0.0561}{0.94} = 5.9\%$$

(b) If the proposed growth rate is 12%, we can solve for the new profit margin necessary to make this happen. Let's call the new profit margin X. Therefore

$$12\% = \frac{(X)(1.3)(1.66)(0.65)}{[1-(X)(1.3)(1.66)(0.65)]}$$
$$x = 7.5\%$$

11.9 Weaknesses of accounting-based management

The primary purpose of any financial plan is to determine whether the plan maximises shareholder value. The problem with the approach we have adopted above (i.e. accounting-based management) is that it is based on accounting concepts (e.g. profits, balance sheets, earnings per share, etc.) and this approach can fail to maximise shareholder value. In particular the accounts-based management approach ignores some basic aspects of firm value, i.e. incremental cash flow, risk and timing (i.e. present values).

Example 11.3 Earnings quality

Growth in earnings per share may not take account of the increased investment needed to achieve the EPS growth.

Two companies, A and B, may achieve the same 20% increase in earnings. Based on accounting information, both companies give the same value. However, let's suppose that company B was much more generous in granting credit to its customers. This helped them achieve the sales necessary to generate a 20% increase in earnings. In other words, company B invested more than company A, yet both achieved the same increase in earnings. Company B will have a higher debtors figure in its balance sheet than company A, and it will have spent more cash to support this higher debtors figure. Current assets will be higher in B's balance sheet, but its profit and loss account will not contain any additional cost for the increased cash outflow.

From a value-based management perspective, company A has created more value for its shareholders because it has generated more cash flow.

Table 11.5 Comparison of A and B – earnings and cash flow

	Company A (€000)		Company B (€000)	
Year	1	2	1	2
Profits	100	120	100	120
Increase in debtors	0	5	0	30
Cash flow	100	115	100	90
% change		15%		(10%)

Even though both companies see a 20% increase in earnings, company A is creating more shareholder value because it is generating more cash flow.

It is not wise to rely on accounts-based management. It is all very well for management to say that they have achieved a 20% increase in after-tax profits. What shareholders want is a maximisation of wealth. For example, a 20% increase in sales is only good news for the shareholders if the increase in investments required to boost sales have a **positive net present value**. This would happen only if the return on investment is greater than the cost of capital (which includes opportunity cost, i.e. the cost of equity capital).

11.9.1 What's wrong with accounting-based management?

In any introductory course to financial accounting, the bottom line figure or net profit is calculated by taking the annual revenues for operations and deducting the costs used up in generating this revenue.[2] The earnings figure calculated is divided by the weighted average number of shares outstanding to give earnings per share, which is then used as a company valuation measure.[3] Earnings per share determine the economic health of a company.

However relying on earnings-based management can result in a reduction in shareholder wealth rather than what should be the main objective of financial management, which is the **enhancement of shareholder value**. Accounting-based management can lead to the destruction of shareholder value because of distortions and manipulation of accounting methods. The first is the problem of revenue recognition:

(a) **Trade loading**: refers to the practice of pulling next year's deliveries into the last period of the current accounting year. With long-term contracts, revenues can span different accounting periods and turnover becomes more difficult to determine. The problem is when to recognise turnover on the company's profit and loss account. This is usually done as a percentage on completion basis. There are different methods used in calculating the percentage completion and this will give different turnover figures.

(b) **Charging costs**: There are two kinds of costs: invoiced costs (actual costs that require an invoice, e.g. rent and rates, etc.) and paper costs that do not require an invoice, e.g. bad debts and depreciation. Calculating paper charges requires a lot of judgement and this can result in charges being made that alter profits. For example, interest payments can be capitalised, i.e. charged to the balance sheet and not to the profit and loss account. The capitalisation of interest payments has the effect of improving profit and asset values. Furthermore, changing depreciation policy can result in profit manipulation. For example, extending the life of an asset reduces the depreciation charge and boosts profits. Similarly, increasing residual values will lower the depreciation charge. In addition, firms will differ in the treatment of research and development costs. Cross-company comparisons are difficult because some companies will write off the research and development expenditure against profits and consequently have lower asset values than companies that do not write off the research and development expenditure.

(c) **Stock valuation**: Changing the method of stock valuation can have important effects on reported profits.

(d) **Provisions**: Markets don't like surprises. They prefer a non-volatile growth in profits. Announcing a profit figure this year of €100m suggests that the market will expect €110m next year. If the market expects, say, €90m in profits this year, should the company report the actual profit figure of €110m? There's a tendency for companies to make large provisions in good years and low provisions in bad years. The effect will be to smooth out profits over the years.

(e) **Risk**: Earnings-based management doesn't take into account the risk inherent in different investment projects. For example, the manager whose objective is to increase earnings will select projects that offer the highest expected profits, even though the same projects may have a higher risk. In order to adequately compare two companies, A and B, that show the same growth and earnings per share, and therefore on an earnings basis would appear to offer the same attractiveness, it would be necessary to consider the levels of investment needed to generate that growth. The company that has invested more in terms of working capital and/or fixed assets will generate less shareholder value. For example, if company A has had to provide longer payment periods to its customers in order to boost sales than company B, then it will cost A more to support higher debtors. Company A may also have to invest more in stock and fixed assets in order to increase sales. Consequently the higher investment in working capital and fixed assets is shown in the balance sheet, but the additional costs are not shown in the profit and loss account. Company B will be generating more in cash flow and therefore more shareholder value than company A.

(f) **Short-termism**: It is clear therefore that focusing on accounting-based management can lead to short-termism. Concentrating on reported operating profit and balance sheet figures for capital invested can be worthless in calculating shareholder value. Judging the performance of management by looking at accounting rates of return can lead to management decisions which result in reductions in shareholder value. For example, an investment in plant and machinery that would lead to financial gain in the long term could be postponed because it may lead to a fall in the accounting rates of return in the short term. This is because it raises the denominator in the accounting rate of return calculation. This is what happens if managers are judged based on accounting rates return. In the long term, however, such an investment could raise shareholder value.

(g) **Agency theory**: In Chapter 1 we introduced the student to agency costs. Managers can claim benefits from the company and in doing so can reduce shareholder value. These could include using expensive company cars where a smaller inexpensive car would do, taking Wednesday afternoon off for golf, and anything else that is essentially for the managers' pleasure but does not increase shareholder value.

11.10 How is shareholder wealth maximised?

From the preceding discussion we can conclude that rather than maximising profits the objective of management should be to maximise shareholder value.

In essence, shareholder wealth is maximised by maximising share prices. A shareholder's wealth is the number of shares held by that shareholder multiplied by the share price. A shareholder, in order to increase her wealth, will want an increase in share prices. In Chapter 8 we saw how the valuation of a share depends on:

- the ability of the company (more precisely the ability of the company's assets) to generate cash flows
- when the cash flows are received – cash flows received sooner are better because they can be reinvested or paid out as dividends
- the firm's risk – if a firm's risk falls, investors will, all else being equal, pay a higher price per share for cash flows that are more certain than for a share whose cash flows are risky.

Therefore, the key to creating shareholder value is to increase the cash flows and get them into the company as quickly as possible and by minimising the riskiness of the cash flows.

11.10.1 Free cash flow

More specifically, the way for managers to maximise shareholder value is to increase their free cash flows. This is why free cash flow is the most important determinant of shareholder value. Free cash flow is what is available for distribution to the shareholders after the company has made all the reinvestment in working capital and fixed assets necessary to maintain the business. In other words, having made a provision for depreciation to cover the annual cost of existing assets, expanding companies will make further investments in working capital and fixed assets. That is, they make a net investment. If the company's net earnings are greater than net investment, the free cash flow is positive. If net earnings are less than net investment, free cash flows are negative. Focusing on cash flow, which is more difficult to manipulate than accounting profits, makes cross-border comparisons of companies easier. Different countries can have different ways of dealing with depreciation, valuations of assets, etc. A classic example was provided by Daimler-Benz, which became the first German firm to list its shares on the New York Stock Exchange. Under German accounting rules, it reported a $372 million profit. However, under American accounting rules it had losses of $1.1 billion.[4] (We discussed how to calculate free cash flow in Chapter 2.)

11.10.2 Company valuations using free cash flows[5]

We can therefore use free cash flows to value the entire company. Value is created when the rate of return on capital invested is greater than the cost of that capital, i.e. the required rate of return. The difference between actual rates of return and required rates of return is the investment spread. If the actual rates of return is greater than the required rates return, the investment spread is positive. So, for example, if ABC Ltd invests €1m which requires a rate of return of 10% and the actual return is 15%, then the value of ABC Ltd would have increased by €50,000, i.e. €1m × (15% − 10%). If the investment spread is positive, then value is created. If the investment spread is negative, then value is diminished. Positive investment spreads signify growth stocks. Examples of growth stocks include (at the time of writing) companies such as Elan, Microsoft and Amazon.com. However at some time in the future growth stocks will settle into competitive equilibrium. As more companies enter the industry and competition becomes intense, the scope for investment spread and hence supernormal growth will evaporate. The time when this occurs is referred to as the horizon or terminal period where subsequent growth or value creation opportunities are zero. The positive performance spread will evaporate and rates will return to minimum acceptable levels. General Motors, for example, was the Microsoft of the 1960s – a supernormal growth stock. Competition eventually forced it into competitive equilibrium, so that it has now settled into a state of steady growth. Intel currently enjoys a sort of competitive advantage in that the costs of entry into the industry are excessive – it can cost an excessive amount to build a wafer fabrication plant. As long as this competitive advantage remains, Intel will remain a growth stock, other things being equal.

When companies reach this stage of their life cycle and where opportunities for further growth are zero, this period is called the **horizon period**. In the following example, we will see how a company, which goes through these different stages of growth, can be valued.

Example 11.4 Valuation based on free cash flow

Table 11.6 gives the summarised balance sheet and summarised profit and loss account for Extra Value Ltd.

Table 11.6 Summarised balance sheet for Extra Value Ltd

(Actual and projected)	Actual	Projected			
Year	2008	2009	2010	2011	2012
Net fixed assets	140	150	180	185	190
Marketable securities	30	35	40	40	45
Net operating working capital	100	120	140	145	150
	270	305	360	370	385
Financed by:					
Debentures	130	145	180	180	190
Equity	140	160	180	190	195
	270	305	360	370	385

Summarised profit and loss account for Extra Value Ltd

(Actual and projected)	Actual	Projected			
	2008	2009	2010	2011	2012
Net sales	1000	1220	1427	1529	1574
Operating costs	872	1068	1248	1339	1378
Depreciation	28	30	36	37	38
PBIT	100	122	143	153	158
less interest	5	6	7	8	8
PBT	95	116	136	145	150
Tax (25%)	23.75	29	34	36.25	37.5
PAT	71.25	87	102	108.75	112.5
Dividends	—	—	—	65.25	67.5
Retained earnings	71.25	87	102	43.5	45
Number of shares	50	50	50	50	50

The horizon for Extra Value is after 2012 and sales are expected to grow at a constant rate of 2% afterwards.

Table 11.7 Calculation of free cash flows

	Actual	Projected			
Year	2008	2009	2010	2011	2012
NOPAT = (PBIT)(1–tax rate)	75	91.5	107.25	114.75	118.5
less Incremental investment in fixed capital		10	30	5	5
less Incremental investment in operating working capital		20	20	5	5
FCF		61.5	57.25	104.75	108.5

An alternative method of calculating free cash flows is to use gross investment in operating fixed assets and deducting depreciation from fixed assets:

	2008	2009	2010	2011	2012
NOPAT	75	91.5	107.3	114.8	118.5
plus Depreciation	28	30	36	37	38
Operating cash flow	103	121.5	143.3	151.8	156.3
less Gross investment in fixed assets		(40)	(66)	(42)	(43)
less Increase in operating working capital		(20)	(20)	(5)	(5)
Free cash flow		61.5	57.3	104.8	108.5

Table 11.7 shows the calculation of free cash flows. In 2009, for example, Extra Value Ltd would generate €91.5m in after-tax operating profit and it would invest a further €30m in additional assets. Therefore the free cash flows for 2009 are €91.5 *minus* €30 = €61.5.

Process for finding corporate valuation

1. Find the present value of the expected free cash flows for each year within the horizon period. Extra Value's cost of capital is 12%.

$$PV = \frac{61.5}{1.12} + \frac{57.25}{(1.12)^2} + \frac{104.75}{(1.12)^3} + \frac{108.5}{(1.12)^4} = €244.6m$$

2. Calculate the present value of the free cash flows after the horizon period. Because growth is expected to be constant after 2012, we can use the constant growth formula to calculate the value of operations as at the end of 2012. First, we can use the free cash flow for 2012 to find the free cash flow for 2013.

$$FCF_{2013} = FCF_{2012}(1 + g)$$
$$= €108.5(1 + 0.02)$$
$$= €110.67$$

Therefore the value of operations at the end of 2012 is

$$\frac{€110.67}{0.12 - 0.02} = €1,106.7$$

We now discount the year 5 value back to the present to get the present value:

$$\frac{€1215.2}{(1.12)^4} = €772.3$$

3. The sum of the present values got in 1 and 2 is €947.9m. This represents the current value (2001) of its operating assets. This is illustrated in Figure 11.2.

Figure 11.2 Valuation of whole company using free cash flows and non-constant growth rates

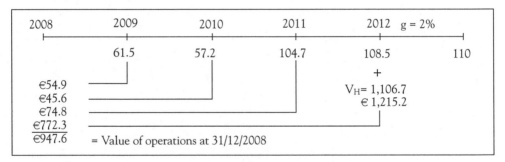

2008	2009	2010	2011	2012 g = 2%	
	61.5	57.2	104.7	108.5	110
				+	
€54.9				V_H= 1,106.7	
€45.6				€ 1,215.2	
€74.8					
€772.3					
€947.6	= Value of operations at 31/12/2008				

4. The total value of the company is the value of its operating assets *plus* the value of its non-operating assets, in Extra Value's case marketable investments of €30m. Therefore Extra Value's total valuation at the end of 2008 is €947.6m + €30m = €977.6m.

5. The value of equity (i.e. shareholders' value) is the value of operations *less* debt. This is:

Total value of operations (€977.6m) less value debt (€130m) = €847.6m

Summary (€millions)
Value of operation assets   €947.6
Value of non-operating assets   €30
Total value of operations   €977.6
less value of debt   €130
equals value of equity   €847.6

One of the benefits of value-based management (projecting financial statements into the future), in addition to giving us a current valuation of the business, is that it allows us to identify ways of increasing shareholder value. Furthermore, we can compare the pro forma statements and the financial plan to see if the targets set out in a financial plan are met. For example, the value of shareholders' funds is €847.6m. There are 50 million shares outstanding, which means that the value of a single share is €16.96. If the current market price is greater than €16.96, it would clearly not be acceptable. Management will therefore have to make adjustments to and *revise their financial plan*. They could start by improving the company's actual financial ratios (profitability, acid management, expenses, debtors collection periods, payment periods) that are lagging behind some benchmark like the industry average. The company may have higher costs to sales ratios, and below average accounts receivable to sales and stock to sales ratios. The company will need to revise its financial plan to minimise its investments in working capital so that it can increase its overall return on assets. It could possibly do this by scrapping low-profit products and lowering operating costs. It might need to be more aggressive in cutting the debtors collection period and in reducing the stock to sales ratio. The overall effect will be to increase the NOPAT and improve the net operating working capital. The result will be an improvement in free cash flows. This of course would have the effect of improving company and shareholder value. Therefore, the benefit of value-based management is that it helps increase shareholder value.

11.11 Economic value added (EVA)

Another way to assess the economic performance (value creation) of management and the company is economic value added. This focuses on 'adjusted accounting information' rather than cash flows. While some top executives' bonus packages are based on share price performance, earnings per share and other accounting measures are also important, particularly for divisional and lower level management. As discussed earlier, focusing on accounting measures as a performance yardstick has obvious drawbacks. Managers whose compensation packages depend on end of term profits can manipulate short-term earnings at the expense of creating longer-term difficulties. Earnings-based bonus payments can result in managers offering huge discounts which require employees working overtime to produce and distribute extra product (trade loading). These practices consume vast amounts of extra capital (for warehousing, additional working capital, etc.) and the extra costs do not appear on the income statement. Economic value added attempts to prevent this type of problem. Whereas traditional profit and loss accounts only deduct the cost of debt capital to arrive at the bottom line, economic value added deducts the cost of all capital (including the cost of equity capital) to arrive at the bottom line figure (see Box 11.1). For example if a company has invested €100m in capital and its cost of capital is 10%, its required rate of return is €10m. If the company's actual rate of return is €30m, its EVA is €20m. The company will have enhanced shareholder value by €20m. If the company's actual return is €5m, its EVA is *minus* €5m and it will have diminished shareholder value by €5m. The formula for economic value added is

$$\text{Economic value added (EVA)} = \text{NOPAT} - \text{WACC}$$
$$= \text{PBIT}(1 - T) - \begin{bmatrix} \text{Adjusted} \\ \text{invested} \\ \text{capital} \end{bmatrix} \begin{bmatrix} \text{After-tax} \\ \text{cost of} \\ \text{capital} \end{bmatrix} \quad (11.7)$$

where WACC = weighted average cost of capital

T = tax rate

Alternatively,

$$
\text{Economic value added (EVA)} = \begin{bmatrix} \text{Adjusted} \\ \text{operating profits} \\ \text{after tax} \end{bmatrix} - \begin{bmatrix} \begin{pmatrix} \text{Adjusted} \\ \text{invested} \\ \text{capital} \end{pmatrix} (\text{WACC}) \end{bmatrix} \qquad (11.8)
$$

Example 11.5 Economic value added calculation

Using the data from the income statement and the balance sheet we can calculate Extra Value Ltd's economic value added.

Table 11.8 Extra Value Ltd's economic value added calculation

PBIT	€100
Tax rate	25%
NOPAT	€75
Invested operating capital	€240
WACC	12%
Cost of capital	€28.8
EVA = NOPAT less WACC	€46.2

In calculating economic value added, we use the term 'adjusted' in describing capital invested and adjusted operating profits after tax. The term 'adjusted' is used because, according to Stern Stewart, the arbiters of EVA, over 160 adjustments may need to be made to the accounting data before calculating economic value added. The main adjustment is to include a cost for equity supplied capital. Equity capital has a cost called opportunity cost because shareholders give up the opportunity of investing funds elsewhere and receiving a more favourable rate of return. The rate of return they could receive, if they invested the capital elsewhere in companies of similar risk, is the cost of equity capital. While the cost of equity capital is the main difference between economic value added and accounting profit, there are other adjustments needed to accounting earnings before calculating economic value added. The following is a list of some of the most common adjustments:

- Goodwill: If it is the practice of a company to write off goodwill to the profit and loss account, then it should be added back to shareholders' funds when calculating economic value added. This is because the goodwill payment represents what the acquisition is actually worth. Therefore, in calculating EVA, the current period's goodwill amortisation is added back to net operating profit after tax (NOPAT) and goodwill amortised in past years is added back to capital.
- Research and development costs: Again, if the practice is to write off research and development costs to the profit and loss account then these should also be treated as

an asset and added back to shareholders' funds. This is because the research and development is obviously an investment in future products and will generate future cash flows. Accounting rules state that all research and development costs should be immediately deducted from earnings. For companies that spend a lot of money on research and development, such as high-tech pharmaceutical companies, this treatment reduces one of their most valuable assets to nothing. The economic value added treatment is to capitalise research and development costs. This of course is the correct treatment for such a valuable asset.

• Minority interests:[6] Since all capital is working in the company, regardless of where it comes from, minority interests and total debt are added to shareholders' funds.

• Expenses and revenues: Many companies spend money on marketing in order to enter new markets, gain new market share and establish brand names. Following the deregulation of the telecommunications market in Ireland, emerging companies spend a lot of money on winning customers, which is an investment that will lead to future profitability. However, accounting rules state that these expenses must be written off and deducted from earnings. Economic value added companies capitalise customer acquisition costs and amortise them over the appropriate period.

• Depreciation: With economic value added the capital charge for depreciation declines in line with the depreciation value of the asset. So companies using the straight-line method of depreciation, which has the same capital charge each year, will have to make the appropriate adjustment under economic value added. The effect of EVA adjustment, however, is to make old assets look cheap and new assets look expensive, and managers may therefore be reluctant to replace old equipment with new.

• Taxes: For the purpose of calculating EVA (and consequently NOPAT) companies should only deduct the cash taxes they pay. Deferred taxes that were deducted from earnings in the past should be taken out of the liability section of the balance sheet and added to shareholders' funds for calculating cost of capital.

• Passive investments: Passive investments such as marketable securities are deducted from capital because they are not used in the operating activities of the company. The income from these investments should be subtracted from the net operating profit after tax (NOPAT). In addition, any form of free capital (e.g. accrued wages, trade creditors) should be subtracted from capital.

Box 11.1 EVA and performance pay

Economic value added can be used to determine value creation at all levels and divisions as well as for the company as a whole.

Research in Britain and the US suggests there is little correlation between performance and chief executive salaries . . . A key performance criterion centres on shareholder value. Capitalism proposes share price as an anchor indicator for other types of performance measures, especially profitability.

Profitability, in turn, is deemed to result from superior management decisions and practices. If share price is a good proxy for performance, it should be tightly correlated to profitability and management behaviour. Unfortunately, a link up among these criteria is

⟶

not apparent. In the present bull market, relatively mediocre profitability performers have enjoyed rising share prices. The tenuous link between profit and share price highlights the tendency to speculation and the astronomical price/earnings ratios of some companies. Often companies are valued not for their intrinsic value creation, through products and services to customers, but on the fervent hope that they will attract a takeover bid, especially if in a trendy industry, viz. many Internet and biotechnology companies have never posted a profit. Why was Telecom so oversubscribed?

An increasingly accepted performance criterion is economic value added (EVA). This measure seeks to assess the intrinsic value created by the company rather than merely its 'paper' value. EVA subtracts cost of capital from after tax profit. Cost of capital includes interest paid, dividends and the cost of equity through capital gains to shareholders.

Published EVA figures for Irish and UK companies in 1997 show that of the 20 Irish listed companies, eight had negative EVAs, while 141 of 200 UK companies had negative EVAs. According to Stern Stewart, the arbiters of EVA, these companies would be better off if they were taken over or if they installed new management.

Extracted from an article by Dr Eleanor O'Higgins (UCD)
'Spotlight on pay-for-performance system'
The Irish Times, 20 October 1999

11.12 Market value added

One of the problems with EVA is that it tells us nothing about how current management strategies are likely to affect future shareholder value. To resolve this problem, Stern Stewart have come up with market value added (MVA), which deducts the total equity capital supplied by shareholders from the market value of its shares. Increasing EVA will increase the share price (other things being equal) and MVA will therefore increase because of an increase in share price.

$$
\begin{aligned}
\text{Market value added (MVA)} &= \begin{bmatrix} \text{Market value} \\ \text{of equity} \end{bmatrix} - \begin{bmatrix} \text{Equity capital supplied} \\ \text{by shareholders} \end{bmatrix} \\
&= \begin{bmatrix} \text{Number of shares} \\ \text{outstanding} \end{bmatrix}\begin{bmatrix} \text{Share} \\ \text{price} \end{bmatrix} - \begin{bmatrix} \text{Total common} \\ \text{equity} \end{bmatrix}
\end{aligned} \tag{11.9}
$$

Since the primary objective of companies is the maximisation of shareholders' wealth, MVA is the definitive measure of wealth and wealth creation. Market value added is the difference between the capital invested by shareholders and the market value of that capital at today's market price. It is therefore a measure of how the company has enhanced or diminished shareholder value.

MVA is risk adjusted because the market automatically incorporates judgements on risk into stock prices. Therefore we can use MVA to compare different companies in different industries and countries. The company with the highest MVA is the one that has created most wealth for its shareholders. If we think of a company as a whole series of investment projects, then MVA is equivalent to the company's net present value (NPV). MVA is the difference between gross market value and the cumulative capital investment. This is the net present value. However we cannot use accounting book values to estimate MVA. Accounting rules tend to understate the amount of capital a company has invested. Various adjustments have to be made similar to those discussed under EVA, for example adding back research and development costs and goodwill to shareholders' funds. (See Box 11.2)

EVA shows the value added during a given year, whereas MVA shows the value added over the company's entire existence. Unlike EVA, there is no MVA for business units, divisions or subsidiaries. Therefore, unlike EVA, MVA cannot be used to assess annual internal performance.

Box 11.2 Company valuation issues still unresolved

by Chris Johns

In 'how to' manuals of investing, we are often exhorted to focus on the underlying fundamentals of a company's business. This sounds sensible enough although it is rarely straightforward in practice.

One problem is that investors need to become acquainted with rudimentary elements of accountancy in order to get to grips with the various ways in which financial information is presented.

A basic understanding of profit and loss accounts and balance sheets is of obvious importance; from these we can glean information about many of the key numbers that analysts believe are essential inputs into any investment decision.

For a long time the humble P/E ratio held sway as the most important number in the investors' toolkit. This ratio has the virtue of simplicity and it is easy to calculate. Indeed the P/E ratio is widely used for these very reasons. Unfortunately it has a number of drawbacks, not least of which is the issue of precise and proper measurement of earnings, and relatedly, the ability of the company, or any analyst of the company, to manipulate (properly or improperly) the way in which profits are counted to suit a particular story.

To get a more accurate grip on underlying profitability, analysts come up with a whole raft of measures, many of which try to focus on the pure amount of cash generated by the firm in its day-to-day operations. Different bits of a company's information were focussed on and concepts such as free cash flow and earnings before interest, tax depreciation and amortisation (EBITDA) entered the lexicon . . .

As the ways of looking at financial information proliferated, so did confusion grow over just how to value the worth of a company . . .

A leading UK analyst called Terry Smith once famously lost his job (with investment giant UBS) for writing a book on how accounts can be manipulated. Some of Smith's criticisms have been dealt with by regulatory changes but much of what he wrote remains apposite . . .

There are too many measurement issues surrounding earnings to be listed here, but a few examples will suffice. Most obviously there are international problems – different countries employ different accounting standards.

Firms with listings on several different stock exchanges will sometimes present different measures of earnings to comply with local rules. A common example is a

$\longrightarrow$

European company that presents its profits according to home country conventions as well as earnings according to US GAAP for its US investor base.

Some of these issues will be resolved if proposals to unify standards under the auspices of the International Accounting Standards Board come to fruition.

In the US pro-forma earnings came to notoriety during the bubble years of the late 1990s when, in one or two extreme cases, some companies simply excluded as much of the negative profits items as they could get away with. This measure, although still in use, has become discredited, and along with some other ways of looking at profits, has been christened in some quarters as EBBS (earnings before bad stuff) . . .

Problems common to many countries include acquisition accounting, the appropriate of capital spending and the appearance of so-called extraordinary items . . .

One upshot of all of this is that the ratios used by analysts to value companies go in and out of fashion . . .

(Extract) *The Irish Times*, 3 September 2004

SUMMARY

- Financial planning involves the conversion of the corporate plan into quantitative terms. This will involve projected financial statements that show the effect the corporate plan has on corporate profits.
- Financial forecasting begins with the budgeting process, which identifies the assets that are required and the revenues that will be generated from the use of these assets.
- The sales budget is the most important budget of all, because all other budgets will depend on the volume of sales activity.
- One method used to assess the effect the forecasted growth in sales has on the income statement and balance sheet is the 'per cent of sales method'. Here items on the profit and loss account and balance sheet are divided into two groups – those that vary directly with sales and those that do not.
- Additional finance needs (AFN) are the additional funds the company needs if the increase in assets required to finance the increase in sales is greater than the spontaneously generated funds produced from the sales increase.
- The equation approach is another method used to estimate the AFN.
- The maximum internal growth rate is the growth the firm can achieve without recourse to external funds.
- The maximum sustainable growth rate is the rate that can be achieved without recourse to additional equity financing, while keeping a constant debt:equity ratio.
- The weakness of accounting-based management is that it is based on accounting concepts and this approach can fail to maximise shareholder value.
- The objective of financial management is to maximise shareholder value rather than maximising profits.
- Specifically, shareholder value is maximised by maximising the company's free cash flows (FCF). FCF is the most important determinant of shareholder value. Free cash flow is what is available for distribution to shareholders and lenders after the company has made all the reinvestment in working capital and fixed assets necessary to maintain the business.

- Shareholder value is created when the actual rate of return is greater than the required rate of return (positive investment spread). Shareholder value is destroyed when the actual rate of return is less than the required rate of return (negative investment spread).
- Economic value added focuses on adjusted accounting information rather than cash flows. EVA is defined as NOPAT *minus* WACC.
- Market value added is the market value of equity *minus* the capital supplied by shareholders.

WEB LINKS

www.businessfinancemag.com
For budgeting and reporting.

www.sternstewart.com
A look at EVA. Which companies earn less than their cost at capital?

www.jaxworks.com/zscore2.htm
For business planning; the small-business spreadsheet factory.

QUESTIONS

1. Describe pro forma financial statements and explain the use of pro forma statements in creating shareholder value. Why is forecasting necessary?
2. Explain the term 'competitive advantage period'. Is it possible to have positive NPV where it has no competitive advantage?
3. Outline the deficiencies in accounting-based management as a performance measure.
4. ✦ Companies can grow too fast. Explain.
5. Explain the terms 'maximum internal growth rate' and 'maximum sustainable growth rates'.
6. Financial plans have qualitative and quantitative inputs. Explain.
7. The sales forecast is the most important input in financial plans. Why?
8. Explain the terms 'spontaneously generated funds' and 'AFN'.
9. What is value-based management?
10. ✦ The following are the summarised financial statements of XYZ Ltd for the year ended 2007:

Profit & loss account	
Turnover	€20,000
Costs	€16,000
Profit before tax	€4,000
Tax (20%)	€800
Profit after tax	€3,200
Dividends	€500
Retained earnings	€2,700

Balance sheet	
Assets	€140,000
Financed by	
debt	€28,000
Equity	€112,000
	€140,000

Sales for the year are expected to be €23,000. Calculate the additional financial needs based on the following assumptions:

(a) The company wishes to maintain a constant payout ratio.

(b) Both assets and costs are directly proportional to sales.

11. The following is a list of assets and liabilities of Coolroe Ltd and its profit and loss account for year end 2008.

Assets	
Fixed assets	€6,000
Current assets	€1,050
Total assets	€7,050
Liabilities	
Creditors	€300
Short-term loans	€60
Debentures	€4,500
Ord. shareholders' funds	€900
Retained earnings	€1,290

Sales for the year were €3,000 and they are expected to grow by 50% during 2009 and operating costs should increase at the same rate. The net profit margin is 14.8% and the company has a policy of paying out 50% of its profit for ordinary shareholders. The company can expand its sales to grow without further investment in fixed assets. Net current assets should increase at the same rate as sales.

Calculate the additional finance needs using balance sheet method.

12.♦ Explain how the capital intensity ratio affects the AFN.

13. What are the weaknesses in using the AFN formula in forecasting financial requirements?

14.♦ The following is the balance sheet of Clashmore Ltd for the year ended 2007:

Fixed assets	€100,00
Current assets	€75,00
Total	€175,000
Financed by	
Creditors	€10,000
Short-term loans	€5,000
Ord. shares	€160,000
	€175,000

All of the company's profit for ordinary shareholders is paid out as dividends and the company has excess capacity. Sales for 2007 were €175,000 with a net income of €35,000. Sales for 2008 are expected to be €350,000. Calculate the AFN for 2008. Assume that the short-term debt is paid off during the year.

15. Sales for Ring Ltd last year were €1m. The ratio of required assets to sales is 2:1. The ratio of liabilities that change spontaneously with sales is 0.6:1. The payout ratio is

50% and the profit margin is 12%. What is the maximum growth rate that Ring Ltd can expect to accomplish without having recourse to non-spontaneous external capital?

16. Dunmore Enterprises is currently not paying dividends. Sales for the year just gone were €20m. Current assets are €4m and current liabilities are €0.6m. Sales are forecasted to increase by 20% next year. What are the additional finance needs (AFN) if the profit margin is 7%?

17. Portlaw Technologies Ltd – summarised income statement and balance sheet
    Using the percentage of sales method prepare a pro forma balance sheet and income statement for December 2008 basing your answer on the following assumptions:

Profit & loss acc. for year ended 31 Dec. 2007		
Turnover	€504,000
Operating costs	€454,160
PBIT	€4,9840
Interest	€7,840
PBT	€42,000
Tax (20%)	€8,400
PAT	€33,600
Dividends (40%)	€13,440
Retained earnings	€20,160

Balance sheet for year end 2007		
Fixed assets (net book value)		€176,400
Current assets		
Debtors	€90,720	
Stocks	€126,000	
Cash	€15,120	
		€231,840
		€408,240
less Current liabilities		
Creditors	€60,480	
Prepayments	€40,320	
Short-term loans	€29,400	
		€130,200
Total net assets		€278,040
Financed by		
Debentures	€49,000	
Ord. shareholder funds	€49,000	
Retained earnings	€180,040	
		€278,040

(a) Sales are expected to grow by 20% during 2008.
(b) Assets, spontaneous liabilities and operating costs are expected to increase by the same percentage as sales.
(c) The company is operating at full capacity.
(d) The company has decided to borrow any additional finance as short-term debt.
(e) Interest rates on short-term debt is 5%.
(f) You should incorporate any financing feedbacks into your answer.

18. From the following information calculate (a) the return on equity and (b) the sustainable growth rate.

Net profit	€16,500
Profit margin	8%
Debt:equity ratio	50%
Capital intensity ratio	70%
Dividends	€5,000

19.◆ A firm has been operating successfully (it thinks) and wants to maintain its growth rate of 10% per annum. The ratio of total assets to sales is 170% and it has a net profit margin of 5%. Its total assets are financed with 40% debt in its capital structure. Advise the company on its growth rate.

NOTES

1. Remember that the equity multiplier is

$$\frac{\text{Total assets}}{\text{Total equity}} = \frac{1}{0.6} = 1.66$$

   The debt:equity ratio is: $\dfrac{0.4}{0.6} = 0.66$

   Therefore $1 + 0.66 = 1.66 = $ Equity multiplier

2. This is the accruals concept underlying financial accounting.
3. Investment ratios are discussed in Chapter 14.
4. This particular fact was extracted from an article titled 'A Star to Sail by', *The Economist*, 2 August 1997.
5. There are different methods of calculating free cash flow. The method used here is that used by Brigham, Gapenski and Ehrhardt, *Financial Management: Theory and Practice*.
6. When companies consolidate subsidiaries that are not wholly owned, some of the profits shown on the profit and loss account do not belong to the shareholders. That part of the profits that does not belong to the parent company's shareholders is shown as minority interests.

12

Investment Appraisal

CHAPTER OBJECTIVES

At the end of this chapter the student should be able to:
1. identify the drawbacks and attractions of the main techniques available to appraise capital investment projects
2. appreciate why discounted cash flow methods are preferred to payback and accounting rate of return
3. explain why net present value is preferred to internal rate of return from an academic point of view
4. have an awareness of the empirical evidence of the techniques used in practice
5. understand the concept of capital rationing and the use of the profitability index
6. know when to use nominal discount rates and real discount rates on cash flow projections
7. incorporate risk into the investment appraisal decision
8. know how to deal with taxation liabilities and benefits
9. evaluate asset replacement decisions for projects with unequal project lives
10. appreciate the different reasons for, and methods of, international investment
11. understand the types of real option that might be embedded in a capital investment decision.

INTRODUCTION

From an investor's perspective, investment can be defined as any application of funds which is intended to provide a return by way of interest, dividend or capital appreciation; whereas viewed from a business perspective it is an outlay of cash now, in return for cash inflows over future periods. The allocation of funds among alternative investment projects is a crucial decision for a company. Investment opportunities often involve major funding and influence the future profitability of the company. A capital investment project is a proposed investment in a long-term asset. Examples include the purchase of new buildings and equipment, expenditure on research and development programmes, asset replacement decisions, etc.

Investment appraisal is the evaluation of proposed investment projects involving capital expenditure. The purpose of investment appraisal is to make a decision about whether the capital expenditure is worthwhile and whether the investment project should be undertaken. Investment appraisal or capital budgeting techniques are used to evaluate proposed projects and in this chapter we will look at these appraisal techniques including the payback period, the discounted payback period, the accounting rate of return, the net present value, the profitability index and the internal rate of return. After assessing the techniques available we will look at their application and the impact of inflation, taxation and risk.

Before looking at the various techniques available it is important to look at the capital budgeting process and this can be divided into six stages.

1. **Identification.** This involves searching for possible projects that the company could undertake and the initial screening of such projects to identify likely candidates. Factors such as the amount of expenditure involved, associated risks, strategic fit and management competence in the business area would all be looked at before the short-listed projects would qualify for further analysis. It may also involve a search within the company to identify opportunities for efficiencies.
2. **Estimating cash flows.** This stage requires estimates of projected cash flows related to the project and would involve forecasts of many variables such as demand, price, variable cost, fixed cost, depreciation charges allowable, corporate tax rates, etc.
3. **Evaluation.** At this stage the various appraisal techniques are used in the evaluation process. Where the objective of the business is to maximise shareholder wealth the net present value method of investment appraisal is the most suitable.
4. **Selection.** This process involves decision-making for the selection committee based on information on the level of risk inherent in the project, the finance available, the appraisal technique used and the type of project.
5. **Funding.** The company needs to identify how to finance the project selected. This involves selecting an appropriate source of finance to suit the timeframe of the project and how it fits with the company existing capital structure. This area is addressed in Chapter 13.
6. **Post-audit.** The last stage is an important one and reviews the performance of the projects adopted. Cash flow variances are assessed based on actual versus forecasted. This continuous monitoring of projects determines if they should be continued or abandoned by the company.

Projects that were rejected previously can be reassessed, to see if they are now viable. This could be based on more favourable economic conditions prevailing or less capital rationing, etc.

The quantitative assessment of projects is just the culmination of the process of identifying possible projects. The company should formulate a strategic plan to identify the direction in which the company needs to go, in terms of products, markets, financing, etc., to best generate profitable investment opportunities. This process requires considerable management talent.

In this chapter we will concentrate on the appraisal techniques involved and how they are applied to projected cash flow forecasts, starting with payback.

12.1 Payback

The payback period is the time that it takes cash inflows from an investment project to equal cash outflows and is usually expressed in years. **Payback is measured by cash flows and not profits.** When deciding between two or more competing projects which are mutually exclusive (only one can be chosen), the decision rule is to accept the one with the shorter payback. Companies who have a target payback would reject a project unless its payback period is less than a target number of years.

Example 12.1 Payback

A company is faced with two **mutually exclusive** projects with the following forecasted cash flows in €s.

	Project A Cash flow	Project A Cumulative	Project B Cash flow	Project B Cumulative
Year 0	(60,000)	(60,000)	(60,000)	(60,000)
Year 1	20,000	(40,000)	50,000	(10,000)
Year 2	50,000	10,000	20,000	10,000
Year 3	40,000	50,000	10,000	20,000
Year 4	50,000	100,000	5,000	25,000
Payback		1.8 years		1.5 years

The payback period for both project **A** and project **B** is less than two years. Payback period for **A** occurs in $1 + 40/50 = 1.8$ years and for **B** in $1 + 10/20 = 1.5$ years.

Strengths
- Payback is easy to calculate, understand and communicate.
- It has an implicit assumption that the risks of cash flow forecasts are directly related to the length of time into the future. If funds are limited there is an advantage to receiving returns earlier and the payback method focuses on the early years.
- Finally, the payback method is one of the most common initial methods of investment appraisal in use, because companies place a major emphasis on liquidity. It is not, however, often used exclusively but rather as a screening method or in conjunction with other techniques.

Weaknesses
- It does not take into account the time value of money. In our example above, most of project **B** is paid back in year 1, while in the case of **A** it is delayed until year 2.
- Cash inflow beyond the payback period is ignored altogether and in the example above project **A** has substantial cash inflows after year 2.
- A final weakness relates to the selection of the payback duration, which can be an arbitrary decision without theoretical foundation.

12.2 Accounting rate of return (ARR)

ARR is also known as the **return on capital employed (ROCE),** or the **return on investment (ROI)** and expresses the accounting **profits** from a project as a percentage of the capital cost. The decision rule is that if the ARR of the project is greater than the company target rate the project is acceptable. The ratio can be calculated in a number of ways with the most common method having the following definition.

$$\text{ARR} = \frac{\text{Average annual accounting profit}}{\text{Initial capital cost}} \times 100\% \qquad (12.1)$$

Accounting profit is based on profit before interest and tax after depreciation. Accounting profits are not the same as cash flows, since depreciation is an accounting adjustment and not an annual movement of cash.

   If we use project A above and assume a depreciation charge of €15,000 per annum, then average annual profit is (5 + 35 + 25 + 35)/4 in €000s, i.e. €25,000

$$\text{ARR} = \frac{€25,000}{€60,000} \times 100\% = 41.67\%$$

Another measure of ARR is $\dfrac{\text{Average annual accounting profit}}{\text{Average capital invested}} \times 100 \qquad (12.2)$

Here the ARR is $\dfrac{€25,000}{€30,000} \times 100\% = 83.33\%$

Average capital invested is simply based on half of the initial investment. If a scrap value exists at the end of the project, then the average capital invested becomes (initial outlay + scrap value)/2, using straight-line depreciation.

Strengths
- The ARR technique is easy to calculate, managers are familiar with this form of profitability measure and unlike the payback method it looks at the full life of the investment.

Weaknesses
- The different definitions that exist for profits and assets are a weakness of ARR and may tempt management to manipulate the technique to suit their purposes.
- It fails to take account of the timing of profits within the project's life and again the cut-off or hurdle rate is an arbitrary decision. ARR is not based on cash, but on accounting profit and profit figures are not as transparent as cash flow. Cash is what ultimately counts and profits are only a guide to cash availability.
- A decision has to be made about what the minimum target ARR should be. There is no rational economic basis for setting this target and it will usually be a subjective decision.

Both payback and ARR suffer a major weakness in not taking into account the time value of money, the effect of which can be stated as the following general rule:

There is a time preference for receiving the same sum of money sooner rather than later. Conversely, there is a time preference for paying the same sum of money later rather than sooner.

The reasons for time preference are threefold:
Consumption preference – money received now can be spent on consumption.
Risk preference – risk disappears once money is received.
Investment preference – money received can be invested now.

Discounted cash flow (DCF) is an investment appraisal technique, which takes into account the time value of money and the cash flows over the entire life of the project. Discounting is the reverse of compounding which is a concept based on finding the future value of a sum of money invested at a given rate of return for a number of years. Although covered in Chapter 4, a quick reminder using the following example illustrates the technique.

Example 12.2 Discounting

If you invest €10,000 at 10% for four years, what will the future value of the investment be worth?

Solution

$$FV = PV \, (1 + r)^n \tag{12.3}$$

where **FV** is the future value, **PV** is the present value, **r** is the rate of return and **n** is the number of years or time periods.
   In this case the future value = €10,000$(1 + 0.1)^4$ = €10,000 × 1.4641 = €14,641 where 1.4641 is the compound factor.

Box 12.1 Money and time

If you invested €100 for 200 years at 8% per annum, what do you think the investment would be worth?

$$€100 \times 1.08^{200} = €100 \times 4{,}838{,}949.585 = €483{,}894{,}958.50$$

i.e. nearly €484 million! Unfortunately you will not be around to enjoy it!

The basic principle of discounting is finding the present value of a future sum of money if a certain rate is available. Using the last example, try to find the present value of €14,641 in four years' time when rates are 10% per annum.

In this case the **present value** = $FV \, (1 + r)^{-n}$ or $\dfrac{FV}{(1 + r)^n}$ $\qquad$ (12.4) and instead of a compound factor we have a **discount factor** of $(1 + 0.10)^{-4} = 0.6830$ to four decimals. These discount factors are easily found in the present value **discount tables** provided at the end of the textbook.

Present value = €14,641 $(1 + 0.1)^{-4}$ = €14,641 × 0.6830 = €10,000 approximately.

Two of the most important measures of investment appraisal using DCF techniques are the Net Present Value (**NPV**) and Internal Rate of Return (**IRR**). Both of these techniques are derived from the theories of two economists, namely Irving Fisher and John Maynard Keynes.

12.3 Net Present Value (NPV)

The NPV method works out the present values of all cash inflows and outflows of an investment at a given target rate of return or cost of capital, and then works out a net total. A positive NPV indicates that an investment is expected to give a return in excess of the cost of capital and will therefore lead to an increase in shareholder wealth. Cost of capital, put simply, is the opportunity cost of funds used to finance the project. The decision rule here is **projects with a positive NPV are deemed acceptable or viable**. Projects that exhibit a negative NPV are considered to be unacceptable. The NPV is also a measure of the value of a company. For example, if a company invests in a project that has an NPV of €3.5 million, then the value of the company should increase by €3.5 million.

In DCF analysis all cash flows are assumed to occur at the end of the year. If a cash flow occurs early during a particular year, it is assumed that it will occur at the end of the previous year.

Example 12.3 Net present value

Find the NPV of the following cash flows if the company's target rate of return is 19%.

Year	Cash flow
0	(€20,000)
1	€6,000
2	€6,000
3	€6,000
4	€6,000

Solution

1 Year (n)	2 Cash flow	3 19% Discount factor	2 x 3 Present value
0	(€20,000)	$(1 + 0.19)^0 = 1$	(€20,000)
1	€6,000	$(1 + 0.19)^{-0} = 0.8403$	€5041.8
2	€6,000	$(1 + 0.19)^{-2} = 0.7062$	€4237.2
3	€6,000	$(1 + 0.19)^{-3} = 0.5934$	€3560.4
4	€6,000	$(1 + 0.19)^{-4} = 0.4987$	€2992.2
		Net Present Value =	(€4,168.40)

The net present value is negative with a value of (€4,168.4).

The present value of the outflow exceeds the present value of the inflows resulting in a negative NPV of €4,168.4. The project is not viable, as the return on the €20,000 is less than 19%.

If a company has a choice of projects which are mutually exclusive, **the project with the highest NPV should be chosen.**

An **annuity** is a constant cash flow over a number of time periods. In the example above the cash inflows are in annuity form and instead of using a separate discount factor for each cash inflow, a compound factor or an annuity factor can be used. The formula for an annuity factor is given below

$$\text{Annuity discount factor} = \frac{1 - (1 + r)^{-n}}{r} \qquad (12.5)$$

where **r** is the discount rate and **n** is the number of time periods. **Annuity discount tables** are also available at the back of the book.

If the annuity is a **perpetuity,** i.e. a constant cash flow that lasts for ever, the discount factor tends in the limit to r^{-1}.

$$\text{Perpetuity discount factor} = 1/r \text{ or } r^{-1} \qquad (12.6)$$

In the example above the cash flows can be rewritten as

Year	Cash flow	19% Discount factor	Present value
0	(€20,000)	1.000	(€20,000)
1 to 4	€6,000	$\dfrac{1 - (1 + 0.19)^{-4}}{0.19} = 2.639$	
			€15,832
		Net present value	(€4,168)

Strengths
- The NPV takes into account the time value of money and the discount rate can be adjusted to reflect the level of risk associated with the cash flows explicitly.
- It is expressed in today's money terms and can be used to assess the value of the investment project.
- The NPV uses cash flow rather than accounting profits over the entire life of the project.

Because of these advantages NPV is the academically preferred method of investment appraisal.

Weaknesses
- Net present value is not as easily understood as payback or ARR.
- A more fundamental criticism relates to the discount factor used. The company's cost of capital is normally used as a basis for the discount factor. The company's cost of

capital may be difficult to find (see Chapter 13) and may change over the life of the project.

12.4 Internal rate of return (IRR)

This is an alternative to the NPV method of investment appraisal. The NPV method determines whether the investment earns a positive or negative NPV when discounted at the company's target rate of return. If the NPV is zero, the return for the project is the same as the discount factor and this is what the IRR method tries to find. The IRR method tries to find the discount factor that gives an NPV of zero, i.e. it tries to find the rate of return on an investment.

The decision rule is that **if the IRR exceeds the company's target rate of return the project is viable**. The IRR method, also known as the DCF yield method, involves finding two NPVs at two discount rates and then using a linear interpolation technique to find an approximate IRR. The process is illustrated in the following example.

Example 12.4 Internal rate of return

Estimate the IRR for the following project using an initial discount rate of 12%.

Year	Cash flow	Discount factor 12%	Present value
0	(€75,000)	1.000	(€75,000)
1	€20,000	0.893	€17,860
2	€30,000	0.797	€23,910
3	€50,000	0.712	€35,600
		Net Present Value =	€2,370

The positive NPV indicates that the return on this investment is greater than the discount rate (12%), so the IRR of this project must be greater than 12%.

0	(€75,000)	1.000	(€75,000)
1	€20,000	0.877	€17,540
2	€30,000	0.769	€23,070
3	€50,000	0.675	€33,750
		Net Present Value =	(€640)

Now let us try a higher discount rate, 14% for example.

The negative NPV indicates that the IRR is lower than the discount rate (14%) and so the IRR must lie somewhere between 12% and 14%.

There is an interpolation formula based on the two discount rates and the two NPVs found that gives an approximate value of the IRR.

Internal rate of return approximation

$$a + \frac{AX}{(A - B)} \times (b - a) \% \qquad (12.7)$$

where   **a** = lower discount rate   **A** = NPV at the lower discount rate
             b = higher discount rate   **B** = NPV at the higher discount rate

In the example above **a** =12%, **b** = 14%, **A** = €2370 and **B** = (€640).

$$IRR = 12\% + \frac{2{,}370}{(2{,}370 + 640)} \times (14 - 12)\% = 13.6\%$$

If this IRR is above the company's target rate of return, the project will be accepted.

The interpolation formula assumes a linear relationship between the discount rate and the NPV. In calculating the two values for NPV, the closer they are to the actual IRR, the more accurate the interpolation approximation becomes. If the two discount factors used lead to negative NPVs or result in two positive NPVs, the interpolation formula will still work.

It is important to remember that the IRR calculated using the interpolation formula is only an approximation of the true IRR.

The following diagram illustrates this fact.

Figure 12.1 IRR as an approximation

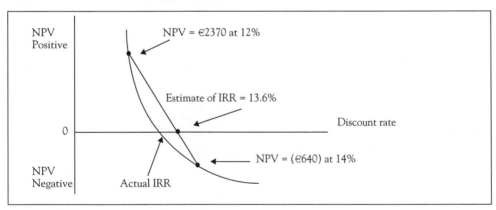

The diagram above shows that the IRR calculated using two discount factors and associated NPVs gives only an approximate value of the true IRR. The interpolation technique is a linear approximation whereas the relationship is in fact curve-like. A statistical computer package or spreadsheet package can easily perform the calculations necessary to get an accurate NPV or IRR.

Strengths
- Like the NPV method the IRR considers both the magnitude and the timing of the project's cash flows over the entire life of the project.
- The IRR is measured as a percentage, which is easy to understand.

Weaknesses

• There are, however, serious disadvantages concerning the IRR method, which the following four examples illustrate.

1. It ignores the relative size or scale of investments. Both of the following investments have an IRR or DCF yield of 18%.

	Project A	Project B
Cost in year 0	(€3.5 million)	(€350,000)
Cash inflow years 1–6	€1 million	€100,000

Project A is ten times as big and more profitable, but on the basis of an IRR of 18% they are both equal.

2. More than one IRR may result if the cash flows from projects are 'not conventional'. Most projects have **conventional cash flows** that consist of an initial negative cash flow followed by positive cash inflows in later time periods. If negative cash flows arise in later time periods, multiple IRRs may occur.

   The following cash flows are non-conventional and give two values (5% and 50%) for IRR.

Year	Cash flow
0	(€400)
1	€1,020
2	(€630)

There will be as many IRR rates as there are changes in the direction of cash flows. The NPV method can accommodate non-conventional cash flows whereas the IRR cannot.

3. The IRR cannot accommodate changes in the discount rate over the life of the project whereas the NPV method can. This is another reason why the NPV is the preferred method of investment appraisal.

4. The **IRR method should not be used to assess mutually exclusive projects**, as the IRR assumes the rate at which funds generated by the projects can be reinvested is the same rate as the IRR. This is an unrealistic assumption in many cases. NPV assumes reinvestment can occur at the company's cost of capital, which is a more realistic assumption. When mutually exclusive projects are available, the IRR of the **incremental cash flows** can be used to decide which project to accept.

Example 12.5 Incremental cash flow

Two mutually exclusive projects have the following cash flow forecasts.

Year	Project A	Project B
0	(€10,200)	(€35,250)
1	€6,000	€18,000
2	€5,000	€15,000
3	€3,000	€15,000

At a cost of capital of 16%, the NPV for project A is €610, and project B is €1,026.

However, the IRR is 20% for project A and only 18% for project B.

Using NPV criteria project B would be chosen and using IRR criteria project A would be chosen. However, to make a rational decision it is necessary to calculate the **incremental cash flows** and discount these at the company's cost of capital.

Solution
The incremental cash flows are

Year	Project A	Project B	Incremental cash flow
0	(€10,200)	(€35,250)	(€25,050)
1	€6,000	€18,000	€12,000
2	€5,000	€15,000	€10,000
3	€3,000	€15,000	€12,000

The NPV of the incremental cash flows at 16% is €416, which means it is worth investing the extra amount involved in project B, to get the extra benefit.

In this example the IRR of the incremental cash flows is over 17%, which again indicates that project B is preferred.

When projects are mutually exclusive, the NPV is a better criterion for making investment decisions and the simple decision rule is to accept the project with the highest NPV.

If the IRR method of investment appraisal is used, you must also find the IRR of the incremental cash flows to make the correct evaluation.

12.5 Spreadsheet solutions

Below is an extract from an Excel spreadsheet showing how to input cash flows relating to a project to find the net present value. The example is of a four-year project with a discount factor of 15%.

Table 12.1 Spreadsheet calculation of NPV

1	A	B
2	Year	€ Cash flow
3	0	−100,000
4	1	60,000
5	2	80,000
6	3	40,000
7	4	30,000
8	NPV	€56,119

The cell with the solution (B8) contains the formula = NPV(15%,B3:B7).

Spreadsheets take out all the hard work associated with DCF calculations.

The same investment example can be used to show how easy it is to calculate the IRR of a project. In Excel all you do is input =IRR(B3:B7) into cell B8 and the result is given immediately.

Table 12.2 Spreadsheet calculation of IRR

1	A	B
2	Year	€ Cash flow
3	0	−100,000
4	1	60,000
5	2	80,000
6	3	40,000
7	4	30,000
8	IRR	44.48%

Spreadsheets can be used to carry out all sorts of financial calculations such as annuities, mortgages, etc.

12.6 Profitability index and capital rationing

When a company has insufficient funds available for investment in projects with a positive NPV, the company is said to be in a capital-rationing situation.

If the limitation on available funds is external to the firm this is called **hard capital rationing**, for example the inability of the company to obtain funds from existing shareholders or financial markets.

If the restriction is internally imposed, this is known as **soft capital rationing**. Management may not want to raise more capital so as not to undertake projects which could overstretch the company's existing resources.

When this occurs absolute NPV cannot be used to rank the better projects, because a project with a large NPV would be ranked ahead of a combination of smaller projects, which together would collectively offer a higher NPV. A more appropriate technique to adopt here is the **profitability index**, which shows NPV per €1 of scarce capital.

The profitability index assumes that projects cannot be deferred to a subsequent time, projects are divisible (portions of projects can be undertaken) and capital is rationed in the initial period only. The index shows how much is received in present value terms per € invested.

$$\text{Profitability index} = \frac{\textbf{Present value of future cash flow}}{\textbf{Value of initial investment}} \qquad (12.8)$$

If there is no capital rationing then all projects with a ratio greater than one should be accepted. This is consistent with a positive NPV.

If capital rationing exists and projects are **divisible**, then projects should be ranked according to their profitability index. Those projects with the **highest ranking** should be undertaken before those with a lower ranking, until the available funds are depleted.

If the projects are **not divisible**, then the projects should be looked at differently. The selection of projects should be based on the combination of projects giving the highest NPV within the budget available.

Example 12.6 Profitability index

A company has maximum funds available of €1,500 and the following projects are to be considered:

Project	A	B	C	D
Initial Cost	€500	€600	€700	€800
PV future cash flow	€1100	€1300	€1500	€1550
NPV	€600	€700	€800	€750
Profitability Index	2.2	2.17	2.14	1.94
Ranking by NPV	4	3	1	2
Ranking by PI	1	2	3	4

Which investments should be chosen if the investments are: (a) divisible, and (b) non-divisible?

Solution

(a) If we assume that investments are divisible, the optimum investment is all of projects A and B and 57% (i.e. 400/700) of project C. The combined investment of €1,500 is made up of €500 in A, €600 in B and €400 in part of project C. The total NPV is €1,757, which is better than just C and D with a total NPV of €1,550.

(b) If the projects are not divisible the optimum choice would be projects C and D as they would give the highest total NPV and use up all available capital.

The above capital rationing examples assume that funds are limited initially for **single period** only. If this were not the case, the problem becomes more complex and involves the application of **multiple-period** linear programming techniques.

Multiple-period capital rationing implies that funds are limited over a number of years and the company may be faced with a choice of investments. Linear programming is a technique for solving such problems.

Example 12.7 Multiple-period capital rationing

Suppose a company is considering four investment projects and has a required rate of return of 12%. The cost commitments and NPVs associated with the four projects are as follows (all figures are in € millions)

Time	Project 1	Project 2	Project 3	Project 4
0	(22)	(17)	(8)	(3)
1	(10)	(4)	(2)	(3)
2	(10)	(7)	(3)	(5)
3	(12)	(7)	(8)	(6)
NPV	22.44	11.1	16.45	24.39

If we assume the company has €15 million, €14 million, €16 million and €20 million available in each of the next four years, the following linear programming model can be formulated.

Let a = the number of units of project 1 that are accepted
        b = the number of units of project 2 that are accepted
        c = the number of units of project 3 that are accepted
        d = the number of units of project 4 that are accepted

Maximise $22.44a + 11.1b + 16.45c + 24.39d$ (in NPV)
Subject to: $22a + 17b + 8c + 3d \leq 15$
                $10a + 4b + 2c + 3d \leq 14$
                $10a + 7b + 3c + 5d \leq 16$
                $12a + 7b + 8c + 6d \leq 20$

where a, b, c and d satisfy the non-negativity constraint.

This problem can be solved using what is known as the **simplex technique**. If this procedure were applied the solution to this problem would be $a = 0$, $b = 0$, $c = 0.1818$ and $d = 3.0909$. This is interpreted as follows: 'Do not invest in projects 1 or 2, invest in 0.1818 of a unit in project 3 and 3.0909 units of project 4.' The NPV that corresponds to this solution is $(16.45)(0.1818) + (24.39)(3.0909)$ = €78.378 million. If the restrictive assumptions of projects being divisible and undertaken more than once are relaxed, the solution to this problem becomes more complicated and is beyond the scope of this text.

12.7 Relevant and irrelevant costs

We are now in a position to apply the techniques learned, but before applying these, it is important to look at the cash flows that are relevant to the appraisal. The concept of cash flow is critical.

The real cost to a business of any new project is the actual net amount of cash that flows out of the business as a result of the investment decision. The real return is the actual amount of cash which is earned for the business from the project during its life.

The cash flows to be considered are those which arise as a consequence of a decision. It therefore follows that any costs incurred in the past, or any committed costs, which will be incurred regardless of whether or not a project is undertaken, are **irrelevant** items and should be **excluded.**

Examples of items to **exclude** are as follows:

- **Depreciation** is a purely accounting expense – it is not a cash flow. It represents an accounting regulation, whereby the cost of a capital asset is charged to profit as it is used up rather than as it is paid for. This is not a cash flow and any depreciation charges should be excluded from calculations. So if profit figures after depreciation are given, the profit needs to be increased by adding back the depreciation charge to get to a cash approximation.
- **Apportioned fixed costs** – production costs may include an apportionment of factory or other fixed costs using some standard basis for absorption. These should be excluded as they do not arise directly from the project, i.e. they are not relevant. Fixed costs may appear in cash flow calculations only if it is known that they will increase directly as a result of accepting the project. These relevant fixed costs are normally referred to as incremental fixed costs.
- **Interest payments** – in most cases it can be assumed that the cost of interest has already been taken into account in the discounting process as the discount factor should reflect the cost of funds for the company. The same applies to the cost of dividend payments.
- **Book value of assets** – these are not cash flows and fall into the same category as depreciation. The relevant value of an existing fixed asset is the sale value.
- **Sunk costs** – these are costs already incurred and should be ignored, as they are not affected by and do not vary with the investment decision about to be undertaken.

The **relevant costs** and benefits required for decision-making are only those that will be affected by the decision. These are the future cash flows, which will differ between the various alternatives being considered. These **differential or incremental cash flows** should be taken into account and cash flows that are that will be the same for all alternatives are irrelevant.

Relevant costs include:

- **Incremental working capital** related to the project, such as increased levels of stock, debtors and trade creditors, which represent a cash outflow, must be included in the investment appraisal. At the end of the project these levels will fall and any investment in working capital will be recovered and this cash flow must be accounted for.

- The **opportunity cost** of using an asset for one purpose rather than another. For example using raw materials, already available in stock, in the new project, which could have been used elsewhere.

In cash flow calculations the various cash flows are assumed to occur at the end of the time period in which they arise. For example, if revenues are earned or costs incurred throughout the course of a year, they are assumed to occur at the end of the year in question. Making this assumption of treating cash flows later than they actually occur introduces a bias, which tends to understate the NPV, as future cash flows tend to be inflows. If cash flows occur at the beginning of a year they are assumed to occur at the end of the previous year. However, using a spreadsheet package, there is nothing difficult in timing the cash flows in intervals of months, weeks or days.

Finally, when a company has already started a project and wants to establish whether it should abandon the project during its life, the only relevant costs are future costs related to the decision to abandon. Past costs are again irrelevant to any decision regarding the future of the project. Management is often reluctant to abandon a project, as it may reflect a poor past decision. However if it was a bad decision, it would even be worse to compound the mistake by making another bad decision. Projects must therefore be continuously monitored and kept under review.

Example 12.8 Investment appraisal application

Scribes plc has over the past four years spent €3 million on the development of a new silicon chip and is now considering whether to manufacture this silicon chip. An initial investment of €5 million in plant and machinery will be needed at the end of December this year. Additional working capital of €2.1 million will be required when production starts in early January. Sales and selling prices are expected to be as follows:

Year	1	2	3	4	5
Sales (000s of units)	100	100	100	80	80
Price per unit €	120	120	120	100	90

The company depreciates plant and machinery over five years, using the straight-line method and assumes a zero scrap value. Variable costs per unit are expected to be €65. Fixed costs, including depreciation, are €3 million per year. Assume all revenues and costs occur at the end of the year in question.

(a) Calculate the cash flows relevant to a decision to manufacture the silicon chips, assuming it is now December.

Solution
The €3 million already invested in the development of the silicon chip is an irrelevant cost.

The cash outflow now is €7.1 million. This is made up of €5 million in plant and machinery and €2.1 million in working capital. The end of December and early January can be considered as the same time period and as they both occur at the start of the project they can be considered to occur in time period zero.

The recovery of working capital of €2.1 million is entered as a cash inflow at the end of year 5.

Fixed costs are €3 million less a depreciation charge of €1 million per annum over the five years, i.e. €2 million cash outflow.

The contribution each year is (price − variable cost)(sales units). In the case of year 1 the contribution is (€120 − €65)(100,000) = €5,500,000.

All figures in € million.

Year	0	1	2	3	4	5
Total Contribution	0	5.5	5.5	5.5	2.8	2
Less fixed costs		(2)	(2)	(2)	(2)	(2)
Profit		3.5	3.5	3.5	0.8	0
Plant and equipment	(5)					
Working capital	(2.1)				2.1	
Net cash flow	(7.1)	3.5	3.5	3.5	0.8	2.1

Developing the example above further, suppose Scribes plc has a second option for this silicon chip project.

Option 2: Sell the know-how associated with the development of the silicon chip for a royalty of €10 per unit to another company. If this second option is taken, the company will not manufacture the chips itself. Assume the anticipated sales are the same as above. The company discounts projects at the WACC, which is 12%. Assume all revenues and costs occur at the end of the year in question.

(b) Calculate the net present value of each option.

Solution
Option 1

Year	€ million	Discount @ 12%	Present value
0	(7.1)	1.000	(7.1)
1	3.5	0.893	3.126
2	3.5	0.797	2.790
3	3.5	0.712	2.492
4	0.8	0.636	0.509
5	2.1	0.567	1.191
			€3.008 million

The NPV of the net cash flows above at 12% is €3.008 million.

Net cash flow for **Option 2** is just sales in units by €10 per unit. There is no initial investment in plant and machinery and no working capital necessary.

Year	1	2	3	4	5
Total royalty in €million	1	1	1	0.8	0.8

The present value of these cash inflows at 12% is €3.364 million.

The option with the higher present value is **option 2** and using NPV decision-making criteria, option 2 should be chosen.

12.8 Inflation and investment appraisal

Inflation generally alters the cash flows associated with projects by reducing the real value of future cash flows and increasing their uncertainty. There are two approaches appropriate to dealing with inflation.

1. Adjust future cash flows to reflect inflationary impact to find the nominal or money values and discount these nominal values at the nominal cost of capital.
2. Deflate the nominal cash flows by the inflation rate to express cash flows in real terms (adjusted for inflation) and discount these real cash flows at the real cost of capital.

The real cost of capital (**r**) is the nominal amount adjusted for inflation using the following formula

$$r = \frac{(1 + m)}{(1 + i)} - 1 \qquad (12.9)$$

where **m** and **i** are the money and inflation rates respectively.

Example 12.9 Inflation and investment

A project has the following cash flows before allowing for inflation:

Year	Real cash flow in € millions
0	(7.5)
1	3.3
2	2.42
3	5.32

The discount rate including an allowance of inflation of 5% per annum is 15.5%.

Evaluate the project using the NPV criteria.

Solution
Using nominal values the future cash flows need to be inflated by 5% per annum and then discounted by 15.5% to give a NPV of €1.5 million.

If we are using real values we need to calculate the real discount rate.

$$r = \frac{(1 + 0.155)}{(1 + 0.05)} - 1 = 0.1 \text{ and so r} = 10\%$$

The real cash flows above are then discounted at 10% to give an NPV of €1.5 million. The result is the same in both cases and the project is viable.

Inflation affects costs and revenues differently and this must be taken into account. This is much more easily dealt with using nominal cash flows and discount rates. In a survey carried out by Drury, Braund, Osborne and Tayles on 260 UK manufacturing firms, the majority of companies did not account for inflation appropriately in the investment appraisal process and often got misleading results.

12.9 Taxation and investment appraisal

Taxation plays an in important role in investment decisions with after-tax returns being the decision breaker. Thus, in calculating the cash flows for analysis, taxation flows must be considered. In a comparison of investments, taxation can be ignored if both are subject to the same rules and rates. However, this will not be the case if comparing investments in different regions or types of business. It is useful therefore to have some knowledge of how corporation tax systems work in terms of how the tax liability is calculated and the rates to which it is subject. A detailed list of international tax systems is beyond the scope of this text but let us look at the Irish system in brief.

Capital gains are taxed differently from revenue gains/profits. Capital gains are taxable at 25%, after allowing deductions for acquisition cost, improvements and disposal costs, as adjusted for inflation, over the life of the asset (up to December 2001, no relief for inflation thereafter).

Revenue gains are taxable at a standard rate of 12.5 % (with the exception of certain 'exempted' trades, taxable at 25%) after deduction of all revenue expenses which can be shown to be 'wholly and exclusively incurred for the purposes of the trade', provided not prohibited by statute. Accounting depreciation is never allowable and no deduction is available for capital expenditure, with the exception of relief in the form of 'capital allowances' given only on certain very specific types of capital expenditure as follows:

Expenditure	Plant and machinery	Industrial buildings	Hotels buildings	Farm
Annual capital allowance (straight line)	12.5% of cost	4% of cost	4% of cost	15% of cost

However, on sale of an asset on which capital allowances have been claimed, a balancing allowance or charge must be calculated. This is the difference between the tax written down value (TWDV) (cost − allowances claimed) and the sales proceeds. If positive − an additional allowance is available; if negative − a clawback of allowances previously claimed is made.

The impact of the above on cash flows means that in calculating the tax flows associated with the investment, adjustments must be made to the accounting profit to adjust it for the different treatment of expenses under taxation and accounting rules. It is only then that the appropriate tax rate is applied and the tax liability for inclusion in the cash flows is calculated, e.g. accounting depreciation must always be added back to accounting profit and in its place, if relevant, capital allowances deducted. The appropriate rate is then a function of whether the receipts are capital (25%) or revenue (12.5%/25%) in nature, e.g. sale of investments is taxable at 25% and trading profits are taxable at 12.5%.

Example 12.10 Taxation and capital allowances

A company is considering buying a machine for €200,000. This machine would generate the following pre-tax cash flows from the sale of the resulting goods produced.

Year	1	2	3	4	5	6
Cash flow	€85,000	€65,000	€75,000	€70,000	€50,000	€40,000

The machine will be sold at the end of year 6 for €20,000. Corporation tax is paid at 12.5% per year one year in arrears and the company is able to claim capital allowances at 12.5% on a straight-line basis.
(a) Calculate the capital allowances and tax liability for each year.
(b) If the company, after tax cost of capital is 10%, calculate the NPV of this investment.

Solution
(a) Capital allowances for each year are given on a straight-line basis at 12.5% of cost, i.e. 12.5% of €200,000 = €25,000.
In year 6, a balancing allowance is claimed, i.e. [€200,000 − (€25,000 × 5)] − €20,000 = €55,000. The resulting tax is as follows:

Year	Cash flow	Capital allowance	Tax at 12.5%
1	85,000	(25,000)	(7,500)
2	65,000	(25,000)	(5,000)
3	75,000	(25,000)	(6,250)
4	70,000	(25,000)	(5,625)
5	60,000	(25,000)	(4,375)
6	60,000	(55,000)	(625)

(b) Tax is paid in year 2, based on taxable profit in year 1, and the NPV is calculated as follows:

Year	Cash flow	Tax	Net	10% disc. factor	Present value
0	(200,0000)		(200,000)	1.000	(200,000)
1	85,000		85,000	0.909	77,265
2	65,000	(7,500)	57,500	0.826	47,485
3	75,000	(5,000)	70,000	0.751	52,570
4	70,000	(6,250)	63,750	0.683	43,541
5	60,000	(5,625)	54,375	0.621	33,767
6	60,000	(4,375)	55,625	0.564	31,373
7		(625)	(625)	0.513	(321)
				NPV =	€85,680

Changes in taxation are one of the ways in which governments (through fiscal policy) try to change investment patterns in an economy. Governments can also operate through giving direct grants and having special regional policies to encourage investment in particularly underdeveloped locations, e.g. the Border Midlands and Western (BMW) region, in which various tax incentives are available.

Box 12.2 Investment in mobile phone licences

The bids of more than €50 billion for the next generation of mobile phone licences are already having a damaging impact on world stock market prices. The valuations being attached have not been calculated on the basis of any recognised criteria. There has been no evidence that the assets have been properly valued, that discounted cash flow projections have been employed or that even subjective models of future consumer behaviour have been used to forecast profit, loss and cash flow.

Instead the licences have been bought almost on instinct. It is a huge gamble, perhaps the biggest gamble in the history of capitalism, and it has been a feature of several markets in recent weeks and months – London, Amsterdam and Frankfurt. It is as if conventional means of assessing risk have been thrown out the window.

Editorial comment, *Sunday Business Post*, 27 August 2000

12.10 Asset replacement with unequal lives

If a company has a choice between two machines with different asset lives, then it would be a mistake to simply choose one machine on the basis of net present value alone without considering the timescales of the investments. When choosing between mutually exclusive projects with unequal lives an investment appraisal technique that is often used is the equivalent annual cost method.

$$\text{Equivalent annual cost (EAC)} = \frac{\text{Present value cost over one replacement cycle}}{\text{Annuity factor for that cycle}} \quad (12.10)$$

Example 12.11 Unequal lives

A company has a choice between two machines with unequal lives and the following cash outflows:

Year	Machine A	Machine B
0	(€60,000)	(€75,000)
1	(€15,000)	(€10,000)
2	(€15,000)	(€10,000)
3	(€15,000)	(€10,000)
4		(€10,000)
Present value at 12%	(€96,030)	(€105,370)

Which machine has the lower equivalent annual cost method?

Solution
The cumulative present value factor for three years at 12% is 2.402 and 3.037 for four years.

$$\text{Machine A } \textbf{EAC} = €96{,}030/2.402 = €39{,}979 \text{ and}$$
$$\text{machine B } \textbf{EAC} = €105{,}370/3.037 = €34{,}695.$$

The machine with the lowest equivalent annual cost should be chosen, and machine B in this example is the better choice.

12.11 Lease or buy

Once a decision has been made to acquire an asset for an investment project, a decision has to be made on how to finance it. One of the major choices in financing the asset is whether to lease or buy it.

If the asset is leased, it is never owned by the user company. The implications are that the user receives no written down allowances on the asset but is able to offset the full rental payments against tax. The relevant cash flows would be the lease payments and any tax relief on the lease payments.

If the asset is bought, the user will receive written down allowances on the asset and tax relief for the interest payable on any loan involved. Here the relevant cash flows would be the purchase cost, any residual value and any associated tax implications of the written down allowances. If the investment is approved, the appropriate course for appraisal is to calculate the net present values of the two sets of cash flows associated with leasing and buying and to choose the one with the lower cost.

12.12 Empirical evidence of appraisal techniques

The empirical literature relating to investment evaluation techniques used in business is extensive and the following is a brief summary of the main findings.

1. Payback is the most popular technique used as it focuses on liquidity.
2. The IRR technique is the most commonly used DCF method as it is the most easily understood.
3. Companies prefer to use a combination of payback and DCF.
4. The use of qualitative judgement is an important complement to the quantitative techniques available.
5. The ARR is still very popular despite its limitations.

12.13 Risk and project appraisal

Management do not have precise forecasts about the future cash flows related to a particular project and a certain level of risk exists in all forecasting. Risk describes a situation where there is more than one possible outcome in the future. Risk, however, also implies a likelihood or probability associated with each potential outcome. Risk should not be confused with uncertainty, which implies that it is not possible to assign such probabilities. There are six common methods used to adjust the project appraisal technique and incorporate some form of risk assessment.

1. **Discounted payback:** The payback evaluation technique can be modified, by discounting cash flows at the company's cost of capital, to give a discounted payback timeframe. Consider the payback example again (Example 12.1) and assume a discount factor of 10%. The discounted payback period is now longer for project **A**, reflecting the fact that the significant cash inflows are more distant, whereas the non-discounted payback was under two years. The discounted payback has the same advantages and disadvantages as before, except that the weakness associated of failing to take into account the time value of money is now addressed.

Example 12.12 Discounted payback

Year	Project A €	Project A PV@ 10% D.F.	Project B €	Project B PV@ 10% D.F.
0	(€60,000)	(€60,000)	(€60,000)	(€60,000)
1	€20,000	€18,182	€50,000	€45,456
2	€50,000	€41,322	€20,000	€16,529
3	€40,000	€30,053*	€10,000	€7,513
4	€50,000	€34,151	€5,000	€3,415
Normal payback		1.8 years		1.5 years
Discounted payback		2.017 years		1.88 years

Project **A** now has more than a two-year discounted payback. The discounted payback is found by adding up the present values until the initial investment is recovered. In the case of project **A**, the first two years' present values do not add up to €60,000, i.e. €60,000 − (€18,182 + €41,322) = €596. The payback occurs early in the third year, i.e. 2 years + 596/30,053 = 2.017 years.

(The discounted payback for project B is 1 + (€60,000 − €45,456)/€16,529 = 1.88 years.)

Another term that has become popular in recent years is breakeven time (BET). This is the time from when the initial concept for a new product is approved by management until the time that the discounted cash flows break even. It is considered more important for companies that experience rapid technological change. These companies want to recoup their investments quickly; before the product becomes obsolete (shorter product life cycles have made products obsolete more rapidly). By counting time from the point at which management approves a project, BET penalises project delays to take account of lost opportunities from failing to develop products quickly.

2. **Risk-adjusted discount rate:** This method handles the risk of a project by adjusting the cost of capital or discount rate and using the new rate as the required rate of return on the project. The advantages associated with this technique are:
   - It is easy to understand.
   - Different rates can be applied to different projects exhibiting different risk profiles.
   - It adjusts for the timing of cash flows, while simultaneously incorporating risk into the analysis.

The disadvantage is mainly concerned with the arbitrary/subjective nature of the adjustment process.

Example 12.13 Adjusting the discount rate

Referring back to Example 12.4, in which an IRR was calculated:

Year	Cash flow
0	(€75,000)
1	€20,000
2	€30,000
3	€50,000

The NPV at a discount rate of 12% was a positive score of €2,370 and the project is therefore viable if the company's required rate of return is 12%. Risk could be incorporated into the decision-making process by adjusting the discount rate, for example increasing the discount rate to incorporate a safety cushion for risk. By adding 2% to reflect risk and again appraising the project using the NPV criteria, the result is negative score of (€640) and the company would therefore reject this project.

   The capital asset pricing model can be used to calculate the risk-adjusted discount rate (see Chapter 13).

3. **Certainty equivalents:** This method takes into account the risk of a project by adjusting (multiplying) the expected cash flows, by a factor known as the certainty equivalent (**CE**) coefficient. The CE coefficient has a value between 0 and 1 and the more risky a cash flow the lower will be the CE coefficient. More distant cash flows tend to exhibit greater degrees of uncertainty and therefore attract lower CEs. The technique has the advantage of:

   - Adjusting for both the timing and the risk associated with expected future cash flows.
   - It also adjusts for risk by modifying separately the net cash flow for each period and incorporates the decision-maker's utility preference with respect to risk directly.

The major disadvantage of this method lies with the estimation of the CE's, which may be arbitrary scores displaying the decision-makers' bias.

Example 12.14 Certainty equivalent

Using Example 12.4 again:

Year	Cash flow	CE score	Adjusted cash flow
0	(€75,000)	1	(€75,000)
1	€20.000	0.9	€18,000
2	€30,000	0.8	€24,000
3	€50,000	0.7	€35,000

The cash flows are then discounted at the company's target rate of return and if the NPV is still positive the project is accepted.

4. **Sensitivity analysis:** This is a procedure which measures the impact that a change in one or more input variables may have on the investment appraisal. It asks by what percentage could an assumption or parameter change for the worse before there would be an NPV of zero. For example, input variables such as initial investment, price per unit, variable cost per unit, corporate tax rates, the discount rate, etc. could be altered to identify new NPVs. Sensitivity analysis is useful in identifying the variables which, if changed, have the greatest impact on the NPV or IRR of a project. It is also useful in monitoring marginally accepted investment projects, in order to determine whether they should be continued or terminated. The difficulties associated with sensitivity analysis are identifying precisely the relationships between variables and the NPV, and the final decision is again a subjective one.

Example 12.15 Sensitivity analysis

Dugeen plc is considering a project with the following cash flows:

Year	Initial cost	Running cost	Savings
0	(€7,000)		
1		(€2,000)	€6,000
2		(€2,500)	€7,000

(a) Measure the sensitivity of the project to changes in the levels of expected costs and savings if the company cost of capital is 8%.

(b) Calculate by how much the cost of capital would have to increase before there would be an NPV of zero.

Solution
All of the cash flows are discounted at 8% to present value.

Year	DF 8%	Initial cost	Running costs	Savings	Net cash flow
0	1.000	(€7,000)			(€7,000)
1	0.926		(€1,852)	€5,556	€3,704
2	0.857		(€2,143)	€5,999	€3,856
Total		(€7,000)	(€3,995)	€11,555	€560

(a) The project has a positive NPV of €560 and is therefore viable.
   The changes in the cash flows necessary to have an NPV of zero are as follows:
   - The initial cost would need to increase by €560/€7,000 or 8%.
   - The running costs would need to increase by €560/€3,995 or 14%.
   - The savings would have to fall by €560/€11,555 or 4.8%. The savings are the most sensitive variable.
(b) The IRR here is 13.7% and therefore the cost of capital or discount factor would have to increase from 8% by 5.7 percentage points (or 5.7/8 = 71.25%) to have an NPV of zero.

5. **Probability distributions and decision trees:** When considering an investment decision it may be possible to make several predictions about alternative future outcomes and to assign probabilities to them. This approach generates a probability distribution of NPVs from the yearly probability distributions of net cash flows. In its simplest form these alternatives would include optimistic, most likely and pessimistic estimates. Statistical measures of expected value (return) and standard deviation (risk) can then be used to identify the expected NPV of a project and the probability of a negative NPV of a project. (See Chapter 6.)

   A **decision tree** is a graphical method of showing all the possible outcomes that may result from a particular situation and their probabilities of occurrence.

   The probability distribution approach specifies a risk profile associated with a project in a quantifiable fashion, helping to identify the expected value of NPV and the probability of a negative NPV. However, it is not easy to understand, it is difficult to estimate probability distributions accurately, and again, subjective estimates may be biased towards the personal beliefs of the decision-maker. Decision trees facilitate the process by giving a visual dimension to the decision-maker.

Example 12.16 Probability and expected values

Find the expected value of the NPV if the following project has an initial investment of €11,000 and the company's cost of capital is 15%.
   The cash flows and probability estimates for the project are given below.

Outcome	Probability	Year 1	Year 2	Year 3	Year 4
Optimistic	0.3	€5,000	€6,000	€4,500	€5,000
Most Likely	0.5	€3,500	€4,000	€3,800	€4,500
Pessimistic	0.2	€3,200	€3,600	€3,100	€4,000

Solution

The expected value in year 1 is found by multiplying the cash flows by their associated probabilities and adding the results

$$(0.3)(€5,000) + (0.5)(€3,500) + (0.2)(€3,200) = €3,890 \text{ etc.}$$

Year	1	2	3	4
Expected Value	€3,890	€4,520	€3,870	€4,550

The NPV is found by discounting each of these expected cash flows as follows:

Year	Cash flow	Discount factor 15%	Present value
0	(€11,000)	1	(€11,000)
1	€3,890	0.870	€3,384.3
2	€4,520	0.756	€3,417.12
3	€3,870	0.658	€2,456.46
4	€4,550	0.572	€2,602.6
		NPV =	€860.48

6. **Simulation:** This is a risk analysis method that involves utilising predetermined probability distributions and random numbers to estimate, using a computer, a distribution of possible NPVs. The approach requires the construction of a probability distribution for each factor affecting net cash flows. Then, using a computer, a random observation from each probability distribution is selected and a net cash flow is created. These random net cash flows are then used to estimate a distribution of possible NPVs. This distribution is then analysed using statistical information of expected value and standard deviation to determine whether or not to accept the project. The technique is a sophisticated one but it does not give clear investment advice. The rational investment decision would be to accept projects with the highest expected return and lowest risk. It does not offer a decision rule to indicate whether a project's expected NPV is sufficient to compensate for its risk as measured by the standard deviation of the distribution of possible NPVs.

12.14 Empirical evidence of risk assessment

There have been several empirical studies carried out to ascertain evidence on the risk assessment methods used in practice. A positive trend has been developing in the adoption of risk evaluation techniques, facilitated in no small means by the availability of financial software packages, and the most common method used is sensitivity analysis, followed by the risk-adjusted discount rate and the adjusted payback method. A more recent development in the area of risk analysis in investment appraisal is the application of options theory to enhance the decision-making process.

12.15 Capital investment and real options

Investment appraisal based on the calculation of NPV usually assumes that the investment being analysed is on an 'accept/reject' and a 'now or never' decision basis. However, with a lot of projects companies are not making all or nothing decisions, and they are able to respond to changing circumstances as they happen over the project life. Companies sometimes undertake projects with negative NPVs for strategic reasons. For example, Irish companies may have offices in China or India which are not presently viable, but in the long term the potential market is considered so valuable that the current losses are justified.

An option is a choice which need only be exercised if it is to the investor's advantage. A **real option** is such a choice or opportunity which exists because of a capital investment. The choice may involve being able to change plans once the project is undertaken.

Options theory can be applied to investment appraisal when deciding whether to wait, abandon a project or make follow-on investments. Foreign currency and interest rate options are discussed in Chapter 19, but here we will identify some of the basic application of options theory as it applies to investment appraisal. Real options give the right, but not the obligation, to take an action in the future. The significance of these options is that they add value to the project and should be taken into account in the investment appraisal. Options are usually described as calls (the right to buy something) or puts (the right to sell something). In investment appraisal real options include:

- **Follow-on investment options**
  Investing in a project may lead to other possibilities or opportunities that companies can take advantage of and which will not be reflected in a conventional NPV analysis. It is essentially a call option to make follow-on investments in the future. New technology investment is very difficult to evaluate and intangible benefits may accrue to such investment decisions. They may offer further investment opportunities or greater flexibility in the future.
- **Abandon options**
  Sometimes once an initial investment is made, it may be impossible to abandon it. Where the benefit streams from a project are highly uncertain, the option to abandon a project when things do go wrong could be of great value. It is this policy to pursue investments with greater flexibility (i.e. offering the choice to abandon without high penalties) that may be favoured. Any project that permits management to extract value when things go wrong has an embedded put option, and to ignore this is to undervalue the project.
- **Wait and see options**
  Here the option is to wait and see in the expectation of gaining more relevant information before making a decision or to defer until economic and other conditions improve. Usually, there is a time period over which a project can be postponed and this can correspond to the period in which the option can be exercised. In effect this amounts to viewing the decision as a call option that is about to expire – the capital investment outlay being the exercise price of the option. The company needs to balance the benefits of cash flows foregone in the period of postponement with the

value of potential new market information obtained during that period. For example, establishing a new drug patent allows the owner of the patent to wait and see how market conditions develop before manufacturing the drug, without the potential downside of competitors entering the market.

Other option formats include:

- **Staging options**
  Instead of investing in one lump, the investment can be made in phases. Each of the stages can be viewed as an option on the value of later stages.
- **Growth options**
  These are small investments that may lead to potential bigger investments at a later date, e.g. setting up an agency in China to promote your product for potential demand in the future
- **Switching options**
  This sometimes involves switching from an expensive input to a cheaper one or from a current output to a more profitable one. For example, traditional production lines were set up to make one product whereas more flexible manufacturing systems allow the product output to be changed to match consumer requirements.

Example 12.17

Bagger P. Browne, a property developer, buys a prime site in the centre of town and applies for planning permission to develop the site. As planning permission can take years, the developer has the option of selling the site (**abandonment**) or selling the site with planning permission when permission is granted. The planning could be drafted in such a way as to make it possible to switch from offices to apartments (**switching**). If the developer waits for a few years then the prospects for office space and apartments could be more accurately assessed (**wait and see**). In this example the developer has the ability to allow for flexibility. In such a project, value can be enhanced because of the alternatives that exist.

The practical problem of calculating the value of these options are based on not being able to measure the degree of uncertainty, and also assessing how long the option value will be available to the company. However, although these valuations are difficult, even a rough estimate is better than no estimate at all and can enhance the decision-making process by explicitly stating their reality. The total NPV of a project being undertaken should include some representation of the values of the various options associated with the decision, i.e.

Total NPV = NPV of the project + NPV of potential option formats that
exist with this investment.

If the project itself has a positive NPV then it is already viable. However, if the NPV of the project itself is negative, then it may be worthwhile looking at the present value of potential options that may enhance the present value of future cash flows leading to a positive NPV. Some academics believe these option values can be estimated using the Black-Scholes option pricing model, which is outside the scope of this text.

12.16 International investment

Many Irish companies are attracted to international business by starting projects or investing in other countries. A company seeking to maximise shareholder wealth may find it worthwhile to increase its foreign business and there are several possible motives for a company becoming more internationalised.

Some of the more important motives are:

1. **Attract new sources of demand**

   Companies often reach a stage where growth is limited in their home country because of intense competition or because market share has reached its potential peak. A possible solution is to consider foreign markets where there is potential demand.

2. **Fully benefit from economies of scale**

   A company that sells its products in new markets may increase earnings and shareholder wealth due to economies of scale (lower average cost per unit resulting from increased production). Many multinational companies (MNCs) are manufacturing more homogeneous products in EU countries, rather than differentiating them to meet specific needs for each country.

3. **Use foreign factors of production**

   Labour and land costs vary dramatically among countries and MNCs often attempt to set up production in a location where land and labour are cheap. Japanese companies have, in the past 15 years, used countries such as Mexico to relocate production facilities and take advantage of lower costs.

4. **Exploit monopolistic advantages**

   Companies may become more internationalised if they possess resources or skills not available to competing companies. A common example of monopolistic advantage is technology. For example, if a company possesses advanced technology and has exploited this advantage successfully in local markets, it may attempt to exploit it internationally as well. There may also be the need to protect patents and intellectual property by locating abroad.

5. **Diversify internationally**

   A domestic company may reduce its cash flow variability by diversifying its product mix, i.e. if revenues are down for one product there may be a compensating increase in other product revenues. However, demand for all products in that country tends to be influenced by the economic state in that country. This systematic exposure to economic conditions cannot be diversified away in that country. The company can, however, reduce such risk by marketing its product mix among many countries. By diversifying sales internationally a company can make its cash flow less volatile.

6. **React to trade restrictions**

   Sometimes direct foreign investment is used as a defensive rather than an aggressive strategy, e.g. Japanese car manufacturers established production facilities in the US in anticipation that their exports might be subject to more stringent trade restrictions such as tariffs and quotas. Additional foreign investment to Europe was enhanced due to a fear of increased trade barriers to imports into Europe.

7. **Government incentives**

Companies may benefit from grants or tax incentives given by governments to encourage inward investment. The Irish government has attracted many leading-edge software companies partially because of the grants available to them. Many multinational companies try to position some of their operations in what are called 'tax havens'. This is a term used to describe a country with lenient taxation rules and taxation rates which are designed to attract foreign direct investment.

12.16.1 Methods of going international

If a company wishes to increase its foreign business, there are several methods available.

1. **Exporting** – Here any increase in production occurs at the existing production plants. Exporting is a safer way to break into a new market since there is less to lose if the strategy fails. The initial cost of production at home, and exporting, is low relative to establishing a subsidiary. However, selling and distribution costs will be higher with exporting when compared to local production.

2. **Licensing** – A local firm in the host country could produce the goods to the licensing company's specifications. As the goods are sold, a portion of the revenues as specified by the agreement would be sent to the licensor.

   Advantages:

   (a) since exporting is not necessary, transportation costs are avoided, and (b) because a local firm handles production in the host country, direct foreign investment is not necessary.

   Disadvantages:

   (a) it can be difficult to ensure quality control of the local firm's production process, and (b) the local firm may turn out to be a competitor in the future.

3. **Franchising** – A firm allows an individual to sell its product in a specific territory. The firm normally receives an initial fee plus periodic royalty payments in return, e.g. Pizza Hut and McDonald's, etc.

4. **Joint Venture and Foreign Direct Investment** – If the market shows strong consistent demand, a company might decide to initiate a joint venture or set up a wholly owned subsidiary. Foreign direct investment is a long-term investment in an economy other than that of the investing company, where the investing company has control over the business invested, e.g. in a foreign subsidiary.

   This method of increasing international business is generally expensive. The investment made to build or purchase a plant in a foreign country is irreversible. If the project fails it may have difficulty in selling the plant.

   Regardless of what form of investment and risk assessment is taken, an international investment will require forecasts of extra financial variables related to the investment. These new variables include forecasting international tax rates, inflation rates, political risks and foreign currency exchange rates, etc. – these variables will increase the risk in the assessment process. The investment decision may be evaluated from more than one point of view (see question 13).

Example 12.18 International investment

An Irish-based company is evaluating an overseas project in the US. The investment will cost $5 million and is expected to earn post-tax cash inflows as follows:

Year	1	2	3	4
$million	1.2	1.5	2.2	2.2

Exchange rate forecasts under two different scenarios are as follows:

	Year	1	2	3	4
1	€1 =	$1.28	$1.25	$1.20	$1.15	$1.10
2	€1 =	$1.28	$1.35	$1.40	$1.45	$1.50

The company requires a 12% target rate of return based on its cost of capital. Calculate the € NPV of the project under each exchange rate scenario and comment on the results.

Solution

Year	$	Scenario 1 €1 = $	€	Scenario 2 €1 = $	€
0	(5,000,000)	1.28	(3,906250)	1.28	(3,906,250)
1	1,200,000	1.25	960,000	1.35	888,889
2	1,500,000	1.2	1,250,000	1.4	1,071,429
3	2,200,000	1.15	1,913,043	1.45	1,517,241
4	2,200,000	1.10	2,000,000	1.5	1,466,667
		NPV =	€517,936	NPV =	(€220,024)

The stronger the US dollar is in the future (scenario 1) the better the result.

In international investment the tax systems in each country are likely to be different and double taxation relief is usually available due to double taxation agreements or treaties that exist between countries. The net effect of a double taxation treaty is that the parent company will pay in total the higher of the local tax or domestic tax on profits generated by the subsidiary. Political risks may also arise when a company invests internationally. Many foreign governments, particularly those in less developed economies, may be less stable than those in Europe. A change in government may lead to a change in policies to businesses – especially a foreign business. An extreme policy change may involve nationalisation or expropriation (government seizure) of certain businesses. All of these risks make estimating future cash flows and choosing an appropriate discount rate more complicated in an international investment than for a domestic investment.

12.17 Qualitative factors

It is not always easy to quantify the benefits of a project in monetary terms. A company may invest in improved safety facilities for its employees or improving the recreational facilities available to employees. Company policies of this nature have a cost that is quantifiable, but the resulting benefits may be difficult to put a figure on. A **cost benefit analysis** can be carried out on these types of projects. This type of analysis includes a wider range of factors than would be involved in the traditional investment appraisal. Cost benefit analysis was applied on the ring road in Dublin with qualitative factors such as travel time saved and reduction in gridlock assessed as benefits. It is important to be aware of projects that may be a lot more difficult to appraise due to the nature of the extra qualitative variables involved.

Other forms of corporate investment may be undertaken for strategic reasons without any quantifiable appraisal used. The introduction of advanced manufacturing techniques forced companies to change their production techniques to achieve manufacturing excellence. This leads to reduced labour costs, defective production costs, delivery times and inventory levels as well as improved quality and greater flexibility due to **economies of scope**. Economies of scope is the potential for low-cost production of high-variety and low-volume products.

The development of Internet companies has added a new dimension to business and investment appraisal. Development of a website became not so much a choice for a company, but a necessary strategy for survival and growth. Internet online business is growing at a rapid pace, and right across all business sectors, new ways of doing business are emerging, new markets are opening and new opportunities are coming on stream. This type of investment decision may not lend itself to traditional investment appraisal techniques, as the benefits associated with developing Internet business, although very real, may be difficult to quantify.

The concept of ethical shareholder wealth creation has become increasingly important in financial management over recent years. Environmental concerns such as controlling pollution, protecting wildlife, fair wages for employees in less developed countries and product safety are important ethical issues for companies. Acting in an ethically responsible way can have a direct detrimental affect on expected cash flows and net present value. However, shareholders are increasingly expecting companies to act ethically and if they do not, adverse publicity can sway investors away and depress share value.

12.18 Conclusion

In this chapter methods of investment appraisal were assessed with the net present value technique considered the soundest academically. The problems associated with inflation, taxation, capital rationing, unequal project lives, incorporating risk into the investment appraisal, as well as options and international investment, were all discussed.

Empirical evidence indicates a difference in preferences between the academic world and the real world. Successful investments usually rest more on quality management in the earlier stages of the decision-making process rather than the pure quantitative stages of the appraisal stage. Issues of human communication, enthusiasm and commitment are vital components in the successful company.

SUMMARY

- Investment appraisal techniques include payback, accounting rate of return, net present value, internal rate of return and discounted payback.
- Each of these techniques has advantages and disadvantages.
- Empirical evidence suggests that payback is the most commonly used technique, usually in conjunction with other techniques. Academics prefer NPV.
- In a single period capital rationing situation the profitability index provides a ranking of investments assuming investments are divisible, non-deferrable and non-repeatable.
- Only relevant cash flows should be included in the appraisal of an investment.
- Inflation, taxation and risk should be accounted for in the appraisal.
- Options theory can be applied to investment appraisal
- Asset replacement with unequal lives decisions can be accommodated applying the equivalent annual cost method.
- Companies have a variety of motives for foreign investment decisions
- Companies can conduct international operations through exporting, licensing, franchising, joint ventures and foreign direct investment.
- Sometimes investments are made for strategic reasons, which do not lend themselves to traditional investment appraisal techniques.
- Companies must be aware of the ethical issues involved in investment.

QUESTIONS

1. The ARR method has weaknesses, but is still a popular technique. Explain.
2. What is the difference between soft and hard capital rationing?
3. What is the equivalent annual cost method and where is it useful?
4. Explain four techniques of investment appraisal and comment on the strengths and weaknesses of each method.
5.♦ IOU Systems plc is considering four projects at present and the following information is available:
   Project A
   This would involve an initial cash outflow of €20,000 and a further cash outflow of €20,000 after one year. Cash inflow thereafter would be as follows:
   Year 2   €15,000
   Year 3   €12,000
   Years 4–8   €8,000
   Project B
   This is a long-term project, involving an initial cash outflow of €32,000 and annual cash inflows of €4,500 in perpetuity.
   Project C
   This would involve an initial cash outflow of €50,000 on equipment and €15,000 on working capital. The investment in working capital would be increased to €21,000 at the end of the first year. Annual cash inflows would be €18,000 per annum for five years starting in year 1, at the end of which time the investment in working capital would be recovered.

Project D

This involves an initial cash outflow of €20,000 and annual cash inflows as follows:

Years 1–5	€5,000
Years 6–10	€4,000
Years 11 to infinity	€3,000

The company discounts all projects of ten years duration or less at a cost of capital of 12%, and all other projects at a cost of 15%. Calculate the payback and net present value of each project and comment on the results that you have found.

6. The Rightyoke, a labour saving machine, costs €60,000 and will save €24,000 per annum at current wage rates. The machine is expected to have a three-year life and a zero scrap value. The company discounts all investment projects at 10%. Calculate the project's NPV if there is no inflation. Calculate the project's NPV if general inflation in wage rates is 15% per annum.

7. Nuts Corner plc is considering buying a new machine and has two mutually exclusive projects available to it. The following data is available to assess this investment project.

	A	B
Cost (immediate outlay)	€93,000	€60,000
	Expected annual net profit (loss)	
Year 1	€29,000	€18,000
Year 2	(€1,000)	(€2,000)
Year 3	€9,000	€8,000

The company discounts all projects at its weighted average cost of capital of 10%. In calculating net profit the company uses the straight-line method of depreciation and both machines have a zero residual value. Calculate for each project the payback period, the net present value and comment on your results.

8. ♦ Brass Monkey plc is a company which has just received a quotation of €100,000 for the installation of insulation in its building during December this year. The following information is available to assist in the evaluation of this project.
   1. The fuel bill for this year is expected to be €200,000. Fuel prices are expected to increase by 10% per year.
   2. The insulation is expected to save 15% of the fuel bill.
   3. The company is moving premises in 4 years' time and because of the uncertainties involved, the company has decided to ignore any effect of the improvement on the sale value of the building.
   4. The annual depreciation charge is €25,000 each year with no residual value.
   5. The company has an ARR target of 20% based on average annual accounting profit/average investment.
   6. The company discounts all projects at its weighted average cost of capital of 12%.
   7. Assume that all cash flows arise at the end of the year in which they occur.

   Calculate the accounting rate of return, the payback period, the net present value and the approximate internal rate of return for the project and make a recommendation based on your results.

9.♦ DodgyJab plc has invested €500,000 to date in developing a new vaccine. The vaccine is now ready for production and the marketing director estimates that 150,000 units will be sold per annum over the next five years. The selling price of the vaccine will be €5 and the variable costs are €3 per vaccine. Fixed costs are expected to be €200,000 per annum. This figure is made up of €160,000 additional fixed costs and €40,000 fixed costs relating to existing business which will be apportioned to the new product.

In order to produce the vaccine, machinery costing €520,000 will be purchased today. The estimated residual value of the machinery in five years time is €100,000. The company calculates depreciation on a straight-line basis. The cost of capital for the company is 12%.

(a) Calculate the net present value of the vaccine.

(b) Carry out sensitivity analysis to show how much the following factors would have to change, before the vaccine ceased to be worthwhile:

1. The discount rate.
2. The initial outlay on machinery.
3. The operating cash flow.
4. The residual value of the machinery.

10. You have been asked by a client, Dalton Commuter, who is the prospective purchaser of a second-hand car, to write a report on the following four financing options available to him.

(a) €10,500 cash now.

(b) Three consecutive annual payments of €4,000, with the first one now (discount factor 12% p.a.).

(c) €1,200 deposit now, and 35 monthly payments of €300, the first one in exactly one month from now (discount factor = 1% per month).

(d) 36 monthly payments of €330, the first one now (discount factor = 1% per month).

Using the criteria of present value, evaluate these four methods and, in your report, identify the most economical method of paying for the car. Use the discount formulae and not discount tables to calculate the discount factors required.

11.♦ Keegan Ballycumber plc has €620,000 available to invest and has identified six possible projects. The projects are non-divisible and may not be postponed until a future period.

Expected net cash inflows in €000s

Project	Year 1	Year 2	Year 3	Year 4	Year 5	Initial Outlay
A	70	70	70	70	70	246
B	75	87	64			180
C	48	48	63	73		175
D	62	62	62	62		180
E	40	50	60	70	40	180
F	35	82	82			150

Projects A and E are mutually exclusive and all projects are consistent with the company's existing operations. Any surplus funds may be invested in the money market at 9% per annum. Keegan's cost of capital is 12%.
(a) Calculate the expected net present value for each project.
(b) Calculate the expected profitability index for each project.
(c) Rank the projects according to both of these investment appraisal methods and make a recommendation as to which projects should be selected.

12.♦ Clonown plc, an Irish multinational corporation, has a strong export trade to the US and is considering the development of a subsidiary there. All relevant information follows:
(a) The initial investment is $30 million and the existing spot rate is €1 = $0.85
(b) The price, demand and variable cost are as follows:

Year	Price	Demand	Variable Cost
1	$350	60,000	$200
2	$350	60,000	$200
3	$360	100,000	$250
4	$380	100,000	$260

(c) The fixed costs are estimated to be $1 million per year.
(d) The $/€ exchange rate is expected to be $0.90 at the end of year 1, $0.95 at the end of year 2, $1.00 at the end of year 3 and $1.05 at the end of year 4.
(e) The US government will impose corporation tax of 20% on income. The Irish government will allow a tax credit on remitted earnings and will not impose any additional taxes as the Irish rate of corporation tax is 12.5%.
(f) All cash flows received by the subsidiary are to be sent to the parent at the end of each year.
(g) The plant and machinery are depreciated over ten years using the straight-line method, i.e. $3 million per year.
(h) At the end of four years the subsidiary is to be sold and the parent company expects to receive $20 million net of all taxes.
If the company requires a 15% rate of return, determine whether the project is viable using net present value technique.

13. Orson Cart plc is an Irish company that produces and sells farm equipment and is thinking of expanding its subsidiary in the US. The company believes the subsidiary could also develop an equipment-repair business.
The following projections and relevant data have been compiled for the analysis.
(a) The initial investment is $8.5 million now.
(b) Current exchange rate €1 = $1.30.
(c) Cash profits $3 million for the first year increasing by 5% per annum over the following 4 years.
(d) All cash flows received by the subsidiary are to be sent to the parent at the end of each year.
(e) US corporation tax 20%. The Irish government will allow a tax credit on remitted earnings and will not impose any additional taxes.
(f) The required rate of return (WACC) is 12%

Forecasted exchange rate starting at the end of year 1:

	Year 1	Year 2	Year 3	Year 4	Year 5
€1 =	$1.28	$1.15	$1.00	$0.95	$0.90

Find the net present value of this project from both the subsidiary and the Irish parent company's perspective and make a recommendation.

14. DolanMcConigly plc have developed a new product they have named the 'Langer' and the following information is available to help make a final decision on whether to produce the product.

(i)   The development costs to date have been €1 million and the company is committed to spending a further €350,000 within the next three months.

(ii) To produce the product, new machinery will be purchased now costing €4.7 million and this will have a scrap value of €700,000 in four years' time.

(iii) Total fixed costs of production of the Langer are €1.75 million per year. This includes a depreciation charge of €1 million per year and a charge allocated to represent a fair share of the fixed assets of the business as a whole of €250,000 per year.

(iv) Langers will sell for €10,000 each and sales are expected to be 800 per year over the next four years.

(v)   Variable costs of production are €7,000 per unit.

(vi) If the business decides not to manufacture the product, it can sell the patents associated now for €1.3 million.

(vii) The company has a weighted average cost of capital of 12%.

   (a) Prepare the relevant cash flows and find the NPV of producing the Langer.
   (b) Carry out sensitivity analysis on the following input variables:
      1   The residual value of the machinery.
      2   The discount rate.
      3   The initial investment on machinery.
      4   The annual net operating cash flows.
      Comment on your results.

15. Athlone plc has two courses of action open to it.

(a) Sell the company for an offer of €200 million. This offer was received today informally for the company's shares.

(b) Continue with existing operations and no further capital investment. Projected financial data for the next five years including inflation are as follows:

Projected cash flows (€ millions)					
Year	1	2	3	4	5
Sales	260	275	255	215	185
Variable costs	150	160	145	125	105
Fixed costs	45	45	45	45	45
Depreciation charge	40	30	25	20	10

Tax may be assumed payable in the year that the income arises and the tax rate is expected to remain at 12.5% for the duration of the project. Projections continue on an annuity basis after year 5, for a further 5 years, based on the results in year 5. The

company has 50 million shares with a market value of €3.50 each. The company discounts all future cash flows at a weighted average cost of capital of 13%.
Calculate the present value of the cash flow projections above and make a recommendation.

16. ◆ Right Price Joe plc has to replace a number of machines and is faced with a choice – machine A with a life of 12 years and machine B with a life of 6 years. If machine B is used it will be replaced at the end of 6 years by another of the same type. The pattern of maintenance and running costs differ between the two types of machine and relevant data are shown below:

	Machine A	Machine B
Purchase price	€19,000	€13,000
Trade-in value	€3,000	€3,000
Annual repair costs	€2,000	€2,600
Overhaul costs	€4,000 end of year 8	€2,000 end of year 4
Financing costs	10% p.a.	10% p.a.

Calculate the equivalent annual cost of using either machine a make a recommendation.

17. Olive Grove plc is considering the installation of new machinery in its production line. The existing machinery was bought three years ago for €27,000 and is being depreciated straight line over a ten-year period at €2,500 per annum. The current market value of its old machinery is €6,000. The new machinery has a lifespan of seven years but using it would improve current production capacity. The machinery will cost €175,000 and will have a scrap value at the end of seven years of €5,000. Information on the two pieces of machinery is as follows:

	New machinery	Existing machinery
Annual running costs	€1,700	€2,200
Annual production capacity	150,000	130,000
Variable costs per unit	€0.75	€0.90
Fixed overhead absorption rate per unit	€0.80	€0.92

Any increase in output is not expected to affect the current selling price of €2 per unit. The company target rate of return/cost of capital is 10% and corporate tax can be ignored.
Calculate the payback period, net present value and internal rate of return on an incremental basis.

18. Kinahan Mobiles plc is considering whether to invest in a project costing €40,000 now. Expected sales from the project are as follows:

Probability	Sales volume (units)
0.10	2,000
0.25	6,000
0.40	9,000
0.15	10,000
0.10	14,000

Once sales are established at a certain volume in the first year, they will continue at the same volume in later years. The unit price will be €10 and the unit variable cost will be €5. Additional fixed costs will be €20,000. The project will have a life of six years, after which the equipment will be sold for €3,000. The company's cost of capital is 10%.

(a) What is the expected value of the NPV of this project?

(b) Assuming the cost of the equipment and scrap value are correct, calculate the minimum annual volume of sales required the get a NPV of zero.

19. Konfused plc has a choice of two machines which have different life expectancies as follows:

	Machine 1	Machine 2
Initial cost	€50,000	€90,000
Residual value	€5,000	€7,000
Annual running cost	€10,000	€8,000
Useful life	4 years	7 years

The two machines are identical in terms of quality of work and capacity. The company cost of capital is 10% per annum.

Illustrate, using equivalent annual cost, which machine is the most economical.

How much would the cost of machine have to change for both machines to be equally economical?

20. ◆ Hugh De Mann plc is considering an investment project which will involve purchasing a new machine for €20,000 with a four-year life and a terminal value of €5,000. Profits before depreciation from the project will be €8,000 per annum. An investment in working capital of €2,000 will be required for the duration of the project. Tax allowances on the machine are 25% per annum on a reducing balance basis with a balancing allowance equal to the difference between the scrap value and the tax written-down value. Tax of 12.5% on cash profits occurs in the same year as the profits rise. If the company required rate of return is 15%, calculate:

(a) The effects on cash flows of the capital allowances.

(b) The actual project net cash flows for each year.

(c) The NPV of the project from the net cash flows.

21. Wayne Dwops plc has identified a project with the following real cash flows:

Year	Cash flow
0	(€750,000)
1	€330,000
2	€242,000
3	€532,000

The rate of inflation is expected to be 5% per annum and the cost of capital including inflation is 15.5%.

(a) Calculate the real discount rate and the appropriate NPV.

(b) Calculate the money cash flows and the appropriate NPV.

13

The Cost of Capital and Capital Structure

CHAPTER OBJECTIVES

At the end of this chapter the student should be able to:

1. calculate the cost of the different sources of finance available to a company
2. understand why sources of finance are weighted using market values in calculating the weighted average cost of capital
3. appreciate the problems associated with WACC calculation in practice
4. calculate the required rate of return of a security using the capital asset pricing model and risk-adjusted discount rates for use in investment appraisal
5. discuss the concept of financial gearing and capital structure
6. discuss the traditional and Modigliani/Miller approaches to capital structure, and the value and limitations of their theories
7. identify the practical considerations and influences on the optimal capital structure debate
8. appreciate the interaction of investment and financing decisions using adjusted present value.

INTRODUCTION

The purpose of this chapter is twofold:

1. To explain how to calculate the costs of the different sources of finance used by a company and, in working out an overall average cost, to weight them according to their relative importance.
2. To look at the theories related to the capital structure debate and as to whether an ideal capital structure exists that can maximise the value of a company.

The cost of capital for a company represents the cost of the different sources of finance that a company uses, and is therefore the **minimum** required rate of return on company investments. When a company uses investment appraisal techniques such as net present value, its cost of capital should be used as a minimum guide to the discount rate.

Capital structure relates to the various combinations of the different sources of finance that a company uses. The concept of an optimal capital structure is an ideal mix of finance with the lowest cost of capital, i.e. the lowest overall rate of return that needs to be paid on funds provided. If the cost of capital is low, the discounted value of future cash flows generated by the company is high, resulting in a high overall value for the company. If a company raises capital by the cheapest and most efficient means, the cost of capital will be minimised and the company value is maximised.

13.1 The cost of different sources of finance

Companies are rarely financed by just one source of capital and in the main tend to use a mixture of both debt and equity capital. In this section we consider each of the different sources of long-term finance available to a company and how to calculate their cost.

13.1.2 Equity

Equity capital can be raised by issuing new shares, or by using the retained earnings of a company. Although retained earnings do not have any servicing costs, they have an opportunity cost equivalent to the ongoing cost of equity, since if these funds were returned to the shareholders they could make good use of these funds by investing in other firms and obtaining a return.

The fundamental theory of share values states that the market price of a share should reflect its future income stream discounted, i.e. it assumes that the share price is the present value of all future dividends. The discount rate that equates the present value of these future dividends to the market price today is the rate of return that investors require or the shareholders cost of equity (K_e).

$$P_0 = d/(1 + K_e) + d/(1 + K_e)^2 + d/(1 + K_e)^3 \ldots \ldots \text{ in perpetuity}$$

The sum of the discount factors tend in the limit to the finite value of $1/K_e$

This implies in the limit

$$P_0 = d/K_e \qquad \text{and therefore} \qquad K_e = d/P_0 \qquad\qquad (13.1)$$

where P_0 is the market price of the share ex dividend and d is a constant dividend in perpetuity. The share price ex dividend implies the current dividend has been paid out and is not reflected in the current share price.

Like all theoretical models the theory is based on several assumptions:

1. New funds are invested in projects with similar business risk to existing operations.
2. There is no change in the capital structure of the company.

3. Shareholders have perfect information about future dividends.
4. Dividends are paid annually with the next dividend payable in one year.
5. Shares are perpetuities in themselves, i.e. investors may buy or sell them, but only exceptionally are they redeemed by the company.

Example 13.1 Cost of equity
A company has in issue equity with a current price ex dividend of €3. Dividends recently paid were 45c per share and this is expected to remain constant in perpetuity. What is the cost of equity capital?

Solution

$$K_e = d/P_0 = 45c/300c = 0.15 \text{ or } 15\%$$

The issue of **new shares** costs money and these costs can be considered in two ways:
1. One approach is to deduct the issue costs as a year zero cash outflow of the project for which the share capital is being raised.
2. An alternative approach is to calculate the cost as follows:

$$K_e = \frac{d}{(P_0 - X)}$$

where X represents the issue costs per share. If the issue cost above was 19c per share then the cost of equity

$$= \frac{45c}{(300c - 19c)} = 0.16 \text{ or } 16\%.$$

Cost of capital, regardless of what type of finance, is given as a percentage.

Dividend growth model (Gordon's)
Shareholders will normally expect dividends to increase over the years and not to remain constant in perpetuity.
   Myron Gordon developed the model to reflect dividend growth over time.

$$P_0 = d(1 + g)/(1 + K_e) + d(1 + g)^2/(1 + K_e)^2 + d(1 + g)^3/(1 + K_e)^3 \cdots \text{in perpetuity}$$

$$P_0 = \frac{d(1+g)}{(Ke - g)} \qquad \text{(see proof in \textbf{Appendix 13A})}$$

This implies $$K_e = \frac{d(1 + g)}{P_0} + g \qquad \text{or} \qquad K_e = \frac{d_1}{P_0} + g \qquad (13.2)$$

where K_e is the cost of equity
   d is the current dividend (to be paid shortly or just paid)
   g is the annual growth rate
   d_1 is next year's dividend
   P_0 is the market price of the share ex dividend.

Here it is also assumed that **g** must be less than K_e and that, while in practice growth rates may vary, they are assumed to be relatively constant.

Example 13.2 Dividend growth formula

A company has in issue equity with a current price ex dividend of €9. Dividends recently paid were 45c per share and this is expected to rise by 10% per annum. What is the cost of equity capital?

Solution

$$K_e = \frac{45c(1 + 0.10)}{900c} + 0.10 = 0.155 \text{ or } 15.5\%$$

If past performance of dividends indicate growth over a number of years, it may be necessary to work out the annual growth rate before finding the cost of equity.

Example 13.3 Dividend growth rate and cost of equity

An Irish company has issued share capital of 3 million shares with a current market value of €3.27 per share cumulative of dividend. An annual dividend of €810,000 is due for payment shortly, on 31 December. Over the past five years, dividends (in €000s) have been as follows:

Year	1	2	3	4	5
Dividends	620	650	710	770	810

Calculate the cost of equity.

Solution
The current dividend is €810,000/3,000,000 = 27c
The five years' figures indicate four years' growth from the base year, and the annual growth rate is calculated as follows:

$$\text{Four years compounded} = (1 + g)^4 = 810/620 = 1.3065$$

By getting the fourth root of either side this implies

$$1 + g = (1.3065)^{1/4} = 1.069 \text{ and therefore } g = 6.9\% \text{ per annum.}$$

$$K_e = \frac{27c(1.069)}{300c} + 0.069 = 0.165 \text{ or } 16.5\% \text{ approximately.}$$

The **capital asset pricing model** (which was more thoroughly examined in Chapter 6) is an alternative model to find the cost of equity, based on the risk-free rate of return plus an equity risk premium. The equity risk premium reflects both the systematic risk of the company and that generated by the market, relative to risk-free investments. The cost of equity is given by the following linear relationship:

$$K_e = R_f + [E(R_m) - R_f]\beta \qquad (13.3)$$

The development and application of the capital asset pricing model was more thoroughly examined in Chapter 6.

Example 13.4 CAPM *and cost of equity*

A company has a share beta of 1.5. The risk-free rate is 4% and the expected market return is 12%. What is the cost of equity?

Solution

$$K_e = 4\% + (12\% \text{ - } 4\%)\ 1.5 = 16\%$$

13.1.2 Debt

Preference shares are often included in the debt capital of the company because they have a prior charge on the company returns, i.e. preference shareholders receive dividend before the ordinary shareholders. Dividends on preference shares, like ordinary share dividends, are distributed out of after-tax earnings. Preference shares are usually irredeemable with a constant dividend based on a percentage of the nominal value of the share. This implies the cost of preference shares, like the basic equity model above, is given by the expression

$$K_p = d/P_0 \qquad (13.4)$$

where K_p is the cost of preference shares.

Example 13.5 Cost of preference shares

A company has in issue 8% preference shares with a nominal value of €1. The shares are currently trading at 50c ex dividend. Calculate the cost of preference shares.

Solution
In this case the K_p = 8c/50c = 0.16 or 16%.

Debt is more usually associated with interest-bearing securities known as **debentures**. There are three major types of debenture (also known as loan stock or corporate bonds): **irredeemable, redeemable and convertible** debentures. In the case of interest-bearing securities, **the interest payments are an allowable deduction for purposes of taxation. This reduces the after-tax cost of the debt.**

As with equity, the basis for the calculation of the cost of debt will be the dividend valuation model with the interest payments replacing dividends. If the debentures are irredeemable and the corporate tax rate is **T**, then the cost of debt (K_d) after tax is

$$K_d = \frac{Int(1 - T)}{P_0} \qquad (13.5)$$

where K_d is the cost of irredeemable debt after tax
        Int is the interest to be paid annually
        P_o is the market price of the debenture ex interest.

The cost of irredeemable debt represents the cost of continuing to use the finance rather than redeem the security at its current market price ex interest.

Redeemable debentures have a specific redemption date and are usually repaid in full, i.e. redeemable at par value. The arithmetic becomes more complicated when allowing for the repayment of the principal at some time in the future. The cost is simply the internal rate of return on the after-tax cash flows of the debenture. **The interest payable is tax deductible, but the capital repayment or redemption value is not.** Here again the internal rate of return (IRR) represents the cost of continuing to use the finance rather than redeem the security at the current market price.

Example 13.6 Debenture cost

A company has in issue 10% debentures with a nominal value of €100 (par value). The market price is €90 ex interest. The corporate tax rate is 12.5%. Calculate the cost of capital if the debenture is (a) irredeemable and (b) redeemable at par in 10 years.

Solution

(a) $K_d = \dfrac{€10(1 - 0.125)}{€90} = 0.0972 \text{ or } 9.72\%$

(b) In this case you need to identify the time frame and the cash flows involved and then calculate the internal rate of return.

Relevant cash flows	Year	Cash flow
P_0	0	(90)
Interest $(1 - T)$	1 – 10	8.75
Redemption value	10	100
	IRR = K_a =	10.41%

Example 13.7 Cost of redeemable debenture

A company has 8% securitised debenture stock (nominal value €100) on which the interest is to be paid annually on 31 December. The stock is due for redemption at par in three years' time (on 1 January).The market price of the debenture at 28 December is €103 cumulative of interest. Calculate the cost of debenture stock if the rate of corporation tax is 12.5%.

Solution
The ex-interest market price is €103 − €8 = €95. If this was irredeemable debt the after-tax cost of the debentures would be €8(1 − 0.125)/€95 = 7.4%.

As it is redeemable, work out an IRR on the after-tax cash flows.

Year	After-tax cash flow
0	(95)
1–3	7
3	100
IRR =	8.97%

The model is based on ex-interest market value (€103 − €8 = €95 ex interest) and the debenture being redeemable at par, i.e. same as nominal value(€100).

If you are calculating the IRR manually and not using a spreadsheet package, a good initial discount factor to use in calculating an initial net present value is:
(a) Work out the irredeemable cost, and (b) adjust it by the annualised capital gain or loss.

$$(a) \quad \frac{\text{Interest }(1-T)}{\text{Price ex interest } P_0} \quad + \quad (b) \quad \frac{(\text{Redeemable value} - P_0)/\text{years to maturity}}{\text{Price ex interest }(P_0)}$$

$$\frac{€8\,(1-0.125)}{€95} \quad + \quad \frac{(€100 - €95)/3}{€95} \quad = 0.0913 \text{ or } 9\% \text{ approximately}$$

A good initial discount factor to use is approximately 9%.
  Using a spreadsheet package like **Excel**, the IRR generated is 8.97% after tax.
  Companies are legally entitled to buy back their redeemable debentures at any time. Management should constantly appraise the cost of their redeemable debentures against other sources of finance and identify redemption opportunities if they are of benefit to the company.

Example 13.8 Redemption opportunity

A company has 8% debentures with a market value of €80 which are redeemable at par (nominal value €100) in 8 years. Alternative funds are available at an after-tax cost of 9% (tax rate is 12.5%). Ignoring issue and redemption costs, should the debentures be redeemed?

Solution
Find the internal rate of return of the existing debentures and compare it with the alternative at 9%.

Year	After tax @ 12.5%
0	(80)
1–8	7
8	100
IRR =	10.9%

The alternative funds should be used as they are cheaper than the existing debentures.

To find the cost of **convertible debentures** you must first ascertain whether conversion is likely to occur. If conversion is likely, you replace the redemption value with the conversion value and again find an IRR on the after-tax cash flows. If conversion is not likely, you treat the convertible as a redeemable debenture.

Example 13.9 Cost of convertible debenture

A company has convertible debenture stock at an 8% coupon or interest rate, with a market value of €106 per cent. An interest payment has been made recently. The debentures will be convertible into equity shares, at a rate of 40 shares per €100 nominal stock in three years' time. The shares are expected to have a market value of €3.50 each at that time, and all the debenture holders are expected to convert their debentures.

Calculate the cost of capital to the company if corporation tax is at the rate of 12.5%. Assume that tax savings occur in the same year that the interest payments arise.

Solution
Using an Excel spreadsheet format.

The initial cash flow is the market value of the debenture ex interest, i.e. €106.

The final year cash flow is based on the future market value of conversion into equity, i.e. €3.50(40) = €140.

Year	After tax @ 12.5%
0	(106)
1–3	7
3	140
IRR =	15.77%

Several obvious questions are posed based on the above calculation.
1. How do you know what the share price will actually be in the future?
2. When will investors convert? (Normally several conversion dates exist.)
3. Will the company redeem the debenture, as early redemption on the part of the company is possible?

Other sources of funds include eurobonds (see **Appendix 13B**), deep discounted bonds, overdrafts and floating rate loans or fixed rate bank loans. Deep discounted bonds are those where the coupon rate being offered is below the market rate at the time of issue. There might even be no annual interest payment, i.e. zero coupon bonds. Overdrafts are not normally a source of capital in a company, unless the overdraft is a long-term facility.

If the finance raised involves interest payments, you must allow for their tax deductibility. If, for example, the interest rate is variable on a loan (floating rate loan), base the cost on the current interest rate after tax. This is only appropriate if the company is in a **non-tax-exhaustion position**, i.e. it has taxable profits against which to set its interest payments.

Bank loans are not a tradeable security and as such do not have a market value. The cost of a bank loan is the after-tax cost of the interest payable by the company, i.e. $K_L =$

interest rate $(1 - T)$. The interest rate can be found by dividing the interest paid after tax on bank borrowings by the amount of the loan for the year (interest after tax/loan amount). Alternatively, the cost of existing debentures can be used as an approximate value for the cost of the debt.

Example 13.10 Cost of a bank loan

A company has a five-year term loan from a bank at floating rate of interest. If the current interest rate is 8% what is the pre-tax and after-tax cost of the loan if the tax rate is (a) 25%, and (b) 12.5%?

Solution

Pre-tax = 8%.

(a) The after-tax cost when the tax rate is 25%, $K_L = 8\%(1 - 0.25) = 6\%$.

(b) The after-tax cost when the tax rate is 12.5%, $K_L = 8\%(1 - 0.125) = 7\%$. Note that the higher the rate of corporation tax, the lower the after-tax cost.

Leasing also provides finance on a medium- to long-term basis and again it seems appropriate to treat the cost of leasing as being similar to that of secured debt finance, given that leases are secured on the leased assets.

13.1.3 General comment

Equity finance represents the highest risk category of finance to investors (and tends to be the highest cost of finance to a company), as it is at the bottom of the creditor hierarchy should a company go into liquidation. Preference shares should cost less because they are paid dividends before ordinary share dividend (less risk) and rank higher in a liquidation situation. Debentures and loans are further up the creditor ladder than equity or preference shares implying a lower cost again. This lower cost is more pronounced if the interest-bearing debt is secured and if rates of corporate tax are high.

13.2 Weighted average cost of capital (WACC)

Having looked at different sources of finance, it is now necessary to work out the overall cost of capital. In reality companies are rarely financed by any one particular source of finance, and use a mixture of debt and equity. Because of this it would seem appropriate to calculate an average cost of finance. However, to reflect the extent of each source, a weight should be attached to each separate type of finance.

The weighting of each source of finance should be based on **market values**, as book values are of doubtful economic significance. Book values are historical and rarely reflect the current required return of providers of finance. In the case of a company using only equity and irredeemable debt, the following formula expresses the overall cost of finance for a company.

$$\text{WACC} = \frac{E}{D + E} (K_e) + \frac{D}{D + E} K_d (1 - T) \qquad (13.6)$$

where **E** and **D** represent the market values of equity and debt.

The equation can be expanded according to the number of different sources of finance used.

The major assumptions behind the WACC and its application as a discount rate in investment appraisal are:

1. That companies continue to invest in projects of a standard level of business risk, i.e. the business risk of the proposed investment is similar to the business risk of existing operations. If the business risk is different, a project specific discount rate that reflects the business risk should be considered.
2. New funds are raised in the same proportion as its existing capital structure and financial risk. If this is not the case, an investment appraisal technique called the adjusted present value (APV) should be used.
3. The project is small relative to the overall size of the company. If this is not the case, the scale of the investment could cause a change to occur in the perceived risk of the investing company, which renders the existing WACC an inappropriate discount rate.

WACC is not a static concept, as over time the market value of the securities and the cost of the various sources of finance will change. Companies should recalculate their WACC regularly to reflect any significant changes. This implies that WACC is both difficult to calculate and to apply in investment appraisal. Although you rarely find cost of capital calculations in the company financial statements, a lot more attention is being paid to the value of WACC due to its close association with concepts of economic value added.

Example 13.11 Calculation of WACC

The current capital structure of a company is as follows:

Ordinary shares (25c par)	€50 million
12% (four-year redeemable) debentures	€71 million

The company shares are trading at €2.20 ex dividend and the debentures at €105.50 ex interest. The company equity beta is 1.25, the risk-free rate of return is 6% and expected market return is 15%. The debentures are redeemable at a par of €100 in four years and the corporate tax rate is 12.5%.

Calculate the cost of capital for the company.

Solution

E = 200m × €2.20 = €440 million D = €71m × 1.055 = €74.91 million

K_e = 6% + (15% − 6%)1.25 = 17.25%

K_d is based on the IRR of the after-tax cash flows as follows:

Year	After tax @ 12.5%
0	(105.50)
1–4	10.5
4	100

K_d = IRR = 8.8%

$$\text{WACC} = \frac{440(17.25) + 74.91(8.8)}{440 + 74.91} = 16\%$$

13.2.1 Practical problems in calculating WACC

There are a number of problems in calculating the WACC in practice.

1. Choosing which model to use in calculating the cost of equity. One could use either the dividend valuation model or the capital asset pricing model – both rely on different assumptions. CAPM seems to be the preferred option, as it does not rely on estimating the dividend growth rate of a company using historical data and the assumption that past growth will be replicated into the future.
2. The market values of both debt and equity may be difficult to find. There may not be a continuous trading market and some forms of debt may not trade at all.
3. Many forms of debt exist, and company accounts may not always state the interest they are paying, or the maturity date. Debt may have split redemption dates or be in foreign currency form. Which redemption date should be used and at which exchange rate should the debt be converted into €?
4. Convertible debt starts out as debt (K_d) and then potentially reverts to equity (K_e). The difficulty is in knowing if redemption will occur! By assuming a redemption value, the K_d may be underestimated and if the conversion takes place and the conversion value is used, it may be overestimated.
5. Floating rate debt rates can be difficult to identify. What is the current rate as compared to previous rates in the accounts?
6. Where interest rates are subject to swap agreements, should the cost of debt reflect the interest rate when the loan was raised or the rate agreed in the swap? Foreign currency swaps also create difficulties.
7. Short-term debt should not be included in the WACC calculation as it is usually associated with financing short-term assets and a working capital issue. However, if an overdraft is used on an ongoing basis, it can be argued that it is being used to finance long-term assets and therefore should be included in the WACC.
8. Leasing provides finance on a medium- to long-term basis and while lease payments (after tax) may be identified, the capital value to which these payments should be related is more difficult to determine.

Very few, if any, companies include cost of capital calculations in their financial statements. The outsider trying to accommodate all the potential complexities listed above faces a difficult problem and results will vary with the arbitrary interpretation of the observer. However, the corporate treasury department within the company has access to more accurate information, which should lead to a more informed estimate.

13.3 CAPM and WACC

The capital asset pricing model (CAPM) was looked at in Chapter 6 and it was shown that the CAPM can be used instead of the dividend valuation model to establish an equity cost of capital. However, the CAPM can also be used to find the required rate of return which directly reflects the risk profile of a specific project. The formula restated is as follows:

$$K_e = E(R) = R_f + (E(R_m) - R_f)\beta$$

where K_e = cost of equity capital.

Example 13.12 CAPM and WACC

Scobie plc is financed by €3 million of equity and €1 million of irredeemable debt capital. The debt capital has a coupon rate of 6% before tax and is considered risk-free. The beta value of the company's equity is 1.25, the market return is expected to be 15%. The rate of corporation tax is 12.5%.

Solution
Ke = 6% + (15% − 6%) 1.25 = 17.25% using CAPM.
Kd = 6%(1 − 0.125)= 5.25% the after-tax cost.
WACC = ¾ (17.25%) + ¼ (5.25%) = 14.25%.
The WACC above would be an appropriate discount rate to use in the appraisal of projects with the same systematic risk as Scobie's current investments, i.e. the company stays in the same line of business.

Example 13.13 CAPM and DVM

Company A has a share beta of 1.5. The risk-free rate is 4% and the expected market return is 12%.
(a) What is the cost of equity?
(b) Continuing the example and assuming two different dividend policies:
    1. If the company has a policy of paying a constant dividend of 20c each year.
    2. If the dividend per share over the past number of years was as follows:

Year	1	2	3	4	5
Dividend	10c	11c	12c	13c	14c

Calculate the theoretical share price using the dividend valuation models.

Solution
(a) The CAPM can be used to find the cost of equity and the dividend valuation can be used to find a theoretical price for the share. Expected return = 4% + (12% − 4%) 1.5 = 16% and this also represents the cost of equity.

(b)   By using the constant dividend valuation model $K_e = div/P_o$ or $P_o = d/K_e$ this implies share price $= 20c/0.16 = €1.25$ in theory.

   Using the dividend growth model:

$$P_o = \frac{d(1 + g)}{(K_e - g)} = \frac{14c(1.0878)}{(0.16 - 0.0878)} = €2.11$$

13.4 Gearing, beta and the cost of capital

The greatest potential use of the capital asset pricing model in the financial management of a company is the ability to set risk-adjusted discount rates for new investment projects. The risk level associated with an equity investment has two elements, namely the business risk and the gearing or financial risk. The gearing of a company will affect the risk of the equity. If a company is geared its financial risk will be higher than a company that is all equity financed. This financial risk is an element of systematic risk and should be reflected in the beta value of a company's shares if that company is geared. The beta value of a geared company will be higher than the beta of a company that is identical in every respect except it is an ungeared company. This is because of the extra financial risk involved. The relationship between the level of gearing and equity betas is firmly based on the theories of Modigliani and Miller with corporate taxation (discussed later). The mathematical expression to show the relationship between geared and ungeared betas is as follows.

$$\beta a = \beta e \left[\frac{E}{E + D(1 - T)} \right] + \beta d \left[\frac{D(1 - T)}{E + D(1 - T)} \right] \tag{13.7}$$

where β_a is the asset beta or beta of an ungeared company. The asset beta represents only the business risk profile of the company and incorporates no financial risk at all.

β_e is the equity beta of a similar company that is geared. β_d is the beta of the debt in the geared company (sometimes considered risk-free or = 0).

D is the market value of the debt capital.

E is the market value of the equity.

T is the rate of corporation tax.

The formula above is an expression of the company's asset beta (or all equity beta) as a weighted average of its equity and debt betas. If the assumption is made that companies do not default on their interest payments, the beta of debt can be assumed to be zero and the formula is simplified.

   In this case the formula reduces to:

$$\beta a = \beta e \left[\frac{E}{E + D(1 - T)} \right] \tag{13.8}$$

From the formula a company's equity beta will always be greater than its asset beta (ungeared beta), unless a company is all equity financed – this ties in with the Modigliani and Miller formulae. The asset beta measures purely business risk as the finance is in all equity form and no financial risk exists.

The formula above can be used to estimate the beta of an unquoted company, by adjusting the beta of a quoted company in the same industry with similar operating characteristics.

Example 13.14 *Gearing and beta*

Company X is an all equity company that has just gone public and insufficient data is currently available about its own equity performance in order to calculate the company's equity beta. Company X is essentially a mobile phone sales company and a similar type of company (company Y) has a published beta of 1.15.

Company Y has a capital structure at market value of 30% debt and 70% equity. If the corporate tax rate is 12.5%, and the beta of debt is zero calculate the equity beta for company X.

Solution

$$\beta a = \beta e \times \left[\frac{E}{E + D(1 - T)} \right]$$

$$\beta a = \frac{1.15\ (70)}{70 + 30(1 - .125)} \qquad = 0.84$$

The above beta estimate could then be used to find the cost of equity in company X. If company X were a geared company, the same formula could be used to adjust 0.84 to reflect the financial risk associated with the level of debt capital in the company.

Example 13.15 *Gearing and beta*

If company X has a capital structure made up of 60% equity and 40% debt, what would be the geared beta for company X?

Solution
The ungeared beta for company X is 0.84, so this must now be regeared to reflect the new capital structure.

$$\beta a = \beta e \times \left[\frac{E}{E + D(1 - T)} \right]$$

$$0.84 = \beta_e \times \frac{60}{60 + 40(1 - 0.125)}$$

Calculating for the equity beta, the result is $\beta_e = 1.324$. In this case the beta has increased to reflect the increased financial risk.

There are problems associated in calculating beta factors using data about other companies:

1. It is difficult to find companies with identical operating characteristics.
2. Estimates of beta values are based on a statistical analysis of past data and may not be accurate.
3. Estimates using one company's data may differ from estimates using other companies.
4. Debt capital may not be risk-free.

If a company plans to invest in a diversification project outside its normal range of business expertise, the investment will involve a different level of systematic risk. The company's existing WACC would not be an appropriate discount factor to apply in investment appraisal. A discount rate should be calculated which is specific to the new project, and which takes into account both the projects systematic risk and the company's gearing level (financial risk).

This is a three-stage process:

1. Obtain published information on the beta values of companies in the industry into which the company is planning to diversify.
2. Adjust these beta values to reflect the company's capital structure.
3. Use the CAPM to find the cost of equity and the WACC.

Example 13.16 Diversification discount rate

Scobie plc (in Example 13.12 above) was financed by €3 million of equity and €1 million of irredeemable debt capital. The risk-free debt capital had a coupon rate of 6% before tax. The beta value of the company's equity was 1.25, the market return was 15% and the rate of corporation tax is 12.5%. The existing WACC was calculated at 14.25%.

Assume that the company is now proposing to invest in a project, which would involve diversification into a new industry, and the following information is available about a company in this industry.

This company has a beta of 1.59 and a debt:equity ratio of 1:2 based on market values.

Solution

The existing beta factor (1.25) and the WACC (14.25%) calculated before are of no use because one of the fundamental assumptions underpinning the application of WACC in investment appraisal is that the company remains in the same line of business. A new discount rate is needed to reflect the new business risk involved.

First adjust the beta.

$$\beta a = \beta e \quad \times \quad \left[\frac{E}{E + D(1-t)} \right]$$

$$= \quad \frac{1.59 \ (2)}{2 + 1(1 - .125)} \quad = 1.106$$

This is equivalent to the ungeared beta of a company in the same industry.

The next step is to gear this all equity beta to Scobie's capital structure (€3 million equity and €1 million debt).

$$\beta a = \beta e \quad \times \quad \left[\frac{E}{E + D(1-t)} \right]$$

$$1.106 = \beta_e \times \quad \frac{(3)}{3 + 1(1 - 0.125)}$$

$1.106 = 0.7742 \beta e$ and therefore $\beta e = 1.43$.

We can now get a project specific cost of equity using CAPM.

$$K_d = 6\% + (15\% - 6\%) \, 1.43 = 18.87\%.$$

The required rate of return calculated by this method is an appropriate discount rate for appraising the new project if it is being wholly financed by equity or retained earnings. If the project is being financed by a mixture of debt and equity finance, however, the required rate of return on equity will need to be combined with the cost of the new debt finance to give a project-specific weighted average cost of capital.

Using the existing capital structure above the WACC is calculated:

$$K_d = 6\%(1 - 0.125) = 5.25\%$$

Finally:

$$\text{WACC} = \tfrac{3}{4} \, (18.87\%) + \tfrac{1}{4} \, (5.25\%) = 15.47\%.$$

The application of CAPM in finding a target rate of return specific to individual projects is that it can be used to compare projects of all different risk classes. It is therefore superior to an NPV approach, which uses only one discount factor for all projects regardless of risk While the application of the CAPM may lead to better investment decisions, practical problems exist.

1. Companies may have difficulty identifying surrogate companies with similar systematic risk characteristics. Many companies have diversified activities rather than a specific area related to the project being appraised.
2. Capital structures measured by market values may be difficult to ascertain.
3. CAPM is a single period model, usually one year, whereas project duration tends to be over a number of years.
4. CAPM assumes that all investors are mean variance efficient.
5. The beta adjustment formulae are based on the theories of Modigliani and Miller and are therefore subject to the limitations of their theory particularly at very high gearing levels.

Example 13.17 WACC and capital structure change

The directors of a company are considering the feasibility of issuing 12% debentures at par to raise €1,000,000 for an investment to broaden their product range. The new plant is expected to produce a return of €240,000 per year indefinitely before tax and interest charges.

The company's existing capital structure is:
Issued ordinary shares (€0.50 nominal)	€3 million
Issued 5% preference shares (€1 nominal)	€6 million

The current market value of ordinary and preference shares are €2 and €0.80 respectively (ex dividend). The company's current earnings before corporation tax of 50% are €3,840,000 per year.

Earnings have been constant for the last few years and are always fully distributed.
(a) Calculate the current weighted average cost of capital (WACC).
(b) If there are no changes in the cost of equity or preference capital, what would you expect the market value of the ordinary shares and WACC to be after the issue of the debentures?

Solution (a)

Market value of equity = 6,000,000 × €2 = €12,000,000
Market value of preference shares = 6,000,000 × €0.80 = €4,800,000
To find the cost of equity, you need to find the dividend available.

Annual pre-tax profit	€3,840,000
Less tax at 50%	€1,920,000
Profit after tax	€1,920,000
Less preference dividend	€300,000
Available to equity	€1,620,000

Cost of equity = Dividend available/market value of shares
              = €1,620,000/€12,000,000 = 13.5%

Cost of preference shares = €300,000/€4,800,000 = 6.25%

$$\text{WACC} = \frac{\text{€12million} \times 13.5\% + \text{€4.8million} \times 6.25\%}{\text{€16.8million}} = 11.43\%$$

This is the current WACC and the minimum target rate of return for the company, providing it stays in the same line of business and maintains its present capital structure.

Solution (b)
Again to find the cost of equity, you need to find the dividend available.

New pre-tax profit	€4,080,000
Less debenture interest	€120,000
Profit before tax	€3,960,000
Less tax at 50%	€1,980,000
After tax	€1,980,000
Less preference dividend	€300,000
Available to equity	€1,680,000

If the cost of equity is constant at 13.5%, the market value can be calculated as follows:

Market value of shares = Dividend available/cost of equity
                   = €1,680,000/13.5% = €12,444,444 giving a share value of
                   approximately €2.07 per share
Cost of new debentures = 12%(1 − .5) = 6%

$$\text{WACC} = \frac{\text{€12.44million} \times 13.5\% + \text{€4.8million} \times 6.25\% + \text{€1million} \times 6\%}{\text{€18.244million}} = 11.18\%$$

The answer assumes K_e, K_p and the market value of preference shares remain constant. This is an unrealistic assumption, as the issue of debt increases the financial risk of the shareholders. This idea of increasing cost of equity because of financial risk is a core element in the capital structure debate, which is now introduced.

13.5 Capital structure

Before discussing the concept of an optimal capital structure we need to explain the term **financial gearing**. Gearing refers to the amount of debt finance versus equity finance that a company has in its capital structure. As in the case of the WACC, it is based on market values rather than book values. A company's gearing can be measured using a number of ratios, for example

$$\text{Gearing ratio} = \frac{\text{Market value of debt}}{\text{Market value of debt + Market value of equity}}$$

Preference shares are treated as debt.
Another measure of financial risk is interest cover:

$$= \frac{\text{Profit before interest and taxation}}{\text{Interest}}$$

Example 13.18 Financial gearing

Using the information in Example 13.17 part (b), calculate the gearing ratio and the interest cover.

Solution
The results would be as follows

$$\text{Gearing ratio} = \frac{\text{€4.8 million + €1 million}}{\text{€12.444 million + €4.8 million + €1 million}}$$

$$= \quad 0.3179 \times 100\% = 31.79\%$$

$$\text{Interest cover} = \frac{\text{€4.08 million}}{\text{€120,000}} = 34 \text{ times}$$

When comparing ratios it is very important to compare like with like. If you are given figures of gearing for two companies, make sure that both figures are compared on the same ratio basis.

A high level of gearing creates financial risk and this risk is borne by the ordinary shareholders. For equity holders, financial risk is evident in the variability of earnings after deducting payments to holders of debt capital. The higher the gearing of a company, the greater will be the amount of interest payments, and the less the proportion of earnings available to equity, leading to a perceived financial risk for ordinary shareholders. This financial risk requires a reward in the form of a risk premium and is reflected in a higher cost of equity. At very high levels of gearing a company may get into difficulty meeting its interest commitments and may face the risk of bankruptcy. If gearing levels are going to affect the cost of equity then it follows that a company's gearing could have a bearing on its WACC. The relationship can be expressed as follows:

$$\text{Cost of equity} = \text{risk-free rate of interest} + \text{risk premium}$$
$$\text{where the risk premium} = \text{business risk} + \text{financial risk} + \text{bankruptcy risk}$$

Be careful not to mix up operational gearing and financial gearing. Operational gearing represents the relationship of the fixed cost to the total cost of an operating unit. Both forms of gearing have a common feature in that an increase in either – i.e. higher fixed cost or higher debt – reduces the earnings available to shareholders and therefore increases their risk (see Chapter 3).

Example 13.19 Operational gearing

	Company X	Company Y
Sales	€5 million	€5 million
Variable Costs	€3 million	€1 million
Fixed costs	€1 million	€3 million
EBIT	€1 million	€1 million

What is the impact of a 10% increase in sales volume on the EBIT of both companies?

Solution
X EBIT = (€5m – €3m) × 1.1 – 1m = €1.2 million or a 20% increase.
Y EBIT = (€5m – €1m) × 1.1 – 3m = €1.4 million or a 40% increase.

$$\text{Operational gearing} = \frac{\%\text{ change in EBIT}}{\%\text{ change in sales}}$$

X = 20%/10% = 2 and Y = 40%/10% = 4.

Here Y has a higher operational gearing because it has higher fixed costs and its operating earnings are more volume-sensitive. There is a trade-off between operational gearing and financial gearing. When a company has a high degree of operational gearing, unless sales are quite stable it would prefer to avoid financial gearing, and vice versa.

13.6 Theories on gearing

There has been a lot of academic literature on the subject of whether an ideal capital structure exists, and the theory can be summarised with the following two major models – the traditional (relevancy) theory and the Modigliani and Miller (irrelevancy) theory.
    Both theories are based on the following assumptions:

1. All earnings are paid out in interest and dividends and are constant in perpetuity.
2. The gearing of a company can change by issuing debt for equity or issuing equity for debt.
3. No transaction costs exist in buying or selling shares.
4. No taxes exist, either personal or corporate.
5. Business risk is constant over time.
6. Companies can only issue irredeemable debt finance or ordinary equity shares.
7. Shareholders have perfect knowledge of all information.

13.7 The traditional approach to capital structure

The proposition here is that an optimal capital structure exists and that a company can increase its market value by using the best mix of equity and debt.

The WACC is saucer-shaped and thus an ideal capital structure exists. Selecting a particular method of financing projects is therefore important.

Figure 8.1 Traditional view of gearing

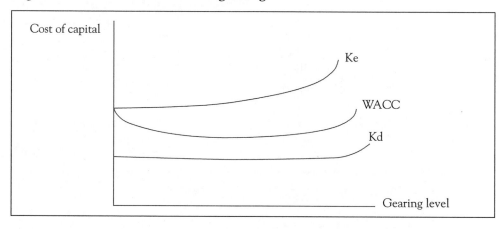

The cost of equity rises as debt increases (financial risk). The cost of debt remains unchanged up to a certain level of gearing and then the cost of debt increases. The WACC does not remains constant, but rather falls initially as the proportion of cheaper debt capital increases, and then begins to increase as the rising cost of equity (and possibly debt because of default risk) becomes more significant. The implication is that an optimal level does exist and is found where the WACC is at a minimum. A company should therefore try and locate a combination of debt and equity that minimises its overall cost of capital and maximise shareholder wealth. Minimising the weighted average cost of capital and maximising market value are identical concepts.

Example 13.20 Traditional view illustrated

Suppose a company is all equity financed with K_e =20% (=WACC). Now suppose it introduces debt capital (K_d = 10%) and its debt to equity ratio is 3:7. If the cost of equity rises because of perceived financial risk to 22%, what is the new WACC?

Solution

WACC = 7/10(22%) + 3/10(10%) = 18.4%. The WACC has been lowered with the introduction of debt.

Now suppose the company increases the proportion of debt to give a debt to equity ratio of 1:1. If the cost of equity now rises to 28%, what is the WACC?

In this case the WACC = ½(28%) + ½(10%) = 19% and so the WACC has started to rise again, indicating that the gearing is above the optimal level.

The traditional view has no underlying theory to show how much the cost of equity would rise due to increases in gearing, or how the cost of debt should rise because of default risk. It is purely a descriptive viewpoint. This 'common sense' view of capital structure was accepted until in 1958, when the ideas of Franco Modigliani and Merton Miller opened up a whole new debate on capital structure and corporate value.

13.8 The net operating income approach of Modigliani and Miller

The proposition put forward by Modigliani and Miller (M&M) flew in the face of the traditional model. Their seminal paper in 1958 proposed that, for a given operating or business risk, the WACC remains unchanged at all levels of gearing, implying that that no optimal capital structure exists and that how a company was financed was irrelevant. Their view is that companies which operate in the same type of business, with similar earnings and which have similar operating risks, must have the same total value, irrespective of their capital structures.

The simple idea is that how an asset is financed is irrelevant. For example, if you purchase a house through a bank loan (debt) or savings (equity), the value of the house is not based on the way in which the house has been financed. What gives the house value is the income it can potentially generate, i.e. how the house was financed has no impact on its resale value.

Figure 13.2 Modigliani and Miller theory of gearing without tax

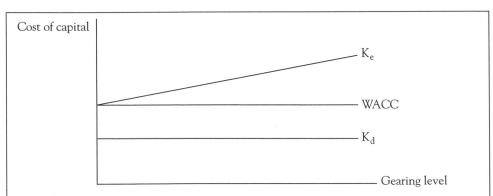

Here the cost of debt **(K_d)** remains unchanged as the level of gearing rises. The **WACC** is unchanged as gearing levels change. As gearing increases, the cost of equity **(K_e)** increases in such a way as to exactly offset the greater proportion of cheaper debt capital.

As the WACC remains constant, this implies the method of financing projects is irrelevant. M&M came to this conclusion based on the assumptions above, but added an extra assumption that capital markets are perfect, i.e. bankruptcy costs were zero.

Their starting point was that if two firms had similar operating and business risk, and similar earnings, then they must have the same overall value and the same WACC.

Proposition 1   Market value of the firm is independent of capital structure.

$$V_g = V_u \qquad (13.9)$$

Proposition 2   Cost of equity in a geared firm is higher than that of an ungeared firm, or $K_{eg} > K_{eu}$.

$$K_{eg} = K_{eu} + \text{Premium for financial risk}$$

$$K_{eg} = K_{eu} + (K_{eu} - K_d)\ D/E \qquad (13.10)$$

Unlike the traditional view, this second proposition allows a way of computing the increase in the cost of equity resulting from an increase in gearing.

V_g is the value of the geared company
V_u is the value of the ungeared company
K_{eg} is the cost of equity of the geared company
K_{eu} is the cost of equity of the ungeared company
K_d is the cost of debt pre-tax
D and E are the market values of debt and equity respectively
$V_g = D + E$ and $V_u = E$

M&M developed a defence of their approach based on investor arbitrage, i.e. switching through buying/selling shares between companies. In this arbitrage process, however, investors would substitute personal gearing for corporate gearing and continue to do so, selling shares in one company and buying shares in another, until the market value of each firm is equal.

M&M argued that two companies identical in every respect except their capital structure should not have different costs of capital and therefore market valuations.

The argument is best illustrated with an example.

Example 13.21 Modigliani and Miller's theory illustrated

Suppose we have two companies A and B who are identical in every respect except for the way in which they are financed. Both are in the same risk class and have the same operating characteristics, however A is all equity financed and B has €40,000 worth of irredeemable debt at 8% interest included in its capital structure. Both companies have the same annual earnings before tax of €20,000 and these earnings are assumed constant in perpetuity. The cost of equity is higher in B to reflect the financial risk associated with debt capital.

The market value of both companies is as follows:

	Company A	Company B
1. Annual earnings (PBIT)	€20,000	€20,000
2. *Less* interest	—	€3,200
3. Available to equity (and distributed)	€20,000	€16,800
4. Cost of equity	13.5%	14%
5. Market value of equity (3/4)	€148,148	€120,000
6. Market value of debt	—	€40,000
7. Market value of company (5 + 6)	€148,148	€160,000
8. **WACC** (PBIT/Market value)	**13.5%**	**12.5%**
9. Gearing ratio D/(D + E)	0%	25%

As you can see, the above conforms to the traditional model, in that the two companies have different market values purely because they have different capital structures. Modigliani and Miller believed this was a short-term disequilibrium and could not last, because investors in company B could improve their return by switching companies. They would consider company A to be undervalued and company B to be overvalued.

If we assume an investor owns 10% of company B and receives 10% of the dividends, i.e. 10% of €16,800 = €1,680, the **arbitrage process** would occur as follows:

1. Sell shares in B for €12,000 (10% of €120,000).
2. Borrow €4,000 at 8%. By doing this, the investor is replicating personal gearing for the corporate gearing that exists in B (10% of €40,000). The annual interest cost is €320.
3. Invest the €16,000 in company A.

The annual return will now be

$$\frac{€16,000}{€148,148} \ (€20,000) \text{ less interest of } €320 = (€2,160 - €320) = €1,840$$

This is an improvement of (€1,840 − €1,680) = €160. This risk-free surplus of €160 is called an arbitrage profit. Investors will continue to practice arbitrage, buying **A** shares and increasing their value (excess demand), selling **B** shares and depressing their value (excess supply), until the market values of the two companies are the same and no further opportunity for arbitrage exists.

Since both the market values and the earnings in both are the same, it follows that the WACC is the same despite the difference in gearing.

Example 13.22 Modigliani and Miller and cost of equity

Crumlin is an all equity company with a 16% cost of equity. Kimmage is similar to Crumlin in all respects, except that it is a geared company financed by €1,000,000 of 5% debentures with a current market price of €50 per cent ex interest. Kimmage also has one million ordinary shares with a current market value of €1.50 ex dividend. Using the propositions of M&M, what is the cost of equity in Kimmage and what is its WACC?

Solution

Here K_d = €5/€50 = 10%, D = €500,000 and E = €1,500,000

$$K_{eg} = K_{eu} + (K_{eu} - K_d) \, D/E = 16\% + (16\% - 10\%) \; \frac{€500,000}{€1,500,000} = 18\%$$

The company has a total market value of €2 million made up of ¼ debt and ¾ equity.

$$WACC = \frac{1}{4} \times 10\% + \frac{3}{4} \times 18\% = 16\%$$

Here, as gearing is introduced the cost of equity rises, but in such a way as to maintain the same WACC.

The **weaknesses** associated with M&M are as follows:
1. It is impossible in practice to find identical firms with different financial structures.
2. The cost of borrowing tends to be higher for an individual than for a company.
3. Transaction costs can impede the arbitrage process.
4. It ignores taxation, particularly corporate taxation.
5. Earnings may be retained in practice.
6. It ignores growth and possible changes from year to year.
7. Investors are not necessarily rational and may not use arbitrage to maximise return.
8. In company A above, the investors' stake is €16,000 not €12,000.
9. As gearing levels reach extremely high levels (with potential default in interest payment obligations being met), debenture holders will require higher coupon rates.

Modigliani and Miller did ignore the possibility of bankruptcy and its costs, so at high levels of gearing their theory may not be valid. Bankruptcy costs relate to the fact that when a company is liquidated, its assets are usually sold for less than the going concern value. This loss in value can often be borne by debt holders, who may seek a higher coupon rate to reflect this potential risk. Also, in potential bankruptcy situations, suppliers may refuse to supply trading stock and customers may refuse to buy if they perceive a risk that the after sales service will not be there in the future. These operating problems will reduce future cash flows and company value.

13.9 Modigliani and Miller with taxation

In M&M's second paper on capital structure in 1963, the earlier model was amended, by recognising the existence of corporate taxation. Because interest is an allowable deduction for the purposes of corporate tax, the more debt a company takes on, the more of their profits the company will shield against tax. The after-tax cost of debt capital is cheaper than equity finance, and therefore the WACC will fall as debt capital is introduced. Based on this theory the balance shifts in favour of debt capital and the implication is that companies should borrow as much as possible.

Geared companies pay less tax than ungeared companies and will, therefore, have a greater market value and a lower weighted average cost of capital.

Figure 13.3 Modigliani and Miller theory of gearing with tax

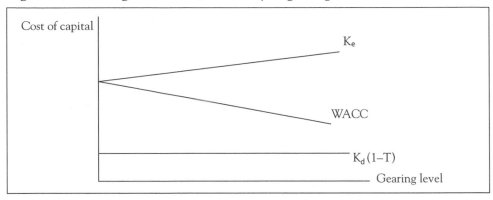

T is the rate of corporation tax.

M&M adjusted their formulae to allow for taxes:

(1) $\qquad V_g = V_u + DT$ $\qquad\qquad\qquad\qquad\qquad$ (13.11)

(2) $\qquad K_{eg} = K_{eu} + (1 - T)(K_{eu} - K_d)\, D/E$ $\qquad\qquad$ (13.12)

This implies that the WACC continues to fall up to 100% gearing levels and by implication

$$V_g > V_u \qquad \text{[by DT]}$$

Consider **Example 13.22** on capital structure and assume a corporate tax rate of 20%. The propositions above would imply that the WACC should be less than the 16% found previously.

Solution

Here K_d after tax = €5$(1 - 0.2)$/€50 = 8%, D = €500,000 and E = €1,500,000

$$K_{eg} = 16\% + (1 - 0.2)(16\% - 10\%)\ \frac{€500,000}{€1,500,000}\ = 17.6\%$$

WACC = $^1/4$ X 8% + 3/4 X 17.6% = 15.2% i.e. WACC is reduced.

If we were to increase gearing and switch the proportions so that the company was 75% debt financed the result would be a further reduction in the WACC.

$$K_{eg} = 16\% + (1 - 0.2)(16\% - 10\%)\ \frac{€1,500,000}{€500,000}\ = 30.4\%$$

WACC = 3/4 × 8% + 1/4 × 30.4% = 13.6%, i.e. the higher the gearing the lower the WACC.

There is an alternative formula to find the WACC without having to find the cost of equity in the geared company.

$$\text{WACC} = K_{eu} \left[1 - \frac{DT}{E + D} \right] \qquad (13.13)$$

Take the example of Kimmage and Crumlin with tax at 20%.

$$\text{WACC} = 16\% \left[1 - \frac{€500,000 \ (0.20)}{€1,500,000 + €500,000} \right] = 15.2\%$$

Modigliani and Miller argued that since the WACC falls as gearing rises, and the value of the company rises as WACC falls, the value of a geared company will always be higher than that of an ungeared company. The difference in value is based on the amount of debt-associated tax saving of the geared company (**DT**).

The positive tax effects of debt finance will be exhausted, however, where there is an insufficient tax liability to use the tax relief that is available (tax exhaustion). M&M defended their model using the arbitrage process. However, in substituting personal gearing for corporate gearing you must allow for tax relief on corporate debt (see question 16).

Taking the earlier example of company A and company B, let us assume tax at 12.5% and adjust personal gearing for tax relief. In this case the investor should borrow €4,000(1 − 0.125) = €3,500.

Companies do not follow all-debt policies, which indicates the existence of factors that undermine the tax advantages of debt finance, the most obvious being the risk of bankruptcy.

This is the risk of interest rate charges actually putting the company into liquidation and from the shareholders' point of view, the possibility of losing the value of their initial investment, due to the position they occupy in the creditors' hierarchy.

M&M's second model ignored the market imperfection associated with bankruptcy costs. In reality there is a possibility of a company defaulting on its interest payments at high gearing levels. The costs of bankruptcy include the costs of paying lenders higher rates of interest to compensate for higher risk, the costs of employing lawyers and accountants to manage the liquidation process and the costs of having to sell off assets below their market value. By combining the tax shield advantage of gearing with the bankruptcy costs associated with high gearing, the concept of an optimal capital structure appears again. The problem of tax exhaustion mentioned earlier is another reason why companies might try to avoid very high gearing levels.

13.10 Pecking order theory

This theory, first introduced by Donaldson (1961) and developed further by Myers (1984), suggests that financial managers **do not pursue an optimal capital structure** but that funds are raised along the line of least resistance. Consequently, funds are raised in the following order:

1. **Internally generated:** Retained earnings are the easiest to raise with very little external scrutiny. Retained earnings, however, are limited by the amount of cash generated from operations, and by the need to pay a dividend.

2. **Debt capital:** If insufficient funds are available from retained earnings etc. to finance new projects, various forms of debt are introduced due to low issue costs. This source of funds is limited by the company's gearing position, the probability of financial distress and the limit on borrowing imposed by lenders in restrictive covenants.

3. **Equity:** This is the last resort source of external finance, due to higher issue costs and the increased disclosure of information.

Myers suggested the order of preference relates to a form of asymmetry of information between a company and the markets. For example, suppose a company needs finance for a new project that the market undervalues. The management, with their inside information about this project, will want to finance this project through retained earnings so that, when the market finally sees the true value of the project, existing shareholders will benefit. If the retained earnings are insufficient, the management will issue debt finance in preference to equity finance, as they consider the equity to be undervalued

The consequence of this theory is that profitable companies borrow the least, as they have no need for external funds and not because they desire low gearing levels, which is in sharp contrast to the idea of an optimal capital structure. Baskin also found a negative correlation between high profit levels and gearing. Pecking order theory does not explain the influence of taxation, issue costs, financial distress on the capital structure decision, or whether there is an ideal capital structure. Because of these limitations, it is often used as a complement to Modigliani and Miller rather than as an alternative theory.

13.11 Practical factors that influence a company's capital structure

1. **Tax rates:** The higher the level of corporate taxes the more tax-efficient and attractive debt capital becomes. If, however, the company becomes tax-exhausted, it will not be as attracted to higher gearing levels. At a certain level of gearing companies may discover that they have no taxable income left, against which to offset interest charges. After this point companies will experience all the problems of gearing and none of the advantages.

2. **Asset base:** Companies with high levels of tangible assets will find it easier to take on debt, since they are in a better position to offer security in the event of bankruptcy than companies with a high level of intangible assets. Intangible assets such as capitalised research and development expenditure do not provide security for further borrowing. The nature of the asset base has been shown empirically to affect the capital structure. In practice, companies know it is easier to borrow money on the basis of land and buildings than it is on trademarks, etc.

3. **Cash flow volatility:** A company with a stable cash flow can service debt capital easier than a company with a volatile cash flow. The greater the potential variability in the projected cash flows, the more difficult it will be for a company to take on high debt levels. High-risk ventures are normally financed by equity, as there is no legal obligation to pay equity dividends.

4. **Interest rate levels:** Debt capital issues are attractive when interest rates are low. When interest rates are high it will be relatively expensive to attract investors in a debt issue.

5. **Stock market performance**: Where a bull market exists, with high share values, it may be attractive to issue equity as a smaller number of shares may generate the finance needed.

6. **Articles of association**: This indicates what types of finance are authorised in a company. The articles can be changed by the company through the stock exchange.

7. **Foreign currency operations**: A company may want to obtain finance in a foreign currency and service the capital out of their foreign currency earnings in order to minimise foreign currency exposure or to protect against political risk. This is even more attractive if the interest rates in the foreign country are lower than domestic rates.

8. **Issue costs:** Debt tends to have a cheaper issuance cost than equity and no issue is needed in the case of retained earnings. Arrangement costs on bank loans are significantly lower than flotation costs of new issues of equity.

9. **Management preference:** Retained earnings are often preferred over debt and equity issues (pecking order). This is partly due to the transaction cost involved in raising finance, but is also due to the balance of ownership and control.

10. **Industry norms:** Substantial deviations from the industry norm may send the wrong signal to investors. Behavioural theory or 'herd migration' theory was first proposed by Zeckhauser, Patel and Hendricks and they found that in 70% of industries studied, more than 15% of companies changed their capital structure 'with the herd', i.e. they followed what other companies in the industry were doing. There is also the occasional tendency of banks to refuse to lend to companies whose debt:equity ratio is higher than the industry average. Credit-rating agencies often compare companies gearing ratios to that of other companies in the industry when deciding credit ratings.

11. **Agency costs:** These are the direct or indirect costs that try to ensure the agents (managers) act in the interests of equity and debt holders. Examples of agency costs include covenants written into debt contracts. Borrowing money often entails certain obligations for the borrower over and above repaying the interest and principal. These are known as covenants. These include restrictions on the use of the assets financed by the loan, restrictions on dividend payments (to prevent the capital base being run down and thereby increasing the risk to the lenders) and restrictions on further borrowing. These agency costs may restrict the level of debt in a company.

12. **Dilution of earnings:** Large issues of equity could lead to the dilution of EPS, if profits from new investments are not immediate. This may upset shareholders and lead to falling share prices.

13. **Operating gearing:** Companies with high operating gearing (high proportion of fixed assets) tend to have volatile operating profits. If sales increase, operating profit increases by a larger percentage and if sales volume falls operating profit falls by a higher percentage. Generally, it is a high-risk policy to combine high financial gearing with high operating gearing.

Many of these factors can have a huge impact on how a company is financed. Although the list of practical factors above may indicate that capital structure management is more art than science, it indicates the basic considerations that go into making capital structure decisions.

> **Box 13.1 Man Utd's profits will just cover Glazer debts**
>
> While Manchester United have regained its position as the richest club in Britain with record financial results for last year, almost all of its profits will be required by the Glazer family to repay loans associated with the takeover of the club. According to the club's year-end financial results for 2007, United's gross turnover rose 21% to €245 million, compared to €202 million in 2006. Profits before tax rose to €59.6 million, a 93% increase on the previous year. Match-day revenue was up 30% to €92.5 million, following the expansion of Old Trafford to a 76,000 capacity. Media revenue was up 35% to €61.5 million boosted by the team's UEFA Champions League semi-final spot, FA cup final appearance and the Premier League win. There was also a 15% increase in commercial revenues to €56 million, mainly due to the world record jersey sponsorship with AIG and accompanying financial services deals. The club's after-tax profits were €42.3 million.
>
> However, this is just over the €42 million required for the annual interest payments of 8% on a €525 million loan secured against the club's assets by Red Football, the Glazer-owned holding company. Malcolm Glazer and his family also have to cover a further €20 million annually on another €135 million in borrowing.
>
> 'The amount of debt repayment we are responsible for is comfortably serviced by the business and that will remain the case' said David Gill, chief executive of Manchester United.
>
> Linda Maher, *Sunday Business Post*, 13 January 2008

13.12 The capital structure debate

The traditional and Modigliani and Miller theories of capital structure should be viewed as a starting point for appreciating the problems faced by a company in determining its appropriate capital structure. Debt attracts tax relief but high levels of debt can cause financial distress in a company and a financial manager must try to balance these opposing effects. The traditional model suggests an ideal capital structure exists, but gives no analytical mechanism for finding it.

In their first paper Modigliani and Miller suggested that capital structure was irrelevant, but then adjusted their model to show that with market imperfections, such as taxation and bankruptcy risk, a company should use debt capital, but avoid extremely high levels of gearing (they lead to a higher WACC).

When you look at the practical factors that a company would take on board in deciding their capital structure, it seems likely that there is a range of capital structures that could minimise WACC, rather than one optimal capital structure. Empirical research has failed to identify any unique capital structure applicable to any industry or company type. Hamada found that announcements of increased gearing levels were associated with equity value increases and reductions in gearing tend to have an adverse effect on share values. Homaifar, Zeitz and Benkato found that gearing levels tend to be higher in firms exposed to higher levels of corporate tax and that the larger the company the higher the gearing level. Most companies are attracted to some level of gearing, but very high levels of gearing are rarely seen. The evidence seems to suggest that Modigliani and Miller are correct up to a point and that WACC falls as cheaper debt capital is introduced, but beyond which, by increasing gearing towards a 100 per cent level, the WACC begins to rise again.

Companies should perhaps pursue sensible levels of gearing, i.e. use the tax advantages of debt capital but avoid levels of debt that could cause problems of bankruptcy.

SUMMARY

- The cost of capital for a company is a fundamental determinant of its market value, as it is the basis for the discount rate in investment appraisal methods such as net present value.
- The cost of equity can be calculated based on dividend models, or risk using the capital asset pricing model.
- The cost of debt capital must be adjusted to take into account the tax-deductibility of interest payments.
- The costs of individual sources of finance must be weighted according to market value if possible.
- The WACC is appropriate for appraising investments if the company's capital structure remains stable and the business risk associated is similar to existing company operations.
- The beta factor for a share reflects both business and financial risk. The CAPM can be used to calculate the required rate of return of a security and, more important, an appropriate discount rate for a company which is diversifying away from its core business.
- Theories of capital structure include the traditional, Modigliani/Miller (pre- and post-corporate tax) and Donaldson's pecking order models.
- Empirical evidence suggests many practical factors influence capital structure and that the existence of an optimal capital structure is open to debate.

WEB LINKS

www.londonstockexchange.com
www.ise.ie
www.ft.com/companies/financial
www.irishtimes.com/business/
www.sbpost.ie/

QUESTIONS

1. Are retained earnings a free source of finance?
2. Define capital gearing. What is meant by a highly geared company?
3. Describe the traditional viewpoint on capital structure and its relationship with cost of capital.
4. The calculation of the weighted average cost of capital (WACC) is straightforward in theory, but in practice it is not that easy. Outline the possible difficulties that might be experienced when trying to calculate the WACC.

5.♦ (a) A convertible 8% loan stock of Photocopy Bernie plc currently trades at €140 per €100 nominal. The stock may be converted in five years' time at 50 ordinary shares per €100 of nominal stock. The debentures will be redeemed at €120 if conversion does not take place. The present price of ordinary shares is €2.20 and is expected to grow by 5% per annum over the next five years.

What is the cost of capital to the company if corporation tax is at the rate of 12.5%? Assume that tax savings occur in the same year that the interest payments arise.

(b) Kavanaugh Joe plc has issued €10 million of 7% convertible debentures. The nominal value of the debentures is €100 and they are convertible into 45 shares per €100 nominal in 5 years. The share price is expected to be €4 in 5 years' time. The investors required rate of return is 15%. Estimate the current market value of the debentures using present-value methods, assuming conversion takes place, and comment on any reservations you may have with your evaluation.

(c) Lou Pole plc has issued 8% debentures (nominal value €100) paid semi-annually on 30 June and 31 December each year. The debentures are redeemable at par in seven years' time and have a current market price ex interest of €89. Calculate the cost of the debentures.

6.♦ Soft Stout plc has annual earnings before interest and tax of €15 million. These earnings are expected to remain constant. The market price of the company's ordinary shares is 86 cents per share cumulative of dividend and €105.5 per debenture ex interest. An interim dividend of six cents per share has been declared.

Corporation tax is at the rate of 12.5% and all available earnings are distributed as dividends.

The long-term capital structure of the firm is as follows:

Ordinary shares (25 cents par value)   €12.5 million
16% debentures 31/12/2011 nominal €100   €23.697 million

Calculate the cost of capital of the company assuming it is now 31 December 2008.

7. Spare Me plc is currently financed entirely by equity with 2 million shares currently trading at €4.20 ex dividend. This company proposes to issue €4 million of fixed debt at 10% per annum interest and the finance raised will be used to repurchase ordinary shares. The corporate tax rate is 12.5% and current earnings before interest and tax are €2.5 million. These earnings are not expected to change for the foreseeable future and earnings are fully distributed.

Using Modigliani and Miller's model, in a world of corporate tax, estimate the impact on Spare Me's cost of capital.

8.♦ Doarunner plc is an all-equity company with an equilibrium market value of €32.5 million and a cost of capital of 18% per year. The company proposes to repurchase €5 million of equity and replace it with 13% irredeemable loan stock. Doarunner's earnings before interest and tax are expected to be constant for the foreseeable future. Corporate tax is at a rate of 12.5%. All profits are paid out as dividends.

Using the assumptions of Modigliani and Miller explain and demonstrate how this change of capital structure will affect (a) the market value (b) the cost of equity and (c) the WACC of Doarunner plc.

9. Dropkick plc is an all-equity-financed company with a market value of €45 million. Earnings are constant and are fully distributed. The current share price ex dividend is €2 and the current dividend is 38c. Dropkick is considering buying back €8 million of equity by issuing 10% irredeemable loan stock. The current rate of corporate tax is 12.5%.

    Using Modigliani and Miller's model, in a world of corporate tax, calculate the capital structuring impact on Dropkick's cost of equity, WACC and market value.

10. The government has just announced that corporation tax is to be reduced from 24% per year to 20% per year and the directors of your company wish to know the likely effect of this change on the company's share price and cost of capital.

    The company's current capital structure is

	€m
Ordinary shares (50c par value)	30
Share premium	48
Other reserves	62
Shareholders equity	140
10% debentures (irredeemable)	40
	180

    The company's shares are trading at €3.20 ex dividend, and the debentures at €125 ex interest. The company's current cost of equity is 14% and the tax cut is expected to increase the net present value of the company's operating cash flows by €15 million. Assume that the cost of debt and the market price of debt do not change as a result of this tax change.
    (a) Estimate the company's current weighted average cost of capital.
    (b) Using M&M's theory of capital structure (with tax), find the expected share price after the tax change.
    (c) What is the company's expected weighted average cost of capital after the tax change?

11. You have been asked to calculate the weighted average cost of capital (WACC) of Temple Villa plc based on the following information.

    ### Balance sheet as at 31 December 2008

	€ Million
Fixed assets	445
Current assets	185
Current liabilities	(110)
	520
Ordinary share capital (25c shares)	90
9% preference shares (€1 shares)	50
Reserves	145
11% loan stock (redeemable 31/12/2013)	80
10% irredeemable loan stock	95
Bank loan	60
	520

The ordinary share price ex dividend is €1.76. The company equity beta is 1.1, the risk-free rate is 6% and the estimated market return is 16%. Preference shares are priced at €0.76 cumulative of dividend. The 11% stock priced at €95 ex interest. The 10% stock priced at €72 ex interest. Bank interest is currently 10% and corporation tax is at 12.5%.

(a)   Calculate the WACC for the company.

(b)   Comment briefly on the practical factors a company may take into account when determining capital structure.

(c)   If the company had annual earnings before interest and tax of €50 million this year, calculate the earnings per share (EPS).

12.   Hugo First plc is an engineering company, which has just announced its final results for the year 5 ended 31 December. Earnings per share (EPS) and dividends per share (DPS) for the past five years have been as follows:

Year	1	2	3	4	5
EPS in cents	61	64	71	73	76
DPS in cents	38	40	41	42	44

The board of directors believes that the annual growth rate in dividends will be consistent with the average growth rate in dividends above. The company beta factor is 1.4, the risk-free rate of return is 7% and the market return is expected to be 12% for the next year.

(a)   Use the capital asset pricing model and Gordon's growth model to calculate the share price (€) that might be expected.

(b)   Give reasons why the share price might react differently.

13.   (Ref. Appendix 13B) An Irish multinational company Gerties plc has $100 million of eurobonds issued at 6%, and redeemable at par in three years' time. The eurobond issue has a nominal value of $1,000 and is currently trading at $900 ex interest. The current rate of exchange is €1 = $1.10. The corporation tax rate is 12.5%.

(a)   What is the cost of capital to the company if the exchange rate remains stable?

(b)   What is the cost of capital if the dollar is expected to appreciate by 15% per annum?

(c)   What is the cost of capital if the dollar is expected to depreciate by 5% per annum?

(d)   What is the current market value of the eurobond issue in euros?

14.   The cost of debt in Caulry plc varies according to the level of gearing in the company as follows:

% debt = (debt)/(debt + equity)	Pre-tax cost of debt
0%	Not relevant
20%	6.5%
40%	8.5%
60%	10%

The company's ungeared equity beta (asset beta) is 0.85. The risk-free rate is 6% per annum, and the market return is 14% per annum. Corporate tax is at 12.5%.

Estimate the WACC under the gearing levels specified and suggest an appropriate level.

15.   Scribes plc is a food and drink company with 15 million shares in its capital structure. The current share price is €2.75 ex dividend. Past performance of dividends is as follows:

Year	2004	2005	2006	2007	2008
Div. per share (cents)	24	28	32	35	38

Scribes plc also has the following debt in its capital structure as at 31 December 2008. All interest has just been paid.

Type	Book value	Market value per €100	Redemption value
7% Irredeemable	€10 million	€70	–
5% Redeemable 31 December 2016	€5 million	€80	par

(a)   Calculate the cost of each type of finance and the weighted average cost of capital for Scribes plc assuming no corporate tax.

(b)   Under what circumstances is it not appropriate to use the WACC as a target rate of return in investment appraisal?

16.♦   Rodge and Podge are two companies in the electronics industry. The companies have the same business risk and are almost identical in all respects except for their capital structures and market valuations. The capital structure of Rodge is entirely equity financed with 80 million shares with a market value of €1.40 per share. Podge has 25 million shares with a share value of €4 each and €25 million of 12% irredeemable debentures currently valued at par.

Annual earnings before interest and taxation are €25 million. Corporation tax is at 20%.

If you owned 4% of the equity of Podge and you agreed with the theories of Modigliani and Miller, explain what action you would take to improve your financial position and calculate the financial improvement.

17.   The board of directors of Mulroy Ballinahown plc is considering whether to alter the company's capital structure. The board is proposing to issue €5 million of new debentures at par, and to use the funds to repurchase ordinary shares. A summary of the company's current balance sheet is shown below.

	€000s
Fixed assets (net)	24,500
Current assets	12,300
Less current liabilities	(8,600)
	28,200
Financed by	
25c ordinary shares	4,500
Reserves	14,325
	18,825
5% Debentures redeemable at par in 10 years	9,375
	28,200

The company's ordinary share price is €1.67 ex dividend, and the dividend is expected to be constant at 28.5c per year in the future. The debentures are currently priced at €80 ex interest. The price of the ordinary shares and debentures are not expected to change as a result of the proposed issue of new debentures. Issue costs and transaction costs may be assumed to be zero. The corporate tax rate is 12.5%.
(a) Calculate the current weighted average cost of capital (WACC).
(b) Evaluate the likely effect on the WACC if the company restructures its capital and comment on any weaknesses that you identify in your analysis.

18.♦ (Ref. Appendix 13C)
Dod & Cuso plc is considering an investment of €25 million in a diversification project away from its core business. The investment will be financed as follows:

- €6 million of the investment will be financed by internal funds, €10 million by a rights issue and €9 million by long-term loans (€4 million of which is a governmental subsidised loan at 2% below the cost of long-term finance, which is 8%).
- The investment is expected to generate pre-tax net cash flows of €5 million per year, for a 10-year period. The residual value at the end of 10 years is expected to be €5 million.
- The company is currently financed entirely be equity with a cost of equity of 10%. The risk-free rate is 5.5% per annum.
- Issue costs are estimated to be 1% for debt financing (excluding the subsidised loan), and 4% for equity financing. These costs are not tax allowable and the rate of corporate tax is 12.5%.

Estimate the adjusted present value (APV) of the proposed investment.

19. Baylin plc, operating in the transport industry, is considering whether to diversify by investing in a project in the insurance industry. The company has a gearing ratio of 30% debt and 70% equity with an equity beta of 1.254. Its debt capital is considered risk free. The insurance industry has an average beta of 1.584 and the average gearing for the industry is 40% debt and 60% equity.

The risk-free rate of return is 3%, the expected market return is 8% and the rate of corporate tax is 12.5%. The project has the following cash flow projections

Year	Cash flow
0	€600,000
1–3	€250,000

(a) Calculate the base case net present value.
Assume the company finances the project using €400,000 of new equity and €200,000 of new debt. The debt is in the form of a three-year amortising loan at 3% interest. Issue costs are 5% for equity and 2% for debt.

(b) Calculate the adjusted present value (**APV**) of the project and assess whether the project is viable.

20. Sean's De Castle plc is considering diversifying into a different type of business and has collected financial information about four companies in that business. An extract of that information is as follows:

Company	A	B	C	D
Debt in € millions	10.3	17.6	23.2	9
Equity in € millions	9	10	4	10
Turnover in € millions	40.2	47.7	52.3	33.4
Nominal share value	25c	50c	25c	€1
Current share price	€2	€3	€1.5	€1.70
Beta	1.3	1.5	1.1	1.05

The risk-free rate is 7% and the company can borrow at 2% above this. The market risk premium is 8% and the corporate tax rate is 12.5%.

Sean's Castle has a debt to equity ratio of 4:6.

Estimate the discount rate Sean's Castle should use in assessing the risk of its new project.

21. ◆ Gobshy has produced a draft guidance manual to assist in estimating the cost of capital to be used in investment appraisal.

Extracts are given below:

1. The discount rate should reflect the weighted average cost of capital of the company.
2. The cost of equity can be based on book or market values.
3. The capital asset pricing model or the dividend valuation model may be used in estimating the cost of equity.
4. The cost of redeemable debt is based on the redemption yield of existing debt.
5. Always round the solution up to the nearest whole percentage. This is a safeguard if the cost of capital is understated.

Illustrative examples

	Book Value (€ million)	Market Value (€ million)
Equity (100 million shares)	280	428
Debt €80 million of 10% debentures redeemable in 4 years' time	80	90

	Per share	Annual growth rates
Dividends	24c	9%
Earnings	77c	10%

The asset beta of the company is 1.1, market return is 14%, risk-free rate is 6% and the tax rate is 12.5%.

Illustration 1: Expanding existing operations

$$Ke = \frac{d}{Po} + g = \frac{24}{428} + 0.09 = 0.146 \text{ or } 14.6\%$$

Using the CAPM

Ke = Rf + (Rm − Rf) beta = 6% + (14% - 6%) 1.1 = 14.8%

Cost of debt is based on the following cash flows:

Year	Cash flow
0	(€80 million)
1 to 4	€8 million
4	€80 million

The internal rate of return here using the interpolation method is 10%.

Market value of equity €428 million and debt €90 million.

$$\text{The WACC} = \frac{428 \, (14.8\%) + 90 \, (10\% \,)}{518} = 13.97\%$$

Illustration 2: A company is diversifying

The asset beta of a similar sized company (with a debt to equity ratio of 4:6) is 0.9 and this company is in the same industry into which Gobshy is about to enter.

To find the cost of equity we need to adjust this beta as follows:

$$\text{Asset beta} = \text{beta of equity} \times \frac{E}{E + D(1 - T)} = 0.9 \times \frac{6}{6 + 4(1 - 0.125)} = 0.5684$$

Using CAPM Ke = Rf + (Rm − Rf)beta = 6% + (14% - 6%) 0.5684 = 10.55%

The cost of debt remains the same at 10% and the WACC is as follows:

$$\text{WACC} = \frac{428 \, (10.55\%) + 90 \, (10\%)}{518} = 10.45\%$$

Produce a revised version of the draft manual for estimating the cost of capital. Revisions should be made, where appropriate, to both the written guidance notes and the illustrations.

22. Spondulix plc is a company which has two divisions, X and Y, and they account for one-third and two-thirds respectively of the company's total market value.

The long-term capital structure at 31 December 2008 is as follows:

14% bond redeemable at par December 2017 (nominal value €100)	€2 million
Ordinary shares (10c nominal)	€1.2 million
The bonds are currently priced at €129 ex interest and the current share price ex dividend at 53c.	

The company has an overall beta of 1.25. The overall beta of other firms in the same industry as the division Y is 1.35 with an industry average market-weighted debt to equity ratio gearing of 50%:50%.

The risk-free rate of return is 6% and the expected market return is 12%. The rate of corporation tax is 12.5% and the debt is considered risk free.

(a)   Use the capital asset pricing model to find the cost of equity in both X and Y.
(b)   Calculate a discount rate (weighted average cost of capital) for both the X and Y divisions.

23.   AIT plc is looking at its capital structure and its weighted average cost of capital. If company gearing changes then the interest covers will change along with the cost of long-term debt as follows:

Interest cover	Cost of long-term debt
More than 6	8%
3–6	9%
1–4	11%

Summarised financial data	€ million
Earnings before interest and tax	90
Interest	27
Taxable income	63
Tax at 12.5%	7.875
Net income	55.125

The market vale of equity is €450 million and of debt €300 million. The company equity beta is 1.4 and the beta of debt is assumed zero. The risk-free rate is 5.5% and the market return is 14%.

Any change in capital structure is achieved by borrowing to repurchase existing debt, or by issuing equity to redeem existing debt.

(a)   Determine the effect on the WACC if the company capital structure was:
      (i)   80% equity and 20% debt by market values.
      (ii) 60% equity and 40% debt by market values.
      (iii) 40% equity and 60% debt by market values.
      Recommend which capital structure should be selected.
(b)   List any reservations you may have about the WACCs calculated.

24.   Clonown Carrots plc has the following capital structure:

€0.50 ordinary shares	€2,000,000
5% irredeemable debenture stock	€7,000,000

The company has constant annual profit before interest of €6 million each year and all income is distributed. The company has a current weighted average cost of capital of 12% and the debentures (€100 nominal) are trading at €100 ex interest (at par). Assume no corporate tax.

(a) Calculate the cost of equity and the current market price per share.

(b) The company has decided to issue additional 5% irredeemable debenture stock and use it to buy back 1 million shares. Ignoring transaction costs and using the net operating income approach of Modigliani and Miller in a world without corporate tax, demonstrate the effect of the share repurchase on the market value per share, the cost of equity and comment on the results you have found.

(c) Explain how the introduction of corporate tax would affect the results in parts (a) and (b).

APPENDIX 13A Dividend growth model proof

Equation 1:

$$P_0 = d(1 + g)/(1 + K_e) + d(1 + g)^2/(1 + K_e)^2 + d(1 + g)^3/(1 + K_e)^3 + \dots d(1 + g)^n/(1 + K_e)^n$$

For the series above to converge and be finite, discounting must more than compensate for the growth in dividends. Therefore Ke must be greater than g.

If equation 1 is multiplied by $(1 + g)/(1+K_e)$ the result is equation 2

Equation 2:

$$P_0 (1 + g)/(1 + K_e) = d(1 + g)^2/(1 + K_e)^2 + d(1 + g)^3/(1 + K_e)^3 + \dots d(1 + g)^{n+1}/(1 + K_e)^{n+1}$$

Subtract equation 2 from equation 1 to get the following

$$P_0 - \frac{P_0 (1 + g)}{(1 + K_e)} = \frac{d(1 + g)}{(1 + K_e)} - \frac{d(1 + g)^{n + 1}}{(1 + K_e)^{n + 1}}$$

If Ke is greater than g, then the right term above $\dfrac{d(1 + g)^{n + 1}}{(1 + Ke)^{n + 1}}$ approaches zero as n approaches infinity.

Therefore the equation simplifies to

$$P_0 - \frac{P_0 (1 + g)}{(1 + K_e)} = \frac{d(1 + g)}{(1 + K_e)}$$

Multiply both sides by $(1 + K_e)$ and solve for P_0

$$P_0 (1 + K_e) - P_0 (1 + g) = d(1 + g)$$
$$P_0 [1 + K_e - (1 + g)] = d(1 + g)$$
$$P_0 (K_e - g) = d(1 + g)$$

to give

$$P_0 = \frac{d(1 + g)}{K_e - g}$$

And re-arranging this expression gives us the cost of equity formula

$$K_e = \frac{d(1 + g)}{P_0} + g$$

APPENDIX 13B Cost of international sources of finance

Small and medium-sized companies and other small enterprises are usually limited to their domestic markets in their search for sources of finance. Large companies and multinationals have access to a wide range of international sources. The international money markets relate to short and medium sources, and include the **eurocurrency** market (not to be confused with the euro). The international capital markets relate to long-term sources of finance and include the **eurobond** market.

When an Irish company borrows in a foreign currency from an Irish bank, the loan is known as a eurocurrency loan. The eurocurrency markets involve the depositing of foreign currency with a bank, and the bank re-lending these funds for a short term, which is typically three months.

A eurobond is a bond which is issued in a capital market, denominated in a currency which often differs from that of the country of issue, and is sold internationally. Eurobonds are long-term loans raised by international companies or other institutions in several countries at the same time. Eurobonds can be sold by one bond-holder to another, i.e. a secondary market exists. The term of a eurobond issue is typically 10 to 15 years. Eurobonds would only be used by a company to raise large sums of money (above €10 million) and are very suitable for an organisation with an excellent credit rating, such as a successful multinational company. The interest rate on the bond may be fixed or variable; a variable bond is called a floating rate note. Many variable rate issues guarantee the bondholder a minimum interest rate, even if the market rates fall below this level (drop-lock floating rate bonds). Other variants are zero coupon (deep discount) bonds, convertibles and multi-currency used to reduce the risks of currency movements.

Example of eurobond cost
Greenbacks plc, an Irish company, has $40 million of eurobonds issued at 10% and redeemable at par in four years' time. The eurobond issue has a nominal value of $1,000 and is currently trading at $800 ex interest. The current rate of exchange is €1 = $1.
(a) What is the cost of capital to the company if the exchange rate remains stable?
(b) What is the cost of capital to the company if the dollar is expected to appreciate by 10% per annum (ignore taxation)?

Solution
The cash flows need to be identified from the company point of view.

The current dollar market value is $800 and each year the interest payment in dollars is 10% of the nominal value ($1,000) or $100. At the end of year four, there is an interest payment and also the redemption value of $1,000 or $1,100.

The exchange rate is currently €1 = $1 and as the dollar appreciates by 10% each year, the exchange rate in year 1 is $1/1.10 = $0.909 the exchange rate and year 2 is $0.909/1.10 = $0.826 etc.

The solution to the IRR is calculated on an Excel spreadsheet as follows.

Year	$ cash flow	€ cash flow	Exchange rate	€ cash flow
0	− 800	− 800	1.000	− 800
1	100	100	0.909	110
2	100	100	0.826	121
3	100	100	0.751	133.1
4	1,100	1,100	0.683	1,610.51
		(a) 17.34%		(b) = 29.07%

The cost of the eurobond increases dramatically due to the appreciation of the dollar.

APPENDIX 13C Adjusted present value (APV)

An alternative approach to investment appraisal to the net present value technique is the adjusted present value (**APV**). This is an application of Modigliani and Miller propositions. The difference between the APV and NPV methods is that the APV tries to show explicitly the financial side effect of how an investment is financed. The APV suggests that the NPV of a project can be increased or decreased by the side effects of financing.

The finance of a major project may change the risk profile of the existing capital structure, in which case the APV method is more appropriate.

The APV technique is applied by taking NPV as a first stage (called the base case NPV), in which the project is evaluated as if it were totally financed by equity. Then the APV is introduced at a second stage, by making adjustments to the base case NPV to allow for the side-effects of the intended method of financing.

Method

1. Discount the project cash flows at K_{eu} (i.e. as if it were all equity financed). This is known as the base case NPV.
2. Make adjustments to reflect the impact of the actual financing method used. These impacts could include issue costs, tax shields, loan subsidy, spare debt capacity, etc. All adjustments should be in present value terms and the discount rate is usually the cost of debt or the risk free rate.

   The end result is the same as using the net present value technique, but more information is obtained because the APV shows financial side effects explicitly.

Example 1(basic)

An Irish company is about to invest €1.9 million on new machinery, which will provide cost savings of €300,000 per annum indefinitely. The company is currently all equity financed with a cost of capital of 16%. The company proposes to finance the project with irredeemable debt with a 9% coupon rate. The costs of issue, which are not tax-deductible, are 5% of the gross proceeds. Corporate tax is at 12.5%. Find the adjusted present value of the investment.

Solution

A. Base case NPV = (€300,000/0.16) − €1.9 million = −**€25,000**
B. Now adjust the base case to reflect the finance used.
   Amount raised €1.9 million/0.95 = €2 million
   Issue cost = €2 million − €1.9 million = −**€100,000**
   Tax benefit = €2 million × 9% × 12.5% = €22,500 per year in perpetuity. This is discounted at 9%.

   €22,500/0.09 = **€250,000**. Alternatively, using MM formula, the tax benefit is the tax shield DT = €2 million × 0.125 = €250,000

   Finally the APV = − €25,000 − €100,000 + €250,000 = €125,000 and the project is viable.

APV Example 2 (advanced)

A company has an investment project that costs €20 million, and will generate cash flow over 4 years. The project will be financed with a €10 million 4-year bank loan (at 10%) and a rights issue. The tax rate is 30% and payable one year in arrears. The risk-free rate is 8%. All adjustments should be in present value terms and the discount rate is the risk-free rate. Because the project is deemed environmentally friendly, the loan is subsidised at 2% below the cost of 10%. This project increases borrowing or debt capacity by €6 million. The rights issue costs are 5% of the equity issued and the issue costs are allowable for tax purposes.
   What are the financial side effects of the intended method of financing this project?

Tax shield
Annual interest €10 million × 8% = €0.8 million
Tax relief = €0.8 million × 0.3 = €240,000
Discount factor years 2–5 at 3.067 = **€736,080**

Subsidy effect
= €10 million × (10% − 8%) × (8% DF years 1–4)
= €10 million × 2% × 3.312 = **€662,400**

Debt capacity effect
= €6 million × 8% × 0.3 × 3.067 (years 2–5) = **€441,649**

Issue costs effect
= 5% of amount issued, leaving €10 million
Issue €10 million/0.95 = €10,526,316 or 5/95 × €10 million = **(€526,316)**

The tax effect of issue costs
= 0.3 × 526,316 × 0.926 = **€146,211**

The financial side-effects or adjustments to the base case NPV are
= €736,080 + €662,400 + €441,649 + (€526,316) + €146,211 = €1,460,024

This style of appraisal has several advantages over the traditional use of WACC to find an NPV.

1. The normal WACC treatment of debt assumes that the amount of debt supported by the project is proportional to the present value of the project so that the gearing ratio does not change. This is unlikely as creditors lend in relation to the initial cost of the investment rather than the future cash flows.
2. APV can handle problems of changing capital structure and can incorporate the tax shield on any size of loan.
3. APV can also value other financial side effects, subsidised loans issue costs, etc. This step-by-step procedure may lead to a clearer understanding of all the elements of a decision.

However, some limitations do exist, namely:

1. Finding the ungeared cost of equity for the base case NPV may involve using Modigliani and Miller equations which assume debt is risk free.
2. The discount rates for the various side effects can be difficult to determine. For example, using the risk-free rate for the tax shield is only valid if the company is certain that it will be earning sufficient profits to take advantage of tax relief. If not, a higher discount rate should be used and this adjustment may be subject to the arbitrary interpretation of the observer.
3. Adjusting for various side effects can become very complex.

Part 5

Long-term
Sources of Finance

14

Raising Equity Finance

CHAPTER OBJECTIVES

At the end of this chapter the student should be able to:

1. outline the features of common shares
2. understand primary markets, secondary markets and initial public offerings (IPOs)
3. explain the concept of underpricing
4. understand different methods of issuing shares
5. analyse venture capital as a source of long-term funds
6. understand the different stock market indices and why Irish companies get listed on more than one exchange
7. understand the trading systems and the regulation of the Irish Stock Exchange
8. calculate various stock market ratios
9. gain an appreciation of the concept of the 'efficient market hypothesis'.

INTRODUCTION

Companies raise new equity capital in the market all the time. In Chapter 8 we discussed share valuation techniques. In this chapter we look at equity capital as a source of long-term finance. This includes why firms sell shares and the methods used in selling shares, the impact of issues of shares on the price of shares and different theories relating to market efficiency.

14.1 Ordinary shares and shareholder rights

Ordinary shares or common stocks are shares that have a claim to the financial success of the company and have no preferential treatment in terms of dividends or in cases of bankruptcy. The owners of these shares have control over the company along with the right to vote at company meetings and elect company directors. They have the right to either accept or reject company strategic moves such as company merger plans or other major capital investment decisions. In the area of voting rights, the rule is one share, one vote. Therefore, a shareholder with 100 shares can cast 100 votes. Shareholders must receive as much information as is sensible and must receive a copy of the company's annual report. Common shareholders have the right to purchase any new shares (in proportion to their existing holding) issued by the company. This is called the **pre-emption right**. This right is enshrined under the Irish Company's Amendment Act 1983. This enables existing shareholders to maintain control. For example, if new shares issued were purchased by management, control of the company would be seized by management away from the shareholders. In addition, the pre-emption right works to protect shareholders from a dilution in their wealth. Suppose for example there are 100 shares in issue and each share has a market value of €10 giving a market capitalisation of €1,000. If the company issues an additional 100 shares at €5 per share, the new market capitalisation will be €1,500 giving a share price of €7.50. Therefore, the existing shareholders will have suffered a 25% dilution in their shares. Effectively the new share issue has transferred wealth away from the existing shareholders to the new shareholders.

Shareholders do not receive any interest on their shares, and they have no legal right to any return on their investment. However, once all other costs have been paid, e.g. interest on debt, taxes to the government and payments made to other creditors, common stockholders have the right to whatever is left over – if anything. This may be paid out to the shareholders as a dividend or it may be reinvested in the company at the discretion of the company's directors.

Furthermore, shareholders do not have the right to take their money out of the company. If they want to 'liquidate' their investment, they can do so by selling their shares to other investors who may want to buy them. Remember that shares do not have a fixed price. The price of a share is determined in the market place by supply and demand. Liquidity refers to the ability to convert assets into cash at short notice. Even if companies are doing very well, investors are unlikely to commit their money to shares in that company if they believe they will not be able to liquidate (sell for cash) their shares.

Many companies continue to exist as successful private firms and have no desire to go public. Indeed some of Ireland's biggest companies are private, e.g. Dunnes Stores and Clery's. Furthermore, there have been many notable examples of companies that **delisted** and went from being public companies back to being private. Examples of these include James Crean and Clondalkin.

14.2 Primary markets, secondary markets and initial public offerings (IPOs)

Some companies are privately owned. This means that the shares in these companies are not traded. They are owned by the family members who own the company or perhaps by the managers of the company. When the shares of a company are actively traded, they are called publicly owned companies. The shares of large companies are listed on organised security exchanges like the ISEQ or FTSE. These shares are said to be listed. Shares of smaller companies are not listed on organised exchanges. They trade in the over-the-counter market (OTC market) and are said to be unlisted. We will explain more about the various markets later on in the chapter.

14.2.1 *Advantages and disadvantages of selling shares in the company to the public (going public)*

Advantages
- Liquidity: Privately owned firms do not have a ready market for their shares. Selling shares to raise cash is difficult and it is even more difficult to establish a fair price for the shares. Publicly owned firms do not have these liquidity problems.
- Valuation: It establishes a market valuation of a firm.
- No obligation to pay dividends: Corporations do not have an obligation to pay a dividend on the shares. Interest on debt must be paid.
- Debt:equity ratio: If a company's debt:equity ratio is too high, borrowing more may be too expensive. Companies may see equity financing as the cheaper option. It would also bring the debt:equity ratio down to more acceptable levels. This could facilitate further borrowing in the future.
- Status: Listed companies will get an amount of free advertising and being listed gives a certain amount of prestige.

Disadvantages
- Issuing new stock means sharing power and profits with new shareholders.
- Flotation costs: Fees paid to bankers, lawyers and advisers are very high. Flotation costs associated with equity issues are higher than the costs associated with debt issues.
- Signalling: Selling shares may send the wrong signal to the market. We discuss this in a later section.
- Cost of reporting: Quarterly and annual reporting is expensive.
- Disclosure: Privately held firms can operate in such a way as to pay high salaries and show favouritism in promoting employees (nepotism). These are more difficult to do when the company is public. In addition, operating data must be reported in annual reports which become available to competitors.
- Stock price: The market may not be putting a fair price on the company's shares. Indeed this is one of the reasons cited why companies delist and revert back to being private concerns. An example is Clondalkin plc, discussed in Chapter 10.

When a publicly owned firm wishes to raise new finance, it can do so by selling securities (shares and bonds) to investors. This is the **primary market**. When the owners of these shares wish to liquidate or sell these shares to other investors, they do so in the **secondary market**. The secondary market is where shareholders sell their shares to other investors. When privately held firms wish to **go public** to raise equity capital by selling shares to the public, we refer to this as an **initial public offering**. IPOs also describe the privatisation programmes of governments around the world, where government-owned utilities such as telecommunications are **sold off** to the public. Examples include Telecom Éireann (now Eircom), Deutsche Telecom (Germany), Nippon Telephone and Telegraph (NTT, Japan) and British Telecom. Going public provides companies with an immediate market valuation of their company. Employees are usually offered share options. We discuss share options later in the chapter.

14.3 Initial public offerings and underpricing

IPOs generate many headlines, particularly in the areas of the so-called new economy stocks and government privatisations. New economy stocks are described as technology or dot.com stocks.

If IPOs are oversubscribed, the share price will go up on the first day of trading. The investment bankers who deal with the issue will usually favour the large institutional investors like pension funds that will get the bulk of the shares. The smaller investor will usually have to wait until the after market to buy up shares after they have been initially sold. The **after market** is defined as the period after the issue is sold to the public. The problem is, as evidence shows, that IPOs tend to underperform the market in the long run.[1] IPOs are costly if the shares are issued at a price below their true value. Investors who buy these shares gain at the expense of the original shareholders. This is as true for a government-owned utility (the taxpayer loses out) as it is for a privately owned firm (the existing shareholders lose out). This is called the **cost of underpricing**. On the other hand, it can also be costly if the shares are priced too high, because the issue may be unsuccessful. Another reason for underpricing is what economists call the **winner's curse**. If you buy a house at an auction, you could say that you have won. You beat off all the others to buy the house. However, it could be that everybody else in the auction room thought that the house was overpriced. It seems that you have overpaid. The same reasoning applies to stock issues. If you apply for every IPO you will have no difficulty getting whatever stock you apply for in companies whose stock is overpriced (that nobody else wants). However, in issues that are underpriced you will only get a fraction of what you want. It would be better therefore if you apply for IPOs that are underpriced. So underpricing will counteract the winner's curse. Thus if you are offered all the shares you want, it is more than likely that the issue is overpriced and smart investors will stay away. This is seen as a rationale for underpricing. (See Box 14.1.)

Underpricing of IPOs occurs in all countries.[2] In America the average age of IPO companies is about seven years, whereas in continental Europe it is about 50 years. Research by American economists Roger Ibbotson, Jody L. Sindelar and Jay R. Ritter[3] shows significant underpricing of IPOs from 1960 to 1998. Only 5 of the 36 periods witnessed overpricing. Between 1960 and 1992, the average underpricing of IPOs was 15%. Interestingly, the number of IPOs tended to increase around the same time as the underpricing. This is because underpricing signals high returns to investors and companies react to the positive sentiment among investors by going public. However the research also shows that much of the underpricing occurs in companies that are high-risk, very young companies with low sales growth. Underpricing is necessary therefore to attract investors for these types of companies.

> **Box 14.1 IPOs and the winner's curse**
>
> Sean and Mary are both investors. Two IPOs are coming on the market, company X and company Y. Mary is a smart investor and considers company X to be overpriced and company Y to be underpriced. Sean on the other hand considers that share prices tend to rise after an initial issue of shares. He therefore invests in all IPOs. Because company Y is underpriced, the issue will be oversubscribed and neither Sean nor Mary will get all the shares they wanted. However, because Mary, the smart one, correctly considered company X to be overpriced, she did not invest any of her money in company X shares. Therefore Sean gets all the shares he asked for in company X. Therefore the moral of the story is that if you are offered all of the shares you wanted, it is likely that the IPO is overpriced and the smart investor will stay away. Therefore, you should only subscribe for shares in IPOs that are underpriced. Avoiding the winner's curse is a rationale for underpricing.

In addition to the cost of underpricing, there are administrative costs which involve legal, financial and underwriter costs. **Underwriters** perform three functions: (a) they provide advice to the company; (b) they buy the new issue of shares; and (c) they resell the shares to the public. They make their money on the spread. This means that they buy the shares from the company at a price below which they resell them to the public.

14.4 Ways of selling common shares

There are five ways of raising cash through the sale of common stock. These are:

1. through a public offering to the general public
2. through a private placement or a stock exchange placing of shares to a single investor or a small group of investors
3. through a rights issue to existing shareholders in proportion to their existing holdings of shares
4. through stock purchase plans to employees.

14.4.1 *Going public*

This is mainly used for larger companies where shares are offered to institutional investors and the public.

Prospectus and underwriting

The prospectus or the listing particulars are critical to the success of any new listing. It serves the requirements of the stock exchange and it acts as a marketing instrument that will raise the awareness of the company. A summary of the listing requirements is given in section 14.6.

Methods used in public issues of shares

(a) Bookbuilding: Most issues in the US are priced using the bookbuilding procedure. Investors indicate to the underwriters how much of the stock they wish to buy and indicate the maximum price they wish to pay. Others will indicate that they just want to invest a certain amount of money regardless of the price of the issue. So, for example, they might say that they will take $10,000 of shares. This is used by the underwriters to give an estimate of the issue price. They will also take into consideration the share price of similar companies in the same industry and will, in addition, undertake discounted cash flow analysis.

(b) Fixed Price: Companies undergoing IPOs in the UK do so on a fixed price basis or by auction. The selling price is fixed and the number of shares to be issued is advertised. If the issue is overpriced, not all the shares on offer will be sold and the underwriters will buy the shares that were not sold. If the issue is underpriced and oversubscribed, each investor will get a proportion of the shares s/he applied for. As explained earlier, the fixed price offer leaves investors open to the winner's curse.

(c) Auction: With an auction system, investors are invited to submit their bids on the number of securities they want to buy and how much they are prepared to pay for them. The securities are then issued to the highest bidders. Unlike the bookbuilding system used in the US, the bids made under an auction system are binding. The auction system can bypass the underwriters because there are no unsold securities, unless of course the seller imposes a minimum bid price, in which case underwriters could be used to buy any securities that remain unsold at this minimum price. There are two types of auctions – **discriminatory price** and **uniform price**. An example will illustrate.

Example 14.1 Issuing securities and auctions

Suppose that 5 million securities are being issued by auction. Suppose that three investors apply for the issue. Investor A applies for 2 million securities and is willing to pay €100 each. Investor B wants 3 million securities at €90 each and investor C has applied for 1 million securities at €80 each.

Investors A and B are the winners. Investor C loses out and gets no allocation. If the auction was a discriminatory auction, the total proceeds would be €470m, i.e. (€100 × 2m) + (€90 × 3m) = €470m. On the other hand if the auction was a uniform auction, the total proceeds would be €450m, i.e. (€90 × 2m) + (€90 × 3m) = €450m. Under a discriminatory price auction the investors are required to pay whatever price they bid, while under a uniform price system all investors will pay the lowest winning bid, in this example €90 bid by investor B (see Box 14.2).

Box 14.2 A note on auctions and the winner's curse

In Example 14.1 the uniform price system yielded lower proceeds than the discriminatory price system. However, there is a hidden cost here, which we have not imputed. It seems that the uniform price auction acts as an insurance against the winner's curse. Under uniform pricing the issue is less likely to be overpriced. In the example, investor B pays €90 per security, whereas investor A pays €100 per security. The discriminatory price leaves investors exposed to the winner's curse. If investors recognise this, then the proceeds from a uniform price issue could possibly yield more. In fact, some government bond issues in the US have switched from discriminatory pricing to uniform pricing.

Share issues and the effect on share price

There have been some famous examples of share price fluctuations and collapses following IPOs down through the years. One of the most memorable of recent times is the flotation of the Internet stock, lastminute.com. (See Box 14.3.)

Supply and demand analysis indicates that a share issue (an increase in supply) will depress share price. However, evidence suggests that share prices do not fall **in proportion** to the size of the stock issue. There are other factors at work. Share issues send signals (information) to the market about the company's intentions. If the prospects for the company are good, it will not want to share the fruits of future successes with new shareholders. For this reason the issue will not be seen as a favourable development by investors and the share price will fall when the announcement of the issue is made. Effectively what happens is that investors see the issue as being risky and consequently assign a higher cost of capital to the company's shares to compensate for the higher risk and the share price falls. Similarly, companies are more likely to issue shares when they believe their shares are overvalued. This information feeds into the market and investors mark down the price the shares are offered at because of this information. In other words, if companies have discretion when to issue shares, they are more likely to do so when it is advantageous to them, i.e. when the shares are overvalued. This doesn't fool the market and prices drop. However, it appears that the market is not as efficient as we might like to think it is. Studies conducted by Loughran and Ritter[4] have shown that for both IPOs and issues from established companies, share prices have underperformed, in terms of average returns, than portfolios of similar stocks by a significant margin. This can be to the tune of 30% over a five-year period.

Box 14.3 How to sink flotation opportunity

If somebody ever gets around to writing a worthy paper on how not to float a company on the stock market, the shambles of the recent lastminute.com flotation is sure to be one of the case histories. Quite simply this is a company that was floated on little more than dot.com hype.

But for the moment, let's forget whether this online corner sweetie shop should have been floated in the first place. Let's look instead at how the flotation turned sour with lastminute.com now left with a veritable army of small shareholders who are seriously cheesed off.

First, punters were so sure of the dot.com revolution that 189,000 of them signed up with lastminute.com to make sure that they qualified for an allocation for the website's shares.

The promoters – obviously convinced democrats – decided that everybody would get the same allocation and this meant that the punters ended up with a grand total of just €235 worth of shares each.

They should be thankful that €235 was all they got given the way lastminute.com shares have tanked in the past couple of weeks. From a float price of 380p sterling and a post-float high of 555p, the shares this week have been trading below 200p. The words 'bubble' and 'burst' spring to mind.

⟶

> And then to make matters even worse, the company's registrars IRG were forced to issue a cringing apology to investors for mistakes which led to mistakes in getting share certificates to investors. Bit of a problem this – no certificate meant that punters couldn't take advantage of the very brief jump in the shares and may now be left with lastminute.com shares worth half what they paid for them.
>
> Problem number two came when some refund cheques sent to punters who didn't get their full allocation bounced! In a statement IRG said: 'IRG wish to emphasise that these errors did not result from lastminute.com and wishes to apologise.'
>
> Indeed.
>
> *The Irish Times*, 7 April 2000

Setting the price of shares in publicly quoted firms

For companies that are already publicly owned, the new issue share price will be based on the existing market price of the share. Investment bankers will usually quote a price below the last price quoted on the day before the issue. Like IPOs, seasoned issues tend to be followed by a decline in the share price. The reasons are similar to those discussed above for IPOs. First, there is the information signalling reason. Managers will try to fool the market by issuing shares when they believe that the share price is overvalued. The market anticipates this and marks the prices of the share down. Secondly, the market might take the view that if the company is so confident about the future, why would it want to let new shareholders share in the rewards? Existing shareholders could have all the gain and the company could finance its expansion plans by issuing debt.

Maintaining a secondary market in shares of small companies

The market for **blue chip** companies such as Smurfit, Bank of Ireland, AIB, Cement Roadstone Holdings, Intel, etc. is liquid. Buyers and sellers of these shares are easily matched. The transactions volume of such securities is high, which makes it easier for these shares to be bought and sold. This creates liquidity.

However, smaller companies have fewer transactions and it is therefore more difficult to match buyers and sellers. This does not mean that the market for such shares is illiquid. These shares usually trade in the **over-the-counter market**. The investment bankers or dealers will usually agree to **make a market** in such stocks to keep them liquid. They do this by holding an inventory of such stock and when a buyer surfaces the shares are pulled from the inventory and sold over the counter – hence the term 'over the counter'. Therefore, an active secondary market is maintained in such securities.

Table 14.1 Summary of costs of public offerings

Spread: The difference between the price the issuer receives and the offer price. This is the spread, the fee charged by the underwriter.

Expenses: These include legal fees, costs of filing the issue, and administrative and management time spent on the issue.

Underpricing: The losses that arise from selling stocks below their intrinsic or true value.

Abnormal returns: On the announcement of the issue, the price of existing stock falls in relation to overall stock market or other similar companies.

14.4.2 Private placements

This is the most frequently used method in Ireland of bringing a new company to listing. In a private placement, securities are sold to a single investor or a small group of investors. These are usually institutional investors like insurance companies or pension funds. Private placements have the main advantage in that they can avoid the costs of selling securities to investment bankers, which can be very significant. One of the drawbacks of the private placement of equity is its liquidity. Investors will find it difficult to resell the investment. **A stock exchange placing** is the process by which the company gets a stockbroking firm to sell shares to its various clients. Another example of a private placement is the process of firms taking out equity holdings in other companies. This might be a company in which it has a stake, e.g. a supplier or a company in which there is a joint venture in operation. For example, Eircom have taken out a number of joint ventures with companies aimed at supplying services to Eircom. These joint ventures centre on Eircom's **access network** which links customers to telephone exchanges. Fiat and General Motors, in September 2000, announced a $2.4 billion joint venture alliance aimed at reducing the two car makers' costs.

14.4.3 Rights issues

Earlier in the chapter, we described **pre-emptive rights** which gives existing shareholders the right to purchase any additional issue of stock in proportion to their existing shareholding in the company. We also illustrated how pre-emptive rights help to prevent the dilution of existing shareholder wealth. More formally, a rights issue allows shareholders the right to purchase a certain number of shares for a specified price within a specified period. If the current shareholders do not wish to exercise their rights, they can sell their rights in the market.

The number of rights needed to buy one new share

To illustrate the procedure of a rights issue we take the following example. Suppose that Decies Ltd needs to raise an additional €4m to finance further expansion and it plans to raise this capital from a rights issue. It has 4,000,000 shares outstanding, each with a current market price of €10. Decies has set the price of the subscription at €5 per share.

How many rights are needed to purchase one new share? The company will have to issue an additional 800,000 shares (€4m/€5 = 800,000 shares). Therefore the number of rights needed to purchase one new share is 5 (old shares/new shares = 4,000,000/800,000 = 5). This is a 1 for 5 rights issue. To buy one new share the shareholder will need to give up 5 rights plus the price of the new share of €5.

The value of each right

Existing shareholders have the right to purchase a share that has a current market value of €10 for €5. This right therefore has value. What is this value? Suppose that a shareholder owns 100 shares. The value of her existing holding is €1,000 (number of shares × price per share = 100 × €10 = €1,000). The rights issue gives this shareholder who has 100 shares the rights to purchase 20 new shares for €5 each. If the shareholder exercises her rights and buys the new shares, she will now have 120 shares. Her total investment in the company will now be €1,000 + €100 = €1,100. Therefore the price per share is now €1,100/120 = €9.17 per share. The difference between the old share price of €10 and the new share price of €9.17 is the value of one right, that is €10 − €9.17 = €0.83. The old shares carry a right to subscribe for new shares. Therefore the difference between the old share price and the new share price must be equal to the value of one right, i.e. €0.83. The old shares are called **cum-rights** shares and the new shares are called **ex-rights** shares. We can confirm this as the correct price of a right by imagining an investor who has no shares in the company and wishes to get some. She can do so by buying 5 rights at a cost of €0.83 and then exercising her rights by investing another €5 to buy the share. Her total investment will be €9.15 (allowing for rounding errors), which is what we calculated to be the ex-rights price.

Theoretical ex-rights price

The price of the share after the rights issue, or the ex-rights price of the share in the above example, is €9.17. The ex-rights price is below the market price of the share before the issue was announced and above the price the rights were offered at. If the rate of return on the new funds is the same as that on the existing capital of the company, the ex-rights price can be calculated using the following equation:

$$\text{TXRP} = P_0\,\frac{N_0}{N} + P_n\,\frac{N_n}{N} \qquad\qquad (14.1)$$

where
TXRP = theoretical ex-rights price
P_0 = original price of share
N_0 = original number of shares
N_n = number of new shares
P_n = price of new shares being issued
N = total number of shares in issue following the rights issue.

Therefore: $$\text{TXRP} = €10 \ \frac{100}{120} \ + \ €5 \ \frac{20}{120} = €9.17$$

The value of a right can be got using the equation

$$\text{Value of a right} \ = \ \left[\frac{\left(\begin{array}{c}\text{Ex-rights} \\ \text{price}\end{array}\right) - \text{Rights price}}{\begin{array}{c}\text{Number of rights needed} \\ \text{to buy one new share}\end{array}} \right]$$ (14.2)

$$\frac{€9.17 - €5}{5} = 83 \text{ cents}$$

The actual ex-rights price of the share will depend on the reaction of the market to the rights issue. If the rights issue is seen in a positive light and investors are sure that the proceeds from the issue will be invested in positive net present value projects, the market price may not drop, if at all. The result could be an overall gain in shareholder value. If on the other hand the market views the rights issue in negative terms and if investors expect the proceeds from the issue to be used to simply repay some outstanding debt, for example, then the price will fall more than that predicted by the theoretical ex-rights price.

Rights issues and the effect on shareholders' wealth

Suppose that Decies Ltd offered a 1 for 10 rights issue instead of a 1 for 5 rights issue. The new issue price will be €2.50 instead of €5. In other words, it issues twice the number of shares at half the price. Therefore, to raise €4m it will need to issue 1,600,000 shares (€4m/€2.50). The theoretical ex-rights price of the share will be €7.86, i.e. €10 (4m/5.6m) + €2.50(1.6m/5.6). The value of the right in this case is the cum-rights price €10 less the ex-rights price €7.86 = €2.14.

A shareholder can exercise her rights or sell them on the open market. In either of these two cases, the shareholder's wealth is not affected. In the Decies example our investor who had 100 shares had shareholder value of €1,000, i.e. 100 shares × €10 each. After exercising her rights she has 120 shares and her wealth is €1,100. In other words she buys 20 extra shares at €5 each for a total additional investment of €100. Her wealth increases by the amount of her investment. Therefore, she is neither better nor worse off. This is explained in Table 14.2.

Table 14.2 Effect of rights issue on shareholder wealth

Number of shares	Original value	New value	Gain/loss
100	€1,000	€917	– €83
20	€100	€183	+ €83
120	€1,100	€1,100	—

The shareholder's gain from the discount price is offset by the fall in the market price of the share. The shareholder receives rights (which have value) and these rights are offset by the fall in the market price of the share.

Instead of exercising her rights, the investor could sell her rights. If she sells her rights she will receive €83 (100 × €0.83). She will then have her original 100 shares at the ex-rights price of €9.17 each or €917. So the cash received from selling her rights of €83 *plus* the new market value of her holding of €917 is €1,000, which is exactly the value of her holding before the rights issue. She will not make or lose any money.

Note that it is not possible to underprice a rights issue. As long as the issue price is greater than zero and less than the market price, it is irrelevant what the subscription price is. It is irrelevant because there is no transfer of wealth from the existing shareholders and it does not affect existing shareholders' claims on the assets of the company.

If for some reason the shareholder fails to exercise her rights, her percentage holding in the company falls and suffers a loss because of the fall in the market value of the shares. This failure to exercise valuable rights is probably due to lack of knowledge of the issue or indifference. Stock exchange rules permit companies to sell any rights that are not taken up and the proceeds to be distributed to the shareholders concerned.

14.4.4 Employee stock ownership plans

These are stock option plans that allow employees to purchase shares on favourable terms. This provides employees with a stake in the performance of the company and as a result, if the company does well, the share price increases and the stock options increase in value. See Box 14.4 and Box 14.5 for a very succinct definition of the terms and the different ways of obtaining shares.

Box 14.4 Defining the terms of financial participation

Profit Sharing: involves employees receiving a proportion of their income from profits. Share-based profit sharing involves allocating shares to employees based on profits.

Employee share ownership: This refers to the arrangements that provide for the broadly based ownership of shares by employees in their own firm. It may involve employee share ownership plans (ESOPs), where shares are held for employees in a trust, or it may consist of reserving a proportion of company shares for employees, which are offered at privileged terms and limited to a worker's period of employment.

→

Gainsharing: is a group incentive scheme in which employees receive a bonus related to the performance of the group. This may be based on cost savings or productivity improvements within a production line or sales team, for example.

Formal gainsharing plans have been used in the US since the 1930s. Research is under way into the potential of some form of gainsharing in the public sector.

Clare O'Dea, *The Irish Times*, 9 June 2000

Box 14.5   Variety of ways to get a share

Approved profit sharing schemes (APSS)
Incentives to promote approved profit sharing schemes were first introduced in 1982. Employees in a company may be given shares worth up to €12,697 in that company per annum tax-free. In the 1999 Finance Act, the €12,697 annual limit was increased to €38,000 on a once off conditional basis. To qualify, shares must have been held in the Employee Share Ownership Trust (ESOT) for 10 years.

Employee share ownership plans (ESOPs)
First introduced in 1997, the basic idea of an ESOP is that a trust acquires shares in the company for the benefit of employees. They are being introduced mainly in commercial State enterprises undergoing privatisation.

Save-as-you-earn (SAYE) share option schemes
Under this scheme, employees agree to save for a fixed time and are given the option to buy shares at a predetermined discount price. At the end of the savings period employees can: (a) take their savings and a tax-free bonus or (b) avail of the option to purchase the shares at the initial fixed price.

Gains depend on the share price performance and profits made on the exercise of the share option are subject to capital gains tax on disposal rather than income tax.

To date (April 2000) 28 SAYE schemes have been approved by the Revenue Commissioners and there are 30 applications awaiting a decision.

Tax relief
An employee may claim full tax relief on shares purchased in his or her employer's company up to a lifetime of €6,337. The shares must be retained for a minimum of three years.

Tax relief can be claimed on the interest on loans taken out to purchase shares in an employer's company. Tax relief can also be claimed on loans made by employees to a company that is not publicly quoted.

Clare O'Dea, *The Irish Times*, 9 June 2000

14.5 Venture capital

Venture capital is **zero-stage financing** or financing for start-up, often high-risk ventures. If you have a good idea for a business venture but have no money and no assets to your name, you might think of going to a bank to get some capital to get started. Not all banks, however, are willing to help fund a new venture that doesn't have any equity capital of its own. You may need to look at other individuals or firms that specialise in this type of financing. Some venture capitalists specialise in **seed capital**. This is referred to as **initial stage financing**. Other venture capitalists will specialise in **secondary financing** or **mezzanine finance** (the floor above the ground floor).

In addition, companies such as Intel have made venture capital investments in Irish technology companies such as Baltimore Technologies, Iona Technologies, Enba and International Financial Services. Because 75% of Irish IT output is exported, companies like Intel are looking at a much greater market. Intel has a global investment technology fund of circa $5 billion. Much of this is invested in European technology companies in an effort to stimulate demand for PC and communications products.

Venture capital companies take an equity holding in companies that can be anything up to 40%. They seek investment opportunities in companies that have the potential for high rates of return. They do not seek security on their investment, so if the venture fails they lose their investment. Venture capitalists may have seats on the board of directors and may even appoint members to operational management. This, along with the high equity holding in the company, makes venture capital very expensive. The venture capitalists will also add their arrangement fees, which could be as high as 2.5%, and similar amounts will be incurred for legal and professional fees. In Ireland and in other countries the fastest growing companies in terms of employment and profitability have a venture capital shareholder. In Ireland, venture capital is also used for acquisition, mergers and management buy-outs. At the time of writing, venture capital from Irish venture capitalists comes to about €253m with individual investments ranging from €250,000 to about €6m. Venture capitalists will exit the company when they feel it is the right time to do so and when they feel they can get an adequate return. From the client's point of view it is important to know how and under what circumstances the venture capitalist will exit the company.

The most important first step in seeking venture capital is the **business plan**. We discussed financial planning in Chapter 11, which is part of the overall business plan. In addition to the financial aspects of the plan it will be important for the budding entrepreneur to show the venture capitalists that he has the managerial ability to propel the business forward.

Table 14.3 Comparison of average annual growth rates % (1991–1995)

	Venture backed companies	FT-Extel top 500 European companies
Employment	15	2
Share capitalisation	36	15
Sales revenue	35	14
Pre-tax profits	25	17
Fixed assets	27	11
Long-term debt	14	13

Source: Baker, Peter, 'Economic Impact of Venture Capital in Europe', *Strategic Development Options for Ireland's Capital Markets in a Comparative Context.*

14.5.1 *Venture capital markets and economic growth*

Research has found an important link between venture capital and economic growth.[5] A study by the European Venture Capital Association (EVCA) shows that between 1991 and 1995 employment increased by 15% per annum in companies funded by venture capital, compared to just 2% for the top 500 largest companies. The jobs created in venture capital companies were shown to be high-quality jobs. A study by the National Venture Capital Association (NVCA) found that the number of scientists, engineers and managers employed in venture capital companies was 61%, compared to 15% for the US labour force. This would indicate that innovative companies tend to employ highly skilled and professional workers with consequent higher pay scales. In addition, a study by Cognotec found that between 1995 and 1996 young venture capital-backed companies called **gazelles** accounted for 80% of job growth, even though they represented just 3% of the firm population.

14.6 Stock markets

Earlier in the chapter we distinguished between primary and secondary markets. The most important secondary market is the stock market. The stock market determines the share prices of individual shares and since it is the primary goal of financial management to maximise shareholder wealth, knowledge of how the stock market works is important.

We have already seen that stock markets are divided into two types: (a) the organised and (b) the over-the-counter market.

(a) **Organised markets:** have a physical existence and location, their own building and an elected board of governors. There are organised stock exchanges around the world. In Ireland there is the Irish Stock Exchange (ISE), in London there is the London Stock Exchange (LSE) and in New York there is the New York Stock Exchange (NYSE).

14.6.1 *The Irish Stock Exchange*

Companies seeking a listing of their securities on the Irish Stock Exchange may do so on the official list, the developing companies market or exploration securities market. The official list is the main market for listed companies and Irish Government bonds. The developing companies market is for new and developing companies. The exploration securities market is confined to exploration and mineral companies.

14.6.2 *Eligibility requirements for admission to the official list*

There are basic minimum requirements for companies that apply to have their shares admitted to the official list:

*   Incorporation: The company must be organised and be operating in conformity with its own articles of association.

- Three-year record: The company must have been independently carrying on its main revenue-earning activity for at least three years.
- Audited accounts: This three-year record must be supported by published audited accounts with unqualified audit reports.
- Profits and assets: There are no minimum profitability or net asset requirements.
- Directors: The board of directors and senior management must have appropriate expertise and experience for the management of the business.
- Controlling shareholders: The company must be capable of carrying on its business independently of any shareholder which controls 30% or more of the company's voting rights or which is able to control the board.
- Conflicts of interests: The company must ensure that all the directors are free from any conflicts between their duties to the company and any other interests or responsibilities.
- Working capital: The company must confirm that it has sufficient working capital for at least the next twelve months from the date of the prospectus.
- Free transfer of shares: Shares must be freely transferable.
- Shares in hands of the public: At least 25% of shares must be held outside the hands of the directors, major shareholders owning more than 5% of the company's shares, or the trustees of any employee share scheme or pension fund established for the benefit of directors or employees of the issue.

(b) **The over-the-counter market:** The over-the-counter market does not have a physical location. It is a market driven by computer screens and telecommunications. For shares that are new, or traded infrequently, some means of maintaining liquidity in these shares is necessary. This is achieved by dealers who keep an inventory of these stocks and when an order comes in, they simply sell the security over the counter. The brokers who deal in such securities are said to be **market makers** in these securities. The over-the-counter market today is a generic term incorporating the market makers and the computer-driven electronic trading system which brings investors and dealers together. Dealers will quote **bid** prices and **ask** prices over the computer screen for whatever stocks they are making a market in. The bid price is the price the dealer will pay for the stock, or the price they are willing to buy the stock. The ask price is the price at which the dealer will sell the stock. The difference between the bid and the ask price is the **spread** and it constitutes the dealer's profit. When a dealer finds that her inventory levels in a particular stock are rising, she will lower both her bid price and her ask price. As a result investors will be more likely to buy and less likely to sell the stock. On the other hand if the dealer's inventory of a security is falling, she can raise both the bid price and the ask price. This will encourage more selling and less buying. The supply and demand for a particular security determines its price. The NASDAQ computer system is an example of an over-the-counter market. NASDAQ stands for National Association of Securities Dealers Automated Quotation System. It was first introduced in 1971 and, in terms of the number of companies listed, is bigger than the New York Stock Exchange. The OTC market consists of stocks that generally have less trading volume than companies listed on organised exchanges. There used to be a tendency for NASDAQ companies to move from the NASDAQ to the organised exchanges whenever they became large enough. However, companies like Microsoft and Intel, which are huge international companies, have remained on the NASDAQ. There are a number of Irish companies listed on the NASDAQ, such as Ryanair Holdings, Iona, Riverdeep and Elan Corporation. There is a European equivalent to the NASDAQ called the EASDAQ or the European Association of Securities Dealers Automated Quotation, which raises finance for fast growing high-tech firms. It is possible to list on both the NASDAQ and the EASDAQ. In London there is the Alternative Investment Market (AIM), in Germany the Neuer Market, in France the Nouveau Marché and the DCM in Dublin, all designed to generate finance for small developing companies.

14.7 Stock market indices

A stock market index shows the weighted average price of shares making up the index. It is a summary of what is happening to a group of similar shares. So, for example, the ISEQ is a summary of what is happening to the share prices of the 91 companies listed on the Dublin Stock Exchange. Indices are useful because they allow the investor to see what is happening to an individual share compared to the index as a whole. For example, it is possible for the share price of an individual stock to fall on a particular day when the index for all the companies quoted on the index goes up. In other words, a share can do badly compared to the rest of the market. Stock market indices are benchmarks that allow individual shares to be compared to a market index. The characteristics of some of the better-known indices are given below:

14.7.1 ISEQ

The Irish Stock Exchange Quotation (ISEQ) is a broad-based index representing all publicly quoted companies. Companies that are large and relatively safe are referred to as blue chip companies. The index is weighted in such a way that a change in the largest capitalisation stocks will have a bigger impact on the index than a change in smaller capitalisation stocks. In other words, a 1% change in Smurfit will have a greater impact on the index than a 1% change in Abbey plc.

Membership of the stock exchange has been beneficial to companies such as Kerry and Ryanair. Kerry was initially quoted on the USM (unlisted securities market) in October 1986 with a market capitalisation of €9.175m. By July 1999 it was a member of the full list, the number of shares in issue had risen tenfold from 18.3m to 172.05m, the share price had risen from 50p to 849p and as a result the market capitalisation had reached €1,850m. Ryanair was on the official list in 1997 with a market capitalisation of €522.5m (€662.23). Two years later its share price had doubled, giving a market capitalisation of €1,646.4m.

14.7.2 FTSE 100

The 'footsie' 100 is based on the largest (in terms of market capitalisation) 100 companies listed on the UK stock market. The market capitalisation of companies on the footsie is usually greater than Stg £1.8bn.

The London Stock Exchange and the Deutsche Börse had planned to merge in May 2000 to form the €X international exchange. Combined, the two would have more than half of Europe's trading in blue chip stocks and over 56% of Europe's derivatives trading.[6] However (at the time of writing) this proposed merger seems to have failed.

Nevertheless, a merger of some description is likely and, along with the other merger forming the Euronext (discussed below), Europe's stock exchanges are likely to be transformed because it is likely that exchanges currently outside these two will eventually join them.

14.7.3 Dow Jones

The Dow Jones Industrial Average index (DJIA) (after Charles H. Dow who created the index) is an index composed of 30 blue chip industrial companies. The editors of the *Wall Street Journal* select the companies that make up the index. The difficulty is that the index is narrowly based (only 30 companies). Most broader based indices (e.g. the NASDAQ) give a better indication of the overall performance of the market. Other international benchmark indices include the Japanese Nikkei 225 index, the German Dax, the Hong Kong Hang Seng index and the French CAC-40.

14.7.4 FTSE all-share index

This is the UK's broadest based index and therefore the most accurate in assessing the performance of the market because it comprises 900 companies. In addition to the overall market index, the index is also subdivided into sectors such as media, engineering, retail, etc. This allows you to compare companies that are similar and in the same industry. An entire industry can be doing very poorly while the rest of the market can be flying high.

14.7.5 Euronext

The stock exchanges of Paris, Amsterdam and Brussels merged in March 2000 to create Euronext and it represented the first formal step towards a single European stock market. The Euronext provides for a common trading platform, common settlement system and clearance and a common rule book. A consolidation of European bourses is developing to provide greater liquidity and lower transaction costs to combat increasing competition from online trading and by the competition expected from the arrival of the NASDAQ in Europe.[7]

14.8 Listing on more than one exchange

Many Irish companies are listed not just on the Irish Stock Exchange but also on the London stock market and in New York on the NASDAQ. The Smurfit group, CRH and Iona are some examples. High-tech companies such as Iona are better understood and more highly valued in the US[8] and get a better price on a major market like the NASDAQ. In Ireland's case, the domestic market is too small and companies such as Smurfit have no choice but to seek a quote on larger markets such as London and the

NASDAQ. Instead of issuing shares in the US, companies outside the US issue American Depository Receipts (ADRs), which are claims on their shares. ADRs are administered by American banks. They trade on US stock exchanges. So, for example, Smurfit plc with trading shares in foreign countries is indicative of the globalisation of the international economy. ADRs have become a means whereby foreign companies tap into the capital markets of the US.

Furthermore, the advent of EMU has meant that institutional investors such as pension fund managers have taken advantage of the abolition of exchange rate controls and the single currency to invest in overseas markets. The consequence of this has been to depress the overall ISEQ index.

14.9 Regulation

The Irish Stock Exchange operates a system of self-regulation in the supervision and the operation of the stock market. Ultimate responsibility for the supervision of the stock market is placed with the Central Bank. The stock exchange was given day-to-day authority over the securities market. The exchange has to produce rules that ensure fairness in the market but at the same time does not prevent or restrict competition any more than is necessary to protect investors. The exchange has responsibility for the regulation of listed companies and their disclosure requirements.

14.10 Trading system

The order-driven system is how trading in equities in Ireland is conducted and this is how most stock exchanges in the world operate. When a stockbroker receives a buy or sell order from an investor, the broker will try to match the investor with another investor with whom to trade. When a broker receives an order, s/he will try to match the order to one of his/her own clients. For example, if a broker receives an order from an investor to sell a security the broker will see if one of their own clients wishes to buy the security. This is an in-house deal and the transaction is known as a **put-through**. Obviously there are restrictions on brokers who want to conduct such a trade, and permission is required from the exchange to do so.

Alternatively, the order is put on a central system and a deal is done where a buyer and seller are matched. In addition, most Irish securities are traded on the London market, and the Irish broker may contact his/her London counterpart to conduct a trade. All deals must be reported to the exchange and this information is then made available to all other market participants. After the deal has been struck, the settlement must take place, which transfers the ownership of shares from seller to buyer. **CREST** is the real-time settlement system for Irish and UK shares. Investors normally pay for shares five days after the transaction is completed. The previous system was known as the talisman system and it involved a long paper-chase between investors, brokers, company registrars and the exchange's talisman. The CREST system is electronic and paperless.

14.10.1 Introduction of electronic trading system

On 6 June 2000 the Irish Stock Exchange changed over to electronic trading. This allows Irish stockbrokers to offer online Internet trading facilities to customers. Trading is conducted via a screen-based system. This allows brokers to execute buy and sell orders more quickly and this helps improve liquidity. The introduction of electronic trading will allow brokers to bring in execution-only online dealing services, which means that customers will have a choice in how they deal with brokers.[9]

14.11 Types of securities traded on the Irish Stock Exchange

There are five types of securities traded on the Irish Stock Exchange:

1. Domestic Irish ordinary shares issued by Irish companies.
2. Overseas equities issued by non-Irish companies.
3. Irish Government bonds which pay regular interest payments and repayment of the fixed sum at a given date in the future.
4. Bonds or fixed interest stocks issued by companies or local authorities.
5. Investment funds that invest in portfolios of investments based on spreading risk. (See Chapter 7.)

Figure 14.1 Securities sold on the Irish Stock Exchange

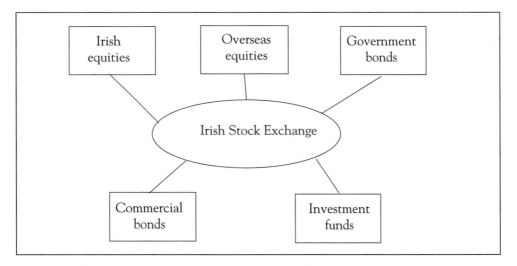

14.12 Stock market ratios

Companies can find it useful to calculate ratios that bring together data from the stock market and from the company's accounts. The following ratios are the most useful.

14.12.1 Dividend yield

As we discussed in more detail in Chapter 9 the overall rate of return on a stock is made up of two components – an annual income in the form of a dividend payment and a capital gain in the form of a rise in the share price. The expected dividend payment as a percentage of the current share price is the dividend yield.

$$\text{Dividend yield} = \frac{\text{Dividend per share}}{\text{Market price of share}} \times 100 \qquad (14.3)$$

Yield is inversely related to price and a rising price will mean a falling yield. A low dividend yield could mean that investors are satisfied with a low rate of return as they can look forward to higher dividends in the future and capital growth in the value of their shares. On the other hand, a low dividend yield could mean the company is in trouble and is unable to pay worthwhile dividends.

In order to compare the dividend yield with the return from other investments (debentures, gilts, etc.), the dividend yield needs to be calculated on a gross basis. This is done by adding back the tax credit to the net dividend.

Example 14.2 Calculating dividend yield

XRH Ltd has just paid out a net dividend of 20 cents per share. The current market price of the share is €7. The basic rate of income tax is 22%. Therefore the gross dividend yield is:

$$\frac{20c \times 100}{78} \quad = 26 \text{ cents}$$

Therefore the dividend yield is

$$\frac{0.26 \times 100}{€7} \quad = 3.7\%$$

14.12.2 Earnings per share

We have discussed earnings per share in other chapters, particularly in terms of the limitations of EPS as an investment ratio. For example in Chapter 11 we saw how the quality of earnings reported is not always reliable and therefore has limitations as a ratio in its own accord and as the denominator in the calculation of the P/E ratio. However, the EPS is always shown in the accounts of publicly quoted firms and is the subject of the Statement of Standard Accounting Practice, number 3 (SSAP 3). Earnings per share is defined as: 'the profit in pence attributable to each equity share, based on the profit (or, in the case of a group, the consolidated profit) of the period after tax, minority interests and extraordinary items, and after deducting preference dividends and other appropriations in respect of preference shares, divided by the number of equity shares in issue and ranking for dividend in respect of the period.'

Therefore, earnings per share are defined as earnings divided by the number of shares. Earnings are defined as profit available to equity shareholders, which are profits after taxation, minority interests, preference dividends and extraordinary items. The number of shares is based on those in issue and ranking for dividend during the period.

$$\text{Earnings per share} = \frac{\text{Profit available for equity shareholders}}{\text{Equity shares issued and ranking for dividend}} \qquad (14.4)$$

The point of SSAP 3 is to standardise the calculation of EPS. It deals with **basic earnings per share** and **fully diluted earnings per share**.

Basic earnings per share

In calculating the basic earnings per share, we use a weighted average number of shares, having taken into account any new shares issued during the year.

Shares can be issued:

(a) at their full market value
(b) as a bonus issue for no consideration
(c) at a discount in a rights issue, and
(d) in exchange for shares in a subsidiary.

Example 14.3 shows the calculation of basic EPS assuming no change in the company's capital. Here EPS are earnings available for ordinary shareholders divided by the number of shares.

Example 14.3 Calculation of basic EPS assuming no change in capital

Portlaw Ltd share capital 1 January	2008 (€000)	2007 (€000)
1,000,000 Preference shares of A1 each	1,000	1,000
6,000,000 Ordinary shares of 20 cents each	1,200	1,200
	2,200	2,200
Profit after tax	600	500
Preference dividends	100	100
Earnings for ordinary shareholders	500	400
Number of ordinary shares	6,000	6,000
EPS	8.33 cents	6.67cents

Example 14.4 below shows the calculation of basic earnings per share after an issue of ordinary shares at full market price. If shares are issued during the year, the number of shares in the calculation of EPS must be adjusted to reflect the fact that this new capital is generating a return (in terms of earnings) for only part of the year. In other words, we use **a weighted average share capital** in the denominator of the EPS calculation.

Example 14.4 Calculation of basic EPS assuming an issue of shares at full market price

Assuming that Portlaw Ltd issued an additional 1m ordinary shares at full market price on 1/10/2008.

	2008 (€000)	2007 (€000)
Profit after tax	600	500
Preference dividends	100	100
Profit for ordinary shareholders	500	400
Weighted average number of shares		
6,000,000 shares for 9 months (6m x 9/12)	4,500	
7,000,000 for 3 months (7m x 3/12)	1,750	
	6,250	6,000
Earnings per share	8 cents	6.7 cents
500/6,250 for 2008 and 400/6,000 for 2007		

Calculation of EPS following a bonus issue of shares

A bonus issue of shares is an issue of shares to existing shareholders free of charge. Because the company is not raising any new capital, the new shares issued do not generate a matching increase in revenue. For a bonus issue, no weighting of shares is necessary. All that is necessary is that the number of shares for the previous year is adjusted so that the EPS figures remain comparable.

Example 14.5 Calculations of EPS following a bonus issue

	2008 €000	2007 €000
Profit after tax	600	500
Preference dividends	100	100
	500	400
Number of shares		
at 1 January	6,000	6,000
Bonus issue	1,200	1,200
	7,200	7,200
Earnings per share	6.9 cents	5.5 cents
500/7,200 for 2008 and 400/7,200 for 2007		

Portlaw Ltd, instead of issuing shares at full market price on 1/10/2008, gives the shareholders a bonus issue on the same date. The terms of the bonus issue is one new share for every five shares already held.

Calculation of EPS following a rights issue

Earlier on in this chapter we discussed rights issues, which are issues of shares to existing shareholders in proportion to their existing shareholding in the company at a discount to the prevailing market price of the share. A rights issue can be separated into a cash issue at full market price plus a bonus issue. To calculate the EPS, the features of the cash issue and the bonus issue must be used. SSAP 3 recommends the following approach for the adjustments necessary to calculate the EPS after a rights issue.

1. Calculate the theoretical ex-rights price of the share and divide it by the market price of the share cum-rights on the last day the shares were quoted cum-rights. This adjusts the previous year's EPS for the effects of the bonus issue in the rights.

$$\frac{\textbf{Theoretical ex-rights price}}{\textbf{Cum-rights price of shares on last day of quotation cum-rights}} \qquad (14.5)$$

2. The number of shares before the issue is multiplied by the fraction of the year which has passed before the date of the issue to give a weighted average share of capital and by the fraction

$$\frac{\textbf{Cum-rights price of share on last day of quotation cum-rights}}{\textbf{Theoretical ex-rights price}} \qquad (14.6)$$

This is the adjustment for the pre-rights share capital.

Example 14.6 Calculation of EPS following a rights issue

On 1 April 2008, Portlaw Ltd made a 1 for 5 rights issue at 50 cents per share. The market price of the share cum-rights is €1.

	2008 €000	2007 €000
Profit after tax	600	500
Preference shares	100	100
Profit for ordinary shareholders	500	400

1. Calculate the theoretical ex-rights price.
   5 shares @ €1 *plus* 1 share @ 50 cents = 6 shares = €5.50
   Therefore TXRP = €5.50/6 = 92 cents

2. Calculate the EPS for 2008.
   Number of shares before issue = 6,000,000. Number of shares issued = 1,200,000.
   6m × 3/12 × €1/€0.92 = 1,630,434
   plus   7.2m × 9/12 = 5,400,000
   Therefore, the weighted average number of shares = 1,630,434 + 5,400,000 = 7,030,434
   $$EPS = €500,000/7,030,434 = 7.1 \text{ cents}$$

3. Calculate the EPS for 2007

Portlaw Ltd's EPS before the rights issue in 2007 was 6.7 cents. Taking the rights issue into consideration the 2007 EPS is €0.92/€1 × 6.7 = 6.16 cents.

14.12.3 *Fully diluted earnings per share*

The EPS of a company can be diluted in the future if it has:

(a) convertible debentures or preference shares convertible into equity shares,
(b) warrants or options which provide the holder with the right to subscribe for equity shares, or
(c) a separate class of equity share which doesn't rank for dividend at present but will at some future date.

Fully diluted EPS is calculated by assuming that **all** possible ordinary shares were in issue from the first day of the accounting period under consideration. The number of shares in issue will increase but these new shares will not generate any new income. Fully diluted EPS is calculated so that the impact of this dilution is shown in the current period.

Example 14.7 Calculating fully diluted earnings per share

The following information is available for Molleran's Ltd for the year ended 31/12/2008

Profit after tax and preference dividend	€100,000
Number of ordinary shares already in issue	300,000

In addition, Molleran's Ltd has €100,000 10% convertible loan stock in issue. These give the holders of this convertible loan stock the right to convert this stock into equity shares. The conversion rights are

Date	Price per share
30/5/2008	€1.20
30/5/2009	€1.30
30/5/2010	€1.40
30/5/2011	€1.50

Calculate the fully diluted earnings per share for 31/12/2008. Assume a corporation tax of 15%.

Remember, when calculating fully diluted earnings per share we assume that all of the convertible loan stock was converted at the beginning of the accounting period. If this was the case then we will need to add back to the profit after tax figure the interest savings that would arise.

The fully diluted EPS is calculated at the end of year 2008. The next conversion will occur on 30/5/2009. Therefore the number of shares to be converted in calculating the fully diluted earnings per share for the end of year 2008 is €100,000/€1.30 = 76,923 shares. The number of shares already in issue is 300,000. Therefore we assume that there are 376,923 shares in issue on 1/1/2008. The fully diluted earnings per share is €108,500/376,923 = 28.8 cents.

14.13 Warrants

Warrants are securities that give the holder the right to buy shares at a fixed price over a certain period. Warrants are sometimes called **equity sweeteners** or **kickers**. They are typically issued with loans or bonds because they make the bond more attractive to the lenders. Warrants cause the number of shares issued to increase. The profit after tax figure is then distributed over a larger number of shares, thus causing a dilution in the EPS. Fully diluted EPS is therefore lower than basic EPS because the numerator in the fully diluted EPS equation is larger.

Warrants give rise to additional future capital, unlike the conversion process in the previous example where loan capital was converted into equity capital. Therefore, if we assume that warrants were exercised during the period, we must have some way of estimating the rate of return on this additional capital. SSAP 3 requires that when warrants are used, the diluted EPS should be calculated on the assumptions that (a) earnings from the period be adjusted, assuming that the proceeds of the subscription were invested in 2.5% consolidated war bonds (consols), and (b) the maximum number of shares are issued under the terms of the warrants.

Example 14.8 Exercising warrants

Glaxis Ltd has 150,000 shares already in issue and has warrants which entitle the holders to subscribe for an additional 100,000 shares in the company. The warrants can be exercised after 31/12 at €1.50 per share. The price of 2.5% consolidated stock on 1/1/2007 was €50. Glaxis has just earned profit after tax of €70,000. The tax rate is 15%.

Subscription income received = 100,000 × €1.50 = €150,000. The yield on 2.5% consolidated stock is 2.5 × 100/50 = 5%. Therefore, we assume that the subscription from exercising the warrants is invested in consols yielding 5%. This is €150,000 × 0.05 = €7,500 *less* tax (15%) = €6,375.

Therefore the total earnings for calculating the fully diluted earnings per share is €76,375. The total number of shares for calculating fully diluted earnings per share is 250,000.

Therefore the fully diluted earnings per share is €76,376/250,000 = 31 cents.

If the dilution is 5% less than the basic EPS, it need not be disclosed.

14.15 Earnings yield

This is the earnings per share divided by the market price per share.

$$\text{Earnings yield} = \frac{\text{EPS}}{\text{Market price of share}} \qquad (14.7)$$

For example, the annual reports of *Independent News and Media* show an EPS of €0.25 in 1998 and an average share price in 1998 of €3.45.[10] This gives an earnings yield of 7.2%.

In general, a low earnings yield would indicate that the company has good growth prospects. A high yield would indicate that investors believe that the share is risky and are unsure about the future prospects of the company.

14.16 Price/earnings ratio

This is the market price of the share divided by the EPS.

$$\text{P/E ratio} = \frac{\text{Market price of share}}{\text{EPS}} \qquad (14.8)$$

It is a measure of the time needed to recover the purchase price, assuming that earnings per share remain constant. It is the inverse of the earnings yield.

Example 14.10 Calculating the P/E ratio

The market price of a share (ex-dividend) is €5. The company's most recent EPS figure is 50 cents. Therefore the P/E ratio is €5/€0.50 = 10 times.

This means that the market is valuing the current earnings of the company at a multiple of 10. Therefore, if the company is currently earning net profits of €1m on a P/E basis, the market value of the company is €10m. Therefore a high P/E ratio would suggest that investors are optimistic about the growth prospects of the company with a low risk.

14.17 Dividend cover

Dividend cover is defined as

$$\text{Dividend cover} = \frac{\text{EPS}}{\text{Dividend per share}} \qquad (14.9)$$

Alternatively,

$$\text{Dividend cover} = \frac{\text{Profit for ordinary shareholders}}{\text{Actual dividends paid to shareholders}} \qquad (14.10)$$

Profits available for distribution (i.e. PAT and preference dividends)/Actual dividends paid to shareholders.

Management may decide not to pay out all after-tax earnings in the form of a dividend. Some of the earnings may be reinvested in the company. A high cover may mean that dividends can continue to be paid even if earnings drop. In this way, it is a measure of the riskiness of the investment.

Furthermore, the dividend cover will show how much of the company's profits are being retained (retention ratio) for further investment. Therefore, for example, a dividend cover of 5 will mean that 80% of the company's profits are being retained.

For example, the dividend per share of Independent News and Media plc in 1998 was €0.11 and the EPS was given as €0.25. Therefore the dividend cover was 2.27 times.

14.18 The efficient market hypothesis

The efficient market hypothesis (EMH) deals with the extent to which share prices reflect all available information about the company and the economy. The market share price reflects the true underlying intrinsic value of the share. If all information is reflected in the market price of the share, it is impossible for any investor to consistently outperform the market. When an investor buys a stock she gets exactly what she pays for and investors and companies who sell shares get exactly what they are worth. The difference between the market value of the investment and its cost is zero. Therefore all investments in the market have zero net present values. Note that because no investor or analyst is better informed than the market, the quest for mispriced stocks is futile. The **rationale for market efficiency** is competition among investors. Investors cannot consistently beat the market because stock markets are extremely competitive. For example, if it was the case that it became well known that companies that reinvested all their after-tax earnings did particularly well, more and more investors would buy stocks in these companies, forcing up the price of these stocks and eliminating any excess profits that were being made. Stocks that are mispriced will become fewer and fewer because of competition. The market will become increasingly efficient. The EMH says that trying to find patterns in stock prices or trying to find 'winners' is a waste of time. The possibility of making excess profits in the stock markets is as rare as finding a sum of money on the street. If a sum of money is lost it will be picked up by somebody very quickly. In the very same way an opportunity to make excess profits will be taken up quickly, so that no such opportunity will exist for long.

14.18.1 Forms of market efficiency

It is generally understood that there are **three** forms of market efficiency. Markets are either **weak form efficient**, **semi-strong form efficient** or **strong form efficient**. The distinction between these three forms of market efficiency depends on the level of information incorporated into the stock price.

Weak form efficiency

If markets were weak form efficient, then all historical information would be reflected in the stock price. It is not possible to make excess returns by using historical information, such as company reports, past prices, or any other information that is readily available on the company. Investors would not be able to benefit from this type of information because it is readily available and doesn't cost very much. Selecting stocks based on historical information would be of no use to investors. The fact that a share price might have risen for the past four days, for example, doesn't give us any information about how the stock price will perform on the fifth day. Analysts who plot past price movements are called chartists. If you believe that weak form efficiency exists, then you believe that chartists are wasting their time. For example, if a chartist finds a pattern which shows that if a stock price falls for three consecutive days and then rises by 5% on the fourth day, investors could make money by buying stocks that fall for three consecutive days. However, no investor would sell a stock that had fallen for three consecutive days if she thinks that it will rise in price the following day. In fact, if the share price is €10 on the third day and if it is expected to rise by 5% on the fourth day, the share price would probably rise to €10.50 on the third day, which will eliminate any opportunity for excess profits.

Semi-strong form efficiency

Could any public information be used to earn excess returns? Markets are said to be semi-strong form efficient if no excess returns can be made using public available information. The semi-strong form of the EMH indicates that market prices reflect all publicly available information. Excess returns cannot be earned by looking at annual reports or any other published data because all such information, good or bad, would have been incorporated into the share price when the information became available. However, any information that is not made available to the public such as that held by company insiders (e.g. directors) can be used to earn excess returns under semi-strong form efficiency. In addition, stock prices will be affected by information that becomes available if the information is different to what was expected. For example, if the company reports a 10% increase in after-tax earnings, the share price won't be affected by this news if that is what the market was expecting. On the other hand, if the market was expecting an earnings increase of an amount greater than 10%, then the share price will drop and the share price will rise if the increase in earnings was greater than 10%.

Strong form efficiency

In strong form efficient markets, **all** information, public and private, is reflected in the share price. Incorporating all private information would seem to be difficult. Some information like a company's sales figures may only be known to the directors of the company. If this information is not divulged, then it doesn't seem possible for the market to incorporate this information into the share price. It might be possible to observe if there was any buying or selling of company shares by insiders acting on privately held information. Remember that some forms of insider trading are illegal (see Chapter 10). If a strong form of market efficiency exists, even insider information cannot be used to earn excess returns.

Empirical tests

Empirical research suggests that stock markets are highly efficient in weak form, moderately efficient in semi-strong form, but the strong form efficient market does not hold and excess returns can be made by insider held information. In the related Box 14.6, the author suggests that few active investors place sufficient weight on the implications of market efficiency.

Box 14.6 Standing out from the crowd

Serious money: market efficiency, or the notion that stock prices are an unbiased reflection of value, underpins modern financial theory, yet few active investors place sufficient weight on its implications.

Active investors implicitly believe markets are inefficient, yet they routinely use financial models that were developed on the assumption that prices do reflect the wisdom of crowds.

Embarking on an investment strategy without a clear understanding of the rules of the game is hardly a recipe for success and calls into question the raison d'être of many active managers.

Investors need to be aware that stock markets satisfy the conditions that are likely to ensure prices reflect the best estimate of fair value. These conditions include: diversity, whereby individuals use different approaches and information to estimate prices; an aggregation mechanism, where individual guesses are converted into a collective estimate; and the existence of incentives that motivate individuals to be right.

Under such conditions the market price or the collective estimate will always outdo the prediction of the individual, and active investment management proves to be largely a function of luck or randomness.

For those who are sceptical, consider the work of Francis Galton. The father of eugenics, Galton was obsessed with measurement and, in a famous 1907 paper, 'Vox Populi', demonstrated convincingly the wisdom of crowds.

The paper detailed his observations at an ox-weighing contest, where almost 800 individuals paid a sixpenny fee to estimate the animal's weight.

The participants were motivated by the chance of winning a prize for the best guess. The average guess came to 1,197 pounds, versus an actual weight of 1,198 pounds. The surprising result has been repeated in several experiments over the years and only one sensible conclusion can be reached: collective wisdom is hard to beat.

The wisdom of crowds seems to suggest that active investment management is a waste of time and resources. However, all is not lost, as markets occasionally go awry. The existence of 'black swans' or rare events, popularised by Nassim Taleb in his best-selling books, means that superior returns are possible.

Stock price movements do not conform to a normal distribution, as suggested by efficient market theory, due to the presence of outliers such as Black Monday in 1987 or the dot.com crash. Stock prices sometimes reach critical points, where a seemingly small change in fundamentals can produce an outsized effect.

Black swans are, by definition, virtually impossible to predict, but there are clues that help detect whether a rare event is a growing possibility.

The reason markets sometimes fail can usually be traced to a breakdown in diversity, when collective behaviour becomes remarkably similar.

$\longrightarrow$

Blake LeBaron has demonstrated how crashes happen. He writes that, 'during the run-up to a crash, population diversity falls' as 'agents begin to use very similar trading strategies as their common good performance begins to self-reinforce'.

He notes that 'this makes the population very brittle, in that a small reduction in the demand for shares could have a strong destabilising impact on the market'. The mechanism is easy to understand in that 'traders have a hard time finding anyone to sell to in a falling market since everyone else is following very similar strategies'.

The existence of such a mechanism in the late 1990s is obvious given the widespread belief that no price was too high for high-flying, loss-making technology stocks. The number of mutual funds dedicated to 'new economy' stocks soared as public enthusiasm grew, and even non-believers in the investment community were forced to participate due to short-term performance concerns.

However, those who left the party early were handsomely rewarded, as the record now shows that stocks have failed to keep pace with US Treasuries over the past decade.

The lesson for investors is clear. It is difficult to beat the collective wisdom of the market most of the time, but occasionally stock prices stray from their fundamentals and no longer reflect an unbiased assessment of value. Mispricing typically arises from a breakdown in diversity, which allows astute investors to benefit. Investors should assess the likelihood of a rare event and, in the presence of a diversity breakdown, panic early.

Charlie Fell
www.sequoia.ie
The Irish Times, 16 May 2008

SUMMARY

- Ordinary shareholders have a claim on the financial success of the company but have no preferential treatment in terms of dividends or in cases of bankruptcy.
- The pre-emption right gives shareholders the right to purchase any new shares, in proportion to their existing holding, issued by the company.
- The shares of privately owned companies are not traded. When the shares of companies are traded, they are publicly owned companies.
- The **primary market** is where publicly owned firms raise finance by selling shares.
- The **secondary market** is the market where the owners of shares sell their shares to other investors.
- An initial public offering (IPO) occurs when a privately owned firm goes public for the first time. It also refers to the privatisation programme of governments.
- IPOs are costly if priced below their true value. This is the cost of underpricing.
- Underpricing avoids the winner's curse.
- There are five ways of raising cash through selling shares: (a) public offering, (b) through a private placing, (c) through a stock exchange placing of shares, (d) through a rights issue, (e) through stock purchase plans to employees.
- Share issues tend to depress share prices. This is partly due to the increased supply of shares and due to signalling, or the information sent to the market about the company's intentions.

- Venture capital is zero stage financing or financing for start-up, often high-risk ventures.
- Stock markets are divided into organised exchanges and over-the-counter markets.
- A stock market index is a summary of what is happening to a group of similar shares.
- The order driven system is how trading in equities in Ireland is conducted.
- Warrants are securities that give the holder the right to buy shares at a fixed price over a certain period.
- The efficient market hypothesis states that share prices reflect all available information about the company and the economy. The rationale for market efficiency is competition among investors.

WEB LINKS

http://cbs.marketwatch.com
Information on the IPO markets.

http://bear.cba.ufl.edu/ritter
Home page of Jay Ritter and IPOs.

www.ise.ie
The Irish Stock Exchange site.

www.123world.com/stockexchanges
Links to worldwide stock exchanges.

www.morningstar.com
Information on mutual funds.

QUESTIONS

1. What are the characteristics of ordinary shares?
2. Distinguish between privately owned and publicly owned companies.
3. What are the advantages and disadvantages of selling shares to the public?
4. Distinguish between the primary and secondary capital markets.
5.♦ Explain IPOs and why they are usually underpriced.
6. Distinguish between the bookbuilding, fixed-price and auction method of issuing shares. Under what circumstances can uniform pricing lead to higher proceeds than discriminatory pricing?
7. What is the difference between organised stock markets and over-the-counter markets?
8. Why do companies list on more than one exchange?
9. What types of securities are listed on the Irish stock exchange?
10. Distinguish between strong form, semi-strong form and weak form efficient markets.
11.♦ It has been consistently shown that the returns from shares outperform the return from bonds. Why is it that investors hold bonds for long periods?

12. Can a market be both semi-strong form efficient and weak form efficient at the same time?

13. ◆ If the market is strong form efficient, what happens when investors try to outperform the market?

14. A company's share is selling at €100 and it has an exercise price of €70 per share. The warrant gives the holder the right to buy five shares at the exercise price. What is the exercise value of the warrant?

15. Crehana Ltd has paid an annual dividend to its shareholders of €1.50 per share. The share price at the start of the year was €20 and the current share price €25. Calculate: (a) the dividend yield, (b) the capital gains yield and (c) the total return.

16. ◆ The sales director of a company has just put together figures with unexpected but positive sales growth. Could the sales director profit by buying shares in the company before the information becomes public? To what form of market efficiency does this refer?

17. Distinguish between value stocks and growth stocks.

18. If you read some of the advertisements in the newspapers, you will be told that some fund managers outperform the average market performance. Does this make market efficiency theory invalid?

19. What effect do you think the elimination of the pre-emptive right would have on the ability of a company to raise new capital? Do you think that in terms of ownership and control, pre-emptive rights are critically important to shareholders of very large publicly owned firms?

20. ◆ Brandon Ltd needs to raise an additional €15m in equity capital. The current market price of Brandon's shares is €10 each. They have decided to employ the expertise of underwriters who inform the company that they must price the issue at 20% below the current market price. The underwriters will receive 3% of the price the shares are issued at and additional costs of the issue to the company amount to €20,000. Calculate the number of shares the company must issue to raise the capital it needs and cover all its costs.

21. Qwelly Quarrepus Ltd has 300,000 shares in issue at €55 each. The company is proposing a rights issue of 50,000 new shares at €45 each.
    (a) What is the new market capitalisation?
    (b) How many rights are needed to purchase one new share?
    (c) What is the theoretical ex-right price of the share?
    (d) What is the value of a right?

22. Tinhallow Ltd needs an additional €10m to finance new investments. It is proposing to sell new Shares at an offer price of €15 per Share. The underwriters of the issue charges a 6% spread. How many shares will need to be sold by Tinhallow Ltd?

23. ABC Ltd has decided on a rights issue. The current price of the share is €20 and there are 3 million shares in issue. The company has decided that the ex rights price will be €17 per share. The rights issue would raise €35 million. At what price can existing shareholders subscribe for additional shares?

NOTES

1. 'The Market's Problem with the Pricing of IPOs', R.G. Ibbotson, J. Sindelar and J.R. Ritter, *Journal of Applied Corporate Finance* 7, Spring 1994.
2. 'IPO Underpricing around the World', J.R. Ritter in *Fundamentals of Corporate Finance*, 5th edn., Ross, Westerfield and Jordan.
3. See note 1.
4. R. Loughran and J. Ritter, 'The New Issues Puzzle', *Journal of Finance* 50, 1995.
5. 'Strategic Development Options for Ireland in a Comparative Context' Peter Bacon & Associates, October 1999.
6. 'Cheap Accessible Cross-border Trading Possible after Merger', Margaret Doyle (of the *Economist*), from *The Irish Times*, 5 May 2000.
7. 'Irish Exchange Faces New Challenge from Euronext', Mary Canniffe, *The Irish Times*, 24 March 2000.
8. 'Foreign Firms Flock to US for IPOs', M.R. Seist, *Wall Street Journal*, 23 June 1995.
9. 'Exchange to Switch to Electronic Trading Tomorrow', Mary Canniffe, *The Irish Times*, 5 June 2000.
10. For simplicity, this average price is got by taking the high and low price for the year and dividing by 2.

15

The Bond Market

CHAPTER OBJECTIVES

At the end of this chapter the student should:

1. be able to calculate bond prices between coupon dates
2. understand the importance of, and be able to calculate, price volatility in relation to fixed-interest bonds
3. be able to calculate price volatility of a callable bond/dual-dated bond
4. understand the factors that determine price volatility
5. understand the concept of the true cost of finance
6. be able to calculate the true cost of finance
7. understand the structure and operation of the Irish Government bond market
8. understand the concept of a unit-linked fund
9. understand the attractiveness of unit-linked funds to small investors
10. be aware of the different types of unit-linked funds
11. understand the concept of a pension fund
12. be able to distinguish between defined benefit and defined contribution pension schemes
13. understand the key investment objectives, criteria and management approaches of pension funds

INTRODUCTION

This chapter builds on the material in Chapter 5 and deals with more advanced aspects of bonds and the operation of the bond market. Appendices 15B and 15C introduce the student to two other investment vehicles, unit-linked funds and pension funds.

15.1 Pricing between coupon dates

Bonds trade every day, not just on exact coupon dates. The price of a bond therefore has to reflect the time which has elapsed since the last coupon payment or, more particularly, the time until the next coupon payment. This section examines the mathematics of pricing the bond between coupon dates.[1]

Example 15.1 Pricing between coupon dates

A government bond with face value of €100 is due for redemption on 1 July 2013. It pays an annual coupon of 15% on 1 July each year to the holder of the bond at the close of trading on 30 June in that year. The redemption value is tax-free, but the coupon income is subject to tax at the holder's marginal rate. Using a net redemption yield (at 20% tax) of 8% p.a., calculate the price of the bond on

- 1 July 2010
- 30 June 2010
- 31 March 2010
- 31 December 2009
- 30 September 2009
- 1 July 2009
- 30 June 2009.

1 July 2010: The price on this date is calculated using 5.2 with the following parameters

$$Pt = 12.00 \ (€15 \ less \ tax \ @ \ 20\%)$$
$$k = 0.08$$
$$n = 3$$

This gives a price of €110.31.

Note that the investor buying the bond on this day does not get the coupon payment on that date, but must wait until one year later to receive his/her first income from the bond.

30 June 2010: An investor buying the bond on this day is getting the same as the person buying it on 1 July 2010 *plus* an extra €12.00 in one day's time. Since they are both parting with their money at virtually the same time, the buyer on 30 June should pay an extra €12.00 for the bond. The price on 1 July 2010 is calculated as above and the extra coupon of €12.00 payable the next day added to it. This produces an answer of €122.31. Strictly speaking this should be discounted for one day, but this is ignored here for simplicity.

31 March 2010: An investor buying the bond on this date gets the same cash flow as the investor buying it on 30 June 2010. However, she has to part with her money three months earlier and so the price paid on this date should be lower to reflect this. Thus the price of the bond on this date should be €122.31 discounted for three months at a rate of 8% p.a. This produces a price of €119.98.

$$\text{Price } 31/03/10 = \frac{\text{Price } 30/06/10}{(1.08)^{\frac{1}{4}}} = €119.98$$

31 December 2009: The same logic holds in this case, except that the price must be discounted for six rather than three months. This produces a price of €117.69.

$$\text{Price } 31/12/09 = \frac{\text{Price } 30/06/10}{(1.08)^{\frac{1}{2}}} = €117.69$$

30 September 2009: The same logic holds in this case, except that the price must be discounted for nine rather than three months. This produces a price of €115.45.

$$\text{Price } 30/09/09 = \frac{\text{Price } 30/06/10}{(1.08)^{\frac{3}{4}}} = \text{€}115.45$$

30 June 2009: The price on this date can be calculated in two ways. Using the same logic as above, with the price discounted for a full year but then adding the extra coupon of €12.00 which would be paid on 1 July 2006, this produces a price of €125.25.

$$\text{Price } 30/06/09 = \frac{\text{Price } 30/06/10}{(1.08)^{1}} + \text{€}12.00 = \text{€}125.25$$

1 July 2009: The price on 1 July 2009 (€113.25) can by calculated using 5.2 as before with the following parameters

$$Pt = 12.00 \ (\text{€}15 \ less \ \text{tax @ } 20\%)$$
$$k = 0.08$$
$$n = 4$$

This gives a price of €113.25.

If, the extra coupon of €12.00 is then added to it as before, this produces the same answer for 30 June 2006 as above, i.e. €125.25.

It can be seen from these prices that the longer the period to the next coupon payment is, the cheaper the bond will be. The bond price will drop immediately after the coupon is paid and rise continuously until the next coupon date. This assumes that redemption yield remains constant.

The prices are summarised in Table 15.1. Figure 15.1 presents a graphical analysis of the price movements.

Table 15.1 Prices between coupon dates

	€
30/06/09	PV = 125.25
01/07/09	PV = 113.25
30/09/09	PV = 115.45
31/12/09	PV = 117.69
31/03/10	PV = 119.98
30/06/10	PV = 122.31
01/07/10	PV = 110.31

Figure 15.1 Bond price between coupon dates

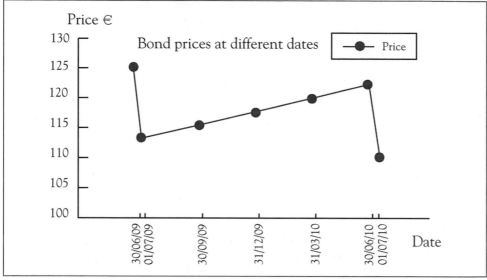

15.2 Price volatility

The general principle is that bond prices fall as the yield rises and vice versa. This is obviously of importance to an investor holding a portfolio of bonds. However, it would be of much greater use to know by **how much** the price of an individual bond and therefore the value of a portfolio of bonds would change for a given change in the yield. This can be estimated if the price volatility of the bond is known.

Price volatility is defined as the % change in price that occurs when the gross redemption yield changes by 1 percentage point.[2]

Example 15.2 Price volatility

A government bond pays an annual coupon of 8%, has face value and redemption value of €100 and has nine years to run. It is currently selling at a gross redemption yield(GRY) of 11% p.a. Calculate the price volatility of the bond for:

(a) a one percentage point fall in the GRY
(b) a one percentage point rise in the GRY.

Solution
First calculate the price at the different GRY using formula 5.2. This gives the following:

GRY	Price
11%	83.39
12%	78.69
10%	88.48

Volatility can be calculated as

$$\text{Price volatility} = \left[\frac{\text{Final price}}{\text{Original price}} - 1 \right] \times 100$$

or as

$$\text{Price volatility} = \left[\frac{\text{Final price} - \text{Original price}}{\text{Original price}} \right] \times 100$$

Using the figures above for a change in the GRY from 11% to 12%:

$$\text{Price volatility} = \frac{78.69}{83.39} - 1 \times 100 = -5.6\%$$

or

$$\text{Price volatility} = \frac{78.69 - 83.39}{83.39} \times 100 = -5.6\%$$

Repeating the same calculation in moving between 11% and 10% GRY gives the following:

GRY	Price
11%–12%	−5.6%
11%–10%	6.1%

Note: The negative measure above simply reflects the fall in the price brought about by a rise in the GRY, i.e. the inverse relationship between price and GRY. A fall in the GRY, e.g. from 11% to 10%, produces a positive volatility measure. The negative sign can be ignored.

If we re-calculate the above volatility measure from the other direction, i.e. from a GRY of 12% to a GRY of 11% and from a GRY of 10% to a GRY of 11%, we get the following:

GRY	Price volatility
12%–11%	6.0%
10%–11%	−5.7%

15.3 Features of price volatility

A number of aspects of volatility should be noted. The last two features are of particular importance in that they will assist in the selection of which bonds to purchase.

Price volatility is not symmetric

In the example above, the absolute measure of price volatility is higher for a one percentage point **fall** in the GRY than for a one percentage **rise** in the GRY, i.e. in going from a GRY of 12% to a GRY of 11% rather than going in the opposite direction, viz. 6.0% compared to 5.6%. This is simply because, while the absolute size of the price change must be the same whichever direction it is measured from, the original price against which the % change is calculated is lower when the GRY is higher and vice versa.

Price volatility is lower, the higher is the starting yield level

In the examples above we see that

GRY	Price volatility
11%–12%	−5.6%
10%–11%	−5.7%

This is simply because increasing the discount rate by one percentage point at a starting discount rate of 10% represents a 10% rise, whereas raising it by one percentage point at a starting rate of 11% only represents a rise of 9%. Thus the impact of a rise in the discount is lower if the starting rate is higher.

Price volatility is not linear

Price volatility is normally defined for a one percentage change in the GRY. Thus it measures the percentage change in price brought about by a one percentage point change in the GRY. If the GRY were to move by half a percentage point the resultant price change will not be half of what it would be for a one percentage point change, or if the GRY were to move by two percentage points the resultant price change will not be double what it would be for a one percentage point change. This is because the relationship between price and yield is convex rather than linear and so a doubling (1% – 2%) in the yield change will lead to a less than doubling in the price change, while a halving (1% – 0.5%) in the yield change will lead to a more than halving in the price change.

GRY	Change in GRY	Price volatility
11%–12%	1%	− 5.6%
11%–11.5%	0.5%	− 2.875%
11%–13%	2%	− 10.85%

These figures can be interpreted as follows:

Starting from a yield of 11%, a one percentage point rise in yield will lead to a fall in price by 5.6%, while a rise in yield of 0.5% will lead to a fall in price of 2.875% (more than half) and a rise in yield of 2% will lead to a fall in price of 10.85% (less than double).

Figure 15.2 Convexity of price volatility

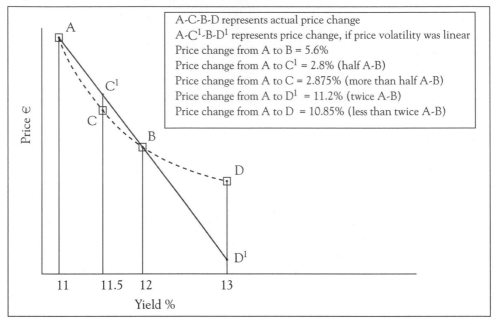

A-C-B-D represents actual price change
A-C^1-B-D^1 represents price change, if price volatility was linear
Price change from A to B = 5.6%
Price change from A to C^1 = 2.8% (half A-B)
Price change from A to C = 2.875% (more than half A-B)
Price change from A to D^1 = 11.2% (twice A-B)
Price change from A to D = 10.85% (less than twice A-B)

Bonds paying lower % coupons are more price volatile than those paying higher % coupons

(a) Consider two bonds A and B.
     The key parameters of the bonds are as follows:

Bond	Time to maturity	Coupon %
A	5	20
B	5	2.5

(b) Suppose the current yield level is 10%.

Price of A			% of value
Coupon element	3.7907 × 20 =	75.81	45 *
Redemption element	0.6209 × 100 =	62.09	55**
Total		= 137.90	100

Price of B			% of value
Coupon element	3.7907 × 2.5 =	9.48	13.2
Redemption element	0.6209 × 100 =	62.09	86.8
Total		= 71.57	100.0

Notes: * 3.7907 is the value of the expression $\dfrac{1 - (1.1)^{-5}}{0.1}$

This value can be read from the annuity tables in Appendix 2.

** 0.6209 is the value of the expression $\dfrac{1}{(1.1)^5}$

This value can be read from the discount tables in Appendix 2.

B is more price volatile than A, 4.16% compared to 3.36%

(c) Suppose the current yield level rises to 11%

Price of A				% reduction in value
Coupon element	3.6959 × 20	=	73.92	2.5
Redemption element	0.5935 × 100	=	59.35	4.4
Total		=	133.27	3.36
Price of B				% of value
Coupon element	3.6959 × 2.5	=	9.24	2.5
Redemption element	0.5935 × 100	=	59.35	4.4
Total		=	68.59	4.16

(d) Explanation

Price/value is equal to the present of the total income stream.

When discounting at 10% p.a., coupon income is discounted at varying rates from 0.9091 (1/1.1) to 0.6209 (1/(1.1)^5), see discount tables in Appendix 2, while the capital value is 'all' discounted at 0.6209.

When discounting at 11% p.a., coupon income is discounted at varying rates from 0.9009 (1/1.11) to 0.5935 (1/(1.11)^5), while the capital value is 'all' discounted at 0.5935.

The first coupon is about 1% lower in present value terms, the second is about 2% lower etc. and the fifth is about 4.4% lower. The capital value is all 4.4% lower.

Therefore the bond which **depends** more on the capital value (i.e. the lower coupon bond) is **harder hit** by a rise in yield to 11%, i.e. a larger chunk of its value is reduced by the full 4.4%.

Therefore the value of that bond falls more than the bond less dependent on the capital value (i.e. the higher coupon bond).

Longer-dated bonds are more price volatile than shorter-dated bonds

(a)   Now consider two other bonds C and D.

Bond	Time to maturity	Coupon %
A	5	20
B	5	2.5
C	10	20
D	10	2.5

(b)   Price/value of bonds

Price	10% yield	11% yield
C	161.44	153.00
D	53.91	49.94

(c)   Price volatility

C	D
5.23%	7.36%

Price volatility of the 10 year bonds in both cases is substantially above the equivalent 5 year bond, i.e. **C** (5.23%) compared to **A** (3.36%) **and D** (7.36%) compared to **B** (4.16%).

(d)   Explanation
      The higher volatility is due to the impact of time on the discount rate

	Capital value		Coupon income cumulative	
	5 year	10 year	5 year	10 year
Yield	Discount factor		Annuity factor	
10%	0.6209	0.3855	3.7907	6.1445
11%	0.5935	0.3522	3.6959	5.8892
% reduction	4.4	8.6	2.5	4.2

Increasing the yield by 1% (10% ⇒ 11%) reduces the present value of the total income stream, but has a proportionately greater effect on the 10 year bond, both for the capital element and the cumulative coupon element.

Summary of the two key factors effecting volatility of bonds

Coupon ⇒	% Price volatility		Conclusion
Maturity ⇓	20%	2.5%	
5 Year	3.36	4.16	Low coupon more volatile
10 Year	5.23	7.36	Low coupon more volatile
Conclusion	Longer maturity more volatile	Longer maturity more volatile	

Therefore in selecting bonds, investors, who are expecting yield levels to fall and thus prices to rise, should choose long-dated low-coupon bonds rather than short-dated, high-coupon ones, since these will experience the greatest price rise for a given fall in yields. The opposite applies if yields are expected to rise and prices are expected to fall.

15.4 Price volatility of callable bonds

As pointed out earlier, callable bonds will invariably be called if it makes economic sense for the issuer to do so. The corollary of this is that they may be called when not in the investor's interest. Because of this, these bonds will normally trade at a higher yield to similarly dated bullet bonds. Also, because of the possibility of early redemption of these bonds, the price volatility may be different to otherwise similar bullet bonds. This is particularly so when the current yield level is close to the coupon rate in the bond. An example will help to elucidate this.

Example 15.3 Price volatility of a callable bond

Two bonds, Capital and Development, pay an annual coupon of 11.5%, have face value and redemption value of €100 and have two and a quarter years to run. The next coupon payment on both bonds is due in three months' time. The issuer of Development bond, however, has the option to redeem it three months from now. Assume for simplicity that both bonds are selling at a gross redemption yield (GRY) of 12% p.a. Calculate the price volatility of the two bonds for a one percentage point fall in the GRY.

While the market yield is 12%, the issuer has no immediate reason to call the bond early, since to reissue would cost more than the existing coupon of 11.5%. Therefore the two bonds are effectively the same at this yield level and will be priced similarly. However, if the market yield were to drop to 11%, the issuer would be wise to redeem Development bond early. It will therefore be priced on the basis of the short date.

The price of both bonds at a 12% yield and 11% yield can be calculated using the normal formula and work out at:

Price at 12% yield *Capital* bond	=	107.56
Price at 11% yield of *Capital* bond	=	109.46
Price volatility of *Capital* bond	=	1.77%

Price at 12% yield *Development* bond	=	107.56
Price at 11% yield of *Development* bond	=	108.63*
Price volatility of *Development* bond	=	0.99%

* The assumption of early redemption results in the redemption value being paid in three months' time along with the normal coupon, but with no further payments thereafter. The price is therefore calculated as:

$$\text{Price} = \frac{111.50}{(1.11)^{0.25}} = 108.63$$

A number of features of the price volatility of callable bonds should be noted:

- The risk of early redemption is greater the closer the % coupon is to current yield levels.
- The longer the option period the greater the possibility that the stock will be redeemed early.

15.5 The Yield Curve

The yield curve refers to the pattern of yields on financial products as the time to maturity lengthens. The normal situation is that the longer the time to maturity the higher is the required yield. This reflects the greater illiquidity of a longer bond (the longer the sacrifice of access to cash) and the greater danger of erosion of the redemption value and later interest payments due to inflation.

The typical yield curve is illustrated below.

Figure 15.3 The yield curve

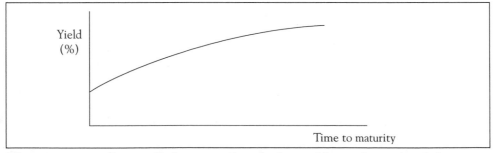

Thus an issuer will normally have to offer a higher yield on a longer bond than on a shorter one.

If the yield on longer-dated bonds is below that on shorter-dated ones, the yield curve is said to be inverted. This reflects the fact that the market expects the rate of interest to fall in the near future, thus exposing those with short-term investments to the risk of re-investing at lower rates. In a sense they are being compensated now for a future reduction in yield. Another way to interpret this is that longer-term investors are locked in to a rate of interest and are not subject to the same risk as short-term investors. They are therefore prepared to accept a lower yield as a result.

Figure 15.4 The inverted yield curve

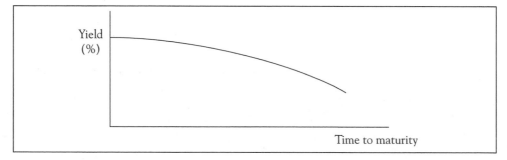

15.6 Rating

A bond issued by a national treasury/exchequer or which is state guaranteed is generally regarded as low risk. This bond will be the most highly rated and the issuer can thus issue it at a relatively low yield. Bonds issued by corporations will receive a rating based on the company's size, stability, reputation, track record, etc. Ratings are issued by a number of established rating agencies. The highest rating of 'AAA', for example, represents a virtually riskless bond and the yield at issue will reflect this. The rating system of each agency is a spectrum with the expected yield increasing as the bond moves out along the risk spectrum. A lower rating might increase the yield required by investors by, say, 50 basis points[3] (50 one-hundreds of a percentage point, i.e. half a percentage point).

15.7 Corporate bonds

The focus up to this point has been on government issued bonds. Most of the mathematical issues are the same for corporate bonds. A key difference concerns the perceived additional risk attached to corporate bonds. This will be manifest in a higher required return for the investor and a higher cost of funds for the company. The yield margin over government stock will vary according to the rating which the company has, either explicitly or implicitly, and will be effected by factors such as

- the size of the company
- the purpose for which the money is being raised
- the existing debt structure of the company
- the guarantees attached to the bond issue, etc.

One specific, technical, aspect of relevance to corporate bond issue, i.e. the true cost of finance, is dealt with in the next section.

15.8 The true cost of finance

If a company issues a fixed-interest bond at par, e.g. an 8% coupon bond with a redemption value of €1,000 at a price of €1,000, then the annual cost of finance is simply equal to the coupon rate of 8%, i.e. the company carries a debt on its balance sheet of €1,000 for, say, 5 years, pays €80 interest per year and repays the debt at the end of the fifth year. In other words the annual cost of finance is the same as the interest paid.

However, if a company issues the bond at a discount or issues a stepped-interest bond, then the annual interest payment is no longer the same as the true finance cost to the company on an annual basis.

Prior to the introduction of Financial Reporting Standard 4 (FRS 4) *Capital Instruments* in 1993, companies could charge to the profit and loss account the **actual** interest paid rather than the underlying true cost of finance. This was referred to as **off-P & L a/c financing** and allowed companies to minimise the charge to the P & L a/c in the early years of the debt and to back-end load the cost of finance on the P & L a/c.

A typical example of this would be a property company developing a new shopping centre which will take two years to build. The company would have no income from the development during the construction phase and so would be in a difficult cash flow position. By back-end loading the interest payment through a stepped-interest, a zero-coupon or a discount bond, the company could structure its debt servicing to coincide with its expected cash inflow from the development.

This introduced the danger of a potential misinterpretation of a company's debt profile by investors or lenders, since it was the P & L a/c and the balance sheet, rather than the cash flow statement, which tended to receive most attention from analysts.

The objective of FRS 4 was 'to ensure that financial statements provided a clear, coherent and consistent treatment of capital instruments' (FRS 4, *Capital Instruments*, Accounting Standards Board, 1993) and to present capital instruments in financial statements in a way that reflected the obligations of the user.

The basic approach of FRS 4 was that the P & L a/c would show the cost of servicing the debt instrument at a constant rate on the carrying amount on the balance sheet. The balance sheet treatment was that an adjustment was made, where appropriate, each year to reflect the change in the carrying amount. The examples below help to explain the approach.

FRS 4 was withdrawn in December 2004 and replaced by FRS 25, *Financial Instruments: Disclosure and Presentation* and FRS 26, *Financial Instruments: Measurement*. These are broadly equivalent to International Accounting Standards IAS 39.

The following examples are based on the examples shown in the 'Application Notes' which accompanied FRS 4. The treatment under the International Accounting Standards is broadly the same. This section is written to show the *numerical treatment only*. It is not intended to explain the required legal treatment under the various standards. Students interested in the full detail of definitions, etc. should consult the relevant standard.

Examples are given for the following situations:

- debt issued with warrants
- index-linked loans
- stepped-interest bonds.

In the cases shown below the true annual cost of finance is given. In practice this will normally be determined by trial and error. This is similar to the derivation of the gross redemption yield on a bond, discussed in Chapter 5. A simple example of the derivation of the true cost of finance is given here as an introduction to the examples below.

Example 15.4 Derivation of the true cost of finance

A company funds a new development through the issue of a four year discount bond. The bonds have a nominal and redemption value of €1,000 and pay an annual interest rate as follows:

End year	% of nominal value
1	3
2	6
3	9
4	12

The bonds are issued at a price of €700.

(a) Calculate the true average annual cost of borrowing for the company over the four year period. (Answer to one place of decimals.)

(b) Verify the answer to (a) above by showing the annual finance cost, annual interest payment and the end-of-year debt position for each of the four years. (Ignore any small rounding error at the end of year 4.)

The cash flow from the bond is as follows:

End-year	1	2	3	4
Cash flow	30	60	90	1,120

The cash flow is discounted at varying rates until two rates are found which give a present value either side of €700. As before, these rates should be one percentage point apart. The true cost of finance can be approximated between these two trial rates by linear interpolation, or by iteration from an approximate answer.

In the example a trial rate of 18% produces a present value of €700.97. A discount rate of 18.1% produces a present value of €698.79. The first answer of 18% is marginally more accurate and taken as the estimated true cost of finance.

The annual cash flow and debt position can be shown as follows:

End-year	Finance cost @18%	Interest paid	Debt
0			700
1	126	30	796
2	143.28	60	879.28
3	158.27	90	947.55
4	170.56	1,120	−1.89

The small positive balance at the end of year 4 is simply a rounding error as the true cost of finance is marginally above 18%.

In all of the following examples, the true annual cost of finance is given.

Debt issued with warrants

An investor who subscribes for this form of capital instrument is buying two separate investments – a bond investment and options on the company equity. The key decision in this situation is how to allocate the proceeds of the issue between the debt and the warrants. The amount attributable to the debt effectively means that, at the beginning of the term of the debt, its value is below the redemption amount by the value of the warrants.

Example 15.5 Debt issued with warrants

A company issues debt with equity warrants attached for a total of €2,200. The redemption value of the debt is €2,200 and the term is 6 years from 1 January 2010. It carries interest at 7.9% p.a. A fair value for the debt and the warrants at the time of issue is €2,000 and €200 respectively.

   The debt is initially valued at €2,000. The interest charge is 7.9% of €2,200 = €173.80. The total finance cost of the debt is the difference between the payments required by the debt which is €3,242.8 ((6 × €173.8) + €2,200) and the deemed proceeds of the debt of €2,000, i.e. €1,242.8. The true finance cost is determined to be 10% p.a.

Table 15.2 Debt issued with warrants

Year ending	Balance at start of year €000	Finance costs for year €000	Cash paid during year €000	Balance at end of year €000
31/12/2010	2,000.00	200.00	173.8	2,026.20
31/12/2011	2,026.20	202.62	173.8	2,055.02
31/12/2012	2,055.02	205.50	173.8	2,086.72
31/12/2013	2,086.72	208.67	173.8	2,121.59
31/12/2014	2,121.59	212.16	173.8	2,159.95
31/12/2015	2,159.95	216.00	2,373.8	2.15

The finance cost for the first year is 10% of the opening debt, i.e. 10% of €2,000 = €200. Since the company only pays €173.80, it underpays by €26.20 and this amount is added to the debt at the end of the first year. The finance cost for the second year is 10% of the debt at the end of the first year, i.e. 10% of €2,026.20 = €202.62. This company again underpays (by €28.82) and this is added to the debt. This process is continued for each successive year.

Note: The balance at the end of the tenth year of €2.15 is simply a rounding error as the true cost of finance is slightly below 10%.

Deep discount bonds

The required treatment is broadly similar to that under debt issued with warrants. Example 15.4 above dealt with this type of instrument.

Index-linked loans

Debts may be issued or loans may be taken out where either the interest payments or the capital value may be determined by reference to an external variable or index, e.g. the interest payments are a mark-up on, say, the inter-bank rate or the capital value is linked to, say, the consumer price index.

Example 15.6 Index-linked loans

A loan of €1,250 is issued on 1 January 2010, on which interest at 6% (€75) is paid annually and the principal amount is repayable based on an index. The balance at the end of each year is found by multiplying the original principal amount by an index at the end of the year. The debt is repayable after 5 years. The index changes as follows:

Date	Index value
01/01/2010	100
31/12/2010	107
31/12/2011	112
31/12/2012	115
31/12/2013	125
31/12/2014	140

The interest paid in the first year was €75. The index rose by 7% in the first year, therefore the debt is adjusted to €1,337.50 (€1,250 × 1.07). The finance cost for the year is 6% interest *plus* the 7% capital adjustment, i.e. 13% of €1,250 = €162.50. The actual payment is €75 and therefore there is an underpayment of (€162.50 – €75 = €87.50). The debt is adjusted upwards by this amount, i.e. €1,250 + €87.50 = €1,337.50. This process is repeated in the subsequent years.

Table 15.3 Index-linked loans

Year ending	Balance at start of year €000	Finance costs for year €000	Cash paid during year €000	Balance at end of year €000
31/12/2010	1,250.00	162.50	75	1,337.50
31/12/2011	1,337.50	137.50	75	1,400.00
31/12/2012	1,400.00	112.50	75	1,437.50
31/12/2013	1,437.50	200.00	75	1,562.50
31/12/2014	1,562.50	262.50	1,825	0.00

Stepped-interest bonds

In this case the interest paid rises in a stepped fashion over the life of the bond (see section 5.4, Chapter 5). The payments are apportioned between a finance charge for each period (at a constant rate on the outstanding debt) and a change in the carrying amount of the debt. The carrying amount of the debt will increase in the periods where the interest payments are below the finance charge (the earlier periods) and decrease in the periods where the payments are higher than the finance costs (the later periods).

Example 15.7 Stepped-interest bond

A company funds a new development through the issue of a four year stepped-interest bond on 1 January 2010. The bonds have a nominal and redemption value of €1,000 and pay an annual interest rate as follows:

Year	% of nominal value
1	3
2	8
3	12
4	18

The bonds are issued at par, i.e. at a price of €1,000. The constant rate works out at 9.7%.

Table 15.4 Stepped-interest bonds

Year Ending	Balance at start of year €000	Finance costs for year €000	Cash paid during year €000	Balance at end of year €000
31/12/2010	1,000.00	97.00	30	1,067.00
31/12/2011	1,067.00	103.50	80	1,090.50
31/12/2012	1,090.50	105.78	120	1,076.28
31/12/2013	1,076.28	104.40	1,180	0.68

The finance charge in the first year is 9.7% of €1,000 = €97. Since the company only pays €30, it underpays by €67. This is added to the debt, which now becomes €1,067. The finance charge in the second year is 9.7% of €1,067 = €103.50. Since the company only pays €80, it underpays by €23.50. This is added to the debt, which now becomes €1,067 + €23.50 = €1,090.50. This process continues for the remaining years of the term of the bond.

Note: The balance at the end of the fourth year of 0.68 is simply a rounding error as the true cost of finance is slightly under 9.7% p.a.

15.9 The Irish bond market

The Irish equity market is discussed in other chapters in this book. This chapter takes a brief look at the structure and operation of the Irish Government bond market.

As pointed out in Chapter 5, bonds normally represent, after equity, the largest asset category in Irish institutional portfolios, though typically not in private individuals' portfolios, where equity and property became the two main asset categories during the height of the Celtic Tiger years. The decline of equity values from about mid-2007 onwards and falling property values in 2008 may lead to some realignment of asset allocations in the future, with a growth in the proportion of the total investment allocated to bonds. Sovereign bonds are perceived as a 'safe haven' when markets are in turmoil and economic prospects are weak.

The bulk of the Irish bond market is in government-issued bonds, with a relatively small market in traded non-government bonds. This part of the chapter deals with the structure and operation of the Irish Government bond market.

The Irish Government bond market has changed significantly over the past 20 years due to a number of factors, the most important of which were:

- the establishment in 1990 of the National Treasury Management Agency (NTMA), and
- the entry of Ireland into the Economic and Monetary Union (EMU) and the consequent replacement of the IR£ with the € as the currency.

Other consequences, discussed below, flowed from these two events.

15.9.1 Bonds currently in issue

There were a total of 8 Irish Government benchmark bonds in issue at the end of April 2009. These benchmark bonds had a total nominal value of approximately €48 billion. This was following the issue of 2 new bonds in January and February 2009 and the redemption of an existing bond in April 2009. The benchmark stocks have maturities ranging from 2010 to 2020. The longest bond matures in April 2020.

All of the bonds are fixed interest, bullet issues with no variable rate or dual-dated stock in the market at present. Coupon income is paid once a year. The coupons on the benchmark bonds range from 3.9% pa to 5% pa.

Gross redemption yield ranges from about 2% at the short end to over 5% at the long end of the maturity range.

Irish national debt stood at just over €50 billion at the end of 2008, with 83% in the form of fixed rate obligation and the remainder at floating rates.

In March 2009, the NTMA commenced a programme of treasury bill issuance. The first three tranches issued had a total value of €12.6 billion. The bills will have maturities ranging from 1 to 12 months. They are issued as zero-coupon instruments at a discount to their redemption value.

The full list of Irish Government benchmark bonds in issue is given in Appendix 15A at the end of this chapter.

The Irish Stock Exchange publishes Clean Price Bond Indices and Total Return Bond Indices each day. There are a total of 12 indices, based on time to maturity. These can be accessed on the Irish Stock Exchange website. The maturity categories are:

- All bonds
- Under 3 years
- Under 5 years
- Under 10 years
- 5 plus years
- 10 plus years.

The base date for all indices is 30 June 2004.

15.9.2 National Treasury Management Agency (NTMA)

The NTMA was established by the Irish Government in 1990 to manage the country's national debt, which at the time stood at about 95% of GDP. The principal objective of the NTMA is to manage the national debt and government funding programmes in a cost-effective manner at acceptable levels of risk and to achieve savings in debt servicing. It is responsible for both the domestic and foreign elements of the funding programme.

Since the inception of the agency a number of changes have been made to the operation of the bond market and a number of other developments have contributed to its growing international status. These include:

- adoption by the agency of a market making system for Irish Government bonds in 1995 and the appointment of primary dealers
- the change from semi-annual to annual coupon payment in line with mainstream European bond markets
- achievement of AAA rated status from all the main rating agencies: these have recently been downgraded somewhat
- the quotation of all benchmark bonds on a number of electronic systems
- the inclusion of Irish Government bonds in global or Euro-wide market indices, e.g.
  — Bloomberg/EFFAS – Euro Bloc Government Bond Index
  — EuroMX – Eurozone Government Bond Indices 1–15+ years
  — CitiGroup – European Government Bond Index
  — Merrill Lynch – Pan-European Government Bond Index II
  — Merrill Lynch – EMU Direct Government Index.

These developments have enhanced the liquidity of the market, which operated on a par with the other middle-ranking Euro government markets, e.g. Netherlands, Belgium, Austria and Finland, until autumn 2008. However, the credit/liquidity crisis in late 2008 led to a significant widening of spreads for Irish bonds relative to the major bond markets.

15.9.3 Participants in the market

Since the advent of the euro as the common currency of, initially, 12 of the then 15 member states of the EU, Irish funds moved to euro denominated benchmarks and switched out of Irish paper, while overseas investors, initially attracted by the greater yields available on the Irish market, switched some of their portfolios into Irish bonds. Ireland's strong economic performance around that time and the upgrading of the state's credit rating to AAA by Standard and Poor's in 2001 also contributed to the greater demand for Irish Government bonds among foreign investors.

Approximately 82% of the debt is held by non-residents, with the remainder held domestically.

There are ten primary dealers who quote two-way prices in designated bonds on both EuroMTS and MTS Ireland. The primary dealers are:
- Barclays Capital, London
- BNP Paribas, London
- Calyon, London
- Citigroup, London
- Davy Stockbrokers, Dublin
- Deutsche Bank, Frankfurt
- Dresdner Bank, London
- HSBC, Paris
- ING Bank NV, Amsterdam
- Royal Bank of Scotland, London.

In addition to the ten primary dealers, a number of other institutions act as market makers for Irish Government bonds on EuroMTS.

15.9.4 Credit ratings

Ratings of Irish Government bonds were downgraded in early 2009 by the main rating agencies. In addition, each of the rating agencies has placed Ireland on 'negative watch', i.e. the outlook for a future ratings is perceived as potentially negative.

	Long-term	Short-term
Moody's	Aaa	P–1
Standard and Poor's	AA+	A–1+
Fitch ratings	AA+	F1+
Rating and Investment Information	AA+	a–1+

Source: NTMA

15.9.5 Taxation of Irish Government bonds

As the bond market is dominated by tax-exempt institutions, taxation issues do not play a critical role. This is particularly the case at the longer end of the market.

There is no withholding tax on Irish Government bonds and non-resident holdings are exempt from Irish taxation (but see the NTMA website for further details). For domestic individual investors, coupon income is liable to tax at the appropriate rate for the particular holder, i.e. the marginal income tax rate for an individual, the corporation tax rate for companies, etc. There is no tax on the redemption value if held to the redemption date, but otherwise the asset may give rise to a capital gains tax liability for some classes of investors.

The tax treatment of government bonds clearly has an implication for the pricing of bonds. Because coupon income is taxed, lower coupon bonds are subject to less tax than higher coupon bonds and therefore tend to trade at a premium to higher coupon stocks. The income flow from low coupon bonds is based more on the redemption value, which is tax-free, whereas with higher coupon stocks, taxable coupon income accounts for a greater part of the total return.

15.9.6 Non-government bonds

The traded corporate bond market in Ireland is small in comparison to the government bond market and relatively under-developed compared to other countries. There are a number of traded bonds issued by the European Investment Bank or state companies (Housing Finance Agency, Electricity Supply Board). Non-government-backed bonds will normally trade at a higher yield to equivalent government bonds to reflect their greater credit risk.

15.9.7 Recent performance of the Irish Government bond market

Irish Government bonds traded at yield levels broadly similar to the middle-ranking Euro government bonds until autumn 2008. The yield relative to the German market widened significantly since then and stood at over 200 basis points (0.2%) in April 2009. This was mainly due to the lower level of liquidity in the Irish market and the deterioration in the Irish public finances.

This section tracks the movement in the Irish bond market over the six-month period mid-March to mid-September 2008 in order to show the pattern of price and yield movements. A medium-term bond is used as an illustration.

Table 15.5 shows the movement in the price and yield of the 5% TRY, 18 April 2013 bond over the period 19 March 2008 to 17 September 2008.

Table 15.5 Price and yield of 5% 2013 bond

Date	Price €	Yield %	Change in Price €	Change in Yield bps
19/03/2008	106.480	3.634		
26/03/2008	105.200	4.842	−1.280	0.208
02/04/2008	104.730	3.959	−0.470	0.117
09/04/2008	104.520	3.974	−0.210	0.015
16/04/2008	104.390	3.961	−0.130	−0.013
23/04/2008	103.570	4.174	−0.820	0.213
30/04/2008	103.700	4.148	0.130	−0.026
07/05/2008	103.780	4.147	0.080	−0.001
14/05/2008	103.500	4.173	−0.280	0.026
21/05/2008	102.950	4.314	−0.550	0.141
28/05/2008	102.560	4.407	−0.390	0.093
04/06/2008	102.470	4.416	−0.090	0.009
11/06/2008	101.130	4.743	−1.340	0.327
18/06/2008	100.270	4.919	−0.860	0.176
25/06/2008	100.600	4.867	0.330	−0.052
02/07/2008	100.170	4.907	−0.430	0.040
09/07/2008	101.350	4.667	1.180	−0.240
16/07/2008	101.620	4.618	0.270	−0.049
23/07/2008	100.320	4.903	−1.300	0.285
30/07/2008	101.700	4.630	1.380	−0.273
06/08/2008	102.440	4.447	0.740	−0.183
13/08/2008	102.500	4.231	0.060	−0.216
20/08/2008	103.490	4.180	0.990	−0.051
27/08/2008	102.940	4.271	−0.550	0.091
03/09/2008	103.120	4.243	0.180	−0.028
10/09/2008	103.420	4.165	0.300	−0.078
17/09/2008	103.760	4.094	0.340	−0.071

Source: Price and Yield data, Irish Stock Exchange

A number of issues should initially be observed about the bond price and yield.

- The price of the bond changed in each of the 26 weeks.
- The trend in the price changed direction nine times over the period.

Figure 15.5 Price and yield of 5% 2013 bond

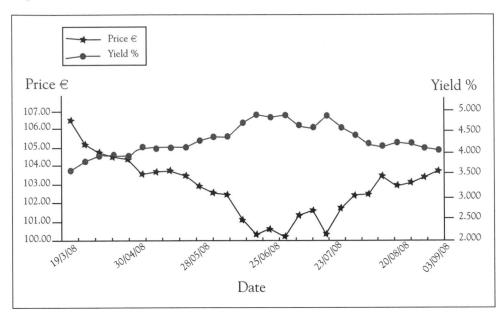

SUMMARY

- Bonds may be priced off the coupon payment date by first pricing at the coupon date and then discounting for the period between the purchase date and the next coupon date.
- Bond prices rise as the coupon payment date approaches and then fall after the coupon is paid.
- Price volatility of bonds is defined as the percentage change in the price brought about by a one percentage point change in the gross redemption yield.
- Price volatility is higher for longer-dated bonds compared to shorter-dated ones.
- Price volatility is higher for bonds with lower coupons rather than those with higher coupons.
- If bond market yields are expected to fall, investors should purchase long-dated, low coupon bonds.
- Callable bonds can be expected to be redeemed as early as possible if it is in the issuer's interest to do so.
- If the market yield falls below the coupon rate on the bond, a callable bond will exhibit lower price volatility than an otherwise similar bullet issue.
- The yield curve normally slopes upwards as the time to maturity lengthens.
- The yield may be inverted if the market expects interest rates to fall in the near future.
- The National Treasury Management Agency (NTMA) is responsible for overseeing the operation of the Irish Government bond market.
- There are 8 Irish Government benchmark bonds in issue.
- Irish Government bonds are now included in a number of international bond indices.
- There are ten primary dealers or market-makers for Irish Government bonds.

- Overseas investors hold over 80% of Irish Government bonds.
- Unit-linked funds have certain attraction for the small investor.
- Exit timing is a key consideration for unit fund holders.
- Equity funds are the dominant type of unit fund.
- The pension fund industry is the subject of increased attention as the population ages and the Irish Government promotes a greater level of private pension provision.
- In a defined benefit scheme, the onus is on the employer to make up any shortfall in investment performance.
- In a defined contribution scheme, the value of the pension payable depends on the investment performance of the fund and the cost of an annuity.
- Investment objectives and management are determined by the age profile of the membership and whether the fund is a defined benefit or defined contribution scheme.

QUESTIONS

1. ◆ Two government bonds, Finance and Treasury, pay an annual coupon of 9.5%, have a face value and redemption value of €100 and have three years and two months to run. The next coupon payment on both bonds is due in two months' time. The government, however, has the option to redeem the Treasury bond two months from now. Both bonds are selling at a gross redemption yield (GRY) of 10% p.a. Calculate the price volatility of the two bonds for a one percentage point fall in the GRY.

2. ◆ A company funds a new development through the issue of a five year discount bond. The bonds have a nominal and redemption value of €1,000 and pay an annual interest rate of 4% of nominal value. The bonds are issued at a price of €800.
   (a) Calculate the true average annual cost of borrowing for the company over the five-year period.
   (b) Verify the answer to (a) above by showing the annual finance cost, annual interest payment and the end-of-year debt position for each of the five years.

3. ◆ (a) A government bond with face value of €100 is due for redemption on 1 July 2015. It pays an annual coupon of 12% on 1 July each year to the holder of the bond at the close of trading on 30 June in that year. The redemption value is tax-free, but the coupon income is subject to tax at the holder's marginal rate. Using a net redemption yield (at 24% tax) of 7% p.a., calculate the price of the bond on
      (i)   1 July 2010
      (ii) 1 May 2010
      (iii) 25 June 2010.
   (b) Using the information in (a) above, what is the gross income yield on the bond on the same three dates?

4. A company funds a new development through the issue of a six year discount bond. The bonds have a nominal and redemption value of €1,000 and pay an annual interest rate of 2% of nominal value. The bonds are issued at a price of €600.
   (a) Calculate the true average annual cost of borrowing for the company over the six-year period.

(b)   Verify the answer to (a) above by showing the annual finance cost, annual interest payment and the end-of-year debt position for each of the six years.

5.   Two bonds, Capital and Development, pay an annual coupon of 12.5%, have face value and redemption value of €100 and have two and a half years to run. The next coupon payment on both bonds is due in six months' time. The issuer of Development bond, however, has the option to redeem it six months from now. Both bonds are selling at a gross redemption yield (GRY) of 13% p.a. Calculate the price volatility of the two bonds for a one percentage point fall in the GRY.

6.   (a)   A government bond with face value of €100 is due for redemption on 1 June 2020. It pays an annual coupon of 8% on 1 June each year to the holder of the bond at the close of trading on 31 May in that year. The redemption value is tax-free, but the coupon income is subject to tax at the holder's marginal rate. Using a net redemption yield (at 24% tax) of 6% p.a., calculate the price of the bond on
      (i)   1 June 2011
      (ii)   1 March 2011
      (iii) 31 May 2018.

      (b)   Using the information in (a) above, calculate the price volatility of the bond on 1 June 2011 for a 1% rise in the gross redemption yield from its current level.

7.♦ A company intends to issue a five year bond to raise funds for a new development. It considers two alternative bonds:

Bond A End year	Interest as % of nominal value
1	2
2	5
3	8
4	12
5	15

Bond A would be a stepped-interest bond which would have a nominal value of €1,000 and pay an annual interest rate as shown above.

Bond A would be issued at a price of €1,000, but would have a redemption value of €1,200, i.e. it would pay a capital bonus of €200 on redemption.

Bond B would have a nominal and redemption value of €1,000 and pay an annual interest rate of 10% of nominal value. Bond B would be issued at a price of €1,000.

Using the true average annual cost of borrowing associated with each bond over the five-year period, determine which of the two bonds is the cheaper from the company's point of view.

8.   (a)   A government bond with face value of €100 is due for redemption on 1 June 2018. It pays an annual coupon of 10% on 1 June each year to the holder of the bond at the close of trading on 31 May in that year. The redemption value is tax-free, but the coupon income is subject to tax at the holder's marginal rate. Using a net redemption yield (at 26% tax) of 9% p.a., calculate the price of the bond on
      (i)   1 June 2011

  (ii) 1 May 2011
  (iii) 20 April 2011.
  (b) Using the information in (a) above, what is the gross income yield on the bond on the same three dates?
9. A company funds a new development through the issue of a five year discount bond. The bonds have a nominal and redemption value of €1,000 and pay an annual interest rate of 3% of nominal value. The bonds are issued at a price of €700.
  (a) Calculate the true average annual cost of borrowing for the company over the five-year period.
  (b) Verify the answer to (a) above by showing the annual finance cost, annual interest payment and the end-of-year debt position for each of the five years. (Ignore any small rounding error at the end of year 5.)
10. (a) A government bond with face value of €100 is due for redemption on 1 June 2021. It pays an annual coupon of 9% on 1 June each year to the holder of the bond at the close of trading on 31 May in that year. The redemption value is tax-free, but the coupon income is subject to tax at the holder's marginal rate. Using a net redemption yield (at 22% tax) of 8% p.a., calculate the price of the bond on
  (i)   1 June 2009
  (ii) 1 February 2009
  (iii) 15 March 2009.
  (b) Using the information in (a) above, what is the gross income yield on the bond on the same three dates?
11. A company funds a new development through the issue of a five year discount bond. The bonds have a nominal and redemption value of €1,000 and pay an annual interest rate of 5% of nominal value. The bonds are issued at a price of €750.
  (a) Calculate the true average annual cost of borrowing for the company over the five-year period.
  (b) Verify the answer to (a) above by showing the annual finance cost, annual interest payment and the end-of-year debt position for each of the five years. (Ignore any small rounding error at the end of year 5.)
12. A government bond with face value of €100 is due for redemption on 1 July 2017. It pays an annual coupon of 7% on 1 July each year to the holder of the bond on 30 June in that year. Using a gross redemption yield of 8% p.a., calculate the price of the bond on
  (a) 6 May 2010
  (b) 31 January 2010
  (c) 6 May 2011
  (d) 1 July 2012.
13. A company funds a new development through the issue of a six year discount bond. The bonds have a nominal and redemption value of €1,000 and pay an annual interest rate of 3% of nominal value. The bonds are issued at a price of €800.
  (a) Calculate the true average annual cost of borrowing for the company over the six year period.
  (b) Verify the answer to (a) above by showing the annual finance cost, annual interest payment and the end-of-year debt position for each of the six years.

14. A company funds a new development through the issue of a four year discount bond. The bonds have a nominal and redemption value of €1,000 and pay an annual interest rate as follows:

End year	% of nominal value
1	0
2	5
3	10
4	15

The bonds are issued at a price of €750.
   (a) Calculate the true average annual cost of borrowing for the company over the four-year period (answer to one place of decimals).
   (b) Verify the answer to (a) above by showing the annual finance cost, annual interest payment and the end-of-year debt position for each of the four years. (Ignore any small rounding error at the end of year 4.)

15.♦ A government bond with face value of €100 is due for redemption on 1 August 2021. It pays an annual coupon of 6% on 1 August each year to the holder of the bond on 31 July in that year.
   (a) Using a gross redemption yield of 9% p.a., calculate the price of the bond on
      (i)   26 May 2013
      (ii) 31 January 2013
      (iii) 26 August 2013
      (iv) 26 May 2014
      (v)   1 August 2017.
   (b) Explain briefly why the bond is cheaper in (a) (ii) above than in (a)(i).
   (c) Explain briefly why the bond is cheaper in (a) (iii) above than in (a)(i).

16. Two bonds, Capital and Development, pay an annual coupon of 10.5%, have face value and redemption value of €100 and have three and a quarter years to run. The next coupon payment on both bonds is due in three months' time. The issuer of the Development bond, however, has the option to redeem it three months from now. Both bonds are selling at a gross redemption yield (GRY) of 11% p.a. Calculate the price volatility of the two bonds for a one percentage point fall in the GRY.

17. A government bond with face value of €100 is due for redemption on 1 November 2019. It pays an annual coupon of 7% on 1 November each year to the holder of the bond on 31 October in that year. Using a gross redemption yield of 10% p.a., calculate the price of the bond on
   (a) 31 October 2012
   (b) 6 June 2012
   (c) 6 November 2012
   (d) 1 November 2017.

18. A government bond with face value of €100 is due for redemption on 1 September 2015. It pays an annual coupon of 9% on 1 September each year to the holder of the bond on 31 August in that year. Using a gross redemption yield of 12% p.a., calculate the price of the bond on

(a) 6 July 2011
(b) 30 April 2011
(c) 6 July 2010
(d) 1 September 2014.

19. A company funds a new development through the issue of a four year stepped-interest bond. The bonds have a nominal and redemption value of €1,000 and pay an annual interest rate as follows:

Year	% of nominal value
1	2
2	5
3	8
4	10

The bonds are issued at a price of €750.
(a) Calculate the true average annual cost of borrowing for the company over the four-year period.
(b) Verify the answer to (a) above by showing the annual finance cost, annual interest payment and the end-of-year debt position for each of the four years.

20. Define price volatility in relation to bonds.
21. Set out the key features of price volatility.
22. Explain why price volatility is higher for longer-dated bonds than for shorter-dated ones.
23. Explain the different price volatility exhibited by a callable bond and an otherwise similar bullet bond.
24. Explain why the yield curve may become inverted.
25. Explain what is meant by bond rating.
26. Explain what is meant by the true cost of finance.
27. Describe the recent changes made to the operation of the Irish bond market.
28. Why do non-government bonds typically trade at a yield premium to government-issued bonds?
29. What are the principal attractions of a unit-linked fund for the small investor?
30. What is the distinction between bid and offer prices?
31. Distinguish between a defined benefit and a defined contribution pension scheme.
32. What is meant by tactical asset allocation?

NOTES

1 For the purpose of the treatment here, it is assumed that the holder of the bond at close of business on the day before the coupon is paid receives the full coupon payment, and that no adjustment is made to the price to reflect accrued interest. In practice price adjustments are made to reflect accrued interest and a distinction is made between *clean* and *dirty* prices. It also obviates the need to consider the ex-dividend period. These assumptions simplify the mathematics without affecting the essence of the argument.

2   The term *duration* is used in many textbooks and market reports. There are a number of different measures of duration. This section deals with it in a simple way.

3   Basis points: A basis point is one-hundredth of a percentage point.

APPENDIX 15 A
Irish government benchmark bonds outstanding April 2009

Bond Title	€bn	Coupon Date
4.0% Treasury Bond 2011	4.4	11 November
3.9% Treasury Bond 2012	4.0	5 March
5.0% Treasury Bond 2013	6.0	18 April
4.0% Treasury Bond 2014	6.3	15 January
4.6% Treasury Bond 2016	5.8	18 April
4.5% Treasury Bond 2018	6.7	18 October
4.4% Treasury Bond 2019	7.0	18 June
4.5% Treasury Bond 2020	7.9	18 April
Total	**48.1**	

Source: NTMA

APPENDIX 15 B
The Irish unit-linked fund industry

Unit-linked investment funds provide a relatively easy way for a small investor to access a wide range of assets, through a pooled investment. This appendix briefly discusses the basic aspects of this type of investment.

Concept of a unit-linked fund

A unit-linked fund is an investment vehicle where the investor takes a stake in a pooled investment and owns the assets of the fund in proportion to the percentage of the overall number of units held.

Types of funds

There are many different types of fund available to the investor largely based on the asset category in which the bulk of the assets are held. There are no precise definitions for the principal categories, but funds are allocated to each category based on the proportion of assets held and the risk stance of the fund:

Equity

- General equity
- Specialist equity
- International equity.

Fixed interest

These funds invest primarily in government gilts or other fixed-interest bonds. They are generally low-risk funds.

Guaranteed

These funds operate by providing a guarantee to the investor that the capital value of the investment will remain intact for a specific period. The fund manager achieves this by placing a proportion of the fund into (risk-free) fixed-interest stock which will have a maturity value equal to the amount invested, e.g. if the redemption yield on a one-year gilt is 5% and the guarantee is for one year, then the fund manager would invest €100/(1.05) = 95.24% of the total amount invested into gilts. This leaves only 4.76% of the investment amount to be placed in other income-earning (risky) assets.

Cash

These funds are generally low risk, but typically low return as they are invested in money market instruments and short-dated government stock. They can be used as a short-term repository for spare cash, perhaps while the investor makes up his/her mind about which sector to commit to.

Property

The investments are normally made in prime property in the retail, office and industrial sectors. Unlike the UK, where funds could have a geographical as well as a sectoral spread, Irish investments are predominantly located in Dublin and to a smaller extent in Cork. This limits the potential for locational diversification although greater investment opportunities have opened up in the past few years in larger provincial towns and cities, especially in the retail sector. Many Irish property funds invest in the UK property market, where opportunities are more plentiful, but which carry exchange rate risk. Property tends to be popular in times of high inflation due to the historical record of outpacing the rate of inflation. **Bricks and mortar** still retain a certain comfort factor for investors. However, the collapse of the commercial property market in Ireland in 2008 may make these funds less popular in the future, at least in the short term.

Mixed/managed funds

These are funds which have a spread across the main asset types. The level of risk will vary across different funds. The higher risk funds will tend to be heavily weighted towards equity and high-risk equity for the most aggressive funds.

Attractions for the small investor

Unit-linked funds are particularly attractive for the small investor. The main advantages for such an investor are:

- They offer a mechanism for the small investor to build a personal diversified portfolio without the time or capital commitment which would normally be required.
- The risk may be spread over a wide range of asset types in the key sectors of the market and across geographical areas.
- They are professionally managed.
- A competitive environment encourages fund managers to perform. This, however, does have the drawback that it can encourage **short-termism** in relation to performance, i.e. fund managers become more concerned with making short-term gains, perhaps at the expense of longer-term growth in the fund. Tactics can become more important than strategy.
- Regular **league tables** of competing funds are available allowing the investor to make comparisons between funds.
- Most assets have a daily or at least weekly valuation. However, with property-based funds, prices may not move as often as with unit funds based on other assets since valuations are only undertaken periodically and market indices are not published very frequently.
- They generally offer a good degree of liquidity. This is particularly important in relation to property-based funds, since the underlying asset itself is highly illiquid.
- Units can be bought or sold but it is generally not profitable to do so over a short period. This is due to the 'spread' between the bid and offer prices (see below). The spread will vary depending on the length of time the unit is held and may be waived as a loyalty bonus if the units are held for a specified period.

  While unit funds are an attractive investment vehicle for the small investor, timing of exit, i.e. the date at which the units are redeemed, is critically important. If the investor intends to use the proceeds as part of a pension, then care should be taken to minimise risk as the exit date approaches, perhaps by switching into lower-risk cash or bond funds. Many investors suffered substantial losses in 2008 due to the sudden and significant fall in both equity and property markets.

Bid and offer prices

The offer price is the price at which units are sold by the fund manager, while the bid price is the price at which the fund manager will buy units back from the unit holders. The pricing structure reflects the value of the underlying assets and is based on a notional figure for establishing or realising the entire fund, tempered to some extent by the manager's pricing policy.

Measuring performance

Performance measurement tables are published regularly and tend to be on an offer-to-offer basis, i.e. the bid-offer spread is ignored for the purpose of performance measurement. Chapter 7 discusses the analysis of fund performance which goes beyond return only and examines the importance of the level of risk inherent in each fund.

APPENDIX 15C
Pension fund structure and management

There is growing attention being paid to the pension fund industry in many countries as populations age and the much-heralded 'pensions time bomb' starts to tick. In Ireland, the scale of the problem is perhaps not as great as elsewhere just yet, due to our younger population profile. Public policy was, however, evolved to deal with the potential cost of pension provision in the future. Measures taken include:

- establishment of the National Pensions Reserve Fund into which, initially, 1% of GNP is invested each year
- increased public awareness campaigns to highlight the importance of private pension provision
- establishment of the Personal Retirement Savings Accounts (PRSA) to encourage private pension provision
- legislative changes which require companies to establish occupational pension schemes for workers.

This appendix deals briefly with the investment objectives of pension funds.

The three pillars of financial provision

Financial provision for old age can be attained through:
- State provision
  This is where the state provides old age pensions to retired and elderly people. In the past it was funded on a **pay-as-you-go** basis, i.e. from current taxation. In recent years a fund, the National Pensions Reserve Fund, has been established to provide for the cost of this pillar in the future.

- Occupational pension provision
  The government has recently legislated to ensure that all workers have an occupational pension scheme available to them, although there is no onus on the employer to contribute to these. These schemes can be either defined benefit schemes or defined contribution schemes.

- Private provision
  This includes a range of schemes including additional voluntary contributions (AVCs), personal retirement savings accounts (PRSAs) and private investments.

Defined benefit schemes

A defined benefit scheme is where the value of the pension is known, in the sense that it is normally based on the finishing salary or average salary over the last few years of work. The pension is normally equal to a fraction of the finishing salary based on the number of years of membership, e.g. one eightieth of the finishing salary for each year of service up to a maximum of 40 years, which produces a maximum pension equal to half the finishing salary. In this instance any shortfall in investment performance is made up by the employer. The employer's liabilities are generally linked to wage inflation. It is normal that the pension is then index-linked to some benchmark, e.g. the consumer price index, the rate of wage inflation in the economy or the rate of wage increase in the company.

Defined contribution schemes

A defined contribution scheme is where the value of the pension is not known with any certainty and is not related to final salary. Instead its value depends on the investment performance over the period of contributions and the cost of establishing an annuity at the start of the pension drawdown. If a shortfall occurs in the sense that the built-up value of the pension fund is insufficient to support the required level of payment, the pension scheme member (the employee) will have to make additional contributions to increase the value of the fund.

Investment objectives and management

Like any investment fund, the objective is to find an acceptable trade-off between return and risk.

The return requirement is informed by the extent to which liabilities are linked to inflation. This is in turn determined by:

- the age profile of the membership
- whether it is a defined benefit or defined contribution scheme
- the contribution rate.

The attitude to risk is largely a function of the maturity match of assets and liabilities, i.e. if the liabilities are primarily long term, then the fund manager may be prepared to take on greater risk, e.g. high-risk equity; whereas if the fund has reached a stage where net outflows will start to occur in a few years' time, then the manager may be risk averse and attempt to consolidate gains already made by investing in low-risk assets such as short-dated bonds.

The need for a satisfactory liquidity position is normally a key objective for investment funds. However, it may be less important for pension funds, especially younger ones, given the long-term nature of the liability structure and also because of the more predictable pattern of outflows.

Diversification both across and within markets is an important strategic objective, particularly where the investment opportunities may be limited domestically. Overseas investment, however, may introduce an exchange rate risk if liabilities are spread across currencies.

There are normally three levels of management:

- long-term **strategic** asset management
- short-term **tactical** asset allocation
- **stock** selection.

Strategic allocation

This refers to the allocation between asset types considered appropriate for the fund over the long term. Clearly for a pension fund this is a critical issue. The most important decision is how to establish the appropriate allocation of assets. There are a number of approaches to this:

- devise a benchmark portfolio
- relate asset distribution to liabilities
- mirror other similar funds.

Tactical allocation

This refers to the short-term deviations from the strategic allocation in an attempt to enhance return. It is predicated on a view of short-term risk and return prospects. The key question is: How wide a range around the strategic weights should tactical allocation cover? It should be narrow if transactions costs are high and market timing skills are poor.

Stock selection

This refers to the process of attempting to identify and invest in winners.

Part 6

Short-term and Medium-term Sources of Finance

16

Working Capital and Cash Management

CHAPTER OBJECTIVES

By the end of this chapter the student should be able to:

1. understand what is meant by working capital policy and the working capital cycle
2. estimate how much should be invested in current assets
3. understand the connection between working capital and sales
4. distinguish between liquidity and profitability
5. understand the concept of overtrading
6. appreciate the concept of zero working capital and the connection between economic value added (EVA) and working capital
7. understand the notion of a minimum cash balance
8. calculate the operating and cash cycles
9. calculate float
10. understand the Baumol model as a theoretical model in estimating optimum cash balances
11. develop a cash flow forecast.

INTRODUCTION

Ask any financial manager about the amount of time they spend on making sure they have the right amount of current assets and they would tell you that it is quite a lot: in particular, making sure they have sufficient cash at the end of each month/quarter to pay the bills. In earlier chapters we discussed long-term financial decisions, dividend policy, investment appraisal, long-term financial planning and capital structure decisions. Yet, even if we get all the long-term financial decisions correct, the company can be knocked out and put into liquidation by not having enough cash to pay current bills.

Working capital policy is a firm's policy regarding the levels of investment in working capital and how this investment should be financed. In this chapter we discuss the first of these issues, namely, how much should be in current asset holdings. Chapter 18 looks at how current asset holdings are financed.

16.1 The cash flow cycle

Figure 16.1 illustrates the working capital cycle for a typical manufacturing firm. Cash comes into the business initially in the form of shareholders' funds and debt capital.

Investments are made in the form of raw material inventories, which are combined with labour and other direct costs of production to produce work-in-progress and finished goods. These finished goods are then sold or held as stock until sold. They are sold as cash sales (in which case the money goes directly back into the cash tank of the business) or on credit (in which case the stock is converted into debtors). Having enough cash in the cash tank of the business is necessary to pay the creditors, interest on loans to the bank and other providers of debt capital, dividends to shareholders and tax to the government. A fall-off in demand for the product or an unnecessary build-up in raw materials would mean that cash will be tied up in stock of finished goods. This is cash which would not come back into the cash tank of the business. The same result would occur if there is an increase in account receivables (debtors). The result will be a shortage of cash to meet the bills that have to be paid. A liquidity crisis develops. Increasing the amount of borrowings would improve the cash position, but this will exacerbate the problem in the long term. The real problem is releasing the cash tied up in stock and debtors. In other words, minimising the amount of cash tied up in working capital will not only enhance company liquidity, it will also increase the overall return on investment (see Example 16.1).

Figure 16.1 Working capital cycle and cash flows

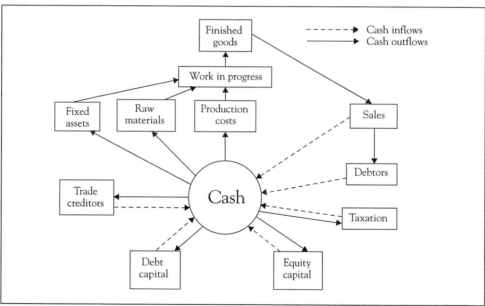

Example 16.1 Minimising investment in working capital

Two companies A and B have invested the same in fixed assets. However, company B has managed to achieve a higher return on capital because it manages to minimise the amount of cash tied up in working capital.

	Company A	Company B
Fixed assets	€400,000	€400,000
Net current assets	€200,000	€100,000
Total capital employed	€600,000	€500,000
Operating profit	€100,000	€100,000
Return on capital employed	16.7%	20%

16.2 Working capital definitions

Gross working capital: refers to investment in current assets. Current assets are those that can be converted into cash in a relatively short period (usually a year). Current assets include cash, debtors and stock.

Net working capital: is current assets *less* current liabilities.

16.2.1 Investments in current assets

How much should be invested in current assets? The answer depends on sales. How much should be carried in current assets to support a given level of sales? Figure 16.2 illustrates the different policies regarding investment in current assets. The top line, or the line with the steepest slope, illustrates a relaxed approach where large amounts of cash, near cash balances and higher stock levels are held, and where sales are made on generous credit terms (i.e. long debtors payment periods). Where there is uncertainty about future sales, a relaxed approach is appropriate. Here, a company will need to keep extra holdings of stocks (safety stocks) and a minimum cash balance to meet likely variations to what might be expected and therefore avoid production stoppages.

In an environment of **certainty**, where sales, creditors and debtors payment periods are known for certain, firms would only need to hold minimal investments in current assets. This is an **aggressive** policy towards management of investments in current assets. Firms would only need to hold minimum cash and stock and would operate tight credit policies. This policy would provide the highest return on invested capital (see Example 16.1 above), but it would also have the highest risk because of the possibility of losing sales. **Operating risk** is low when a company has high holdings in current assets because there is less danger of running short. However, there are opportunity costs and storage costs in holding excessive working capital. The opportunity costs arise because firms must use cash to purchase raw materials. Cash comes from either equity capital or debt capital or a combination of both and, as we know, capital has a cost.

Figure 16.2 Current asset investment policies

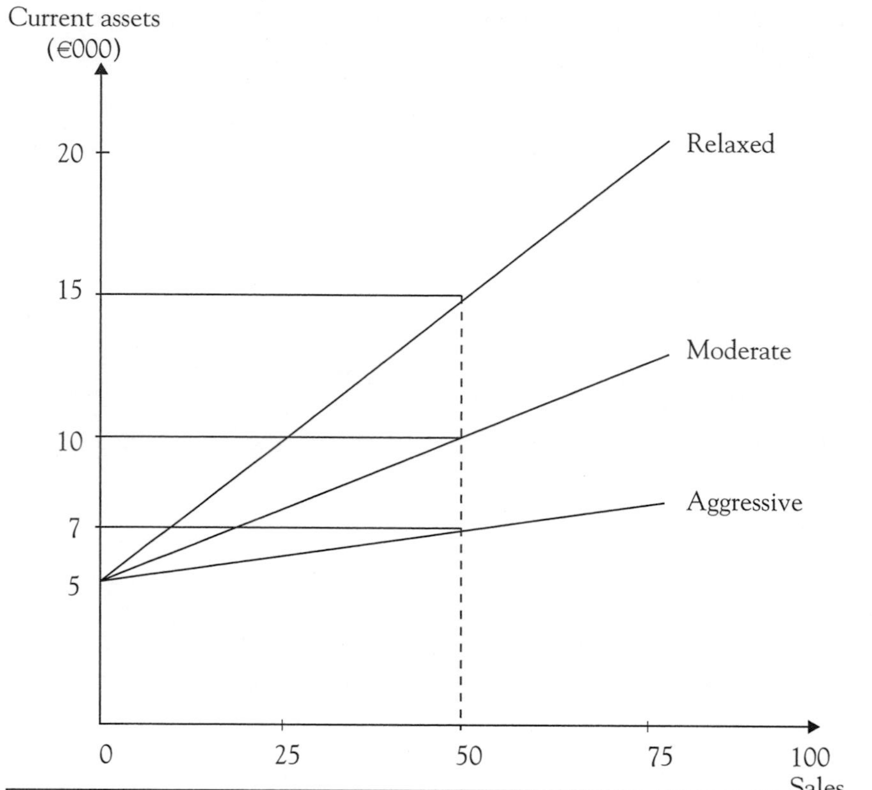

Under a relaxed current asset investment policy €50,000 of sales will demand €15,000 in current assets. A restrictive current asset policy requires only €7,000 in current assets to finance €50,000 in sales.

16.3 Working capital investment and sales

The sales activity a company undertakes will impact on its working capital requirements. In other words, while expansion in sales is good news, the bad news is that the company will require additional working capital to finance the increase in sales. This will be in the form of a rise in raw materials, finished goods and higher debtors to support the increase in sales. Additional working capital will therefore be required to finance the increase in sales. If the additional working capital is not forthcoming, the company is in a situation called **overtrading**. Overtrading occurs when the business experiences an increase in the level of activity in the working capital area of the business, but has insufficient working capital to finance the increased level of activity. Another word for overtrading is under-capitalisation. In other words, the company may have had insufficient start-up equity capital to support the level of activity in terms of cash and in terms of supporting additional borrowing capacity. Therefore, if there isn't enough equity capital there may not be sufficient debt capital forthcoming. To avoid overtrading (illiquidity) is to make sure that increases in sales are matched by increases in the necessary working capital to finance the increase in sales. To rectify an overtrading situation, the company will need to:

(a) increase the capital base in equity capital or organise additional borrowing
(b) minimise the investments in current assets, e.g. by lowering stock or debtor levels.
(c) If it is not possible to either increase the capital base or reduce investments in working capital, then the only solution will be to cut back on sales.

Therefore, it is possible for a company to double sales and profits and still go out of business because of a lack of liquidity. This highlights the possibility that profitable companies can go out of business because of insufficient liquid assets. It illustrates the very important distinction between profitability and liquidity.

16.4 Zero working capital

Some companies (e.g. General Electric in the US) have a policy of zero working capital. Advocates of zero working capital claim that it leads to greater efficiency, generates cash and speeds up production. Zero working capital is defined as

$$\textbf{Zero working capital = Stocks + Receivables − Payables} \qquad (16.1)$$

Reducing working capital (towards zero) as a percentage of sales increases the cash flow and lowers inventories. In other words, releasing cash tied up in stocks or receivables or by increasing payables leads to increased cash flow. As stated earlier, capital has a cost, so reducing the capital tied up in working capital improves profitability because of the savings in capital costs. Because working capital is reduced, companies are consequently forced to speed up production and delivery times (which helps improve sales) and capital tied up in excessive warehousing can be released by selling it off.

The key to zero working capital is **demand-based management** or **demand flow management**. What this means is that the company only produces **after** it has received an order, while still being able to meet customer delivery time. As soon as the product is made, it is delivered immediately. There is no warehousing and no storage costs. Therefore a movement towards zero working capital improves efficiency, leads to higher profitability and improves cash flow.

16.5 Economic value added (EVA) and working capital

The concept of economic value added has been discussed in previous chapters. EVA can be defined as

$$\text{Sales } less \text{ Operating costs } less \text{ Capital costs = EVA}$$

In other words, after the operating profit figure is calculated, an additional deduction is charged. This additional deduction is for the cost of capital. Therefore, by minimising the amount of capital tied up in stock, debtors or cash holdings, more cash will become available which can then be used to buy back shares or pay off debt. The effect of those two policies will be to reduce capital and the cost of financing, thus raising economic value added.

16.6 Cash management

Having cash balances can be a waste of money, particularly if the cash balances themselves earn little or no interest. Still, most companies hold some cash balances to 'grease' the wheels of business. The objective of cash management is to keep the amount invested in cash to a minimum, while keeping enough cash to keep the firm operating as efficiently as possible. In other words, cash is needed to pay for raw materials, to buy fixed assets, to pay taxes and dividends, etc.

16.6.1 Factors affecting the size of the minimum cash balance

The size of the minimum cash balances a firm should hold depends on:

1. The need to meet unexpected cash needs.
    Some of the cash that comes into the business will need to be held to grease the wheels. The rest of the cash will be invested in interest-bearing securities that will generate more income for the firm. The amount of cash held will depend on the opportunity cost of holding cash, i.e. the interest rate, and on the speed at which cash can be obtained. If the opportunity cost is zero (i.e. the cost of borrowing money is zero) and if cash can be obtained at very short notice, then it would not be necessary for a firm (or an individual for that matter) to hold any cash. All the cash that comes into the firm would be immediately invested in income-generating investment.

    However, because borrowing money has a cost (interest rate) and because it takes time, firms must maintain some 'cash on hand'. The more expensive it is to borrow (the higher the interest rate), the more cash the firm needs to keep.
2. The company's need to maintain its credit rating by lenders and trade creditors.
3. The ability to take advantage of trade discounts that become available for cash payments.
4. Business risk: Cash flows can be volatile. For instance, in times of recession sales will be weak, as will cash flows, because companies pay their bills more slowly. Similarly, the unexpected emergence of such things as industrial relations difficulties and strikes will mean that cash must be at hand when it is needed.

16.6.2 Operating cycles and cash cycles

To illustrate the concept of working capital management we can look at the operating cycle and cash cycle. Let us look at the following simple example.

Example 16.2 The operating and cash cycle

Curraghmore Ltd has decided to buy €500,000 worth of inventories on credit. It pays the bill for these 40 days later. Forty-two days later (i.e. on day 82) the inventory is sold for €700,000. The customer will not pay until 50 days later. The effect of these events on the cash cycle can be summarised as follows:

Day	Decision	Effect on cash cycle
0	Buy stock	0
40	Pay for stock	(€500,000)
82	Sell stock	0
132	Receive payment	+ €700,000

From the time stock is acquired to the time payment is received takes 132 days. This is called the **operating cycle**. The operating cycle can be divided into two parts. The first is the **inventory period** – the time it takes to acquire and sell the stock. This is, in this example, 82 days. The second part is the **debtor collection** period – the time it takes to collect the payment for the goods sold. This is 50 days in our example. Therefore the operating cycle of 132 days is:

$$\text{Operating cycle} = \text{Inventory period} + \text{Debtors collection period} \qquad (16.2)$$

Operating cycle	=	Inventory period	+ Debtors collection period
132 days	=	82 days	+ 50 days

16.6.3 The cash conversion cycle

In the above example, the problem for Curraghmore Ltd from a cash flow point of view is that it pays out cash 40 days after it has bought the inventory (payment period), but it doesn't receive any cash flow until day 132. Therefore Curraghmore Ltd will have to find some way of arranging to finance €500,000 for 92 days (132 – 40). This is the cash cycle period. Equation 16.3 shows the cash cycle and Figure 16.3 illustrates the connection between the operating cycle, the cash conversion cycle, the debtors collection period and the inventory period.

$$\begin{pmatrix} \text{Cash cycle} \\ \text{period} \end{pmatrix} = \begin{pmatrix} \text{Stock} \\ \text{conversion} \\ \text{period} \end{pmatrix} + \begin{pmatrix} \text{Debtors} \\ \text{collection} \\ \text{period} \end{pmatrix} - \begin{pmatrix} \text{Creditors} \\ \text{payment} \\ \text{period} \end{pmatrix} \qquad (16.3)$$

(92 days)	=	(82 days)	+	(50 days)	–	(40 days)

Figure 16.3 The operating cycle and the cash conversion cycle

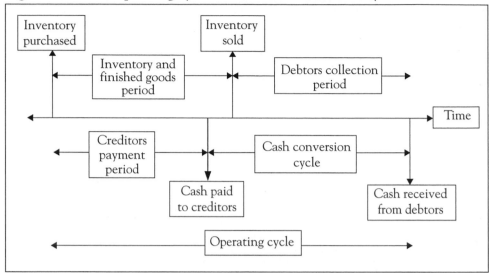

Example 16.3 Calculating the cash conversion cycle

The example above is straightforward and simple. Usually, however, we will have to calculate the cash conversion cycle from the information given in the financial statements. The following example extracts information from the annual report of the Kerry Group 1997:

Table 16.1 Kerry Group 1997 extracts from annual report

	Closing €	Opening €	Average €
Stock	155,681	142,358	149,110
Debtors	155,761	143,750	149,756
Creditors	215,618	185,322	200,470

Cost of goods sold was €965,905 and sales were €1,344,129.

To calculate the cash conversion cycle for the Kerry Group for 1997 we must first calculate the inventory or stock period.

The inventory or stock period is the average time it takes to convert raw materials into finished goods and then to sell the goods. For the Kerry Group in 1997 the average stocks €149,110 and €965,905 was spent on stocks (cost of goods sold). Therefore stock was turned over $\frac{€965,905}{€149,110}$ = 6.5 times. Therefore stock was bought and sold 6.5 times during the year.

Therefore, on average, stock was held for $\frac{365}{6.5}$ = 56 days in warehouses before being sold.

Next, we calculate the debtor collection period. This is the average length of time required to convert debtors into cash, that is, the average length of time it takes debtors to pay. The average debtors figure is €149,756. The average debtors turnover figure is got by dividing credit sales by average debtors.

$$\frac{\text{Credit sales}}{\text{Average debtors}} = \frac{€1,344,129}{€149,756} = 9 \text{ times}$$

The average collection period is

$$\frac{\text{Debtors}}{\text{Sales}} \times 365 = \frac{€149,756}{€1,344,129} \times 365 = 41 \text{ days}$$

Therefore it took, on average, 41 days for customers to pay.

The next step in the process of calculating the cash conversion cycle for the Kerry Group for 1997 is to calculate the creditors' payment period. This ratio might be more accurately referred to as the payables deferral period because it is the length of time between the purchase of materials and labour and the payment for them. In other words, it is the number of days it takes to pay for materials and labour. Average payables is €200,470 and the cost of goods sold (COGS) is €965,905, which means that the payables turnover is

$$\frac{\text{COGS}}{\text{Average payables}} = \frac{€965,905}{€200,470} = 4.8 \text{ times}$$

The payables period is

$$\frac{\text{Average payables}}{\text{COGS}} \times 365 = \frac{€200,470}{€965,905} \times 365 = 76 \text{ days}$$

So, on average, it took the Kerry Group 76 days to pay their creditors.

Finally, the cash conversion cycle is the length of time between the firm's cash payments and its cash receipts from sales. This can be interpreted as the average length of time one euro is tied up in current assets. The cash conversion cycle for the Kerry Group for 1997 is 21 days. In other words, it takes 56 days from the time it buys its raw materials to the time it converts them to finished goods and sells them. It takes 41 days to collect the cash from the sales. However, it takes 76 days before the raw materials are paid for. This gives a cash conversion cycle of 21 days, which is the number of days' finance it needs for its operations. The longer the cash cycle, the more expensive it is, because cash is tied up longer in the cycle. Remember, cash is supplied by shareholders or debt holders and it therefore has a cost. Cutting the cash conversion cycle would therefore be less expensive (in terms of the cost of capital) and more profitable.

16.7 Shortening the cash cycle

It follows therefore that shortening the cash cycle can improve profitability and liquidity and, as we have already discussed, it can enhance economic value added. Therefore management should aim to minimise the cash cycle (without hurting operational activities). It can do this by:

(a) shortening the stock period. This can be accomplished by speeding up the production and selling process.
(b) improving its credit control by getting cash in more quickly from debtors.
(c) slowing down the payment period.

16.8 Reasons for holding cash

John Maynard Keynes in his work, *The Theory of Employment, Interest and Money*, outlined three reasons why cash holdings are necessary:

(a) The transactions motive
It is necessary to hold cash balances to pay debts that are due to be paid, such as wages, creditors, dividends, taxes, etc. Cash inflows from sales should be sufficient to cover cash outflows to pay debts. If inflows are greater than outflows, the balance is reinvested in the business or returned to shareholders in the form of dividends. However, cash inflows and cash outflows are not always synchronised in the sense that inflows are not always sufficient to meet the cash outflows and some **buffer** cash level is needed. (We discuss cash synchronisation later on in the chapter.)

(b) The precautionary motive
Cash inflows and outflows are unpredictable. Firms need to keep some cash in reserve for unforeseen events. The cash balances are called **precautionary balances**. Banks may also require their customers to maintain minimum cash balances with the bank. These are called **compensating balances.**

(c) The speculative motive
This motive for holding cash allows the individual to take advantage of any profitable bargain purchases that might arise from time to time. However, this motive for holding cash can be accomplished (and generally is in business today) by having spare borrowing capacity and/or portfolios of liquid or **near** liquid (cash) balances such as commercial paper or marketable securities.

16.9 Cash management control

Most business is conducted by large firms operating both nationally and internationally. Some of these global companies operate in Ireland, e.g. Dell, Intel, IBM. Having sales and manufacturing points around the globe means that they can have thousands of bank accounts. In some of these accounts, inflows may be greater than outflows, and in others there will be net outflows. Having excess cash in some accounts imposes an opportunity cost because they will be earning rates of return lower than they could if invested elsewhere, e.g. in short-term securities. On the other hand, accounts with net outflows will cost them interest. Cash management of these firms will necessitate transferring funds to where they are needed and investing excess cash immediately. In addition, many payments are made out of central funds such as dividends and taxes, and a system must be in place to transfer funds to central HQ when needed. In Ireland, **repatriation** of profits in 1999 came to almost €20bn, which amounted to 18% of GDP.

Cash flow synchronisation is one method used to control cash flows. By equating cash inflows to cash outflows, firms can be sure of holding their minimum cash balances. Companies such as the ESB and Eircom try to achieve this synchronisation by billing their customers on a regular basis (every two months).

16.10 Cheque clearing system

Delays in the cheque clearing system can work to the advantage of firms. Float occurs because of delays in the bank clearing system. The time that elapses between writing a cheque and when it clears is called the float. Technically, it is the difference between a firm's (or individual's) cheque book balance and the firm's (or individual's) balance in the bank's books.

Disbursement float is when the float works in the firm's favour. When a firm signs a cheque, it credits the amount in the firm's own cash account in its own cash book. However, it can be days before it appears as a debit in the firm's account in the bank's books. The effect of disbursement float is to increase the firm's balance in the bank's books relative to the balance in the firm's own books.

Collection float is when the float works against the firm. It is the delay between the time of receiving a cheque and when the bank credits the firm with the amount. When a firm receives a cheque, it is immediately debited in the cash account of the firm's books, but it can be days before it clears as a credit in the company's account in the bank's books. Collection float reduces the firm's balance in the bank's books relative to the firm's balance in the firm's books.

16.10.1 Net float

Net float is the sum of the disbursement float and the collection float. A company that has to pay bills should be concerned with its balance in the bank rather than with its balance in its own books. It's what's in the bank that pays the bills. So net float is the difference between the firm's book cash balance and the firm's available cash balance in the bank.

Net float = Available cash balance in bank − Firm's book cash balance (16.4)

Example 16.4 Calculating float

A firm pays out an average €20,000 per day in cheques. It takes about four days for these cheques to clear. At the same time suppose the firm receives an average of €20,000 from customers and it takes two days to clear these cheques. The disbursement float is €80,000, that is, the bank will show €80,000 more than will be in the firm's own records. The collection float is €40,000, that is, there will be €40,000 less available in the bank than what appears in the company's books. Therefore the net float is

Net float = Disbursement float (€80,000) + Collection float (−€40,000) = €40,000

Taking the time to manage float can be very profitable. For example, if a company has daily sales of €1m, by accelerating the collection of cheques from customers by just one day, and if the daily interest rate is .0003%, profits could increase by €300 a day or €109,500 a year. Ireland's public electric utility, the Electricity Supply Board (ESB), ran a very successful advertising campaign with a prize draw for customers who paid their bills on time.

16.11 Computing the optimum cash balances

Next, we discuss a theoretical model to compute the optimum cash balances. The theoretical model we will look at is the **Baumol model**. The main assumptions underlying this model are:

1. The firm's consumption of cash is steady and predictable.
2. Both cash outflows and cash inflows occur at steady predictable rates.

For example, suppose that Dunmore Ltd has a weekly cash outflow of €500,000 and a weekly cash inflow of €400,000, leaving it with a net cash flow of minus €100,000. Note that negative cash flows are not unusual for companies that are going through the expansionary phase of their business cycle.

Suppose also that Dunmore Ltd has an initial cash balance of €400,000. Given the initial assumptions of this model, we can conclude that it will take four weeks for this initial cash balance to drop to zero. This is illustrated in Figure 16.4.

Figure 16.4 Cash balances using the BAT model

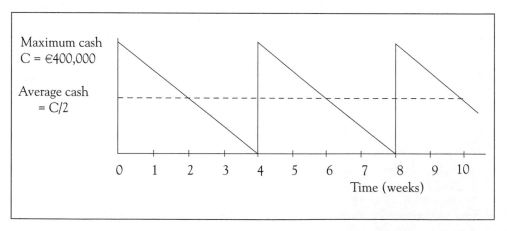

Therefore, at the end of week 4 the firm will have to sell some short-term liquid assets or borrow to replenish its cash balances. If the initial cash balance was higher than €400,000, it would take a longer period of time before it would be necessary to either borrow or sell short-term liquid assets to replenish the cash balance. Conversely, if the initial cash balance was lower than €400,000, there would be a shorter period before it would be necessary to replenish the cash balance.

Borrowing cash or selling securities to replenish cash balances will incur transaction costs, and the more frequently it needs to replenish its cash balances, the higher the total transaction costs. Therefore, the larger the cash balances, the lower the transaction costs. On the other hand, holding cash balances has a cost – opportunity cost. Holding cash balances earns no income. The opportunity cost of holding cash balances is the income (interest) foregone. Therefore, the higher the cash balances, the greater the opportunity cost incurred. This scenario is depicted in Figure 16.5. Note how the transactions costs are high when the firm has to raise more cash to replenish a cash balance. In addition, the opportunity cost curve increases with the size of the cash balance because holding cash does not provide a rate of return.

Figure 16.5 Determining the optimum cash balance

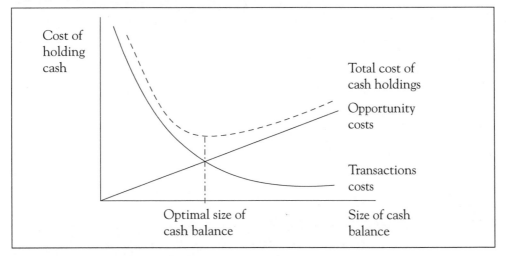

The total cost of holding cash balances is therefore

$$\textbf{Total cost = Opportunity cost + Transactions costs} \qquad (16.5)$$

where

$$\text{Opportunity costs} = \left(\begin{array}{l} \text{Average cash} \\ \text{balance} \end{array} \right) \times \left(\begin{array}{l} \text{Interest} \\ \text{rate (r)} \end{array} \right)$$

$$\text{Average cash balances} = \frac{\text{Maximum cash balance (Q)}}{2} = \frac{Q}{2}$$

Transactions costs = $\left(\begin{array}{c}\text{Number of}\\\text{transactions}\end{array}\right) \times \left(\begin{array}{c}\text{Cost per}\\\text{transaction (C)}\end{array}\right)$

and

$$\text{The number of transactions} = \frac{\text{Total amount of net new transactions needed for the year (N)}}{\text{Maximum cash balance (Q)}}$$

Therefore

$$\text{Total cost} = \frac{Q}{2} \, (R) + \frac{N}{Q} \, (C) \tag{16.6}$$

By differentiating equation 16.6 with respect to Q we can calculate the optimum cash balance (Q*). (To calculate the optimal cash balance equation, differentiate equation 16.6 with respect to Q. Set the derivative equal to zero, and solve for Q = Q*.)

$$Q^* = \sqrt{\frac{2CN}{R}}$$

Suppose in our example the transaction cost for Dunmore Ltd of selling €100,000 of securities or borrowing €100,000 is €300, and if holding costs or opportunity costs (interest forgone) of holding cash is 5%, then the optimum cash balance Q* is:

(Remember that €100,000 is required each week. Therefore N in the equation = 52.)

$$Q^* = \sqrt{\frac{2 \times €300 \times €5,200,000}{0.05}} = €249,800$$

So the company should replenish its cash balances when they reach zero to the tune of €249,800.

The main weakness of the BAT model is that it doesn't allow for uncertainty and seasonal fluctuations in cash disbursements and collections. The student should be aware, however, that the Baumol model, and indeed other optimal cash balance models, is not generally used in practice. In reality, financial managers use experience in judging their optimal cash balance. Nevertheless the theoretical models do provide an insight into the reasoning behind optimal cash balances. The Baumol model illustrated that the higher the interest rate, the lower the target cash balance. Second, the higher the order cost, the higher will be the target balance.

16.12 Cash budgets

In Chapter 11 we investigated long-term financial planning and pro forma statements. In this chapter we discuss short-term financial planning. As we have seen, it is necessary for firms to know when they will have cash surpluses and cash deficits. Knowing when these deficits and surpluses occur will allow the firm to know when they will need to replenish their cash stock or invest their surpluses.

One way of estimating cash balances is the **cash budget**. This is a detailed plan estimating cash inflows and cash outflows on a weekly, monthly or quarterly basis.

16.12.1 Developing a cash flow forecast

The first step in a cash flow forecast is to ascertain the likely cash inflows. The cash inflow forecast will depend crucially on the sales budget. In our chapter on long-term financial planning, we said that the sales budget was the most important budget to get right because the accuracy of all other budgets will depend on the accuracy of the sales budget. The sales budget is equally crucial in short-term financial planning. The **GIGO** effect rules, i.e. **garbage in, garbage out**. If the input into any forecast is garbage, then the output will be garbage. Therefore accuracy in sales forecasting is essential in cash flow forecasting.

In developing a cash flow forecast, the following steps are taken:

Step 1: Estimating the anticipated cash inflow.

Table 16.2 Decies Engineering Ltd projected sales forecast

Nov. 2007	€20,000	May 2008	€30,000	Nov. 2008	€22,000
Dec. 2007	€21,000	Jun. 2008	€32,000	Dec. 2008	€21,000
Jan. 2008	€19,000	Jul. 2008	€34,000	Jan. 2009	€20,000
Feb. 2008	€22,000	Aug. 2008	€31,000	Feb. 2009	€19,000
Mar. 2008	€24,000	Sept. 2008	€28,000		
Apr. 2008	€27,000	Oct. 2008	€25,000		

All of Decies' sales are on credit (i.e. no cash sales). From past experience 20% of debtors will pay their bills at the end of the first month of sale, 50% will pay their account in the month following the sale, and 30% will pay two months after the sale. So, for example, the cash collections for January are as shown in Table 16.3.

Table 16.3 Cash collections for January 2008 (Decies Ltd)

20% of January sales	=	€3,800
50% of December sales	=	€10,500
30% of November sales	=	€6,000
Total	=	€20,300

The cash inflow forecast is presented in Table 16.4.

Step 2: The next step in generating a cash budget is to forecast the cash outflows. The cost of raw materials is 25% of sales. The raw materials are purchased two months prior to the sale of the finished product and will be paid for in full one month after the purchase. For example, the purchase of raw materials for March sales will be made in January and paid for in February. All purchases are on credit. There are no cash purchases. Additional cash outflows are as follows:

- Production expenses are equal to 30% of sales.
- Sales, general and administrative expenses of €4,000 are paid each month.
- Fixed interest charges of €500 are paid at the end of each quarter.
- Taxation of €8,000 for 2008 is paid at the end of each quarter.

Table 16.4 Cash inflow forecast for Decies Ltd 2008 (€000)

	Jan	Feb	Mar	Apr	May	June	July	Aug	Sept	Oct	Nov	Dec
20% in month of sale	3,800	4,400	4,800	5,400	6,000	6,400	6,800	6,200	5,600	5,000	4,400	4,200
50% one month after sale	10,500	9,500	11,000	12,000	13,500	15,000	16,000	17,000	15,500	14,000	12,500	11,000
30% two months after sale	6,000	6,300	5,700	6,600	7,200	8,100	10,000	9,600	10,200	9,300	8,400	7,500
Total cash inflows	20,300	20,200	21,500	24,000	26,700	29,500	32,800	32,800	31,300	28,300	25,100	22,700

Table 16.5 Cash outflow for Decies Ltd 2008 (€000)

	Jan	Feb	Mar	Apr	May	June	July	Aug	Sept	Oct	Nov	Dec
Cost of raw materials	5,500	6,000	6,750	7,500	8,000	8,500	7,750	7,000	6,250	5,500	5,250	5,000
Production costs	5,700	6,600	7,200	8,100	9,000	9,600	10,200	9,300	8,400	7,500	6,600	6,300
Sales, general & admin.	4,000	4,000	4,000	4,000	4,000	4,000	4,000	4,000	4,000	4,000	4,000	4,000
Interest charges			500			500			500			500
Tax			2,000			2,000			2,000			2,000
Total cash outflow	15,200	16,600	20,450	19,600	21,000	24,600	21,950	20,300	21,150	17,000	15,850	17,800

Table 16.6 Cash inflows and outflows and net cash flows 2008 (€000)

	Jan	Feb	Mar	Apr	May	June	July	Aug	Sept	Oct	Nov	Dec
Total cash inflow	20,300	20,200	21,500	24,000	26,700	29,500	32,800	32,800	31,300	28,300	25,100	22,700
Total cash outflow	15,200	16,600	20,450	19,600	21,000	24,600	21,950	20,300	21,150	17,000	15,850	17,800
Net cash flow	5,100	3,600	1,050	4,400	5,700	4,900	10,850	12,500	10,150	11,300	9,250	4,900

Table 16.7 Decies cumulative cash flow 2008 (€000)

	Jan	Feb	Mar	Apr	May	June	July	Aug	Sept	Oct	Nov	Dec
Opening cash balance	20,000	25,100	28,700	29,750	34,150	39,850	44,750	55,600	68,100	78,250	89,550	98,800
Net cash inflow (outflow)	5,100	3,600	1,050	4,400	5,700	4,900	10,850	12,500	10,150	11,300	9,250	4,900

Table 16.8 12 month cash flow summary for Decies Ltd 2008 (€000)

	Jan	Feb	Mar	Apr	May	June	July	Aug	Sept	Oct	Nov	Dec
20% in month of sale	3,800	4,400	4,800	5,400	6,000	6,400	6,800	6,200	5,600	5,000	4,400	4,200
50% one month after sale	10,500	9,500	11,000	12,000	13,500	15,000	16,000	17,000	15,500	14,000	12,500	11,000
30% two months after sale	6,000	6,300	5,700	6,600	7,200	8,100	10,000	9,600	10,200	9,300	8,400	7,500
Total cash inflows	20,300	20,200	21,500	24,000	26,700	29,500	32,800	32,800	31,300	28,300	25,100	22,700
Cost of raw materials	5,500	6,000	6,750	7,500	8,000	8,500	7,750	7,000	6,250	5,500	5,250	5,000
Production costs	5,700	6,600	7,200	8,100	9,000	9,600	10,200	9,300	8,400	7,500	6,600	6,300
Sales, general & admin.	4,000	4,000	4,000	4,000	4,000	4,000	4,000	4,000	4,000	4,000	4,000	4,000
Interest charges		500			500			500			500	
Tax		2,000			2,000			2,000			2,000	
Total cash outflow	15,200	16,600	20,450	19,600	21,000	24,600	21,950	20,300	21,150	17,000	15,880	17,800
Total cash inflow	20,300	20,200	21,500	24,000	26,700	29,500	32,800	32,800	31,300	28,300	25,100	22,700
Total cash outflow	15,200	16,600	20,450	19,600	21,000	24,600	21,950	20,300	21,150	17,000	15,880	17,800
Net cash flow	5,100	3,600	1,050	4,400	5,700	4,900	10,850	12,500	10,150	11,300	9,250	4,900
Opening cash balance	20,000	25,100	28,700	29,750	34,150	39,850	44,750	55,600	68,100	78,250	89,550	98,770
Net cash inflow (outflow)	5,100	3,600	1,050	4,400	5,700	4,900	10,850	12,500	10,150	11,300	9,220	4,900
Cumulative cash flow	21,100	28,700	29,750	34,150	39,850	44,750	55,600	68,100	98,250	89,550	98,770	103,670

The cash outflow forecast is presented in Table 16.5.

Step 3: Calculate the net cash flow. For each month, subtract the cash outflow from the cash inflow. This gives the net cash flow for each month. This is presented in Table 16.6.

Step 4: Calculate the cumulative cash flow. For this example, assume an opening cash flow of €20,000 for Decies Ltd on 1 January 2008. This opening cash balance is added to the net cash flow for January to give the cumulative cash figure for January. The cumulative cash figure then becomes the opening cash position for the next period. Decies Ltd's cumulative cash flow is shown in Table 16.7.

Step 5: Combine steps 1 to 4 to form a complete cash budget, Table 16.8.

In the next chapter we will look at the decision of firms to extend credit to customers. This will have costs and benefits for the firm.

SUMMARY

- Working capital policy is a firm's policy regarding the levels of investments in working capital and how these investments should be financed.
- The cash flow cycle illustrates how cash moves through the business.
- Gross working capital refers to investments in current assets, including cash, debtors and stock.
- Net working capital is current assets *less* current liabilities.
- The level of investments in current assets depends on the level of sales. A relaxed approach to investments in current assets is one where there is uncertainty about future sales and where there are large amounts of investments in current assets. Where a degree of certainty exists about future sales, an aggressive approach is appropriate where the firm keeps minimum investments in current assets.
- Overtrading occurs when the business experiences an increase in the level of activity but has insufficient working capital to finance the increase in sales activity.
- Minimising the amount of capital tied up in working capital can reduce the cost of capital and therefore increase economic value added.
- The operating cycle is the time between acquiring the stock of raw materials and getting paid for the sale of finished goods.
- The inventory period is the time it takes to acquire and sell the stock.
- The debtors collection period is the time it takes to collect payment for the goods sold.
- The cash conversion cycle is equal to the stock conversion period *plus* the debtors collection period *minus* the creditors payments period
- Float occurs because of delays in the bank's clearing system. Disbursement float is when the firm's account in the bank has not been debited with cheques paid out by the firm and credited in the firm's books. Collection float is when the bank has not yet credited cheques lodged to the firm's bank account. Net float is the difference between the two.
- The BAT model determines the amount of cash a firm should hold so that the total costs of holding cash is minimised.
- A cash budget is a detailed plan estimating cash inflows and cash outflows on a monthly, weekly or quarterly basis.

WEB LINKS

www.theICESgroup.com
The Irish Complementary Education System on cash flow games, and financial workshops.

www.intltreasurer.com
For articles on short-term financial management.

QUESTIONS

1. Explain each of the following:
   (a) working capital
   (b) net working capital
   (c) disbursement float
   (d) collection float
   (e) net float
   (f) cash conversion cycle
   (g) target cash balance.
2. Some firms will have longer operating and cash cycles than other firms. Explain.
3. What are the motives for holding cash balances?
4. How does a firm reach the optimal level of current assets?
5. Consider ways in which a firm can increase its liquidity.
6. 'Managing float can be profitable.' Explain.
7. Explain the terms (a) relaxed current asset investment policy, and (b) restricted current asset investment policy.
8. Why is it that working capital policy requires a firm to balance liquidity and profitability?
9. Aggressive working capital policy has low cost but is highly risky. Why?
10. ◆ The following is the summary information provided from the accounts of Comeragh Ltd for the year ended 31 December 2007:

Stock (opening)	€5,000
Stock (closing)	€5,700
Debtors (opening)	€4,300
Debtors (closing)	€4,000
Creditors (opening)	€2,000
Creditors (closing)	€2,200

   Sales for the year came to €20,000 and the cost of goods was €16,000. Calculate and illustrate (a) the cash cycle and (b) the operating cycle.
11. Brickies Ltd has a stock conversion period of 60 days, a debtors collection period of 30 days and a creditors payment period of 25 days. Calculate the firm's cash conversion cycle.
12. Using the BAT model, calculate the target cash balance from the following information:

Total cash required	€300,000
Opportunity cost	10%
Ordering costs	€150

What is the opportunity cost of holding the average cash balance?

13. Pontoon Ltd has a cash need of €30,000 per annum. On average its daily cash balance is €200. The trading cost of obtaining cash is €10 every time the cash needs to be replaced. The annual interest rate is 9%. Calculate the opportunity cost and the total cost. Minimise total cost.

14. You have an original bank balance of €1,000. You then start writing cheques totalling €500 that have not yet cleared the banking system. What is your net float?

15.♦ A company has €2,000,000 in marketable securities which give a rate of return of 3%. It costs €1000 to convert these marketable securities to cash. Annual cash disbursements come to €30m. Using the BAT model, calculate the optimal conversion amount.

16. A firm signs cheques totalling €10,000 each day. The cheques take five days to clear. The firm also receives €7,000 in cheques which take on average two days to convert to cash. Calculate the net float.

17. Why is net disbursement float more desirable than net collection float?

18.♦ Suppose that on 1 September you buy a new computer scanner costing €200 and you write a cheque for this amount. Because you are a student your parents send you a cheque for €100 to help you pay for the scanner. You receive the cheque on 3 February. Suppose it takes seven days for your cheque to clear and five days for your parents' cheque to clear. Before any of the above events occur, you have €100 in your bank account. Calculate the net float on 5 February and your available balance on 7 February.

19. Is it possible to hold too much cash?

20.♦ (a) Using the following information calculate (i) the target cash balance using the BAT model and (ii) the total cost of holding cash.
   Annual interest rate = 10%
   Fixed order costs = €50
   Total cash needed = €30,000.
   (b) What factors are likely to affect a firm's target cash balance?
   (c) How would synchronisation of a firm's cash inflows and cash outflows affect a firm's target cash balance?

21. Ebont Ltd has a debt to asset ratio of 40%. Fixed assets are €1,000,000. The company is considering two alternative working capital policies: 30% or 50% of sales. Projected sales are estimated at €5m and profit before interest and tax is expected to be 12%. The company's cost of debt is 7% and corporation tax is 20%. From a shareholder's point of view what is the **optimum** current asset policy?

22.♦ A large retail outlet has €1m in cash. The cash will not be needed for 24 hours. The annual rate of interest is 8%. What do you think the company should do – hold on to the cash or invest it?

23. You are the treasurer of a company that has a large amount of excess cash. You are required to put a report together outlining the various options available to the company as to what to do with this cash.

24. From the following information draw up the cash budget for Tiffy Ltd. It has a 60-day collection period and it has a minimum cash balance requirement of €100.

	Sales	Opening debtors	Cash outflow	Opening cash balance
First quarter	€200	€350	€220	€50
Second quarter	€250		€240	
Third quarter	€270		€280	
Fourth quarter	€150		€200	

25. The following sales information is given for Widgets Ltd (€000):

2007		2008												2009	
Nov	Dec	Jan	Feb	Mar	Apr	May	Jun	Jly	Aug	Sept	Oct	Nov	Dec	Jan	Feb
200	150	140	150	160	170	200	230	250	200	180	160	150	130	120	120

There are no cash sales. The assumption is that 10% of sales will be paid for in the month of sale, 80% will be pay the amount due in the month after the sale, and the final 10% will pay their bills two months after the sale. The cost of raw material is 20% of sales. The raw material for each month's production will be ordered the month before (i.e. the raw material for January's production is ordered in December). Monthly sales of finished product are made the previous month (i.e. the sale of finished product in February is manufactured in January). Purchases of raw material are paid for in the month after purchase. The following expenses are also incurred and paid for during the month incurred:

(a) Sales and marketing expenses 10% of sales
(b) Production expenses 85% of sales
(c) General expenses €10,000 per month.

An interim dividend of €40,000 is paid in May. A final dividend of €60,000 is paid in December. Interest on loans amounts to €20,000 annually and is paid at the end of each quarter.

Calculate Widget Ltd's net cash flow for the year ended 31 December.

17

Inventory and Credit Management

CHAPTER OBJECTIVES

At the end of this chapter the student should be able to:

1. understand and calculate the optimum inventory level
2. appreciate the inventory management techniques of just-in-time and out-sourcing
3. understand how optimum inventory management can enhance economic value added (EVA)
4. assess the components of credit policy
5. determine the optimum credit policy
6. understand ways of monitoring accounts receivables
7. evaluate a proposed change in credit policy.

INTRODUCTION

Inventories consist of raw materials, work-in-progress and finished goods. All businesses carry inventories of one kind or another. The amount of inventory held at any one point in time will depend on factors such as the production cycle (how long it takes to produce the product). For example, a company that makes fresh cream cakes will have a low inventory relative to sales than, say, a DIY retailer who will carry a vast amount of inventory to satisfy a wide-ranging customer base. Manufacturers of Boeing 737s will have proportionally higher inventory levels than food retail outlets.

17.1 Optimum inventory levels

The objective of inventory management is to determine what level of inventory will maximise shareholder value. This will be settled by a trade-off in the costs of holding low inventories against the cost of having high inventory levels.

Higher inventory levels result in:

- higher storage costs (e.g. rent, insurance, etc., cost of obsolescence and damage)
- higher opportunity costs because of the lost interest in cash tied up in stocks.

Lower inventory levels result in:

- higher reordering costs, e.g. administration costs such as employee time and the processing of each order whenever an order is made
- shortage costs – 'stock-outs' occur when a firm runs out of raw materials, which results in loss of sales, profits and the reputation of the firm.

17.1.1 Inventory and sales

Minimising the cost of inventory (having the lowest cost of inventory) may not lead to the optimum inventory level because more stock on display can boost sales. Therefore, more stock might mean more sales. Consequently, the optimum inventory level is a matter of balancing the costs and benefits of various inventory levels.

17.2 The economic order quantity (EOQ)

This is the most popular approach in estimating the optimum inventory level. The EOQ is illustrated in Figure 17.1. The costs of holding stocks are expressed on the vertical axis and the order size in units is expressed on the horizontal axis. Holding costs (carrying costs) increase and reordering costs decrease as stock levels rise. The total costs of holding inventory are the sum of carrying costs and reordering costs. The total cost curve in Figure 17.1 is u-shaped and is the summation of the carrying costs line and the restocking line. The optimum size of the stock order corresponds to the minimum point of the total cost of holding inventory curve.

Figure 17.1 The economic order quantity (EOQ)

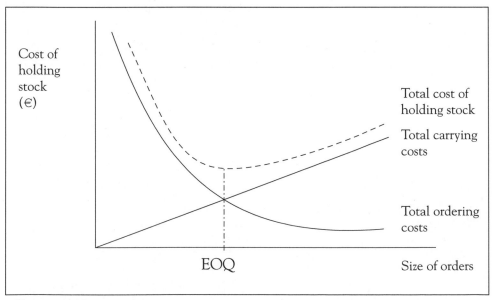

17.2.1 Developing the EOQ model

Suppose that Lismore Ltd sells 20,000 units a month and reorders new inventory once a month. Each time the firm makes an order, it will be for 20,000 units. Assume that it is sold off at a steady rate until it is zero. At this point the firm restocks back to the optimum level. If the firm starts off with 20,000 units of stock and annual sales amount to 240,000 units, or about 4,616 units a week, after four weeks all stock will be sold and the firm will restock by ordering 20,000 units to bring the stock level back up to the optimum level. This is illustrated in Figure 17.2. We can see that the process exhibits a sawtooth pattern for stock holdings. The firm always starts with 20,000 units and ends up with zero. The average stock therefore is 10,000 units. The average investment in inventories depends on the size of each order made and, of course, on how often the order is made. For example, by placing an order once a month, average investment in inventories will be much smaller than if one order a year was placed. Similarly, average investment in inventory will be much smaller if orders are placed every week rather than every month.

Figure 17.2 Stock position for Lismore Ltd

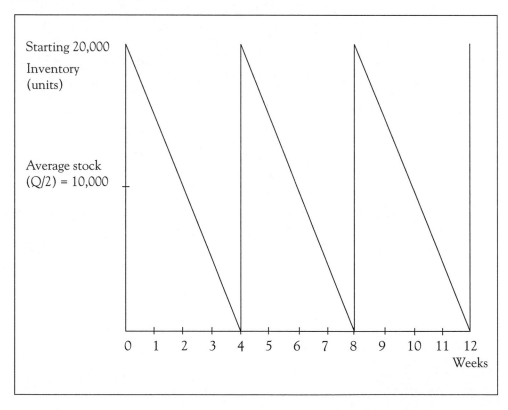

17.2.2 Computing the EOQ model

Carrying costs tend to rise in direct proportion to the average inventory carried. In our example, the firm sells 240,000 units each year (TS) and places orders N times per year.

Therefore $\dfrac{\text{TS}}{\text{N}}$ = the number of units purchased with each order

The average inventory A will be, in our example

$$A = \dfrac{\text{TS}}{\text{N}} \div 2 \qquad\qquad (17.1)$$

where: N = 12
        TS = 240,000

Therefore, the inventory is steadily drawn down from 20,000 units to zero and the average inventory is

$$A = \dfrac{\text{TS}}{2\text{N}} = \dfrac{240{,}000}{(2)(12)} = 10{,}000 \text{ units}$$

Total carrying costs (TCC)

Now consider the cost of inventory and the cost of holding the inventory. Suppose that the cost of purchasing and holding stock for Lismore Ltd is as follows:

Stock price per unit	= €3 (€3 × 10,000 = €30,000)
Taxes, insurance and general storage costs	= €3,000
Depreciation of inventory	= €600
Cost of capital (5%)	= €1,500 (5% × €30,000)
Total carrying cost (TCC)	= €5,100

We can see that average inventory is €30,000. This will need to be financed, and if the cost of short-term debt is 5%, then the cost of financing is €30,000 × 0.05 = €1,500.

So the total cost (TCC) of €30,000 of average stock is €5,100, or 17%.

The total carrying cost is equal to the percentage carrying cost (defined as X%) times the price per unit times the average number of units:

$$\text{TCC} = (\text{X\%}) \times (\text{€P}) \times (\text{A})$$

For Lismore this is TCC = 0.17 × (€3 × 10,000) = €5,100

Total reorder costs

Assume that reorder costs are fixed: in other words, every time an order is made there are fixed costs incurred. For example, the administrative costs incurred in placing an order (telephone calls, paperwork, etc.) are generally fixed so that they don't vary with the size of the order. We refer to these fixed costs with the letter F. Therefore the total reorder costs (TRC) will be the number of orders made per year (N) times the fixed costs per order:

$$TRC = (F)(N) \qquad\qquad (17.2)$$

In equation 17.1 we defined the average inventory (A) as being equal to

$$A = \frac{TS}{N} \div 2$$

We can rearrange equation 17.1 to become $N = \dfrac{TS}{2A}$

By substituting equation 17.1 into equation 17.2 we get

$$TRC = F\left(\frac{TS}{2A}\right)$$

Suppose that Lismore Ltd has fixed restocking costs (F) of €100. We have already established that N = 12 (i.e. 12 orders per year), average inventory (A) is 10,000 units, and sales for the year (TS) = 240,000 units. Therefore the total restocking costs are

$$TRC = €100\left(\frac{240,000}{20,000}\right) = €100\,(12) = €1,200$$

The total cost

The total costs incurred in holding inventory is the sum of the total reorder costs and the total carrying costs:

Total costs (TC) = Total carrying costs (TCC) + Total reordering costs (TRC)

or $\qquad\qquad\qquad$ TC = TCC + TRC

$$(X)(P)(A) + F\left(\frac{TS}{2A}\right)$$

Our objective therefore is to find the value (Q) of the restocking which minimises this cost. For Lismore Ltd we have already established the following:

Purchase price per unit of stock (P)	= €3
Carrying costs as a percentage of average inventory value (X%)	= 17%
Fixed costs of placing an order (F)	= €100
Annual sales in units (TS)	= 240,000

Table 17.1 calculates the total cost for different reordering quantities.

Table 17.1

Reordering quantity Q	Holding costs (X)(P)(A)	+	Reordering costs F (TS/2A)	=	Total costs TC (€)
3,000	765	+	8,000	=	8,765
4,500	1,148	+	5,333	=	6,481
6,000	1,530	+	4,000	=	5,530
7,500	1,913	+	3,200	=	5,113
9,000	2,295	+	2,667	=	4,962
9,700	**2,474**	**+**	**2,474**	**=**	**4,948**
10,000	2,550	+	2,400	=	4,950
12,000	3,060	+	2,000	=	5,060
13,500	3,443	+	1,778	=	5,221
15,000	3,825	+	1,600	=	5,425

For example, when the reordering quantity is 6,000 units, the holding costs are €1,530. Here A or average inventory is 6,000/2 = 3,000 units. At €3 per unit (P = €3) and with X = 17%, we get €1,530.

We can read from the figures that the economic order quantity (EOQ) is that which gives the lowest total cost, i.e. 9,700 units. This is the optimum quantity to be ordered when an order is made. We can see this from Figure 17.3. Note that, diagrammatically, the EOQ is where the total inventory cost curve is at a minimum. This corresponds to the point where the total carrying costs line and the total ordering costs line intersect, i.e. where the total carrying costs and the total ordering costs are the same. This is at a carrying cost and a reordering cost of €2,474. We can verify this algebraically by equating the carrying costs and the reordering costs and then solving for the optimum reordering level Q.

Figure 17.3 The economic order quantity (EOQ) for Lismore Ltd

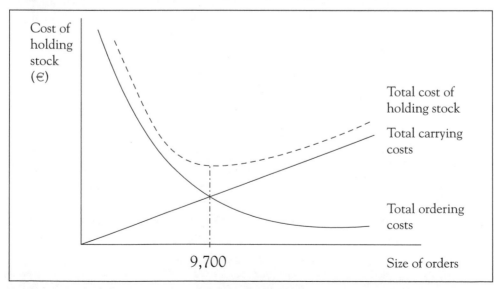

So, by putting carrying costs = reorder costs we get

$$(X) (P) \left(\frac{Q}{2}\right) = (F) \left(\frac{TS}{Q}\right) \qquad (17.3)$$

Remember that average inventory is $\qquad A = \dfrac{Q}{2}$

The point where the total inventory cost is minimised is the economic order quantity. The EOQ formula is found by differentiating equation 17.3 with respect to Q, and setting the derivative equal to zero.

Therefore $\qquad \dfrac{d(TC)}{dQ} = \dfrac{(X)(P)}{2} = \dfrac{(F)(TS)}{Q^2} = 0$

Now solving for Q $\qquad \dfrac{(X)(P)}{2} = \dfrac{(F)(TS)}{Q^2}$

$$Q^2 = \frac{2(F)(TS)}{(X)(P)}$$

$$Q = EOQ = \sqrt{\frac{2(F)(TS)}{(X)(P)}} \qquad (17.4)$$

For Lismore Ltd we have

$$Q = EOQ = \sqrt{\frac{2(100)(240,000)}{(0.17)(€3)}} = \sqrt{94,117,647} = 9,700 \text{ units}$$

Therefore, for Lismore, the reorder quantity is 9,700 units.

17.3 Safety stocks and the EOQ model

To make the EOQ model more realistic some of the assumptions underlying the model are relaxed. For example, the EOQ model assumes that the company will allow stock levels to run down to zero before it reorders. Allowing stocks to drop to zero before reordering may not be something that firms wish to do because it runs the risk of stock outs and the consequent problems of lost sales and customers.

Figure 17.4 illustrates the concept of safety stocks. Safety stocks are the minimum level of stocks that a firm holds. Suppose, for example, that Lismore Ltd sets a safety stock level of 1,000 units so that it initially orders 10,700 units (EOQ of 9,700 units + safety stock of 1,000 units). The consequence of this is that the firm does not run its stock down to zero. Furthermore, because it can take days or even weeks to get stock delivered, a firm will usually place an order **before** the minimum stock levels are reached. Suppose that Lismore uses 1,000 units while it is waiting for the delivery of new stock. Then the company will reorder its EOQ whenever stock levels reach 2000 units (safety stock of 1,000 units + 1,000 units delivery time).

Figure 17.4 Safety stocks and reorder points

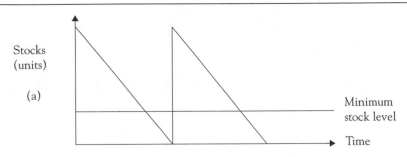

(a) The firm reorders when the stock level reaches the minimum level.

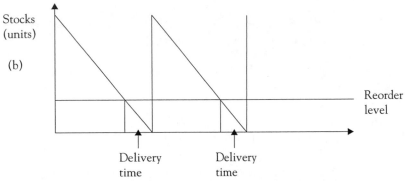

(b) If there are delays in delivery time, the firm reorders when the stock
     level reaches the reorder level.

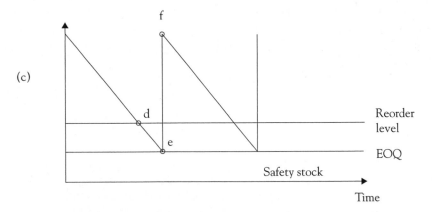

(c) Combined safety and reorder levels: when stock falls to point d an order
     is placed which allows for delivery time. The new stock arrives when the
     inventory has fallen to e. The new stock brings the total inventory back to f.

17.4 Just-in-time (JIT) inventory and out-sourcing

In addition to the theoretical EOQ model, there are other inventory control systems. JIT is a Japanese system of stock delivery that was adopted particularly by large US manufacturing firms in the 1980s, such as General Motors, Hewlett-Packard and Intel. Under this system, production is designed so that stocks of raw materials and parts are delivered to the factory just as they are required. The purpose of JIT is to increase the stock turnover levels and, typically, firms using JIT have higher stock turnover ratios.

Out-sourcing is a system of buying components instead of making the components in-house. Car manufacturing companies around the world use out-sourcing as a means of keeping stock levels, and consequently carrying costs, down.

E-commerce now has the capability of changing the way inventory is managed. There are inventory management advantages of having a web business (see Box 17.1).

Box 17.1 Irish Express Cargo moves into virtual market

While freight forwarding was once simply a delivery business, the advent of e-commerce means that Irish freight companies are moving into providing a physical infrastructure for a virtual market.

One such company is Irish Express Cargo (IEC). They decided to look at adding value along the supply chain as customer demands grew in tandem with developments in technology and the rise in the use of the Internet...

A major development has been a pan European contract which it has with Hewlett-Packard to handle the product logistics for Hewlett-Packard's e-commerce European Shopping Village . . .

IEC's success has been based on providing key information to its clients about the flow of their goods from the manufacturing to supply and consumption stage.

By taking partners in different countries and concentrating on managing the flow of products, IEC has become the largest provider of supply chain management in Europe . . .

Demand from consumers for companies' products varies widely even from week to week. What IEC offers to clients such as Dell, Gateway, Compaq and Hewlett-Packard is a system where they can see at any time what is happening with the products they ordered or supplied, the demand for the products, the numbers being manufactured anywhere in the world.

As technology changes, it makes products more time-sensitive, and so time taken to bring goods to the market becomes even more important.

The advantage of IEC's system is that it reduces inventory to a minimum and avoids fully finished products being outdated by new technology.

Rory Kelleher, *The Irish Times*, 30 January 2001

17.4.1 *Materials requirements planning (MRP)*

The principal idea behind MRP is that it is designed to work backwards. The first item that is estimated is the stock of finished goods. Once this is set, it is then possible to determine the level of work-in-progress stock necessary to meet the requirements for the finished goods. Finally, once the stock levels for work-in-progress are set, it is possible to determine the stock requirements for raw materials that are needed for the work-in-progress.

17.5 Managing accounts receivables

Managing accounts receivables is not just a matter of calculating the average number of days it is taking customers to pay their bills. Granting credit can bring benefits to firms in the form of increased sales. Nevertheless, it also carries costs in the form of increased risk of bad debts and the actual cost of carrying receivables. The amount of trade credit granted will therefore be a trade-off between the benefits and costs associated with granting credit.

17.5.1 *Establishing a credit policy*

A company's credit policy consists of the following factors:

Credit period: This is the length of time customers have before payment is made. This can vary between 30 and 120 days. In granting credit, a customer's (i.e. the buyer's) stock period and credit period will be considered. The stock period or the inventory period is the length of time it takes to buy the raw materials, to turning them into finished goods for sale. The debtors cycle or accounts receivable cycle is the amount of time it takes to collect on the sale. As we discussed in the previous chapter, the stock period *plus* the inventory period is the operating cycle. The longer the buyer's operating cycle, the longer the credit period the buyer will look for. The credit period granted to the buyer helps finance part of the buyer's operating cycle. Consequently, if the credit period granted to a buyer is longer than the buyer's stock period, the supplier ends up financing part of the buyer's capital needs.

If a cash discount is offered, the credit period will have two components – the **net credit period** and the **cash discount period**. The net credit period is the length of time the customer has to pay, and the cash discount period is the length of time for which the cash discount is available.

For example, the terms of sale of 2/10 net 60 means that the customer has 60 days from the invoice date to pay the amount due in full. However, if payment is made in full within 10 days, a 2% cash discount is given. Therefore, if an order for €100 is made and if the terms of sale are 2/10 net 60, the customer has the option of paying €100 (1 − 0.02) = €98 in 10 days or paying the full amount of €100 in 60 days. To see why the discount is important, we can calculate the cost to the customer of **not paying** within 10 days. Effectively, the customer obtains a 50 day loan for 2% of the amount due. This is a loan at a cost of 2% for 50 days. This means the customer is paying €2 to borrow €98 for 50 days.

The effective cost of the loan is €2/€98 = 2.041% and as the 2% is for 50 days there are 365/50 = 7.3 discount periods in the year.[1] Therefore the annual percentage rate (APR) is given by the equation

$$APR = \left[1 + \left(\frac{R}{N}\right)^n\right] - 1$$

where R = quoted rate of interest
N = number of discount periods

Therefore
$$APR = \left[1 + \left(\frac{.149}{7.3}\right)^{7.3}\right] - 1$$

$$= 15.89\%$$

This is also the cost to the seller of the discount allowed to the customer. The cash discount is an inducement given by the seller to speed up its cash collections. From the customer's point of view it is a source of short-term money (with a high cost).

Credit standards: Once a company has decided to offer credit to a customer, it then becomes imperative to find out the creditworthiness of the customer. This involves assessing the financial strength of the customer. What all companies that extend credit will want to find out is which customers are likely to turn out as a bad debt and which of them they will find difficulty in getting money from. **Credit quality** refers to the probability of a customer not paying his/her debts. A company will need to get access to the financial statements of potential customers. Acceptable minimum standards in terms of financial ratios (discussed in Chapter 3) can be used to accept or reject a customer's request for credit. Banks will sometimes provide information on the creditworthiness of firms. In addition, there are some organisations that sell information on the creditworthiness and credit history of firms, the best known being Dun & Bradstreet. Obviously the most readily available information about a customer is the customer's own payment history with the firm.

Profitability of credit sales: Granting credit will have costs – cash discounts and the cost of having more debtors tied up in current assets. If the cash discount **is** availed of by most customers, the company takes in less cash, and this is costly for the company, particularly if it is not accompanied by increased sales revenues. If the cash discount **is not** availed of by most customers, the customer ends up paying more, and consequently more cash is taken in by the company. Forgoing the discount will work to the advantage of the seller. The additional costs incurred in granting trade credit can be offset by the increased revenues in granting credit. If the revenues are greater than the costs, then granting trade credit can be profitable. For example, General Motors offers credit to customers to buy cars. Computer companies adopt a similar approach. Granting trade credit can be very profitable and some of these companies have established very profitable subsidiaries, e.g. Ford Finance.

Cost of debt: An increase in accounts receivable (debtors) must somehow be financed. Therefore the cost of short-term finance must be a factor in a company's credit policy.

The Five Cs of credit: In deciding to whom the company should advance credit, a classic approach is to consider the five Cs:

(a) Character – the ability of customers to pay their bills
(b) Capital – customer's financial capital and liquidity
(c) Conditions – the business environment and business risk of the customer
(d) Collateral – the valuation of the assets that could be sold if the customer does not pay
(e) Capacity – does the customer have the ability to pay?

Credit scoring: This method works by awarding points to customers based on the information provided on their credit worthiness. Points are awarded on different criteria, e.g. the five Cs, net profit history, number of years in business, shareholders' funds, market valuation of fixed assets etc. Scoring could be 10 (excellent) down to 1 (very bad). The company might have a cut-off score below which they will refuse credit.

17.6 The optimum credit policy

The optimum credit policy for a company is where the net cost of receivables is at a minimum. Remember the **cost of granting credit**:

(a) increased risk of bad debts
(b) cost of administration due to increased credit, i.e. increased staff costs of analysing customers, sending out bills, etc.
(c) cost of holding increased amounts of current assets
(d) cost of cash discounts allowed.

All of these costs will increase with the extension of credit granted. This is illustrated in Figure 17.5 as an upward-sloping line. On the other hand, if the firm restricts credit to its customers, sales may be lost with a consequent reduction in profit. Therefore restricting credit has an opportunity cost. The opportunity cost is the lost sales because of refusing credit. Opportunity costs decline as more credit is granted. The net total cost curve combines the carrying costs of advancing credit with the additional income from advancing credit. The point where the carrying cost curve and the opportunity cost curve intersect is the point of optimum credit. By extending credit beyond this level, the total carrying costs exceed the additional net cash flow from increased sales. Below this level the firm is losing out on increased profit.

Figure 17.5 The optimum level of credit

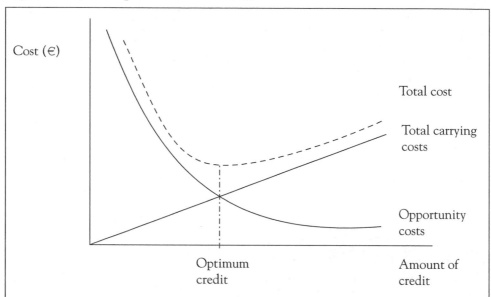

17.7 Monitoring accounts receivable

The accruals concept in accounting implies that as soon as a sale is made for cash or on credit, it is included as an income in calculating profit. Even though the cash from the sale may not have been received, profits will increase and share prices will probably increase. Shareholders should have some idea of a company's accounts receivable policy. Is the company selling goods or services to weak customers just to boost sales and reported profits? An analysis of the accounts receivable will help the shareholder in this regard.

17.7.1 Debtors collection period

For example, the average debtors collection period (DCP) is the number of days, on average, it takes to collect the payment due from customers. Suppose for example that ABC Ltd makes 100,000 bicycles a year which are sold to bicycle shops for €1,000 each. The terms of sale are 2/10 net 40. In other words, if ABC Ltd receives payment within 10 days they give a 2% discount, otherwise the payment is to be paid in full within 40 days. Furthermore, suppose that 60% of the customers take advantage of the discount and the other 40% do not avail of the discount and pay on day 40. The debtors collection period (DCP) is

$$\text{DCP} = 0.6(10 \text{ days}) + 0.4(40 \text{ days}) = 22 \text{ days}$$

ABC's average daily sales (ADS) is

$$\text{ADS} = \frac{100,000 \times €1,000}{365} = €173,973$$

Therefore at any one point during the year the amount of debtors outstanding would be

$$\text{Debtors} = (\text{ADS})(\text{DCP}) = (€273,973)(22) = €6,027,406$$

17.7.2 Ageing schedule

This is another policy firms have in monitoring the quality of a firm's debtors. An ageing schedule is a break-down of the amounts due from debtors arranged by due dates. An example is given in Table 17.2.

Table 17.2 Ageing schedule of debtors

Age of account	Amount	Number of customers
0 to 10 days	€100,000	100
11 to 30 days	€80,000	70
31 to 49 days	€40,000	30
50 to 70 days	€20,000	15
Over 70 days	€5,000	4

If, for example, the terms of trade were 2/10 net 30, 49 customers need watching, while 19 of these need particular attention.

17.7.3 The payment pattern approach to monitoring accounts receivable[2]

The main reason for monitoring debtors is to see if there is a change in the pattern of payment being received. It may be that debtors are paying more slowly and the quality of these accounts may be declining. The debtors collection period (DCP) and the ageing schedule of debtors are useful tools in analysing accounts receivable. However, seasonal fluctuations in sales can distort the information provided in the DCP figures. If there are seasonal fluctuations, the DCP and the ageing schedule will change with the seasonal fluctuations in sales, even though there are no changes in customer payment behaviour.

Example 17.1 Payment pattern approach to monitoring accounts receivable

Fews Ltd, which commenced operations in January 2007, manufactures garden tools. Table 17.3 gives the company's credit sales details for the year 2007. Note the seasonal variation in sales, with the summer months having the highest level of sales. The payment pattern of Fews' customers is as follows: 20% pay in the month of sale, 40% pay in the month following the sale, 30% pay in the second month following the sale and 10% pay in the third month. Therefore at the end of January the debtors figure will be €80, i.e. 0.8(€100) = €80.

At the end of February the debtors figure will be 120, i.e. 40% of January sales and 80% of February sales:

$$\text{Debtors for February} = 0.4\ (\text{€}100) + 0.8(100) = \text{€}120$$

In March the debtors figure will be

$$\text{Debtors for March} = (0.1)(\text{€}100) + (0.4)(\text{€}100) + (0.8)(\text{€}100) = \text{€}130, \text{and so on.}$$

Table 17.3

Month	Credit sales (€000)	Debtors at the end of the month	ADS quarterly (€000)	DCP (quarterly) (days)	ADS (yearly) (€000)	DCP (yearly) (days)
(1)	(2)	(3)	(4)	(5)	(6)	(7)
Jan.	100	80				
Feb.	100	120				
Mar.	100	130	3.3	40	3.3	40
Apr.	100	130				
May	120	146				
Jun.	150	178	4.0	44	3.7	48
July	190	224				
Aug.	180	235				
Sept.	130	195	5.5	36	4.3	45
Oct.	100	150				
Nov.	100	133				
Dec.	100	130	3.3	39	4.1	32

Columns 4 and 5 give the average daily sales (ADS) and the debtors collection period (DCP). So, for example, at the end of March the average daily sales is (€100 + €100 + €100)/91 = €3,300 and the DCP is €130/3.3 = 40 days.

Columns 6 and 7 give the DCP and the ADS on an annual basis. For example, at the end of June the ADS = €670/182 = €3,682 and the DCP = €178/€3.7 = 48 days. The main point here is that **seasonal variations in sales cause the DCP to change even though there is no variation in customer payment pattern. Therefore using the debtors collection period as a tool in monitoring receivables is not reliable enough when there are seasonal variations in sales.**

Introducing the payment pattern approach deals with this problem. Using this approach, **variations in the constant payment pattern would be revealed.** The amount of each month's sales remaining unpaid at the end of each quarter is divided by that month's sales to give a debtors to sales ratio for each month. For example, at the end of March (first quarter) €10,000 of January sales remain unpaid, which is 10%. Therefore at the end of March 10% of January sales have still to be paid. Also at the end of the first quarter 40%

or €40,000 of February sales remain unpaid and 80% (€80,000) of March sales remain unpaid. Therefore the total debtors to sales ratio, or the total uncollected sum, at the end of the first quarter is 130%. This is illustrated in Table 17.4.

We can see that despite the variation in sales throughout the year, the payment pattern does not change. The benefit of the payment pattern approach is that any variation in the payment pattern of customers can be immediately highlighted and shown as a change in the debtors to sales ratio at the end of each month. For example, a slowing down in the payments of customers in the first quarter will be detected in the figures shown in Table 17.5. Because of the slow-down in collections, the total amount of debtors to sales percentage or the total amount of outstanding balances rises from 130% to 175%. Therefore management should take note of the decline in the quality of debts.

Table 17.4

Quarter (€000)	Credit sales	Debtors at the end of quarter (€000)	Debtors as a % of sales
Jan.	100	10	10%
Feb.	100	40	40%
Mar.	100	80	80%
		130	130%
Apr.	100	10	10%
May	120	48	40%
June	150	120	80%
		178	130%
July	190	19	10%
Aug.	180	72	80%
Sept.	130	104	80%
		195	130%
Oct.	100	10	10%
Nov.	100	40	40%
Dec.	100	80	80%
		130	130%

Table 17.5

Quarter 1	Credit sales	Debtors (€000)	Debtors as % of sales
Jan.	100	15	15%
Feb.	100	60	60%
Mar.	100	100	100%
		175	175%

17.8 The cost–benefit of a proposed change in credit policy

What effect will a proposed change in a company's credit policy have on the company's profitability? To evaluate a change in credit policy, consider the case of Nixus Ltd which manufactures computer games. Their current sales policy is to sell for cash only. Nevertheless, they are evaluating the effect on profitability of selling on credit on terms of net 30 days. The current price per package (P) is €100. The variable cost of production (Vc) is €40 and it sells 150 units (Q) per month. Nixus believes that selling on credit will boost sales to 170 units per month (Q*). In addition, when a firm grants credit it must finance the resulting debtors. Therefore a company's cost of short-term finance is a factor to be considered in evaluating its new credit policy. Suppose that the required rate of return (r) is 12% per annum or 1% per month. Should Nixus switch to a new credit policy?

Write down what variables we know:

$$P = €100$$
$$Vc = €40$$
$$Q = 150$$
$$Q* = 170$$

Therefore current monthly sales are $P \times Q = €15,000$

Variable cost per unit per month is $Vc = €40 \times 150 = €6,000$

Therefore, the current policy of cash only gives a cash flow of

$$(P - Vc)Q = (€100 - €40)(150) = €9,000$$

A switch to 30 days' credit will mean monthly sales of

$$(P)(Q*) = (€100)(170) = €17,000$$

The monthly variable cost will be $(Vc)(Q*) = (€40)(170) = €6,800$

Therefore the monthly cash flow under the new policy will be

$$(P - Vc)(Q*) = (€100 - €40)(170) = €10,200$$

Therefore the incremental cash flow of a change in policy is

Cash flow under new policy	–	Cash flow under old policy	=	Incremental cash flow (17.5)
€10,200		€9,000		€1,200

Therefore the present value (PV) of this future incremental cash flow is

$$PV = (P - Vc)(Q^* - Q) \div r$$

$$PV = (€100 - €40)(170 - 150) \div 0.01$$

$$= \frac{€60 \times 20}{0.01} = \frac{1,200}{0.01} = €120,000$$

The costs of the new credit policy are:

(a) increased variable cost (Vc) of producing $(Q^* - Q)$ additional units, and
(b) the sales income that would have been collected under the current policy will not now be collected for one month. Therefore the total cost of the switch in credit policy is

$$PQ + Vc(Q^* - Q) = 15,000 + 800 = €15,800$$

Therefore the NPV of the change in credit policy is

$$- [(PQ + Vc(Q^* - Q))] + [(P - Vc)(Q^* - Q)] \div r$$

$$NPV = - €15,800 + €120,000 = €104,200$$

This says that the cost of switching is €15,800 and the benefit of the proposed switch is €1,200 per month in perpetuity, which is €120,000. Therefore there is a clear advantage in switching to a new credit policy.

SUMMARY

- Optimum inventory is the level of inventory that will maximise shareholder value. This is the result of a trade-off between the cost of holding low inventory levels against the cost of having high inventory levels. The optimum inventory levels are a matter of balancing the costs and benefits of various inventory levels.
- The economic order quantity (EOQ) is the most popular approach in establishing the optimum inventory levels.
- The total carrying costs of holding inventory include the stock price per unit, taxes, insurance, general storage costs, depreciation of inventory and the opportunity cost of investing in stock.
- Restocking costs are the fixed costs incurred when placing an order, e.g. paperwork, telephone calls.
- The total cost of holding inventory is the sum of the total carrying costs and the total reordering costs.
- Safety stocks are the minimum level of stocks that a firm holds.
- Just-in-time (JIT) is a system of production where stocks of raw materials are delivered to the factory just as they are needed.

- Out-sourcing is a system of buying components instead of making the components in-house.
- Minimising the amount of inventory tied up in working capital will enhance economic value added.
- Granting credit can increase the level of sales, but it will also have additional costs in the form of increased bad debt risk, and the cost of carrying receivables. The optimum credit policy will therefore be a trade-off between the costs and benefits associated with granting credit.
- The credit period is the amount of time customers have before payment is made.
- The credit terms of 2/10 net 60 means that customers have 60 days from the time the invoice is received to pay the amount due in full. If payment is made within 10 days, a 2% cash discount is received.
- Credit quality refers to the probability that customers will not pay their bills.
- The five Cs of credit are character, capital, conditions, collateral and capacity.
- Credit scoring is a method of awarding points to customers based on the information provided on their credit worthiness.
- The main reason for monitoring receivables is to see if there is a change in the pattern of payment being received. Using the payment pattern approach to monitoring debtors, variations in the constant payment pattern would be revealed.

WEB LINK

www.creditworthy.com
Resources for credit management.

QUESTIONS

1. Define JIT inventory systems. Explain how JIT inventory impacts on EVA.
2. Define ACP.
3. Explain the following terms: carrying costs; reorder costs; ageing schedule; EOQ; EOQ Range.
4. XYZ Ltd is about to switch to a new credit policy. The current policy is cash only. The new policy will offer credit for 30 days. The current interest rate is 1.5% per month. Under the new policy, sales are expected to increase by 10% from 500 units per month to 550 units per month. The price per unit is €100 and the variable cost per unit is €60. Should the switch be made?
5. ♦ The following information is given for Garravoone Ltd:
   Credit sales = €2m
   Credit control expenses (debt control expenses) = €20,000 p.a.
   Average collection period (ACP) = 40 days
   Bad debts = 1%.

   The company is now considering easing its credit policy such that sales will increase to €2.3m, bad debts will rise to 1.5% and the ACP will be 50 days. Debt collection expenses will fall to €12,000. If the company's cost of funds is 10% and variable costs amount to 75% of sales, is the firm's new policy worthwhile? (Assume tax of 20%.)

6. Windgap Ltd, manufacturer of garden tools, has a variable cost per unit of €10 and a sales price of €15. A customer is looking for a 40 day credit period to buy 1,500 units. You believe there is a 12% chance of default. The required rate of return on a 40 day credit period is 2%. Should credit be given to this customer?

7.♦ Explain the costs involved in carrying debtors, and what are the costs and benefits of granting trade credit?

8. Describe the five Cs of credit.

9. Explain the payment pattern approach to assessing debtor quality.

10. A company always accepts trade credit because it wants to avoid borrowing and never takes a trade discount. The terms of credit are 2/10 net 30. The company's cost of debt is 12%. Should the company accept the discounts?

11. X Ltd begins each period with 100 units of stock. At the end of each period, the stock is depleted and reordered. The carrying cost per unit per annum is €5. The company sells 5,000 units a year, and the restocking cost is €30 per order. Calculate:
    (a) total carrying costs, and
    (b) total restocking costs.
    (c) EOQ

12.♦ Beginning inventory is €200,000 and closing inventory is €20,000. Carrying costs per unit is 20 cents. Calculate the total carrying costs.

13. Syntax Ltd sells 5,000 personal computers per annum. Order costs per PC are €1 and holding costs are 20 cents each. What is the EOQ?

14. Plastics Ltd has 200 units of raw materials in stock at the beginning of each week. The annual carrying cost per head is €20 and the fixed costs are €15. Calculate:
    (a) the restocking costs
    (b) total carrying costs
    (c) the economic order quantity.

15. Fiddler Ltd sells 4,000 fiddles annually. It has a safety stock of 50 fiddles. The cost of each fiddle to the firm is €40. Carrying costs are 15% and ordering cost is €10. Calculate:
    (a) the EOQ
    (b) the maximum inventory of Fiddles Ltd.

16. Flybynight Production, when operating at full capacity, sells 1,000 electronic devices each week. As soon as this happens it orders another 1,000 electronic devices. The company has established that the fixed order cost amounts to €600 and the carrying cost per device is €10. Comment on the company's inventory policy.

17.♦ If carrying costs are €2m per year and restocking costs are €1m per year, what advice would you give to the company?

18. The following information is available for Carrick Ltd:

Carrick Ltd	Industry average
Credit terms = net 60 days	Credit terms = net 30 days
Average collection period = 70 days	Not available

Credit sales for Carrick Ltd amount to €3m. The management of Carrick is concerned about its credit policy. It has estimated that by changing its credit policy to the industry average of 30 days will lead to a reduction in sales to €2.5m. However, the ACP will, as a result of this change, fall to 36 days. Carrick's variable costs come to 75% of sales and short-term debt finance is 10%. Assuming a tax rate of 20%, should Carrick change its credit policy?

19.♦ Sportiris Ltd sells 100,000 football kits per annum. Each kit costs the company €10 and the cost of placing an order is €30. Inventory carrying costs are 15% and the company has an optimal safety stock of 599 kits. Calculate:

    (a) the EOQ

    (b) the number of times the company must order each year

    (c) the maximum inventory of football kits.

20. How will an increase in inflation, interest rates and competition affect average inventory holdings?

NOTES

1. We will discuss effective and annual percentage rates of interest in the next chapter.

2. A very comprehensive treatment of this area can be found in Brigham, Gapenski and Ehrhardt, 'Working Capital Management' in *Financial Management: Theory and Practice*, 9th edn, Chapter 23.

18

Short-term Sources of Finance

CHAPTER OBJECTIVES

Having studied this chapter the student will be able to:

1. understand the difference between the **hedging approach**, the **aggressive approach** and the **prudent approach** to financing current assets
2. appreciate the various sources of short-term finance available to business
3. calculate annual percentage rates (APR)
4. assess the cost of different types of bank loans.

INTRODUCTION

Many factors affect the level of investment in current assets. It will of course depend on the nature of the business. The working capital requirements of a manufacturing business will differ to that of a service company. Companies that have seasonal variations in sales will have different working capital requirements from companies that have the same monthly production levels throughout the year. Construction companies generally will have high working capital requirements during the spring and summer months, and companies that supply construction companies, generally, will tend to follow the construction companies' pattern of working capital. Although possible (see Chapter 16), it is unlikely for working capital to fall to zero. This is because companies tend to have a minimum requirement of stock, cash and debtors and this is maintained over time. This minimum requirement of investment in current assets is called **permanent current assets** (see Figures 18.1 and 18.1A). These current assets are held even during periods of slow demand for the company's product. As the level of sales fluctuates over the business cycle, the level of stock, accounts receivable and cash will also fluctuate. These are referred to as **temporary current assets**. The way in which permanent and temporary current assets are financed is hugely important. Notice from Figure 18.1 how the fixed asset line rises gradually over time. This reflects the increased investment in fixed assets necessary to fund the increase in business activity over time.

Figure 18.1 The build-up of current assets over time

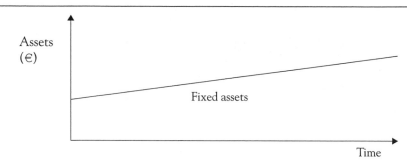

(a) The fixed asset line rises gradually over time as the firm expands.

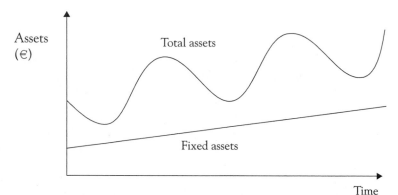

(b) Adding net current assets (current assets *less* current liabilities) to fixed assets. Because of the seasonal variations in sales this total asset line is seen fluctuating over time. The total asset line reflects the total funds required to finance the business at any point in time.

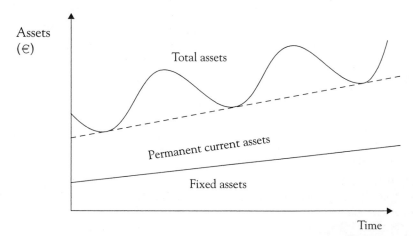

(c) The area between the fixed asset line and the line that is tangential to the valley points of the total assets line represents permanent net current assets.

Figure 18.1A The build-up of current assets over time

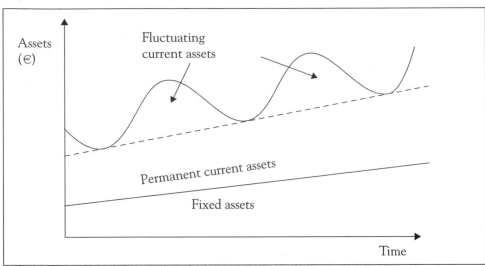

18.1 Financing permanent and temporary current assets

18.1.1 Hedging or matching approach

One system of financing current assets is known as the **hedging** or **matching** approach. It is important that the maturity of the assets is **matched** with the maturity of the liability (debt) used to finance them. Short-term finance should be used to finance short-term assets, medium-term finance should be used to finance medium-term assets, and long-term finance should be used to finance long-term assets. It makes sense therefore to finance short-term assets with short-term debt because short-term assets can be converted into cash in the near term. For example, if stock is to be sold in 40 days, a 40-day loan should be used to finance it. Fixed assets, like buildings, should be financed by, say, a 30-year mortgage. Figure 18.2 illustrates the hedging approach. Note that only the short-term requirement is financed by short-term debt. This is represented by the fluctuations at the top of the diagram. The **permanent** portion is financed by a mixture of long-term debt, equity, medium-term and revolving finance.

Figure 18.2 Hedging approach to current asset financing

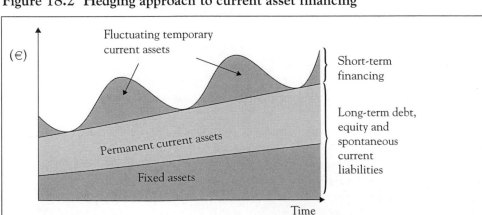

18.1.2 The aggressive approach

Matching the maturity of assets to the maturity of debt is all very cosy in theory. However, some companies adopt a much more aggressive approach to financing. This stems from the fact that short-term debt is usually cheaper than long-term debt (see section 18.2 on the features of short-term finance). Consequently firms will try to take advantage of this and borrow more short term. In other words, some companies will try to finance their fixed assets with long-term debt and part of their **permanent** current assets with short-term debt. However, short-term debt carries higher financial risk because of the short space of time in which the debt must be repaid. Many businesses have gone into liquidation because of this approach. The risk is increased because, while long-term interest rates tend to be relatively stable, short-term interest rates can be more volatile, and companies can be caught up in sharp rises in short-term rates. Furthermore, any downturn in economic activity and demand will result in companies being unable to meet their debt repayments. This aggressive approach to financing is illustrated in Figure 18.3. The dotted line represents a proportion of permanent current assets that are financed by short-term sources of finance. The dotted line could be below (more aggressive) or above (less aggressive) where it is shown in the diagram. If the dotted line was on the fixed asset line, it would mean that all of the permanent current assets were financed by short-term debt.

Figure 18.3 Aggressive approach to financing current assets

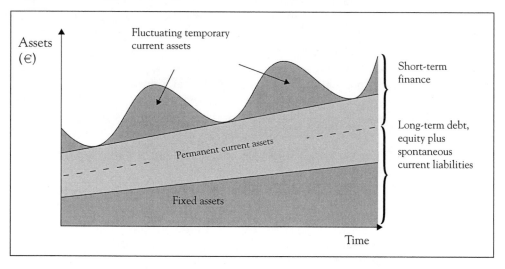

18.1.3 The prudent approach

This is a very cautious approach. Here permanent capital is used to finance not only the permanent assets but also part of the fluctuating needs. Only the very top fluctuations, as depicted in Figure 18.4, are financed by short-term debt. However, part of the fluctuation in current assets is financed by **buffer** liquidity in the form of near cash balances such as marketable securities. This means that the company meets part of its seasonal requirements by **hoarding** liquidity, perhaps in the form of marketable securities. The firm uses a small amount of short-term finance to finance **peak** requirements.

Figure 18.4 Prudent approach to financing current assets

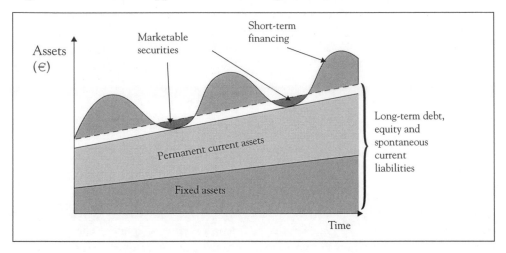

18.2 Features of short-term finance

Relative costs of short-term and long-term debt

The aggressive approach uses the most short-term finance, while the prudent approach uses the least amount of short-term finance. The costs of short-term loans are often cheaper than long-term loans. There are a number of reasons for this:

1. Long-term investments are riskier than short-term investments. It is more difficult to predict how well a company will be doing in 20 years' time than it is to predict how well it will be doing next year.
2. The **liquidity preference theory** suggests that borrowers (who are assumed to be risk averse) prefer to make long-term loans, while lenders prefer to make short-term loans. Therefore borrowers must pay a premium to lenders to entice them to make long-term loans.
3. **Pure expectations theory** holds that interest rates will reflect expected rates of inflation. The interest rate charged on long-term loans would be the average of the interest rates expected throughout each period that the loans span. For example, if interest rates are expected to be 10% over the next twelve months, and 15% over the following twelve months, the 2 year interest will be 12.5% (10% + 15%) = 25%/2. If inflation is expected to increase over the coming years, interest rates in the long term will be higher.

Example 18.1 Interest rates using pure expectations theory

Inflation is expected to increase over the next few years. The financial institutions estimate that annual interest rates will be as follows:

Year	Expected annual interest rate	Expected average annual interest rate
2008	7%	7%
2009	9%	8%
2010	11%	9%
2011	13%	10%

If inflation is expected to increase, long-term interest rates will increase.

On the other hand, long-term rates are more stable. Short-term loans can be riskier than long-term loans because of the risk of increases in short-term interest rates. This makes short-term debt riskier than long-term debt.

Flexibility

In terms of flexibility, short-term debt is more flexible. Flexibility is particularly useful if business activity is seasonal. Some months the firm will borrow to finance additional short-term working capital needs, while for other months its borrowing requirements may be nil.

In general, short-term credit is less restrictive than long-term loan agreements, which may contain provisions on how the funds are used.

Furthermore, lenders will insist on extensive research into the company before advancing long-term loans. Note, however, that small firms do not usually have access to long-term finance – so, in this respect, choice is limited.

18.3 The cost of bank loans

Interest rates vary for different types of borrower. If the risk profile of the borrower is high, the interest rate charged will be correspondingly high. Interest rates can be either fixed or floating.

18.3.1 Fixed-interest rate loans

Interest rates can be fixed for short or long periods, e.g. for 3 months or 10 years. The cost of a fixed-rate loan will depend on:

- the time period for which the funds are required
- the variable interest rate and the forecast for the likely movement in variable rates.

However, the borrower will not benefit if interest rates fall over time. If the borrower wishes to pay off the fixed-rate loan before maturity, s/he is likely to incur penalties.

18.3.2 Variable-interest rate loans

Variable rate simply means that the interest rate the borrower pays will vary in accordance with the rates being paid on the wholesale money markets. The interest rate charged will depend on ECB interest rate policy and on general economic conditions.

18.3.3 *Annual percentage rate*

Consumer legislation in Ireland requires all financial loan products to include the APR.

Quoted interest rates are the rates expressed as the payment made for each period covering the loan. The effective annual interest rate, or the annual percentage rate (APR), is the interest rate expressed as if it was compounded once a year. For example, if a rate is quoted at 6% compounded semi-annually, it implies that it pays 3% every six months. However, this 3% every six months is not the same as 6% per annum. Investing €1 at 6% you will receive €1.06 in 12 months' time. If you invest €1 at 3% every six months, then what you end up with is €1.03 (€1 × 0.03) after six months, *plus* 3% on 3 cents, which is 0.09 cents. Therefore, what you receive after 12 months is 6.09%. Here the 6% is the quoted interest rate, and the 6.09% is the APR.

To convert quoted rates to annual percentage rates proceed as follows:

1. Take the quoted rate and divide it by the number of periods for which the interest is compounded.
2. Add 1 to your answer.
3. Raise the answer to the number of times the interest is compounded.
4. Subtract 1.

These steps are summarised as follows:

$$\text{APR} = \left[1 + \left(\frac{R}{N}\right)\right]^{n} - 1$$

where   R = quoted interest rate
           N = number of times the interest is compounded.

Example 18.2 *Calculating annual percentage rate (APR)*

You are offered a loan at 10% compounded on a monthly basis. What is the annual percentage rate?

Solution

$$\text{APR} = \left[1 + \left(\frac{0.1}{12}\right)\right]^{12} - 1 = 10.47\%$$

Example 18.3 *Calculating annual percentage rate (APR)*

Suppose that a credit card company requires monthly payments and quotes a rate of 18%. This implies that monthly payments will be 0.18 /12 = 1.5% per month. The effective annual rate (APR) will be

$$\text{APR} = \left[1 + \left(\frac{0.18}{12}\right)\right]^{12} - 1 = 19.6\%$$

Therefore, the actual interest rate paid is 19.6%.

18.3.4 *Interest only loans*

Interest is paid by the borrower each period and the original amount of the loan is repaid in the future. This type of repayment schedule is called an interest only loan. For example, a loan of €10,000 at 6% for four years would require an interest payment of €600 at the end of the first three years plus €10,600 at the end of the fourth year. Here the interest is paid once a year. If the interest is paid over a number of periods during the year, the interest payments per period are calculated as follows:

1. Find the interest rate per day. This is got by taking the nominal interest (the quoted rate) and dividing it by the number of days in the year:

$$\frac{\text{Nominal rate}}{365} = \frac{0.06}{365} = 0.00016438356$$

2. The daily rate is then multiplied by the number of days in the period to give the rate per period. For example, if interest is paid monthly (31 days), then the monthly interest payment is

$$(31)\,(0.00016438356)\,(€10,000) = €50.96$$

Incidentally, the more frequently interest has to be paid, the higher the effective interest rate. The reader can satisfy him/herself that this is the case by calculating the effective annual rate in the above example on a quarterly, monthly, weekly and daily basis. You could also compound it on an hourly basis.

Example 18.4 *Annual percentage rates and frequent compounding*

Money is placed on deposit that has a quoted rate of 6%. Calculate the APR on a quarterly, monthly, weekly, daily, hourly and minute basis.

Solution
The APR is as follows:

$$\text{APR} = \left[1 + \left(\frac{R}{n}\right)\right]^{n} - 1$$

Period	Compounding times	APR (%)
Quarter	4	6.136355%
Monthly	12	6.167781
Weekly	52	6.179981
Daily	365	6.183131
Hourly	8,760	6.183632
Minute	525,600	6.183651

The APR keeps getting larger, but as we increase the compounding periods, the difference gets very small.

18.3.5 *Pure discount loan*

With a pure discount loan, the borrower receives the money today and repays a lump sum at some date in the future. **The principal and the interest are lumped into one payment.** This is the same as an interest only loan if there was just one period. For example, a 6% pure discount loan would require the borrower to repay €106 at the end of one year for every €100 borrowed.

18.3.6 *Discount interest loans*

With a discount interest loan, the bank deducts the interest (or discounts the loan) in advance. For example, borrowing €10,000 for one year at 6% on a discount basis means that you only get the use of €9,400, i.e. €10,000 minus (€10,000 × 0.06). The face value of the loan is €10,000, but you only receive €9,600. The funds received are equal to

$$\text{Funds received} = \text{Face value of loan } (1 - \text{Nominal interest rate}).$$

Therefore the face value of the loan is

$$\frac{\text{Funds received}}{1 - \text{Nominal interest rate}}$$

Therefore if you actually need the use of €10,000, with a discount interest loan, you will need to borrow

$$\text{Face value} = \frac{€10,000}{1 - 0.06} = €10,638$$

18.4 Sources of short-term finance

Having discussed financing permanent and temporary current assets, we turn our attention to various sources of short-term finance.

18.4.1 *Bank overdrafts*

Subject to authorised limitations, bank overdrafts allow customers to withdraw more funds from their current account than they have deposited. Individual banks have their own regulations for the use of overdraft facilities.

Features of bank overdrafts

- Repayable on demand. Users of bank overdrafts should bear this in mind. This adds to the risk of using overdrafts as a source of funds. Consequently bank overdrafts should only be used for specific short-term needs. For example, because retailers peak around the Christmas period, bank overdrafts are suitable to pay for Christmas stocks. The Christmas period will usually generate enough cash to repay the overdraft after Christmas. When a loan is used to finance assets that will generate enough cash to repay the loan, we refer to such loans as **self-liquidating loans.**

- An upper limit is put on the overdraft facility and it is allowed to fluctuate within that limit. If the limit is exceeded, penalties will be imposed.
- There is no obligation on banks to renew an overdraft facility.
- Generally, banks will look at balance sheet data over some historical period before granting overdraft facilities.
- Because it is repayable on demand, the financial risk from the bank's point of view is low. This makes it one of the cheapest sources of finance available.
- The actual cost of overdrafts will depend on the prime or base rate of the bank. Overdrafts will be priced at a cost above the prime rate depending on whatever risk the bank attaches to the borrower.
- There is often a requirement that businesses maintain compensating balances, which is usually a credit balance in another account. The effect of having **compensating balances** is to raise the effective interest rate charged to the borrower. For example, if a company needs €8,000 to pay creditors and if the bank requires a 20% compensating balance, how much must the company borrow? The company must borrow the amount that leaves €8,000 after it takes out the 20% compensating balance. Therefore the company must borrow €10,000 for the use of €8000, i.e. €8,000/0.8. The interest paid on €10,000 at 5% is €500. However, since we are only getting €8,000, the effective interest rate is €500/€8,000 = 6.25%. In other words, we are paying 5 cents interest on every 80 cents that we have borrowed. We do not have the use of the 20 cents that is tied up in the compensating balance, i.e. 0.05/0.80 = 6.25%.
- Security in the loan is generally not required. If security is required, it is generally in the form of a mortgage or lien, which of course restricts management from pledging that asset for further finance (unless it gets the bank's permission). However, if there is a good relationship with the bank and if all relevant information is submitted, security will generally not be asked for.
- Interest is charged on the amount outstanding each day.
- There are transaction fees, which can be expensive.

18.4.2 Short-term loans

Short-term loans are provided for specific purposes and repayable by agreed amounts within 12 months. The main features of short-term loans are:

- Short-term loans are for specific purposes and if the terms of the contract are adhered to, it cannot be withdrawn prior to maturity. This makes short-term loans more disciplined than bank overdrafts.
- Term loans are priced at a margin above that of the Euribor. This is usually 1.5% to 3% depending on the risk profile of the borrower.
- A facility to repay the loan early may be available. Repayments can be structured in such a way as to coincide with a time when a company has sufficient cash flow.
- Loans will be interest only or amortised. If interest only, interest is paid only during the life of the loan and the principal is paid at maturity of the loan. **Amortised** means that part of the principal is repaid on each of the repayment dates (sometimes called instalment loans). If repayment is made in one full lump sum, it is called a **bullet loan**.

- Short-term loans are usually secured against some collateral or asset. This prevents the borrower from using the same assets to guarantee other finance.
- Loans borrowed at a fixed rate will be costly if variable rates begin to decline.

18.4.3 Accruals

Income taxes deducted from payrolls, pay-related social insurance and VAT on sales are usually paid on a fortnightly and monthly basis. The company's balance sheet will show some accrued taxes. Similarly, wages are usually paid on a weekly or monthly basis and therefore the balance sheet can show an amount for wages due. Accruals are seen as a spontaneous source of finance, that is, they tend to increase spontaneously as the firm expands its level of sales. Accruals are also a **free** source of short-term finance because no interest is paid on them. Other types of accrued expenses include telephone charges and electricity expenses.

18.4.4 Accounts receivable (debtors)

Next to cash, accounts receivable can be the most liquid asset. Banks can grant loans to companies using receivables as security. In this sense, debtors are collateral for sources of finance, rather than as a source of finance per se. The default risk stays with the borrower. In other words, the bank has recourse to the borrower even if the accounts receivable do not materialise.

18.4.5 Factoring

Factoring is the total sale of a firm's accounts receivable to a financial institution or bank (called a factor). With **recourse factoring**, the risk of bad debts is borne by the business and not by the factor. With **non-recourse factoring**, the risk of the bad debt is borne by the factor. The factoring company takes full control over the debts and advances anything up to 80% of the book value of the debtors to the company. The remaining amount will be given over to the business when the debtor pays (this is after the factor has received his fees, costs, interest and the loan advanced). This type of finance increases spontaneously as the business expands. However, the downside is that it usually costs more than the cost of bank overdrafts.

The cost of factoring can be high. The interest charge can be as high as Euribor plus a margin depending on a customer's risk profile, plus a charge for bad debt risk and a service charge. For companies that have a high quantity of invoices but where each is for a small amount, administrative costs involved could be very high. Furthermore, factoring may be seen as weakening the position in the eyes of creditors who might therefore refuse to sell on credit to the firm.

Finally, when we use a credit card to buy or sell goods, the sellers of these goods are in fact factoring receivables (debtors). The seller receives the amount due, less the fee, the next working day and the buyer of the goods gets usually 30 days to remit the amount due to the credit card company.

Example 18.5 The cost of factoring

Maggie Ltd has made sales of cakes in the past year of €600,000. At the end of the year it has an average debtors figure of €40,000. As a source of finance, Maggie has used a factoring company to factor its accounts receivable. It sells its debtors for 98 cents in the euro. It needs to know what the effective rate of interest is on this source of funds.

Debtors are turned over, on average, €600,000/€40,000 = 15 times a year with an average debtors collection period of 365/15 = 24 days. Maggie receives finance of 98 cents and pays 2 cents in interest on the loan. Therefore the interest rate is 0.02/0.98 = 2.04% per 24 days.

On an annual basis, this is 2.04% × 15 = 30.6%. The annual percentage rate is

$$APR = 1.0204^{15} - 1 = 35\%$$

18.4.6 Invoice discounting

Invoice discounting occurs when a borrower submits or sells selected invoices to a lender. Depending on the risk profile of the borrower, the lender will provide up to 80% of the face value of the invoices. It is estimated that some €114m is advanced through invoice discounting in Ireland, and the business is growing at an annual rate of about 25%. It is estimated that about 600 enterprises accounting for about €1.26 billion of turnover between them were using the facility in the year 2000.[1] The business collects the amount of the invoices and pays the full amount to the lender. The lender will keep whatever amount was advanced plus any interest due on the advanced amount, and give whatever is left back to the business. In invoice discounting, the business decides on the invoices to be sold. An application for invoice discounting can be made through the bank. The cost of invoicing is the bank's cost of funds plus a margin depending on the risk of the customer. The total cost has two elements: the actual cost and a service or administration charge.[2] This actual cost is slightly higher than normal overdraft rates to AA customers, i.e. small and medium enterprises (SMEs). The administration cost is charged as a percentage of the debts purchased, which is usually 0.5% or less. Other important requirements are for a good spread of clean debts. The information the bank needs from the enterprise will include the following:

(a) details of new sales raised
(b) monthly debtor age analysis, which highlights problem accounts.

Like full factoring, the level of financing available will increase as the level of business activity increases. Consequently, business expansion can be financed by increased sales rather than by issuing more and dearer equity. Like recourse factoring, the risk of bad debts is still borne by the business.

Comparing invoice discounting and factoring

Legally, invoice discounting and factoring are the same: each is a financial facility offered through the purchase of debt. The principal differences between the two are as follows:

1. Under invoice discounting, the responsibility for credit management and sales administration remains firmly with the enterprise. In contrast, factoring is for enterprises whose credit management and administration systems are **inadequate**. With factoring, the factoring company (the bank) takes a very active role in the enterprise's credit control function by sending out **reminders** and statements to debtors. The factoring company receives payment from the debtor directly.
2. Invoice discounting has taken over from factoring as the main source of debtor finance. Factoring had become known as a **last chance finance**, and it was often seen in a negative light when the bank got involved in the credit control and administration of the enterprise. In contrast, debtors are not aware of the involvement of banks in invoice discounting because the banks keep a discreet distance in the background.

Box 18.1 Case study[3]

A Dublin-based enterprise, specialising since 1990 in the manufacture and distribution of industrial materials to aid the transport of large consignments, decided in favour of further expansion in 1992 to take advantage of certain opportunities. However, its bankers could not extend any more facilities, as it had no additional security to offer. With demand increasing, for want of working capital the company had to stretch its creditors to the point where the constant supply of materials was threatened. Yet the account for 1992 showed after-tax profit of €27,000 on sales worth €2.1 million in a business employing 18 people.

Eventually, realising that its fastest growing asset was its debtors, the enterprise used this to secure fresh working capital. Under an invoice discounting arrangement, €300,000 was raised against debtors of €500,000, and this revolving facility allowed growth to continue. By the end of 1994, both after-tax profit and turnover had virtually doubled to €52,000 and €4m respectively. A regional depot to co-ordinate national distribution and a subsidiary company to control exports had been established, and a total of 28 were employed. At the same time the discounting facility had increased to €600,000, reflecting the way in which increased sales were converted into cash without having to wait for payment.

18.4.7 Bills of exchange

A bill of exchange is a contract that enables a buyer to postpone payment for a period of up to 130 days. A post-dated cheque is an example. Another example is when the government borrows money by selling **government bonds** – it promises to repay the loan at some stage in the future. **Commercial bills of exchange** are bills of exchange issued by commercial organisations. When goods are sold, the seller draws up a legal document that shows the indebtedness of the buyer. The buyer accepts a bill of exchange by signing it and by writing **accepted** across it. This means that the buyer agrees to pay the amount due at some date in the future. The seller will either hold the bill to maturity or discount it at a bank, and so get immediate cash. In the latter case, if the bill is discounted at a bank, the bank will pay an amount that is lower than would be received by the customer if held to maturity.

Figure 18.5 Bill of exchange: sequence of events

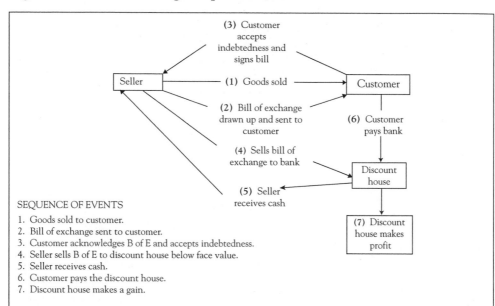

SEQUENCE OF EVENTS

1. Goods sold to customer.
2. Bill of exchange sent to customer.
3. Customer acknowledges B of E and accepts indebtedness.
4. Seller sells B of E to discount house below face value.
5. Seller receives cash.
6. Customer pays the discount house.
7. Discount house makes a gain.

Example 18.6 Discounting bills of exchange

A bill of exchange commits a customer to pay €100,000 in 90 days' time. It is immediately sold to a bank for €95,000. At maturity, i.e. after 90 days, the bank realises a profit of €5,000 on an asset of €95,000. This is a rate of return (interest rate) of 5.26%. This is equivalent to an effective annual percentage rate of

$$(1.0526)^4 - 1 = 22.8\%$$

The result of this process is:

1. The customer receives 90 days' credit.
2. The seller makes a sale and gets cash to the amount of 95% of the amount due.
3. The bank gets a rate of return equivalent to 22.8% per annum. If this is greater than the bank's own cost of capital, the bank will have made a gain.

Acceptance credits are a sort of formal line of credit agreed between the bank and the customer. In a sense, therefore, they are similar to bills of exchange. The company (which needs cash) draws up an acceptance credit document agreeing to pay a sum of money at some date in the future. Once the acceptance credit is drawn up, it is then sent to the bank. The bank accepts, and a commission is paid to the bank. The bank accepts a promise made by the company that it will pay a sum of money at some future date. The company will then sell the acceptance credit to another bank or discount house. The company therefore receives the cash it needs. The bank pays the discount house that bought the acceptance credit the sum due. Finally, the company then pays the bank the accepted amount of money due.

Figure 18.6 Acceptance credits: sequence of events

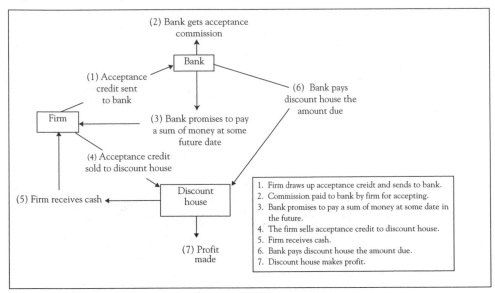

18.4.8 Commercial paper

The main function of banks is to act as intermediaries between lenders and borrowers. The bank profits by charging a higher rate of interest to borrowers than it gives to depositors. Sometimes, however, large well-known companies can bypass the bank and lend directly to borrowers. This type of lending is known as commercial paper. Therefore commercial paper is a sort of unsecured promissory note or IOU issued by large firms and sold to other firms via the money market. The maturity of commercial paper can be up to six months. The interest rate on commercial paper fluctuates with supply and demand conditions in the money market. Issuers can normally issue commercial paper at Euribor + 0.15%. This makes it cheaper than term loans. The principal disadvantage of commercial paper is that if a firm (the debtor) runs into short-term financial difficulties, it will get very little sympathy because of the impersonal nature of the commercial paper market. Banks tend to be more helpful to good customers in times of need. However, the benefit of commercial paper is that it allows businesses to tap into a wider source of finance. The most common type of commercial paper in the Irish market is government guaranteed notes issued by semi-state bodies and bank guaranteed notes issued by major Irish companies. Bank guarantees for commercial finance are off balance sheet contingent liabilities and do not need the same amount of capital backing as traditional bank loans. This allows the bank to offer cheaper funding to the borrower.

18.4.9 Predetermined expense financing

Certain business expenses such as corporation tax, insurance, audit fees and income tax can be discharged by financial institutions and repaid by the business over a period of 6 to 11 months.

18.4.10 Inventory financing

A popular method of short-term finance is inventory financing. Generally, stock is regarded as a liquid asset. Loans (or stock loans) are advanced by financial institutions (mainly by commercial finance companies) with inventory used as collateral. The main features of inventory financing are:

Collateral can be in the form of a **blanket lien** which provides the lending institution with a lien against all the borrower's stock. However, the borrower is free to sell the inventory, which effectively reduces the lien that a lender had at the start of the agreement.

Another instrument of security used in inventory financing is the **trust receipt**. The borrower signs a trust receipt for the stock. The stock is held in trust for the lender. The lender has specific legal control over these items of stock. The goods are held on the borrower's premises on the lender's behalf. Income from the sale of these goods is transferred to the lender. In order to verify the trust receipt, the lender will have to send somebody to the borrower's premises from time to time to verify that the specific items of stock are correct and still on the premises. Automobile dealers can be ideal users of trust receipt financing. However, it is possible for the dealer to sell cars under trust receipt and use the money for purposes other than remitting it to the lender. Further difficulties arise if the borrower has different locations spread over a wide geographical area.

To overcome some of the difficulties of trust receipt financing, **warehouse receipt** financing uses inventory that is under the physical and legal possession of the lender. Unlike the trust receipt the inventory is now in the control of the lender. A **terminal warehousing** agreement is where the stock is stored on the lender's premises and a third party is used to monitor and manage the inventory. A **field warehousing** agreement is where the inventory is stored on the borrower's premises, which is monitored by a third party. Once the loan is being repaid, the lender authorises the third party to release the appropriate amount of inventory held.

The cost of this type of financing is high and the cost of the third party has to be paid for by the borrower. Consequently only large firms use it.

SUMMARY

- Permanent current assets are those that are held even when the demand for the company's product is slow.
- Temporary current assets are those that fluctuate over the business cycle.
- It is important that the maturity of assets is matched by the maturity of liabilities used to finance those assets. This is the hedging approach to financing. For example, if stock is expected to be sold in 40 days, then a 40 day loan should be used to finance it.
- The aggressive approach to financing stems from the fact that short-term finance is usually cheaper than long-term finance. Some firms will therefore try to finance part of their permanent current assets with short-term debt. This is the aggressive approach to financing current assets.
- Bank overdrafts allow customers to withdraw more funds from their accounts than they have deposited.

- Short-term loans are for specific purposes and are repayable by agreed amounts within 12 months.
- Accruals in the form of income taxes deducted from payrolls, PRSI and VAT on sales, wages, etc. are seen as a spontaneous source of short-term finance.
- Banks can grant short-term loans to companies and use accounts receivable as a form of security.
- Invoice discounting is where the borrower submits or sells selected invoices to a lender.
- Factoring is the total sale of a firm's accounts receivable to a financial institution or bank (called a factor). Recourse factoring occurs when the risk of bad debts is borne by the business and not by the factor. With non-recourse factoring the risk of the bad debt is borne by the factoring company.
- A bill of exchange is a contract that enables the buyer to postpone payment for a period of up to 80 days.
- Commercial paper is lending by large well-known companies directly to borrowers. The maturity of this form of loan is usually six months.
- Inventory financing is advancing loans with stock used as collateral.
- The annual percentage rate of interest (APR) is the interest charged per period multiplied by the number of periods in the year.
- Bank loans can be in the form of interest only loans and discount interest loans.

QUESTIONS

1. Explain the following:
   (a) Permanent and temporary current assets
   (b) Current asset financing policies
   (c) Self-liquidating loans
   (d) Bank overdrafts
   (e) Accruals
   (f) Commercial paper
   (g) Compensating balances
   (h) Interest only loans
   (i) Instalment loans
   (j) Pure discount loans.
2. Why is matching the maturities of assets and liabilities so important? What are the benefits of such an approach? What is the downside to such an approach?
3. ◆ Why do you think bank loans are potentially more significant to small firms than to large firms?
4. Quick-Build, a builders' provisions company, has approached its bank with a view to borrowing €100,000 for one year. The bank has provided the following options:
   (a) 10% per annum on a simple interest loan. No compensating balances are required. Interest is paid at the end of the year.
   (b) A simple interest loan @ 7% per annum with interest due at the end of the year. However, under this deal the bank requires a compensating balance of 15%.
   Calculate the effective annual percentage rate of interest under each proposal.
5. You require a loan of €20,000 for one week. The rate of interest quoted is 10% per

annum. The nature of the loan is a discount interest loan. The bank also requires a 12% compensating balance. Calculate the effective annual percentage rate of interest.

6.♦ (a) Explain the trade off between liquidity and profitability.

(b) Distinguish between the conservative, aggressive and matching approach to financing working capital

7. A company adopts a prudent approach to the financing of its assets. An inspection of the company's balance sheet shows that it has permanent current assets of €50,000 and fixed assets of €190,000. It is also shown that the company's temporary current assets fluctuate about €20,000 every month. How should the company finance these assets, assuming that it maintains its prudent policy of financing? Considering the cost element of different types of financing, which policy would provide the most return for shareholders?

8. Companies that have aggressive working capital policies are considered to have higher risk. Why?

9. A company has total assets of €1,000,000 and permanent current assets of €200,000. Its fixed assets amount to €500,000. If the company follows the matching or hedging approach to financing, how much should the firm invest in current assets?

10. The following is information obtained from the accounts of Milo Ltd:

	Aggressive	Prudent (or conservative)
Temporary current assets	€150	€150
Permanent current assets	€150	€150
Fixed assets	€700	€700
	€1,000	€1,000
Current liabilities	€260	€35
Long-term liabilities	€300	€380
Common equity	€440	€585
	€1,000	€1,000

Using the above information, show how working capital policies affect accounting ratios. What are the main conclusions you can draw from the ratios?

NOTES

1. *Bank Brief* – Irish banks' information service, issue no. 9.
2. Ibid.
3. This case study is extracted from the above issue of *Bank Brief*.

Part 7

Special Topics
in Finance

19

Risk Management

CHAPTER OBJECTIVES

At the end of this chapter the student should be able to:
1. identify the nature of interest and exchange rate risks
2. appreciate the difference between internal and external risk management techniques
3. evaluate the types of financial derivatives available
4. select appropriate risk management techniques
5. appreciate the benefits and costs associated with risk management techniques.

INTRODUCTION

There are many aspects to a business that involve risk. When a company invests in a project there will be an element of business risk and when a company uses debt finance in its capital structure there is financial risk to the equity holders. In Chapter 6, measurement of risk was examined in terms of portfolio theory and the capital asset pricing model. In this chapter we look at other types of risk that can affect the profitability of a business, namely risks relating to movements in currency exchange rates and interest rates.

Risk management describes the policies a company may adopt, and the techniques the company may use, to manage these risks. The action a company takes to manage these risks is known as **hedging**.

First we look at the kinds of currency and interest rate risks that companies face and then consider the techniques available to manage these risks. We then look at risk management techniques that are internal to the company, and finally at external techniques available, some of which are quite topical, such as the development of financial derivatives. Derivatives have received a lot of publicity in the past decade, much of it negative, and examples of a few of the more famous derivative disasters are listed in Appendix 19B.

19.1 Currency risk

Prior to 1971 the world had a relatively fixed exchange rate system. In August of that year, the Bretton Woods regime collapsed and the major currencies of the world began, for the first time, to float against each other. This floating exchange rate between two currencies is determined primarily by supply and demand in the foreign exchange markets. The existence of the foreign exchange markets was based on the development of international trade as it required the use of foreign currencies. However, as foreign currency has become a tradable asset in itself, most foreign currency transactions today are based on switching financial assets from one currency to another rather than the direct result of international trade itself. The principal participants in the foreign currency markets are banks who operate on behalf of their customers and also on their own behalf.

Box 19.1 Main trading partners 2007 (Ireland)		
Country	Imports in € millions	Exports in € millions
Great Britain and Northern Ireland	20,516.6	16,594.1
Other EU Countries	18,323.0	39,610.9
US	7,045.0	15,861.2
Rest of the world	16,809.0	16,785.9
Total	62,693.6	88,852.2
Central Statistics Office Ireland		

This floating exchange rate system and the accompanying growth in world trade over the past thirty years have led to the increasing importance of risk management in currency exposure.

Exposure means being open to or vulnerable to risk.

The following different types of currency risk can be identified.

1. **Transaction exposure.** This is the risk of adverse exchange rate movements occurring in the course of normal international trade. When international trade occurs, a company either pays or receives foreign currency at some future date. The amount of local currency paid or received in these foreign currency transactions may change due to floating exchange rates. For example, a sale worth $10,000 when the exchange rate is $1.39 per € has an expected euro value of €7,194.

    If the dollar has depreciated against the euro to $1.44 per € when the transaction is settled, then the euro receipt will have fallen to €6,944. Transaction risk therefore affects cash flows and for this reason most companies choose to hedge or protect themselves against transaction risk.

2. **Translation exposure.** This is the risk that the company will make exchange losses when the accounting results of its foreign subsidiaries are translated into the multinational home currency. Suppose an Irish company buys a subsidiary in the US for $20 million, when the exchange rate is €1 = $1 and the following year the subsidiary is still valued at $20 million, but the exchange rate has moved to €1 =$1.10. In this example on consolidation of the company accounts, the asset value of the subsidiary will be reduced in the balance sheet.

    The cost of the subsidiary was $20 million/1.0 = €20 million and its value in the following year has fallen to $20 million/1.1 = €18.18 million which is a translation loss of €1.82 million. Translation risk does not involve cash flows and so does not directly affect shareholder wealth. However, investor perception may be affected by the changing values of assets and liabilities, and so a company may choose to hedge translation risk by, for example, matching the currency of assets and liabilities (e.g. a dollar-denominated asset financed by a dollar-denominated loan).

3. **Economic exposure.** This refers to the risk of long-term movements in exchange rates undermining the competitiveness of a company. It is quite different from transaction or translation exposure in that the company may not even be involved in international trade at all. Suppose an Irish company was supplying frozen pizzas to the local supermarkets in the domestic market and the euro appreciates against sterling. This may lead to import substitution from similar type companies in the UK. Irish supermarkets would find the local currency has increased buying power in sterling and may begin to source frozen pizzas in the UK. So even though the Irish supplier does not operate internationally, it still has economic exposure to currency movements. Economic exposure is difficult to quantify but a good strategy may be to diversify internationally, in terms of sales, location of production facilities, raw materials and financing. This is likely to reduce the impact of economic exposure and provide much greater flexibility to react to exchange rate changes in the longer term.

Box 19.2 Foreign currency exposure

Sterling fell to its lowest ever level against the euro in trading yesterday. The UK currency closed at €0.7443 against the euro and has now declined by more than 10% against the European currency in the past six months. At the end of June 2007, the euro's exchange rate against sterling stood at €0.6740. The steep decline in sterling's value in recent months will make Irish goods and services more expensive on UK markets.

Paul Tansey, *The Irish Times*, 3 January 2008

In Ireland exchange rates are quoted indirectly, i.e. the number of foreign currency units per €. A direct quotation is the value of one foreign currency unit in terms of the euro. In the case of the euro versus the Swiss franc a **direct quotation** would be of the form €0.80 = SF1 and an **indirect quotation** be quoted as €1 = SF1.25. The tradition in Ireland is to quote currencies indirectly.

The **spot rate** refers to the rate of exchange today and a **forward rate** refers to the rate available from a bank in the future. Banks expect to make a profit from selling and buying currency and this is achieved by quoting a different rate for selling and buying foreign currency.

Example 19.1 Bid and offer rates

The rate of exchange for the dollar versus the euro is as follows:
Spot €1 = 1.4251 – 1.4261
The lower rate is called the **offer rate** and is the rate at which the bank will sell dollars, €1 = $1.4251.

The higher rate is called the **bid rate** and is the rate at which the bank will buy dollars, €1 = \$1.4261.

The difference between the two spot rates is known as the **spread**. In an indirect quotation system the bank '**sells low and buys high**'.

19.2 Interest rate risk

The most obvious form of interest rate risk is that of a company with high levels of variable or floating rate debt. However, interest rate risk can affect companies in many ways and has consequences whether a company is cash rich or cash poor. The incidence of interest rate exposure can impact on corporate performance in the following ways:

1. Companies with floating rate debt are exposed to interest rates rising.
2. Companies with fixed rate debt are exposed to interest rates falling.
3. Companies with cash deposits at fixed rates are exposed to interest rates rising.
4. Companies with cash deposits at floating rates are exposed to interest rates falling.

The interbank market is a market for borrowing and lending large amounts of money between banks for a short term, often overnight (for one day), but possibly for up to a year. The euro interbank offer rate (**Euribor**) is a floating rate of interest based on an aggregate rate of interest at which top-rated banks borrow and lend to each other. Large companies may borrow at a margin above Euribor depending on the company's credit rating. Interest rates may be stated as a number of basis points above Euribor (1% = 100 basis points). So Euribor + 0.5% might be stated as 50 basis points above Euribor. The London interbank offer rate (Libor) is also an important rate in the London markets. It is used as a benchmark interest rate in some derivative markets discussed later in the chapter.

When banks quote interest rates based on interbank rates these rates are quoted on a bid/offer basis, so that a quote of 4.50% − 4.40% means a company can take a borrowing rate at 4.5%(offer rate) and take a deposit rate at 4.4%(bid rate). The offer rate is the higher rate, i.e. the rate at which the bank lends money.

Whether a company is exposed to foreign currency or interest rate risk, it is important to keep the scale of the risk in mind.

Where the magnitude of the risk is immaterial in comparison to the company's overall cash flows, one option is to do nothing and to accept the effects of any exchange/interest rate movements that occur.

19.3 Internal risk management techniques

Before looking at the various techniques applicable to exchange rate and interest rate risk management, it is useful to split the techniques into internal and external.

Foreign currency risk can be managed **internally** as follows:

1. **Invoicing in domestic currency.** One way of avoiding exchange risk is for an exporter to invoice the foreign customer in his domestic currency, or for an importer to arrange with his foreign supplier to be invoiced in his domestic currency. This effectively

means that currency risk is transferred to the other party in each transaction. This would be considered a conservative policy and the company may miss out on trade opportunities and lose out to competitors.

2. **Matching.** A company can reduce its foreign exchange transactions exposure by matching receipts and payments in each foreign currency in which it has exposure. The process of matching is made simpler by having foreign currency accounts with a bank. Foreign currency drafts can then be deposited or cheques drawn through the same account.

   Translation exposure can also be reduced. For example, a company purchasing foreign assets can borrow in a foreign currency to finance such assets and service the loans with the foreign currency revenues received.

3. **Netting.** Although not technically a method of managing exchange risk, netting is used by multinational corporations to reduce transaction costs in foreign currency dealing. Many multinationals engage in intra-group trading (trading between subsidiaries based in different countries) denominated in different currencies. The procedure for netting is usually co-ordinated by the company's own central treasury, which establishes a common currency and the exchange rates to use for netting purposes. The advantage of netting (known as **multilateral netting** if more than two subsidiaries are involved) is that currency purchase and selling costs, including commission and the bid/offer spread between selling and buying rates, and money transmission costs are reduced.

4. **Lead and lagged payments.** Lead payments are payments in advance and would be used by a company that was afraid of a foreign debt becoming expensive due to a currency appreciation. By paying in advance the company hopes to avoid the increased costs of buying the currency later. However, by paying in advance of the due date the company is giving up a credit facility which would have an implied cost. A lagged payment is a payment delayed beyond its due date. If a company believed a currency was weakening over time it might delay the payment as long a possible to avail of the favourable foreign exchange rate movement. Again there may be a cost associated with a loss of goodwill/credit rating on the international markets.

Internal risk management methods used for **interest rates** include:

1. **Mix of fixed to variable rates.** Too much fixed rate debt creates a problem when interest rates fall and too much variable rate debt leads to higher costs when interest rates increase. A company should try to balance these two extremes.

2. **Matching.** Companies can internally match their assets and liabilities when they both have a common interest rate. For example, a financial institution could match interest received from borrowers with interest paid to depositors.

3. **Maturity mix.** It is important not to have too much debt becoming repayable within a short period, as this can lead to difficulties if rates are high on the renegotiation of these debts. It may be a better policy to stagger the debt roll-over on a longer time horizon.

Even where companies have matching assets and liabilities at floating rates, more subtle forms of exposure exist.

(a) The deposits/loans attached may not be determined using the same basis (e.g. one is linked to Euribor and the other to Libor). It is unlikely that both floating rates will move perfectly in tandem and this is known as **basis risk**.

(b) Asset rates may be revised on three-monthly basis while liability rates are revised on a six-monthly basis and this is called **gap exposure**. A **negative gap** occurs when a firm has a larger amount of interest-sensitive liabilities than it has interest-sensitive assets. Both of these forms of exposure are outside the scope of this text.

19.4 External risk management techniques

Because internal techniques are dealt with inside the company they are likely to involve lower costs. In some cases these methods can substantially reduce exposure, however they cannot eliminate exposure. We will now look at external techniques available, known collectively as the derivatives markets, beginning with **forward contracts** and then in turn **futures, options** and **swaps**. There has been an explosive growth in the variety of derivative products available and in the growth of trade volumes over the past few decades.

19.5 Forwards

Forward contracts for commodities are centuries old and commodity futures first emerged in agricultural markets in Chicago in the mid-nineteenth century. Forward contracts exist for both currency and interest rate risk.

A **forward exchange contract (FEC)** is an immediately firm and binding contract between a bank and its customer for the purchase or sale of a fixed quantity of **foreign currency**, at a fixed rate of exchange and for performance at a future time. FECs are traded on an over-the-counter (OTC) market and can be tailor made with respect to maturity and size (OTC are also known as bespoke contracts). There may be an initial small arrangement fee but they give the company certainty about the amount of local currency involved. While a forward contract protects against unfavourable movements in exchange rates, the binding nature of the contract means the company foregoes any potential benefit from favourable currency movements.

The date for performance of the contract can be fixed (**fixed FEC**) or can have option facility (**option FEC**). The latter type of contract means that the customer has the option to call for performance of the contract at any time between two dates.

The bank quotes the US dollar as follows:

€1 =	Offer	Bid
Spot rates	1.5211 – 1.5221	
Two-month forward	1.5231 – 1.5237	
Three-month forward	1.5242 – 1.5249	

Forward rates can also be quoted as adjustments to the spot rates:

	Offer		Bid
Spot rates	1.5211	–	1.5221
Two-month forward	0.20c	–	0.16c dis
Three-month forward	0.31c	–	0.28c dis

In the example above the dollar is at a **discount** (dis) to the euro in the future. To get the forward rate, discounts are added (the three-month forward adjustment to the spot rate is 0.20 cent or $0.0020). The two-month forward offer rate is 1.5211 + 0.0020 = 1.5231. If a currency is more expensive in the future it is said to be at a **premium** (pm) and premiums are subtracted. In an indirect quotation system the bank 'adds discounts and subtracts premiums'.

Example 19.2 Forward exchange contract

Suppose an Irish trader needs to purchase $1 million in three months' time to pay for imported goods from the US. What will it cost the company to use a forward exchange contract, with the rates quoted above?

Solution
The bank's three-month forward offer rate is 1.5242.

The exporter will pay $1 million/1.5242 = €656,081.88 for the required dollars.

Now suppose the exporter was unsure whether the dollars were needed in two or three months. In this case the exporter can arrange an **option** forward exchange contract covering this timeframe.

Here the bank will pick the rate that best suits itself over the option period, i.e. 1.5231, and the customer has the option of going through with the purchase at any time during the option period (the contract is still binding but there is an option as to the performance date). The cost in euros to the exporter will be $1 million/1.5231 = €656,555.71.

The forward rate is the spot rate on the day the forward exchange contract is made plus or minus the **interest differential** for the period of the contract. **It is not a forecast!** It is likely that the difference in interest rates in the two economies will have an impact on future exchange rate movements, i.e. currencies with high interest rates are likely to depreciate in value against currencies with low interest rates.

The difference between spot and forward rates reflects differences in interest rates. If this were not so, then investors holding the currency with the lower interest rate would switch to the currency with the higher rate, ensuring they would not lose on returning to the original currency by fixing the exchange rate in advance at the forward rate.

If enough investors acted in this way (arbitrage dealings), forces of supply and demand would lead to a change in the forward rate to prevent such risk-free profit-making.

Example 19.3 Forward rate determination

Suppose an investor has €5 million to invest for one year and is considering investing in Ireland or the US. The current exchange rate is €1 = $1.4000 and interest rates in Ireland

and the US are 4% and 6% respectively. The obvious choice is to invest in the US where the rate is higher. However, the bank will quote the forward rate calculated on the basis of this potential arbitrage opportunity.

Potential returns in each country are as follows:

In US dollars, €5 million × 1.40 = $7 million and by investing at 6%
= $7 million × 1.06 = $7.42 million.
In Ireland, €5 million invested at 4% = €5 million × 1.04 = €5.2 million.

The forward rate is quoted on the basis of these returns as follows:

Forward rate = 7.42/5.2 = $1.4269 or a 2.69c discount in one year (see Appendix 19A on interest rate parity).

If you have forward rates and spot rates you can work out the interest rate differential between the two currencies, sometimes known as the cost of forward cover.
The approximate cost (annualised %) of forward cover is

$$\frac{\textbf{(Spot rate – Forward rate)} \times \textbf{12} \times \textbf{100}}{\textbf{Spot rate} \times \textbf{number of months cover taken}} \qquad (19.1)$$

Example 19.4 Cost of forward cover

Using the spot and three-month forward rate in Example 19.2 the cost of forward cover is calculated as follows:

$$\frac{(1.5211 - 1.5242)12 \times 100}{1.5211 \times 3} = -0.8152\%$$

The negative value means it is cheaper to buy dollars forward than at the spot rate. Offer and bid differentials are usually averaged in calculating the cost of forward cover.

$$\frac{(1.5221 - 1.5249)12 \times 100}{1.5221 \times 3} = -0.7358\%$$

The average of the two results is 0.7755% and this is the interest differential between the dollar and the euro zone. Here the rate of interest is higher in the US by over 3/4%.

Example 19.5 Forward exchange contract

Dodgy-Tabs plc operating from Balinasloe sells shoes to South Korea. A shipment has just been made to a major South Korean customer, invoiced in South Korean won (W), payable in three months' time. The amount due is W56 million.

Exchange rate W/€	Spot €1 =		W2,320 – 2,322
	3 months forward		15 – 23W dis
Interest rates:		Bid	Offer
	€	6%	8.75%
	SKW	9.25%	12%

(a) Calculate the euro position using a forward exchange contract.
(b) How would your solution change were Dodgy-Tabs to make a payment of W30 million to a South Korean supplier in three months' time?
(c) Calculate and explain what the cost of forward cover represents using bid and offer rates.

Solution
In this example the Irish trader is afraid that the won (SKW) will weaken over time and the trader will receive less euros for the won in the future. By entering into a forward exchange contract the trader will know in advance how much euro will be received in three months' time.

(a) First work out the forward rate = 2322 + 23 = 2345. Dodgy-Tabs agrees to sell W56 million to the bank at an agreed rate of 2345.
     W56 million/2345 = €23,880.60. This is the revenue **in three months time**.
(b) The company could match the W30 million payment and take out a FEC for the W26 million remaining.
     W26 million/2345 = €11,087.42
(c) The annualised cost of forward cover is negative as the won is at a discount to the euro and therefore the interest rate in the South Korea is higher.
The interest rate differential is calculated as an average of the bid and offer rates.

$$\frac{2320 - 2335}{2320} \times \frac{12 \text{ months}}{3 \text{ months}} \times 100\% = -2.586\%$$

and

$$\frac{2322 - 2345}{2322} \times \frac{12 \text{ months}}{3 \text{ months}} \times 100\% = -3.962\%$$

The average of the two scores of the cost of forward cover = −3.274%. By entering into a forward contract, the company is locking in to a lower value of South Korean won (SKW) and is losing about 3.3%, which is the approximate interest rate differential in the two economies.

19.5.1 *Money market operations*

The connection between interest rates, spot rates and forward rates allows the possibility of an alternative hedging technique. This technique is sometimes called a **synthetic forward** or a **money market hedge**. There are a few steps involved in the operation of this type of hedge. Suppose an exporter has a foreign currency receipt (**cash inflow**) in the future. The procedure is as follows:

1. Borrow an *appropriate* amount of foreign currency now.
2. Convert the foreign currency to local currency now.
3. When the foreign currency is received, repay the foreign currency loan.
4. Place this local currency on deposit (optional step) if you need to bring it forward to make a direct comparison to a forward exchange contract in the future.

Example 19.6　Money market hedge

Consider the information in Example 19.5 above and compare the FEC to a money market operation in three months' time.

Solution
Using a forward exchange contract €23,880.60 is the revenue **in three months' time**.

Money market procedure
1. Borrow an amount of won that will leave the exporter owing exactly W56 million in three months' time. Since the annual rate for borrowing won is 12% the quarterly rate is 3%.
   So, borrow W56 million/1.03 = W54.367 million now.
2. Convert at today's bid rate (i.e. sell the won back to the bank) = W54.367 million/2322 = €23,414.73.
   This is the amount of euro available to the exporter today, whereas the FEC value is in three months' time.
3. When the W56 million is received in three months' time, repay the foreign currency loan.
4. To make a direct comparison in the same timeframe as the FEC the €23,414.73 can be placed on deposit at the bid rate in Ireland. The annual deposit rate in euro is 6% and so the quarterly rate is 1.5%. If this euro amount is placed on deposit for three months, the equivalent amount in three months' time is €23,414.73(1.015) = €23,766.73.
In this situation the FEC is better at €23,880.60 by a small amount.

The steps involved in a money market operation for a foreign currency payment (**cash outflow**) are as follows.
1. Buy an appropriate amount of foreign currency today (spot).
2. Place this foreign currency on deposit.
3. When payment is due, pay from the deposit account.
4. Buying the currency spot in step 1 may involve borrowing euro if the company is short of funds and this cost of borrowing can be used to give a direct comparison with the forward contract value.

Example 19.7 Comparison of FEC and money market operation

Again use Example 19.5, but this time assume Dodgy-Tabs plc has to pay W56 million in three months' time. In this situation the trader is afraid that the won will strengthen over time and will cost more in euro in the future.

Compare a forward exchange contract with a money market operation.

Solution

(a) First work out the forward rate = 2320 + 15 = 2335

   W56 million/2335 = €23,982.87 **payment in three months'** time using a forward exchange contract.

(b) Using a money market operation the company would deposit won for three months at the bid rate. The annual bid rate for won is 9.25% and so the quarterly rate is 2.3125%.

The company could buy W56 million/1.023125 = W54,734,270 today and place it on deposit for three months.

   This deposit will grow to W56 million in three months' time.

   The cost of buying the won today is W54,734,270/2320 = €23,592.36 at the spot rate.

   Again, to make this directly comparable, assume Dodgy-Tabs has to borrow the euro to buy the won. The borrowing rate for three months is 8.75%/4 = 2.1875%.

   The cost is €23,592.36(1.021875) = **€24,108.44 in three months' time**. In this example the FEC is better.

19.5.2 Forward rate agreement (FRA)

A forward rate agreement (an FRA) is a contract to borrow or lend money in the future at an interest rate that is agreed today. FRAs are traded on the OTC market so maturity dates and periods can be tailored to the company's requirements. Here again interest rates are quoted on a bid/offer basis, so that a quote of 6.50 – 6.40 means a company can fix a borrowing rate at 6.5% and fix a deposit rate at 6.4%. The rate agreed is based on a notional amount starting on a date in the future and lasting for a specified period (e.g. a 3 v 9 means the FRA starts in 3 months and lasts for 6 months). Banks are able to quote forward rates based on current money market rates available to them now.

Example 19.8 Calculation of forward rate

Suppose a bank wants to quote a 6 month lending/borrowing rate starting in 3 months' time (a 3 v 9 FRA) and can currently borrow at 5% and deposit money at 4.75%. Use the rates quoted to justify an appropriate forward rate.

Solution

Using €1 million for borrowing and lending the results would be as follows:

Cost of borrowing   = €1 million × 5% × 9/12 = €37,500
Deposit return   = €1 million × 4.75% × 3/12 = €11,875

To break even the bank needs to earn interest of €37,500 − €11,875 = €25,625, or an interest rate of

$$\frac{€25,625 \times 12/6 \times 100\%}{€1 \text{ million}} = 5.125\%$$

The bank could base the forward rate knowing they would make a suitable return using the basic analysis above.

The FRA can be arranged with a separate institution as a separate transaction to the company's original exposure. The overall affect of an FRA is that regardless of the actual rate in the future, the company will know in advance what interest is effectively involved, based on a simple compensation mechanism and this compensation occurs at the start of the period of the notional deposit or borrowing. The company will lend/borrow at actual interest rates, and a compensating mechanism between the company and the bank will adjust the effective rates to the agreed amount.

This is illustrated with an example below.

Example 19.9 Forward rate agreement

It is now 1 June and Gazaybo plc uses certificates of deposit (CDs) for its short-term investment. The company currently holds €2 million worth of CDs, which mature in three months' time. The company treasurer intends to replace these CDs when they mature by buying further CDs with three months' maturity, and is afraid that interest rates will fall before the investment is renewed.

The treasurer decides to hedge against a reduction in interest rates by using a forward rate agreement (known as selling a 3 v 6 FRA) which fixes the rate at 6%.

Indicate what outcomes will occur and calculate the resulting payments if on the settlement date the three month CD rate has moved to (a) 4% and (b) 9%.

Solution

(a) If the rate is 4%, the company will receive interest of €2 million × 4% × ¼ = €20,000 at the end of the deposit period.

The bank compensates the company the difference between 4% and 6% for the three-month period.

The amount of interest differential = €2 million (6% − 4%) × ¼ = €10,000.

The settlement date of the FRA is at the start of the notional deposit and the sum involved is discounted at the prevailing interest rate (4%/4 or 1%).

= €10,000 × 1/(1.01) = €9,901.

When this is added to the actual 4% received on deposit, the result is an effective return interest rate of 6%.

(b) If the rate is 9% the company will receive interest of €2 million x 9% × ¼ = €45,000 at the end of the deposit period.

Here the company compensates the bank the difference between 9% and 6% for the three-month period.

The amount of interest differential = €2 million (9% − 6%) × ¼ = €15,000.

The settlement date is at the start and the sum involved is discounted at the prevailing interest rate (9%/4 or 2.25%).

= €15,000 × 1/(1.0225) = €14,670 and this is subtracted from the actual 9% received over the next three months.

The overall effect of the FRA is that regardless of the actual rate of interest the company will receive interest at 6%. The effect is analogous to forward exchange contracts. When using an FRA the company is protected against adverse movements but cannot benefit from favourable movements.

When a company is operating an FRA for a borrowing exposure then the compensation mechanism works in the opposite way. If rates go above the FRA rate, the bank compensates the company and if rates go below the FRA rate the company compensates the bank.

FRA rates are over-the-counter (OTC) agreements quoted by banks that deal in FRAs for various timeframes, for example

3 v 6	4.77% − 4.72%
4 v 7	4.82% − 4.77%
5 v 8	4.89% − 4.84%
4 v 10	4.95% − 4.90%

Example 19.10 *Effective interest rate*

A company needs to borrow €20 million for three months in two months' time and the following FRA rates are available: 2 v 3 at 3.61% − 3.59%, 2 v 5 at 3.67% − 3.63% and 3 v 5 at 3.68% − 3.65%.

If the company can borrow at Euribor + 50 basis points, show how the FRA would operate. What is the effective interest rate if Euribor is 4.5% in two months' time?

Solution

The company needs to buy a 2 v 5 FRA and the quote is 3.67%.

In three months' time, if the rate is 4.5%, the bank will pay the company 4.5% − 3.67% = 0.83%.

Therefore the three-month borrowing rate is 4.5% + 0.5%	=	5%
Less the settlement received in the FRA agreement	=	(0.83%)
The effective borrowing rate	=	4.17%

This rate is the same as 3.67% + 0.5% = 4.17%. The FRA allows the company to fix the rate at the FRA rate + 0.5%.

So, FRAs offer companies the facility to fix future interest rates today for either short-term borrowing (buying an FRA) or short-term lending (selling an FRA) for a specific future period, starting at a future date.

19.6 Futures

Derivatives like futures allow producers, traders and speculators to bet on future price fluctuations in order to speculate on, or protect themselves from, unexpected changes in market prices. A futures contract is like a forward contract, except that the futures contract will be standardised in terms of quantity and delivery dates. From the mid-1970s, the potential offered by futures contracts on financial instruments began to be recognised in areas like stock indices, interest rates, exchange rates and specific shares. Derivatives such as futures were primarily invented to reduce risk and not to fuel speculative activity, however there have been a few famous financial disasters associated with futures in recent years (see Appendix 19B).

A **future** is a standardised contract, covering the sale or purchase of a set quantity of a specific commodity, financial instrument or foreign currency at a set future date, at a price, agreed between two parties. The contracts are binding to both parties. When a person has bought futures without previously having sold any, then the trader holds what is known as a **long position**. When the trader in futures has sold futures without having previously bought them, this is known as a **short position**. Both of these are called **open positions** and can only be closed at, or before, the settlement date associated with the futures involved. For example, the holder of a long position can close that position by selling an equal number of contracts. The original buying price and the selling price to close the position are normally different and there will be an overall gain or loss from the difference between the buying and the selling prices.

Currency futures are traded on a number of futures exchanges around the globe. The most important and the first ever futures exchange is the Chicago Mercantile Exchange. FINEX operating out of the International Financial Services Center in Dublin is the currency futures and options division of the New York Board of Trade (NYBOT) and trades mainly in currency futures. **Euronext N.V.** is a pan-European stock exchange based in Paris and with subsidiaries in Belgium, France, Netherlands, Luxembourg, Portugal and the United Kingdom. In addition to equities and derivatives markets, the Euronext group provides clearing and information services. As of 31 January 2006, markets run by Euronext had a market capitalisation of US$2.9 trillion, making it the fifth largest exchange on the planet. Euronext merged with NYSE Group to form NYSE Euronext in 2007.

19.6.1 Currency futures

These are not nearly as common as forward contracts and have the following characteristics:

1. Not all currencies are traded and the major currencies available are £, ¥, €, C$ and SF. All contracts are priced in dollars.
2. Each currency has a specific contract size:

Currency future	Size or amount	Tick value
US dollar euro	€125,000	$12.50
US dollar sterling	£62,500	$6.25
US dollar yen	¥12.5 million	$12.50
US dollar Swiss franc	SFr125,000	$12.50
US dollar Canadian $	C$100,000	$10

3. The minimum price movement is called a **tick** and it is based on the 4th decimal place of the currency quotation or 0.01% per unit of the contract size.

$$\text{e.g. } \$1.48\underline{81} = €1$$

In the case of a euro contract the tick value is $125{,}000 \times 0.01\% = \$12.50$.

The value of a tick depends on the contract size and these vary according to the currency involved. In the case of the yen the tick movement is per 100 yen as in Example 19.13 below.

4. The contract price is the price at which contracts can be bought or sold and this price is determined by trading on the floor of a futures exchange.

5. Settlement dates for futures contracts are on the third Wednesday of the months of March, June, September and December. It is the date when trading on a particular futures contract stops and all accounts are settled. The maximum cover available is up to 9 months ahead. However, most buyers and sellers of futures close their positions before their contracts reach final settlement date.

19.6.2 The futures exchange clearing house

When a buyer and a seller agree a transaction in futures, the futures exchange takes the role of counterparty to the buyer and the seller in the transaction. Both buyer and seller have a contract with the exchange clearing house and not a contract with each other. The futures exchange clearing house protects itself against credit risk from participants in the exchange by means of a system of margin payments.

When you buy or sell a contract a deposit known as an **initial margin** is paid. This is just a small percentage of the total value of the contract and covers the risk of short-term losses on the position taken. The market is highly regulated and, on a daily basis, a **variation margin** is received or paid depending on the price movement of the future contract and the position you have taken with a futures contract. This process is known as **marking to market**. In this way, all loss positions have been covered by cash payments, and there is no credit risk for the exchange from non-payment of losses by buyers or sellers of futures contracts.

If a trader is afraid of an adverse currency movement, then the trader should take a futures position (i.e. buy or sell futures), that will result in a profit if the spot exchange rate moves against the company.

This should compensate the company for the loss it incurs from the adverse movement in the spot rate.

It is not necessarily a perfect hedge, as will be seen with an example.

Example 19.11 Currency futures

Shades plc, a US company, wants to hedge an appreciation in the € against the $ and owes €125,000 in one month. The current futures price is 1.4245 $/€. Tick value for € contract is $0.01% of 125,000 or $12.50.
(a)   Show how a currency futures hedge would operate.
(b)   Assume the € strengthens and the futures price in one months' time has moved to 1.4370.

Solution
(a)   As the company is afraid of the euro strengthening and the cost rising in dollars, the company should take a position to buy at the current strike price.
   The company should buy one € contract at $1.4245 now and when payment is due sell one € contract (close out the position).
(b)   To realise a futures gain or loss the futures trader must **close out** (make an opposite trade) the futures long position. In this example the trader should sell one euro future in one month's time.
   The profit in this case is calculated as follows:
   (Number of contracts)(Number of ticks)(Tick value)

$$\text{No. of ticks} = \frac{1.4370 - 1.4245}{0.0001} = 125 \text{ ticks}$$

   The profit is therefore 1 contract × 125 Ticks × $12.50 = $1,562.50

The company will, in one month's time, pay its debt buying the €125,000 at the prevailing spot rate at that time, and as the euro has strengthened the company will incur an extra cost.

The futures profit can be then be set off against the loss the company will make when the company buys the € in the spot market.

The prices in the futures market do not necessarily move exactly in line with the spot market (**basis risk**) and this means futures contracts will not necessarily provide a perfect hedge.

The exposure may not equate to an exact number of contracts, which again makes a perfect hedge unlikely.

Settlement date

Currency futures are available for a period of up to 9 months. This implies that there is a choice of date relating to the futures contract needed. To hedge currency receipts and payments a futures contract must have a settlement date **after** the date that the actual currency is needed. Usually the best hedge is achieved by selecting the contract, which matures next after the actual cash is needed.

Example 19.12 Currency futures date

Euro futures: contract size €125,000: price in $ per €

Sept 1.5552   Dec 1.5556   Mar 1.5564

An Irish company will receive $2 million on 13 December and wants to hedge this exposure using currency futures. Show how a futures hedge would operate.

Solution
1. The appropriate futures date in this example is the December contract.
2. To find the number of contracts the dollars are transferred to euros and then multiples of €125,000. $2,000,000/1.5556 = €1.285,678 and dividing by 125,000 = 10.29 or 10 contracts approximately.
3. Today buy 10 euro contracts at $1.5556 and close out on 13 December by selling 10 contracts.

If the dollar weakens, there will be a profit on the futures position, which will help compensate the loss in the value of the dollar cash inflow.

If the dollar strengthens then there will be a loss on the futures position but the company will receive more euros for the dollar inflow.

Transactions not involving $

As the major currency futures are usually priced against the dollar, when a company is not exposed to a future dollar cash flow, the company may need to deal in more than one type of contract. This complication makes use of the currency futures markets much more complex than the use of forward markets and contributes to their lack of popularity.

Example 19.13 Futures and exposure not in dollars

A British company has purchased steel from Japan and needs to pay for this in yen (¥) in 90 days' time.

It can hedge this by buying Japanese yen futures.

However, on the futures market yen are bought with dollars. The company therefore needs to sell sterling futures (to get dollars) and buy yen futures (with dollars).

In 90 days it will close out by buying sterling futures and selling yen futures.

Suppose a UK company needs to buy ¥100 million in 90 days' time. Japanese yen future is trading at $0.8106 per 100 yen and the sterling future is trading at $1.6250 per pound. Show how currency futures can be used to hedge the company's position.

Solution
Contract sizes are ¥12.5 million and £62,500.

The number of yen futures is ¥100 million/¥12.5 million = 8 contracts.

The UK company should buy 8 yen futures contracts.

$$\text{Buy 8 contracts (¥)} = \frac{8 \times 12.5 \times \$0.8106}{100} = \$810,600$$

This amount of dollars needs to be covered using sterling futures.

This is then converted at the sterling futures price i.e. $810,600/1.6250 = £498,831.

This implies the number of sterling contracts is £498,831/62,500 = 7.98 rounded to 8 contracts.

The company should therefore sell 8 sterling futures.

Therefore the futures position to take is: buy 8 yen and sell 8 sterling now, and in 90 days, sell 8 yen and buy 8 sterling contracts.

Interest rate futures

Interest rate futures offer a means of hedging against interest rate risk. They are similar in effect to FRAs, except that the terms, amounts and periods are standardised.

If a company wishes to use an interest rate futures contract as a hedge against interest rate risk, the idea is to take a futures position that will result in a profit if the interest rate moves against the firm. This should compensate the firm for the loss it incurs from the adverse movement in the interest rate.

Short-term interest rate futures (**STIRS**) are notional fixed-term deposits, usually for three-month periods starting at a specified time in the future with standard settlements dates like currency futures. The outlay to buy/sell futures only involves a small initial deposit (margin) and so a company can hedge large exposures with a small outlay. The pricing of STIR futures contract is determined by prevailing interest rates and the price is quoted at a discount to 100. For example, if the rate is 8% the price is quoted as (100 – 8) = 92.00 and if the rate falls to 6.6% the price is quoted as 93.40.

This implies that if a company is afraid of a rate rise, and therefore a falling futures price, it should sell contracts and if a company is afraid of a rate fall it should buy contracts. Most of the interest rate futures are for short-term interest rates in sterling, euro and Eurodollar, etc. (e.g. 3-month sterling and 3-month euro).

These short-term interest rate futures represent interest receivable or payable on notional lending or borrowing for a 3-month period beginning at a standard future date. The contract size depends on the currency in which the lending or borrowing takes place. The 3-month sterling interest rate future is a notional contract of £500,000 in size, with the minimum price movement known as one tick or 0.01% (0.0001) of the contract size. A full 1% move is equivalent to 100 ticks. The tick value for a 3-month sterling interest rate future is (£500,000)(¼)(0.01%)= £12.50. The most commonly traded short-term interest rate futures contracts are as follows:

Contract	Amount	Tick value
3-month Eurodollar	$1,000,000	$25
3-month Euribor	€1,000,000	€25
3-month sterling	£500,000	£12.50

Example 19.14 Interest rate future

In three months' time (June) a company will need to borrow €10 million for a six-month period. Current interest rates for such a loan to the company are 8% per annum (based on Euribor plus a margin). The company treasurer expects interest rates to rise over the next three months. Three-month euro futures €1,000,000 are available, with June futures priced at 92.50. Show how a futures hedge would operate, if interest rates rise by 2% and the futures price moves by 1.8%.

Solution

The number of contracts involved is €10 million/€1,000,000 = 10 contracts, but since cover is needed for six months and the contracts are for a notional 3-month period the number of contracts is doubled to 20. The company should sell 20 contracts at 92.50 and then **close out** the position when the futures price has moved in three months' time.

In this case the 1.8% move is a value of 90.70 (92.50 − 1.80), so buy 20 contracts at 90.70.

The futures profit is (92.50 − 90.70)/0.01 = 180 ticks.

The profit is 180 ticks at €25 and 20 contracts = 180 × €25 × 20 = €90,000 and this €90,000 profit helps compensate for the increased cost of the loan.

The actual cost of the loan increases by (2%)(€10 million)(1/2) = €100,000.

The company pays (10%)€10 million)(½) = €500,000 less the profit on the futures market of €90,000 = €410,000.

In this case there is 90% hedge efficiency, i.e. 90% of the potential increase in cost is covered.

The standardised nature of the contract size is a limitation of their use, as they cannot always be matched with specific interest rate exposures. There is also basis risk in the price movement of the futures contract may not move in tandem with the underlying interest rate move. The difference between the futures price and the spot interest rate is called **basis**. This basis will disappear over time and will be zero at the final settlement date for the futures contract. If this were not the case, speculators would make profits from trading between the futures market and the cash market. When a futures position is opened, it is possible to estimate what the basis will be when the position is closed. It is, however, based on the assumption that the basis risk will disappear overtime in a linear way.

Example 19.15 Expected basis and basis risk

Suppose a company needs to borrow €10 million at the end of April for 3 months, and it is now the end of December. Three-month Euribor June futures are trading at 95.40 and the company decides to sell 10 contracts. The current three-month Euribor rate is 3.4% or 96.60 and June contracts reach final settlement at the end of June. What is the expected basis risk at the end of April assuming basis risk disappears linearly?

Solution

The basis when the hedge is started is 96.60 − 95.40 = 1.2% or 120 ticks. There are six months to the final settlement date and four months to go before the futures position is closed at the end of April. The expected reduction in basis is 120 ticks × 4/6 = 80 ticks and by the end of April, basis is expected to be 40 ticks.

If, for example, the three-month Euribor is 4% in April, then the expected futures price would be 100 − 96 − 0.40 = 95.60.

However, basis risk is the risk that when the futures position is closed, the actual basis may be different from that expected. For example, the futures price above when the position is closed might be 95.45, rather than 95.60, giving an actual basis of 55 rather than 40. In the case of exchange rates and futures, the current price of a currency future and the spot rate, will be different and they will start to converge when the final settlement date for the futures contract approaches.

19.7 Options

Options on commodities have a long history and tulip bulb options were traded in Amsterdam as far back as the seventeenth century. Currency and interest rate options are agreements giving the holder the right, **but not the obligation**, to buy or sell foreign currency at a stated rate of exchange, or borrow or lend at a specific interest rate, at some time in the future. They give the holder flexibility to take advantage of favourable movements in exchange rates or interest rates. Buying an option involves a cost, known as a **premium**. The determination of the option premiums is a complex process because of the number of factors involved. Options come in two forms, namely **over the counter (OTC)** and **exchange traded**.

19.7.1 Currency options OTCs

The main purpose of a currency option is to reduce exposure to adverse currency movements, while allowing the holder to profit from favourable currency movements. They are particularly useful where there is **uncertainty** about foreign currency receipts or payments, either in timing or amount. Every option has an expiry date and unless the option is exercised by its expiry date, the option lapses. For OTC options the expiry date is negotiable. If options can be exercised on their expiry date only, they are known as **European-style** options. If, however, the options can be exercised at any time up to and including their expiry date they are known as **American-style** options.

A **call** option is an option to buy currency and a **put** option is an option to sell currency. The **exercise price** under the terms of the option contract is the stated rate of exchange.

Example 19.16 OTC currency option

Suppose the current spot offer rate is €1 = $1.02 and an Irish company has an outflow (payment) of $100,000 in three months' time. The company arranges an OTC call option contract to buy dollars from its bank, at an exercise price of $1.02. For this option facility the bank charges a premium of €1,000. The OTC contract will be tailor-made to suit the company and should the company exercise the option, because the spot rate turns out to be less than $1.02, the Irish company will pay 100,000/1.02 = €98,039.22 plus the premium of €1,000 = €99,039.22.

If the exercise (strike) price is $1.02, the option is said to be **at the money**.

If the exercise price were less favourable to the company (€1 = $1.01), the option is **out of the money**.

If the exercise price is more favourable (€1 = $1.03) the option is **in the money. An option will only ever be exercised if it is in the money.**

Example 19.17 OTC currency option

An Irish engineering company is tendering for a contract to build a bridge in Switzerland. The company costs the construction project at €18.5 million and tenders a bid at €20 million. The expected profit is therefore €1.5 million.

However, the bid must be priced in Swiss francs. The current exchange rate is €1 = SF 1.6 and so the company prices the bid at SF32 million. The contract is awarded in 6 months' time, and assume for simplicity that the revenue of SF32 million is received up front, if the company is successful with its bid.

This is a classic example of uncertainty with regard to a possible foreign currency receipt. In this example it would be inappropriate to enter into a forward exchange contract, as this is a binding obligation and if the tender is unsuccessful, the company could be faced with an expensive close out. The company would have to buy the currency at the spot rate in six months' time and sell it to the bank under the terms of the FEC.

Assume the company buys an **OTC** option contract at the money (€1 = SF1.6) to sell SF32 million and the bank's premium is €400,000.

There are four possible situations that could occur.

(a) The tender is unsuccessful and the Swiss franc strengthens. Abandon the option and lose €400,000.
(b) The tender is unsuccessful and the Swiss franc weakens. Here the company should buy SF36 million at the cheaper spot rate (€1 > SF1.6) and sell it to the bank under the terms of the option.
(c) The tender is successful and the Swiss franc weakens. The company will have successfully covered this risk and exercise the option.
(d) The tender is successful and the Swiss franc strengthens. The company should abandon the option and sell the SF32 million on the spot market (€1 < SF1.6) and improve its profit on the construction project.

The currency option gives the company a lot of **flexibility**; however, the downside is the cost of the premium, which is an up-front payment or sunk cost.

19.7.2 Exchange traded options

These are standardised (like futures) with respect to the amount of currency and maturity dates. They are available only in certain currencies and are traded on an options exchange. The most important currency options are those on the Chicago Mercantile Exchange and the Philadelphia Stock exchange.

The major currencies available are £, ¥, € and SF and all contracts are priced in dollars. Contract size: £31,250, ¥6.25 million, €62,500, SF62,500.

The following example illustrates their usage.

Example 19.18 Traded currency option

An Irish company expects to receive $6 million in three months' time. The company wants to use currency options to hedge its position. Since it needs to buy € using $ the company can buy September euro **call** options. The prices of these calls are as follows:

€62,500 contracts	September calls	
	Exercise price	Cents per €
	$1.4500/€	5.70
	$1.5000/€	1.45

The current spot rate $/€ is 1.4850 − 1.4900.

   Show how currency options could be used at a strike price of $1.450/€.

Solution

The company first needs to identify the number of contracts involved.

   At $1.450 the company would buy $6 million/1.45 = €4,137,931.

   This amount of euro is then divided by €62,500 to give 66.206 or approximately 66 contracts.

   The contracts will cover 66 × 62,500 × 1.45 = $5,981,250 and the remaining $18,750 will be sold at the spot rate.

   The **premium cost** here is 5.7 cents per € or €62,500 × 66 × 5.7 cents = $235,125 and this will cost $235,125/1.4850 = €158,333 at spot rate.

   The company policy will then be:

(a) If the spot rate is above 1.45, the option will be exercised and the net outcome will be: $5,981,250/1.45 less €158,333 = €3,966,667, and extra dollars ($18,750) need to be sold at the prevailing spot rate in three months time.

(b) If the September spot rate is less than $1.45 the option would not be exercised and the dollars received would be sold on the spot market.

For example, if the spot rate is $1.35 the net outcome would have been

$6 million/1.35 less €158,333 = €4,286,111 receipt.

In the OTC and exchange traded examples above, the companies involved faced foreign currency cash inflows. The fear in both cases was that the foreign currencies would weaken. The companies were in effect buying an upper limit on the exchange rate. This is known as a **cap**. If the foreign currencies were cash outflows, the fear would have been that the currencies would strengthen and therefore give a lower amount of foreign currency. In this case a lower limit option can be bought called a **floor**.

Figure 19.1 Cap floor and collar

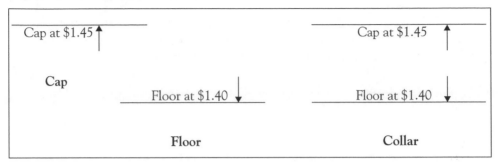

Caps and floors can be combined to produce what is known as a collar. The idea behind a collar is to reduce the cost of the premium, by sacrificing some of the potential gains. A collar involves buying a call and selling a put, or buying a put and selling a call.

Example 19.19 OTC currency collar

A company in Ireland has to pay £300,000 sterling in three months' time and is afraid that sterling will strengthen over that time. It decides to use an OTC option contract to cover its exposure. The current exchange rate is €1 = £0.65 sterling and the company arranges with its bank an OTC call at €1 = £0.64 for the purchase of £300,000 sterling in three months' time. The bank charges a premium of 3 cents per € giving a premium cost of 300,000 × €0.03 = €9,000.

The company considers the premium to be too expensive and to reduce the cost of the premium it writes a put at £0.67, for which the bank agrees to pay a premium of 2 cents per £. The company is telling the bank that if the rate goes above £0.67, the company will still accept £0.67 per euro.

The company is now guaranteed to operate between £0.64 and £0.67. In this case the company has sacrificed some of the potential gains beyond €1 = £0.67, but has reduced the cost of the premium to 300,000 × €0.01 = €3,000.

The net premium in a collar depends on the exercise prices for both call and put. A zero cost collar is possible and both options in a collar are for the same amount of foreign currency.

19.7.3 Option premium

An option is bought from the option seller or writer and the purchase price is called the **option premium**. For an OTC option the premium is negotiated between the buyer and the writer, usually a bank. With an exchange traded option, the premium is the market price of the option at the time it is purchased.

The factors that will determine the option premium for a currency include the current spot rate, the exercise price, the volatility of the exchange rate (measured as a standard deviation) in the past, the time duration to expiry and the interest rate differential between the currencies.

This premium value (price) of an option is usually broken down into two main elements: 1. **The intrinsic value**; and 2. **The time value**.

The **intrinsic value** is the difference between the strike price for the option and the market price (spot rate) of the underlying item. This can be positive or negative depending on whether the strike price is in the money or out of the money.

The **time value** reflects the likelihood that the market price of the underlying item (spot rate) will move. This time value depends on the period of time remaining, the volatility of the market price and the interest rate for the base currency.

The calculation of an option premium can be found by means of a pricing model. The **Black-Scholes** pricing model for the valuation of European-style options was developed in 1973. However, options valuation is outside the scope of this text.

Example 19.20 Traded options complications

The following example looks at some of the complications that arise when choosing options.
1. Choosing call or put, exercise price and number of contracts.
2. Dealing with surplus/deficit foreign currency.
3. Closing out American-style options.
4. Use of collars to reduce premium cost.

Suppose an Irish company has a $10 million inflow in June and the following information is available.

June euro options €62,500 ($cents per €)		
Exercise price	Calls	Puts
1.400	5.74	7.89
1.425	3.40	9.06
1.450	1.94	11.52
1.475	0.89	14.69

Solution
1. As it is a $ inflow we need to buy €, i.e. buy € **calls**.
   At 1.400 the number of contracts = $10m/1.40/62,500 = 114.29 or 114 contracts.
   At 1.475 the number of contracts = $10m/1.475/62,500 = 108.47 or 108 contracts etc.
2. Suppose you bought 114 calls at **$1.40**, then the amount of dollars covered = 114 × 1.40 × 62,500 = $9,975,000 and the extra $25,000 must be sold at the spot rate if the options are exercised.
3. **American-style options** can be **closed out** at any time up to the exercise final date. Assume on the transaction date the spot rate is $1.55 (i.e. the intrinsic value is 15 cents) and the options are trading at a premium of 15.35 cents and the call strike price is 1.40.
   If the option is exercised the gain is 15 cents (intrinsic value) and if the option is sold the gain is 15.35 cents. So close out, i.e. sell the option.

Alternatively, suppose the spot rate is $1.35 and the premium is 0.43 cents. This implies no intrinsic value, but you can still sell the option and make a gain of $0.0043 × 62,500 × 114 = $30,637.50

4. **Collar**: The idea here is to reduce the cost of the premium by sacrificing some of the potential gains in the option facility. For a €10 million inflow the appropriate strategy would be to buy a call and sell a put. If this was a $ cash outflow, then the strategy would be to buy a put and sell a call.

The net premium depends on the exercise prices and a zero-cost collar is possible. Both options in a collar are for the same amount of foreign currency.

19.7.4 Interest rate options

These again can be subdivided into OTCs and exchange traded. Interest rate options grant the buyer the right but **not the obligation** to deal at an agreed rate of interest (strike rate) at a future maturity date. The term interest rate guarantee (**IRG**) is used for an option for a single period of up to one year. An interest rate option is an option on a notional amount of principal, and is not the option to take out an actual loan or make an actual deposit. In this respect they are similar to FRAs and short-term interest rate futures.

Tailor-made OTCs can be purchased from the major banks, with specific values, periods of maturity and rates of agreed interest. The cost of the option involves the up-front payment of a premium, as in currency options.

An interest rate **cap** is an option, which sets an interest rate ceiling. A **floor** is an option, which sets a lower limit to interest rates. A **collar** is an arrangement involving a cap and a floor.

Example 19.21 OTC interest rate option collar

Cabbage plc is an Irish company needing to borrow €10 million in three months' time for a period of six months. The current rate of interest for company borrowings is 5.5% and the company treasurer wants to avoid rates above 7%. The treasurer decides to buy a cap at 7% from her bank, for a premium of 0.25% of the size of the loan. The premium is thought to be too expensive (€25,000) and so the treasurer sells a floor at 6% to the bank for a premium for 0.2%.

The company now knows that if rates go above 7% the company will only pay 7%. However, if rates are below 6%, the company will have to pay 6%, because the company has sacrificed the potential gain of reduced rates below 6%. The net cost of the premium is much reduced, however, at 0.05% of the amount borrowed (€5,000), and the company knows its cost of borrowing will be between 6% and 7%. In the case of options the cash settlement is made at the end of the notional period, not the beginning (as in FRAs) and as a consequence, the cash settlement is not discounted to present value.

Exchange-traded interest rate options are available as options on interest rate futures. They give the buyer the right to buy (call) or sell (put) a futures contract on or before the expiry of the option at a specified price.

Example 19.22 Traded interest rate option

If we use Example 19.14, in which a company, in March, needs to borrow A10 million in three months' time for a period of six months and an extract from the *Financial Times* on June short sterling options is as follows:

Strike price	Calls	Puts (premium based on points of 1%)
92.50	0.05	0.10
93.00	0.02	0.35

Show how an interest rate options hedge would operate at a strike price of 92.50, if interest rates rise by 2% and the futures price moves by 1.8%.

Solution

Since the company is afraid of a rise in interest rates and hence a fall in the futures price, the futures position to take is to sell now (June puts) and buy back at a lower futures price if rates rise.

The premium is set at points of 1%, so the put futures price of 92.50 has a premium cost of 0.10 (of 1%) to sell contracts. As explained (**in solution 19.14**), the number of contracts is 20 and in buying 20 put options the premium involved is €1,000,000 × 1/4 × 0.10/100 × 20 = €5,000 or 10 ticks × €25 × 20 = €5,000.

If interest rates rise by 2% and the futures price falls by 1.8%, the company will exercise its right to sell the futures at 92.50 and buy them at 90.70 (92.50 − 1.80 = 90.70).

The resulting profit is €90,000 (180 × €25 × 20)less the premium cost of €5,000 and this will help compensate the company for the increased cost of borrowing.

The company will actually pay €10 million × 10% x ½ less the futures profit of €85,000 = €415,000.

If the interest rate falls and the futures price will rise and the company will abandon its put options. It will have a reduced cost of borrowing but will have lost the premium of €5,000.

The advantage of options is that they allow the option holder to benefit from the favourable movement in the underlying item (e.g. Euribor or Libor), whilst providing protection against adverse movements. Futures do not allow this flexibility. Futures can guarantee the future cost of a loan, but they do not give any participation in favourable movements in the interest rate.

19.8 Swaps

This is an arrangement whereby two organisations contractually agree to exchange payments on different terms, for example in different currencies or at different interest rates. The currency swap market was developed in the 1980s. Companies often found they could borrow one currency relatively cheaply and the currency they needed was relatively expensive. By finding a counterparty in the opposite position, they could get together and arrange a swap in which both companies would be better off. Swaps are used extensively by large companies and banks to capitalise on their comparative advantages in different debt markets.

Currency swaps usually involve an initial exchange of principal, a periodic exchange of interest payments during the life of the swap and finally a re-exchange of principal at the end of the term of the swap. They are traded on the OTC market on terms that are negotiated individually, by the counterparties to the swap.

Example 19.23 Currency swap

A US multinational company needs a €100 million loan to finance a new subsidiary in Ireland. It has been offered a dollar loan from its bank at 6% and a euro loan at 7.5%. The company has identified with the help of a merchant bank an Irish multinational company which needs to raise $135 million to finance a major expansion in the US.

The Irish company has been offered a dollar loan at 6.5% and a euro loan at 6.7%. All the interest rates are fixed rates (**a fixed to fixed rate swap**). Assume the exchange rate is €1 = $1.35 at present.

The two companies agree to raise five-year loans, for the amounts mentioned, in their respective home currencies, to obtain the most favourable rates. They sign a currency swap contracts at an exchange rate of €1 = $1.35, in which each company agrees to hand over the proceeds of the loans.

In this simplistic example they both receive the currency they need, but at more favourable rates. The US company pays a rate of 6.7%, not 7.5%, and the Irish company pays 6% and not 6.5%. The merchant bank mentioned above would receive a fee for its services, which would reduce some of the interest savings.

Swaps are flexible since they can be arranged in any size and are reversible. The transaction costs are low, only amounting to legal fees, since there is no premium to be paid. Liability on the principal is not transferred in a swap and the parties are liable to **counterparty risk** (if one party defaults on the agreement to pay interest, the original borrower remains liable to the lender). Currency swaps can be fixed to fixed rate, fixed to floating rate and floating to floating rate.

Interest rate swaps in the same currency are transactions that exploit different interest rates in different markets for borrowing, to reduce interest costs for either fixed or floating rate loans. An interest rate swap is an arrangement whereby two companies swap interest rate commitments with each other and can have a term or duration ranging anywhere between one year and 30 years. A company which has debt at a fixed rate of interest can make a swap so that it ends up paying interest at a variable rate and vice versa (this is known as a plain **vanilla** swap). The parties to the swap retain their obligations to the original lenders. This means the parties must accept counterparty risk.

Example 19.24 Interest rate swap

Company A has a good credit rating and can borrow at a fixed rate of 5% or at a variable rate equal to Euribor. It wants to borrow at a variable rate.

Company B is a company with a lower credit rating and it wants to borrow at a fixed rate. Company B can borrow at a fixed rate of 6.5% or at a variable rate of Euribor plus 0.5%.

Without a swap company A would borrow at Euribor and company B would borrow at 6.5%. While company A has absolute advantage in both the fixed and variable rates, the disequilibrium in differentials mean the savings can be made if a swap is entered into, rather than each borrowing their desired style directly from the bank.

(a) Show what benefit is available to both companies (**arbitrage opportunity**) if they engage is a swap arrangement.
(b) Suggest a swap arrangement.

Solution

(a) In this example the arbitrage opportunity can be identified as follows:

	A	B	Difference
Fixed	5%	6.5%	1.5%
Floating	Euribor	Euribor + 0.5%	0.5%
Difference in differences or arbitrage opportunity			1%

This represents the potential gain which can be made out of a swap arrangement. Each company must borrow at the rate in which it has comparative advantage (fixed rate for **A** and floating rate for **B**).

There are an infinite number of swap arrangements that can occur, depending on the negotiating skills of the respective treasurers.

(b) **Suggested swap**

With a swap and based on the law of comparative advantage **A** should borrow at 5% fixed and **B** should borrow at Euribor + .5%.

To determine the terms of the swap above the following pro forma can be used to move from the original interest paid to the desired result.

	Company A	Company B
	(5%)	(Euribor + 0.5%)
Pays to the bank		
Pays in the swap		
Receives in the swap		
Net interest cost	(Euribor − 0.5%)	(6%)

By entering any figure into any slot of the pro forma the other figures must automatically balance out.

Here is one of many possible solutions: Both companies could agree a swap in which **A** will pay **B** a variable interest rate of Euribor and **B** will pay **A** a fixed interest rate of 5.5%.

	Company A	Company B
	(5%)	(Euribor + 0.5%)
Pays to the bank	(5%)	(Euribor + 0.5%)
Pays in the swap	(Euribor)	(5.5%)
Receives in the swap	5.5%	Euribor
Net interest cost	(Euribor − 0.5%)	(6%)

Another alternative swap could be:

	Company A	Company B
Pays to the bank	(5%)	(Euribor + 0.5%)
Pays in the swap	(Euribor + 0.5%)	(6%)
Receives in the swap	6%	Euribor + 0.5%
Net interest cost	(Euribor − 0.5%)	(6%)

Without a swap **A** would have borrowed at a variable rate of Euribor and so the cost is reduced by 0.5%. Without a swap **B** would have borrowed at the fixed rate of 6.5% and again the cost is reduced by 0.5%.

The benefits in the above example could be rearranged to divide the gains (1%) differently between the two companies. However, the basic principle is that there must be a gain for both parties to attract them to engage in a swap.

Banks that specialise in swaps quote rates at which they will pay the fixed rate or receive the fixed rate of interest over different time frames in a swap agreement. For example:

Duration	Bid	Ask
1 year	4.53%	4.56%
5 years	4.98%	5.03%
10 years	5.37%	5.42%
20 years	5.57%	5.70%

The bid rate is the fixed rate that a bank will pay in a swap in exchange for Euribor and the ask rate is the fixed rate that the bank would want to receive in exchange for Euribor. The banks make a profit from the difference between the bid and the ask rates.

A major advantage of swaps over other derivatives such as traded options, forwards and futures is that they can be used to lock into interest and exchange rates for much longer periods of time.

Other advantages include:
1. Access to capital markets that a company may be unable to approach directly.
2. They allow a company to change the strategic mix of fixed and floating loan arrangements (**capital restructuring**) without having to redeem the loans.
3. Foreign currency loans may be cheaper if raised by another company in the foreign country involved.
4. They can be reversed by re-swapping with other counterparties.
5. Transaction costs are low – just based on legal and arrangement fees.

Apart from the obvious danger that the counterparty to the swap may default before the end of the swap period and fail to carry out agreed obligations, once the swap is entered into, it can be difficult to get out of early. This may expose the company to a substantial penalty or may involve the arrangement of an equal and opposite swap with another party, both of which may be problematic and expensive. In the case of foreign currency swaps with a corporate in another jurisdiction, there is the exposure to sovereign risk. Sovereign risk covers political instability and the possibility of exchange controls being introduced apart from the exchange rate moving unfavourably against the company.

19.9 Swaptions

Many hybrid derivatives now exist and one of the most popular is the swaption. As the name suggests, they are a combination of an option and a swap. They give the holder the option to become involved in a swap. For example, a company might buy an OTC swaption from its bank, giving it the right, but not the obligation, to enter into an interest rate swap with the bank at or before a specified time in the future. A European-style swaption is exercisable only on the maturity date, whereas the American-style swaption is exercisable on any day during the exercise period.

Example 19.25 Swaption

Today is 1 January 2009 and your company has a variable rate loan of €2 million which is due for renewal on 30 June 2012. The current rate of interest is 7% and the company is afraid that rates will rise in the near future. The bank the company deals with has offered an American-style swaption as follows:

Interest rate 7.75%, exercise period 1 July 2009 to 31 December 2009, maturity date 30 June 2012. The premium is €40,000.

Under what circumstances would your company gain from exercising the swaption?

Solution

This swaption would be exercised if the interest rate rose above 7.75% in the next six months. The cost over the remaining three years is (€2 million × 7.75% × 3) + €40,000 = €505,000.

This represents an effective rate of €505,000/3/€2 million = 8.417%.

The average rate of interest would have to exceed 8.417% over the next three years for the swaption to be beneficial. If the interest rate falls over the maturity period the swaption would not be exercised and the company would take advantage of the lower interest rate. The premium is lost however, and should be viewed as the price paid for the possibility of taking advantage of lower interest rates.

19.10 Issues arising

Companies should have a clear strategy concerning how much foreign currency and interest rate risk they are prepared to take. A highly risk-averse or defensive strategy of hedging all transactions is expensive in terms of commission costs but recognises that floating rates are very unpredictable and can cause major losses. When formulating hedging strategies, it is important for companies to be clear about their objectives, **to identify and quantify exposures and select appropriate risk management techniques**. A sensible strategy to adopt may be to hedge as much as possible using internal hedging techniques and cover any remaining exposures with appropriate external techniques. Bank created products, or OTCs, may be more suitable for smaller companies as they are likely to lack the experience and knowledge associated with traded derivatives.

Risk management introduces greater certainty to the exchange and interest rates that companies face and, while recent derivative disasters have occurred, they stemmed from their misuse and lack of understanding rather than fundamental problems with the instruments themselves.

SUMMARY

- Both foreign currency and interest rate risks need to be managed in a company owing to recent instability of interest and exchange rates.
- Exchange rate risks include transaction, economic and translation exposure. Transaction risk and translation risk are faced only by companies with overseas operations, whereas economic risk is faced by all companies.
- Interest rate risks are faced by companies with cash surpluses and borrowings.
- Companies should form policies to manage these risks internally as much as possible.
- External techniques include forwards, futures, options, swaps and swaptions.
- Companies should specify hedging objectives, quantify exposures and select appropriate hedging techniques.
- Recent derivatives disasters have stemmed from derivatives misuse and poor controls rather then problems with the derivative instruments themselves.

WEB LINKS

www.cboe.com
Chicago Board Options Exchange

www.euronext.com
New York Stock Exchange Euronext

www.sgx.com
Singapore Stock Exchange

www.ifsconline.ie
The International Financial Services Centre, Dublin

www.ise.ie
Irish Stock Exchange

www.ft.com
The *Financial Times* online (London)

QUESTIONS

1. What is transaction exposure to foreign currency movements?
2. What is the difference between a forward exchange contract and a forward rate agreement?
3. Describe techniques available to reduce foreign exchange risk.
4. What is the difference between an OTC option and a traded option?
5. Describe four techniques available to hedge interest rate risk.
6.◆ McConigly Conway plc has bought goods from a US supplier, and must pay $10 million for them in three months' time. The company's finance director wishes to hedge against the foreign exchange risk and has asked you to help out. Assume that the company needs to borrow to make any payments (cash poor).

    The following annual interest rates and exchange rates are currently available.

US dollar rates		Euro rates		$/€ exchange rate	
Bid	Offer	Bid	Offer	Spot	1.0625 – 1.0635
7%	8%	3%	4%	3 months forward	1.10 – 1.05c dis.

    (a) Ignoring commission costs, assess whether a money market hedge, a forward market hedge or a lead payment should be used.
    (b) Using the spot and forward rates, calculate the cost of forward cover and explain your result.
    (c) Assuming that, instead of a payment, McConigly Conway plc is to receive $10 million from a US importer in three months' time, assess whether a forward exchange market hedge or a money market hedge is more efficient.

7. Assume it is now 1 December and Harney Macko plc has to make a $4.3 million payment to a US supplier in three months.

Spot rate €1 =	$1.4692 – 1.4735				
3 month forward	$1.4632 – 1.4668				
Options prices and premiums in cents per € (contract size €125,000)					
	Calls			**Puts**	
Price	March	June		March	June
1.46	2.55	2.95		1.99	2.51

    Illustrate the possible outcomes of forward market and currency options hedges if the currency rates in 3 months' time are:
    (a) $1.4350 – 1.4386
    (b) $1.4780 – 1.4820
8.◆ Juan F. Deesdays plc wants to borrow €10 million in six months' time for a three-month period and normally borrows at Euribor + 0.5%. The current three-month Euribor is 5.25% and the company is worried that the interest rates may rise. A bank quotes the following FRA rates:
    3 v 9: 5.45% – 5.40% and 6 v 9: 5.30% – 5.25%

(a) How can the company establish the hedge using a forward rate agreement?

(b) What is the effective borrowing rate for the company assuming that on the settlement date the Euribor has moved to (i) 6.5%, and (ii) 4.5%?

9.♦ Janice Saykwa plc is a group of companies controlled from France which has subsidiaries in the UK, South Korea and Switzerland. At 14 February, inter-company indebtedness is as follows:

Debtor	Creditor	Amount
UK	South Korea	W240 million
UK	Switzerland	SF480,000
Switzerland	South Korea	W180 million
South Korea	UK	£74,000
South Korea	Switzerland	SF375,000

The central treasury of the French MNC uses the following exchange rates for netting off inter-company imbalances.

$$€1 = W1,680 = £0.68 = SF1.88$$

Calculate the net payments to be made between the subsidiaries after netting off the imbalances.

10. Squagmullins plc has bought goods from a US supplier, and must pay $1 million for them in three months' time. The company's finance director wishes to hedge against the foreign exchange risk and has asked you to help out. You are asked to assess the use of futures contracts and forward exchange contracts.

€ futures are currently priced at $0.8600 with a contract size of €125,000 and tick value of $12.50.

	$/€
Spot	0.8625 – 0.8635
3 months forward	0.80 – 0.75c pm

Compare a forward exchange contract as against futures contract. Assess both methods, if with hindsight, the spot turns out to be 0.9450 – 0.9460 and the futures price, has moved to 0.9400.

11.♦ (a) An Irish company, Mog and Gerry plc, trades with several countries. Much of this trade involves credit. Today is 1 June and the following data relate to existing future trade.

	Date	Receive	Pay
Australia	1 Sept.	A$120,000	€40,000
Japan	1 Sept.	¥400million	¥320million
UK	1 Sept.	£1million	Nil
Exchange rates versus the €			
Spot	$2.1400–2.1425	¥128.5–129.3	£0.6850–0.6870
3 Month	2–2.5c dis	1–1.5¥ dis	0.5–0.45p pm

Interest Rates	Offer	Bid
Ireland	6%	5%
Australia	8%	7%
Japan	9%	8%
UK	5%	4%

Find the Irish € position on 1 September using forward exchange contracts and the international money markets.

(b) Assume the above trades were reversed as follows:

	Date	Pay	Receive
Australia	1 Sept.	A$120,000	€40,000
Japan	1 Sept.	¥400million	¥320million
UK	1 Sept.	£1million	Nil

Find the Irish € position on 1 September using forward exchange contracts and the international money markets.

12. Assume it is now 1 June and Owen Monie plc is to borrow €12 million in five months' time for a period of four months. The company can currently borrow at Euribor + 100 basis points and the current Euribor is 7.5%. Euro futures of €1 million are priced as follows:

September	92.60
December	92.10

(a) Illustrate how futures hedging would operate.

(b) Calculate the basis risk for the hedge now and the expected basis at the time the contract is likely to be closed out.

13. Melinn plc wishes to borrow €3 million on a fixed interest rate basis for a period of three years. The company can borrow at Euribor plus 100 basis points or issue three-year debentures at 6.5%. Cusack plc also wishes to borrow €3 million for three years, but is seeking a floating rate deal. The treasury department advises that it could issue fixed debentures at 6% or borrow at Euribor plus 75 basis points.

Show how an interest rate swap would work to reduce borrowing costs for Melinn and Cusack plc. Assume that any arbitrage benefits are equally distributed to the two companies. Ignore any associated fees for arrangement/administration by a third party.

14. Joe DeBookie plc needs to borrow €6,500,000 for a period of six months commencing in six months' time. Today is 1 December and the company may be assumed to be able to borrow at the 3-month Euribor rate.

Euribor Futures prices (€1 million contract size)

March   95.56
June   95.29

Options on futures prices are as follows:

€1 million contract size. Premiums are annual %.

	Calls		Puts	
	March	June	March	June
95250	0.445	0.545	0.085	0.185
95500	0.280	0.390	0.170	0.280
95750	0.165	0.265	0.305	0.405

The three-month EURIBOR is currently 4.5%.

Illustrate the possible results of futures and options hedges if interest rates in six months' time have increased by 0.75%. Assume the basis risk decreases in linear fashion.

15. Drew Blood plc has a €10 million variable rate loan at Euribor + 2%. The interest rate is set every six months and is applied to the borrowing for the following six months. This borrowing has a further 3 years to run before redemption at par. A group of consultants forecast Euribor rates over the next three years as follows:

Time in months	6	12	18	24	30	36
Forecasted rate %	8	9	10.5	12	7.2	5

The current Euribor rate is 8%. The company bank has offered Drew Blood a three-year cap at 8.9% for an additional annual interest cost of 0.5%.

Using the consultant's estimates of Euribor, show the cash flows on the loan with and without the cap.

16. ◆ It is now 1 March and at the end of June the treasury department of Du-geen plc may need to advance its US subsidiary $15 million. This depends on whether the subsidiary is successful in winning a franchise. The department's view is that the $ will strengthen over the next few months and wants to hedge its position.

Exchange rates US$/€
1 March spot 1.4461 – 1.4492; 4 months forward 1.4310 – 1.4351
Futures market €125,000 tick $0.0001 per €
March contract 1.4440; June 1.4302

Currency options €62,500 (cents per €)

	Calls	Puts
	June	June
Exercise price		
$1.400	3.40	0.38
$1.425/€	1.20	0.68
$1.450/€	0.40	2.38

Assuming the franchise is won, illustrate the results of using forward, future and option currency hedges if the $/€ spot exchange rate at the end of June is $1.3500 and the difference between the futures and spot price is the same at the end of June as now.

17. Today is 1 December and Deyank plc is an Irish company which has substantial trade with a company in New York. On 1 August the company expects to receive $20 million and has a dollar outflow of $17 million. Today's spot rate is €1 = $1.2300 and the August forward rate is quoted at a premium of 2.10 cents per €. September futures are quoted at $1.1950 per € and the contract size is €125,000.

    Assume that on 1 August the spot rate is $1.1860 per € and the September futures price is $1.1640 per €.

    (a) Calculate the net amount received in euros using a forward contract.

    (b) Calculate the total profit/loss arising from using futures contracts and the net amount to be received in euros.

18. Dympna Guest plc has to pay $250,000 to DeJogger plc, a sports equipment supplier, in six months' time. The financial manager wants to hedge this currency outflow. The following data is available:

	Offer	Bid
Spot rate ($ per €)	1.4980 ± 0.002	
Six months forward	1.4790 ± 0.004	
One year € interest rate	6.1%	5.4%
One year $ interest rate	4.0%	3.5%

Evaluate the cost in six months' time on whether a money market hedge, a forward market hedge or a lead payment should be used to hedge the foreign currency payment. Assume the company has no surplus cash and has to borrow to make any payments.

19. In three months' time (June) Buccaneers plc will need to invest €20 million for a six-month period.

    Current interest rates for such deposits are 8% per annum. The company treasurer expects interest rates to fall over the next three months.

    Three-month futures €1,000,000 points of 100% are available, with June futures priced at 92.50.

    Show how a futures hedge would operate, if interest rates rise by 2% and the futures price moves by 2.2%.

20. Tumbledown Shack plc wants to borrow €1 million in six months' time for a period of three months. It can borrow at Euribor + 0.50% from its bank and Euribor is currently 5.25%. The company is worried about interest rates increasing and the following FRA rates are available to hedge its position:

3 v 9 5.45%–5.40%
6 v 9 5.30%–5.25%
3 v 6 5.40%–5.35%.

    (a) Show how the company could hedge its exposure using an FRA.

    (b) If Euribor is 6.5% in six months' time what will be the effective rate of interest?

21. WalshPower plc has €20 million borrowed at a floating rate of Euribor + 0.75%, with a three-month rollover. The company treasurer has decided to look at alternative techniques for hedging this exposure. The four alternatives available to the company are as follows:

    (a) Buy a cap at 10%, for a premium of 1% per annum.

    (b) Buy a collar between 8% and 10% for 0.25% per annum.

    (c) The company bank has offered a forward rate agreement at 10% interest.

    (d) Do not hedge the exposure.

Show the effective interest rate paid in the next quarter if the Euribor moves to 6.25%, 8.25% or 10.25%.

22.◆ Assume it is now 1 December, and Xavier Monie plc expects to receive €7.5 million in five months' time and can deposit this at a rate of Euribor + 0.6% for a period of 4 months. Euribor is currently 4% and the treasurer wants to hedge the risk of falling interest rates by using futures or forward rate agreements.

    June €1 million three-month euro futures are available at 96.60 with a tick value of €25. A 5 v 9 FRA is available at 3.50 – 3.45.

    (a) Indicate a futures hedge to protect the interest yield of the short-term investment and the expected basis risk.

    (b) If Euribor fell by 0.5% over the next 5 months show the expected outcomes of the cash market, futures market and the FRA market.

    (c) Give two reasons why a futures market outcome might differ from that expected.

23.◆ Al Beback plc is an Irish company with the following trades over the next 6 months:

Purchases in three months	€116,000	
Sales in three months	$197,000	
Purchases in six months	$547,000	
Sales in six months	$254,000	
Exchanges rates	Offer	Bid
Spot rate ($ per €)	1.4106	1.4140
Three months forward	0.82c	0.77c
Six months forward	1.39c	1.34c
Money market rates	Offer	Bid
One year € interest rate	7.5%	4.5%
One year $ interest rate	6.0%	3.0%

    (a) Calculate the € position using forward exchange contracts.

    (b) Calculate the € position using a money market hedge.

APPENDIX 19A Theories of exchange rate determination

There are many factors which influence a currency's exchange rate, such as a country's balance of payments position, government policy carried out by central banks, the activity of speculators (the sentiment of the market participants in respect of future economic prospects) and the comparative differences in inflation rates and interest rates in trading countries, etc. Both inflation and interest rate differentials have formal theories attached.

Purchasing power parity (PPP) theory states that the exchange rate of a foreign currency depends on the relative purchasing power of each currency in its own country and that spot exchange rates will move over time according to relative price changes (inflation rates). Countries with relatively high inflation rates tend to depreciate over time.

Purchasing power parity can be expressed in the following formula

$$\text{Future rate of \$/€} = \text{Spot rate \$/€} \times \frac{(1 + \text{\$ inflation rate})}{(1 + \text{€ inflation rate})} \qquad (19.2)$$

Example
Suppose the spot rate is €1 = \$1.2 and inflation in the US and Europe are expected to be 12% and 5% respectively over the next year. What is the expected spot rate next year using PPP theory?

Solution
Expected spot rate = $1.20 \times \dfrac{(1.12)}{(1.05)}$ = 1.28 or €1 = \$1.28 next year

So the dollar is expected to be weaker. The PPP is sometimes known as the law of one price, i.e. the same goods sold in different countries should sell for the same price if all of the different prices are expressed in terms of the same currency. Inflation will erode the purchasing power of any currency and its exchange rate must adhere to the PPP relationship over time. Unfortunately, however, exchange rate determination is affected by more than just inflation differentials.

Interest rate parity (international Fisher effect) links the forward exchange markets and the international money markets. Currencies with relatively higher interest rates than their trading partners are expected to depreciate, and hence foreign investors see the high interest rates as a compensating payment for the future currency depreciation. The international Fisher effect shows how differences in interest rates indicate the difference between the spot rate and the forward rate as follows:

$$\text{Forward rate of \$/€} = \text{Spot \$/€} \times \frac{(1 + \text{nominal \$ interest rate})}{(1 + \text{nominal € interest rate})} \qquad (19.3)$$

If the same example above is used and the differential rates relate to nominal interest rates instead of inflation rates, the result will be a forward rate of €1 = \$1.28. The forward rate is also considered to be an unbiased predictor of the spot rate at a time in the future.

Unbiased simply means it is equally consistent in over-estimating and under-estimating the future spot rate.

APPENDIX 19B Risk management disasters and value at risk (VAR) analysis

There have been a number of high-profile risk management disasters in past twenty years. Among these were:

1. Metallgesellschaft. A subsidiary built up large positions in oil futures and the resulting fall in oil prices lead to massive losses ($1.3 billion).
2. Barings Bank. The infamous Nick Leeson, a trader working out of Barings' subsidiary in Singapore, built up a huge unauthorised position in futures and options. The bank lost $1 billion.
3. Daiwa bank. Toshihide Iguchi, a bond trader, lost $1.1 billion over an eleven-year period.
4. Sumitoma Corporation. Yasuo Hamanaka, a copper trader, lost $1.8 billion over a ten-year period on unauthorised trades.
5. Allied Irish Banks. John Rusnak was sentenced in 2003 to over seven years in jail for hiding €691 million in trading losses while working for Allfirst Financial, a subsidiary of Allied Irish Banks.
6. Shell. A single employee working in the Japanese subsidiary lost $1 billion in unauthorised trading in currency futures.
7. Mizuho Bank. A broker wanted to sell one share for 600,000 yen (around €3,000). However, the unfortunate broker sold 600,000 shares for one yen each and Mizuho Bank lost €128 million in 2005.
8. Societé General. In January 2008, €4.9 billion was lost due the trades of Jerome Kerviel working in the bank's European equities derivatives desk.

These examples would seem to indicate that risk management using derivatives is a dangerous game and should be avoided. The argument based on the above examples, however, is not that no risks should be taken. A treasurer working for a company or a fund manager in a financial institution should be allowed to take positions on the future direction of relevant currency and interest rates. The argument is that the size of the positions that can be taken should be limited and the systems in place should accurately report the risks being taken. The board of directors in a company should set out strict controls, such as limiting involvement in derivatives for hedging purposes only. They should set authorisation levels on transactions beyond which the board has to be informed of a transaction and they should prepare, and continuously review, control procedures. Risk management is one of the most important topics in the finance world and quantifying risk is an important function of the financial manager. These examples invariably reflect poor control systems and even where risk control systems are appropriate these control systems are only as good as the people operating them.

One of the more recent developments has been value at risk (**VAR**) analysis. In the past decade the value at risk system was developed to help quantify such risks and the use of VAR is continuing to grow among financial institutions and large companies.

Value at risk is a technique for measuring risk as a single number. VAR models produce a probability distribution for expected losses, and this probability distribution can be used to identify the maximum amount that a company can lose over a target period at a given level of probability or confidence level – the maximum likely loss. So VAR refers to a particular amount of money, the maximum amount a company is likely to lose over period, at a given level of confidence. There is a VAR estimation procedure, a numerical or statistical procedure to produce VAR figures.

Example

A bank may predict that the maximum loss from bad debts in any one week is €20 million at the 95% confidence level, or that the maximum loss on the bank's current market positions in any one day is €300 million. The bank can also set VAR limits to control risk. The same bank might have a policy that its monthly VAR for bad debts must not exceed €40 million at the 95% level of probability. Stress testing by banks is a form of VAR analysis. They use it for mortgages and company loans to see if the borrower can handle an interest rate increase of, say, 2%.

VAR has its roots in the portfolio theory developed by Markowitz in the 1950s, but is applicable across a range of different corporate exposures. These exposures include investment decisions, hedging decisions, managing portfolios, credit risk, liquidity risk, operational risk and strategic risk management.

One of the problems with VAR analysis is that it attempts to forecast future losses using past data, i.e. it assumes the past is replicated in the future. If there is a major disturbance like a stock market collapse or a global credit crunch losses may be much greater than VAR would predict. VAR models, like all models, are based on assumptions that may not be valid in certain circumstances. The important point of the criticisms is to be aware of the limitations of any system when interpreting results.

A detailed look at the value at risk techniques is outside the scope of this textbook.

20

Loans and Mortgages

CHAPTER OBJECTIVES

At the end of this chapter the student should be able to:

1. understand the various types of mortgage loans available
2. in particular, understand the difference between an annuity (repayment) and an endowment-linked mortgage
3. calculate the gross (monthly) payment for both the annuity and endowment-linked mortgage
4. calculate the net (monthly) payment for each year of the mortgage term for both the annuity and endowment-linked mortgage
5. calculate the outstanding balance on a loan/mortgage at any point during the term
6. construct an amortisation schedule
7. calculate the new payment on a loan if the rate of interest changes
8. understand the concept of refinancing a loan
9. calculate the cost of servicing a loan before and after refinancing
10. construct a savings fund schedule
11. calculate the new deposit required in a savings fund if the rate of interest changes
12. understand the basic criteria used by banks in assessing loan applications.

INTRODUCTION

This chapter deals with a number of important mathematical issues in relation to loans and mortgages. It also examines the different types of mortgage packages available in Ireland, mainly focused on the residential mortgage market. Numerical examples are given for the main types and a range of examinable questions, e.g. the impact of changing rates of interest and the impact of missed or additional payments, are provided at the end of the chapter. As the material in this chapter draws on material in earlier chapters, and the latter part of the chapter draws on the earlier part, the solutions to questions assume that the student has mastered this earlier material and will benefit from working through the examples with less hand-holding than earlier. Solutions are therefore not displayed in step-by-step detail in every case.

A short section examines briefly the lending criteria applied by commercial banks.

20.1 The Irish mortgage market

The residential mortgage market in Ireland was traditionally the preserve of the building societies, with only limited market presence by the commercial banks. This changed during the 1980s when the banks aggressively targeted this form of lending. The building societies responded by becoming more customer-oriented. With the passing of the Building Societies Act in 1989, the distinction between the two became effectively redundant from the point of view of service provision. Access to the wholesale money markets improved the consistency of funding to the building societies and **mortgage famines** became a thing of the past.

Since then a number of the largest building societies have become public limited companies and/or merged with other financial institutions. The market has become extremely competitive both in terms of cost (interest rates) and availability of finance. There has been an explosion in the range and type of finance packages available. The potential borrower is presented with a sometimes bewildering array of mortgage products. These include

- standard annuity (repayment) mortgage
- endowment-linked mortgage
- pension mortgage
- slow/low start mortgage
- payment holidays
- lump sum payments
- fixed versus variable rate.

Each of these is described in section 20.2 below.

Coupled with the general increase in loan-to-value ratios, the net result has been that consumers had far greater access to finance than ever before both for first-time buyers, for those trading up and also for residential investors. This contributed, in no small way, to the massive growth in residential prices in Ireland during the Celtic Tiger years.

20.2 Types of mortgage loans

Annuity/repayment

This is the traditional method of repaying a mortgage in which a fixed periodic payment is made for the duration of the mortgage term. The payment is made up of capital and interest, with the bulk of the payment meeting the interest charge at the beginning of the period, with only a very small capital contribution. By the end of the term the same payment is primarily being used to repay the capital debt with only a small interest component.

Prior to the 2009 Irish Budget, the interest content of the mortgage payments qualified as a tax allowance at the standard rate of tax (tax credit), up to a limit of €10,000 interest p.a. for a single first-time mortgagor in the first seven years of the mortgage and €3,000 for other single borrowers, and double these amounts for married or widowed persons.

Following the 2009 Irish Budget, first-time buyers can claim tax relief on the interest paid, up to the above limits, at the rate of 25% in years 1–2, 22.5% in years 3–5 and at

20% in years 6–7. First-time buyers relief expires after 7 years. With the exception of first-time buyers, relief can be claimed at 15% in any year of the mortgage. The effect of this is shown in section 20.5 below.[1]

Endowment-linked mortgage

With an endowment mortgage, the mortgagor only pays interest on the loan and the capital value of the loan remains constant for the duration of the term. At the same time the borrower takes out an endowment policy (effectively an investment policy). This is targeted to mature at a value which is at least as high as the loan size. The proceeds of the endowment policy are used to redeem the loan.

Up to the early 1990s these loans could be more tax-efficient than the annuity mortgage since the premium on the endowment policy could also be set off against the tax liability, and they became very popular for a period of time. They are far less popular now due to poor investment performance and the removal of the tax relief on premium payments.

This type of mortgage loan carries additional risks compared with the traditional mortgage. If the rate of interest rises during the term, the full capital value is exposed to the increased charge, whereas with the annuity mortgage some of the capital will have been paid off and the increased interest rate will be against a smaller loan balance. Clearly the opposite applies if the rate of interest falls during the mortgage term. There is also the danger (unless it is a full-cost endowment policy) that if the investment returns are not high enough, the terminal value of the policy will not reach the mortgage loan size and the borrower will have to make up the shortfall. Again this can work both ways, with the possibility of a capital bonus at the end of the term when the mortgage has been redeemed. Section 20.3 below provides a number of numerical examples.

Pension mortgage

This is similar in concept to the endowment mortgage, in that the borrower only pays interest on the mortgage loan and simultaneously contributes to a pension plan. The loan is repaid at the end of the period from the proceeds of the pension lump sum. Since pension contributions are tax allowable and the cash lump sum from a pension is tax-free, this can be a tax-efficient way to repay a mortgage. It is aimed primarily at the self-employed and those not in an occupational pension scheme.

20.2.1 New variants

Payment holidays

Breaks in repayments can be taken, say, for up to three months for particular family needs, e.g. the birth of a child, house renovations, etc. The missed payments can be dealt with by increasing the term of the mortgage or by increasing the size of the remaining payments in order to pay off the mortgage in the original time frame. This facility may not be available if the loan is at a fixed rate. A related facility is where repayments are made 10 or 11 times a year rather than the normal 12, with the payment being missed at, say, Christmas and at summer holiday time.

Slow/low start mortgage

This is aimed at the first-time buyer, either a single person or a couple who may be trying to furnish a home at the same time as starting to pay off the mortgage. It allows for reduced payments for a period of time to give the borrower(s) some breathing space to meet other expenses. It may simply be a moratorium on capital payments, e.g. the borrower only meets the interest charge and the capital value of the loan remains the same until the payments are increased. If the payment doesn't meet the interest charge, then this will be capitalised, i.e. added to the loan size. The borrower then faces an increased payment later.

Lump sum payments

Here the borrower can make occasional lump sum payments which will reduce the capital debt and therefore reduce the interest charge on the loan. This will lead to the term of the mortgage being shortened. It is of particular benefit to individuals who may occasionally make abnormal or windfall gains, e.g. end-of-year bonuses. This type of lump sum payment facility may not be available if the mortgage is at a fixed rate of interest.

20.3 Calculating the mortgage payment

Endowment

In the case of the endowment mortgage, the payment is simply the rate of interest applied to the capital value of the loan plus the endowment policy premium.

Example 20.1 Calculating the payments for an interest only mortgage

A loan of €200,000 is taken out over a 15-year period. The rate of interest is 6% p.a. payable monthly and the endowment policy premium costs €875 per month. The monthly cost of servicing the mortgage is therefore

Payment to bank: €200,000 × 0.005 =	1,000
Endowment policy premium	875
Total	1,875

Note: the interest charge per month is 0.06/12 = 0.005

The endowment policy is targeted to reach a terminal value of at least €200,000 at the end of 15 years.

Example 20.2 Calculating the mortgage payment for an annuity mortgage

The cost of an annuity mortgage for the same amount as above, where the interest is charged on a reducing balance basis, can be calculated using the ordinary simple annuity formula introduced in Chapter 4. (Note: The precise formula used by the lending institutions for calculating the size of the periodic payment is somewhat more complicated. This formula provides a close approximation where the interest is charged on a reducing balance basis.)

Using the figures from the example above

$$€200,000 = P_t \left[\frac{1 - (1.005)^{-180}}{0.005} \right]$$

solving for Pt gives a figure of €1,687.71

This payment is broken into interest and capital components.

In the first month the interest charge is €200,000 × 0.005 = €1,000.

The amount available for capital payment is therefore €687.71.

This will be used to reduce the capital debt which now reduces to €200,000 − €687.71 = €198,312.29.

The interest charge in the second month is €198,312.29 × 0.005 = €991.56.

The amount available for capital payment in the second month is therefore €1,687.71 − €991.56 = €696.15.

This process continues for each payment period, with the interest component declining and the capital component rising.

20.4 Amortisation schedule

The amortisation schedule shows the manner in which the debt is written down over the life of the loan. The schedule is drawn up as described above. The amortisation schedule is shown in Table 20.1 below.

Using the data in Example 20.2 above, it can be seen from the amortisation schedule that the interest element is declining and the capital element is rising over the course of the repayment term. The final payment is slightly smaller than the previous one since the monthly payment was rounded up to the nearest cent.

The total paid over the first year can be divided into interest and capital payments.

It can also be seen that the amount of capital paid in the first year can be calculated either as the sum of the capital payments column or by subtracting the outstanding balance at the end of the 12th month from the opening balance.

Table 20.1 Amortisation schedule

Time	Payment	Interest	Capital	Balance
0				200,000
1	1,687.71	1,000.00	687.71	199,312.29
2	1,687.71	995.56	691.15	198,621.14
3	1,687.71	993.11	694.60	197,926.54
4	1,687.71	989.63	698.08	197,228.46
5	1,687.71	986.14	701.57	196,526.89
6	1,687.71	982.63	705.08	195,821.82
7	1,687.71	979.11	708.60	195,113.22
8	1,687.71	975.57	712.14	194,401.07
9	1,687.71	972.01	715.70	193,685.37
10	1,687.71	968.43	719.28	192,966.08
11	1,687.71	964.83	722.88	192,243.20
12	1,687.71	961.22	726.49	191,516.71
Year 1	20,252.52	11,769.23	8,483.29	8,483.29
177				5,013.96
178	1,687.71	25.07	1,662.64	3,351.32
179	1,687.71	16.76	1,670.95	1,680.37
180	1,688.77	8.40	1,680.37	0.00

It can also be seen that the total paid over the first year can be divided into interest and capital payments. The summary shown for the first year is used in section 20.5 to determine the amount of tax relief available and the resultant net payment.

Outstanding balance during the term

The schedule could be completed for all 180 months. To avoid doing this, the balance at the end of the 177th month is calculated and the last three months are shown. The outstanding balance at any point in time can be calculated from either of the following two formulae:

(a) **Retrospective method**

$$OB_h = PV\,(1+k)^h - P_t \left[\frac{(1+k)^h - 1}{k} \right] \qquad (20.1)$$

where
PV = present value(loan size)
P_t = periodic payment
k = interest rate per conversion period
h = number of payments already made

The logic of the above formula is:

- The first term represents the value that the loan would have reached if no payments had been made against it, i.e. it is the original balance compounded by the rate of interest for the relevant number of periods.
- The second term represents the value of a notional savings fund into which the payments have been lodged and which pays the same rate of interest as the charge on the loan.
- The loan balance is the difference between the two. It can be shown that, where h = n, i.e. the end of the loan term, the balance is zero.

(b) Prospective method

$$OB_h = P_t \left[\frac{1 - (1 + k)^{-(n-h)}}{k} \right] \qquad (20.2)$$

where
P_t = periodic payment
k = interest rate per conversion period
n = planned total number of payments
h = number of payments already made

This method requires that the final payment be the same as previous payments, otherwise an adjustment has to be made to the formula.

The logic of this formula is that the balance at any point has the same value as a loan which could be taken out at that point, to be repaid at the same rate of interest, with the same size and number of payments remaining. This is just the present value at that point of the $(n - h)$ remaining payments. The formula is the same as the formula for the present value of an ordinary simple annuity.

Example 20.3 *Finding the outstanding balance using the retrospective method*

Using the data in Example 20.2 find the outstanding balance at the end of the
(a) 12th month
(b) 177th month

(a)
$$OB_{12} = 200{,}000\,(1.005)^{12} - 1687.71\,\frac{(1.005)^{12} - 1}{0.005}$$

$$= 212{,}335.56 - 20{,}818.85 = 191{,}516.71$$

(b)
$$OB_{177} = 200{,}000\,(1.005)^{177} - 1687.71\,\frac{(1.005)^{177} - 1}{0.005}$$

$$= 483{,}529.44 - 478{,}515.48 = 5{,}013.96$$

Example 20.4 Finding the outstanding balance using the prospective method

Using the data in Example 20.2 find the outstanding balance at the end of the
(a) 12th month
(b) 177th month

(a) $$OB_{12} = 1,687.71 \, \frac{1 - (1.005)^{-168}}{0.005} = 191,516.25$$

(b) $$OB_{177} = 1,687.71 \, \frac{1 - (1.005)^{-3}}{0.005} = 5,012.92$$

Note that using the prospective method the answers are slightly incorrect. This is because
the final payment is not the same as all the previous ones. This can be corrected by
omitting the final payment from the calculation and discounting it separately.

20.5 Gross versus net payments

Interest payments on mortgage loans qualify for tax relief at varying rates. The 2009 Irish
Budget made some changes to mortgage interest tax relief.
    The relief in force from January 2009 was as follows:

Relief – First-time buyers (FTB)

Year	Rate of relief
1	25%
2	25%
3	22.5%
4	22.5%
5	22.5%
6	20%
7	20%

After 7 years, the FTB status lapses and all mortgagors are deemed to be non-FTB. Non-
FTB relief was at 15% in all years.[2]

Maximum allowable interest

	Single	Married
FTB	€10,000	€20,000
Non-FTB	€3,000	€6,000

The tax allowance is the amount of interest paid, subject to the maximum values shown
above. The maximum annual tax relief for a:

- single FTB was €10,000 × 25% = €2,500.
- single non-FTB was €3,000 × 15% = €450.

Tax relief for married or widowed persons is double the above amounts. Relief is deducted at source by lenders.

To introduce the concept of tax relief in a simple way, the examples below assume a single first-time mortgagor and assume that the mortgage is held for the full term.

20.5.1 Endowment Mortgage

In the case of the endowment mortgage, assuming no change in the rate of interest, the amount of interest paid each year remains constant, therefore the tax relief for the first seven years drops down in line with the percentage relief available. It then steps down to a new level based on a lower available interest, at which it remains constant for the rest of the term. The net payment (gross payment less tax relief) therefore steps up a little over the first seven years but then significantly after seven years. Using the information in Example 20.1 above, this can be calculated as follows:

Annual tax relief

Years	1–2	3–5	6–7	8–15
Interest paid (€)	12,000	12,000	12,000	12,000
Allowable interest (€)	10,000	10,000	10,000	3,000
Relief @	25%	22.50%	20%	15%
Tax relief (€)	2500	2250	2000	450

Monthly equivalent

Monthly relief *	208.33	187.50	166.67	37.50
Gross payment **	1875.00	1875.00	1875.00	1875.00
Tax relief	208.33	187.50	166.67	37.50
Net payment	1666.67	1687.50	1708.33	1837.50

* = Annual tax relief/12
** = €1,000 interest on loan + €875 endowment premium

20.5.2 Annuity Mortgage

Using the information in Example 20.2 above produces the results shown in Table 20.2. It can be seen that the tax relief diminishes from €208.33 per month in the first year to €8.04 per month in the last year, and that the net payment rises from €1,479.38 per month in the first year to €1,679.67 per month in the last year.

Table 20.2 Annuity mortgage payments

Loan	Term	Interest Rate
200000	180	0.005
Payment = 1687.71		

MONTHLY

Year	Gross Payment	Tax Relief	Net Payment
1	1687.71	208.33	1479.38
2	1687.71	208.33	1479.38
3	1687.71	187.50	1500.21
4	1687.71	187.50	1500.21
5	1687.71	177.65	1510.06
6	1687.71	146.83	1540.88
7	1687.71	135.07	1552.64
8	1687.71	37.50	1650.21
9	1687.71	37.50	1650.21
10	1687.71	37.50	1650.21
11	1687.71	37.50	1650.21
12	1687.71	37.50	1650.21
13	1687.71	35.69	1652.02
14	1687.71	22.28	1665.43
15	1687.71	8.04	1679.67

The working calculations are shown in the accompanying table.

Working calculations

End Year	Outstanding Balance	Year	Capital Paid	Interest Paid	Interest Allowable	Annual Tax Relief	Monthly Tax Relief
0	200000.00						
1	191516.71	1	8483.29	11769.23	10000.00	2500.00	208.33
2	182510.19	2	9006.52	11246.00	10000.00	2500.00	208.33
3	172948.17	3	9562.02	10690.50	10000.00	2250.00	187.50
4	162796.38	4	10151.79	10100.73	10000.00	2250.00	187.50
5	152018.45	5	10777.93	9474.59	9474.59	2131.78	177.65
6	140575.77	6	11442.69	8809.83	8809.83	1761.97	146.83
7	128427.32	7	12148.45	8104.07	8104.07	1620.81	135.07
8	115529.58	8	12897.74	7354.78	3000.00	450.00	37.50
9	101836.34	9	13693.24	6559.28	3000.00	450.00	37.50
10	87298.53	10	14537.81	5714.71	3000.00	450.00	37.50
11	71864.07	11	15434.47	4818.05	3000.00	450.00	37.50
12	55477.63	12	16386.43	3866.09	3000.00	450.00	37.50
13	38080.52	13	17397.11	2855.41	2855.41	428.31	35.69
14	19610.39	14	18470.13	1782.39	1782.39	267.36	22.28
15	0.00	15	19610.39	643.19	643.19	96.48	8.04

The pattern of the gross and net payments under the two mortgage types is shown in the graph below.

Figure 20.1 Gross and net monthly mortgage payments

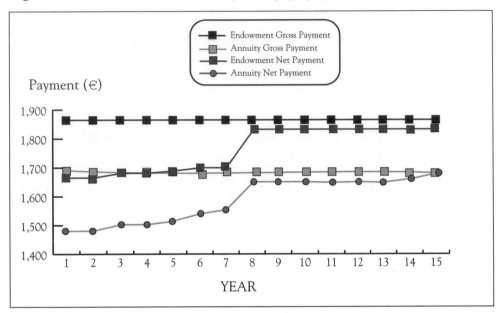

It can be seen that the net payment under the annuity mortgage rises over the course of the term and almost equals the gross payment in the final year, whereas the net payment under the endowment mortgage peaks in the 8th year and remains at that level thereafter.

20.6 Missed payments

If payments are missed in a loan repayment schedule (either through default or through an agreed payment holiday), the borrower must either increase the remaining payments or increase the term of the loan.

Example 20.5 Missed payments

A borrower is repaying a loan of €60,000 subject to interest at a rate of 13.2% p.a. compounded monthly with equal monthly payments over a period of ten years, the first payment one month after the loan is taken out. The payments due at the end of the 70th, 71st, and 72nd months are missed.

(a) If the borrower continues with the same monthly payment as before at the end of the 73rd month, calculate the number of payments required to clear the loan.
(b) If the borrower increases the remaining payments starting at the end of the 73rd month in order to repay the loan in the same time as originally scheduled, find the size of these new payments.

The parameters required to find the original payment and the outstanding balance after 69 payments are:

PV = 60,000
n = 120 months
k = 0.011 per month.

The original payment works out at €902.96. The outstanding balance after the payment at time 69 is made is got from formula 20.1 above and works out at €35,100.90.

Since the borrower makes no payments in time 70, 71 and 72, this balance will be charged interest at the rate on 1.1% per month for the next 3 months (i.e. until time 72). The balance at time 72 will therefore be €36,272.02.

(Note that the interest in month 73 should not be calculated as it will be taken into account in the ordinary simple annuity formula.)

(a) The required number of payments can be calculated using the following parameters. The situation is effectively treated as a new loan from this point on with an 'opening' balance equal to 36,272.02.

PV = 36,272.02
Pt = 902.96
k = 0.011
n = unknown number of payments to be calculated.

This produces an answer of 53.3. This can be interpreted as 53 full payments and one final smaller payment.

(b) The required payment can be calculated using the following parameters:

PV = 36272.02
k = 0.011
n = 48 (120–72)
Pt = unknown payment size to be calculated.

This produces an answer of €976.69.

Therefore the borrower can either stick with the existing payment of €902.96 and pay the loan off in 54 more months (with the final payment somewhat smaller) or increase the payment to €976.69 and pay the loan off in the term originally intended.

20.7 Additional payments

Additional payments will have the opposite effect of a missed payment, in that they will decrease the outstanding balance at any point and lead to either a shortening of the term or a decrease in the remaining payments.

Example 20.6 Additional payments

A borrower is repaying a loan of €60,000 subject to interest at a rate of 13.2% p.a. compounded monthly with equal monthly payments over a period of ten years, the first payment one month after the loan is taken out. Suppose the borrower made an additional payment of €2,000 at the end of the 69th month.

If the borrower continues with the same monthly payment as before at the end of the 70th month, calculate the number of payments required to clear the loan.

If the borrower reduces the remaining payments starting at the end of the 70th month in order to repay the loan in the same time as originally scheduled, find the size of these new payments

(a)   The balance after 69 payments is known from the previous example and equals €35,100.09. This is now reduced by €2,000. The required number of payments can be calculated using the following parameters:
PV = 33100.09 (35,100.09 − 2,000)
Pt = 902.96
k = 0.011
n = unknown number of payments to be calculated.

This produces an answer of 47.2. This can be interpreted as 47 full payments and one final smaller payment. This is almost 4 payments less than the original 51 remaining payments.

(b)   This is similar to part (a) above except that the unknown factor is now the periodic payment. The required payment can be calculated using the following parameters:
PV = 33,100.09
k = 0.011
n = 51 (120 − 69)
Pt = unknown payment size to be calculated.

This produces an answer of €851.48.

Therefore the borrower can either stick with the existing payment of €902.96 and pay the loan off in 48 more months (with the final payment somewhat smaller) or reduce the payment to €851.48 and pay the loan off in the term originally intended.

20.8 Change in the rate of interest

All of the examples discussed so far assume that the rate of interest remains the same for the duration of the loan term. In practice this will rarely be the case and rates of interest can be expected to change a number of times over the course of a normal mortgage term, i.e. 15, 20 or 25 years. If the borrower opts for a fixed rate loan this will overcome the issue of changing rates, but a fixed rate would normally not be available for 15 or 20 years. The example below looks at the impact of a change in the rate of interest on both the gross and net payment for an annuity and endowment mortgage.

Example 20.7 Change in the rate of interest

You are a first-time buyer and taking out a €160,000 mortgage loan repayable over 15 years. The local bank is quoting an interest rate of 4.8% p.a. compounded monthly on an annuity mortgage and a rate of 5.4% on an endowment-linked mortgage. The premium payable on the endowment policy would be €550 per month, payable at the same time as the mortgage payment. The interest content of mortgage repayments (up to a maximum interest of €10,000 per annum for the first seven years of the mortgage and up to a maximum of €3,000 otherwise) qualifies as a tax allowance. Tax relief can be claimed on the interest paid, up to the above limits, at the rate of 25% in years 1–2, 22.5% in years 3–5, 20% in years 6–7 and 15% in subsequent years.

Calculate for both options:

(a) the gross monthly repayment
(b) the net monthly repayment in the first year
(c) the net monthly repayment in the twelfth year
(d) the net monthly repayment in the twelfth year, if the nominal rate of interest on both options rose by 0.6% p.a. compounded monthly at the end of the eleventh year and the gross monthly repayments for the remaining four years of the mortgage were reduced to a new equal value to reflect the new interest rate.

Annuity
The monthly payment is calculated from 4.8 above as €1,248.66.

Endowment

The monthly payment to the bank is calculated as €160,000 × 0.0045	=	720
Add the endowment policy premium	=	550
Total	=	1,270

(b) and (c) Net payments
Interest paid (annuity)

		Year 1		Year 12	
Outstanding balance	Time 0	160,000.00	Time 132	54,435.07
	Time 12	152,533.23	Time 144	41,788.21
Capital paid	Year 1	7,466.77	Year 12	12,646.86
Total paid	Year 1	14,983.92	Year 12	14,983.92
Interest paid	Year 1	7,517.15	Year 12	2,337.06

Endowment
Interest paid = $720 \times 12 = 8{,}640$

Tax Relief

Annual	Annuity		Endowment	
	Y1	Y12	Y1	Y12
Interest paid	7,517.15	2,337.06	8,640.00	8,640.00
Allowable int.	7,517.15	2,337.06	8,640.00	3,000.00
Tax relief	1,879.29	350.56	2,160.00	450.00
Monthly Relief	156.61	29.21	180.00	37.50
Gross payment	1,248.66	1,248.66	1,270.00	1,270.00
Tax relief	156.61	29.21	180.00	37.50
Net payment	1,092.05	1,219.45	1,090.00	1,232.50

(d) Change in the rate of interest
>   The rate of interest changes at the end of the 11th year.
>   Calculate the loan balance at this point.

Annuity
Outstanding balance @ time 132 using 20.1 = 54,435.07

Endowment
Balance = original loan size = 160,000

New monthly payment
Annuity
The outstanding balance is treated conceptually like a new loan at this point. The periodic payment can be found using 4.8.

>   PV = 54,435.07*
>   k = 0.0045
>   n = 48
> P_t = unknown payment size to be calculated.

* Balance at the time the new interest rate becomes operational.

The monthly payment works out at €1,263.49.

Endowment

The monthly payment to the bank is calculated as €160,000 × 0.005	=	800
Add the endowment policy premium	=	550
Total	=	1,350

Net payments:
Interest paid:
Annuity – Year 12

Outstanding balance	Time 132	54,435.07	(start of 'new' loan)
	Time 144	41,905.60	(use h = 12)
Capital paid	Year 12	12,529.47	
Total paid	Year 12	15,161.88	
Interest paid	Year 12	2,632.41	

Endowment – Year 12
Interest paid = $800 \times 12 = 9,600$

Tax relief
Year 12

Annual	Annuity	Endowment
Interest paid	2,632.41	9,600.00
Allowable interest	2,632.41	3,000.00
Tax relief	394.86	450.00
Monthly tax relief	32.91	37.50
Gross payment	1,263.49	1,350.00
Tax relief	32.91	37.50
Net payment	1,230.58	1,312.50

20.9 Refinancing loans

Borrowers are sometimes presented with opportunities to refinance existing loans, i.e. borrowing from a second financial institution and paying off the first. If the new financial package is at a lower rate of interest than the existing loan, then the borrower stands to gain. Against that, however, there may be a penalty or other charge imposed by the original lender. The borrower would then have to borrow more than is currently owed in order to redeem the existing loan. Therefore it becomes a trade-off between a higher loan balance at a lower rate of interest versus a lower loan balance at a higher rate of interest. The refinancing option is worth taking if the periodic payment required to clear the new loan is lower than the existing periodic payment or, alternatively, if sticking with the existing payment, the second loan would be paid off more quickly than the first.

Example 20.8 Refinancing a loan

Using the information in Example 20.2 above, suppose the borrower is offered an alternative source of finance at the end of the fifth year at a rate of interest of 4.8% p.a., but the original bank charges an early repayment penalty of €500 plus the amount of interest which was paid in the previous six months. Should the borrower refinance the loan?

Calculate the balance on the loan at the time the refinancing option becomes available using 20.1 with h = 60.

Balance at time 60 = €152,018.45

The borrower needs to borrow this amount plus the penalty in order to redeem the loan.

Penalty	€
OB at time 60	= 152,018.45
OB at time 54	= 157,488.04
Capital paid (time 55–60)	= 5,469.59
Total paid (time 55–60)	= 10,126.26
Interest paid (time 55–60)	= 4,656.67
Penalty	= 4,656.67 + 500 = 5,156.67
Need to borrow	152,018.45 + 5,156.67 = 157,175.12

The choice is now between continuing an existing loan valued at 152,018.45 at a rate of interest of 6% p.a. compounded monthly, or a loan of 157,175.12 at a rate of interest of 4.8% p.a. compounded monthly, each to be paid off over 10 years with monthly payments.

The new periodic payment can be calculated with the following parameters:

PV = 157,175.12
n = 120
k = 0.004

This produces a payment of €1,651.76.

Since 1,651.76<1,687.71 the borrower should re-finance the loan.

20.10 More complex loan analysis

Example 20.9 Loan analysis – a more complex example

A company is borrowing €50,000 for a period of 12 years. The bank charges interest at a rate of 1.2% per month. The bank agrees to the following repayment schedule:
(a) A payment of €2,500 at the end of each year starting one year after the loan is taken out.
(b) An equal payment at the end of each month , starting one month after the loan is taken out. The monthly payment would be made even in those months when the annual €2,500 payment is made.
   (i) Show the first three and last three lines of the amortisation schedule.
   (ii) Suppose the rate of interest above changed to 1.1% per month at the end of the seventh year, and the company reduced the monthly payment to a new equal value but continued to make the annual €2,500 payment. Show the last three lines of the amortisation schedule.

Solution

(i) The repayment stream involves two separate annuities:

- an annual payment of €2,500
- a monthly payment to be determined.

First find the value of the loan which the annual payment stream can support. To do this the annual effective rate of interest must be determined. With a monthly rate of 1.2%, the annual effective rate is 15.39%.

The loan size sustainable by these payments is found from the following parameters:

$Pt = 2,500$
$n = 12$ years
$k = 0.1539$ per year.

This gives a loan size of €13,329.01. The remainder of the total loan of €50,000 must be repaid with monthly payments. The size of this 'second' notional loan is €50,000 – €13,329.01 = €36,670.99. The monthly payment required to pay this off can be found from the following parameters:

$PV = 36,670.99$
$n = 144$ months
$k = 0.012$ per month.

This produces a monthly payment of €536.31.

Amortisation schedule

Time	Payment	Interest	Capital	Balance
0				50,000.00
1	536.31	600.00	– 63.69*	50.063.69
2	536.31	600.76	– 64.45	50,128.14
3	536.31	601.54	– 65.23	50,193.37

* Note that the capital payment is negative, i.e. the payment made does not even cover the interest and so the loan balance will increase rather than decrease. This arises because the annual payments are relatively high and the resultant monthly payments are accordingly lower. The interest in the first month is against a loan balance of the full €50,000, whereas the monthly payment of €536.31 is designed to amortise a loan of €36,670.99.

An interesting test for the student is to determine for how long the loan balance will rise and from what point it will start to fall continuously each month. The answer is that the balance will rise each month until the end of the third year (with the exception of a temporary reduction in the balance at the end of the first year and the end of the second year) and then fall continuously thereafter.

Time	Payment	Interest	Capital	Balance
141				3,981.65**
142	536.31	47.78	488.53	3,493.12
143	536.31	41.92	494.39	2,998.73
144	534.71 + 2,500	35.98	2,998.73	0.00

** The outstanding balance at time 141 involves two calculations.

The outstanding balance on the 'monthly' loan can be found from the following parameters:

PV = 36.670.99
Pt = 536.31
h = 141 months
k = 0.012 per month.

This produces an outstanding balance of €1,569.53.

The balance on the 'annual' loan can be found by simply discounting the remaining payment of 2,500 back for three months, i.e.

$$\frac{2,500}{(1.012)^3} = 2,412.12$$

The total outstanding balance is the sum of the two components, i.e. 1,569.53 + 2,412.12 = €3,981.65.

(ii) Outstanding balance at end year 7 is calculated in two parts as shown above.

PV = 36,670.99
Pt = 536.31
h = 84 months
k = 0.012 per month.

This produces an outstanding balance of €22,844.12.

The balance on the 'annual' loan can be found from the following parameters:

Pt = 2,500
n = 12 years
h = 7 years
k = 0.1539 per year.

This produces a value of €8,303.58.

The total outstanding balance is therefore €31,147.70.

First find the value of loan which the remaining annual payments can support. To do this the annual effective rate of interest must be determined. With a monthly rate of 1.1%, the annual effective rate is 14.03%.

The loan size sustainable by these payments is found from the following parameters:

Pt = 2,500
n = 5 years
k = 0.1403 per year.

This gives a loan size of €8,576.52. The remainder of the total outstanding balance on the loan of €22,571.18 (€31,147.70 − €8,576.52 = €22,571.18) must be repaid with monthly payments. The monthly payment required to pay this off can be found from the following parameters:

PV = 22,571.18
n = 60 months
k = 0.011 per month.

This produces a monthly payment of €515.88.

Amortisation schedule

Time	Payment	Interest	Capital	Balance
141				3,933.29***
142	515.88	43.27	472.61	3,460.68
143	515.88	38.07	477.81	2,982.87
144	515.68 + 2,500	32.81	2,982.87	0.00

*** The outstanding balance at time 141 involves two calculations.

The outstanding balance on the 'monthly' loan can be found from the following parameters:

PV = 22,571.18
Pt = 515.88
h = 57 months
k = 0.011 per month.

This produces an outstanding balance of €1,514.01.

The balance on the 'annual' loan can be found by simply discounting the remaining payment of €2,500 back for three months, i.e.

$$\frac{2,500}{(1.011)^3} = €2,419.28$$

The total outstanding balance is the sum of the two components, i.e. €1,514.01 + €2,419.28 = €3,933.29.

20.11 Savings fund schedule

Another mechanism through which a debt, due to be paid at some time in the future, may be discharged is by establishing a fund into which regular payments are made. The fund is targeted to reach an amount sufficient to repay the debt at the appropriate time. The fund grows in value through both the payments made into it and the interest earned on the fund. The advantage of this method of discharging a debt for an individual is that it creates a discipline of setting aside a regular or periodic amount, rather than having to meet the entire debt at the end. For a company redeeming, say, a zero coupon bond, it could lead to a well-structured cash-flow management procedure.

Savings fund schedule

This shows the manner in which a savings fund is built up over time.

Payments into the fund may be equal, though this is not necessary. For the purposes of the presentation here, it is assumed that regular equal payments are made.

Recall from Chapter 4 the ordinary simple annuity, which is where an equal payment/deposit is made into a fund, paying interest at the same frequency as the payments and at the same time that the payments are being made. The formula for the future value of an ordinary simple annuity was given as formula 4.7.

$$FV = Pt\left[\frac{(1 + k)^n - 1}{k}\right] \tag{20.3}$$

Each period the fund grows as a result of:

- interest earned on existing fund
- new deposits made.

Over the term of the fund the interest earned each period increases.

Example 20.10 Savings fund schedule

John has promised to give his grandson €30,000 when he leaves college in four years' time and goes off on his round-the-world trip. He can invest in a fund which will pay 0.25% per month. He intends to deposit an equal amount into the fund at the end of each month for the next four years starting at the end of this month. Show the savings fund schedule each month for the first year and for the final three months.

Using 4.7 with:

n = 48
k = 0.0025
FV = €30,000.

This gives a monthly deposit of €589.03.

Suppose that the payment is rounded down to €589.00 for convenience.

The savings fund schedule is shown below:

Table 20.3

	Target	Term	Interest Rate
	30,000	48	0.0025
	Payment =	589.03	
	Round =	589.00	

Time	Payment	Interest	Increase in Fund	Balance
0				0
1	589.00	0.00	589.00	589.00
2	589.00	1.47	590.47	1,179.47
3	589.00	2.95	591.95	1,771.42
4	589.00	4.43	593.43	2,364.85
5	589.00	5.91	594.91	2,959.76
6	589.00	7.40	596.40	3,556.16
7	589.00	8.89	597.89	4,154.05
8	589.00	10.39	599.39	4,753.44
9	589.00	11.88	600.88	5,354.32
10	589.00	13.39	602.39	5,956.71
11	589.00	14.89	603.89	6,560.60
12	589.00	16.40	605.40	7,166.00
45				28,016.41
46	589.00	70.04	659.04	28,675.45
47	589.00	71.69	660.69	29,336.14
48	590.52	73.34	663.86	30,000.00

Each line of the schedule is calculated as follows:

- Using the fund value at the end of the previous period, calculate the interest in the current period by multiplying by the rate of interest per period. In line 4 of this example the relevant calculation is €1,771.42 × 0.0025 = €4.43.
- Add this interest amount to the regular payment to get the total addition to the fund in this period. In line 4 of this example, the relevant calculation is €589.00 + €4.43 = €593.43.
- Add this amount to the fund value in the previous period to get the fund value in this period. In line 4 of this example, the relevant calculation is €1,771.42 + €593.43 = €2,364.85.

In the schedule above it can be seen that the amount of interest earned increases in each period, and therefore the total addition to the fund each period is growing.

Example 20.11

Change the term of the saving fund in Example 20.10 above to 36 months, round the deposit up to the nearest € and show the first five and last five lines of the schedule.

Solution:

Table 20.4 Savings fund schedule

	Target	Term	Interest Rate		
	30,000	36	0.0025		
	Payment =	797.44			
	Round =	798.00			

Time	Payment	Interest	Increase in Fund	Balance
0				0.00
1	798.00	0.00	798.00	798.00
2	798.00	2.00	800.00	1,598.00
3	798.00	3.99	801.99	2,399.99
4	798.00	6.00	804.00	3,203.99
5	798.00	8.01	806.01	4,010.00
31				**25,688.49**
32	798.00	64.22	862.22	26,550.71
33	798.00	66.38	864.38	27,415.09
34	798.00	68.54	866.54	28,281.63
35	798.00	70.70	868.70	29,150.33
36	776.79	72.88	849.67	30,000.00

Finding the fund value at a given point in time

In Example 20.10 above, the fund value after 5 deposits is 2,959.76. Suppose you wish to know the value after 45 deposits. It would take too long to work through 45 lines of the schedule, but the amount in the fund can be calculated by using the FV formula (4.7).

Example 20.12 Finding the fund value

Using the information in example 20.10 above, calculate the fund value after 5 deposits and again after 45 deposits.

Using 4.7 with
n = 5 and n = 45 gives
FV_5 = €2,959.76 and
FV_{45} = €28,016.41

These are the figures given in the schedule shown in Table 20.3.

The final line of the schedule is calculated slightly differently from the other lines. The sequence of steps shown below should be followed:

- Using the fund value at the end of the second last period, calculate the interest in the final period as normal.
- Add this interest to previous fund value.
- Subtract this from target.
- This gives the final deposit required.

In some cases the interest alone in the final period may carry the total over target. If so, no deposit is required in the final period.

Example 20.13 Savings fund schedule – a more complex example

A couple are saving for a deposit on a new holiday home. They wish to have €80,000 four years from now. They lodge €5,000 now into a fund paying interest at 3.6% p.a. compounded monthly and intend to make the following payments into the fund:

- annual deposits of €10,000 at the end of each of the next four years
- 48 monthly deposits starting one month from now.

(a) Show the first three and last three lines of the savings fund schedule.
(b) Suppose the rate of interest changed to 3% p.a. compounded monthly at the end of the second year, and the monthly deposits for the last two years was increased to a new value, which ensured that the target of €80,000 would be achieved at the end of the fourth year. Calculate the size of the new monthly deposit.

(a)

The savings fund is made up of three different components:

- the initial deposit of €5,000
- the 4 annual deposits of €10,000
- the 48 monthly deposits.

First find the value that the initial deposit of €5,000 will grow to by the end of the 4th year (48th month).

This is a compound interest calculation.

PV = €5,000
n = 48
k = 0.003 (note that this is the monthly rate of interest)

This produces FV = €5,773.18

Note that the annual effective rate of interest (3.66%) could have been used with n = 4 years.

Next find the value at the end of year 4 of the 4 annual deposits of €10,000.
   This is the future value of an ordinary simple annuity and can be found using formula 4.7 with:

P_t = €10,000
n = 4
k = 0.0366 (note that this is the annual effective rate of interest)

This produces FV = €42,250.07

These two amounts sum to €48,023.25. Therefore the monthly deposits must make up the remaining €31,976.75 (€80,000 – €48,023.25). The required monthly deposit can then be found from formula 4.7 with:

FV = €31,976.75
n = 48
k = 0.003 (note that this is the monthly rate of interest)

This produces Pt = €620.37

The sinking fund schedule is shown below:

Table 20.5 Savings fund schedule

Time	Payment	Interest	Increase in Fund	Balance
0	5,000.00		5,000.00	5,000.00
1	620.37	15.00	635.37	5,635.37
2	620.37	16.91	637.27	6,272.64
3	620.37	18.82	639.18	6,911.82
45				67,523.78
46	620.37	202.57	822.94	68,346.71
47	620.37	205.04	825.41	69,172.12
48	10,620.37	207.52	10,827.88	80,000.00

In order to show the final three lines, the fund value at time 45 must be calculated. This requires three separate calculations.

Initial deposit

The value of the initial deposit of €5,000 at time 45 can be calculated from the compound interest formula with:

PV = €5,000
n = 45
k = 0.003 (note that this is the monthly rate of interest)

This produces FV = €5,721.53.

Note that in this instance the annual effective rate of interest (3.66%) could not have been used since the time period is not an exact number of years.

Annual deposits

Only 3 of the annual deposits will have been made by the end of the 45th month (i.e. at times 12, 24 and 36). To find the value of these at time 45, first find the value at time 36 from formula 4.7 with:

Pt = €10,000
n = 3
k = 0.0366 (note that this is the annual effective rate of interest)

This produces FV = €31,111.40.

Nine months compound interest must now be added to this to get the value at time 45. Using the compound interest formula with:

PV = €31,111.40
n = 9
k = 0.003 (note that this is the monthly rate of interest)

This produces FV = €31961.55.

Monthly deposits

The value of the monthly deposits at time 45 can be found using formula 4.7 with:

Pt = €620.37
n = 45
k = 0.003

This produces FV = €29,840.70.

Adding the three amounts together gives €67,523.78 as shown on the savings fund schedule.

(b)

The value of the fund at the time of the change in the rate of interest must be calculated. This again involves three separate calculations.

Applying the same approach as above, the values at time 24 are:

Initial deposit	€5,372.70
Annual deposits	€20,366.00
Monthly deposits	€15,413.90
Total	€41,152.60

The rate of interest now changes to 3% p.a. compounded monthly.

The amount above can be notionally placed into a separate account in which it will earn compound interest for the next two years. Its value at time 48 can be found from the compound interest formula with:

$PV = €41,152.60$
$n = 24$
$k = 0.0025$ (note that this is the new monthly rate of interest)

This produces $FV = €43,694.06$.

The value at time 48 of the two remaining annual deposits can be calculated from formula 4.7 with:

$Pt = €10,000$
$n = 2$
$k = 0.0304$ (note that this is the new annual effective rate of interest)

This produces $FV = €20,304.16$.

These two amounts sum to €63,998.22
  Therefore the monthly deposits must make up the remaining €16,001.78 (€80,000 − €63,998.22). The required monthly deposit can then be found from formula 4.7 with:

$FV = €16,001.78$
$n = 24$
$k = 0.0025$ (note that this is the monthly rate of interest)

This produces $Pt = €647.77$.
  Note that the new deposit is higher than the original deposit, since the rate of interest has fallen and so more of the target value of €80,000 has to be generated from the deposits to the fund.

20.12 Bank lending criteria

This section discusses the criteria applied by the lending institutions in assessing loans both for personal mortgages and also for commercial borrowing. The commercial lending criteria are presented in the context of lending to the property sector.

20.12.1 Personal mortgage lending criteria

The principal lending criteria relate to:

- the loan-to-value ratio (LTV)
- ratio of loan size to income (combined income) of the borrower(s)
- % of net income required to service the loan
- stability/security of borrower's income.

Loan-to-value ratio (LTV)

LTV refers to the proportion of the value of the property which the lender is prepared to lend. This may range from 75% to 90% although it can be higher. The typical figure for first-time buyers is about 90%, leaving the borrower(s) to make up the remaining 10% themselves. The LTV serves a number of purposes:

- It caps the lender's risk.
- It forces an input from the borrower's own resources.
- It acts as a buffer for the lender in a time of falling property values.
- It helps to prevent the possibility of a negative equity position for the borrower if property values fall.

If the value of the property rises, and the loan is being written down, the ratio in practice is being reduced from the start. It is a particularly important ratio from the bank's point of view if property values are at the top of a cycle at the time the loan is taken out.

Ratio of loan size to income

This is typically at a maximum of 2.5–3 times the annual earnings of the (higher earning) borrower plus one and a half times the earnings of the second borrower, in the case of a joint application. The purpose is to ensure that the loan is repayable from current earnings and does not represent too large a burden to the borrower. Clearly, as the income of the borrower(s) increases and the loan is partially redeemed, this ratio will fall. It is thus normally at its maximum at the beginning of the loan period, assuming all payments are kept up to date and income levels don't fall.

Percentage of net income required to service the loan

The lender will normally place a cap on the % of net income which should be used to service the loan. This is now one of the key measures of housing affordability used by lenders in Ireland and abroad (and also by local authorities in Ireland in exercising their housing provision function). It can be used to determine the maximum loan size that can be afforded by a borrower. A typical cap operated by lenders is in the range 30–35%, but at the height of the residential property boom in Ireland it rose to 40% and possibly higher.

Box 20.1 Sub-prime lending

Sub-prime is widely believed to have been one of the root causes of the global financial crisis which started at the latter end of 2007 and deepened dramatically in the autumn of 2008.

Borrowers who do not meet the standard credit criteria and therefore cannot access the mortgage market under normal conditions are either excluded from the residential market or seek to borrow from lenders who are prepared to loosen the criteria.

The basis of sub-prime lending is that banks lend to borrowers who don't meet the normal credit criteria. This may be because of income levels which are too low, insecurity of employment, a poor credit history, etc. In the case of poor credit histories, this form of lending is often referred to as second-chance.

As the banks are taking on an increased risk, they will add a risk premium to the interest rate charged. This increases the cost of servicing the mortgage for the borrower and exacerbates the affordability difficulties that they faced in the first place.

Sub-prime lending is often characterised by an automatic increase in the interest rate after a certain point in the mortgage term. The expectation is that either the borrower's economic circumstances will have improved before then or that the property value will have increased, allowing the loan to be refinanced on terms that are more favourable to the borrower.

The default rate with sub-prime borrowers is higher than with other borrowers. This may lead to bad debt for the banks and repossession of the property.

The global financial crisis arose partly out of the repackaging of sub-prime debt into **mortgage-backed securities** (MBS), i.e. banks raised extra capital by selling bond-like investments to investors, which were backed by sub-prime mortgages. When the rate of default on these mortgages rose, the MBS investments defaulted in turn.

20.12.3 Commercial lending criteria

This section is primarily concerned with the criteria used by the banks to assess commercial loan applications. It is presented in the context of the property sector. However, most of the criteria would be applicable to all sectors of the economy.

The property sector competes with other sectors of the economy for a share of the available lending from the financial institutions. Depending on the overall availability of funds, the property sector may find it more or less difficult to borrow money from the banks. In an environment of easy availability of bank finance, the financial institutions may compete to lend to property companies/projects. It is clear that, no matter how competitive the lending environment is, the banks will apply certain criteria in assessing loan applications.

General criteria

As with personal lending the banks will also apply general criteria to the assessment of loan applications by companies. These include:

- trading history
- equity exposure of borrower
- security offered.

Trading history of borrower

This is concerned with the borrower's track record in relation to finishing developments on time and within the original cost.

Equity exposure of borrower

This relates to how much equity the borrower is prepared to put up and whether or not it is provided from the borrower's own resources or whether there is an outside equity involvement.

Security offered

This relates to the security being offered by the borrower, its current value and potential realisable value. It is also concerned with whether or not there is a parent company guarantee and whether the loan is of a limited or non-recourse nature. Non-recourse lending is where the lender's only recourse is to the project being funded and not to other assets of the borrower.

To these general criteria could be added the lender's overall relationship with the borrower, i.e. **relationship banking**. Relationship banking refers to the ongoing business relationship that exists between borrower and lender which has been built up over time. Relationship banking works both ways. On the one hand a lender will take a more benign view of a long-established client and so the borrower benefits in having easier, perhaps less restrictive access to funds. It does, however, confer certain obligations on the borrower, e.g. not to walk away from a failed project, to prepare realistic cash flow projections for project proposals and to inform the lender at an early stage if things start to go wrong.

Specific lending criteria

In addition to the general criteria that the lender will apply there are a number of specific, technical criteria that may be enforced. These are similar in some instances to those described for personal lending, but are reproduced here in a different context.

Loan-to-value ratio (LTV)

This is one of the key criteria used by lenders. LTV refers to the proportion of the value of the project/property which the lender is prepared to put up, e.g. if a project has an expected value of €10 million, a €6 million loan would represent an LTV of 60%. While LTVs can range to higher levels, e.g. 90%, the norm would be of the order of 70%. The gap between the LTV and 100% serves a number of purposes:

- it caps the lender's risk
- it forces an equity input
- it acts as a buffer for the lender in a time of falling property values where the property is used as collateral.

Clearly the initial valuation must be realistic from the lender's point of view or else the LTV will offer a less effective safety net. In a time of inflated property values, where the only direction that values can realistically go is downwards, the banks may be prudent in reducing the LTV in order to improve the safety factor.

In a time of easy access to funding, where the banks are competing with each other to lend money, there is a danger that the LTV will be pushed upwards. While this might appear to be positive from a property development/investment point of view, it may help to over-inflate the market and/or decrease the quality of banks' loan books and hence increase the risk taken.

A loan-to-cost ratio (LTC) may be used for speculative projects as it may offer a better protection than LTV.

Income-to-interest cover

The income-to-interest cover refers to the ratio between the operating income generated by the project and available to service the interest payments on the loan, and the size of these interest payments, e.g. if a project generates an annual operating income of €1 million and the annual interest required on the loan is €800,000, then the income-to-interest cover is 1.25:1

Income-to-interest cover is sensitive to the LTV, i.e. as the LTV rises, the income-to-interest cover will fall. Lower cover ratios will probably be acceptable if the rate of interest is fixed.

20.12.4 Repayment structure

There is a wide variety of repayment structures, e.g.

- interest only with bullet payment at end of term
- regular capital and interest payment (annuity)
- interest payment with some capital payment (partial amortisation)
- deferred interest or capital payments.

20.12.5 Loan security

The quality of the collateral offered may affect either the availability or the cost of finance. The lender will be interested in the following aspects of the security offered:

- It must be capable of being valued.
- There must be a market for the asset if the lender is forced to realise it.
- The value of the security exceeds the value of the loan and it is capable of maintaining or increasing its value.

SUMMARY

- In an annuity mortgage, the regular payment is made up of capital and interest components.
- In an annuity mortgage, the capital component rises and the interest content of the payment falls as the mortgage moves through the term.
- In an endowment mortgage, interest only is paid to the lender, with a separate payment made into an endowment policy.
- The maturity value of the endowment policy is used to redeem the mortgage.
- If the rate of interest rises, endowment mortgages are more exposed than annuity mortgages as none of the capital has been paid off.
- The opposite applies in the case of falling interest rates.
- The outstanding balance on a loan can be calculated as the discounted value of the remaining payments (the prospective method).
- It can also be calculated using the retrospective method. This method adds compound interest to the loan as if no payments have been made and then nets off the value of a notional fund into which payments have been made.
- If the rate of interest on an annuity loan rises, either the payment can be increased in order to pay off the loan in the original term, or the same payment can be continued but the term of the mortgage lengthens.
- The key lending criteria applied by banks to personal lending are:
  - percentage of net income required to service the loan
  - loan-to-value ratio
  - ratio of loan size to income.
- The key lending criteria applied by banks to commercial lending are:
  - trading history of borrower
  - equity input of borrower
  - security provided
  - loan-to-value ratio
  - loan-to-cost ratio
  - income-to-interest cover.

QUESTIONS

Note: In all questions below dealing with net (after-tax) payments on mortgage loans, it is assumed that the mortgagor is a single first-time buyer and that the tax relief is as follows:

Year	Rate of relief
1	25%
2	25%
3	22.5%
4	22.5%
5	22.5%
6	20%
7	20%
Subsequent years	15%*

The maximum allowable annual interest for tax relief is €10,000 for FTB and €3,000 for non-FTB.

* After 7 years, the FTB status lapses and all mortgagors are deemed to be non-FTB. Non-FTB relief is at 15% in all years.

1.♦ Ann is due to repay a loan of €25,000 subject to interest at a rate of 9.6% p.a. compounded monthly with equal monthly payments over a period of twelve years, the first payment one month after the loan is taken out.

   (a) If the payments due at the end of the 49th, 50th and 51st months are missed, and Ann continues with the same monthly payment as before at the end of the 52nd month and the bank agrees to extend the term of the loan, show the last three lines of the amortisation schedule.

   (b) If following the missed payments as in (a) above, the rate of interest rose to 10.8% p.a. compounded monthly at the end of the 54th month, and Ann continues with the same monthly payment as before at the end of the 55th month, show the last line of the amortisation schedule.

   (c) Suppose Ann is offered an alternative source of finance at the end of the fourth year at a rate of interest of 8.4% p.a., but the original bank charges an early repayment penalty of €200 *plus* the amount of interest which would have been paid in the next six months if the loan repayment had gone ahead as usual. Should Ann refinance the loan?

2.♦ You are a first-time buyer and taking out a €200,000 mortgage loan repayable over twenty years. The local bank is quoting an interest rate of 9% p.a. compounded monthly on both an annuity mortgage and an endowment-linked mortgage. The premium payable on the endowment policy would be €400 per month, payable at the same time as the mortgage payment. The interest content of mortgage repayments (up to a maximum interest of €10,000 per annum for the first seven years of the mortgage and up to a maximum of €3,000 otherwise) qualifies as a tax allowance. Tax relief can be claimed on the interest paid, up to the above limits, at the rate of 25% in years 1–2, 22.5% in years 3–5, 20% in years 6–7, and 15% in subsequent years.

   Calculate for both options:

    (a) the gross monthly repayment.
    (b) the net monthly repayment in the first year.
    (c) the net monthly repayment in the twelfth year.
    (d) the net monthly repayment in the twelfth year, if the nominal rate of interest on both options fell by 1.2% p.a. compounded monthly at the end of the eleventh year and the gross monthly repayments for the remaining four years of the mortgage were reduced to a new equal value to reflect the new interest rate.

3. ◆(a) A small company is borrowing €35,000 for a period of seven years. The bank charges interest at a rate of 1.1% per month. The bank agrees to the following repayment schedule:

    (i) a payment of €1,500 at the end of each year starting one year after the loan is taken out.

    (ii) an equal payment at the end of each month, starting one month after the loan is taken out. The monthly payment would be made even in those months when the annual €1,500 payment is made.

    Show the first three and last three lines of the amortisation schedule.

    (b) Suppose the rate of interest in (a) above changed to 1.2% per month at the end of the third year, and the company increased the monthly payment to a new equal value but continued to make the annual €1,500 payment. Show the last three lines of the amortisation schedule.

4.   You are taking out a €240,000 mortgage loan repayable over twenty-five years. The local bank is quoting an interest rate of 4.2% p.a. compounded monthly on an annuity mortgage and a rate of 4.8% p.a. compounded monthly on an endowment-linked mortgage. The premium payable on the endowment policy would be €650 per month, payable at the same time as the mortgage payment. The interest content of mortgage repayments (up to a maximum interest of €10,000 per annum for the first seven years of the mortgage and up to a maximum of €3,000 otherwise) qualifies as a tax allowance. Tax relief can be claimed on the interest paid, up to the above limits, at the rate of 25% in years 1–2, 22.5% in years 3–5, 20% in years 6–7, and 15% in subsequent years.

    Calculate for both options:
    (a) the gross monthly repayment.
    (b) the net monthly repayment in the first year.
    (c) the net monthly repayment in the tenth year.
    (d) the net monthly repayment in the tenth year, if the nominal rate of interest on both options rose by 0.6% p.a. compounded monthly at the end of the ninth year and the gross monthly repayments for the remaining sixteen years of the mortgage were increased to a new equal value to reflect the new interest rate.

5.   (a) A company is borrowing €50,000 for a period of twelve years. The bank charges interest at a rate of 1.2% per month. The bank agrees to the following repayment schedule:

    (i) a payment of €2,500 at the end of each year starting one year after the loan is taken out.

    (ii) an equal payment at the end of each month, starting one month after the loan is taken out. The monthly payment would be made even in those months when the annual €2,500 payment is made.

Show the first three and last three lines of the amortisation schedule.

(b)   Suppose the rate of interest in (a) above changed to 1.1% per month at the end of the seventh year, and the company reduced the monthly payment to a new equal value but continued to make the annual €2,500 payment. Show the last three lines of the amortisation schedule.

6.   Tom is due to repay a loan of €20,000 subject to interest at a rate of 13.2% p.a. compounded monthly with equal monthly payments over a period of fifteen years, the first payment one month after the loan is taken out.

(a)   If the payments due at the end of the 120th, 121st and 122nd months are missed, and Tom continues with the same monthly payment as before at the end of the 123rd month and the bank agrees to extend the term of the loan, show the last three lines of the amortisation schedule.

(b)   If following the missed payments as in (a) above, the rate of interest rose to 14.4% p.a. compounded monthly at the end of the 124th month, and Tom continues with the same monthly payment as before at the end of the 125th month, show the last line of the amortisation schedule.

(c)   Suppose Tom is offered an alternative source of finance at the end of the eighth year at a rate of interest of 12% p.a., but the original bank charges an early repayment penalty of €200 *plus* the amount of interest which was paid in the previous three months. Should Tom refinance the loan?

7.   You are taking out a €300,000 mortgage loan repayable over thirty years. The local bank is quoting an interest rate of 6% p.a. compounded monthly on an annuity mortgage and a rate of 6.6% p.a. compounded monthly on an endowment-linked mortgage. The premium payable on the endowment policy would be €450 per month, payable at the same time as the mortgage payment. The interest content of mortgage repayments (up to a maximum interest of €10,000 per annum for the first seven years of the mortgage and up to a maximum of €3,000 otherwise) qualifies as a tax allowance. Tax relief can be claimed on the interest paid, up to the above limits, at the rate of 25% in years 1–2, 22.5% in years 3–5, 20% in years 6–7, and 15% in subsequent years.

Calculate for both options:

(a)   the gross monthly repayment.

(b)   the net monthly repayment in the first year.

(c)   the net monthly repayment in the fifteenth year.

(d)   the net monthly repayment in the fifteenth year, if the nominal rate of interest on both options fell by 1.2% p.a. compounded monthly at the end of the fourteenth year and the gross monthly repayments for the remaining sixteen years of the mortgage were reduced to a new equal value to reflect the new interest rate.

8.◆   A company has to repay a debt (inclusive of interest) of €60,000 in five years' time. It lodges €7,000 now into a fund paying interest at 4.2% p.a., compounded monthly, and intends to make the following payments into the fund:

•   annual deposits of €8,000 at the end of each of the next five years
•   60 equal monthly deposits starting one month from now.

(a)   Show the first three and last three lines of the savings fund schedule.

(b) Suppose the rate of interest changed to 4.8% p.a., compounded monthly, at the end of the third year, and the monthly deposit for the last two years was reduced to a new value which ensured that the target of €60,000 would be achieved at the end of the fifth year. Calculate the size of the new monthly deposit.

(c) Following on from (b) above, calculate the amount of interest earned in the fourth year.

9. A company has to repay a debt (inclusive of interest) of €50,000 in six years' time. It lodges €7,000 immediately into a fund paying interest at 7.2% p.a. compounded monthly, and intends to lodge €8,000 after one year, €9,000 after two years and €10,000 after three years. It also intends to make 72 equal monthly deposits starting one month from now. Show the first three and last three lines of the savings fund schedule.

10. A company has to repay a debt (inclusive of interest) of €180,000 in seven years' time. It lodges €12,000 now into a fund paying interest at 4.8% p.a. compounded monthly, and intends to make the following payments into the fund:
    • annual deposits of €15,000 at the end of each of the next seven years
    • 84 equal monthly deposits starting one month from now.

    (a) Show the first three and last three lines of the savings fund schedule.

    (b) Suppose the rate of interest changed to 5.4% p.a., compounded monthly, at the end of the third year, and the monthly deposit for the last four years was reduced to a new value which ensured that the target of €180,000 would be just achieved at the end of the seventh year. Calculate the size of the new monthly deposit.

    (c) Following on from (b) above, suppose the company was in a position to increase the annual payment to €17,000 for each of the last four years (i.e. end of year 4 to end of year 7 inclusive), and the monthly deposit for the last four years was reduced to a new value which ensured that the target of €180,000 would be just achieved at the end of the seventh year. Calculate the size of the new monthly deposit.

11. Discuss the main lending criteria applied by banks in relation to personal mortgage lending.

12. Discuss the main lending criteria applied by banks in relation to commercial lending.

13. Distinguish between an annuity and an endowment mortgage.

14. Distinguish between the retrospective and prospective method for calculating the outstanding balance on a loan.

15. Discuss the new features of personal mortgages now available in Ireland.

NOTES

1. Just prior to going to press on this text, the Irish Government published a supplementary Budget for 2009 (delivered to Dáil Éireann on 7 April, 2009), which altered the tax relief on mortgage interest. This appeared to redraw tax relief from all non-first-time buyers. At the end of April 2009 however, the Government announced that the Revenue Commissioners were examining the issue and that a clarification would be published during May 2009.

    The text of this chapter therefore is based on that which was announced in the original 2009 Budget (October 2008).

2. See Note 1.

Appendix 1
Solutions to Selected End of Chapter Questions

CHAPTER 1

Question 13

Because if an investor borrows long term they will fear the damage caused by increasing interest rates and this outweighs any benefit they would get from falling rates. The liquidity preference theory states that lenders prefer to lend short term and borrowers prefer to borrow long term. Borrowers pay a premium for long-term debt because there is less exposure to the risk of having to repay the debt under adverse conditions. On the other hand, lenders demand a higher return on long-term debt because they are exposed to more interest rate risk. In other words, lenders are assumed to have a liquidity preference for holding cash and therefore borrowers must offer an interest rate high enough to induce lenders to abandon their preference for holding cash. Therefore, because lending long term means giving up more liquidity, long-term rates should be higher than short-term rates.

Question 14

Because this is a treasury security both the default risk premium (DRP) and the liquidity premium (LP) are zero.

The yield	=	k
The risk free rate	=	k_{rf}
Interest rate in year one	=	R_1
Interest rate in year 2	=	R_2
Interest rate in year 3	=	R_3
DRP	=	Default Risk Premium
MRP	=	Maturity Risk Premium
LP	=	Liquidity Premium

$K = k_{rf} + LP + DRP + LP + MRP$

On a two-year treasury the inflation premium is:
$IP_2 \quad = (3\% + 5\%)/2 = 4\%$
Therefore the yield on a two-year treasury is:
$K = k_{rf} + IP + DRP + LP + MRP = 3\% + 4\% = 7\%$

On a three-year treasury security the inflation premium is:
$IP_3 = (3\% + 5\% + 5\%)/3 = 4.3\%$
Therefore the yield on a three-year treasury is:
$K = 3\% + 4.3\% = 7.3\%$

Question 17

While the shape of the yield curves would be the same the corporate security yield curve will lie above the treasury yield curve because of the default risk premium.

CHAPTER 2

Question 2

NOPAT is net income if the company had no debt and had no financial assets. NOPAT is a better indicator of the operating performance because debt reduces income.

Question 7

Net working capital = Current assets – Current liabilities = €10,000 – €3,000 = €7,000.
Net worth = Total assets – Total liabilities = €40,000 – €18,000 = €22,000.

Question 9

Profit & Loss Account	
Sales	€1,000,000
Cost of sales	€600,000
Gross profit	€400,000
Depreciation	€12,000
PBIT	€388,000
Interest	€5,000
PBT	€383,000
Tax (15%)	€57,450
Pat	€325,550

Operating cash flow (OCF) = PBIT (1 – T) + Depreciation
= €388,000 (0.85) + €1,200 = €341,800.

Question 12
(a)

Profit & Loss Account	
Sales	€1,000,000
COGS	€600,000
PBDIT	€400,000
Depreciation	€10,000
PBIT	€390,000
Interest	€3,000
PBT	€387,000
Tax	€58,050
PAT	€328,950

(b) Operating cash flow = NOPAT + Dep = €PBIT (1 – T) + Dep. = €341,500
(c) Change in operating working capital = €6,000 – €2,500 = €3,500
     Change in fixed capital = €30,000
     Gross capital expenditure = €30,000 + €10,000 = €40,000
     Change in total operating capital = €40,000 + €3,500 = €43,500
     Free cash flow = €341,500 – €43,500 = €298,000.

Question 13

Profit after tax (PAT) = €1m
Profit before interest and tax (PBIT) = €3m
Tax (T) = 15%
Interest = ?

Tax = €1m/1 – T = €1m/ (1 – 0.15) = €176,470
Interest = PBIT – PBT = €3,000,000 – €1,176,470 = €1,823,530

PBIT	€3,000,000
Interest	a'X'
PBT	€1,176,470
Tax	€176,470
PAT	€1,000,000

CHAPTER 3

Question 2

Manufacturing companies will have much larger inventories. Service companies (e.g. financial services) will not have much stock at all since financial products are paper transactions between companies. It is important therefore in analysing accounts to look at the particular business in question.

Question 4

Effects of inflation:
  (i) Earnings will rise without a corresponding increase in the volume of sales.
  (ii) Depreciation and the book value of the assets used in generating sales will remain at historic figures. However, the cost of replacing these assets is not reflected in the depreciation charged and in the book values.
 (iii) Consequently, a ratio such as earnings to total assets (ROA) will increase even though the assets are generating the same volume of sales.
 (iv) Companies whose assets have been purchased at inflated prices will have higher asset values than companies who purchased their assets earlier. Therefore, two companies with the same sales and the same physical assets will have different ROAs.

Question 8

Sales	100%
COGS	65%
Depreciation	10%
Total Operating Costs	75%
PBIT	25%
Interest	5%
PBT	20%
Tax (15%)	3%
PAT	15.5%

Question 9

(a)   (i)   Current ratio = 0.52; Acid test = 0.33
       (ii) Stock turnover = 8.8 times
     (iii) Debtors turnover = 14 times
    (iv) Days sales outstanding = 26
     (v) Cash ratio = PBIT + Depreciation / Interest = 3 times
    (vi) Times interest earned = PBIT/Interest = 1.8 times
   (vii) Total debt ratio = Total assets minus Total equity/ Total assets = 0.56.

(b)   The ROE is the ratio of net profit to total equity. This is €10/€88 = 11.3.
     With the Du Pont identity, we can write the ROE as:
     ROE = Profit margin x Total assets x Equity multiplier
           = (€10/€126) x (€126/€204) x (€204/€88)
           = 7.9 x .62 x 2.3.
           = 11.35%.

Question 13

M/B ratio = market price per share/ Book value per share.

If the market price per share is greater than the book value per share, the market expects the present value of future earnings are worth more than the company's liquidation value. The difference between the future earnings value and the liquidation value is the going concern value. The higher the M/B ratio the greater is the value based on its going concern value.

With a M/B value <1 it is sometimes assumed that the company's liquidation value is greater than its going concern value. However, we must remember that M/B ratios are accounting based values. In reality, it is likely that liquidation values will be greater than book values. The liquidation value of assets may be greater than their book values. In addition, the market value of a company's bonds can be greater than their book values.

Question 17

ROA = 11%; ROE = 16% and Net margin (NM) = 3%.
ROA = Net income/assets
Profit Margin = Net income/sales
ROE = Net margin/Equity
ROA = Profit Margin × Sales/Total assets
Net Income/Assets = (Net Income/Sales) × (Sales/Total assets)
11% = 3% × Sales/Total assets
Therefore Sales/Total assets = 3.7 times.
ROE = Profit margin × (Sales/Total assets) × (Total assets/Equity.)
Net Income/Equity = (Net income/Sales) × (Sales/Total assets) × (Total assets/Equity)
= 16% = 3% × 3.7 × Total assets/Equity
Therefore Total assets/Equity or the Equity multiplier = 1.44.

CHAPTER 4

Question 2

This question is an example of discounting a future value back to a present value. Note that in this example 'today' means 'the future'.

(a)   Here:
     FV = €10,000
     k = 1% per month
     n = 84 months

     PV represents the value of the fund seven years ago.

     Using 4.5
$$PV_{(7 \text{ years ago})} = \frac{€10,000}{(1.01)^{84}} = €4,335.15$$

(b)   Here: FV = €10,000
                k_1 = 1% per month for 48 months
                k_2 = 5% per half-year for 6 half-years
      Using 4.5

$$\text{PV (4 years ago)} = \frac{€10,000}{(1.01)^{48}} = €6,202.60$$

$$\text{PV (7 years ago)} = \frac{€6,202.60}{(1.05)^6} = €4,628.48$$

Note that the answer to part (b) is higher than that to part (a). This is because the effective rate of interest in the first three years of the investment is lower in (b) than in (a), 10.25% p.a. compared to 12.68% p.a., and therefore in order to have the same amount today, (b) must start from a higher value.

The solution could also be found using annual effective rates

(a)   PV (7 years ago) $= \dfrac{€10,000}{(1.126825)^7} = €4,335.15$

(b)   PV (4 years ago) $= \dfrac{€10,000}{(1.126825)^4} = €6,202.60$

      PV (7 years ago) $= \dfrac{€6,202.60}{(1.1025)^3} = €4,628.48$

Question 6

This is an example of an ordinary simple annuity.

Here: PV = €8,000
          k = 1.1% per month
          n = 84 months

To calculate the amount of interest paid over the life of the loan, the periodic payment must first be calculated.

Find P_t using 4.8

$$8,000 = P_t \left[\frac{1-(1.011)^{-84}}{0.011} \right]$$

Solve for the periodic payment as shown in example 4.15.
   This produces Pt = €146.41.
   Since payments are part interest and part capital (see Chapter 20), the total payments made equals the total interest paid plus the total capital paid.
   Total payments over course of loan term = 84 x €146.41 = €12,298.44
   Subtract original loan value (capital) = €8,000.00
   Interest paid = €4,298.44

Question 7

This question combines an ordinary simple annuity and a compound interest calculation.
(a)   It is useful to notionally separate the initial deposit and the annuity into two different accounts.
      Before the monthly payment can be calculated, the target value for the annuity must be determined. This in turn requires that the future value at time 36 of the initial deposit be determined.
      This is an example of a compound interest calculation.

      Here: PV = €5,000
                k = 1% per month
                n = 36 months

Using 4.4 the initial deposit of €5,000 will grow over 36 months to:

FV= €5,000$(1.01)^{36}$ = €7,153.84
(time 36)

Since the target at time 36 is €15,000 and the initial deposit provides €7,153.84 of this, the annuity must provide the remaining €7,846.16. Thus:

FV = €7,846.16
k = 1% per month
n = 36 months

$$7,846.16 = P_t \left[\frac{(1.01)^{36} -1}{0.01} \right]$$

Solve for the periodic payment as shown in Example 4.13.
This produces P_t = €182.14

(b)   Calculate the total value of the savings at time 30. This involves two calculations:

Compound interest
FV = €5,000$(1.01)^{30}$ = €6,739.24
(time 30)

Annuity
$$FV = 182.14 \left[\frac{(1.01)^{30} - 1}{0.01} \right] = €6,335.72$$

Total value at time 30 = €6,739.24 + €6,335.72 = €13,074.96

This will grow through compound interest.

Here: PV = €13,074.96
        FV = €15,000.00
        k= 1% per month

To find the time required to reach the target of €15,000 use the approach as in Example 4.7.

€15,000 = €13,074.96$(1.01)^{n}$

This produces n = 13.8

The fund will reach the target of €15,000 between 13 and 14 months after month 30.
To complete the answer fully, calculate the value 13 months after month 30.

FV = €13,074.96$(1.01)^{13}$ = €14,880.52

Finally use the simple interest calculation to find the fraction of the next month required to reach the target.

PV = €14,880.52
FV = €15,000.00
k = 1% per month

Using 4.3
€15,000 = €14,880.52(1 + (0.01)   n)
This produces n = 0.8 of a month. To express this in days multiply by 30, i.e. 24 days

The final answer is thus 43 months and 24 days.

(c)   Calculate the total value of the savings at time 24. This involves two calculations:

Compound interest
$FV = €5,000(1.01)^{24} = €6,348.67$
(time 24)

Annuity
$$FV = 182.14 \left[\frac{(1.01)^{24} - 1}{0.01} \right] = €4,912.95$$

Total value at time 24 = €6,348.67 + €4,912.95 = €11,261.62
This will grow through compound interest.

Here: PV = €11,261.62
         n = 12 months
         k = 1% per month
To find the value of this fund at time 36 use the approach as in Example 4.6.

$FV = €11,261.62(1.01)^{12} = €12,689.88$

Since the target at time 36 is now €18,000 and the payments made to date will provide €12,689.88 of this, the annuity must provide the remaining €5,310.12. Thus:

FV = €5,310.12
k = 1% per month
n = 12 months

$$€5,310.12 = P_t \left[\frac{(1.01)^{12} - 1}{0.01} \right]$$

Solve for the periodic payment as shown in example 4.13.
This produces $P_t = €418.70$.

Question 9

This question deals with the comparison of two different payment streams by expressing both in present value terms.
(a)   Calculate the PV of the payment stream and compare it to the once-off payment option of €200,000 now. The rate of interest can either be expressed as the monthly equivalent of 14.4% p.a., i.e. 1.2% p.m. or as an annual effective rate using 4.6 above. If the monthly rate is used then the time should be expressed in months, while if the annual effective rate is used, then the time should be expressed in years.

$$PV = €100,000 + \frac{€30,000}{(1.012)^{12}} + \frac{€30,000}{(1.012)^{24}} + \frac{€30,000}{(1.012)^{36}} + \frac{€30,000}{(1.012)^{48}} + \frac{€30,000}{(1.012)^{60}}$$

This gives a value of €199,644.25. Since this is below €200,000 then the stream of payments should be chosen.
Alternatively the payment stream can be treated as an ordinary simple and the present value calculated using 4.8.
The appropriate rate of interest is the annual effective rate which from 4.6 is 15.3894%.

Thus: P_t = €30,000
        k   = 15.3894% p.a.
        n   = 5

PV is calculated using 4.8. This gives €99,644.40. The €100,000 is added to this to give approximately the same value as above.

(b)   Since the rate of interest changes over the 5 years, the annuity formula cannot be used. The rate of interest should be expressed in monthly/quarterly form and the number of months/quarters used to calculate the present value or alternatively, the annual effective rate for each year may be calculated and the present value found using the number of years as the appropriate time factor.

$$PV = £100,000 + \frac{€30,000}{(1.012)^{12}} + \frac{€30,000}{(1.012)^{24}} + \frac{€30,000}{(1.012)^{24}(1.013)^{12}} + \frac{€30,000}{(1.012)^{24}(1.013)^{12}(1.033)^{12}} + \frac{€30,000}{(1.012)^{24}(1.013)^{12}(1.033)^{8}}$$

This gives a value of €199,655.40. Since this is below €200,000 then the stream of payments should be chosen.

Question 15

This is an ordinary simple annuity.

Here: PV = €700,000
P_t = €100,000
n = 10

Using formula 4.8:

$$700,000 = 100,000 \left[\frac{1 - (1 + k)^{-10}}{k} \right]$$

Trial values of k are inserted into the equation above.

Using k = 7% produces PV = €702,358.15. This means that at a rate of interest of 7%, 10 annual payments of €100,000 would pay of a loan of €702,358.15. Since the loan is only €700,000, the rate of interest must be above 7%.

Using k = 8% produces PV = €671,008.14. This is below the loan size and so the required rate is below 8%. The rate is therefore between 7% and 8%. The answer can be approximated using linear interpolation.

A one percentage point rise in k from 7% causes the present value to fall by €31,350.01 (€702,358.15 – €671,008.14). What fraction of a 1 per cent increase in k from 7% would cause the present value to fall by €2,358.15 (€702,358.15 – €700,000.00)? This is calculated as follows:

$$\frac{x}{1} = \frac{2,358.15}{31,350.01} = 0.075 \approx 0.1$$

The answer is therefore approximated as 7.1%. This can be checked by using 7.1% as the value of k in 4.8 and calculating PV. This produces PV = €699,122.97 which is €877.03 short of the given loan size. Since this is nearer to the loan size of €700,000 than when 7% was used (€702,358.15), the answer is therefore k = 7.1% correct to one place of decimals.

Question 16

This can be treated as a compound interest calculation applied to a reducing balance over the life of the loan.
The annual effective rate for each year should initially be calculated from 4.6.

This gives:

Year	Effective rate
1	16.08%
2	12.68%
3	9.38%
4	12.55%

Time	Borrow	Interest	Repay	Balance
0	14,000			–14,000
1		2,251.20	4,000	–12,251.20
2		1,553.45	5,000	–8,804.65
3		825.88	6,000	–3,630.53
4		455.63	4,086.16	0.00

The final payment is calculated as 3,630.53 + 455.63, i.e. the amount required to clear the debt at the end of the previous year and the interest charge for the final year.

CHAPTER 5

Question 1

This can be solved as shown in example 5.7 in the text.
The price is first calculated using 5.2 above

$$PV = 12 \left[\frac{1 - (1.09)^{-8}}{0.09} \right] + \frac{100}{(1.09)^8} = 116.60$$

Price @ GRY of 9% = €116.60

The net redemption yield is found by equating the present value of the future net receipts from the bond with this price of €116.60. This is done, as before, through a process of trial and error, i.e. the future net cash flow is discounted at varying rates, until two answers, one above €116.60 and the other below €116.60 are found, using discount rates which are one percentage point apart. Remember that the net redemption yield will be less than the gross redemption yield, here less than 9% p.a.
    The net cash flow from the bond is:

€12 per annum less tax at 24% i.e. €12 – (0.24 x €12) or 0.76 x €12 = €9.12 for 8 years plus €100 at the end of the eighth year.

$$116.60 = 9.12 \left[\frac{1 - (1 + k)^{-8}}{k} \right] + \frac{100}{(1. + k)^8}$$

Following trial and error, discount rates of 7% and 6% produce present values of €112.66 and €119.37 respectively.
    Since the current price is €116.60, the investor is getting a yield somewhere between 6% and 7%.
    The answer can be approximated using linear interpolation.
    A one percentage point rise in the discount rate from 6% causes the bond price to fall by €6.71 (€119.37 – €112.66). What fraction of a 1 per cent increase in the discount rate from 6% would cause price to fall by €2.77 (€119.37 – €116.60)? This is calculated as follows:

Discount Rate	Price
6%	119.37
6+x%	116.60
7%	112.66

$$\frac{x}{1} = \frac{2.77}{6.71} = 0.41$$

where x = fractional interest rate increase required to decrease price by €2.77 at this point.
Therefore NRY to a 24% taxpayer is estimated at 6 + 0.4% i.e. 6.4%.

Question 2

This can be solved as shown in Example 5.9 in the text.
    The price is first calculated using 5.2 above.
    The appropriate cash flow to be discounted is the net coupon at 42% tax, i.e. €9 per annum less tax at 42%, i.e. €9 – (0.42 x €9) or 0.58 x €9 = €5.22 for 6 years plus €100 at the end of the sixth year.

$$PV = 5.22 \left[\frac{1 - (1.08)^{-6}}{0.08} \right] + \frac{100}{(1.08)^6} = 87.15$$

Price @ NRY (@ 42% tax) of 8% = €87.15

The net redemption yield at 20% tax is found by equating the present value of the future net receipts from the bond with this price of €87.15. This is done, as before, through a process of trial and error, i.e. the future net cash flow is discounted at varying rates, until two answers, one above €87.15 and the other below €87.15 are found, using discount rates which are one percentage point apart. Remember that the net redemption yield at the lower tax rate (20%) will be higher than the net redemption yield at the higher tax rate (42%).

The net cash flow from the bond is:

€9 per annum less tax at 20% i.e. €9 – (0.20 × €9) or 0.80 × €9 = €7.20 for 6 years plus €100 at the end of the sixth year.

$$87.15 = 7.20 \left[\frac{1-(1+k)^{-6}}{k} \right] + \frac{100}{(1.+k)^6}$$

Following trial and error, discount rates of 11% and 10% produce present values of €83.92 and €87.81 respectively.

Since the current price is €87.15, the investor is getting a yield somewhere between 10% and 11%.

The answer can be approximated using linear interpolation,.

A one percentage point rise in the discount from 10% causes the bond price to fall by €3.89 (€87.81 – €83.92). What fraction of a 1 per cent increase in the discount rate from 10% would cause price to fall by €0.66 (€87.81 – €87.15)? This is calculated as follows:

Discount Rate	Price
10%	87.81
10+x%	87.15
11%	83.92

$$\frac{x}{1} = \frac{0.66}{3.89} = 0.17 \approx 0.2$$

where x = fractional interest rate increase required to decrease price by €0.66 at this point.

Therefore NRY to a 20% taxpayer is estimated at 10 + 0.2% i.e. 10.2%.

Question 3

This can be solved as shown in Example 5.10 in the text.

The price is first calculated using 5.2 above.

The appropriate cash flow to be discounted is the net coupon at 44% tax, i.e. €9 per annum less tax at 44% i.e. €9 – (0.44 x €9) or 0.56 x €9 = €5.04 for 8 years plus €100 at the end of the eighth year.

$$PV = 5.04 \left[\frac{1-(1.05)^{-8}}{0.05} \right] + \frac{100}{(1.05)^8} = 100.26$$

Price @ NRY (@44% tax) of 5% = €100.26
The income yields can be found using 5.1
(a) The gross annual coupon is €9

$$\text{Gross income yield} = \frac{9}{100.26} \times 100 = 8.98\%$$

(b) The net coupon is €9 less tax at 22% = €7.02

$$\text{Net income yield} = \frac{7.02}{100.26} \times 100 = 7\%$$
$$\text{(@22\% tax)}$$

CHAPTER 6

Questions 1 to 5 are explained in the text.

Question 6

(a) Assuming the return for the market was (5150 – 4750)/4750 plus 4% = 12.42%, the Rf = 4% and beta = 0.97.

Therefore the share return = 4% + (12.42% – 4%)0.97 = 12.17%

Actual return = (23 + 9)/167 = 16.16% implying the return was very satisfactory.

(b) Only one period was chosen in the analysis. Does one past year of ISEQ return represent the market? Is the risk-free rate appropriate? The beta value may not be stable.

Question 7

(a) Expected value of High stool = 0.3(25%) + 0.45(22%) + 0.25(12%) = 20.4%
Expected value of Low stool = 17.3%
Variance of High stool = $0.3(25 - 20.4)^2 + 0.45(22 - 20.4)^2 + 0.25(12 - 20.4)^2 = 25.14$

Standard deviation = $\sqrt{25.14}$ = 5.014
Variance of Low stool = 5.310 and standard deviation = 2.304

(b) Covariance = 0.3(25 – 20.4)(14 – 17.3) + 0.45(22 – 20.4)(18 – 17.3) + 0.25(12 – 20.4)(20 – 17.3)
= – 9.72

Correlation coefficient = $\dfrac{\text{Covariance High and Low}}{\text{SD High SD Low}}$

$= \dfrac{-9.72}{5.014 \times 2.304} = -0.84$

The two securities are negatively correlated.

(c)

State	Probability (P)	Portfolio return (R)	P × R
A	0.3	0.7(25) + 0.3(14) = 21.7%	6.51
B	0.45	0.7(22) + 0.3(18) = 20.8%	9.36
C	0.25	0.7(12) + 0.3(20) = 14.4%	3.60
			19.47%

Expected value = 0.7(20.4%) + 0.3(17.3%) = 19.47%
Variance = $0.3(21.7 - 19.47)^2 + 0.45(20.8 - 19.47)^2 + 0.25(14.4 - 19.47)^2 = 8.714\%$
Or variance = 0.49(25.14) + 0.09(5.310) + 2(0.3)(0.7(–0.84)(5.014)(2.304) = 8.714% and standard deviation
= 2.95%

Question 8

(a) The correlation coefficient = $\dfrac{\text{Covariance xy}}{\text{SDx SDy}}$

M and N = 12.2/(2.4)(6.2) = 0.82
M and O = 8.1/(2.4)(4.3) = 0.78
N and O = –4.5/(6.2)(4.3) = –0.17, the lowest risk on correlation criteria.
(b) Expected value   M and N = 0.5(15%) + 0.5(18%) = 16.5%
M and O =16% and N and O = 17.5%
Variance M N = $0.5^2(2.4)^2 + 0.5^2(6.2)^2 + 2(0.5)(0.5)(0.82)(2.4)(6.2) = 17.1508\%$

Standard deviation M and N = $\sqrt{17.1508}$ = 4.14%

Standard deviation M and O = 3.18%
Standard deviation N and O = 3.46%
In this example portfolio M and N are inferior to portfolio N and O on both expected value and standard deviation measures.
However, conflicting results are found for both portfolio M and O and portfolio N and O and it is therefore difficult to say which portfolio is the most efficient.

Question 9

The options available in using up all €800,000 are as follows:

1 & MM   2 & MM   3 & MM   4 & MM   1 & 2   2 & 3   2 & 4 MM

If the return must be greater than 16%, then 1 & MM, 2 & MM, 1 & 2 and the money market as an option on its own are not viable.
Portfolio 3 & MM is inferior to portfolio 4 & MM.
Portfolio 2 & 3 is inferior to portfolio 2 & 4.
Using expected values and standard deviation for two asset portfolios, the following results are obtained:

Portfolio	Expected value	Standard deviation
4 & MM	20.25%	5.03%
2 & 4	21.373%	5.29%

She should invest in project 4 and place the remaining funds into project 2 or the money market. Project 2 offers a higher return but is associated with higher risk.

Question 11

(a) Portfolio return = 73/5 = 14.6% as there is an equal investment in each.
   Portfolio variance is based on a sum of the squared weights by standard deviations or variances, as there is no correlation, i.e. r = 0.
   $0.2^2\ 8^2 + 0.2^2\ 10^2 + 0.2^2\ 7^2 + 0.2^2\ 4^2 + 0.2^2\ 16^2 = 19.4$

   Standard deviation $= \sqrt{19.4} = 4.4\%$

(b) Diversification has reduced portfolio risk. The portfolio risk reduction is quite large because of the lack of correlation between the investments. The further away from +1 the greater the risk reduction.

Question 12

$\text{Beta} = \dfrac{n\Sigma xy - \Sigma x\Sigma y}{n\Sigma x^2 - (\Sigma x)^2} = \dfrac{12(13.4) - .8(5.7)}{12(23.45) - .8^2} = 0.5565$

(b) 6% + (12% − 6%)0.5565 = 9.34%

Question 14

$\text{Profitability index} = \dfrac{\text{Present value of cash flows}}{\text{Capital outlay}}$

$1.4 = \dfrac{\text{Present value of cash flows}}{\text{Capital outlay}}$ and PV of cash flows = €16.8million

The annuity factor = €16.8/€5.3 = 3.170
From tables annuity factor 3.170 for four years = 10%
10% = 6% + (11% − 6%) Beta
Beta = 4%/5% = 0.80

Question 16

Expected return
(16% x €3.8M + 6% x 5.2M + 10% x 6.1 + 13% x 2.9)/18M = 10.59%
Weighted average Beta
= (1.4 x 3.8 + 0 x 5.2M + 0.7 x 6.1M + 1.1 x 2.9M/18M) = 0.71
Required return = 5.5 + (12.5 − 5.5)0.71 = 10.47%
As the expected return is greater than the required return, the investment looks good.

CHAPTER 7

Question 1

(a) Roy's criterion
   $R_l = 7\%$

Fund	A	B	C
Mean return	13	17	21
Standard Deviation (σ)	5	9	12
Difference From 7% (σ)	−1.2	−1.11	−1.17
Probability of Return <7%	11.51%	13.35%	12.1%

A has an 11.51% chance of delivering a return of 7% or less, B has a 13.35% chance of such a return, while C has a 12.1% chance. Therefore A is the preferred portfolio.

(b) Kataoka's criterion
   $\alpha = 13\%$.

From the standard normal distribution tables it can be seen that the bottom 13% of the distribution (13% in the left-hand tail of the distribution) occurs at 1.13 standard deviation below the mean. This holds for all normal distributions. Thus the value of R_l can be calculated for each fund as 1.13 standard deviations below the mean i.e.

$R_l = \bar{R}p - 1.13\sigma$

Portfolio	A	B	C
$\bar{R}p$	13	17	21
σp	5	9	12
$R_l=$	7.35	6.83	7.44

The results indicate that 13% of the time fund A will fall below 7.35% return, fund B will fall below 6.83% while fund C will fall below 7.44%. Since fund C produces the highest floor it is the preferred portfolio.

(c) Telser's criterion
    R_l = 7% (minimum desired return)
    α = 13% (acceptable risk level)

Fund	A	B	C
Mean return	13	17	21
Standard Deviation (σ)	5	9	12
Difference From 7% (σ)	–1.2	–1.11	–1.17
Probability of Return <7%	11.51%	13.35%	12.1%
Obeys constraint?	Yes	No	Yes

Fund B fails the constraint since it has a greater than 13% (13.35%) chance of falling below a 7% return in any period. Both funds A and C meet the constraint. Of these two, fund C has the highest average return and is therefore the preferred portfolio.

Question 2

(a) Roy's criterion
    R_l = 5%

Fund	A	B	C
Mean return	12	15	20
Standard Deviation (σ)	4	7	10
Difference From 5% (σ)	–1.75	–1.43	–1.5
Probability of Return <5%	4.01%	7.64%	6.68%

A has an 4.01% chance of delivering a return of 5% or less, B has a 7.64% chance of such a return, while C has a 6.68% chance. Therefore A is preferred portfolio.

(b) Kataoka's criterion
    α = 8%.
    From the standard normal distribution tables it can be seen that the bottom 8% of the distribution (8% in the left-hand tail of the distribution) occurs at 1.41 standard deviation below the mean. This holds for all normal distributions. Thus the value of R_l can be calculated for each fund as 1.41 standard deviations below the mean, i.e.

$R_l = \bar{R}p - 1.41\sigma$

Portfolio	A	B	C
$\bar{R}p$	12	15	20
σ_p	4	7	10
$R_l =$	6.36	5.13	5.90

The results indicate that 8% of the time fund A will fall below 6.36% return, fund B will fall below 5.13% while fund C will fall below 5.90%. Since fund A produces the highest floor it is the preferred portfolio.

(c) Telser's criterion
    R_l = 5% (minimum desired return)
    σ= 8% (acceptable risk level)

Fund	A	B	C
Mean return	12	15	20
Standard Deviation (σ)	4	7	10
Difference From 5% (σ)	−1.75	−1.43	−1.5
Probability of Return <5%	4.01%	7.64%	6.68%
Obeys constraint?	Yes	Yes	Yes

Each of the funds A, B and C meet the constraint. Since fund C has the highest average return it is the preferred portfolio.

Question 4

The Sharpe measure
R_f = 4%
R_A = 11%
σ_A = 5%
R_B = 14%
σ_B = 7%

The Sharpe measure for the two funds is:

Fund A $\quad \dfrac{11 - 4}{5} = 1.4$

Fund B $\quad \dfrac{14 - 4}{7} = 1.43$

Fund A earned 1.4 % return for each 1% of risk carried while Fund B earned 1.43% return for each 1% of risk carried. Fund B, is delivering a greater return for the level of risk attached and is therefore the preferred fund.

Question 5

The Treynor measure:

R_f = 6%
R_m = 9%
R_a = 13%
β_a = 1.1
R_b = 14%
β_b = 1.2

The Treynor measure for the two funds and the market average is:

Market average $\quad \dfrac{9 - 6}{1} = 3$

Fund A $\quad \dfrac{13 - 6}{1.1} = 6.36$

Fund B $\quad \dfrac{14 - 6}{1.2} = 6.67$

Both funds are paying excess returns higher than the market average. Fund A earned an excess return of 6.36% when the risk level is neutralised to the market average while Fund B earned an excess return of 6.67% when the risk level is neutralised to the market average. Fund B is therefore paying an excess return higher than Fund A. Fund B is therefore the preferred fund.

Question 6

Differential return (total risk) measure

R_f= 6%
$\bar{R}_m$ = 11%
σ_m = 5%
$\bar{R}_A$ = 16%
σ_A = 8%
$\bar{R}_B$ = 9%
σ_B = 6%

$$E(R_i) = R_f + (E(R_m) - R_f) \times \frac{\sigma_i}{\sigma_m}$$

The expected return on Fund A is:

$$6 + (11 - 6) \times \frac{8}{5} = 14\%$$

The actual return on Fund A was 16%.
The differential return is therefore 16% – 14% = 2%.
Fund A has therefore achieved a return 2% above that which could have been achieved by simply borrowing at the risk-free rate and investing in the market portfolio.
The expected return on Fund B is:

$$6 + (11 - 6) \times \frac{6}{5} = 12\%$$

The actual return on Fund B was 9%.
The differential return is therefore 9% – 12% = – 3%.
Fund B has therefore achieved a return 3% below that which could have been achieved by simply borrowing at the risk-free rate and investing in the market portfolio.
Fund A is therefore the preferred portfolio.

Question 7

Jensen measure

R_f = 7%
$\bar{R}_m$ = 10%
$\bar{R}_A$ = 11%
β_a = 1.4
$\bar{R}_B$ = 13%
β= 1.6

$$E(R_i) = R_f + \beta_i(E(R_m) - R_f)$$

The expected return on Fund A is:

$$7 + 1.4(10 - 7) = 11.2\%$$

The actual return on Fund A was 11%.
The differential return is therefore 11% – 11.2% = –0.2%.

Fund A has therefore achieved a return 0.2% below that which could have been achieved by simply borrowing at the risk-free rate and investing in the market portfolio.
The expected return on Fund B is:

$$7 + 1.6(10 - 7) = 11.8\%$$

The actual return on Fund B was 13%.
The differential return is therefore 13% – 11.8% = 1.2%.

Fund B has therefore achieved a return 1.2% above that which could have been achieved by simply borrowing at the risk-free rate and investing in the market portfolio.

Fund B is therefore the preferred.

CHAPTER 8

Question 3

The value of a share is the expected value of future cash flows. This does not mean that the share price can be increased simply by increasing the dividend. Shareholders are concerned about all of their dividends – dividends paid now and dividends paid in the future. Companies that pay out high dividends now will have less money to reinvest in the company and this will lower expected future dividends. This will have the effect of lowering share price.

Question 9

(a) Current price of the share: (P_o)

€1/1.08 + €1.5/$(1.08)^2$ + €2/$(1.08)^3$ + €2.08/$(8\% - 4\%)$/$(1.08)^3$

P_o= €0.93 + €1.29 + €1.6 + €41.27 = €45

(b) The price of the share in one year's time: (P_1)

= (P_1) = €1.5/(1.08) + €2/$(1.08)^2$ + €2.08/.04/$(1.08)^2$.

= €1.38 + €1.7 + €44.6 + €48.

(c) Capital gain:

(€48 – €45)/€45 = 6.25%.

(d) Dividend yield

€1/€45 = 2.2%.

Question 14

P_o = (€5 + €60)/1.1 = €59.

Question 16

P_A = Div_1/K_e = €5/0.08 = €62.5

P_B = Div_1 $(K_e - g)$ = €6/(0.08 – .005) = €200.

P_C = $Div_1/(1.08)$ + $Div_2/(1.08)^2$ + $Div_3/(1.08)^3$ + $Div_4/(1.08)^5$ +Div$(1.08)^5$ +$(Div_6/.08)(1/(1.08)^5$:

€2/(1.08) + €2(1.15)/$(1.08)^2$ + €2.3(1.15)/$(1.08)^3$ + €2.64(1.15)/$(1.08)^4$ +(€3.45/.08)(1/1.08)^5:

= €1.85 + €1.97 + €2.11 + €2.24 + €2.37 + €29.32 = €39.85.

Stock B is most valuable.

Question 18

P_o = D_o $(1 + g)/K_e - g)$ = €3(0.9)/(0.14 – .10) = €2.7/0.04 = €67.5

Question 19

P_o = FCF $(1 + g)/(K_e - g)$ = €200,000 $(1 + 0.05)/(0.12 - 0.05)$ = €3m.

Value of equity = Total value of operating activities less value of debt.

€3m – €500,000 = €2.5m.

CHAPTER 9

Question 9

Modern corporations do not follow a residual dividend policy. Some people think that cash dividends are what is 'left over' after everything else has been paid. If this were the case then a 'residual' dividend policy would lead to volatile dividend payments. This would adversely affect share prices.

Question 10

P/E ratio = 10. The earnings per share (EPS) = €2,000,000/100,000 = €20.

Therefore the P/E ratio = 10 = ?/20, which means the price of the share is €200.

Dividend pay-out ratio = Dividends/Net income
    = €8 per share × 100,000 = €800,00
    = €800,000/2,000,000 = 40%.

Question 11

(a) Murphy's debt:equity ratio is 0.6/0.4 = 1.5. By reinvesting all of its earnings, it would need to borrow €100,000 × 1.5 = €150,000 to maintain its debt: equity ratio. Therefore, it can spend €250,000 (€100,000 earnings + €150,000 borrowings) on capital projects without raising new equity. The company's planned investment is €200,000. This will be financed with 40% equity. This is €200,000 × 40% = €80,000.
(b) Profits after tax are €100,000. Therefore it can pay €100,000 = €80,000 = €20,000 in dividends.

Question 13

Dividend policy can be irrelevant even when the share price rises following an increase in dividends. The change in the price of the share is due to the change in the dividend, not in dividend policy.

Question 18

The value of equity is €230,000 and with 10,000 shares this gives a market value per share of €23. Paying a dividend of €3 per share, the price of the share, ex-dividend, will be €20 per share. Total assets decrease €30,000 (cash), and equity is now 10,000 × €20 = €200,000, i.e. fall of €30,000. Incidentally, the EPS after the dividend is the same as it is before the dividend, i.e. €2. However, the P/E ratio is €20/€2 = 10, compared to 11.5 before the dividend (€23/€2).

CHAPTER 10

Question 5

Some possible reasons:
(a) Usually the acquiring company is much bigger with a larger number of shares. Therefore, the gains made from mergers are spread more sparsely among shares.
(b) The managers of the acquiring company may not be acting in the best interest of the shareholders.
(c) The merger may have been anticipated, and the gains incorporated into the share price before the merger.
(d) In an era of 'merger mania', the demand for takeovers may be pushing the price (cost) of acquisition up to the point where the NPV = zero.

Question 7

The main reason is that 'reverse synergy' is possible. This is possible because the smaller entity can manage and focus more clearly on its core business, and, of course, performance evaluation is now easier, financial reports and stock prices are now separated from the mire of consolidated accounts.

Question 10

(a) $K_e = R_{fr} + RP_m(\beta)$
    $= 0.07 + 0.08(0.8) = 13.4\%$

Therefore the current price of Patterson is:
$= D_1/K_e - g = €1.50/0.134 - 0.06 = €20.27.$

(b) $K_e = R_{fr} + RP_m(\beta)$
    $= 7\% + 8\%(1.1) = 15.8\%$

Therefore, the value of Patterson to Murphy (per share) is:
$= D_1/K_e - g = €1.50/0.158 - 0.07 = €17.04$

Range in values per share: €20.27 to €17.04.

Question 14

The value of firm Y to Firm X is:

$V_b^* = \Delta V + V_b$

$= €1m + (2,500,000 \times €40)$

$= €101m.$

Firm Y wants €50 per share. Firm X would have to pay €50 x 2,500,000 = €125,000,000.

The NPV is:

$NPV = V_b^* - Cost$

$= €101m - €1.25m$

$= (€24m).$

This is a negative NPV, so Firm X should not purchase the share at €50.

CHAPTER 11

Question 4

It is possible for a company to grow too fast. A company's growth can be greater than the company's ability to generate the capital to fund growth. Quality may also suffer because of rapid growth. A company might decide to limit distribution or it might increase prices to slow down growth.

Question 10

Dividends = €575
Addition to RE = €3,105

XYZ Ltd Pro Forma Profit and Loss Account 31 December 2000	
Sales	€23,000
Costs	€18,400
PBIT	€4,600
Interest	—
Tax (20%)	€920
PAT	€3680

Pro Forma Balance Sheet 31 December 2000	
Assets	€161,000
Debt	€28,000
Equity	€112,000
Addition to retained earnings	€3,105
	€143,105

AFN = €161,000 – €143,105 = €17,895.

Question 12

The capital intensity ratio is the amount of assets that are required per euro of sales, i.e. A/S_0 in the AFN formula. If a firm is capital intensive (a high A/S_0 ratio), a small increase in production and output will require much additional external funds. A low capital intensity ratio will mean output and sales can grow without much additional capital.

Question 14

Pro Forma Balance Sheet (2001) Clashmore Ltd.	
Fixed assets	€100,000
Current assets	€150,000
Total assets	€250,000
Financed by creditors	€20,000
Short-term debt	€0
Equity	€160,000
	€130,000
Therefore the AFN = €70,000.	

Question 19

First, we need to discover if the current growth rate is possible.
Remember from chapter 3 that the ROE = ROA × Equity Multiplier.

        = ROA × (1 + Debt:Equity)

        5% × 1/1.7 × (1 + 0.4) = 4.11%.

The sustainable growth rate is given as 10%.

        = 0.1 = [0.0411 (b)]/ [1 − 0.0411(b)] where 'b' is the retention ratio.

        = 0.0411(b) = 0.1 − 0.00411(b)

        = 0.03521(b) = 0.1 = 2.2 = 'b'.

Therefore the retention ratio is 2.2 and the pay-out ratio is (1 − b) = −1.2. Since the retention ratio plus the pay-out ratio must equal 1, it is impossible to have a pay-out ratio of −1.2 or minus 120%. If all earnings are retained, the dividend pay-out will be zero, which is the lowest possible pay-out.
Therefore the maximum sustainable growth rate for the firm is:

        'g' = 0.0411/(1 − 0.0411) = 4.2%.

CHAPTER 12

Questions 1 to 4 are explained in the text.

Question 5

(a) Payback occurs in year 5. The NPV using EXCEL is as follows:

Year	Cash flow €	Discount rate 12%	Present value €
0	−20,000	1	−20,000
1	−20,000	0.893	−17,857
2	15,000	0.797	11,958
3	12,000	0.712	8,541
4 to 8	8,000	2.566	20,528
			NPV = €3,170

Project A is viable using NPV.

(b) Payback never occurs. The NPV using EXCEL is as follows:

Year	Cash flow €	Discount rate 15%	Present value €
0	−32,000	1	−32,000
1 to infinity	4,500	1/0.15	30,000
			NPV = −€2,000

Project B is not viable.

(c) Payback occurs in year 4. The NPV using EXCEL is as follows:

Year	Cash flow €	Discount rate 12%	Present value €
0	−65,000	1	−65,000
1	−6,000	0.893	−5,357
1 to 5	18,000	3.605	64,890
5	21,000	0.567	11,907
			NPV = €6,440

Project C is viable.

(d) Payback occurs in year 4. The NPV using EXCEL is as follows:

Year	Cash flow €	Discount rate 15%	Present value €
0	−20,000	1	−20000
1 to 5	5,000	3.352	16,760
6 to 10	4,000	1.667	6,668
11 to infinity	3,000	1.648	4,944
			NPV = €8,372

Project D is viable.

Question 8

Year	Cash flow €	Account profit €
0	(100,000)	
1	33,000	8,000
2	36,300	11,300
3	39,930*	14,930
4	43,923	18,923
Total		**53,153**
Average		**13,288**

Average annual accounting profit = 13,288/50,000 = 0.2658 or 26.58%
Payback occurs in year 3*.

Year	Cash flow €
0	(100,000)
1	33,000
2	33,600
3	39,930
4	43,923
NPV	14,765

The project is viable with a positive NPV of €14,765
Using EXCEL the IRR is 18%.
The ARR is greater then 20%, the NPV is positive, the IRR is greater than 12% and the project is viable.

Question 9

(a) Sales = €750,000, VC = €450,000, FC = €160,000 and initial cost = €520,000.
   Annual cash inflow €140,000 and extra €100,000 in year 5.

Year	€ Cash flow	DF 12%	Present value
0	−520000	1.000	−520000.00
1	140000	0.893	125000.00
2	140000	0.797	111607.14
3	140000	0.712	99649.23
4	140000	0.636	88972.53
5	240000	0.567	136182.45
			NPV = 41411.35

NPV = €41,411 approximately €41,000
Using Excel IRR = 14.93%

(b) 1.   IRR = 15% approx or 25% increase in discount rate.
    2.   €41,411/€520,000 = 7.96% increase
    3.   C × annuity factor − NPV = 0
          C × 3.605 = 41,411 and C = €11,487 or fall 8.2%.
    4.   R × DF − NPV = 0, R × 0.567 = 41,411 or R = €73,035 or fall 27%.

Question 11

(a) and (b)

Project A

Year	Cash flow €000s	Discount factor 12%	Present value	Profitability index
0	(246)	1	(246)	
1 to 5	70	3.605	252.35	6.35/246
			NPV = 6.35	PI = 0.026

Project B

Year	Cash flow €000s	Discount factor 12%	Present value	Profitability index
0	(180)	1	(180)	
1	75	0.893	66.975	
2	87	0.797	69.339	
3	64	0.712	45.568	1.882/180
			NPV = 1.882	PI = 0.10

Project C

Year	Cash flow €000s	Discount factor 12%	Present value	Profitability index
0	(175)	1	(175)	
1	48	0.893	42.864	
2	48	0.797	38.256	
3	63	0.712	44.856	
4	73	0.636	46.428	(2.596)/175
			NPV = (2.596)	PI = (0.015)

Project D

Year	Cash flow €000s	Discount factor 12%	Present value	Profitability index
0	(180)	1	(180)	
1 to 4	62	3.037	188.294	8.294/180
			NPV = 8.294	PI = 0.046

Project E

Year	Cash flow €000s	Discount factor 12%	Present value	Profitability index
0	(180)	1	(180)	
1	40	0.893	35.72	
2	50	0.797	39.85	
3	60	0.712	42.72	
4	70	0.636	44.52	
5	40	0.567	22.68	5.49/180
			NPV = 5.49	PI = 0.031

Project F

Year	Cash flow €000s	Discount factor 12%	Present value	Profitability index
0	(150)	1	(150)	
1	35	0.893	31.255	
2	82	0.797	65.354	
3	82	0.712	58.384	4.993/150
			NPV = 4.993	PI = 0.033

Ranking	NPV	Profitability index
1st	D	D
2nd	A	F
3rd	E	E
4th	F	A
5th	B	B
6th	C	C

The rankings differ because the capital outlays differ. NPV shows the absolute benefit from a project, while the profitability index scales that benefit according to the project's size.

(c) Project C should not be undertaken. The company cannot afford to undertake more than three projects given the amount of money available. It cannot undertake A and E simultaneously. The choices available are as follows:

Projects	Capital outlay	NPV in total
DFE	€510,000	€18,777
DFA	€576,000	€19,637
DFB	€510,000	€15,169
DEB	€540,000	€15,666
DAB	€606,000	€15,526
FAB	€576,000	€13,225
FEB	€510,000	€12,365

Money should not be invested in the money market as the return is 9% and the cost of capital is 12%. **The company should invest in D, F and A with an outlay of €576,000 in total.**

Question 12

Year 1 Cash flow

Total revenue =	60,000($350)	$21,000,000
Total variable cost =	60,000($200)	($12,000,000)
Fixed cost =		($1,000,000)
Depreciation =		($3,000,000)
Total expenses =	VC + FC + Dep	($16,000,000)
Before-tax earnings =	Revenue − Expenses	$5,000,000
Host tax @ 20% =		($1,000,000)
After-tax earnings =		$4,000,000
Cash flow remitted =	* Add back deprec. expense	$7,000,000

Exchange rate	€1 = $0.9 €7,777,778	
Initial investment	$60 million/0.85	€35,294118
Year 3 cash flow	Add $20,000,000	

Year	Net cash flow $ millions	Net cash flow €
0	(30)	(35,284,118)
1	7	7,777,778
2	7	7,368,421
3	8.6	8,600,000
4	29.4	28,000,000
	NPV @ 15% =	**(€1,282,000)**

The project is not viable.

Question 16

Equivalent annual cost (EAC) = $\dfrac{\text{PV cost over one replacement cycle}}{\text{Cumulative PV factor for that cycle}}$

Year	Cash flow machine A	Year	Cash flow Machine B
0	(€19,000)	0	(€13,000)
8	(€4,000)	4	(€2,000)
12	€3,000	6	€3,000
1–12	(€2,000)	1–6	(€2,600)
	NPV at 10% = (€33,540)		**NPV at 10% = (€23,996)**

EAC for machine A = €33,540/6.814 = €4,922. EAC for machine B = €24,016/4.355 = €5,510.
Machine A is more efficient, assuming the cash flow estimates are correct, they occur at year end and machine reliability is the same for both machines.

Question 20

(a) Capital allowances based on a four-year 25% reducing balance are:

	Year 1	Year 2	Year 3	Year 4
	€5,000	€3,750	€2,813	€2,109 + €1,328*
Tax saved	€625	€469	€352	€430

* The balancing written-down value at the end of year 4 is €6,328 less €5,000 = €1,328.

(b) Net cash flows from the project

Year	Machine	Working capital	Project profit	Tax	Tax saved	Net cash flow
0	(20,000)	(2,000)				(22,000)
1			8,000	(1,000)	625	7,625
2			8,000	(1,000)	469	7,469
3			8,000	(1,000)	352	7,352
4	5,000	2,000	8,000	(1,000)	430	7,430

(c)

Year	Net cash flow	15% Discount factor	Present value
0	(22,000)	1.000	(22,000)
1	7,625	0.870	6,634
2	7,469	0.756	5,647
3	7,352	0.658	4,838
4	7,430	0.572	4,250
		NPV =	(€631)

The NPV at 15% of the net cash flows is (€631) and the project is not worthwhile.

CHAPTER 13

Questions 1 to 4 are explained in the text.

Question 5

(a) The current market value of the convertible is €140 assuming it is ex-interest. The conversion value is $(€2.20)(1.05)^5(50) = €140.39$ and as this is greater than €120 conversion will take place.

The after-tax interest cost is $€8(1 - 0.125) = €7$ and so the relevant cash flows and IRR are as follows:

Year	Cash flow after tax
0	(€140)
1 to 5	€7
5	€140.39
IRR	**= 5.05%**

(b) Discounting the future cash flows at 15% will give a current market value.

Year	Cash flow
1	7
2	7
3	7
4	7
5	7 + 180

NPV at 15% = €112.96

Reservations relate to share price, tax rates and discount rate.

(c)

Six-month periods	Cash flow
0	(89)
1–13	4
14	104

If an initial discount factor of 10% per annum is chosen then 10% implies $(1.1)^{0.5} - 1 = 0.0488$ per 6 months.

6 month	Cash flow	DF 10%	PV	DF 15%*	PV
0	(89)	1	(89)	1	(89)
1–13	4	9.462	38	8.245	33
14	104	0.651	53	0.376	39
	NPV		2		(17)

*15% implies $(1.15)^{0.5} - 1 = 0.0724$ per 6 months
IRR = 10% + (2/19)(5%) = 10.5%

Question 6

The cost of equity can be found using the constant dividend formula
K_e = Dividend available/market value.

Constant earnings	€15,000,000
Less Interest	€3,791,520
Earnings before tax	€11,208,480
Less Tax at 12.5%	€1,401,060
Dividend available	€9,807,420

Market value of equity = 50 million shares @ €0.80 = €40 million
K_e = €9,807,420/€40,000,000 = 0.2452 or 24.52%
The cost of the debentures is found as follows:

Year	Cash flow before tax	Cash flow after tax
0	−€105.5	−€105.5
1	16	14
2	16	14
3	16	14
3	100	100
IRR =	13.65%	11.72%

Market value of the debentures = €23.697(1.055) = €25 million

$$WACC = \frac{€40 \text{ million } (24.52\%) + €25 \text{ million } (11.72\%)}{€65 \text{ million}} = 0.196 \text{ or } 19.6\%$$

Question 8

(a) Vg = Vu + DT = €32.5 + €5 (0.125) = €33.125 million and market value has increased by **€0.625 million.**

(b) K_d = 13% D = €5 million and E = €33.125 − €5 = €28.125 million.
$K_e = K_u + (1 - T)(K_u - K_d)D/E = 18\% + (1 - 0.125)(18\% - 13\%)5/28.125 = \textbf{18.78\%}$
The cost of equity rises to reflect increased financial risk.

(c) K_e = 18.78% K_d after tax = 13% (1 − 0.125) = 11.375% D = €5 million and E = €28.125 million.

$$WACC = \frac{18.78\% \ (28.125) + 11.375\% \ (5)}{28.125 + 5} = 0.1766 \text{ or } \textbf{17.66\%}$$

The WACC falls as debt capital is introduced.

Question 16

Value of Rodge = 80 million (€1.40) = €112 million
Value of Podge = 25 million (€4) + €25 million = €125 million
M & M would say **Vg = Vu + DT** = €112 + €25 million (0.2) = €117 million and so Podge is overvalued.
A rational investor should sell shares in Podge, substitute personal gearing for corporate gearing and buy shares in Rodge.
Current earnings = (€25 million − €3 million)(1 − 0.2) = €17.6 million and 4% of this is **€704,000.**
Sell Podge shares = 4% of €100 million = €4 million and borrow 4% of €25 million (1 − 0.2) = €0.8 million.
Stake available = €4.8 million and buy €4.8 million/€112 million of Rodge, i.e. 4.286%

New earnings = €25 million (1 − 0.2)(0.04286)	=	€857,143
Less interest of €0.8M(12%)	=	€96,000
New earnings		€761,143

This is an improvement in earnings of **€57,143.**

Question 18

Find base case NPV and adjust for financial side effects of tax shield, loan subsidy and issue costs.

Base case NPV

Year	Cash flow	DF 10%	PV
0	(€25 million)	1	(€25 million)
1 – 10	€4.375 million	6.145	€26.884375 million
10	€5 million	0.386	€1.93 million
		Base case NPV =	€3,814,375

Tax shield – €5 million @ 8% = €400,000
With tax relief at 12.5% = €50,000
€4 million @6% = €240,000 with tax relief at 12.5% = €30,000
The present value @ 5.5% = €80,000 X 7.538 = €603,040

Loan subsidy – Saves 2% × €4 million each year = €80,000

After tax = €80,000(1 – 0,125) = €70,000
The present value   @ 5.5% = €70,000 × 7.538 = €527,660
Issue costs – Less 1% of €5 million = €50,000 and 4% of €10 million = €400,000
APV = €3,814,375 + €603,040 + €527,660 + (€450,000) = **€4,495,075**
The project is viable

Question 21

Statements
1. This is correct as long as the company stays in the same line of business and maintains its current capital structure. Use CAPM to find a diversification discount rate and use APV if there are substantial financial side affects of a capital structure change.
2. The cost of equity should be based on market values. Book values are historic and of doubtful economic significance.
3. This is correct although the two models may give different results due to the nature of the inputs in each model. CAPM is normally considered to be the better alternative.
4. The cost of redeemable debt is based on the internal rate of return/redemption yield of the corporate cash flows and the market value of debt should be used in this calculation. If the company is in a tax-paying position, the cost of debt should be estimated net of any tax relief on interest paid on the debt.
5. There is no need to round up.

Expanding existing operations – use existing WACC
Cost of equity incorrect

$$Ke = \frac{d_1}{Po} + g = \frac{24(1.09)}{428} + 0.09 = 0.151 = 15.1\%$$

Asset beta should be geared

$$\text{Asset beta} = \text{Beta of equity} \times \frac{E}{E + D(1 - T)}$$

$$1.1 = \text{Beta of equity} \times \frac{428}{428 + 90(1 - 0.125)} = 1.3$$

Using the CAPM Ke = Rf + (Rm – Rf) beta = 6% + (14% – 6%) 1.3 = 16.4%
Cost of debt is based on the following set of cash flows

Year	Cash flow in millions
O	(€90)
1 to 4	€7
4	€80

The internal rate of return here using the interpolation method is 5%.
The market value of equity and debt are €428 million and €90 million.
The CAPM estimate will be used in calculating the WACC.

$$\text{The WACC} = \frac{428\,(16.4\%) + 90\,(5\%\,)}{518} = 14.42\%$$

The discount rate to be used in investment appraisal is 14.42%

Diversifying activities

No ungearing is necessary as the asset beta is given. This needs to be regeared however.
Asset beta should be geared

$$0.9 = \text{Beta of equity} \times \frac{428}{428 + 90(1 - 0.125)}$$

Beta of equity = 1.066
Using CAPM Ke = Rf + (Rm − Rf)beta = 6% + (14% − 6%)1.066 = 14.52%
The cost of debt remains the same at 5% and the WACC is as follows

$$\text{The WACC} = \frac{428\ (14.52\%) + 90\ (5\%)}{518} = 12.87\%$$

The discount rate to be used in investment appraisal when diversifying into the new industry is 12.87%
This question covers material in chapters 6, 12 and 13.

CHAPTER 14

Question 5

Setting the offer price is the most difficult part of an IPO. If the offer price is set too low, the issuing firm is faced with a potential loss. On the other hand, set the price too high and the issue may be unsuccessful.

Underpricing helps new shareholders get a higher rate of return on the shares they buy. Existing shareholders will experience a loss.

Much of the underpricing is concentrated on smaller and very speculative issues with little or no sales record. They must be underpriced in order to attract investors.

Another reason why IPOs have such a large initial return is because of the 'winner's curse'. The only way in which the winner's curse can be avoided is by 'underpricing'.

Finally, underwriters could possibly be sued if they consistently got the offer price wrong. Therefore, underpricing could be seen as an insurance against being sued.

Question 11

The only reason is that some investors are completely risk averse.

Question 13

If markets are efficient, all available information is incorporated into the share price. Therefore, in order for you to outsmart the market, you must have information that *nobody else* has. If you believe this then the market will end up outsmarting you.

Furthermore, don't try to predict what the future holds. Past price performance is no evidence of future prices. If the stock market rises for 15 days in a row, it doesn't mean that it will continue to rise.

Investors who try to find good deals can spend a lot of money buying and selling securities hoping for abnormal returns. The transactions costs alone can push up the required rate of return necessary for you just to break even. It would be wise for the investor to minimise transactions costs by investing long term.

In summary, with efficient markets, investors will, on average, earn what the market offers. When we include trading costs, these investors will loose out by the amount of the transactions costs.

Question 16

Yes. This violates strong form market efficiency, because the sales director can make a profit by using insider information.

Question 20

Proceeds per share = 8(1 − 0.03) = €7.76. This is the net proceeds per share sold. In addition, it has to pay additional expenses of €20,000. Therefore, the total number of shares it must issue is = (15m + 20,000)/€7.76 = 1,935,567.

CHAPTER 15

Question 1

The price of both bonds at a 10% yield and 9% yield can be calculated using 5.2 (chapter 5) and the procedure in section 15.1. This gives the following results:

Price at 10% yield *Finance* bond	=	106.55
Price at 9% yield of *Finance* bond	=	109.19
Price volatility of *Finance* bond	=	2.48%

Price at 10% yield *Treasury* bond	=	106.55
Price at 9% yield of *Treasury* bond	=	107.94*
Price volatility of *Treasury* bond	=	1.30%

*The assumption of early redemption results in the redemption value being paid in two months' time along with the normal coupon, but with no further payments thereafter. The price is therefore calculated as

$$\text{Price} = \frac{109.50}{(1.09)^{0.16}} = 107.94$$

Question 2

(a) The cash flow from the bond is as follows:

End-Year	1	2	3	4	5
Cash flow	40	40	40	40	1040

The cash flow is discounted at varying rates until two rates are found which give a present value either side of €800. As before, these rates should be one percentage point apart. The true cost of finance can be approximated between these two trial rates by linear interpolation.

Since the payments of €40 form an annuity, the present value can be found using 5.2 (Chapter 5).

A discount rate of 9% produces a present value of €805.52. A discount rate of 10% produces a present value of €772.55. The answer is therefore between 9 and 10%. The answer can be approximated by linear interpolation:

$$\frac{x}{1} = \frac{5.52}{32.97} = 0.17$$

The answer is approximated at 9.2%

(b) The annual cash flow and debt position can be shown as follows:

End-Year	Finance Cost @9.2%	Interest Paid	Debt
0			800.00
1	73.60	40	833.60
2	76.69	40	870.29
3	80.07	40	910.36
4	83.75	40	954.11
5	87.78	1040	1.89

The small positive balance at the end of year five is simply a rounding error as the true cost of finance is slightly below 9.2%.

Question 3

(a) 1 July 2010

The price on this date is calculated using 5.2 (chapter 5) with the following parameters

$P_t = 9.12$ (€12 less tax @ 24%)
$k = 0.07$
$n = 5$

This gives a price of €108.69

Note that the investor buying the bond on this day does not get the coupon payment on that date, but must wait until one year later to receive her first income from the bond.

1 May 2010

An investor buying the bond on this day is getting the same as the person buying it on 1 July 2010 plus an extra €9.12 in two months' time. The price paid should reflect this extra payment, but also the fact that it is purchased earlier. The price is therefore:

$$\text{Price } 31/05/10 = \frac{\text{Price } 01/07/10 + €9.12}{(1.07)^{1/6}} = €116.49$$

25 June 2010
This is similar to the above except that the discount period is 6 days rather than two months. The price is therefore:

$$\text{Price } 25/06/10 = \frac{\text{Price } 01/07/10 + €9.12}{(1.07)^{6/365}} = €117.68$$

(b) 1 July 2010

$$\text{Gross income yield} = \frac{12.00}{108.69} \times 100 = 11.04\%$$

1 May 2010

$$\text{Gross income yield} = \frac{12.00}{116.49} \times 100 = 10.30\%$$

25 June 2010

$$\text{Gross income yield} = \frac{12.00}{117.68} \times 100 = 10.20\%$$

Question 7

Since Bond B is issued and redeemed at par, the true average annual cost of finance is equal to the coupon rate, i.e. 10%. It is sufficient therefore to determine whether the true average annual cost of finance of Bond A is above or below 10%. The cash flow from the bond is as follows:

Bond A					
End-Year	1	2	3	4	5
Cash flow	20	50	80	120	1350

A discount rate of 10% produces a present value of €1,039.81. A discount rate higher than 10% would be required to bring the present value down to €1,000. Therefore the true average annual cost of finance of Bond A is above 10%. Bond B is cheaper from the company's point of view.

Question 15

(a) First find the price on 1/08/13.
The price on this date is calculated using 15.2 (chapter 15) with the following parameters:

$P_t = 6.00$
$k = 0.09$
$n = 8$

This gives a price of €83.40.
Note that the investor buying the bond on this day does not get the coupon payment on that date, but must wait until one year later to receive her first income from the bond.

Next calculate the price on 31 July 2013.
An investor buying the bond on this day is getting the same as the person buying it on 1 August 2013 plus an extra €6.00 in one day's time. Since they are both parting with their money at virtually the same time the buyer on 31 July should pay an extra €6.00 for the bond. The price on this date is therefore €89.40.

(i) 26 May 2013
An investor buying the bond on this date gets the same cash flow as the investor buying it on 31 July 2013. However, she has to part with her money about 66 days earlier and so the price paid on this date should be lower to reflect this. Thus the price of the bond on this date should be €89.40 discounted for 66 days at a rate of 9% p.a. This produces a price of €88.02.

$$\text{Price } 26/05/13 = \frac{\text{Price } 31/07/13}{(1.09)^{66/365}} = €88.02$$

(ii) 31 January 2013

An investor buying the bond on this date gets the same cash flow as the investor buying it on 31 July 2013. However, she has to part with her money about 6 months earlier and so the price paid on this date should be lower to reflect this. Thus the price of the bond on this date should be €89.40 discounted for 6 months at a rate of 9% p.a. This produces a price of €85.63.

$$\text{Price } 31/01/13 = \frac{\text{Price } 31/07/13}{(1.09)^{1/2}} = \text{€}85.63$$

(iii) 26 August 2013

First find the price on 31 July 2014 as shown above but changing n to 7. This gives a value of €90.90. An investor buying the bond on the 26 August 2013 gets the same cash flow as the investor buying it on 31 July 2014. However, she has to part with her money 339 days earlier and so the price paid on this date should be lower to reflect this. Thus the price of the bond on this date should be €90.90 discounted for 339 days at a rate of 9% p.a. This produces a price of €83.91.

$$\text{Price } 26/08/13 = \frac{\text{Price } 31/07/14}{(1.09)^{339/365}} = \text{€}83.91$$

(iv) 26 May 2014

Similarly to part (iii), the price on 31 July 2014 should be calculated and then discounted for 66 days. An investor buying the bond on this date gets the same cash flow as the investor buying it on 31 July 2014. However she has to part with her money 66 days earlier and so the price paid on this date should be lower to reflect this. Thus the price of the bond on this date should be €90.90 discounted for 66 days at a rate of 9% p.a. This produces a price of €89.49

$$\text{Price } 26/05/14 = \frac{\text{Price } 31/07/14}{(1.09)^{66/365}} = \text{€}89.49$$

(v) 1 August 2018

The price on this date is calculated using 5.2 with the following parameters:
$P_t = 6.00$
$k = 0.09$
$n = 3$
This gives a price of €92.41.

Note that the investor buying the bond on this day does not get the coupon payment on that date, but must wait until one year later to receive her first income from the bond.

(b)

	Date	Price
(a) (i)	26/05/13	88.02
(a) (ii)	31/01/13	85.63

(a) (ii) < (a)(i) because the cash flow is similar irrespective of the date, but the purchaser has to part with his/her money earlier in (a)(ii) and so the cash flows are discounted for a longer period.

	Date	Price
(a)(i)	26/05/13	88.02
(a)(iii)	26/08/13	83.91

(a)(iii) < (a)(i) because purchase on 26/05/13 generates an extra coupon payment of €6 (on 01/08/13). This outweighs the effect of earlier purchase.

CHAPTER 16

Question 10

Stock Turnover = Cost of goods sold/Average stock
$$= €16,000/[€5,000 + €5,700/2] = €16,000/€5,350$$
$$= 2.99 \text{ times}$$
Debtors Turnover
Sales/Average Debtors
€20,000/[€4,300 + €4,000/2]
€20,000/€4,150
$$= 4.8 \text{ times}$$
Creditors turnover
$$= \text{Cost of goods sold/Average creditors}$$
$$= €16,000/[€2,000 + €2,200/2]$$
$$= €16,000/[€2,100] = 7.6 \text{ times.}$$
Therefore:
Stock period = 365/2.99 = 122 days
Debtors period = 365/4.8 = 76 days
Creditors period = 365/7.6 = 48 days
Consequently, it takes 122 days to acquire and sell stock. It takes 76 days to collect the cash from debtors. The operating cycle is therefore 122 + 76 = 198 days.
The cash cycle is 198 days – 48 days = 150 days.

Question 15

$Q^* = [(2)(\text{annual cash disbursements})(\text{cost per sale of securities})/\text{interest rate}]^{.5}$.
$Q^* = [2 \times €30m \times €1,000/ 0.03]^{5}$.
$Q^* = [€60m \times €1,000/ 0.03]^{5}$.
$Q^* = €1,414213$.

Question 18

Net float is the difference between the balance available at the bank and your own book balance.

The available balance will be €100, what you started with. The €200 cheque will not have cleared, and the cheque sent by your parents will not have cleared either. Your book balance on 5 February is:
€100 + €100 – €200 = €zero.
Therefore, your net float is:
€100 – €Zero = €100.
Your cheque will be presented on 7 February. So it is necessary for the available balance to be at least €200 on that date. Your parents cheque will be presented on February 8th. The available balance on 7 February is €100 – €200 = –€100. The cheque will bounce.

Question 20

(a) $Q^* =[(2 \times €30,000 \times €50)/0.1].\ 5 = €5,477.2$.
What this means is that the initial balance should be €5,477.2. If the balance drops to zero, a further €5,477.2 should be put into cash.
The average cash balance is:
$Q^*/2 = €5,477.2/2 = €2,738.6$.
The opportunity cost is:
$(€2,738.6)(0.1) = €2,737.8$.
In addition, there will be €30,000/€5,477 = 5.5 orders during the year. Therefore the total trading costs are:
$(5.5)(€50) = €274$.
The total costs are:
Opportunity costs + Trading costs
€2,73.8 + €274 = €5,476.6

(b) (i)   Synchronisation.
(ii) Increase in the forecast sales which leads to lower target cash balances.
(iii) Reduce marketable securities, which would increase firm's cash balances.
(iv) Arranging an overdraft will allow the firm to hold less cash.

(c) Synchronisation of cash flows is a plan to keep cash balances to a minimum by improving the firm's forecasting so that cash inflows occur simultaneously with cash outflows.

Question 22

The daily interest rate is about .022 basis points. The rate of return earned on €1m per day is €1,000,000 x 0.00022 = €220. This is the opportunity cost. The order cost will usually be much less than this. Therefore, large firms will buy and sell short-term securities regularly rather than leave cash lying around.

CHAPTER 17

Question 5

Profit and Loss Account under Old and New Policies		
	Old Policy	New Policy
Turnover	€2,000,000	€2,300,000
Variable Costs	€1,500,000	€1,725,000
Gross Profit	€500,000	€575,000
Cost of Carrying Debtors*	€16,437	€23,630
Credit Control Expenses	€20,000	€12,000
Bad Debts	€20,000	€23,000
Profit Before Tax	€443,563	€516,400
Tax (20%)	€88,713	€103,280
Profit After Tax	€354,850	€413,120

Therefore, the new policy will improve the profit after tax figure.
* Cost of carrying debtors is the average collection period by the variable cost percentage by the cost of the funds used to carry debtors. Note the variable costs represent the costs of goods sold.
Cost of carrying debtors:
(Debtors Collection Period)(Daily Sales)(VC: Sales ratio)(Cost of Funds)
(40 days)(€5,479)(0.75)(0.1) = €16,437 = Old policy.
(50 days)(€6,301)(0.75)(0.1) = €23,630 = New policy

Question 7

The cost of debtors:
   (i)   Probability of default
   (ii) The actual cash discount
   (iii) Cost of debt.
By not granting credit there is the cost of lost sales. Firms that give credit have the cost of running credit departments. This job is often factored out to outside companies.
   Total carrying costs are the costs that are incurred when credit is granted. These are positively related to the amount of credit that is granted.
   Opportunity costs are the sales that are lost by not granting credit. Opportunity costs decline when credit is given.

Question 12

(0.2)(110,000) = €22,000

Question 17

Remember an optimum inventory policy requires restocking costs to equal carrying costs. Since this is not the case, the company does not have optimum inventory. Furthermore, since carrying costs are high compared to restocking costs, the company should reduce its stock levels.

Question 19

(a) EOQ = $[2(F)(TS)/(X)(P)]^{0.5}$.
    =$[2(30)(100,000)/(0.15)(10)]^{0.5}$ = 2000 units
(b) 100,000/2000 = 50 orders a year or 365/50 = 7.3 days.
(c) The maximum stock is the stock that is available immediately a new order is received is 2,000 + 599 (safety) = 2,599.

CHAPTER 18

Question 3

Larger firms generally have greater access to the financial markets in terms of issuing shares and bonds. In addition, older and more mature companies will have built up a substantial level of retained earnings over their lifetime. Smaller firms are therefore more dependent on short-term finance.

Question 6

(a) Investors who lend money to a company would prefer if the company had a healthy current ratio, i.e. a sizeable excess of current assets over current liabilities.

However, from the point of view of the company, it is wasteful if the current ratio is too high. Having money tied up in cash, stock, debtors, etc. does not provide a return. Having cash in a current account usually doesn't pay interest. Stock on hand provides no return because the company hasn't sold it. Debtors are customers who owe money to the company, which cannot be used until it is received.

On the other hand, fixed assets generate the income that earns profit, but they are not very liquid. The decision for companies is whether they should invest in long-term assets that generate returns (profit), and consequently have low investments in current assets, or whether they should keep a high level of cash and other current assets and stay liquid.

(b) Aggressive working capital policy finances temporary current assets, possibly all of its permanent current assets and maybe some of its fixed assets with short-term debt.

If it finances its temporary current assets and most of its permanent current assets with current liabilities (short-term debt), it will have very little net working capital. In other words, there is only a small difference between liquid assets and the amount due for current liabilities. Therefore, this policy is very risky. As described in Chapter 13, zero working capital results from financing all current assts with short-term debt. Negative working capital is the situation where all current assets and part of the fixed assets are financed with short-term debt.

Conservative working capital policy involves using long-term debt to finance all fixed assets, permanent current assets, and part of the temporary current assets. Only a small portion of the current assets is financed with current liabilities. The current ratio is therefore very high. This is a low-risk strategy. However, because long-term funds are more expensive than short-term loans, a conservative working capital policy is expensive to the firm.

The moderate or matching approach to financing is where temporary current assets are financed with current liabilities, and all permanent current assets and fixed assets should be financed by long-term liabilities and equity. The level of net working capital is larger than under the aggressive policy and smaller than under the prudent or conservative policy. The level of risk is therefore medium.

CHAPTER 19

Questions 1 to 5 are explained in the text.

Question 6

(a) **Lead payment – \$10,000,000/1.0625 = €9,411,765**

Money market – Deposit \$10,000,000/1.0175 = \$9,828,010 at a cost of 9,828,010/1.0625 = €9,249,892

FEC – Forward rate = 1.0625 + 0.0110 =1.0735.
FEC = \$10,000,000/1.0735 = €9,315,324 in three months.
To make a direct comparison discount at the cost of borrowing in euros, i.e. €9,315,324/1.01 = €9,223,093. The FEC is the lowest cost.

(b) The cost of forward cover

$$\frac{-0.011 \times 12 \times 100}{3 \times 1.0625} = -4.14\%$$

$$\frac{-0.0105 \times 12 \times 100}{3 \times 1.0635} = -3.96\%$$

The cost of forward cover is approximately −4% (dollar cheaper in the future) and this also reflects the difference in interest rates in the two economies, i.e. € rates are lower by 4%.

(c) Forward exchange contract: Forward rate = 1.0635 + 0.0105 =1.074. FEC = $10,000,000/1.074 = €9,310,987 in three months.
Money market – borrow $10,000,000/1.02 = $9,803,922 and transfer into euros at 1.0635 – 9,803,922/1.0635 = €9,218,544. To compare in the same timeframe as the FEC this can be deposited at 3/4%, i.e. €9,218,544(1.0075) = €9,287,683.
The FEC is the higher revenue value.

Question 8

(a) The company should buy an FRA on the notional principal amount of €10 million at the 6 v 9 at 5.3%.

(b) (i)   If Euribor is 6.5% at settlement, the FRA bank must pay
€10 million × (6.5% – 5.3%)3/12 × 1/(1.01625) = €29,520 to the company.
In each case the company will borrow at Euribor + 0.5% = 7%
Interest cost = €10 million × 7%/4 = €175,000 less €29,520
= €145,480 and €145,480/€10 million for 3 months = 5.8%
(ii) If Euribor is 4.5% at settlement the company must pay
€10 million × (5.3% – 4.5%) 3/12 × 1/(1.01125) = €19,778 to the FRA bank.
In each case the company will borrow at Euribor + 0.5% = 5%
Interest cost = €10 million × 5%/4 = €125,000 plus €19,753
= €144,778 and €144,778/10 million for 3 months = 5.8%
The FRA allows the company to fix the borrowing at the FRA rate plus 0.5%.

Question 9

Multilateral netting is carried out by first changing all values to €.
W240 million/1680 = €142,857
SF480,000/1.88 = €255,319
W180 million/1680 = €107,143
£74,000/0.68 = €108,824
SF375,000/1.88 = €199,468
Then net them off in the following table:

Receiving €	Paying € UK	Paying € SK	Paying € SW	Total
UK € receipts		108,824		108,824
SK € receipts	142,857		107,143	250,000
SW € receipts	255,319	199,468		454,787
Total payments €	(398,176)	(308,292)	(107,143)	
Total receipts €	108,824	250,000	454,787	
Net cash flow €	(289,352)	(58,292)	347,644	

The UK subsidiary pays the Switzerland subsidiary €289,352.
The South Korean subsidiary pays the Switzerland subsidiary €58,292.

Question 11

(a)
FEC $A120,000/2.1675 = €55,363.32
MM $A120,000/1.02 =$A117,647/2.1425 = €54,911 and to make this directly comparable to the FEC on 1 September place this on deposit at 1.25% = €54,911 × 1.0125 = €55,598. The money market operation is better.
FEC   80 million/130.8 = €611,621
MM   80 million/1.0225/129.3 = €605,101 deposit at 1.25% = €612,665
Again the money market operation is better.
FEC   €1 million/0.6825 = €1,465,201
MM   €1 million/1.0125/0.6870 = €1,437,634 and deposit at 1.25%
= €1,437,634 × 1.0125 = €1,455,604 and here the FEC is better.
The net cash inflow on 1 September = €55,598 – €40,000 + €612,665 + €1,465,201 = €2,093,464

(b)
FEC $120,000/2.16 = €55,556*
MM   120,000/1.0175 = $117,936. This costs $117,936/2.14 = €55,110 at 1.5% cost of borrowing = €55,937 cost in three months
FEC   80 million/129.5 = €617,761*
MM   80 million/1.02 = 78,431,373 at 128.5 = €610,351 and borrowing cost of 1.5% = €619,516 in three months.
FEC   €1 million/0.68 = €1,470,588
MM   €1 million/1.01 = €990,099. This costs €990,099 /0.685 = €1,445,400 today and at 1.5% = €1,467,081* in three months.
The net cash outflow on 1 September = €40,000 – €55,556 – €617,761 –€1,467,081= (€2,100,398)

Question 16

Forward contract will cost $15m/1.4310 = **€10,482,180** in four months' time.
Futures position is to sell June futures. The number of contracts = $15m/1.4302/125,000 = 83.9 or 84 contracts. Tick size = 0.0001 × 125,000 = $12.50. As the futures price is in the same relationship to the spot price the futures price = 1.3500 – (1.4302 – 1.4461) = 1.3341
        Sell 84 contracts at 1.4302 now
        Buy 84 contracts at 1.3341 in four months
Profit = 961 ticks × 84 × $12.50 = $1,009,050
The net outcome = ($15,000,000 – 1,009,050)/1.35 = **€10,363,667** in four months. This solution ignores the time value of money and the fact that there were not an exact number of contracts.
Options position is to buy euro puts. There are three choices available
1.4000 less premium 0.0038 = 1.3962 net
1.4250 less premium 0.0068 = 1.4182 net
1.4500 less premium 0.0238 = 1.4262 net. Choose 1.4500
Number of contracts = 15m/1.45/62,500 = 165.52 or 166. Tick value = 62,500 × $0.0001 = $6.25
Premium cost = $0.0238 × 62,500 × 166 = $246,925 at 1.4461 = €170,752
If the spot turns out to be $1.35 then exercise the put options. Buy 166 at 1.4500 and sell at 1.35.
The profit on the options = 1000 × 166 × $6.25 = $1,037,500.
The net outcome = (15,000,000 – 1,037,500)/1.35 less $170,752 = **€10,171,841** in four months.
The options are the best choice.

Question 22

(a) The company is afraid of rates falling and futures price rising, therefore buy futures at 96.60.

$$\text{The number of contracts} = \frac{7.5 \text{ million} *4/3}{1 \text{ million}} = 10 \text{ contracts}$$

The company should buy 10 June futures @ 96.60 today.
Current Euribor = 4% = 96.00 and basis risk = 96.60 – 96.00 = 0.6%.
June futures have 7 months to run and as close out occurs in 5 months, the basis risk = 2/7 × 0.60%.
Basis risk = 0.171% and Euribor lock-in rate = 96.60 – 0.171 = 96.429 or 3.571%.
(b) The FRA available = 3.45% and if Euribor falls by 0.5% the results will be as follows:
Cash market rate = 3.5% + 0.6% = 4.1% or 7.5 million × 4.1% × 4/12.
Total = €102,500 or 4.1%
Futures market If rate = 3.5% then price = 96.50 + 0.171 basis = 96.671.
1 Dec buy 10 June futures @   96.60
1 May sell 10 June futures @   <u>96.671</u>
                              0.071 or 7.1 ticks
Profit = 7.1 × $25 × 10 = €1,775. Cash market = €102,500.
Total = €104,275 or 4.171%
FRA rate 3.45% and actual Euribor is 3.5%. The company will compensate the bank. Amount is €7.5 million × (3.5% – 3.45%) × 4/12 = €1,250
This is discounted at the prevailing interest rate of 3.5%
= €1250/1.016667 = (€1071). Cash market = €102,500
Total = €101,429 or 4.05%
The future gives the best outcome in this case.

(c) The number of contracts may not be an exact number.
Basis risk may be different from that expected above.
Gains and losses are market-to-market base daily which ignores the time value of money and transactions costs are ignored.

Question 23*

The forward exchange rates are as follows:

Exchange rates	Offer	Bid
Spot rate ($ per €)	1.4106	1.4140
Three months forward	1.4024	1.4063
Six months forward	1.3967	1.4006

Three month position
$197,000 inflow
FEC 197,000/1.4063 = €140,084*
MM (197,000/1.015/1.4140) × 1.01125 = €138,806. Here the FEC is better.
Net cash flow = €140,084 − €116,000 = €24,084

Six month position = $547,000 − $254,000 = $293,000 outflow
FEC = 293,000/1.3967 = (€209,780)*
MM (293,000/1.015/1.4106) × 1.0375 = €212,318. Here the FEC is better.

CHAPTER 20

Question 1

(a) This is similar to Examples 20.5 and 20.8 in the text.
   The parameters required to find the original payment and the outstanding balance after 48 payments are

PV = 25,000
n = 144 months
k = 0.008 per month

The original payment is got from 4.8 and works out at €293.02. The outstanding balance after the payment at time 48 is made is got from 20.1 above and works out at €19,582.70.
   Since Ann makes no payments in times 49, 50 and 51, this balance will be charged interest at the rate on 0.8% per month for the next 3 months (i.e. until time 51). The balance at time 51 will therefore be €20,056.46.
   The required number of payments can be calculated from 4.8 using the following parameters.

PV = 20,056.46
P_t = 293.02
k = 0.008
n = unknown number of payments to be calculated

This produces an answer of 99.5. This can be interpreted as 99 full payments and one final smaller payment.
   The last three lines of the amortisation schedule are therefore months 98, 99 and 100 of a new schedule when the payments resume. To show the last three lines, the outstanding balance after 97 payments must be calculated. Using 20.1 with the following parameters:

PV = 20,056.46
P_t = 293.02
h = 97 months
k = 0.008 per month

This works out as €733.54.

Amortisation Schedule

Time	Payment	Interest	Capital	Balance
97				733.54
98	293.02	5.87	287.15	446.39
99	293.02	3.57	289.45	156.94
100	158.20	1.26	156.94	0.00

(b) The balance at time 51 is, from (a) above, equal to 20,056.46. The balance at time 54 can be got be drawing up three lines of the amortisation schedule as follows:

Time	Payment	Interest	Capital	Balance
51				20,056.46
52	293.02	160.45	132.57	19,923.89
53	293.02	159.39	133.63	19,790.26
54	293.02	158.32	134.70	19,655.56

The rate of interest now changes to 0.009 per month. Since the payment stays the same as before, the term of the loan must be increased further. The required number of payments can be calculated from 4.8 using the following parameters:

PV = 19,655.56
P_t = 293.02
k = 0.009
n = unknown number of payments to be calculated

This produces an answer of 103.3. This can be interpreted as 103 more full payments from this point and one final smaller payment.

The last line of the amortisation schedule is therefore month 104 of a new schedule starting at time 55. To show the last line, the outstanding balance after 103 payments must be calculated. Using 20.1 with the following parameters:

PV = 19,655.56
P_t = 293.02
h = 103 months
k = 0.009 per month

This works out as €89.86.

Amortisation Schedule

Time	Payment	Interest	Capital	Balance
103				89.86
104	90.67	0.81	89.86	0.00

(c) Calculate the balance on the loan at the time the re-financing option becomes available using 20.1 with h = 48.

Balance at time 48 = 19,582.70

The borrower needs to borrow this amount plus the penalty in order to redeem the loan.

Penalty
OB at time 48 = 19,582.70
OB at time 54 = 18,748.01 (if payments continued as originally agreed)
Capital paid (time 49–54) = 834.69
Total paid (time 49–54) = 1,758.12
Interest paid (time 49–54) = 923.43
Penalty = 923.43 + 200 = 1.123.43

Need to borrow 19582.70 + 1123.43 = 20706.13

The choice is now between continuing an existing loan valued at 19582.70 at a rate of interest of 9.6% p.a. compounded monthly or a loan of 20706.13 at a rate of interest of 8.4% p.a. compounded monthly each to be paid off over 8 years with monthly payments.
The new periodic payment can be calculated from 4.8 with

PV = 20,706.13
n = 96
k = 0.007

This produces a payment of €296.94.

Since 296.94 > 293.02 the borrower should not re-finance the loan.

Question 2

(a) Gross payment
Annuity
The monthly payment is calculated from 4.8 above as €1,799.45.
Endowment

The monthly payment to the bank is calculated as €200,000 x 0.0075	= 1,500
Add the endowment policy premium	= 400
Total	= 1,900

(b) and (c) Net payments
Interest Paid
Annuity

	Year 1		Year 12	
Outstanding balance	Time 0	200,000.00	Time 132	132,870.84
	Time 12	196,254.60	Time 144	122,828.27
Capital paid	Year 1	3,745.40	Year 12	10,042.57
Total paid	Year 1	21,593.40	Year 12	21,593.40
Interest paid	Year 1	17,848.00	Year 12	11,550.83

Endowment
Interest paid = 1,500 x 12 = 18,000

Tax Relief

	Annuity		Endowment	
Annual	Y1	Y12	Y1	Y12
Interest paid	17,848.00	11,550.83	18,000.00	18,000.00
Allowable int.	10,000.00	3,000.00	10,000.00	3,000.00
Tax relief	2,500.00	450.00	2,500.00	450.00
Monthly Tax Relief	208.33	37.50	208.33	37.50
Gross payment	1,799.45	1,799.45	1,900.00	1,900.00
Tax relief	208.33	37.50	208.33	37.50
Net payment	1,591.12	1,761.95	1,691.67	1,862.50

(d) Change in the rate of interest
The rate of interest changes at the end of the 11 year.
Calculate the loan balance at this point.

Annuity
Outstanding Balance @ time 132 using 20.1 = 132,870.84

Endowment
Balance = original loan size = 200,000

New monthly payment
Annuity
The outstanding balance is treated conceptually like a new loan at this point. The periodic payment can be found using 4.8.

PV = 132,870.84*
k = 0.0065
n = 108
P_t = unknown payment size to be calculated.

* Balance at the time the new interest rate becomes operational.

The monthly payment works out at €1,716.06.

Endowment
The monthly payment to the bank is calculated as €200,000 x 0.0065 = 1,300
Add the endowment policy premium = 400
Total = 1,700

Net Payments
Interest Paid:
Annuity
Year 12

Outstanding balance	Time 132	132,870.84 (start of 'new' loan)
	Time 144	122,268.33 (use h = 12)
Capital paid	year 12	10,602.51
Total paid	year 12	20,592.72
Interest paid	year 12	9,990.21

Endowment
Interest paid = 1,300 x 12 = 15,600

Tax relief

Annual	Year 12 Annuity	Endowment
Interest paid	9,990.21	15,600.00
Allowable interest	3,000.00	3,000.00
Tax relief	450.00	450.00
Monthly tax relief	37.50	37.50
Gross payment	1,716.06	1,700.00
Tax relief	37.50	37.50
Net payment	1,678.56	1,662.50

Question 3

(a) The repayment stream involves two separate annuities
   • an annual payment of €1,500
   • a monthly payment to be determined.

First find the value of a loan which the annual payment stream can support. To do this the annual effective rate of interest must be determined. With a monthly rate of 1.1%, the annual effective rate is 14.03%.
   The loan size sustainable by these payments is found from 4.8 with the following parameters:

P_t = 1,500
n = 7 years
k = 0.1403 per year

This gives a loan size of 6,426.57. The remainder of the total loan of €35,000 must be repaid with monthly payments. The size of this 'second' notional loan is €35,000 − €6,426.57 = €28,573.43. The monthly payment required to pay this off can be found from 4.8 with the following parameters:

PV = 28,573.43
n = 84 months
k = 0.011 per month

This produces a monthly payment of 522.92.

Amortisation Schedule

Time	Payment	Interest	Capital	Balance
0				35,000.00
1	522.92	385.00	137.92	34,862.08
2	522.92	383.48	139.44	34,722.64
3	522.92	381.95	140.97	34,581.67
81				2,986.26*
82	522.92	32.85	490.07	2,496.19
83	522.92	27.46	495.46	2,000.73
84	522.74 + 1,500	22.01	2,000.73	0.00

*The outstanding balance at time 81 involves two calculations.

The outstanding balance on the 'monthly' loan can be found from 20.1 with the following parameters:

PV = 28,573.43
Pt = 522.92
h = 81 months
k = 0.011 per month
This produces an outstanding balance of 1,534.69.

The balance on the 'annual' loan can be found by simply discounting the remaining payment of 1,500 back for three months, i.e.

$$\frac{1,500}{(1.011)^3} = 1,451.57$$

The total outstanding balance is the sum of the two components i.e. 1,534.69 + 1,451.57 = 2,986.26

(b) Outstanding balance at end year three is calculated, in two parts as shown above.

PV = 28,573.43
P_t = 522.92
h = 36 months
k = 0.011 per month
This produces an outstanding balance of €19,419.90.
    The balance on the 'annual' loan can be found by using 20.2 with:

P_t = 1,500
n = 7
h = 3 years
k = 0.1403 per month

This produces a value of €4,367.88.
The total outstanding balance is therefore €23,787.78.
    First find the value of loan which the remaining annual payments can support. To do this the annual effective rate of interest must be determined. With a monthly rate of 1.2%, the annual effective rate is 15.39%.
    The loan size sustainable by these payments is found from 4.8 with the following parameters:

P_t = 1,500
n = 4 years
k = 0.1539 per year

This gives a loan size of 4,248.90. The remainder of the total outstanding balance on the loan of €23,787.78 must be repaid with monthly payments. The size of this 'second' notional loan is €23,787.78 – €4,248.90 = €19,538.88. The monthly payment required to pay this off can be found from 4.8 with the following parameters:

PV = 19,538.88
n = 48 months
k = 0.012 per month

This produces a monthly payment of €537.86.

Time	Payment	Amortisation Schedule Interest	Capital	Balance
81				3,022.73*
82	537.86	36.27	501.59	2,521.14
83	537.86	30.25	507.61	2,013.53
84	537.69 + 1,500	24.16	2,013.53	0.00

*The outstanding balance at time 81 involves two calculations.
    The outstanding balance on the 'monthly' loan can be found from 20.1 with the following parameters:

PV = 19,538.88
P_t = 537.86
h = 45 months
k = 0.012 per month

This produces an outstanding balance of 1,575.46.

The balance on the 'annual' loan can be found by simply discounting the remaining payment of 1,500 back for three months, i.e.

$$\frac{1500}{(1.012)^3} = 1,447.27$$

The total outstanding balance is the sum of the two components i.e. $1,575.46 + 1,447.277 = 3,022.73$

Question 8

(a) The savings fund is made up of three different components:
- the initial deposit of €7,000
- the 5 annual deposits of €8,000
- the 60 monthly deposits.

First find the value that the initial deposit of €7,000 will grow to by the end of year 5 (month 60).

This is a compound interest calculation and can be found from 4.4 with

PV = €7,000
n = 60
k = 0.0035 (note that this is the monthly rate of interest)
This produces FV = €8,632.58.

Note that the annual effective rate of interest (4.28%) could have been used with n = 5 years.

Next, find the value at the end of year 5 of the 5 annual deposits of €8,000.

This is the future value of an ordinary simple annuity and can be found from 4.7 with

P_t = €8,000
n = 5
k = 0.0428 (note that this is the annual effective rate of interest)

This produces FV = €43,575.28.

These two amounts sum to €52,207.86. Therefore the monthly deposits must make up the remaining €7,792.14(€60,000 – €52,207.86).The required monthly deposit can then be found from 4.7 with

FV = €7,792.14
n = 60
k = 0.0035 (note that this is the monthly rate of interest)

This produces P_t = €116.94.

The sinking fund schedule is shown below:

Savings Fund Schedule

Time	Payment	Interest	Increase in Fund	Balance
0	7,000.00		7,000.00	7,000.00
1	116.94	24.50	141.44	7,141.44
2	116.94	25.00	141.93	7,283.37
3	116.94	25.49	142.43	7,425.79
57				51,109.43
58	116.94	178.88	295.82	51,405.25
59	116.94	179.92	296.85	51,702.11
60	8,116.94	180.96	8,297.89	60,000.00

In order to show the final three lines, the fund value at time 57 must be calculated.

This requires three separate calculations.

Initial deposit
The value of the initial deposit of €7,000 at time 57 can be calculated from 4.4 with

PV = €7,000
n = 57
k = 0.0035 (note that this is the monthly rate of interest)

This produces FV = €8,542.57.

Note that in this instance the annual effective rate of interest (4.28%) could not have been used, since the time period is not an exact number of years.

Annual deposits
Only 4 of the annual deposits will have been made by the end of the month 57 (i.e. at times 12, 24, 36 and 48). To find the value of these at time 57, first find the value at time 48 from 4.7 with

P_t = €8,000
n = 4
k = 0.0428 (note that this is the annual effective rate of interest)

This produces FV = €34,114.56.
Nine months' compound interest must now be added to this to get the value at time 57. Using 4.4 with

PV = €34,114.56
n = 9
k = 0.0035 (note that this is the monthly rate of interest)

produces FV = €35,204.34.

Monthly deposits
The value of the monthly deposits at time 57 can be found from 4.7 with

P_t = €116.94
n = 57
k = 0.0035

This produces FV = €7,362.53.

Adding the three amounts together gives €51,109.43, as shown on the savings fund schedule.

(b) The value of the fund at the time of the change in the rate of interest must be calculated. This again involves three separate calculations.

Applying the same approach as above the values at time 36 are

Initial deposit	€7,938.23
Annual deposits	€25,042.30
Monthly deposits	€4,478.07
Total	€37,458.60

The rate of interest now changes to 4.8% p.a. compounded monthly.

The amount above can be notionally placed into a separate account in which it will earn compound interest for the next two years. Its value at time 60 can be found from 4.4 with

PV = €37,458.60
n = 24
k = 0.004 (note that this is the new monthly rate of interest)

This produces FV = €41,225.00

The value at time 60 of the two remaining annual deposits can be calculated from 4.7 with
P_t = €8,000
n = 2
k = 0.0491 (note that this is the new annual effective rate of interest)

This produces FV = €16,392.56

These two amounts sum to €57,617.56

Therefore the monthly deposits must make up the remaining €2,382.44 (€60,000 – €57,617.56). The required monthly deposit can then be found from 4.7 with

FV = €2,382.44
n = 24
k = 0.004 (note that this is the monthly rate of interest)

This produces P_t = €94.78

Note that the new deposit is lower than the original deposit, since the rate of interest has increased and so more of the target value of €60,000 will be generated from the interest earned on the existing fund and less from the deposits into the fund.

(c) To calculate the interest earned in the fourth year, it is first necessary to determine the total increase in the fund in that year and then subtract the value of the deposits made into the fund during the year.

The value at time 48 can be found as follows

Applying the same approach as above the values at time 48 are

Amount in fund at time 36	€39,296.70
1 annual deposit	€8,000.00
12 monthly deposits	€1,162.69
Total	€48,459.39

Increase in fund in year 4   €11,000.80   (€48,459.39 – €37,458.60)

Less payments made	
Annual	€8,000.00
12* monthly	€1,137.34
Interest earned in year 4	€1,863.46

Appendix 2
Mathematical Tables

Table A2.1

Future value of €1 at the end of n periods = $(1 + k)^n$

Period (n)	Interest Rate (k)								
	1%	2%	3%	4%	5%	6%	7%	8%	9%
1	1.0100	1.0200	1.0300	1.0400	1.0500	1.0600	1.0700	1.0800	1.0900
2	1.0201	1.0404	1.0609	1.0816	1.1025	1.1236	1.1449	1.1664	1.1881
3	1.0303	1.0612	1.0927	1.1249	1.1576	1.1910	1.2250	1.2597	1.2950
4	1.0406	1.0824	1.1255	1.1699	1.2155	1.2625	1.3108	1.3605	1.4116
5	1.0510	1.1041	1.1593	1.2167	1.2763	1.3382	1.4026	1.4693	1.5386
6	1.0615	1.1262	1.1941	1.2653	1.3401	1.4185	1.5007	1.5869	1.6771
7	1.0721	1.1487	1.2299	1.3159	1.4071	1.5036	1.6058	1.7138	1.8280
8	1.0829	1.1717	1.2668	1.3686	1.4775	1.5938	1.7182	1.8509	1.9926
9	1.0937	1.1951	1.3048	1.4233	1.5513	1.6895	1.8385	1.9990	2.1719
10	1.1046	1.2190	1.3439	1.4802	1.6289	1.7908	1.9672	2.1589	2.3674
11	1.1157	1.2434	1.3842	1.5395	1.7103	1.8983	2.1049	2.3316	2.5804
12	1.1268	1.2682	1.4258	1.6010	1.7959	2.0122	2.2522	2.5182	2.8127
13	1.1381	1.2936	1.4685	1.6651	1.8856	2.1329	2.4098	2.7196	3.0658
14	1.1498	1.3195	1.5126	1.7317	1.9799	2.2609	2.5785	2.9372	3.3417
15	1.1610	1.3459	1.5580	1.8009	2.0789	2.3966	2.7590	3.1722	3.6425
16	1.1726	1.3728	1.6047	1.8730	2.1829	2.5404	2.9522	3.4259	3.9703
17	1.1843	1.4002	1.6528	1.9479	2.2920	2.6928	3.1588	3.7000	4.3276
18	1.1961	1.4282	1.7024	2.0258	2.4066	2.8543	3.3799	3.9960	4.7171
19	1.2081	1.4568	1.7535	2.1068	2.5270	3.0256	3.6165	4.3157	5.1417
20	1.2202	1.4859	1.8061	2.1911	2.6533	3.2071	3.8697	4.6610	5.6044

	Interest Rate (k)								
Period (n)	10%	12%	14%	15%	16%	18%	20%	24%	28%
1	1.1000	1.1200	1.1400	1.1500	1.1600	1.1800	1.2000	1.2400	1.2800
2	1.2100	1.2544	1.2996	1.3225	1.3456	1.3924	1.4400	1.5376	1.6384
3	1.3310	1.4049	1.4815	1.5209	1.5609	1.6430	1.7280	1.9066	2.0972
4	1.4641	1.5735	1.6890	1.7490	1.8106	1.9388	2.0736	2.3642	2.6844
5	1.6105	1.7623	1.9254	2.0114	2.1003	2.2878	2.4883	2.9316	3.4360
6	1.7716	1.9738	2.1950	2.3131	2.4364	2.6996	2.9860	3.6352	4.3980
7	1.9487	2.2107	2.5023	2.6600	2.8262	3.1855	3.5832	4.5077	5.6295
8	2.1436	2.4760	2.8526	3.0590	3.2784	3.7589	4.2998	5.5895	7.2058
9	2.3579	2.7731	3.2519	3.5179	3.8030	4.4355	5.1598	6.9310	9.2234
10	2.5937	3.1058	3.7072	4.0456	4.4114	5.2338	6.1917	8.5944	11.806
11	2.8531	3.4785	4.2262	4.6524	5.1173	6.1759	7.4301	10.657	15.112
12	3.1384	3.8960	4.8179	5.3503	5.9360	7.2876	8.9161	13.215	19.343
13	3.4523	4.3635	5.4924	6.1528	6.8858	8.5994	10.699	16.386	24.759
14	3.7975	4.8871	6.2613	7.0757	7.9875	10.147	12.839	20.319	31.691
15	4.1772	5.4736	7.1379	8.1371	9.2655	11.974	15.407	25.196	40.565
16	4.5950	6.1304	8.1372	9.3576	10.748	14.129	18.488	31.243	51.923
17	5.0545	6.8660	9.2765	10.761	12.468	16.672	22.186	38.741	66.461
18	5.5599	7.6900	10.575	12.375	14.463	19.673	26.623	48.039	85.071
19	6.1159	8.6128	12.056	14.232	16.777	23.214	31.948	59.568	108.89
20	6.7275	9.6463	13.743	16.367	19.461	27.393	38.338	73.864	139.38

Note: €1 deposited at start of first period

Table A2.2

Present value of €1 to be received after n periods = $1/(1+k)^n$

Period (n)	Interest Rate (k)								
	1%	2%	3%	4%	5%	6%	7%	8%	9%
1	0.9901	0.9804	0.9709	0.9615	0.9524	0.9434	0.9346	0.9259	0.9174
2	0.9803	0.9612	0.9426	0.9246	0.9070	0.8900	0.8734	0.8573	0.8417
3	0.9706	0.9423	0.9151	0.8890	0.8638	0.8396	0.8163	0.7938	0.7722
4	0.9610	0.9238	0.8885	0.8548	0.8227	0.7921	0.7629	0.7350	0.7084
5	0.9515	0.9057	0.8626	0.8219	0.7835	0.7473	0.7130	0.6806	0.6499
6	0.9420	0.8880	0.8375	0.7903	0.7462	0.7050	0.6663	0.6302	0.5963
7	0.9327	0.8706	0.8131	0.7599	0.7107	0.6651	0.6227	0.5835	0.5470
8	0.9235	0.8535	0.7894	0.7307	0.6768	0.6274	0.5820	0.5403	0.5019
9	0.9143	0.8368	0.7664	0.7026	0.6446	0.5919	0.5439	0.5002	0.4604
10	0.9053	0.8203	0.7441	0.6756	0.6139	0.5584	0.5083	0.4632	0.4224
11	0.8963	0.8043	0.7224	0.6496	0.5847	0.5268	0.4751	0.4289	0.3875
12	0.8874	0.7885	0.7014	0.6246	0.5568	0.4970	0.4440	0.3971	0.3555
13	0.8787	0.7730	0.6810	0.6006	0.5303	0.4688	0.4150	0.3677	0.3262
14	0.8700	0.7579	0.6611	0.5775	0.5051	0.4423	0.3878	0.3405	0.2992
15	0.8613	0.7430	0.6419	0.5553	0.4810	0.4173	0.3624	0.3152	0.2745
16	0.8528	0.7284	0.6232	0.5339	0.4581	0.3936	0.3387	0.2919	0.2519
17	0.8444	0.7142	0.6050	0.5134	0.4363	0.3714	0.3166	0.2703	0.2311
18	0.8360	0.7002	0.5874	0.4936	0.4155	0.3503	0.2959	0.2502	0.2120
19	0.8277	0.6864	0.5703	0.4746	0.3957	0.3305	0.2765	0.2317	0.1945
20	0.8195	0.6730	0.5537	0.4564	0.3769	0.3118	0.2584	0.2145	0.1784

Period (n)	Interest Rate (k)								
	10%	12%	14%	15%	16%	18%	20%	24%	28%
1	0.9091	0.8929	0.8772	0.8696	0.8621	0.8475	0.8333	0.8065	0.7813
2	0.8264	0.7972	0.7695	0.7561	0.7432	0.7182	0.6944	0.6504	0.6104
3	0.7513	0.7118	0.6750	0.6575	0.6407	0.6086	0.5787	0.5245	0.4768
4	0.6830	0.6355	0.5921	0.5718	0.5523	0.5158	0.4823	0.4230	0.3725
5	0.6209	0.5674	0.5194	0.4972	0.4761	0.4371	0.4019	0.3411	0.2910
6	0.5645	0.5066	0.4556	0.4323	0.4104	0.3704	0.3349	0.2751	0.2274
7	0.5132	0.4523	0.3996	0.3759	0.3538	0.3139	0.2791	0.2218	0.1776
8	0.4665	0.4039	0.3506	0.3269	0.3050	0.2660	0.2326	0.1789	0.1388
9	0.4241	0.3606	0.3075	0.2843	0.2630	0.2255	0.1938	0.1443	0.1084
10	0.3855	0.3220	0.2697	0.2472	0.2267	0.1911	0.1615	0.1164	0.0847
11	0.3505	0.2875	0.2366	0.2149	0.1954	0.1619	0.1346	0.0938	0.0662
12	0.3186	0.2567	0.2076	0.1869	0.1685	0.1372	0.1122	0.0757	0.0517
13	0.2897	0.2292	0.1821	0.1625	0.1452	0.1163	0.0935	0.0610	0.0404
14	0.2633	0.2046	0.1597	0.1413	0.1252	0.0985	0.0779	0.0492	0.0316
15	0.2394	0.1827	0.1401	0.1229	0.1079	0.0835	0.0649	0.0397	0.0247
16	0.2176	0.1631	0.1229	0.1069	0.0930	0.0708	0.0541	0.0320	0.0193
17	0.1978	0.1456	0.1078	0.0929	0.0802	0.0600	0.0451	0.0258	0.0150
18	0.1799	0.1300	0.0946	0.0808	0.0691	0.0508	0.0376	0.0208	0.0118
19	0.1635	0.1161	0.0829	0.0703	0.0596	0.0431	0.0313	0.0168	0.0092
20	0.1486	0.1037	0.0728	0.0611	0.0514	0.0365	0.0261	0.0135	0.0072

Note: €1 received at end of period

Table A2.3

Present value of an ordinary simple annuity of €1 per period for n periods
$= [1-1/(1 + k)^n]/k$

Periods (n)	Interest Rate (k)								
	1%	2%	3%	4%	5%	6%	7%	8%	9%
1	0.9901	0.9804	0.9709	0.9615	0.9524	0.9434	0.9346	0.9259	0.9174
2	1.9704	1.9416	1.9135	1.8861	1.8594	1.8334	1.8080	1.7833	1.7591
3	2.9410	2.8839	2.8286	2.7751	2.7232	2.6730	2.6243	2.5771	2.5313
4	3.9020	3.8077	3.7171	3.6299	3.5460	3.4651	3.3872	3.3121	3.2397
5	4.8534	4.7135	4.5797	4.4518	4.3295	4.2124	4.1002	3.9927	3.8897
6	5.7955	5.6014	5.4172	5.2421	5.0757	4.9173	4.7665	4.6229	4.4859
7	6.7282	6.4720	6.2303	6.0021	5.7864	5.5824	5.3893	5.2064	5.0330
8	7.6517	7.3255	7.0197	6.7327	6.4632	6.2098	5.9713	5.7466	5.5348
9	8.5660	8.1622	7.7861	7.4353	7.1078	6.8017	6.5152	6.2469	5.9952
10	9.4713	8.9826	8.5302	8.1109	7.7217	7.3601	7.0236	6.7101	6.4177
11	10.3676	9.7868	9.2526	8.7605	8.3064	7.8869	7.4987	7.1390	6.8052
12	11.2551	10.5753	9.9540	9.3851	8.8633	8.3838	7.9427	7.5361	7.1607
13	12.1337	11.3484	10.6350	9.9856	9.3936	8.8527	8.3577	7.9038	7.4869
14	13.0037	12.1062	11.2961	10.5631	9.8986	9.2950	8.7455	8.2442	7.7862
15	13.8651	12.8493	11.9379	11.1184	10.3797	9.7122	9.1079	8.5595	8.0607
16	14.7179	13.5777	12.5611	11.6523	10.8378	10.1059	9.4466	8.8514	8.3126
17	15.5623	14.2919	13.1661	12.1657	11.2741	10.4773	9.7632	9.1216	8.5436
18	16.3983	14.9920	13.7535	12.6593	11.6896	10.8276	10.0591	9.3719	8.7556
19	17.2260	15.6785	14.3238	13.1339	12.0853	11.1581	10.3356	9.6036	8.9501
20	18.0456	16.3514	14.8775	13.5903	12.4622	11.4699	10.5940	9.8181	9.1285

Periods (n)	Interest Rate (k)								
	10%	12%	14%	15%	16%	18%	20%	24%	28%
1	0.9091	0.8929	0.8772	0.8696	0.8621	0.8475	0.8333	0.8065	0.7813
2	1.7355	1.6901	1.6467	1.6257	1.6052	1.5656	1.5278	1.4568	1.3916
3	2.4869	2.4018	2.3216	2.2832	2.2459	2.1743	2.1065	1.9813	1.8684
4	3.1699	3.0373	2.9137	2.8550	2.7982	2.6901	2.5887	2.4043	2.2410
5	3.7908	3.6048	3.4331	3.3522	3.2743	3.1272	2.9906	2.7454	2.5320
6	4.3553	4.1114	3.8887	3.7845	3.6847	3.4976	3.3255	3.0205	2.7594
7	4.8684	4.5638	4.2883	4.1604	4.0386	3.8115	3.6046	3.2423	2.9370
8	5.3349	4.9676	4.6389	4.4873	4.3436	4.0776	3.8372	3.4212	3.0758
9	5.7590	5.3282	4.9464	4.7716	4.6065	4.3030	4.0310	3.5655	3.1842
10	6.1446	5.6502	5.2161	5.0188	4.8332	4.4941	4.1925	3.6819	3.2689
11	6.4951	5.9377	5.4527	5.2337	5.0286	4.6560	4.3271	3.7757	3.3351
12	6.8137	6.1944	5.6603	5.4206	5.1971	4.7932	4.4392	3.8514	3.3868
13	7.1034	6.4235	5.8424	5.5831	5.3423	4.9095	4.5327	3.9124	3.4272
14	7.3667	6.6282	6.0021	5.7245	5.4675	5.0081	4.6106	3.9616	3.4587
15	7.6061	6.8109	6.1422	5.8474	5.5755	5.0916	4.6755	4.0013	3.4834
16	7.8237	6.9740	6.2651	5.9542	5.6685	5.1624	4.7296	4.0333	3.5026
17	8.0216	7.1196	6.3729	6.0472	5.7487	5.2223	4.7746	4.0591	3.5177
18	8.2014	7.2497	6.4674	6.1280	5.8178	5.2732	4.8122	4.0799	3.5294
19	8.3649	7.3658	6.5504	6.1982	5.8775	5.3162	4.8435	4.0967	3.5386
20	8.5136	7.4694	6.6231	6.2593	5.9288	5.3527	4.8696	4.1103	3.5458

Note: €1 paid/received at end of each period

Table A2.4

Future value of an ordinary simple annuity of €1 per period for n periods
$= [(1 + k)^n - 1]/k$

Periods (n)	Interest Rate (k)								
	1%	2%	3%	4%	5%	6%	7%	8%	9%
1	1.0000	1.0000	1.0000	1.0000	1.0000	1.0000	1.0000	1.0000	1.0000
2	2.0100	2.0200	2.0300	2.0400	2.0500	2.0600	2.0700	2.0800	2.0900
3	3.0301	3.0604	3.0909	3.1216	3.1525	3.1836	3.2149	3.2464	3.2781
4	4.0604	4.1216	4.1836	4.2465	4.3101	4.3746	4.4399	4.5061	4.5731
5	5.1010	5.2040	5.3091	5.4163	5.5256	5.6371	5.7507	5.8666	5.9847
6	6.1520	63081	6.4684	6.6330	6.8019	6.9753	7.1533	7.3359	7.5233
7	7.2135	7.4343	7.6625	7.8983	8.1420	8.3938	8.6540	8.9228	9.2004
8	8.2857	8.5830	8.8932	9.2142	9.5491	9.8975	10.260	10.637	11.028
9	9.3685	9.7546	10.159	10.583	11.027	11.491	11.978	12.488	13.021
10	10.462	10.950	11.464	12.006	12.578	13.181	13.816	14.487	15.193
11	11.567	12.169	12.808	13.486	14.207	14.972	15.784	16.645	17.560
12	12.683	13.412	14.192	15.026	15.917	16.870	17.888	18.977	20.141
13	13.809	14.680	15.618	16.627	17.713	18.882	20.141	21.495	22.953
14	14.947	15.974	17.086	18.292	19.599	21.015	22.550	24.215	26.019
15	16.097	17.293	18.599	20.024	21.579	23.276	25.129	27.152	29.361
16	17.258	18.639	20.157	21.825	23.657	25.673	27.888	30.324	33.003
17	18.430	20.012	21.762	23.698	25.840	28.213	30.840	33.750	36.974
18	19.615	21.412	23.414	25.645	28.132	30.906	33.999	37.450	41.301
19	20.811	22.841	25.117	27.671	30.539	33.760	37.379	41.446	46.018
20	22.019	24.297	26.870	29.778	33.066	36.786	40.995	45.762	51.160

Periods (n)	Interest Rate (k)								
	10%	12%	14%	15%	16%	18%	20%	24%	28%
1	1.0000	1.0000	1.0000	1.0000	1.0000	1.0000	1.0000	1.0000	1.0000
2	2.1000	2.1200	2.1400	2.1500	2.1600	2.1800	2.2000	2.2400	2.2800
3	3.3100	3.3744	3.4396	3.4725	3.5056	3.5724	3.6400	3.7716	3.9184
4	4.6410	4.7793	4.9211	4.9934	5.0665	5.2154	5.3680	5.6842	6.0156
5	6.1051	6.3528	6.6101	6.7424	6.8771	7.1542	7.4416	8.0484	8.6999
6	7.7156	8.1152	8.5355	8.7537	8.9775	9.4420	9.9299	10.980	12.136
7	9.4872	10.089	10.730	11.067	11.414	12.142	12.916	14.615	16.534
8	11.436	12.300	13.233	13.727	14.240	15.327	16.499	19.123	22.163
9	13.579	14.776	16.085	16.786	17.519	19.086	20.799	24.712	29.369
10	15.937	17.549	19.337	20.304	21.321	23.521	25.959	31.643	38.593
11	18.531	20.655	23.045	24.349	25.733	28.755	32.150	40.238	50.398
12	21.384	24.133	27.271	29.002	30.850	34.931	39.581	50.895	65.510
13	24.523	28.029	32.089	34.352	36.786	42.219	48.497	64.110	84.853
14	27.975	32.393	37.581	40.505	43.672	50.818	59.196	80.496	109.61
15	31.772	37.280	43.842	47.580	51.660	60.965	72.035	100.82	141.30
16	35.950	42.753	50.980	55.717	60.925	72.939	87.442	126.01	181.87
17	40.545	48.884	59.118	65.075	71.673	87.068	105.93	157.25	233.79
18	45.599	55.750	68.394	75.836	84.141	103.74	128.12	195.99	300.25
19	51.159	63.440	78.969	88.212	98.603	123.41	154.74	244.03	385.32
20	57.275	72.052	91.025	102.44	115.38	146.63	186.69	303.60	494.21

Note: Future value calculated just as last payment/deposit is made

Table A2.5

Standard Normal Distribution

Z	0.00	0.01	0.02	0.03	0.04	0.05	0.06	0.07	0.08	0.09
0.0	0.5000	0.5040	0.5080	0.5120	0.5160	0.5199	0.5239	0.5279	0.5319	0.5359
0.1	0.5398	0.5438	0.5478	0.5517	0.5557	0.5596	0.5636	0.5675	0.5714	0.5753
0.2	0.5793	0.5832	0.5871	0.5910	0.5948	0.5987	0.6026	0.6064	0.6103	0.6141
0.3	0.6179	0.6217	0.6255	0.6293	0.6331	0.6368	0.6406	0.6443	0.6480	0.6517
0.4	0.6554	0.6591	0.6628	0.6664	0.6700	0.6736	0.6772	0.6808	0.6844	0.6879
0.5	0.6915	0.6950	0.6985	0.7019	0.7054	0.7088	0.7123	0.7157	0.7190	0.7224
0.6	0.7257	0.7291	0.7324	0.7357	0.7389	0.7422	0.7454	0.7486	0.7517	0.7549
0.7	0.7580	0.7611	0.7642	0.7673	0.7704	0.7734	0.7764	0.7794	0.7823	0.7852
0.8	0.7881	0.7910	0.7939	0.7967	0.7995	0.8023	0.8051	0.8078	0.8106	0.8133
0.9	0.8159	0.8186	0.8212	0.8238	0.8264	0.8289	0.8315	0.8340	0.8365	0.8389
1.0	0.8413	0.8438	0.8461	0.8485	0.8508	0.8531	0.8554	0.8577	0.8599	0.8621
1.1	0.8643	0.8665	0.8686	0.8708	0.8729	0.8749	0.8770	0.8790	0.8810	0.8830
1.2	0.8849	0.8869	0.8888	0.8907	0.8925	0.8944	0.8962	0.8980	0.8997	0.9015
1.3	0.9032	0.9049	0.9066	0.9082	0.9099	0.9115	0.9131	0.9147	0.9162	0.9177
1.4	0.9192	0.9207	0.9222	0.9236	0.9251	0.9265	0.9279	0.9292	0.9306	0.9319
1.5	0.9332	0.9345	0.9357	0.9370	0.9382	0.9394	0.9406	0.9418	0.9429	0.9441
1.6	0.9452	0.9463	0.9474	0.9484	0.9495	0.9505	0.9515	0.9525	0.9535	0.9545
1.7	0.9554	0.9564	0.9573	0.9582	0.9591	0.9599	0.9608	0.9616	0.9625	0.9633
1.8	0.9641	0.9649	0.9656	0.9664	0.9671	0.9678	0.9686	0.9693	0.9699	0.9706
1.9	0.9713	0.9719	0.9726	0.9732	0.9738	0.9744	0.9750	0.9756	0.9761	0.9767
2.0	0.9772	0.9778	0.9783	0.9788	0.9793	0.9798	0.9803	0.9808	0.9812	0.9817
2.1	0.9821	0.9826	0.9830	0.9834	0.9838	0.9842	0.9846	0.9850	0.9854	0.9857
2.2	0.9861	0.9864	0.9868	0.9871	0.9875	0.9878	0.9881	0.9884	0.9887	0.9890
2.3	0.9893	0.9896	0.9898	0.9901	0.9904	0.9906	0.9909	0.9911	0.9913	0.9916
2.4	0.9918	0.9920	0.9922	0.9925	0.9927	0.9929	0.9931	0.9932	0.9934	0.9936
2.5	0.9938	0.9940	0.9941	0.9943	0.9945	0.9946	0.9948	0.9949	0.9951	0.9952
2.6	0.9953	0.9955	0.9956	0.9957	0.9959	0.9960	0.9961	0.9962	0.9963	0.9964
2.7	0.9965	0.9966	0.9967	0.9968	0.9969	0.9970	0.9971	0.9972	0.9973	0.9974
2.8	0.9974	0.9975	0.9976	0.9977	0.9977	0.9978	0.9979	0.9979	0.9980	0.9981
2.9	0.9981	0.9982	0.9982	0.9983	0.9984	0.9984	0.9985	0.9985	0.9986	0.9986
3.0	0.9987	0.9987	0.9987	0.9988	0.9988	0.9989	0.9989	0.9989	0.9990	0.9990

Mean = 0

Standard Deviation = 1

Number in body of table gives probability of occurrence between minus infinity and the relevant z value

Example: The probability of finding an observation between minus infinity and 1.73 is 0.9582 or 95.82%

To find the probability of an observation below a negative number, subtract the probability shown in the table for the equivalent positive number, from 1

Example: The probability of an observation below −1.4 is found by $1 - 0.9192 = 0.0808 = 8.08\%$

Glossary of Terms

Abnormal return: A return which is greater than the market return after adjusting for systematic risk.

Accounting rate of return: The average annual accounting profit generated by an investment relative to the required capital outlay. Also known as return on capital employed.

Accounts payable period: The time between receiving stock and paying for it.

Accounts receivable financing: Short-term loans involving the factoring of accounts receivable.

Accounts receivable period: The time between the sale of stock and the collection of the amount due.

Accrued interest: Interest earned but not yet paid.

Acid test ratio: *See* Quick ratio.

Additional funds needed (AFN): The external funds required when the forecasted growth in assets exceeds the forecasted growth in liabilities and equity.

Ageing schedule: A schedule used to show the proportion of debtors balance outstanding for a particular period.

Agency costs: Costs incurred by principals (shareholders and/or creditors) to monitor (prevent or minimise) agency problems and therefore to contribute to the maximisation of shareholder value.

Agency problem: The conflict of interest between managers (agents) and principals (shareholders and/or creditors).

Alpha value: A share's alpha value is a measure of its abnormal return, which is the amount by which the share's returns are currently above or below the required return, given the level of systematic risk.

American depository receipt (ADR): Securities issued in the US which represent shares of a foreign company and which therefore allow those shares to be traded in the US.

American option: An option that can be exercised at any time before the final exercise date.

Annual compounding: Computing future values where interest is earned on interest that is paid each year.

Annual percentage rate: The true annual interest rate charged by the lender, taking into account the timing of interest payments and capital.

Annuity: A stream of equal annual cash flows for a limited number of periods.

Annuity due: An annuity where the cash flow payments occur at the beginning of the period.

Arbitrage: The simultaneous buying and selling of assets or securities in different markets in order to make a risk-free gain.

Ask price: The price a dealer is willing to accept for a security, i.e. the price at which a dealer is willing to sell a security.

Authorised share capital: The maximum amount of share capital that a company is allowed to issue.

Average collection period: The average number of days it takes to collect debts from customers.

Balance sheet: A statement showing an economic unit's assets, liabilities and equity at a given point in time.

Balloon payment: Most of the repayment of a loan is made near or at the maturity date.

Base rate: The reference rate of interest that forms the basis for interest rate on bank loans, deposits and overdrafts.

Basis point: 0.01 per cent.

Basis risk: The risk that a specific percentage movement in the cash market will not be matched by an equal move in the futures market when hedging interest and exchange rate risk.

Bearer: The owner of a share or security.

Beta: A measure of the sensitivity of a security's returns to systematic risk.

Bid-ask spread: The difference between the bid price and the asked price.

Bid price: The price a dealer is willing to pay for a security.

Bill of exchange: A commitment in writing to pay a certain sum of money at a certain specified point in time. A bill of exchange can be sold (discounted) before its maturity date at less than face value.

Bird in the hand theory: A theory on dividend policy which states that investors prefer (place a higher value on) €1 of dividends than €1 reinvested in the company.

Bonds: Securities that pay the owner of the security a certain amount at some time in the future and which may pay interest at regular intervals over the life of the security.

Bonus issue: The issue of additional shares to existing shareholders in accordance to their current holding of shares.

Book building: Underwriters ask financial institutions to provide non-binding indications as to the number of shares they are interested in purchasing and the price they are willing to pay in a new or secondary issue of shares.

Book-to-market value: The ratio of balance sheet value (book value) to market value of shares.

Book value: Balance sheet value.

Bootstrapping game: This is the 'price-earnings' game where a company can increase its earnings per share by acquiring another company with a lower earning per share.

Broker: A person who assists in bringing buyers and sellers together.

Buffer stock: The level of stock that is held to prevent 'stock-outs'.

Business risk: The equity risk that arises because of fluctuations in operating income.

Buy-back: Repurchase of shares.

Call option: The option to buy an asset at some specified date or exercise price on or before a specified exercise date.

Cap: An agreement setting the upper limit on the interest rate on a floating rate note.

Capital asset pricing model (CAPM): The relationship between the required rate of return and the beta coefficient or the nondiversifiable risk of the firm.

Capital budgeting: The evaluation of long-term investment proposals discounting all cash flows to the present.

Capital market: Financial market that trades long-term securities.

Capital market line (CML): The risk-return combinations available when the market portfolio and risk-free borrowing or lending is combined.

Capital rationing: The procedure that sets a limit on the amount of cash available for any new investment project.

Capital structure: The mix of equity capital and long-term debt capital.

Carrying cost: The variable cost per unit of carrying an item of stock for a specific period of time.

Cash conversion cycle: The time between cash disbursement and cash collection.

Certificate of deposit: A tradable security issued by banks to investors who deposit a given amount of money for a specified period.

Clientele dividend theory: The dividend theory that states that firms should set their dividends in a way that matches their clients' (shareholders') consumption or tax position.

Collar: An agreement that keeps either a borrowing or a lending rate between specified upper and lower limits.

Commercial paper: Short-term unsecured debt issued by large corporations or financial institutions.

Conglomerate merger: Where two firms that operate in unrelated areas combine.

Conversion price: The share price at which convertible bonds may be converted.

Convertible bonds: Bonds that give the right to the holder to exchange the bonds at some future date for ordinary shares at some predetermined price.

Corporate valuation: The sum of the present value of free cash flow during the horizon period and the present value of the free cash flows after the horizon period.

Cost of capital: The rate of return required by providers of capital to compensate for the risk they take on.

Coupon interest payments: Interest payments made at regular intervals as promised at the time when the bond was issued.

Credit period: The time it takes, on average, between the purchase of inputs and the payment for them.

Credit rating: A procedure in which those seeking credit are compared to some standard indicators of creditworthiness and scored accordingly.

Creditor: A person to whom a debt is owed.

Cum-rights: Shares that are purchased prior to the ex-rights date, giving the purchaser the right to subscribe for new shares under the rights issue.

Current assets: Liquid assets that can be converted into cash, usually within a year.

Current liabilities: Liabilities due to be paid, usually within one year.

Current yield: The interest paid on a bond divided by the current price of the bond.

Dawn raid: In acquisitions, the acquirer acts with such alacrity in buying the shares of the target company that the raider builds up a substantial holding in the target company before the target company's management has time to react.

Dealer: A person who makes a living buying and selling assets.

Debenture: A bond with specified redemption dates and usually secured against specific assets (mortgage debenture) or against a floating charge on the company's assets.

Debtor collection period: The number of days it takes on average to collect debts from customers.

Default risk premium: That part of a bond yield or nominal interest rate that represents compensation for the possibility of default on the promised interest and principal payments.

Degree of operating leverage (DOL): The proportionate change in operating income divided by the proportionate change in sales.

Derivative security: Financial asset that represents a claim on another financial asset.

Derivatives: Financial securities whose values are based on the values of other securities or assets such as bonds, shares, commodities, interest rates and currencies.

Dilution: Existing shareholders suffer a loss in value in relation to book value, market value, ownership of shares, or earnings per share.

Discount loan: A loan in which the interest is paid in advance by deducting it from the amount borrowed.

Discount rate: The rate used when calculating the present value of future cash flows.

Discount yield: The yield an investor receives by purchasing a security at less than face value and redeeming it at maturity at face value.

Discounted cash flow valuation: The process of valuing an investment by calculating the sum of the present value of all future cash flows.

Discounted payback: The time needed to recover initial cash outflows after discounting cash inflows at the appropriate required rate of return.

Diversification effect: The process of portfolio selection where the fluctuations of the assets offset each other, reducing the overall volatility or risk of the portfolio.

Divestiture: To divest or remove assets from a company.

Dividend: The proportion of profit paid to ordinary shareholders, at the discretion of the board of directors.

Dividend cover: The number of times the profit available for distribution to shareholders exceeds the actual dividend paid.

Dividend payout ratio: The ratio of dividends paid to net income.

Dividend valuation models (DVM): The value of a share is the sum of the present value of the expected future cash flows (dividends) from holding that share.

Dividend yield: A shares annual dividend divided by its current market price.

Du Pont formula: This relates the firm's net profit and total asset turnover to its return on total assets (ROA).

EASDAQ: European Association of Securities Dealers Automated Quotation. A stock exchange aimed at fast-growing companies.

Economic order quantity (EOQ): A model to determine an item's optimal order quantity. The order quantity that minimises carrying costs and order costs.

Economic value added (EVA): This is net operating profit after taxes (NOPAT) – after tax euro cost of capital (including the cost of equity capital).

Efficient market hypothesis (EMH): Asserts that organised capital markets are efficient.

Security prices reflect all public information available, and prices react immediately to new information. Securities are fairly priced and therefore investors need not waste time looking for stocks that are 'mispriced'.

Employee share ownership plans (ESOPs): Devices to promote employee share ownership in their company.

Equity multiplier: The ratio of total assets to equity.

Equity sweetener: Gives bond holders the right to participate in the favourable performance of the company by exercising an option to purchase shares.

Euribor: The European inter-bank offer rate is the key inter-bank money market rate.

Euro: The name of the single European currency.

Eurobonds: Long-term debt securities denominated in a currency outside the control of the country of its origin.

European option: Options that can only be exercised on the expiration date.

Exchange rate: The units of one currency needed to purchase one unit of another currency.

Exchange rate risk: The risk associated with having international business where relative currency values can vary.

Ex-dividend: A share that is trading without having entitlement to forthcoming dividend.

Expected return: The return expected to be generated on a risky asset.

Ex-rights: A share that is trading without the entitlement to the forthcoming rights issue.

Face value: also par value. The amount that is promised to be paid to the holder of a bond at maturity.

Factoring: The management practice of selling accounts receivable (debtors) to another firm or factor.

Financial leverage: A change in operating income causes a more than proportionate change in net income because of the fixed nature of financial costs.

Financial risk: The risk of the firm being unable to cover the fixed financial obligations of interest payments, lease payments.

Firm-specific risk: Risk associated specifically with individual firms, such as poor management and industrial relations problems.

Fisher effect: The relationship between nominal returns, real returns and inflation.

Five 'Cs' of credit: Character, capacity, capital, collateral and conditions.

Fixed assets: Assets that are normally held for long periods of time.

Floating rate note (FRN): A note whose interest rate varies with short-term interest rates.

Floor: An agreement that fixes a minimum rate of interest at which a party can borrow.

Flotation: The issue of company shares for the first time on the stock exchange.

Flotation costs: Fees that are paid to bankers when new securities are issued.

Forward rate: The exchange rate used for future delivery of an asset.

Forward rate agreement (FRA): An agreement struck between two parties about the future level of interest rates. If the market interest rate deviates from the agreed level, compensation is paid by one party to the other.

Free cash flow: Cash flow that is free to distribute to shareholders and creditors because it is not needed for investment in fixed assets or working capital.

Friendly mergers: When two companies agree to a proposed merger.
Future value: The value an asset will have in the future.

Gearing: (leverage) The proportion of debt in the overall capital structure.
Gilts: Fixed interest government bonds traded on the stock exchange.
Going concern value: The value of a business if it continues to operate.
Golden parachutes: A stipulation that managers will receive very large payments if the firm is acquired. Used as a defensive tactic in mergers.
Goodwill: The difference in the amount paid for a firm (the purchase price) and its book value.
Gordon's growth model: The dividend valuation model using the assumption of constant growth.
Greenmail: Shareholders will offer to sell their shareholding to the company at a substantial premium in return for not selling to a hostile bidder for the company.
Growth stock: Shares in a company that can invest money that will earn more than the opportunity cost of capital.

Hedging: The mitigation of risk exposure by undertaking equal and opposite transactions.
Holding company: A company whose only purpose is to hold shares in other companies.
Homemade dividend: Individual investors make their own dividends by selling shares.
Horizontal merger: Merger between two companies that operate in the same line of activity.
Hostile merger: Where the target company's management is opposed to the merger.
Hurdle rate: The required minimum acceptable rate of return management needs from a project before the project is accepted.
Hybrid finance: A financial security exhibiting the characteristics of both equity and debt.

Income stock: Shares of companies that provide high dividend payouts but have very few (if any) profitable investment opportunities.
Incremental cash flow: Cash flows that only occur if a particular project is undertaken.
Incremental cost: The change in costs as a result of a small change in output.
Incremental revenue: The change in revenue as a result of a small change in output.
Indenture: The contract between the company issuing a bond and the purchaser of the bond.
Index trackers: A managed investment fund such as unit-linked funds, designed to match the returns on a stock market index.
Initial public offering (IPO): A private company issues new shares to the public to become a publicly quoted company.
Insider trading: Trading in shares on the basis of privileged information, i.e. information not in the public domain.
Institutional investor: Financial institutions that invest other companies' shares.
Inter-bank market: A money market that facilitates banks' short-term borrowing.
Interest cover: The number of times the income of a company exceeds the interest paid to service the company's debts.

Interest rate parity (IRP): The interest rate differential between two countries is equal to the percentage difference between the forward and the spot exchange rate.

Interest rate risk: The risk of an adverse change in interest rates on the company's performance.

Interest rate spread: The difference between the interest rate charged by a bank on loans and the rate it pays on deposits.

Interim dividend: Dividends paid on the basis of half-yearly results.

Internal growth rate: The maximum growth rate a company can achieve without resorting to outside finance.

Internal rate of return (IRR): The discount rate where investment projects have zero net present value.

Inventory financing: Using inventory as collateral for a loan.

Inventory period: The time between acquiring stock and selling stock.

Inverted yield curve: A yield curve that is downward sloping, indicating that long-term borrowing costs are cheaper than short-term borrowing costs.

Issued share capital: Total amount of the authorised share of capital that is issued.

Junk bond: Debt with below 'investment grade bond' ratings.

Just-in-time (JIT) inventory: A system of inventory control in which stock items needed are delivered 'just-in-time' to be used as they are needed.

Lead-time: The time between placing an order and the order being delivered.

Leveraged buyouts (LBOs): The acquisition of a company, unit or subsidiary in which a large percentage of the money used to buy the shares is borrowed. Usually involving incumbent management.

LIBOR: The London Inter-Bank Offer Rate is the rate of interest applying to wholesale money-market lending between London banks.

Lien: The claim by lenders on specified assets.

Liquidation: The ending of the firm as a going concern.

Liquidity: The ability of a firm to meet its short-term obligations at the fall due.

Liquidity preference theory: Theory suggesting that longer-term interest rates are higher than short-term interest rates, causing the yield curve to be upward sloping.

Liquidity risk premium: The additional interest demanded by lenders to compensate for holding an asset that is not easy to sell at a fair price.

Marginal cost of capital (MCC): The weighted average cost of capital (WACC) of the next euro amount of capital that is raised.

Market maker: A dealer who creates a market in securities by either buying or selling them.

Market risk: Also called systematic risk or nondiversifiable risk. The risk that cannot be diversified away.

Market value added (MVA): The difference between the market value of a firm and its book value.

Matching principle: The maturity of debt matches the maturity of the projects financed by that debt. Short-term assets are financed by short-term debt and long-term assets are financed by long-term debt.

Maximum sustainable growth rate: The growth rate a firm can maintain without adding equity capital.

Merger: Where two firms combine under one ownership.

Mezzanine finance: Unsecured debt that carries high risk and the possibility of high returns.

Moderate working capital financing: The approach to financing in which temporary current assets are financed with short-term finance, and permanent current assets and fixed assets are financed with long-term finance.

Money market: Wholesale financial markets in which short-term securities are traded.

Mutual fund: A managed investment fund, the shares of which are sold to investors.

Mutually exclusive projects: Projects that compete against each other and where only one of the mutually exclusive projects may be accepted.

Net present value (NPV): The project's initial investment minus the present value of its cash inflows discounted at the firm's appropriate cost of capital.

Net working capital: Current assets less current liabilities.

Net worth: The book value of a company's ordinary shares, share premium and retained earnings. Total assets minus total liabilities.

Nominal rate of interest: The real rate of interest plus various premiums. The actual interest rate charged by the supplier of funds.

Noncash items: Expenses charged against company earnings that do not involve a movement of cash, e.g. depreciation.

Nondiversifiable risk: That part of total risk that cannot be diversified away. Nondiversifiable risks include inflation and interest rate risk.

Off balance sheet financing: Any financing that is not shown as a liability on the company's balance sheet.

Offer for sale: A method used in selling shares in a new issue.

Offer price: The price market at which makers sell shares.

Official List: The list of securities admitted for trading on the Irish Stock Exchange.

Operating cash flow: Cash flow generated from the normal operating activities of the business.

Operating cycle: The time between buying stock and the collection of cash from debtors.

Operating leverage: The extend to which a company or a project relies on fixed costs.

Opportunity cost: The most productive or most valuable alternative sacrificed if a particular investment is undertaken.

Option: A contract that gives the owner the right to buy or sell a specified asset at a fixed price on or before a given date.

Order-driven trading system: Buy and sell orders are entered on a central computer system, and the computer automatically matches buyers and sellers according to the price and volume they entered.

Ordinary shares: This is the equity capital of a firm. Ordinary shareholders are the owners of the company and are therefore entitled to all distributable profits after debt holders have been paid.

Over the counter: This term refers to derivatives that are tailor-made by banks to suit the requirements of their customers.

Over-the-counter market (OTC): An intangible market used for the purchase and sale of securities not traded on organised markets. Most notable of the OTC market is the NASDAQ.

Overtrading: When the company has insufficient working capital to finance the level of trading activity.

Par value: Also 'face value'. The stated value of an ordinary share shown on the share certificate.

Partnership: An unincorporated business owned by two or more people.

Payback period: The amount of time a capital project will take to generate sufficient cash flows to cover the initial cash outflow.

Payout ratio: Dividends as a proportion of earnings per share.

Pension fund: Financial institutions that obtain money from workers, invest the funds and provide a pension upon retirement.

Performance spread: The percentage difference between the actual rate of return and the required rate of return on an investment.

Perpetuity: An investment that provides a level stream of cash flows into perpetuity.

Placing: A method of issuing shares in the primary market where shares are offered to the broker's private clients or a selected group of financial institutions.

Poison pill: An issue of securities that are convertible into ordinary, if the merger goes ahead. Designed to make the firm unattractive to the hostile acquiring firm.

Portfolio: A selected group of assets.

Pre-emption right: The right of existing shareholders to subscribe for any additional issue of shares.

Preference shares: Securities issued by a company providing a given dividend to be paid before any dividends are paid to holders of common shares.

Present value: The current euro value of a future amount.

Price/earning (P/E) ratio: The number of times the current market price of a share covers the earnings per share. It indicates the amount investors are willing to pay for each euro of a firm's earnings. Share price divided by earnings per share.

Primary market: The financial market in which securities are initially issued.

Principal-agent problem: Problem shareholders (principals) have in ensuring that managers (agents) act in the interest of the shareholders.

Profitability index: A ratio of the present value of the cash inflows from a project to the present value of the cash outflows.

Pro forma financial statements: Projected financial statements.

Promissory note: A legal document signed by the borrower agreeing to the terms of the loan.

Proprietorship: An unincorporated business owned by one person.

Prospectus: A document issued to provide information about a company during an IPO.

Proxy battle: An attempt by a group of shareholders (non-management) to gain control of the management of the firm by soliciting a sufficient number of proxy votes.

Public offering: The sale of bonds or shares to the general public.

Put option: An option to sell a given number of shares on or before a specified future date at a specified price.

Quick ratio: The ratio of current assets less stock to current liabilities. Also 'acid test' ratio.

Random walk theory: Share price movements are independent of one another. The share price on any particular day cannot be predicted by looking at the previous day's price.

Real rate of interest: The nominal interest rate adjusted for inflation.

Redemption: The repayment of the principal amount at maturity.

Redemption yield: The return required by an investor over the life of a security, taking into account both revenue and capital gains.

Relevant cash flows: The incremental after-tax cash outflow and the consequent cash inflows that result from a particular capital investment.

Required return: The rate of return required by investors to compensate for the level of risk.

Residual theory of dividends: The theory that the dividends paid by a firm should be what are left over after all acceptable investment projects have been undertaken.

Restrictive covenants: Clauses included in bond deeds designed to place restrictions on a company's future financing in order to protect existing creditors' interests.

Retained earnings: The cumulative amount of all earnings that have been retained (after dividends have been paid) since the company's inception.

Return on equity (ROE): The rate of return earned by the owners on their investment.

Return on total assets (ROA): The rate of return management generates on its assets.

Reverse stock split: Used as a method of increasing the share price by exchanging a certain number of outstanding shares for one new ordinary share.

Rights issue: An invitation to existing shareholders to purchase additional shares in the company in proportion to their existing holdings.

Risk-free rate of return: The rate of return an investor looks for to take on a project where there is no risk other than the risk of inflation.

Risk-return trade-off: The higher the risk, the higher the rate of return required to compensate for that risk; and the lower the risk, the lower the rate of return required to compensate for the lower risk.

Safety stocks: Extra stocks that can be drawn down when usage rates and lead times are greater than was expected.

Seasoned equity offering: A new issue of securities to the public by a company that has previously issued securities.

Secondary market: The market where securities previously issued are traded.

Securitisation: The process whereby companies, instead of raising finance by borrowing from financial institutions, convert assets into securities for sale.

Security market line (SML): An upward sloping straight line representing the relationship between expected return and beta.

Semi-annual compounding: Compounding of interest over two periods in the year.

Sensitivity analysis: Assessing the effect on NPV when one variable is changed.

Share dividend: The payment of a dividend in the form of shares instead of cash.

Share split: This is a free issue of shares to existing shareholders, commonly used to lower the share price.

Simple interest: Interest earned on the principal amount only.

Sinking fund: Regular payments into a fund in order to repay a debt.

Spontaneous financing: A form of financing that arises from the normal operations of the firm, e.g., creditors and accruals.

Spot market: The market for immediate transactions, e.g. spot interest rates, spot exchange rates. This is the opposite to arranging transactions to take place some time in the future, e.g. options and future markets.

Straight bond: A bond that is not convertible and has no conversion features.

Straight bond value: The price at which a convertible bond would sell without its conversion feature.

Striking price: The exercise price of an option.

Strong form efficiency: All relevant information, both public and private, is reflected in the market price of the share.

Subordinated debt: Also junior debt. Debt over which senior debt takes priority.

Subsidiaries: Companies controlled by holding companies.

Sunk costs: Costs that have already been incurred and cannot be reversed. Sunk costs should be ignored in investment appraisal.

Swap: A procedure where two companies lend to each other on the basis of different terms, e.g. one on a fixed rate and the other on a floating rate. With an interest rate swap one company arranges with another company to swap interest rate payments.

Swaption: An option to have a swap at some later date.

Syndicate: A group of underwriters who are formed to share the risk and sell the issue together.

Synergy: Where the combined entity will have a value greater than the sum of the individual parts.

Systematic risk: See Market risk.

Tangible assets: Physical assets such as plant and machinery, vehicles, fixtures and fittings.

Target cash balance: The optimum or desired cash holdings a company should have, determined by the trade-off between carrying costs and shortage costs.

Tender offer: A public offer to buy securities.

Term loans: Loans of usually one to five years.

Term structure of interest rates: The relationship between the interest rate and the time to maturity.

Time interest earned ratio: Measures the ability of a company to meet its fixed interest obligations. Profit before interest and tax divided by payments.

Total shareholder return (TSR): The total return a shareholder receives from holding a share. This is dividend income plus capital gains from the increase in the share price, divided by the initial share price.

Underpricing: When securities are issued below their current market price.

Underwriting: The procedure where an underwriting firm (investment bank) buys a security issue from the company issuing the security at a price below which the underwriting firm plans to sell it to the market. The issuer gets a guaranteed amount of cash and the underwriter takes on the risk of price changes between the time of purchase and the time of sale.

Uniform price auction: An auction system where all successful bidders will pay the same price for the shares.

Unit trusts: An investment organisation which attracts funds from individuals in return for units of investment in shares and bonds.

Unsecured loan: Loans that have no assets pledged as collateral in the event of default.

Unsystematic risk: The risk that is specific to a company and hence can be diversified away using a portfolio of investments.

Value-based management: The approach to management which states that the primary purpose is shareholder value maximisation.

Variable cost: Costs that change as a result of changes in output.

Variable rate bond: The interest rate payable varies with variations in short-term interest rates.

Venture capital: Capital to finance new firms.

Vertical merger: Merger between a customer and a supplier.

Warehouse receipt: A document providing evidence that a company owns stocks of goods held in a warehouse.

Warrant: The holder of a security is given the option to purchase a certain number of shares in the issuing company, at a certain price, at some specified date.

Weighted average cost of capital (WACC): The weighted average of the components of the capital structure, i.e. the cost of equity and the after-tax cost of debt.

Winner's curse: This is the problem faced by investors who are not well informed. The average investor will find difficulty in getting an allocation of shares in a successful IPO (one whose share price goes up) because there won't be enough shares to go around. If the average investor 'wins' and gets his/her entire allocation, it could be because the more informed investors avoided the issue.

Withholding tax: A tax levied by an overseas country on profits repatriated to the home country.

Working capital: A company's short-term assets and short-term liabilities.

Yield: Income from a security expressed as a percentage of its market price.

Yield curve: A graph showing the time to maturity of a bond and the interest rate. The term structure of interest rates.

Zero coupon bond: Bonds that do not pay regular interest. They are issued at a discount to their par value and redeemed at par, providing a capital gain.

References and Further Reading

CHAPTER 1

The *Economist* magazine, *The Irish Times*, the *Sunday Business Post*, *The Financial Times* — all have very useful sections on finance and should be regular reading material for students of finance.

Brigham, E.F., Gapenski, L.C. and Erhardt, M.C., *Financial Management: Theory and Practice*.

Eakins, S., *Finance, Investments Institutions & Management*.

Gallagher, T.J. and Andrew, J.D., *Financial Management, Principles and Practice*.

Kelly, K., *New Rules for the New Economy*.

Quinlan, J. and Stevens, K., *101 Trends Every Investor should Know about the Global Economy*.

For a discussion on agency theory, see:
Jensen, M.C. and Meckling, W.H., 'Theory of the Firm, Managerial Behaviour, Agency Costs and Ownership Structure', *Journal of Financial Economics*, October 1976.

Seitz, N., 'Shareholder Goals, Firm Goals and Firm Financing Decisions', *Financial Management*.

CHAPTER 2

Brigham, Gapenski and Ehrhardt, *Financial Management: Theory and Practice*.

Copeland, T., Koller, T. and Murrin, J., *Valuation: Measuring and Managing the Value of Companies*, Wiley & Sons 1992.

Stewart, G. Bennett, *The Quest for Value*, HarperCollins 1991.

CHAPTER 3

There are many sources of financial information available, some of which are:

The Internet – Some companies make their annual reports available on the Internet.

Extel – a company that specialises in providing financial information on an entire range of companies.

Stockbroking firms provide information on a regular basis on the companies they analyse.

Newspapers – news articles, market data along with daily prices of securities. *The Irish Times* and the *Sunday Business Post* along with *The Financial Times* are important sources of up-to-date financial information.

The Irish Stock Market Annual.

Chen, Kung, H. and Shimerda, T.A., 'An Empirical Analysis of Useful Financial Ratios', *Financial Management*, Spring 1981.

Dun & Bradstreet, *Key Business Ratios.*

McKenzie, W., *Guide to Using and Interpreting Company Accounts*, 2nd edn, *Financial Times*/Pitman Publishing.

Ross, S., Westerfield, R. and Jordan, B., *Fundamentals of Corporate Finance*, 5th edn, Irwin McGraw Hill.

Brigham, Gapenski and Ehrhardt, *Financial Management: Theory and Practice.*

Gallagher, A., *Principles of Financial Management*, Prentice-Hall.

CHAPTER 4

Most introductory financial textbooks include a section on the time value of money. Two useful texts are:

Bradley, T. and Patton, P., *Essential Mathematics for Economics and Business*, 2nd edn, John Wiley & Sons 2002.

Swift, L., *Mathematics and Statistics for Business, Management and Finance*, Macmillan Press Ltd 1997.

A more advanced treatment is available in:

Ross, S.A., Westerfield, R.W. and Jaffe, J.F., *Corporate Finance*, 7th edn, Irwin McGraw Hill 2005.

The Irish Financial Regulator website.

CHAPTER 5

Bradley, T. and Patton, P., *Essential Mathematics for Economics and Business*, John Wiley & Sons 2002.

Swift, L., *Mathematics and Statistics for Business, Management and Finance*, Macmillan Press Ltd 1997.

Elton, E.J., Gruber, M.J., Brown S.J. and Goetzmann, W., *Modern Portfolio Theory and Investment Analysis*, 6th edn, John Wiley & Sons 2004.

Ross, S.A., Westerfield, R.W. and Jaffe, J.F., *Corporate Finance*, 7th edn, Irwin McGraw Hill 2005.

CHAPTER 6

Arnold G., *Corporate Financial Management*, FT Pitman Publishing 2007.

Dimson, E., Marsh, P. and Staunton, M., 'Global Evidence on the Equity Risk Premium', *Journal of Applied Corporate Finance*, vol. 15, no. 4, 27–38, 2003.

Fama E. and Macbeth J., 'Risk Return and Equilibrium: Empirical Tests', *Journal of Political Economy*: 81: 607–636, May 1973.

Lintner, J., 'The Valuation of Risk Assets and the Selection of Risky Investments in Stock Portfolios and Capital Budgets' *Review of Economics and Statistics*: 47, 13–37, February 1967.

Markowitz, H., 'Portfolio Selection', *Journal of Finance* 7: 77–91, March 1952.

Pike, R.H. and Neale, C.W., *Corporate Finance and Investment: Decisions and Strategies*. Prentice-Hall 2007.

Roll, R., 'A Critique of the Asset Pricing Theory's Tests Part 1: On Past and Potential Testability of the Theory', *Journal of Financial Economics*, 4 March 1977, 129–76.

Ross, S., 'The Arbitrage Theory of Capital Asset Pricing', *Journal of Economic Theory*, 13: 341–360, December 1976.

Sharpe, W., 'Capital Asset Prices: A Theory of Market Equilibrium under Conditions of Risk', *Journal of Finance*, 19: 425–442, September 1964.

Solnick, B.H., 'Why Not Diversity Internationally rather than Domestically?', *Financial Analysis Journal*, July–August 1974, 48–54.

Watson, D. and Head, T., *Corporate Finance: Principles and Practice*, FT Pitman Publishing 2007.

CHAPTER 7

Many textbooks on investment cover the area of risk-adjusted return analysis in some detail. The area of safety-first investment is not normally covered as well. For an excellent treatment of both topics see:

Elton, E.J., Gruber, M.J., Brown, S.J. and Goetzmann, W., *Modern Portfolio Theory and Investment Analysis*, 6th edn, John Wiley & Sons 2004.

CHAPTER 8

For an excellent treatment of company valuations and the use of FCF and DCF, see:
Brigham, Gapenski and Ehrhardt, *Financial Management: Theory and Practice*.

For further reading on company valuations and the concept of the 'horizon period', see:
Brealey and Myers, *Principles of Corporate Finance*, Irwin McGraw Hill.

For advanced studies on company valuation methods, see:
Copeland, Koller and Murring, *Valuation*.

For a clear exposition of cash flow valuation methods, see:
Rappaport, A., *Creating Shareholder Value*, New York Free Press 1986.

Gordon, M.J. and Shapiro, E., 'Capital Equipment Analysis: The Required Rate of Profit', *Management Science*, 3 October 1956.

CHAPTER 9

The classic article, which is often quoted but seldom read, on dividend policy is:
Miller, Merton and Modigliani, 'Dividend Policy, Growth and the Valuation of Shares', *Journal of Business*, October 1961.

For a discussion on optimum investment policy, see:
Gordon, Myron J., 'Optimal Investment and Financing Policy', *Journal of Finance*, May 1963.

For a discussion on the clientele effect and taxes, see:
Richardson Pettit, R., 'Taxes, Transactions Costs and the Clientele Effect of Dividends', *Journal of Financial Economics*, December 1977.

See also:
Elton and Gruber, 'Marginal Stockholder Tax Rates and the Clientele Effect', *Review of Economics and Statistics*, February 1970.

For the classic article on the way firms set their dividend policy, see:
Litner, John, 'Distribution of Incomes of Corporations Among Dividends, Retained Earnings and Taxes', *American Economic Review*, May 1956.

On the relevancy of dividend policy, see:
Hayes, Linda S., 'Fresh Evidence that Dividends Don't Matter', *Fortune*, 4 May 1981.

For a review of the 'bird in the hand' theory, see:
Gordon, 'Dividends, Earnings and Stock Prices', *Review of Economics and Statistics*, May 1956.

For a study on the information content of dividends, see:
Bhattacharya, S., 'Imperfect Information, Dividend Policy and the Bird in the Hand Fallacy', *Bell Journal of Economics and Management Science*, Spring 1972.

The Bank of England produced a special on dividend policy:
Bank of England Quarterly Review, August 1993.

Of special interest to students who would like to take a further look at dividend policy, see an excellent series of articles in:
Financial Management, Autumn 1998.
Bingham, Gapenski and Ehrhardt, *Financial Management: Theory and Practice*.
Brealey and Myers, *Principles of Corporate Finance*.
Gallagher and Andrew, *Financial Management: Principles and Practice*.
Ross, Westerfield and Jordan, *Fundamentals of Corporate Finance*.

CHAPTER 10

For a discussion on acquisitions that offer no economic gain, see:
Myers, S.C., 'A Framework for Evaluating Mergers', in S.C. Myers (ed.), *Modern Developments in Financial Management*, F.A. Praeger, Inc. Publishers 1976.

For a discussion on the effect of increased borrowing on merger gains, see:

Lewellen, W.G., 'A Pure Financial Rationale for the Conglomerate Merger', *Journal of Finance*, 26 May 1971.

For a discussion on post-merger share price performance, see:

Franks, J.R., Harris, R.S. and Titman, S., 'The Postmerger Share-Price Performance of Acquiring Firms', *Journal of Financial Economics*, 29 March 1991.

For a discussion on proxy contests, see:

Dodd, P. and Warner J., 'On Corporate Governance: A Study of Proxy Contests', *Journal of Financial Economics*, 2 April 1985.

For a discussion of the 1980s merger wave, see:

Shleifer, A. and Vishney, E.W., 'The Takeover Wave of the 1980s', *Journal of Applied Corporate Finance*, Autumn 1991.

See also:

'The Best and Worst Deals of the 1980s: What We Learned from All Those Mergers, Acquisitions and Takeovers', *Business Week*, 15 January 1990.

For a discussion on whether the shareholders of the acquiring firm or the acquired firm benefit most from mergers, see:

Black, B. and Grundfest J., 'Shareholder Gains from Takeovers and Restructurings between 1981 and 1986: $162 billion Is a Lot of Money', *Journal of Applied Corporate Finance*, Spring 1988.

Elgers, P. and Clarke, J., 'Merger Types and Shareholder Returns: Additional Evidence', *Financial Management*, Summer 1980.

Manson, S., Stark, A. and Thomas, H.M., 'A Cash Flow analysis of the Operational Gains from Mergers', Chartered Association of Certified Accountants – Research Report 35, London 1994.

Meeks, G., *Disappointing Marriage: A Study of the Gains from Mergers*, Cambridge University Press.

Rappaport, *Creating Shareholder Value* (Chapter 9).

For discussions on LBOs, the spring 1989 edition of the *Journal of Applied Corporate Finance* provides a number of articles.

For a discussion on the cultural and personnel side of mergers, see:

Cartwright, S. and Cooper, C., *Mergers and Acquisitions: The Human Factor*, Oxford: Butterworth Heinemann.

Also, on societal costs and benefits of mergers, see:

Cowling, K., Stoneman, P. and Cubbin, J., *Mergers and Economic Performance*, Cambridge: Cambridge University Press.

For a discussion on the UK experience of mergers and acquisitions, see:
Coopers & Lybrand and OC & C, 'A Review of Acquisition Experience of Major UK Companies', London: Coopers & Lybrand, 1993.

For a case study on mergers, see:
Baker, G.P., 'Beatrice: A Study in the Creation and Destruction of Value', *Journal of Finance*, July 1992.

For more detailed textbook treatment of mergers and acquisitions, see:
Brealey and Myers, *Principles of Corporate Finance*.
Ross, Westerfield and Jordan, *Fundamentals of Corporate Finance*.
Brigham, Gapenski and Ehrhardt, *Financial Management: Theory and Practice*.

CHAPTER 11

For an advanced discussion and a clear exposition of company valuations see:
Brealey and Myers, *Principles of Corporate Finance*.
Brigham, Gapenski and Ehrhardt, *Financial Management: Theory and Practice*.
Copeland, Koller and Murrin, *Valuation, Measuring and Managing the Value of Companies*.

For additional reading on financial forecasting and planning, the following texts are excellent:
Eakins, Stanley G., *Finance, Investments, Institutions & Management*, Addison-Wesley.
Ross, Westerfield and Jordan, *Fundamentals of Corporate Finance*.

An excellent discussion on EVA and MVA is given in:
Ehrbar A., *Stern Stewart's EVA: The Real Key to Creating Wealth*.

CHAPTER 12

Arnold, G. (2007) *Corporate Financial Management*. FT Prentice Hall.
Diacogiannis, P.G. and Lai, R. (1989) 'Survey on the Investment and Financing of the Companies in the USM', Warick Paper in *Management*, No. 33, April.
Drury, C., Braund, S., Osborn, P. and Tayes, M. (1993) 'A Survey of Managing Accounting Practices in UK Manufacturing Companies', Certified Research Report 32, ACCA.
Fisher, J. (1930) *The Theory of Interest*, Macmillan.
Keynes, J.M. (1936) *The General Theory of Employment Interest and Money*, Macmillan.
Madura, J. (1998) *International Financial Management*, South-Western College Publishing, Cincinnati, Ohio.
McLaney, E. (2006) *Business Finance*, FT / Prentice Hall.
Pike, R.H. and Neale, C.W. (2003) *Corporate Finance and Investment: Decisions and Strategies*, Prentice-Hall.
Solnick, B. (2000) *International Investments*, Addison Wesley.
Watson, D. and Head, T. (2007) *Corporate Finance (Principles and Practice)*, FT / Pitman Publishing.

CHAPTER 13

Arnold, G. (2007), *Corporate Financial Management.*

Donaldson, G. (1961) *Corporate Debt Capacity*, Harvard University Press.

Hamada, R. (1969) 'Portfolio Analysis, Market Equilibrium and Corporate Finance', *Journal of Finance*, vol. 24, 13–31.

Homaifar, G., Zeitz, J. and Benkato, O. (1994) 'An Empirical Model of Capital Structure: Some New Evidence'. *Journal of Business Finance and Accounting* (January).

Miller, M. (1991) 'Debt and Taxes', *American Economic Review*, vol. 32, 261–75.

Modigliani, F. and Miller, M. (1958) 'Cost of Capital, Corporation Finance and the Theory of Investment', *American Economic Review*, vol. 48, 261–96.

Modigliani, F. and Miller, M., (1963) 'Corporate Income Taxes and the Cost of Capital: A Correction', *American Economic Review*, vol. 53, 433–43.

Myers, S. (1984) 'The Capital Structure Puzzle', *Journal of Finance*, vol. 39, 575–92.

Watson, D. and Head, T. (2007) *Corporate Finance (Principles and Practice)*, FT / Pitman Publishing).

Zeckhsnser, R., Patel, J. and Hendricks, D. (1991) *Nonrational Actors and Financial Market Behaviour*, National Bureau of Economic Research.

CHAPTER 14

Arnold, *Corporate Financial Management.*

Brealey and Myers, *Principles of Corporate Finance.*

Brennan, Pierce, *Irish Company Accounts – Regulation and Reporting*, Oak Tree Press.

Brigham, Gapenski and Ehrhardt, *Financial Management: Theory and Practice.*

Dixon, *Financial Management*, Longman.

Eakins, *Finance, Investments, Institutions & Management.*

Westerfield, Ross and Jordan, *Fundamental of Corporate Finance.*

CHAPTER 15

Information on the operation of the Irish bond market is available from the National Treasury Management Agency (NTMA) and from the banks and stockbroking companies.

Information on the Irish pension fund industry is available from the Irish Association of Pension Funds (IAPF) and from the National Pensions Board.

Information on the Irish unit-linked fund industry is contained in the MoneyMate database from Moneymate at www.moneymate.com.

Bradley, T. and Patton, P., *Essential Mathematics for Economics and Business*, 2nd edn, John Wiley & Sons 2002.

Elton, E.J., Gruber, M.J., Brown, S.J. and Goetzmann, W., *Modern Portfolio Theory and Investment Analysis*, 6th edn, John Wiley & Sons 2004.

Ross, S.A., Westerfield, R.W. and Jaffe, J.F., *Corporate Finance*, 7th edn, Irwin McGraw Hill 2005.

CHAPTER 16

Arnold, G, 'Corporate Financial Management'.

Baumol, William, 'The Transactions Demand for Cash: An Inventory Theoretic Approach', *Quarterly Journal of Economics*, November 1952.

Brigham, Gapenski and Ehrhardt, *Financial Management: Theory and Practice*.

Davis, E.W. and Collier, P.A., *Treasury Management in the UK*, Association of Corporate Treasurers.

Gallagher and Andrew, *Financial Management – Principles and Practice*.

Gentry, J., Vaidyanathan, R. and Hei Wai Lee, 'A Weighted Cash Conversion Cycle', *Financial Management*, Spring 1990.

Gentry, J.A., 'State of the Art of Short-run Financial Management', *Financial Management*, Summer 1988.

Journal of Cash Management (US).

Ross, Westerfield and Jordan, *Fundamentals of Corporate Finance*.

CHAPTER 17

For further additional textbook reading:

Arnold, *Corporate Financial Management*.

Department of Enterprise, Trade and Employment, *How to Finance your Business*, Government Publications Office, Molesworth St, Dublin 2.

Eakins, *Finance, Investments, Institutions and Management*.

Ross, Westerfield and Jordan, *Fundamentals of Corporate Finance*.

CHAPTER 18

Arnold, *Corporate Financial Management*.

Brigham, Gapenski and Ehrhardt, *Financial Management*.

Carty, P., 'The Economics of Expansion', *Accountancy*, March 1994 (on sources of finance).

Central Bank of Ireland Bulletin, for information on various deposit and other selected interest rates.

Davies, H., 'Finance for Small Firms', *Bank of England Quarterly Bulletin*, February 1994.

Department of Enterprise, Trade and Employment, *How to Finance your Business*.

European Central Bank, *Monthly Bulletin* – useful for main interest rate trends in the euro zone and other monetary aggregates.

Gallagher and Andrew, *Financial Management – Principles and Practice*.

O'Kane, B., *Starting a Business in Ireland*, 2nd edn, Oak Tree Press.

Ross, Westerfield & Jordan, *Fundamentals of Corporate Finance*.

Wynn, G.L., Sources of UK Short-term and Medium-term Debt', *Handbook of Corporate Finance*, London.

CHAPTER 19

Arnold, G. (2007) *Corporate Financial Management*, FT / Pitman Publishing.

Buckley, A. (2004) *Multinational Finance*, FT / Prentice-Hall.

Eiteman, D.K., Stonehill, A.I. and Moffett, M.H. (2004) *Multinational Business Finance*, 10th edn, Pearson Addison Wesley.

O'Loughlin, B. and O'Brien, F. (2006) *Fundamentals of Investment – an Irish Perspective*, Gill and Macmillan.

Watson, D., Head, T. (2007) *Corporate Finance (Principles and Practice)*, FT / Pitman Publishing.

CHAPTER 20

The Irish Financial Regulator, especially *Mortgages made easy*.

www.itsyourmoney.ie

Bradley, T. and Patton, P., *Essential Mathematics for Economics and Business*, John Wiley & Sons 2002.

Swift, L., *Mathematics and Statistics for Business, Management and Finance*, Macmillan Press Ltd 1997.

Information on the products and services offered by Irish mortgage providers is available from the main banks and building societies.

Index